GREAT BASEBALL WRITING

SPORTS ILLUSTRATED
1954 - 2004

EDITED BY ROB FLEDER
SPORTS ILLUSTRATED BOOKS

Copyright 2005
Time Inc. Home Entertainment

Published by
Sports Illustrated Books

Time Inc.
1271 Avenue of the Americas
New York, NY 10020

ISBN: 1-932994-02-5

Sports Illustrated Books is a trademark of Time Inc.

CONTENTS

CONTENTS

Giants

God's Squads

Opposite Fielders

Good Stuff

You Could Look It Up

INTRODUCTION

Introduction

BY MICHAEL LEWIS

I T'S A MEASURE OF THE QUALITY OF THIS COLLECTION THAT THE weakest piece in it is by Robert Frost; it's a measure of its honesty that the editors left out pieces by William Saroyan and Ted Williams in favor of better ones by writers you may never have heard of. It's as if SPORTS ILLUSTRATED has thrown a quixotic, half-century–long dinner party, and seated faces in the crowd beside the world's most clever conversationalists—only to have the unknowns dazzle with their wit and charm as the legends eat their meals in slack-jawed silence. Here baseball writing is shown to share the egalitarian quality of baseball: On any given day you never can tell who will be the star.

The writing here reflects the game in other ways, too. It reflects, for instance, the tension between the space on the field, and the space just off it. There is a willful distance between baseball insiders and baseball outsiders, between the people playing the game and the people watching the game, writing about the game, even owning and running the business end of the game. The players sense that they are better off if the fans don't really get to know them, and the fans, in an odd way, approve of the instinct. The loneliest piece in this collection is Jim Bouton's account of his attempt to reinvent himself as a knuckleball pitcher after he has published the most famous of all insider memoirs, *Ball Four*. The poor man has done nothing but inform outsiders of the way insiders actually behave when outsiders aren't watching. He's sold a lot of books—and given a lot of people a lot of innocent pleasure—but he now writes from what is clearly a growing sense of isolation. The mere fact of having spoken honestly to the outsiders has turned Bouton into one of them—except that he isn't. He's caught between the two nation states, the Player's Kingdom and the Republic of Fandom. A baseball exile.

This tension between insiders and outsiders exists in all sports—indeed in all public life—but in baseball it is especially noticeable. The reason for this is that baseball has more to hide. Or, to put it another way, the difference between what baseball is, and what many of its customers want it to be, is still vast. Movie stars who play loving husbands are now allowed to sleep around in real life. Politicians are permitted to feign honesty; at this point we don't know how to respond if they are truly honest. But catch a baseball player lacking respect for the game and you have a scandal. Baseball is capable of deeply upsetting people because its fans actually have illusions about it. And one of their illusions is that baseball shouldn't ever be any different than it's always been.

This presents an obvious problem. Baseball changes often, usually in response to economic pressure. The most obvious recent sources of change are the demands of television and the fantastic increase in what players are paid. (The most jarring line in Roy Blount's wonderful 1974 piece on Reggie Jackson is the one that reveals that Reggie is being paid the shockingly large sum of $135,000 a year.) As the money gets bigger, so does the cost of failure. What an ordinary ballplayer might not do for a living he might well do for a fortune. The scramble to find the winning formula has reshaped not just players' bank accounts but also their bats, their strategies, their medical care, their pharmacists, their bodies, and maybe even their characters. Baseball on the inside is a very American story of technology answering challenges posed by the market. Baseball from the outside is another very American story, of people lamenting change, or pretending that it never happened. Of longing for a different, and better, past. The professional baseball diamond is a conflicted space—not merely an arena of American ambition but a place defined by its uneasiness with American ambition.

Really, it's an impossible situation—a backward looking sport in a forward looking nation—and it is one of the baseball writer's job is to make everyone feel a bit better about it. To that end many of the pieces here look back nostalgically on some great event, or anticipate the nostalgia with which the current event under consideration will be looked back upon. The most obvious of these is Rick Reilly's letter to his granddaughter, meant to be read in 40 years' time, about the purity and simplicity of Mark McGwire's new home run record. (It certainly reads differently now.) But there are others. Steve Rushin's piece on his preference for listening to baseball on the radio to watching baseball on television, for instance. That the writer's beloved old delivery mechanism is radio is sheer historical

accident. Had baseball come of age with the carrier pigeon, some gifted essayist would now be making the case for receiving box scores from a bird.
These writers know their reader; they know that his obsession with the past
is his distinctive trait—the thing that sets him apart from the football and
the basketball fan.

Still, the reader of these articles may sense a contradiction. How does
the plain old present ever become the glorious past? The modern baseball
player as he is depicted in a few of the articles, and the two about Barry
Bonds, does not appear to be the sort of character future generations will
wax poetically nostalgic about. Harold Peterson's interesting piece on the
origins of baseball—which informs us that the fellow we were all taught, by
baseball's authorities, had invented the game in fact had nothing to do
with it—suggests one solution. Any game capable of inventing its own in-
ventor can easily manufacture whatever else it needs. With the passage of
time, the home runs will travel farther, the fastballs will gain in velocity,
the characters of today's players will improve. The seeds for a Barry Bonds
Was Misunderstood movement, though it may take another 50 years to
gain strength, can be found at the back end of Steve Cannella's splendid
piece about Bonds' private bat maker. Here we find a genuinely humble
and great-souled Bonds, new owner of the single season home run record,
paying tribute to another human being. ("You know, it's my record, but
it's still your bat.")

Actually, in these pages, there is a perfect, if chilling, example of outsiders shaping the present they dislike into a past they can embrace: Peter
Gammons's piece on Bill Buckner. It is one of Gammons's many attractive
traits that when he sees a mob gathering he leaps in to stick up for its intended victim. He does it again here, though perhaps unknowingly. The
Red Sox have just lost the 1986 World Series, which they might have won
had Buckner fielded cleanly a slow ground ball that rolled between his
legs; but that's not the story Gammons has come to tell. In light of what
happened later—death threats, Buckner and his family driven out of Boston
by rabid Red Sox fans—it's shocking to read about Buckner's warm reception at the time. The piece reminds us that what Red Sox fans now regard as a species of moral failure was in fact a moment of great courage. But
that is not the history that Red Sox fans wanted for themselves, so they
created another: Buckner as villain.

These articles have been chosen by the editors of SPORTS ILLUSTRATED
mainly for their ability to still give pleasure, and they do. If you're holding

the book you can see for yourself what's in it, so there's no need for me to tell you. What's interesting is what is not in it—apart from a handful of failed pieces by famous writers. In the half century since the magazine's creation there have been some great changes in baseball, and a few go very nearly unmentioned here. There is little about the entrance of foreign players, apart from Esmeralda Santiago's inspiring piece about Vladimir Guerrero. There's nothing about the increased professionalization of amateur baseball; indeed, there's nothing at all about amateur baseball. And there is only the faintest whiff of the intellectual movement that appears to be changing the way the game is run and understood by thoughtful fans.

Mainstream baseball writing tends to take the view that the game is chiefly an emotional experience and that "emotional" is antithetical to "intellectual." Hard thinking, even if it improves the game, threatens to spoil the feeling in the air. But there's no denying that such thinking has been done—is still being done. Once upon a time it was done by lone statheads in their home basements; now it is done also by teams of researchers in offices beneath major league ballparks. The one article about this strange movement—Dan Okrent's profile of Bill James— sort of explains why there is only one article: New knowledge in a past-drenched game is about as welcome as a cat at a fish dinner. SPORTS ILLUSTRATED initially rejected Okrent's article because its fact-checkers refused to believe, among other things, that Nolan Ryan didn't boost attendance figures. Even Okrent, as fantastically prescient as he was, puts a bit of distance between himself and James's biggest, and most revolutionary, ideas. James's attempt to create a formula for measuring a player's contribution to a baseball offense, for example. "Not all of his analysis is lucid," writes Okrent before his faintly dismissive paragraph on James's runs-created formula. Twenty-five years later I know of at least six front offices in baseball that evaluate their own hitters with something very close to this formula.

The other line of inquiry unpursued here is the story of the ordinary player. We read about baseball, apparently, to read about the stars. The experience of the vast majority of baseball players would appear to be of little interest to the average reader; the just good enough, and the just not good enough, don't swing on the page. (Where is the poetry in the Tampa Bay Devil Rays? Where is the nostalgia?) One of two delightful exceptions is Jimmy Breslin's piece about the '62 Mets. ("The Mets are bad for many reasons, one of which is that they do not have good players.")

The other is George Plimpton's piece about his experience of pitching to the 1960 National League All-Stars. Plimpton entered professional sports in a way that no writer of his caliber ever has, or perhaps ever will. His secret was that, unlike a lot of famous writers, he never condescended to his subject; rather, he routinely allowed his subject to condescend to him. A lot of readers missed just how fine a writer George Plimpton was. The quality of his prose tended to be overshadowed by the quality of his stunts. But how the man could write! Here he has taken an experience that millions of American men dream of having and turned it into a nightmare. He has dared to offend the Baseball Gods—his offense is the reverse of Jim Bouton's—and thus the Gods must punish him. Behold, he tells us, here is what becomes of the outsider who dares to trespass on the sacred turf of the insider.

INSIDE THE PARK

❧

Spring Has Sprung

BY FRANK DEFORD

*It's Opening Day, so buy me some peanuts and Cracker Jack, remember
to hold the label up, and please, please tell me Who's on First.*

OPENING DAY: THERE IS ONLY ONE, AND IT'S IN
baseball. The theater has opening nights scattered here
and there about the calendar, and there are various
opening days of . . . the fishing season, the race meeting, the NFL season. But there is only one Opening Day, when grand-
mothers drop like flies and dreams are born anew.

Opening Day means spring. It means, literally, an opening: of buds spreading and jackets unbuttoning; of little birds' mouths gaping; of rubber bands
being released from neat's-foot-oiled baseball mitts that have been held tight
around a ball all winter. The Louisville Slugger sends painful jolts up your
arms if you don't connect properly in the chill air. It will be better soon:
warmer, and the wind will die down. But even now, if you keep the label up,
you can knock that old horsehide clean and far and feel nothing but warmth.

The beginnings of the other major sports seasons have no connection with
the natural rhythms of life. To be sure, they arrive according to an annual schedule, but so do subscription renewals and visits to the dentist. If anything, the starting dates for football, baseball and hockey are reminders to look back. The beginning of football heralds the conclusion of summer; it goes hand-in-glove

with—ugh!—back-to-school. And winter sports? If they're starting, then it must soon be—oh, no—winter. It is significant that of all the sports seasons, hockey and basketball most sneak up on us; if you are not attentive to the fellow with the blond teeth on the TV news, you will suddenly open the paper one day late in October and discover that the Celtics have already played four games.

But baseball. Opening Day. To have picked up the newspaper one fine day in April and seen this:

W L Pct. GB
Washington 1 0 1.000 --
Boston 0 0 .000 ½
New York 0 0 .000 ½
Detroit 0 0 .000 ½
Chicago 0 0 .000 ½
Cleveland 0 0 .000 ½
St. Louis 0 0 .000 ½
Philadelphia 0 1 .000 1

Why, that told you better than anything that God had truly kissed the land again, that a whole life lay ahead. Play them one at a time? Ridiculous. There were 154 to play, a number that overwhelmed a child's mind. Where would we be when the season was done? In a new grade, for certain. And perhaps our team would win. That, too. Not believe in Opening Day? Why, you might as well have said you didn't believe in Tinker Bell.

So, if you cannot bury your poor grandmother one more time, here is an article for Opening Day. It is not really about baseball. There are no bunts and round-trippers and sliders and curves. We have a whole summer for that. No, this is about Opening Day, about baseball sensations, about throwing out the first ball, about Cracker Jack, and Louisville Sluggers and about *Who's on First?* Let's start off with a quiz. The answers will be found buried in the article. If you bat .300—get five or more correct—you pass. You are also stamped as a strange person for knowing such foolishness.

1) Everybody knows that Taft was the first president to throw out a first ball. You think I'm going to ask a simple question like that? Who caught the first ball that Taft threw?
a. Clark Griffith, the Senators' owner
b. Gabby Street, the Senators' catcher

c. Walter Johnson, the Senators' pitcher

d. Vice President Sherman

2) Cracker Jack was invented in Chi by:

a. The Wrigley Gum Company

b. The head concessionaire at Comiskey Park

c. Two German immigrants with a sidewalk popcorn popper

d. Pop Norworth, the older brother of Jack Norworth, who wrote, *Take Me Out to the Ball Game*

3) Louisville Sluggers are now made in:

a. Where else, dummy? Louisville

b. Hong Kong and Haiti

c. Slugger Park in Indiana

d. North Louisville, U.S.A., which is in the great ash forests of Ontario

4) Only two real players are mentioned in *Who's on First?* They are:

a. Joe DiMaggio and Ted Williams

b. Mickey Owen and Ralph Branca

c. Dizzy and Daffy Dean

d. Babe Ruth and Ty Cobb

5) From 1910 through 1971, when the Senators left Washington for good, only two nongovernment officials threw out the first ball. They were:

a. Perle Mesta, the famous hostess, and Clark Griffith, Sr.

b. Mrs. Calvin Coolidge and Shirley Povich, *Washington Post* sports editor

c. David Eisenhower and a returned Vietnam POW

d. Duke Zeibert, the restaurateur, and Sammy Baugh

6) Every prize at Cracker Jack must pass:

a. An esthetic test administered by the National Candy Coupon Council

b. A screening by the baseball commissioner's office

c. A simulated esophagus test conducted by Cracker Jack's "prize lady"

d. Samplings personally undertaken by the chairman of the board and his grandchildren

7) The Old Gladiator was:

a. Wilson R. Keeney, a fabled blind woodturner who made 162,000

Louisville Sluggers

b. Bud Hillerich, former president of Hillerich & Bradsby Company, who is said to have made the first Slugger

c. Pete Browning, star of the Louisville Eclipse, who reputedly used the first Slugger

d. The Slugger that Joe Sewell used for fourteen seasons

8) Lou Costello was 5' 4" and weighed 195 pounds, but he had many sporting interests. He:

a. Had fourteen professional prizefights

b. Was a movie stunt man

c. Owned a 2-year-old colt named Bold Bazooka that equaled the world record at five and a half furlongs

d. Spent $5,000 on a personal campaign to get the Dodgers moved to Los Angeles in 1953

9) Walter Johnson pitched 12 presidential openers, the first in 1910, when Taft started the tradition. The Big Train lost a no-hitter in that game because:

a. An easy grounder nicked a Philadelphia baserunner, Ira Thomas, who had walked

b. While President Taft bellowed "Let it roll!" a bunt by the A's Rube Oldring stayed fair for a scratch single

c. Embarrassed for having unintentionally brushed back Home Run Baker, the easygoing Johnson grooved the next pitch and Baker, startled, poked an opposite-field triple

d. Washington rightfielder Doc Gessler tripped over a child who was sitting in front of the outfield ropes, and that allowed an easy fly to drop for a double

10) For sure, popcorn is this old:

a. 126 years

b. 360 years

c. 560 years

d. 5,600 years

11) When he hit number 715, Henry Aaron used this player's bat model:

a. Stan Musial

b. Eddie Mathews

c. Eddie Waitkus

d. Babe Ruth

12) The last player mentioned in *Who's on First?* is the shortstop. He's:

a. Never Mind

b. Because

c. Why

d. I Don't Care

13) In the past decade only three politicians have thrown out the first ball for two teams. They are:

a. John Lindsay, Richard Nixon, Richard Daley

b. Jimmy Carter, Spiro Agnew, Hubert Humphrey

c. Nelson Rockefeller, John Connally, John Gilligan

d. Gerald Ford, Ronald Reagan, Henry Jackson

14) The model for Sailor Jack, the little boy on the Cracker Jack package, is:

a. R.W. (Boots) Rueckheim III, grandson of the company founder, who later became chairman of the board and is now retired in Lake Wales, Florida, where he lives next door to Red Grange

b. An unknown street urchin who was paid his "fee" in Cracker Jack and was bitten by the mutt Bingo while posing for the artist

c. A former minor league baseball player, Freddie Trail, who later gained brief notoriety when he was suspected of kidnapping the Lindbergh baby

d. The Cracker Jack board chairman's grandson, who was a childhood pneumonia victim and whose gravestone bears a carving of the Sailor Jack-Bingo drawing.

15) This Louisville Slugger model is the current best seller:

a. Johnny Bench

b. Reggie Jackson

c. Henry Aaron

d. Jackie Robinson

16) When Abbott got the phone call telling him that Costello had died, he was:

a. Packing to go to Cooperstown to present the *Who's on First?* script to the Hall of Fame

b. In Walter O'Malley's box at a Dodger-Giant game
c. Talking to his manager about performing *Who's on First?* at the White House when President Eisenhower entertained Canadian Prime Minister John Diefenbaker
d. Watching the *Who's on First?* routine in an old movie being rerun on TV

EXTRA CREDIT: Name the rightfielder in *Who's on First?*

OPENING DAY seems to have attained a certain ceremonial status long before presidents got into the act. Christmas found its arbitrary December slot on the calendar because there was already cause for celebration: the lengthening of the days, which had been the reason for the pagan festival of Saturnalia for centuries before Jesus' birth. In the same way, Opening Day fit right in as a welcome to spring. Of course, the vernal equinox always came before Opening Day, but in the northeastern quadrant of the country, where major league baseball was contained until 1957, consistently mild weather did not arrive until sometime in April. Moreover, it is worth remembering that in those days people did not gambol on indoor tennis courts all winter, or watch golf tournaments from the desert on TV, or fly off to Barbados and the Yucatan. Baseball was the only game in town, except maybe for some basketball over at the Y, and its return was a true renaissance of life.

We do not know exactly when politicians began to exploit this afternoon of goodwill, but it was surely by the Gay Nineties, perhaps earlier. When President Taft threw out the first ball on April 14, 1910 at National Park, a contemporary account noted that he was usurping the "time-honored" role of the District of Columbia's city commissioners.

But it has been the presence of presidents that has made Opening Day very special. No other private enterprise has ever been accorded such cachet. Indeed, except for sporadic appearances at the Army-Navy football game, incumbent presidents have rarely gone to stadiums for sporting events and never to arenas. But Opening Days have been treated by all presidents with an annual deference given only two other nongovernmental functions, posing with the March of Dimes poster child and lighting the White House Christmas tree.

FROM TAFT in 1910 through 1971 (when the Senators left for Texas), the 11 presidents went 45 for 62 on Opening Days. Given wars, death depression, Communists, and what-have-you, this is an incredible record. When the chief executives could not make it, they invariably called in their top relievers, the vice-presidents. Only in the Senators' final two seasons did somebody other than a government official fire the first pitch. David Eisenhower did the honors in 1970, and in 1971 a released POW, Master Sergeant Daniel I. Pitzen, became the last man to throw out the first ball in the capital.

Most presidents quite enjoyed the task. Only Wilson (3 for 8) batted less than .500 but he attended other Senator games during the season, parking his limousine in deep right, where a substitute catcher was stationed by a fender to snare incoming line drives. Harding, Truman (7 for 7), and Kennedy never missed an Opening Day; Roosevelt made eight. Coolidge hated baseball. He had to be reminded every damn time why it was that everybody stood up in the seventh inning—something he remedied late in his term by leaving in the second inning. Still, Cal made four of his five Opening Days, and the missus was nuts about baseball. Grace Coolidge would not only pop up at Senator games during the season, but it is also on record that she kept score and stayed through rain delays.

Harding bet on the games to make them more interesting. Truman practiced surreptitiously on the White House lawn before his second opener in 1947 and then startled the photographers and everybody else by chucking the old apple southpaw. Ike was a good baseball fan, but shortly before his first Opening Day (1953) he announced that he would have to pass it up for a golfing vacation. All hell broke loose. The country club over the national pastime? Mercifully, old Jupiter Pluvius saved Ike; Opening Day was rained out, and he made it back from the links in time for the rain date. After that, Ike didn't mess around, boy; he made all openers until 1959. Next question.

How did Taft come to start this great tradition?

Sorry, the folds of history have hidden that earthshaking story. When the Griffiths were running the Senators, the fable—in the best tradition of Parson Weems writing about Geo. Washington and the cherry tree—had it that old Clark Griffith dropped by to see Taft, presented him with a gold pass, and invited him to throw out the first ball. Because Taft had been a pitcher in his svelter, salad days, he leapt at this opportunity. This is a great story except that Taft first threw out the first ball in 1910. Griffith did not become an owner of the Senators until 1912.

In fact, there was no advance warning of Taft's appearance; "The opening will not be attended by any ceremony," reported *The Washington Post* that morning. It is quite possible that Taft just up and went to the game on the spur of the moment. He did very little as president except eat and fret that he could not be Chief Justice, so what follows would be consistent with history. One can visualize Taft as he sat in the breakfast nook that morning, looking out of the window and saying, "Besides lunch, what are we gonna do today?"

It was a sweetheart of a day, "sun-kissed," according to eyewitnesses.

"Well," said a chum, General Clarence Edwards, spreading some marmalade, "It's Opening Day at the ball yard."

"Yeah, who are the Nationals playing," asked the president, reaching for another apricot Danish.

"The Mackmen," piped up Secretary of State Philander Knox, polishing off the home fries.

"District Commissioner Rudolph will be chucking out the first ball," added Mrs. Taft.

"Hmmm, said the president, finishing his Western omelet. "That gives me an idea. Let's pack a picnic and pop over."

And thus, as the *Post* reported, did there come about "the auspicious union of official Washington and baseballistic Washington."

On the diamond the Big Train was mowing 'em down. All told, he was to start a dozen presidential openers, winning nine with six shutouts, but he would never again pitch as well as he did in his first. He would have had the first Opening Day no-hitter (Bob Feller finally got one 30 years later) but for the overflow multitude that settled in the outfield grass. With two gone in the seventh, Baker lifted an easy fly to the rightfielder, Doc Gessler. The swarm of fans seated along the perimeter of the outfield was supposed to dutifully scatter under these circumstances, but one boy was not nimble enough. Gessler tripped over the tyke, and the ball fell for a double, the A's only hit of the game.

But no sense crying over spilt milk. Taft and Johnson put on such a show of arms that even should diamond scholars "go back to the very inception of the national game—there will be found no day so altogether glorious, no paean of victory changed by rooters and fanatics half so sweet as that witnessed yesterday." Perhaps proudest of all were the two managers, the storied Cornelius McGillicuddy (a.k.a. Connie Mack) of the Athletics (a.k.a. Mackmen) and James McAleer of the Nationals. They went to Taft's box to meet him, and while he greeted both courteously, the president disclosed his allegiance for the home nine by saving "a subtle wink and a double-action smile" for McAleer.

Despite his girth, Taft was no slouch when it came time to deliver the mail. Let the *Post* correspondent recapture that moment for us: "A mighty cheer swept across the crowd as President Taft showed such faultless delivery. . . . He did it with his good, trusty right arm, and the virgin sphere scudded across the diamond, true as a die to the pitcher's box, where Walter Johnson gathered it in. . . . "

In a sense, the presidential tradition started that day by Taft has outlasted the Senators, because the consecutive-president streak goes on. Jimmy Carter served up the opening pitch twice in Atlanta (1972 and '73), and Gerald Ford is one of only three politicians in the last decade to have first-balled two clubs, working Cincinnati as vice president in '74 and Texas as president in '76. (Senator Henry Jackson pitched the first ball for both Seattle franchises, Pilots and Mariners, and Ronald Reagan did the honors for the A's and the Angels.)

But then, politicians are not as fashionable as they used to be, especially in the National League, which is ahead of the American even in this department. The most somber openers occur in Milwaukee, which always has the county executive throw out the first ball, and in Detroit, where gaiety is manifest when the fire department trots out its traditional floral horseshoe with its clever message "Good Luck Tigers!" and presents it to the manager.

On the other hand, San Diego once had a fellow dressed up like a chicken throw out the virgin sphere, and Philadelphia, which always confuses good humor with tackiness, employs the likes of Kite Man, Cannon Man, Sky Cycle Man and Parachute man to deliver the ball into the park. A number of clubs have taken to using old ballplayers instead of politicians. Poster children are also somewhat in vogue, and two clubs have called upon local centenarians. The Dodgers used an umpire once, Jocko Conlan, and the Angels went with Mickey Mouse.

Predictably, Charlie Finley marched to a different Opening Day drummer. The likes of Governor Reagan aside, Finley often preferred to have singers throw out the first ball, because then he could entreat them to warble the anthem on the cuff. Just imagine how Finley would have gotten the presidents to work freebies if he had owned the Senators: notarize contracts, naturalize players, pardon the ones with paternity suits, lead the pledge of allegiance.

Down in front! Pass the Cracker Jack!

PERHAPS THE best thing about Cracker Jack is that it never goes away, but you think it does, so it is a pleasant surprise when it reappears. This is not just me talking off the top of my head. Ask, say, an unmarried man, age 26 or so, would he like some Cracker Jack, and he will stare at you as if you had just inquired if he would like to watch *The Donna Reed Show* on a Muntz TV. People are bonkers about Cracker Jack as kids, and then they forget about it until they have kids of their own.

It also works this way: After a lousy week, during which no visions of Cracker Jack danced through your aching head, you finally get to a circus or a game, and Cracker Jack pops right into your mind. It would probably do it at the ball park even if a fellow named Jack Norworth had not, in 1908, been fishing around for some confection that rhymes with "back," hence: "Buy me some peanuts and Cracker Jack! I don't care if I never get back." Next question.

Who invented Cracker Jack?

The Rueckheim Brothers, F.W. and Louis, German immigrants. When F.W. came to the Windy City from down on the farm in 1872 with $200 in capital, he and a partner set up a sidewalk popper.

Popcorn was not invented in a movie theater by Thomas Edison. It is the oldest corn going. One ear was found in the Bat Caves of New Mexico. It was 5,600 years old. But nobody had ever done a whole lot with popcorn. Then at the World's Columbian Exposition in 1893, F.W. and his brother (who had bought out F.W.'s former partner) wowed the innocents with a popcorn-peanuts-molasses snack.

Unfortunately, Cracker Jack is a sticky business. It was blob-sized until Louis figured out how to break up the gooey mess—by banking it against baffles in a rotating barrel. Then F.W. gave the new, improved bite-sized confection to a salesman. "Whaddya think of that?" F.W. asked.

The salesman replied, "That's a crackerjack of an idea."

That's a true story. Now do you want to go on with the history or get right into the prizes, the same way everybody does when they buy Cracker Jack?

Yeah, the prizes.

THERE IS a very pretty woman at Cracker Jack, a former art teacher named Susan Reedquist. She is known around the plant as the "prize girl" or the "prize lady," depending on how up-to-date you are. She is in charge of selecting the 1,000 or so prizes that go into 420 million boxes of Cracker Jack each year. No fewer than 400 different prizes are packaged every day, and these are deposited manually—14 prize sorters dropping 128 prizes a minute. It is the only unautomated part of the process, but there are also three mechanized checks to ensure that a prize gets into each package.

Of course, just like you and me and batting averages, the prizes are not what they used to be. The prize lady has a vault that contains virtually every Cracker Jack prize ever produced, back to 1912, when prizes were introduced. Their heyday seems to have been in the 1930s, when the prizes included intricate, metal and wooden toys. Once, during these halcyon days, there was an episode of *Amos 'n' Andy* in which Kingfish went to a ball game and dropped a diamond ring he had bought for Sapphire. It fell into the Cracker Jack box out of which a fellow in the next row was munching. Of course the stranger thought the diamond ring was his prize. Ohhhh me, Andy! Imagine anybody today thinking that even a zircon ring could be included in a Cracker Jack box. Down in front!

But for goodness' sake, let's understand what the prize lady has to put up with. The Food and Drug Administration, for example. Nitpickers, all of them. You can't use sharp metal; you can't have any rough edges; you can't have toys that break into pieces. If it's not one thing, it's another. You could never in your wildest dream imagine what is sitting prominently on the prize lady's desk. A simulated child's esophagus, that's what. If a toy can fit into the simulated esophagus, the prize lady has got to scratch it.

Worse, the prize lady has to accommodate today's TV generation. "The toys have to provide instant gratification," she says. "That's the effect of television."

The prize lady selects the prizes that will be tried out on whole children, as well as on their esophagi, and only the items that score high on the "smile scale" qualify for Cracker Jack. "You've got to remember that these kids have grown up in a paper and plastic world," the prize lady says. What the little shavers don't know won't hurt them.

Cracker Jack is one of the four or five most recognized brand names in the country. Ninety-nine percent of Americans are aware of it. And yet Cracker Jack is hardly in the mainstream in the way Coke and Ford, two other of the most familiar brand names, are. Undoubtedly, Cracker Jack owes much of its fame to its felicitous inclusion in the one sports anthem in the country.

But as you careful readers of *The Wall Street Journal* have learned, there is no such thing as a free lunch. Cracker Jack has been terrific for baseball, too. Why, Cracker Jack is still made with all natural ingredients: popcorn, peanuts, molasses, corn syrup, salt and sugar. There are still the same number of peanuts—nine to 14—in every box. And they use the exact same formula they've always used; connoisseurs can tell that the goo covering the peanuts is different from the goo covering the popcorn. You still get "A Surprise in Every Package." Take a hike, Mom's apple pie.

Think about this: Suppose Norworth had not used Cracker Jack in his song. Has baseball ever thought about that? Suppose Norworth had used

Moxie: "Give me some peanuts and cold Moxie!" Or Sen-Sen. Or JuJuBes. Wouldn't that be a fine how-do-you-do? Every time baseball played its theme song, it would be connecting itself with things that hardly exist anymore. That's all Bowie Kuhn needs, to be defunct-linked. And football. What a time it would have rubbing it in. Ha, ha, ha, baseball and Sen-Sen! Ha, ha, ha! Football would not let baseball hear the end of it.

So it has been a fair trade-off between Cracker Jack and baseball. And if Cracker Jack was struck by dumb luck in getting featured billing in *Take Me Out to the Ball Game*, it has looked out for number one very well indeed. The name itself is a dandy, the prize idea a gem. It has two famous slogans: "A Surprise in Every Package," and "The More You Eat The More You Want." And everybody instantly recognizes the symbol of the little boy and his dog that has graced billions of Cracker Jack packs since 1919.

Actually, Sailor Jack and Bingo (for those are their names) are touched up every now and then, restyled to look more like a modern sailor boy and a fashionably precious mutt. For a number of years Bingo appeared forlorn; his head drooped. Now his puppy countenance has brightened. Jack has put on a white hat in recent years and is saluting much more proficiently than he did in the early going. That's the good news.

The bad news is that Jack is dead.

The sailor boy was modeled after F.W. Rueckheim's young grandson Robert, but alas, shortly after posing, the lad succumbed to pneumonia. He was buried in St. Henry's Cemetery in Chicago. On the child's tombstone is the friendly commercial image of Sailor Jack and Bingo.

WHAT WERE your favorite wirephotos? There were two types I most admired. One was from Election Day and showed the president/governor/mayor emerging from the voting booth in his precinct grade school or church basement. This was democracy's pictorial equivalent of they-put-their-pants-on-one-leg-at-a-time-too. It made all the afternoon editions.

The other wirephoto jewel showed bat-kissing. If a fellow got a clutch bingle, he was shown bussing his lumber. If he hit three round-trippers he was photographed kissing one of a like number of bats, held rather like a bouquet. The most bats I ever remember a hero holding and kissing was four. When the operative number was five to 19 only one symbolic kissing-bat was employed for the wirephoto. (I always imagined these strict canons were spelled out in the UP, AP, and the INP manuals.) From 20 on up, the number celebrated was formed by baseballs, the digits created by dots on the order of a Seurat painting.

Once in a blue moon a player was shown kissing a baseball, but he never was pictured kissing his glove. In wirephoto protocol, glove-kissing was considered kinky. But bats were there to be kissed. And the bats were always Louisville Sluggers. You could see the little oval trademark. So ingrained in the consciousness of American youth was the dictum "Keep the label up" that players made sure to do it even when kissing bats for wirephotos.

In Slugger Park there is a bat museum—tours daily—and amid the display of famous bats is an endorsement for Louisville Slugger from Babe Ruth. He raises a hymn to the cudgel, praising its "driving power and punch that brings home runs." As a child, I never saw such a testimonial, which is just as well, because it would have utterly confounded me. Why would any major-leaguer, Babe Ruth or anybody, bother to endorse a Louisville Slugger? Why, this would be as unnecessary as endorsing food or shelter. "Hello, I'm Julia Child, and I'd like to urge you to eat food!"

Oh sure, I knew there was such a thing as an Adirondack, and whenever anybody's dim-witted visiting maiden aunt bought a bat as a gift for a nephew, she got stiffed with a little brown number named Hanna Bat-Rite. But these were aberrations. A baseball bat was a Louisville Slugger. . . and if you threw it after hitting a ball you were out.

The Slugger is almost a century old. The baseballs are made in Haiti, and it is estimated that 85% of the gloves are manufactured in the Orient, but Louisville Sluggers are constant, immutable. Henry Aaron hit with a slimmed-down version of the model that Babe Ruth used. The official name of the company is still Hillerich & Bradsby, it is still 100% privately held, and a member of the Hillerich family's third generation of bat executives—John A. Hillerich III—presides as president.

The Hillerichs, like the Cracker Jack Ruechkeims, were immigrants from Germany, where J. Frederick Hillerich was born in 1834. By 1859 he was sufficiently established in Louisville to open his own woodcraft shop. It had a reputation for quality manufacture of items like balusters and butter churns. His son Bud, a fan of baseball and an instrument of destiny, soon joined the enterprise.

One day in '84 (so our story goes), Bud was at the ball field, watching the local pro team, the Louisville Eclipse of the (then major league) American Association. The star of the Eclipse, Pete Browning, broke his bat, and young Bud offered to make him a new one. Browning looked askance at Bud (the tale continues), but he accompanied him to the shop. Any port in a storm. Bud turned out an ash bat to Browning's specifications, and as you fable fans might imagine, Browning went 3 for 3 the next day. Soon Browning's teammates, and then visiting opponents, were beating a path to the quaint little woodshop on First Street. The elder Hillerich (the story guffaws) fumed; one can almost hear him bellowing at Bud in a Katzen-jammer dialect, "Vat iss diss mit das crvazy baseball schtick?" Fade out. . . .

Fade in the Slugger factory. Portentous bass voice-over: "Today that quaint little woodshop on First Street makes three and one-half million bats a year!"

The Pete Browning tale is promulgated in all hallowed Slugger chroni-cles. And why not? Browning was a period superstar, lovingly known as the Old Gladiator. But there is a skeleton in the closet. On the wall of the company president's office is a clipping from a 1912 *Louisville Herald*. It relates a story told by Bud Hillerich that does not mention the Old Gladi-ator. Instead, Hillerich explained how he had made his own bat when he was playing on a semipro club. A teammate, Augie Weyhing had asked him to use it, and Bud had made one more for another teammate, Monk Cline. Monk Cline? Augie Weyhing? Down in front!

Anyway, the rest is history. The bat was known as the Falls City Slug-ger until 1894. In 1905 Honus Wagner signed a contract with Hillerich, permitting his signature to be branded on bats. He thus became the first baseball player ever to ink an endorsement pact. In 1911 Frank Bradsby, a sales expert, came on board, and the corporate name was altered in 1916. The factory was moved across the Ohio River to Indiana in 1974. Other-wise, business as usual.

More than 90% of all pros sign up with Slugger. Most join on as minor-leaguers earning a small fee and the promise that Louisville will make them personalized bats for as long as they play for pay. On semiautomat-ic lathes, consumer bats can be knocked out in eight seconds flat, but the pros' personal models are still turned by hand. Bats are never made or cut or formed. They are turned.

In the old days players used to make special trips to Louisville to talk to the craftsmen, to pick out their own timber. Not surprisingly, Ted Williams was the most persnickety. Players tended their bats, "cooling" them in al-cohol, "tightening" the grain by rubbing them with a bone or a pop bot-tle. Today Louisville hears only from agents trying to renegotiate the old service contracts.

Styles change, too. Generally, handles have gotten thinner. Still, the most popular bat with the public is the Jackie Robinson model that has a relatively stout grip. The other retail autograph models are named after Aaron, Clemente, Mantle, Frank Robinson, and 14 current hitters including Pete Rose, who is trying to get out of his Slugger contract so he can Charlie Hustle aluminum bats.

An original model is catalogued in a very simple way—by the initial of the player's surname and a number that indicates how many players with the same initial have had distinct models turned for them. Thus, the first bat made with a concave end is designated as C271 because it was turned for Jose Cardenal, who is the 271st player with the initial C to have had a Slugger model created for him.

A small room at Slugger Park holds file cards on every major-leaguer who ever had a Slugger turned for him. There is an eerie feeling there, a sense of time having stopped. A man can go into that file cabinet and determine what bat it was that Home Run Baker used on April 14, 1910. And in a few minutes a craftsman can turn that exact bat. There are 13 check points on every bat. It is always made from a white ash that has grown for 45 to 50 years in New York or Pennsylvania. The tree has to have grown on a ridge top or have been exposed to the north and east for the right amount of sun. Then it is cut and dried. Finally it is turned by an artisan who does it precisely as one of his predecessors did it decades ago, about the time the seed went into the ground and Home Run Baker took his cuts.

Unfortunately, it is hard to find young men who want to be woodturners. It requires a long time to learn this honest craft, and young people do not want to invest that time. Besides, there are aluminum bats. They already take up 35% to 40% of the total bat market, and their share increases every year. A Slugger will cost you nine bucks tops, but it will break and sting your hands, and you must remember to keep the label up. Aluminum bats sell for as much as $50, but they last and last, whichever way you hold the label. It is also alleged that a baseball jumps off them faster. The sound is different, too. It is more modern, like an automobile crash.

Aluminum bats are now allowed in every game but Organized Baseball. There, as always, the law reads that a bat must be turned out of one solid piece of God's own wood. Someday soon a phenom is going to step to the plate in the majors, fresh out of college, and he is going to be swinging with a wooden bat for the first time. *Que será, será.*

None of this upsets Hillerich & Bradsby as much as you might imagine. Remember, these are the same fellows who got out of butter churns when the time was ripe. Now their brand is pressed on aluminum bats, too. And the Slugger people are especially proud of their top-quality mag-nesium bats. Magnesium bats made by Louisville Slugger! Why, you might as well tell me there is magnesium Cracker Jack.

Bill Williams, Hillerich & Bradsby's vice president of advertising, says, "The crack of the bat doesn't seem to mean that much to kids anymore." He spoke that not in anger but merely in resignation, with a hint of pity. Imag-ine never getting good wood on a ball. Imagine not knowing what a loud foul off Home Run Baker's bat sounded like.

COMEDY IS not the most dependable traveler through time. Many peo-ple now find the mots of the wits of the Algonquin Round Table forced and leaden. And Abbott and Costello, those purveyors of the broad and fool-ish? They appear downright puerile. Consider their horse routine, when Abbott, the tall one (he was 5' 11"), brings Costello to blubbery tears by telling him deadpan about the mudder who had no fodder. Our first reac-tion is wonderment: Did a nation laugh at this?

You bet it did. Except for Laurel and Hardy, there has never been a pair of comics who were so enjoyed for so long. They were Top 10 box-office draws for more than a decade; in 1942 they were No. 1, just ahead of Clark Gable. They struck some simple child-like chord in us and strummed it again and again.

The pair broke up in 1957, and Costello died two years later when he was 50. Abbott, ever the happy wastrel, had to scuffle with the IRS over back taxes for most of his sunset years, but he lasted till age 78, dying four years ago this month. But they remain as much in evidence as ever. Their movies—and they churned out three or four a year for Universal—are every-where on TV, usually during the children's hours, harmlessly washing our minds without leaving a trace upon our consciousness. But hush, my chil-dren, here is the one heirloom of Abbott and Costello that endures:

Costello: I would like to know some of the guys' names on the team. . . .
Abbott: Oh sure. But you know baseball players have funny names. . . .
nowadays.
Costello: Like what?
Abbott: Well, like Dizzy Dean and Daffy Dean.
Costello: Oh yeah, a lot of funny names. I know all those guys.
Abbott: Well, let's see now. We have on our team: Who's on first, What's on second, I Don't Know's on third.

Costello: That's what I want to find out, the guy's names.

Abbott: I'm telling you: Who's on first, What's on second, I Don't Know's on third.

Costello: You're going to be the manager of a baseball team?

Abbott: Yes.

Costello: You know the guys' names?

Abbott: Well, I should.

Costello: Will you tell me the guys' names on the baseball team?

Abbott: I say: Who's on first, What's on second, I Don't Know's on third.

Costello: You know the guys' names on the baseball team?

Abbott: Yeah.

Costello: Well, go ahead—who's on first?

Abbott: Yeah!

Costello: I mean the guy's name.

Abbott: Who.

Costello: The guy playing first.

Abbott: Who!

Costello: The guy on first?

Abbott: Who's on first. . . .

That, of course, is just the beginning of the Who part. Not until considerably later do they introduce What. It goes on and on. Tomorrow is pitching. Today is catching. Why is in left, Because is in center, and finally, I Don't Care is at short. For some reason, there is no rightfielder. The routine could be played at any length. Maybe at one point there was a rightfielder, but it didn't work. No one knows for sure. Strangely, even though *Who's on First?* is far and away the best-known comic bit in American history and even though Abbott and Costello played it more than 15,000 times—including a dozen times for President Roosevelt, who never tired of it—and even though they did it in vaudeville, in burlesque, on radio, on television and in the movies, there seems to be no account of what inspired it, who wrote it or even what Abbott and Costello thought of it.

Studio publicity had it that the comics introduced the routine in 1936 at the Oriental Theater in Chicago, but almost surely its origins date to '31 or '32. The two men had become a team shortly before. William A. Abbott, a theater box-office employee, filled in one night when Louis Cristillo's straight man didn't show. Both men were from New Jersey, although Abbott grew up on Coney Island until, at age 15, he was shanghaied. Slipped a

Mickey Finn, he woke up a seaman in the middle of the ocean. He later returned to show biz, the family profession.

Costello had a more uneventful childhood in Paterson, where, despite his short stature, he played baseball and other sports. Later he had 14 professional prizefights and became a Hollywood stuntman. He was always interested in sports. In 1955 his two-year-old colt, Bold Bazooka, equaled the world record for five-and-a-half furlongs, and two years before that he had spent $5,000 of his own money on a vain campaign to have the Dodgers moved to Los Angeles. (Now you know that number 8 is a trick question: all the answers are correct. The other answers are: questions 1 to 7, *c*; 9 to 16, *d*.)

Given Costello's interest in sports, it is more likely that *Who's on First?* originated with him. Certainly no one claims that anyone but the two comics themselves wrote it. Betty Abbott, Bud's widow, believes that her husband and Costello first performed the routine—a version about one-third as long as the final one—at the Eltinge Theatre in New York late in 1932.

Almost from the first it seems to have been the centerpiece of their act, but it did not receive national attention until 1938, when Abbot and Costello got their big break, appearing on the Kate Smith radio show. Two years later they used *Who's on First?* in their first movie, *One Night in the Tropics* in which Robert Cummings and Allan Jones starred. Because the comedians and the routine were a big hit in this film, Universal signed them, and they later used *Who's on First?* in movies of their own.

"They kept embellishing it," their manager, Eddie Sherman, recalls. "Initially they didn't do the entire routine the way it's been recorded or the way they did it in pictures. They added on a thing they called 'Naturally.' They were always adding things to it over the years."

The official version, if there is such a thing, was enshrined in the Hall of Fame at Cooperstown in 1956. The gold record and script usually are displayed on the second floor, next to the National League centennial exhibit. Recently, Universal bought the rights to *Who's on First?* so it can use the bit in a movie and a TV show. This is business, of course, but it is also altogether silly. You can no more sell the rights to *Who's on First?* without Abbott and Costello than you can sell the rights to Sally Rand's fan dance without Sally Rand, or Babe Ruth's home-run trot without Babe Ruth. Oh well, never mind. Down in front!

It is hard to pin down why *Who's on First?* became so popular and enduring—especially at a time when sports material usually bombed on the stage. For obvious reasons, the bit must have appealed to baseball fans, and probably it also appealed to those who laugh at baseball fans for being so devoted to the sport's minutiae, its names and statistics. It goes without saying that the routine never could have worked for another sport. Who's at Halfback? No way. Baseball is the only popular American sport in which every position is permanently set at a specific location. The one thing you can count on in life is that there is a first baseman and a shortstop and a catcher, and they are right where they were last month. The second base-man is not going to vanish—poof—and materialize down the leftfield line as something known as a nose guard or a power forward. Baseball positions are anchors in a shifting world, and to have given the most indefinite names to the personnel at these most dependable positions is to have made brilliant use of comic irony. That is the genius of *Who's on First?*

Obviously, two burlesque comedians did not sit around and ponder all this, but their routine has a sort of uncultured existentialism. Costello is like a Sartre character in *No Exit*, stymied at every turn despite being on the most familiar, comfortable territory. Abbott is a seminal bureaucratic figure, ever helpful, never helping. Maddening.

The routine was written in the depths of the Depression, a time when the nation was still as confounded by this unforeseen calamity as it was hungry. Without warning, unseen forces were frustrating, then destroying common folk in ways they could not comprehend. Who? What? I don't know. Tomorrow! Why? Because. Economic disaster aside, the modern, impersonal, urban, red-tape society had just begun to crank up. You see, Abbott and Costello were saying, you can't depend on a damn thing anymore, not even baseball.

This is why, I think, they never came up with a rightfielder.

You might say that this is all a lot of gobbledygook. These were two down-town comics who worked bawdy routines out front while the strippers were getting ready backstage. Maybe, but genius pops up in funny places, and those who have it are often unaware of it.

On the afternoon of March 3, 1959, right after the Dodgers went off to spring training, Bud Abbott turned on the television in L.A. to watch an old Abbott and Costello movie. *Who's on First?* was in the film. Near the end of the routine the phone rang, and Abbott answered it. He was told that Lou Costello had died. "Tell me," Abbott would often say after that, "why did I happen to be watching that picture at that time? Will you tell me why?"

Probably because all along, surely, the rightfielder in the routine was God.

A Day of Light
And Shadow

BY JONATHAN SCHWARTZ

*A Red Sox fan, so devoted he listened to their games over the phone
in Paris, recounts the glittering glory and the chilling finale of the one-game
Boston–New York playoff of 1978.*

*I didn't feel much pressure the night before the game, when the manager told
me that even if Guidry went only a third of an inning I'd be the next guy out
there. But I felt the pressure when I actually came into the game. More pressure than I've ever felt. Even in my personal life.*

—Goose Gossage

IN THE KITCHEN IN UPPER MANHATTAN, LUIS TIANT APPEARED
to be in charge of the Red Sox' 162nd game of the year. Boston
had widened a small lead over Toronto to five runs, and Tiant's
impeccable control compelled even the restless woman roam-
ing through the apartment to stop at the kitchen door and admire his performance, as one would admire an exquisitely bound volume of dense the-
ological writing in another language.

In the bedroom, the Yankees had fallen well behind Cleveland and were
hitting pop-ups, always a sign late in the game that things are out of hand.

The woman was restless because her quiet Sunday afternoon was being
assaulted by the babble of baseball and by what she perceived as yet another

increase in my furious tension. She had retreated to the living room to sit sullenly among the Sunday editions of *Newsday*, *The Washington Post* and two interim New York papers born of a strike that was now in its eighth week. She had been told that this was positively *it*; that there was no chance that the Red Sox would advance past this Sunday afternoon; that the baseball season would be over by sundown. She had been told that there would never be a repetition of my impulsive flight to Los Angeles after the Yankees' four-game Fenway Park sweep three weeks before. I had simply up and left the house during the seventh inning of the last humiliating defeat. I had taken nothing with me but a Visa card and $50. I had called home from Ontario, Calif., having pulled my Avis Dodge off the road leading to the desert, though I realized it was well after midnight in New York. "I am filled with regret," I said from a phone booth without a door.

"Over what?" I was asked.

Her question meant this: Was I filled with regret because the Red Sox had lost four consecutive games, or was I filled with regret because I had up and left without explanation and had not bothered to call until the middle of the night—and if you want this relationship to work you're going to have to work at it?

I replied above the roar of traffic from the San Bernardino Freeway that I was regretful about leaving, and about my insensitivity and my inability to put baseball in perspective. "A trip of this kind," I said severely, "will never happen again."

The truth: I was regretful because the Red Sox had lost four consecutive games, had blown an enormous lead and had handed the championship of the Eastern Division of the American League to the Yankees.

Three weeks later, the phone rang for an hour after the Sunday games were over. Congratulations! From California—Palm Springs, Brentwood, San Francisco. From Stamford, Conn., and Bridgehampton, N.Y. From 73rd Street and 10th Street in Manhattan. Congratulations!

Returning from oblivion, the Red Sox had tied for first place on the last day of the season, forcing a playoff game in Boston the next afternoon. Somehow this development had moved people to seek me out with warm feelings, as if my control had been as superb as Tiant's and had contributed to the unexpected Red Sox comeback. My control, of course, had vanished after Labor Day, leaving me infuriated and melancholy. And yet I accepted congratulations that Sunday afternoon as if my behavior during September had been exemplary. In fact, I had wept and raged. Had participated in two fistfights, had terminated a close friendship and had gone out in search of a neighborhood 15-year-old who had written RED SOX STINK in orange crayon on the back window of my car. I had set out after him with vicious intent, only to return home in a minute or so, mortified. The psychiatrist, whom I immediately sought out, said to me, "This is not what a 40-year-old should be doing with his time. *Comprenez-vous?*"

On the triumphant Sunday evening, I drank Scotch and talked long distance. I was asked, "Are you thrilled?" I was thrilled. "Can they do it?" I doubted they could. "Are you going to the game?" Well, maybe.

I had actually thought of trying to use my connections as a radio broadcaster to round up some kind of entrée to Fenway Park for the next afternoon, but the prospect of tracking down people in their homes on a Sunday night was depressing. And there would be the scramble for the air shuttle, an endless taxi ride in a Boston traffic jam, no ticket or pass left at the press window as promised, and a frantic attempt to reach Bill Crowley, the Red Sox' cantankerous P.R. man on the phone—"Bill, the pass was supposed to have been . . . and no one's seen it and they can't . . . and is there any possibility that I could . . . . "

No. I would watch at home, alone. I would have the apartment to myself all day. I would stand in the bedroom doorway and watch with the sound off to avoid Yankee announcer Phil Rizzuto's ghastly shrieking. At home, in the event of a Red Sox victory, I would be able to accept more congratulatory calls, this time for the real thing. "To me, it's the division championship that means the most," I had often said reasonably to whoever would listen. "After the division it's all dessert."

And yet. Had there been a more significant athletic event held in this country during my lifetime? The World Series, like the Super Bowl, is public theater, designed to entertain. Women and children gather around. Aren't the colors on the field pretty? Isn't that Howard Baker?

The NBA playoffs, even the Celtics' wild triumphs of the '60s, are local affairs, presented for small numbers of people in the heat of May. And what, after all, can be seriously expected of a major professional league that has a hockey team in Vancouver?

It occurred to me that perhaps one event had been as significant as the Yankee–Red Sox playoff—the Bobby Thomson game of 1951. The circumstances had been similar: a playoff involving intense rivals home-based in relative proximity; personalities that occupied the mind at four in the morning; and startling rallies through August and September, the '51 Giants having wiped away a 13½-game Dodger lead and the '78 Yankees having fought from 14 back of the Red Sox. The difference in the two games seemed to be a small one: for the Dodgers and Giants it had been the third of a three-game playoff; for the Red Sox and Yankees it would be one game, sudden death.

IN FEBRUARY, with a cable-television bill, a notice had arrived: COMING ATTRACTIONS. EXCITING BASEBALL ACTION. RED SOX BASEBALL ON CHANNEL F. The notice had said nothing else, but it had stopped my heart. Having lived in New York and having been a Red Sox fan since childhood, I had spent hours sitting in parked automobiles on the East Side of the city where reception of WTIC in Hartford, which carries Red Sox games, was the clearest. Eventually I had obtained through a friend in Boston an unlisted air-check phone number that tied directly into WHDH broadcasts. From anywhere in the world one could hear whatever it was that WHDH—and, subsequently WITS, with a different number—was airing at any moment of the day or night. WHDH was—just as WITS is—the Red Sox flagship station, and one had only to be prepared for an exorbitant phone bill to listen to any Boston game, or season. Between 1970 and 1977 I had spent nearly $15,000 listening to Red Sox broadcasts. In a hotel in Paris I had heard George Scott strike out in Seattle. From my father's home in London I had heard George Scott strike out in Detroit. From Palm Springs, Calif., I had listened to at least 100 complete games, attaching the phone to a playback device that amplified the sound. One could actually walk around the room without holding the receiver. One could even leave the room, walk down the corridor and into a bathroom to stare glumly into one's eyes in a mirror and still pick up the faint sound of George Scott slamming into a double play in Baltimore.

The most significant athletic event in my lifetime.

Fifteen thousand dollars in phone bills.

Endless Red Sox thoughts on beaches, and in cables, and while watching movies with Anthony Quinn in them.

And most of the summer of '78 spent in a darkened kitchen with Channel F.

I got on the phone to a guy who works at ABC, the network that would televise the playoff game. Their truck was up there now, I assumed, with everyone's credentials in order. The guy at ABC owed me $150 and a copy of Frank Sinatra's rare *Close to You* album that I had lent him for taping six months before. The guy at ABC was at home asleep.

"I'll try. I'll do my best," he said, "but it's slim city."

He called me at eight in the morning. A press pass would be waiting in my name at the front desk of the Ritz Carlton Hotel in Boston. "If anyone asks, you're with Channel 7 in New York," he said. "But you've got to be dignified, or I'm in the toilet."

"Have I ever *not* been dignified?" I asked.

"Yes," he said. "Yes," he repeated softly.

LOU PINIELLA: *We had dinner around eight, me and Catfish and Thurman. After dinner, we went over to a watering hole, Daisy Buchanan's. We had a couple of drinks, and talked about the game. I remember that we all thought it was ironic justice that these two good teams should wind up like this after 162 games. Like it was just meant to be. Some of the fans in there, they recognized us, and they ribbed us about how we were going to get beat and all. But, you know, we all felt pretty confident because of the series in September when we came up to Fenway and beat 'em four straight. We all love to play at Fenway, and we talked about it that night.*

In the morning I got up early, around nine, and had my usual breakfast: corned beef hash, three eggs over lightly, an order of toast, orange juice. I like to play on a full stomach. It's just the way I am.

I got to the park around noon. I felt nervous, but it's good to feel nervous. It puts an edge on things. In the clubhouse about 12 guys played cards. It kind of relaxed us. I thought about Torrez. I never hit him too well.

I talked to Zimmer before the game. I wished him good luck. He's a very close friend of mine. He lives in Treasure Island, and I live in Tampa. I remember thinking during batting practice, what a beautiful autumn day in Boston. It was a beautiful day. You know?

"It's a game that blind people would pay to hear." Reggie Jackson once said of the prospect of a Frank Tanana-Ron Guidry matchup.

That comment flashed through my mind while I was riding in a taxi to Fenway Park. The season did, too. Specifics: an extra-inning loss to Cleveland in April that concluded a Sunday-afternoon doubleheader at 8:46 p.m.; opening day in Chicago, and the next afternoon there; two games in Texas a few weeks later. All told, five losses that came in the closing inning. Had the Red Sox held on to but one of those games, there'd be nothing cooking at Fenway today—no tie, no playoff. The Yankees would be scattered across the country like the Montreal Expos, and the Red Sox would be in a Kansas City hotel lining up tickets for friends.

I had bought the papers at the Ritz Carlton after picking up my pass, but I hadn't read them and wouldn't now as I approached Kenmore Square. After all, who wanted to stare at Ron Guidry's stats on Storrow Drive?

I arrived on the field at 1:10, exhilarated, the papers left in the taxi, my pass in hand.

I took a look in the Red Sox dugout. At the far end, Ned Martin, the team's chief radio announcer, was fumbling with a small cassette recorder while, next to him, manager Don Zimmer waited patiently in silence. I have known Martin for 15 years and discovered early in our relationship that he has no mechanical aptitude. The tap in a kitchen sink would break away from its stem at his touch. A zippered suitcase would open only in the hands of a hotel maintenance man. The cassette machine, though it was used daily to tape the pregame show with the manager, was apt to defy Martin at any time, before any game. I saw at once that it was defying him now, on this most crucial of crucial afternoons.

Crouching on the top step of the dugout, I stared down at the two men. Perhaps three minutes elapsed, enough time for Zimmer to take notice of me. "Who's that?" he said to Martin, who was tangled in the tape of a broken cassette.

Ned looked up. "Holy Christ," he said, aware that someone who knew him well was scrutinizing his difficulties.

"I'll deal with you later," I said to him.

"Christ," Ned repeated, an utterance that to this day remains the first word on the last pregame program that Martin, a Red Sox announcer for 18 years, would conduct on the teams radio network.

Munson was hitting. Around the batting cage were the faces of the New York press, and those of some Boston writers I had gotten to know through the years. One of the Boston writers told me that moments earlier, in the clubhouse, Carl Yastrzemski had confided that he was "damned scared." A New York broadcaster, who was there only for the pleasure of it, said to me somewhat confidentially, "This is a gala occasion."

Always, when I think of baseball games that have been played, I see them as if they had taken place in the light of day. I have spent a lot of time mentally reshuffling two-hitters and leaping catches that occurred at 10 or 11 in the evening, so that they return to me grandly in afternoon sunshine. The fact that baseball is part of my daily procedure, like getting up for work or eating lunch, inspires me to conjure up sunlight for its illumination.

Forty-five minutes before the 2:30 start, I realized as I looked around the park that in all my years of journeying to Fenway, on all the summer afternoons spent peacefully in the many corners of the stadium, I had never experienced a day of such clarity, of such gentleness. Fluffy cirrus clouds appeared to have arrived by appointment. The temperature of 68° was unaccompanied by even the slightest trace of wind, which made the day seem 10° warmer than it was. For such a majestic encounter there had been provided, despite a less-than-optimistic forecast the night before, a shimmering neutral Monday, as if God, recognizing the moment, had made some hasty last-minute adjustments. It was the afternoon of my imagination, the handpicked sunlit hours during which my perpetual baseball game had always been played.

After a while I made my way up to the press room, which is on the roof of the stadium, behind the press box and the three enclosed rows of seats that stretch down both foul lines. They had been desirable seats to me as a child, because they allowed easy access to foul balls. One had only to lurk in the doorway of one of those roof boxes and await the inevitable. Other lurkers in other doorways were the competition—kids my age, ready to spring into action.

"Here it comes!"

We were off. Under or over a green railing (now red). Across the roof to the brick wall. A slide, a leap, a grapple. A major league baseball in your pocket; if not this time, the next. You always had a shot at getting one on that roof. If I competed 50 times, and surely that is a conservative guess, I emerged from my adolescence with at least 15 souvenirs—and one chipped tooth (the railing).

Before entering the press room, I looked around for a moment. I could see myself outside doorway 25–27 wearing a Red Sox cap. Oh, how quiet it had been when I raced across the top of Fenway Park—just those other feet and the whistling wind shooting me ever so gradually through the years to this very afternoon, to this very press room that I had aspired to for so long, to the tepid piece of ham and half a ring of pineapple that I would be served, to the unexpected sight of Phil Rizzuto making his way toward my table.

"You huckleberry," he said to me with a smile. "I heard what you said."

The morning before, on my radio program in New York, I had spoken harshly of Rizzuto's announcing. "He is shrill," I had said, which is true. "He roots in an unfair and unacceptable way for the Yankees," which is true.

"I heard you," Rizzuto repeated, extending his hand. "You got a nice, calm show. I like it," he continued, surprising me.

Rizzuto is a charmer, an attractive, graying man with the eyes of a child. One imagines that his attention span outside a baseball park is short, but one would like to be included in whatever spare moments he has available. My distaste for his broadcasts was muted at once by the warmth of his radical innocence. Getting up from my seat, I touched his cheek in friendship. I had never met Rizzuto before and had often imagined myself dressing him down before a large and approving assembly. Instead, when he departed to make his way to the radio booth, I found myself regretting the fact that I hadn't told him that I had never come upon a better or more exciting shortstop. Never.

MIKE TORREZ: *I had my usual breakfast, just tea and a piece of toast. I don't like to pitch on a full stomach.*

As I drove to the park, I thought about a couple of games during the year. After those games I had thought that I didn't want them to be the deciding thing. Like a game in Toronto that Jim Wright pitched. It was extra innings. We got a few guys on. I think with no outs. We couldn't score and we got beat. And there was a game in Cleveland when we came back with four in the ninth. Yaz hit a homer, but we blew it. You think about those things.

When I was warming up in the bullpen I felt good. I had good motion. I didn't throw hard until the last two minutes. I looked over at Guidry and waved to him. I wished him good luck and all that. He did the same to me. And I thought about Rivers and Munson. They're the keys. And then the national anthem was played. And then we started to play.

A photographers' box is suspended beneath the roof seats along the first-base line. One descends a metal ladder that is difficult to negotiate. One stands throughout the game, because the early arrivals have captured the few folding chairs scattered around.

As Mickey Rivers, the first batter, approached the plate, I said out loud to no one, "If Torrez gets Rivers right here, the Red Sox will win." I have a tendency to think and speak such notions. "If this light turns green by the time I count three, I won't catch the flu all winter."

Rivers walked on four pitches and promptly stole second. "If Torrez gets out of this with only one run, the Red Sox have a shot," I said aloud.

Torrez got out of it unscored upon, striking out Munson with commanding determination. I was elated. My hands were shaking. I moved to the right corner of the box and stood by myself in a small puddle of water left over from a rainstorm the night before.

Instilled in me from childhood is an awful fear that Whitey Ford created: the fear not only of not winning, but of not even scoring, of not even stroking a modest fly ball to an outfielder. Grounders and strikeouts, and the game would be over in an hour and 40 minutes. Done and done. Ron Guidry is a slim man with shocking velocity and a devastating slider. One does not imagine that one's team will defeat Guidry, or score on Guidry, or make even the smallest contact with Guidry's pitches. What caught my eye in the first three innings as I hung above the field, clasping my hands together to prevent the shaking, was that the Red Sox were not futilely opposing him. The outs were long outs. The hitters were getting good wood on the ball.

I was astounded when Yaz connected with an inside fastball for a leadoff second-inning homer, a blast that from my vantage point looked foul. Fisk and Lynn followed with flyball outs, Lynn's drive propelled to deep center-field. I reasoned that Guidry, after all, was working on only three days' rest, that the he was a fragile guy, that maybe there was a shot at him. . . . Maybe there was a shot at him.

Torrez was getting stronger as the game moved along. When the fourth inning began, my nerves were so jumbled that I felt it impossible to continue standing in that puddle staring out at the field. I wanted to break away from it, soften its colors, lower its volume.

I climbed up the metal ladder and went into the men's room, a separate little building with one long urinal and two filthy sinks above which was written in large, well-formed blue Magic Marker letters and numbers, FATE IS AGAINST '78.

In the press room the ABC telecast was playing to an empty house. I sat down to watch an inning or so and was joined a moment later by Ned Martin, whose partner, an amiable, childlike man named Jim Woods, was handling the fourth. Woods's usual innings were the third, fourth and seventh. Knowing of this arrangement, I had hoped for Ned's appearance. Someone so close to it all, so immersed in it all for so many years, would have the answer. He would reassure me, calm me down.

"Well," I said.

"Torrez," he said.

"Do you think?"

"Can't tell."

Ned is usually more loquacious than he was that afternoon. He is as articulate and as creative a sportscaster as there is in the country. He is often poetic and moving. "The Yankee score is up," he had observed late in September from Toronto, where scores remain only momentarily on the electric board. "Soon it will be gone," he had continued in his usual quiet tone. "It will flash away like a lightning bug into the moist and chilly Canadian night."

From Chicago a number of seasons ago—I wrote it down at the time: "The dark clouds approaching from beyond leftfield look to be ambling across the sky in no apparent hurry. They know what trouble they are and are teasing the crowd with their distant growl."

We sat in silence through the rest of the inning.

"Well," I said finally, hoping for an encouraging word.

"You never know," Ned said.

I walked him back toward the radio booth. On the catwalk outside the visitors' radio booth, Buddy LeRoux, one of the Red Sox' new owners, was in conversation with two men wearing dark suits. I heard LeRoux use the word "cautious." He, too, was wearing a suit, pin-striped and ill-fitting. It was a baggy garment that did not complement a man of position.

I studied his eyes. This same fellow, with a younger, pudgier face, had, as the Celtics' trainer, sat next to Red Auerbach throughout my adolescence, attending thoughtfully to some of the heroes of my youth. His face is lined now, his demeanor formal, suggesting high finance. An owner. What did he know of shaky hands and midnight calls from Ontario, Calif.? There he was in conference, having missed the fourth inning—or so I imagined. I thought: If an owner can take the fourth inning off, what is so important about it all, anyway?

I returned to the puddle for the fifth and sixth innings. The Yankees stirred around against Torrez, but didn't break through. The Red Sox sixth produced a run on a line single by Jim Rice.

It also produced the play that changed the game.

Fred Lynn came to bat with two runners on, two outs and a 2–0 Red Sox lead. It was clear that Guidry was not overpowering. With Torrez so formidable, another run might put the game away. At that moment, it seemed possible to me that the Red Sox would actually win, that the nightmare would end at last.

I paced half the length of the photographers' box. With every pitch I moved a few feet to my right or left, winding up at the foot of the ladder for Guidry's 3–2 delivery.

RON GUIDRY: *I was a little tired and my pitches were up. I threw him a slider on the inside. He must have been guessing inside, because he was way out in front of it and pulled it.*

I watched the ball, trying to judge how deep it was hit. I realized it didn't quite have it, but I envisioned a double. Piniella seemed confused. I wanted the two runs. I felt 4–0 in my heart.

LOU PINIELLA: *Guidry wasn't as quick as usual. Munson told me that his breaking ball was hanging, so I played Lynn a few steps closer to the line than usual. I saw the ball leave the bat and then I lost it in the sun. I went to the place where I thought the ball would land. I didn't catch it cleanly, but kind of in the top of my glove. It would have short-hopped to the wall and stayed in play. Without any doubt two runs would have scored. But it was catchable.*

PINIELLA'S CATCH was an indignity. He had appeared bollixed and off-balance, lurching about under the glaring sun in the rightfield corner. That Lynn had unleashed so potent a smash and would go unrewarded, that I would go unrewarded, that the game itself would remain within the Yankees' reach, struck me as an ominous signal that things would not, after all, work out in the end. The game and the season—the losses in Toronto, Butch Hobson's floating bone chips, Rich Burleson's injury just before the All-Star break, a thousand things that had created this day in the first place—all had spun through the early autumn sky with the ball that Lynn had struck, the ball that Piniella held in his bare right hand all the way in from rightfield, across the diamond, through the third-base coach's box and into the dark sanctuary of the visitors' dugout. He had caught it, he had held on to it, he held it even now sitting there on the bench. The play could not be called back. The score still stood at 2–0.

In the top of the seventh inning I went into the solitary phone booth on the first-base side of the roof. I dialed my secret air-check number, realizing it was the first time I had ever sought it out as a local investment.

It was a Jim Woods inning, which frightened me all the more. Woods, like a child fumbling with a lie, cannot hide the truth of any Red Sox situation. One can tell immediately if Boston is in a favorable or thorny position, if the game is lost or won, or even tied.

Even with a 2–0 lead, Woods was somber. For Pittsburgh, New York, St. Louis, Oakland and Boston, Woods had been broadcasting games ever since Dwight Eisenhower's presidency. The importance of Piniella's catch had not eluded him. Then he was presented with singles by Chris Chambliss and Roy White that brought the lead run to the plate. I had dialed in for the security of the radio's familiar rhythm and was suddenly faced with potential disaster.

I hung up on Woods and ran back to the photographers' box, taking the steps of the ladder two at a time. Jim Spencer was pinch-hitting for the Yankees. I remembered a Spencer home run earlier in the year. Could it have been against the Angels? Jim Spencer, of all people. Spencer hit the ball fairly well to left, but Yaz was with it all the way.

Two outs.

Bucky Dent.

I had a fleeting thought that, through the years, Yankee shortstops had hurt the Red Sox at the plate. Inconsequential men—Fred Stanley, Gene Michael, Jim Mason—no power, .230 hitters. Shortstops. Bucky Dent.

I leaned way over the railing, as if trying to catch a foul ball hit just below me. I was motionless, except for my shaking hands.

Dent fouled the second pitch off his shin.

Delay.

I studied Torrez. He stood behind the mound rubbing up the new ball. He did not pace, he did not turn to examine the outfield. He just rubbed up the new ball and stared in at Dent, who was bent over to the left of the plate, his shin being cared for.

MIKE TORREZ: *I lost some of my concentration during the delay. It was about four minutes, but it felt like an hour. I had thought that they'd pinch-hit for Dent with maybe Jay Johnstone or Cliff Johnson. I felt good. I just wanted to get going. That first inning really helped. My concentration was there, especially on Munson. During the delay, I thought slider on the next pitch. But Fisk and me were working so well together, I went along with his call for a fastball. When Dent hit it, I thought we were out of the inning. I started to walk off the mound. I could see Yaz patting his glove.*

I watched, hanging over the railing. I had seen too many fly balls from the roof seats on the first-base side to be fooled now. This fly ball by a Yankee shortstop with an aching shin was clearly a home run. I had no doubt from the start.

When the ball struck the net, Yastrzemski's whole body trembled for an instant. Then he froze, every muscle drawn tight in excruciating frustration. I said out loud, "God, no! God, no!"

In minutes the Yankees had scored another run.

I climbed the ladder and walked slowly to the press room. I went into the lavatory, closed the door to the one stall and sat on the toilet with my head in my hands, wishing there were a lid on the seat. It was entirely quiet, as if I were alone in the stadium.

"You are emotionally penniless," a girl had shouted at me years before from behind a slammed and locked bathroom door.

That is what came into my mind in my own locked cubicle.

I also thought to leave the park, to take a walk, to just go away. Instead

I decided to change locations, to venture to the far reaches of the left-field roof, out near the wall.

A couple of kids were running mindlessly around, chasing each other as if they were on a beach. They pushed their way through clusters of writers and photographers who were all standing, because there were no seats to be had. I sat down on the roof and crossed my legs. I was no more than a foot from the lip, which was unprotected by a railing or other barrier.

The wind had picked up. Shadows dominated the field, except in right and right center. I noticed that the clouds were just a bit thicker. A rain delay. Would the game revert to the last complete inning? A seven-hour delay and finally a decision. Red Sox win 2–0. I saw it as the only possibility. It had to rain right at this moment. Torrentially. Monumentally. Before the new Yankee pitcher could complete this last of the seventh. The new Yankee pitcher was Gossage, and Bob Bailey was preparing to pinch-hit against him.

Bob Bailey!

I bowed my head.

GOOSE GOSSAGE: *When I saw Bailey coming up, I said to myself, with all respect to Bob, "Thank you."*

Bailey looked at strike three and went away, out of my life, off the team, out of the league, out of the country, away, away.

Reggie Jackson homered in the eighth. I affected bemusement as I watched him round the bases. I thought: Let's see, just for the fun of it, how big it's going to be. What does it matter, anyway? It's only a game.

Official bemusement on the leftfield roof.

A leadoff double by Jerry Remy in the bottom of the eighth. How nice.

A Rice fly-ball out.

Five outs left. It's only a game.

Three consecutive singles.

The score was 5–4, Yankees' favor, with Red Sox runners on first and second. Hobson and Scott, two righthanded hitters, would now face the righthanded Gossage. My bemusement vanished. I stood.

I felt that Hobson had a real crack at it, that he is good two-strike hitter and that he would surely be hitting with two strikes before very long. I felt that if they let Scott hit I would leap from the roof in a suicidal protest. The Boomer vs. Gossage was too pathetic for me even to contemplate.

Hobson's fly-ball out to right set up the Boomer vs. Gossage. I did not leap from the roof. I sat down and rested my chin on my knees. I believe I smiled at the Boomer. I know I said aloud, "Surprise me, baby."

The Boomer did not surprise. Gossage took only a minute or so to strike him out.

I remained motionless as the teams changed sides and as they played the top of the ninth, about which I can remember little. It seems to me that Paul Blair got a hit and Dick Drago pitched. There was base-running of some kind, activity around second. I know there was no scoring.

Just before the start of the last of the ninth, I imagined myself swimming in an enormous pool. I was in the desert in early summer. I thought that it was the dry heat that enabled me to move through the water so rapidly. I hardly had to move my arms or legs in order to cover the length of the pool. It was possible to swim forever.

I spotted Dwight Evans striding quickly, intensely to the plate. For whom was he hitting?

He was hitting for Frank Duffy, who had replaced Jack Brohamer, who had been hit for by Bailey. Duffy had played third in the top of the ninth, and I hadn't even noticed.

Evans was hitting for Duffy.

Why hadn't Evans come to bat instead of Bailey in the seventh?

And where was Garry Hancock? A lefthanded hitter, a slim Gary Geiger kind of guy. Where was Garry Hancock?

It looked to me as if Evans nearly got a hold of one. He missed, by God knows how small a portion of the ball, and flied routinely to left.

Gossage walked Burleson as if it had been his intention. That would give Rice a turn at bat, providing Remy stayed out of the double play.

Remy lined a shot to right. My thought was . . . double play. Piniella catches the ball and throws to Chambliss with Burleson miles off first.

LOU PINIELLA: *I didn't want the ball hit to me. It was a nightmare out there in the sun. I kept telling Blair in center to help me. When Remy hit it, I saw it for a second and then lost it. I knew it would bounce, so I moved back three steps to prevent it from bouncing over me to the wall. I moved to my left a piece. I decoyed Burleson. I didn't want him to know I couldn't see it. If Burleson had tried for third, he would have been out. There's no doubt about it. My throw was accurate and, for me, it had good stuff on it.*

JERRY REMY: *I think Burleson did 100% the right thing. It would have been very close at third. He had to play it safe. I knew I had a hit, but Rick had to hold up for just a moment between first and second. So why gamble?*

I knelt on the roof. I thought, is this actually happening? First and second, one out, last of the ninth. And Rice and Yaz. Is this actually happening?

GOOSE GOSSAGE: *I tried to calm myself down by thinking of the mountains of Colorado, the mountains that I love. I thought that the worst thing that could happen to me was that I'd be in those mountains tomorrow. I had once hiked to a lake in the mountains. It was really quiet. I had pictured seats on the mountainsides. Thousands and thousand of seats looking down on a ball field next to the lake. I imagined myself pitching in front of all those people in the mountains.*

I didn't think Yastrzemski had a chance. I thought about it being late in the day, about his being fatigued, about how he wouldn't get around on Gossage's fastball. My hopes rode with Rice.

LOU PINIELLA: *I played Rice in right center, not deep. It cut the angle of the sun. I saw the ball clean. I caught it maybe 25 feet from the fence.*

GOOSE GOSSAGE: *When I was warming up before I came in in the seventh, I imagined myself pitching to Yaz with two outs in the ninth. The Red Sox would have a couple guys on base, and it would be Yaz and me. When it turned out that way, I thought, here it is. It was ESP.*

I screamed at Yaz from the leftfield roof, "Bunt, goddam it!" I even waved my arms, thinking that I might catch his eye. He'd call time out and wander out to leftfield. "What did you say?" he'd shout up at me. "Bunt!" I'd yell back. "Interesting," he'd say.

Then Yaz would lay down a beauty.

Burleson, who had taken third after Rice's fly ball, would easily score the tying run.

Carl Yastrzemski, nearly my age.

I gazed down at him through tears.

I thought: Freeze this minute. Freeze it right here. How unspeakably beautiful it is. Everyone, reach out and touch it.

AUGUST 20, 1973

⌘

No Place in
The Shade

BY MARK KRAM

*Cool Papa Bell could run, hit, field and all that jazz, but for him and
other players in the old Negro leagues, life was a bittersweet gig.*

I N THE LANGUAGE OF JAZZ, A "GIG" IS AN EVENING OF WORK;
sometimes sweet, sometimes sour, take the gig as it comes, for
who knows when the next will be. It means bread and butter
first, but a whole lot of things have always seemed to ride with the
word: drifting blue light, the bouquet from leftover drinks, spells of odd
dialogue, and most of all a sense of pain and limbo. For more than anything the word means *black*, down-and-out black, leavin'-home black, what-
ya-gonna-do-when-ya-git-there black, tired of-choppin'-cotton-gonna-find-
me-a place-in-de-shade black.

Big shade fell coolly on only a few. It never got to James Thomas Bell,
or Cool Papa Bell as he was known in Negro baseball, that lost caravan
that followed the sun. Other blacks, some of them musicians who worked
jazz up from the South, would feel the touch of fame, or once in a while
have the thought that their names meant something to people outside their
own. But if you were black and played baseball, well, look for your name
only in the lineup before each game, or else you might not even see it there
if you kept on leanin' and dreamin'.

Black baseball was a stone-hard gig. Unlike jazz, it had no white intellectuals to hymn it, no slumming aristocracy to taste it. It was three games a day, sometimes in three different towns miles apart. It was the heat and fumes and bounces from buses that moved your stomach up to your throat and it was greasy meals at fly-papered diners at three a.m. and uniforms that were seldom off your back. "We slept with 'em on sometimes," says Papa, "but there never was 'nough sleep. We got so we could sleep standin' up or catch a nod in the dugout."

Only a half-mad seer—not any of the blacks who worked the open prairies and hidden ball yards in each big city—could have envisioned what would happen one day. The players knew a black man would cross the color line that was first drawn by the sudden hate of Cap Anson back in 1883, yet no one was fool enough to think that some bright, scented day way off among the gods of Cooperstown they would hear their past blared out across the field and would know that who they were and what they did would never be invisible again.

When that time comes for Papa Bell, few will comprehend what he did during all those gone summers. The mass audience will not be able to relate to him, to assemble an image of him, to measure him against his peers as they do the white player. The old ones like Papa have no past. They were minstrels, separated from record books, left as the flower in Grey's *Elegy* to "waste its sweetness on the desert air." Comparisons will have to do: Josh Gibson, the Babe Ruth of the blacks; Buck Leonard, the Lou Gehrig of his game; and Cool Papa Bell—who was he?

A comparison will be hard to find for Papa. His friend Tweed, whom Papa calls *the* Black Historian, a title most agreeable to Tweed, says that you have to go all the way back to Willie Keeler for Papa's likeness. Papa's way was cerebral, improvisational; he was a master of the little things, the nuances that are the ambrosia of baseball for those who care to understand the game. Power is stark, power shocks, it is the stuff of immortality, but Papa's jewellike skills were the meat of shoptalk for 28 winters.

Arthritic and weary, Papa quit the circuit in 1950 at age 47, ending a career that began in 1922. During that time he had been the essence of black baseball, which had a panache all its own. It was an intimate game: the extra base, the drag bunt; a game of daring instinct, rather than one from the hidebound book. Some might say that it lacked discipline, but if so, it can also be said that never has baseball been played more artfully, or more joyously. "Before a game," says Papa, "one of our big old pitchers, he'd say,

'Jist git me a coupla runs, that's all.' You see, we played tricky ball, thinkin' all the time: we git a run they got to git two to beatcha. Right?"

The yellow pages of Tweed's scrapbooks don't tell much about the way it was, and they don't reveal much about Papa, either; box scores never explain. They can't chart the speed of Papa Bell. "Papa Bell," says Satchel Paige, "why he was so fast he could turn out the light and jump in bed before the room got dark!" Others also embellish: he could hit a hard ground ball through the box and get hit with the ball as he slid into second; he was so fast that he once stole two bases on the same pitch. "People kin sure talk it, can't they?" says Papa.

Papa says he did steal two bases on one pitch, which was a pitchout. "The catcher, why he was so surprised the way I was runnin' that he just held the ball," says Papa. "I ask him later what he doin' holdin' that ball, and he say he didn't know, 'cept he *never* seen a man run like that before in his life." It is also a reliable fact that once in Chicago, on a mushy field, he circled the bases in 13.1 seconds, two-fifths faster than Evar Swanson's major league record. "On a dry field," he says, "I once done it in 12 flat."

Papa could run all right and he could hit and field as well. He played a shallow centerfield, even more so than Willie Mays when he broke in. "It doesn't matter where he plays," Pie Traynor once said. "He can go a country mile for a ball." As a hitter Bell had distance, but mainly he strove to hit the ball into holes; he could hit a ball through the hole in a fence, or drag a bunt as if it were on a string in his hand. Bell never hit below .308, and on one occasion when he was hitting .390 on the last day of the season he gave up his batting title; he was 43 at the time.

"Jackie Robinson had just signed with the Dodgers, and Monte Irvin was our best player," says Papa. "I gave up my title so Monte would have a better chance at the majors. That was the way we thought then. We'd do anything to get a player up there. In the final two weeks of the season, a doubleheader, I still needed a few times at bat. I was short of times at bat to qualify for the title. I got two hits in the first game and sat out the second game. The fans were mad, but they didn't know what we were trying to do. After the season I was supposed to git the $200 for the title anyway, but my owner, he say, 'Well look, Cool, Irvin won it, didn't he?' They wouldn't give me the $200. Baseball was never much for me makin' money."

Papa Bell earned $90 a month his first year back in 1922. He would never make more than $450 a month, although his ability was such that later he would be ranked on Jackie Robinson's alltime team in the same outfield with Henry Aaron and Willie Mays. Bill Veeck, who also saw Bell play, puts him right up there with Tris Speaker, Willie Mays and Joe DiMaggio. "Cool Papa was one of the most magical players I've ever seen," says Veeck.

The money never bothered Papa; it was a game, a summer away from the packinghouse. " 'Cept one time," adds Papa, "when one team told me to pay my expenses from St. Louis to Memphis. They'd give it to me back, they said. I git there, and they say no. Owner of the club was a dentist. I say to 'em I didn't come down here 'cause I got a toothache. So I went back home. Owners are owners, whether they blue or green."

Papa spent the winters in the packinghouse until he learned of places like Havana and Vera Cruz and Cuidad Trujillo, which competitively sought players from the Negro League. He will never forget that winter in Cuidad Trujillo. It was in 1937, he thinks, when Trujillo was in political trouble. He had to distract the people, and there was no better way than to give them a pennant. First, Trujillo had his agents all but kidnap Satchel Paige from a New Orleans hotel. Then he used Paige to recruit the edge in talent from the States: namely, Papa Bell and Josh Gibson who, along with Orlando Cepeda, the storied father of the current Cepeda, gave the dictator a pat hand.

The look of that lineup still did not ease Trujillo's anxiety. "He wanted us to stay in pajamas," says Papa, "and all our meals were served to us in our rooms, and guards circled our living quarters." Thousands would show up at the park just to watch Trujillo's club work out, and with each game tension grew. "We all knew the situation was serious, but it wasn't until later that we heard how bad it was," says Papa. "We found out that as far as Trujillo was concerned we either won or we were gonna lose big. That means he was going to kill us." They never did meet Trujillo. They saw him only in his convertible in the streets, all cold and white in that suit of his that seemed to shimmer in the hot sun. "A very frightenin' man," says Papa.

Trujillo got his pennant and his election. A picture of Papa's, taken near a large stream, shows the team celebrating; the dictator had sent them out of the city—along with their fares home and many cases of beer. It had been a hard buck, but then again it had never been easy, whether it was down in Santo Domingo or back up with the St. Louis Stars or the Pittsburgh Crawfords or the Homestead Grays or the Chicago American Giants. East or West, North or South, it was always the same: No shade anywhere as the bus rattled along, way down in Egypt land.

Papa took the bumps better than most. Some, like Josh Gibson, died too young; some got lost to the nights. *Coolpapa*, as his name is pronounced by those who came from the South as he did, well, Coolpapa, he just "went on movin' on." That was the way his mother taught him back in Starkville, Miss., where he was born in 1903; look, listen and never pounce, those were her words, and all of them spelled survival. Work, too, was another word, and Papa says, "If I didn't know anythin', I knew how to work."

Long days in the sun and well after the night slipped across the cotton fields, all that Papa and his friends could talk about was "going off." Papa says, "One day some boy would be there along with us and then he'd be gone. 'Where'd he go?' I'd ask. 'Why that boy, he done gone off!' someone'd say. Next you'd see that fella, why he'd be back home with a hat on and a big, bright suit and shiny shoes and a jingle in his pocket." They would talk of the great cities and what they would have when they, too, went off and only sometimes would they hear about baseball. An old, well-traveled trainman used to sit under a tree with them on Sundays and tell them of the stars he had seen.

"Why, there's this here Walter Johnson," the trainman would say. "He kin strike out anybody who picks up a bat!"

"Is that right?" Papa would ask.

"Sure enough, boy. You'd think I'd lie? Then there is two old boys named Ty Cobb and Honus Wagner. Well, they don't miss a ball and they never strike out!"

"Never miss a ball?" gasped Papa. "Never strike out? Is that right?"

"I'm tellin' ya, boy. I've been to the cities and I know!"

"Well, *mmmm, mmmm,*" Papa would shake his head. "Only one thing botherin' me. What happen when this here Walter Johnson is pitchin', and these other two boys are battin'?"

"Y'all go on!" the old man would yell, jumping up. "Y'all leave me alone. I'm not talkin' anymore. Don't none of ya believe. I should know. I've been to the cities!"

By 16 Papa was up north in St. Louis with several of his brothers and sisters, who were already in the packinghouse. "Didn't want to know 'bout ball then," says Papa. "Jist wanted to work like a man." His brother suggested that he play ball on Sundays. "'James,' he said, 'you a natural. You throw that knuckleball, and there ain't nobody going to hit it.'"

Soon he was getting $20 to pitch, until finally he was facing the lethal St. Louis Stars of the Negro National League. "They were a tough club," says Papa. "And mean! They had a fella named Steel Arm Dicky. Used to make moonshine as mean as he was on the side. His boss killed him when he began to believe Steel Arm weren't turnin' in all the profits."

Bell impressed the Stars, and they asked him to join them. "All our players were major-leaguers," says Papa. "Didn't have the bench to be as good like them for a whole season. We only carried 14, 15 players. But over a short series we could have taken the big-leaguers. That October, I recall, we played the Detroit Tigers three games and won two of them. But old Cobb wasn't with them, 'cause 12 years before a black team whipped him pretty good, and he wouldn't play against blacks anymore. Baseball was all you thought of then. Always thinkin' how to do things another way. Curve a ball on a 3–2, bunt and run in the first innin'. That's how we beat big league teams. Not that we had the best men, but we outguessed them in short series. It's a guessing game. There's a lot of unwritten baseball, ya know."

The Stars folded under the Depression. Papa hit the road. An outfielder now, he was even more in demand. He finally began the last phase of his career with the Washington Homestead Grays; with Josh Gibson and Buck Leonard and Bell, it was one of the most powerful clubs in the black league's history, or anybody's history for that matter. "I was 'bout 45 then," says Papa. "Kinda sick. Had arthritis and was so stiff I couldn't run at times. They used to have to put me in a hot tub. I had to git good and warm before I could move." Yet, he had enough left to convince Jackie Robinson that he should never try to make it as a shortstop

"It was all over the place that Jackie was going to sign with the Dodgers," says Papa. "All us old fellas didn't think he could make it at short. He couldn't go to his right too good. He'd give it a backhand and then plant his right leg and throw. He always had to take two extra steps. We was worried. He miss this chance, and who knows when we'd git another chance? You know they turned him down up in Boston. So I made up my mind to try and show him he should try for another spot in the infield. One night I must've knocked couple hundred ground balls to his right and I beat the throw to first every time. Jackie smiled. He got the message. He played a lot of games in the majors, only one of 'em at short."

Papa was named to manage the Kansas City Monarchs' B team in 1948, the agreement being that he would get one third of the sale price for any player who was developed by him and sold to the majors. He had two prospects in mind for the Browns. "But the Browns," says Papa, shaking his head, "didn't want them. I then went to the Cardinals, and they say they don't care, either, and I think to myself, 'My, if they don't want these boys, they don't want nobody.' " The Monarchs eventually sold the pair: Ernie Banks and Elston Howard. "I didn't get anything," says Papa. "They said I didn't have a contract. They gave me a basket of fruit. A basket of fruit! Baseball was never much for me makin' money."

Life began all over for Papa. He took a job at the city hall in St. Louis as a custodian and then a night watchman. For the next 22 years the routine was the same, and only now and then could he go to a Cardinal game. He would pay his way in and sit there in the sun with his lunch long before the game began; to those who wondered about him, he was just a Mr. Bell, a watchman. He'd watch those games intently, looking for tiny flaws like a diamond cutter. He never said much to anyone, but then one day he was asked by some Dodgers to help Maury Wills. "He could run," he says. "I wanted to help." He waited for Wills at the players' gate and introduced himself quietly.

"Maybe you heard of me," Papa said, "maybe not. It don't matter. But I'd like to help you."

Wills just looked at him, as Papa became uneasy.

"When you're on base," said Papa, "get those hitters of yours to stand deep in the box. That way the catcher, he got to back up. That way you goin' to git an extra step all the time."

"I hadn't thought of that," said Wills, who went on to steal 104 bases.

"Well," Papa smiled, "that's the kind of ball we played in our league. Be seein' you, Mr. Wills. Didn't mean to bother you."

After that year Papa seldom went to the ball park anymore. He had become a sick man, and when he walked his arthritic left side seemed to be frozen. It was just his job now. In the afternoons he would walk up to the corner and see what the people were up to, or sit silently in his living room turning the pages of his books of pictures: all the old faces with the blank eyes; all of those many different, baggy uniforms. There is one picture with his wife Clarabelle on a bench in Havana, she with a bright new dress on, he with a white suit on, and if you look at that picture hard enough it is as if you can hear some faraway white-suit, bright-dress music.

Nights were spent at city hall, making his rounds, listening to the sound of radio baseball by the big window, or just the sound of the hours when winter mornings moved across the window. When it was icy, he would wait for the old people to come and he would help them up the steps. Often, say about three a.m., he would be looking out the window, out across to the park where the bums would be sleeping, their wine bottles as sentries, and he'd wait for their march on the hall. They would come up those steps and place their faces up against the window next to his face and beg to be let in where it was warm.

"We're citizens, old Bell, let us in," they would yell.

"I know," Papa would say.

"It's cold out here," they would say.

"I know," he would answer.

"No, you don't, you. . . . " And Papa would just look away, thinking how cold it was outside, listening to all that racket going on out there, trying to think of all the things that would leave him indifferent to those wretched figures. Then it would be that he sometimes would think of baseball, the small things he missed about it, things that would pop into his mind for no reason: a certain glove, the feel of a ball and bat, a buttoning of a shirt; the sunlight. "You try to git that game out your mind," he says, "but it never leaves ya. Somethin' about it never leaves ya."

Papa Bell is 70 now. He lives on Dickson Street in North St. Louis, a neighborhood under siege: vacant, crumbling houses, bars where you could get your throat cut if you even walked in the wrong way, packs of sky-high dudes looking for a score. They have picked on Papa's house a couple of times, so now when he feels something in the air, hears a rustle outside of his door, he will go to the front window and sit there for long hours with a shotgun and a pistol in his lap. "They don't mess with Papa anymore," says his friend Tweed, looking over at Papa sitting in his city hall retirement chair. "It's a reclinin' one," says Tweed. "Show 'im how it reclines, Papa."

Now the two of them, black historian Tweed and Papa, who sits in his chair like a busted old jazz musician, torn around the edges but straight with dignity, spend much time together in Papa's living room. They mull over old box scores, over all the clippings in Tweed's portable archives. They try to bring continuity of performance to a man's record that began when nobody cared. They argue, they fuss over a figure here, they assemble pictures to be signed for people who write and say that they hear he will be going into the Hall of Fame; the days are sweet.

"Can't believe it," says Tweed. "Kin you, Papa? Papa Bell in de Hall of Fame. The fastest man who ever played the game."

"Ain't happened yet," cautions Papa, adjusting his tall and lean figure in his chair.

"Tell me, Papa," says Tweed. "How's it goin' to feel? De Hall of Fame . . . *mmmm, mmmm.*

"Knew a fella blowed the horn once," says Papa. "He told me. He say, 'Ya got to take de gigs as dey come.' "

JULY 23, 1956

❧

'Perfect Day—A Day Of Prowess'

BY ROBERT FROST

*The All-Star Game is an All-American affair, especially when it's
in Washington, D.C. Appropriately, SI invited America's greatest living
poet to sit in the grandstand as guest columnist.*

AMERICANS WOULD RATHER WATCH A GAME THAN play a game. Statement true or false? Why, as to these thousands here today to watch the game and not play it, probably not one man-jack but has himself played the game in his athletic years and got himself so full of bodily memories of the experience (what we farmers used to call kinesthetic images) that he can hardly sit still. We didn't burst into cheers immediately, but an exclamation swept the crowd as if we felt it all over in our muscles when Boyer at third made two impossible catches, one a stab at a grounder and the other a leap at a line drive that may have saved the day for the National League. We all winced with fellow feeling when Berra got the foul tip on the ungloved fingers of his throwing hand.

As for the ladies present, they are here as next friends to the men, but even they have, many of them, pitching arms and batting eyes. Many of them would prefer a league ball to a pumpkin. You wouldn't want to catch them with bare hands. I mustn't count it against them that I envision one in the outfield at a picnic with her arms spread wide open for a fly ball as for a descending man-angel. Luckily it didn't hit her in the mouth, which was open too, or it might have hurt her beauty. It missed her entirely.

How do I know all this and with what authority do I speak? Have I not been written up as a pitcher in *The New Yorker* by the poet, Raymond Holden?—though the last full game I pitched in was on the grounds of Rockingham Park in Salem, New Hampshire, before it was turned into a race track. If I have shone at all in the all-star games at Breadloaf in Vermont it has been as a relief pitcher with a soft ball I despise like a picture window.

Moreover I once took an honorary degree at Williams College along with a very famous pitcher, Ed Lewis, who will be remembered and found in the record to have led the National League in pitching quite a long time ago. His degree was not for pitching. Neither was mine. His was for presiding with credit over the University of New Hampshire and the Massachusetts College of Agriculture. My great friendship for him probably accounts for my having made a trivial 10¢ bet on the National League today. He was a Welshman from Utica who, from having attended *eisteddfods* at Utica with his father, a bard, had like another Welsh friend of mine, Edward Thomas, in England, come to look on a poem as a performance one had to win.

Chicago was my first favorite team because Chicago seemed the nearest city in the league to my original home town, San Francisco. I have conquered that prejudice. But I mean to see if the captain of it, Anson, my boyhood hero, is in the Hall of Fame at Cooperstown where he belongs.

May I add that one of my unfulfilled promises on earth was to my fellow in art, Alfred Kreymborg, of an epic poem some day about a ball batted so hard by Babe Ruth that it never came back, but got to going round and round the world like a satellite. I meant to begin something like this:

> It was nothing to nothing at the end of the tenth
> And the prospects good it would last to the nth.

It needs a lot of work before it can take rank with *Casey at the Bat*.

In other words, some baseball is the fate of us all. For my part I am never more at home in America than at a baseball game like this in Clark Griffith's gem of a field, gem small, in beautiful weather in the capital of the country and my side winning. Here Walter Johnson flourished, who once threw a silver dollar across the Potomac (where not too wide) in emulation of George Washington, and here Gabby Street caught the bulletlike ball dropped from the top of George Washington's monument. It is the time and the place. And I have with me as consultant the well-known symbolist, Howard Schmitt of Buffalo, to mind my baseball slang and interpret the incidentals. The first player comes to the bat, Temple of the Redlegs, swinging two bats as he comes, the meaning of which or moral of which, I find on application to my consultant, is that we must always arrange to have just been doing something beforehand a good deal harder than what we are just going to do.

But when I asked him a moment later what it symbolized when a ball got batted into the stands and the people instead of dodging in terror fought each other fiercely to get and keep it, Howard bade me hold on; there seemed to be a misunderstanding between us. When he accepted the job it was orally; he didn't mean to represent himself as a symbolist in the highbrow or middle-brow sense of the word, that is as a collegiate expounder of the double-entendre for college classes; he was a common ordinary cymbalist in a local band somewhere out on the far end of the Eeryie Canal. We were both honest men. He didn't want to be taken for a real professor any more than I wanted to be taken for a real sport. His utmost wish was to contribute to the general noise when home runs were made. He knew they would be the most popular hits of the day. And they were—four of them from exactly the four they were expected from: Musial, Williams, Mays and Mantle. The crowd went wild four times.

Howard's story would have been more plausible if he had brought his cymbals with him. I saw I would have to take care of the significances myself. This comes of not having got it in writing. The moral is always get it in writing.

Time was when I saw nobody on the field but the players. If I saw the umpire at all it was as an enemy for not taking my side. I may never have wanted to see bottles thrown at him so that he had to be taken out by the police. Still I often regarded him with the angry disfavor that the Democratic Party showed the Supreme Court in the '30s and other parties have shown it in other crises in our history. But now grown psychological, shading 100, I saw him as a figure of justice, who stood forth alone to be judged as a judge by people and players with whom he wouldn't last a week if suspected of the least lack of fairness or the least lack of faith in the possibility of fairness. I was touched by his loneliness and glad it was relieved a little by his being five in number, five in one so to speak, *e pluribus unum*. Right there in front of me for reassurance is the umpire brought up perhaps in the neighborhood of Boston who can yet be depended upon not to take sides today for or against the American League or the Boston Red Sox belong to. I saw one batter linger perceptibly to say something to the umpire for calling him out on a third strike. I didn't hear what the batter said. One of the hardest things to accept as just is a called third strike.

It has been a day of prowess in spite of its being a little on the picnic side and possibly not as desperately fought as it might be in a World Series. Prowess in about equal strength for both sides. Each team made 11 hits, two home runs and not a single error. The day was perfect, the scene perfect, the play perfect. Prowess of course comes first, the ability to perform with success in games, in the arts and, come right down to it, in battle. The nearest of kin to the artists in college where we all become bachelors of arts are their fellow performers in baseball, football and tennis. That's why I am so particular college athletics should be kept from corruption. They are close to the soul of culture. At any rate the Greeks thought so. Justice is a close second to prowess. When displayed toward each other by antagonists in war and peace, it is known as the nobility of noble natures. And I mustn't forget courage, for there is neither prowess nor justice without it. My fourth, if it is important enough in comparison to be worth bringing in, is knowledge, the mere information we can't get too much of and can't ever get enough of, we complain, before going into action.

As I say, I never feel more at home in America than at a ball game, be it in park or in sandlot. Beyond this I know not. And dare not.

The Ballad Of Joe Moock

BY STEVE RUSHIN

Sailors have the Bermuda Triangle; the Mets have third base. When the author composed this epic tribute, the New Yorkers had, in 36 years, employed 112 different men at the hot corner, none of them all that hot.

IN THEIR 36-YEAR HISTORY THE NEW YORK METS HAVE employed an astonishing 112 men at third base. In other words, the Mets change third basemen as often as most sportswriters change their underwear. Which is to say, as many as five times a year, whether they need to or not.

With that in mind, we commissioned one such housebound scribe to pen a Homeric epic on the Mets' third base jinx. Composed in secret (code name: the Flushing Project), the result is a bold new genre—part Mother Goose, part Dr. Seuss, you might call it Mother Seuss. Or Dr. Goose. Whatever the case, we think it will become an important convention in journalism: the epic nursery rhyme.

> WALLY BACKMAN
> Was a lousy third sackman
> Like 100-odd other Met vets—
> From FELIX MANTILLA
> To BOBBY BONILLA,
> Who cursed like a man with Tourette's.

GARY CARTER
Made third base look harder
Than walking on fresh-waxed linoleum.
BUTCH HUSKEY
Was so often rusty
He whirlpool-bathed in Rust-Oleum.

TEDDY MARTINEZ
And CHICO FERNANDEZ:
Together they gave the Mets nada.
One part rum
And two parts bum
Make a FERNANDO VINA colada.

BILL SPIERS
Seldom inspires
Comparisons to those who played well.
HUBIE BROOKS
Played like a Brooks—
Not Robinson, sadly, but Mel.

CHUCK HILLER
Was worse than KEITH MILLER
Who was worse than ELLIOTT MADDOX.
The two Mr. EDS*
Who played third for the Mets
Were quickly returned to their paddocks.

BOB ASPROMONTE
Was not the full 'monte—
That was his big brother Ken.
TATUM and GRAHAM
Had hands made of ham.
RICH PUIG belonged in a pen.

Ed Bressoud and Ed Charles

TIM BOGAR
Was no Humphrey Bogart—
He was not even Lauren Bacall.
And CARLOS BAERGA
Needed Viagra
Just to get wood on the ball.

JACK HEIDEMANN
Was a Flintstone vitamin—
A man who got eaten alive.
As for WAYNE GARRETT,
He never could snare it—
His vanity plates read E-5.

AMOS OTIS
Eluded the notice
Of baseball's elite Hall of Fame.
While ROD KANEHL
Caused Stengel to squeal,
"Can't anyone here play this game?"

JUNIOR NOBOA
Was not a strong throwa,
He played with the greatest of E's.
BILL PECOTA
Had a strong oda
Reminiscent of moldering cheese.

MIKE CUBBAGE
Excelled at ball flubbage—
He simply could not find the handle.
But TIM FOLI—
After two shots of Stoli—
Looked almost as good as LEN RANDLE.

JOSE MORENO
(For all that we know)
Was really his big sister, Rita.

A NAPOLEON (Danny),
An ALEXANDER (named Manny)—
Neither man was a great leada.

CHICO WALKER,
Clean out your locker,
You're as versatile as a cadaver.
JERRY GROTE,
You reek like a roadie
Who's toured for a year with Blues Traveler.

MATT FRANCO
(In Spanish, "El Ranko")
Was inexpressibly vile.
Along with BOB PFEIL
The two had a style
Historians call Rank-and-Pfeil.

SHAWN GILBERT
Not unlike Dilbert,
Simply could not please his bosses.
They knew for more wins
They'd need fewer DOUG FLYNNS,
And fewer JOE FOYS and BOB KLAUSES.

JEFF KENT
Was prudent to rent:
He was in Queens for what seemed like a day.
PHIL MANKOWSKI
May I have your house key?
It seems you've been waived away.

A. ESPINOZA,
Like Lou (the Toe) Groza,
Was famous for booting the ball.
AARON LEDESMA
Had Al Gore's charisma
And the arm of a Gore—Gore Vidal.

RON HUNT—
Shall we be blunt?—
Was not someone we'd pay to go see.
But BOB BAILOR
Was no total failure:
At least he was not JIM FREGOSI.

TIM TEUFEL—
Though German for "devil"—
Still inspired no terror.
JASON HARDTKE?
We're pretty sure he's
A typographical error.

DON ZIMMER
Has X-rays that shimmer
With stainless-steel plates in his noggin.
CRAIG SHIPLEY
Went downhill so quickly
He must have used a toboggan.

KEVIN COLLINS,
Unbothered by pollens,
Was allergic instead to success.
Nor was BILL ALMON
An accomplished groundballman—
He was swiftly shown the egress.

TOMMIE REYNOLDS
Should have been kenneled
And if you think he was a dog,
Then what of AL WEIS
Who couldn't catch flies
If you turned him into a frog?

TUCKER ASHFORD,
Like a drink on a dashboard,
Lasted only about a half minute.

CLINT HURDLE
Wore fame like a girdle—
He never seemed to fit in it.

PUMPSIE GREEN
Had a name half obscene
And so, in a way, did STEVE SPRINGER.
DAVE KINGMAN
Had a terrible swing, man
But could he ever hit a long dinger.

On AMADO SAMUEL
It is best not to dwell,
He will never hear fans chanting, "Sammy!"
And soft KEVIN MITCHELL,
The slightest leg twitch'll
Cause him to blow out his hammy.

TOM O'MALLEY
Inspired no rally
When stepping into the box.
And then there's FRANK THOMAS,
Who wasn't—we promise—
The one who's on the White Sox.

TED SCHREIBER
Is not a subscriber
So we can say he was swine.
To his kemosabe
A young man named Bobby,
We say, "Don't be our VALENTINE."

KEN BOYER
Like a bad lawyer
Never prepared a defense.
MACKEY SASSER
Was so large in the ass, for
Undies he wore circus tents.

GARY KOLB
Could have been sold
As a bobble-handed Mets' doll.
CHARLEY NEAL
Was not a trained seal:
He had no nose for the ball.

JOHN STEARNS
Had hot-corner burns
Over 90% of his body.
LARRY BURRIGHT
Looked skyward one night
And pleaded, "Beam me up, Scotty."

CHRIS DONNELS
And Chris O'Donnell—
The two have something in common:
Like KELVIN CHAPMAN,
Donnels was crap, man,
While Chris O'Donnell played Robin.

If SAMMY DRAKE
Were a T-bone steak,
He'd require a lot of A-1.
Whereas S. FERRER
Would be medium rare:
Nothing he did was well done.

ALEX TREVINO
Resembled El Nino
In the sense that both of them blew.
If CLIFF COOK
Was a bear in a book
They'd call him Losie the Pooh.

AL MORAN
Is in the Koran
As the first sign of the Apocalypse.

The second sign,
Most scholars find,
Is the unspeakable play of MIKE PHILLIPS.

SANDY ALOMAR
Made like Alydar
And sired a couple of studs.
But he was more awful
Than day-old falafel;
Before long the job was JOEL YOUNGBLOOD's.

PHIL LINZ,
Like other fill-ins,
Never really panned out.
RICK HERRSCHER—
We'll get letters, fer sure—
Was both a dog and a kraut.

RICHIE HEBNER
Was bad with the leather—
BOB HEISE was a terrible stick man.
Add 'em together—
No stick and no leather—
And you get the inept JIMMY HICKMAN.

KEVIN MORGAN,
Like Shea, had one organ,
But the Mets themselves had two JOHNSONS.
There was HOWARD (or "HoJo")
And BOB (never "BoJo"—
His temper was worse than Chuck Bronson's).

CHARLEY SMITH
At third took the fifth
Or his every act would incriminate.
About ROY STAIGER
Even Tony the Tiger
Would have to say, "He's not grrreat!"

Your ROSS JONESES
And ELIO CHACONSES,
JOE MOOCKS and JERRY BUCHEKSES—
If dreadful careers
Were longhorned steers
These four men would be Texas.

JEFF MCKNIGHT
And Slappy White are equally
Lacking in gravitas.
You need three e's
To spell JEFFERIES,
Another third baseman emeritus.

LEO FOSTER
Belongs on this roster
Along with RON GARDENHIRE.
Look what the cat dragged in—
SAUNDERS and MAGADAN—
Two other stiffs for our pyre.

KEN BOSWELL
Alighted in Roswell—
He certainly played like a spaceman.
LOPEZ, STEPHENSON,
RAMIREZ and TEMPLETON:
Stop when we've named a third baseman.

The err apparent
To these (RAY) KNIGHTS errant
Was a kid by the name of PAQUETTE.
He's bad, undesirable.
Unwaiverwireable.
In short, he's a future ex-Met.

As for JOE TORRE,
Now there's a short story—
A bleak one, something by Sartre.

And finally, EDGARDO ALFONZO,
Who wasn't in *Bedtime for Bonzo*—
But we defy you to tell them apart.

❧

An Outfielder for Hiroshima

BY MARK HARRIS

The author of Bang the Drum Slowly *and other baseball novels tells the winning story of Californian Fibber Hirayama, whose dedication to American principles throroughly reoriented his Japanese teammates.*

White are the trodden paths
Of baseball
Among the tall grasses
Of summer.

Far, and beyond
The summer grass,
The baseball players are seen.

—Shiki Masaoka (1867–1902)

THE MOST PORTENTOUS RESIDENT OF THE CITY OF Hiroshima (pop.: 400,000) is the 28-year-old Californian who plays in the outfield for its major league Carp. The city's fans, who in 1958 will pass in record numbers beyond the ticket-takers at the brand new Hiroshima Citizens' Ball Place, call him "Hwee-bah," which is the way the Japanese deliver "Fibber," which in turn was his father's version of "February," the month of Fibber's birth, in Fresno.

If nobody has ever called him by his proper name, Satoshi, which means, in Japanese, wisdom, and which much more accurately defines his character than Fibber, he has not complained. Indeed, although he has borne through life his full share of small disappointments, and—once at least—a measure of pure injustice, he has confounded fate as he confounded the rivals of his football days at Fresno State College, most of whom outweighed him by 50 pounds. "Nobody," he recollects, "ever hit me real solid."

Of Fibber Hirayama's spiritual past, however, the citizenry of Hiroshima hears nothing. His memory is notably weak in the matter of his own considerable achievement. To his father in Lindsay, Calif.—Tokuzo, called George—and to his wife Jean in Hiroshima he has delegated the task of pasting up his scrapbooks, while Fibber himself, in the language of Carp manager Katsumi Shiraishi, "plays baseball *like* baseball."

Therefore, the city's copious affection for him can only be ascribed to its conscious appreciation of his present talents. For three years he has been the Carp's gracefully aggressive rightfielder, leadoff batter and spiritual focus, and in this year of promise he continues to be its vital center, as the Carp, who have never finished higher than fourth in the Central League, point their hopes toward the top brackets.

But this conscious appreciation, like all activity in a city whose devastation is so recent to memory, is in fact an expression of Hiroshima's profound necessity to achieve something much more ennobling than a mere pennant at baseball. Thorstein Veblen might have been describing the aroused temperament of this historic community when he spoke of a people "brought up against an imperative call, to revise their scheme of institutions in the light of their native instincts, on pain of collapse or decay."

A way of life is sought that shall be more humane and democratic than the feudal pattern of the Oriental past. Yet it can be nothing so simple-minded as the blind adoption of all things American. In the person of Fibber Hirayama, whose ancestry is Japanese, whose techniques are American and who contains in fine balance within himself his double heritage, the humiliated but emergent city of Hiroshima glimpses in ideal fusion of West with East.

Three years ago, when Fibber Hirayama arrived with his bride in Hiroshima, he was greeted by 10,000 persons. He paled. "It was something *terrible.*" Informed of the possibility of a small welcoming committee, he had requested translation into Japanese of a speech which he had rehearsed upon the train from Tokyo and which, when silence was established, he delivered at Hiroshima station. When 10,000 people hallooed with laughter he was appalled. In beginner's Japanese he had attempted to say, "I am Satoshi Hirayama. I will do my best," but he afterward learned that he had misused a word, which caused him to say: "I am Satoshi Hirayama and a splendid fellow."

His Carp teammates, still made merry by that incident, console him for his ignorance by reference to his primitive origins: he is only, they say, a piteous California farmer from a woebegone place called Fresno. "Hirayama," they sometimes inquire, "is it true that Fresno will soon have electricity?"

But he has done his best, as promised. Fibber Hirayama, according to the testimony of Takeo Yagi, chairman of Carp Fans (19,600 of whom have thus far this year contributed 200 yen apiece to their club, and who in the dark days of the Carp's infancy paid the team's salaries by public subscription), has become "famous for his constancy and sincerity," which is only to say, of course, that Fibber plays baseball as he learned to play it at Fresno.

At first glance, Fibber's resemblance to an athlete is by no means pronounced. Afflicted by nature with near-sightedness and a slight astigmatism, he wears tortoise-shell eyeglasses, exchanging those when in baseball uniform for silver-rimmed unbreakable lenses which he habitually polishes with a bar of dry soap. Elevated by nature to a height of only 5' 3" (5.22 Japanese *shaku*) he is sometimes indistinguishable from the bat boy, and even in Japan, where folk stand upon the average nearly a shaku shorter than Americans, he presently is the smallest Carp of all.

On the other hand, if he is vertically Japanese, he is horizontally American. Nourished upon eggs, meat and milk, he is broad-shouldered and full-chested, unlike most Japanese baseball players, whose power is predominantly in their legs. In a recent soliloquy in one of the two Hiroshima magazines entitled *Carp*—one in English, one in Japanese—an essayist arrived at the somewhat metaphysical conclusion that Fibber has the "strongest shoulders" of any Carp. And it is a tangible fact that he is the only Carp who can throw to home plate from the farthest reaches of the Ball Place. In a game in Honolulu on a 1951 tour with the Fresno State College baseball team, Fibber retired a runner at home with a heroic throw which moved sportswriter Wallace Hirai to maintain that "other than Joe DiMaggio, no player has come through with such a perfect strike from the outfield in the 25-year history of the stadium."

FIBBER ATTRIBUTES his compact power to "real good wrists" and abundant sleep ("[If] I can get sideways, I can sleep") and a mystic quality he calls "quickness." Characteristically amiable with regard to fine verbal distinctions, he allows "quickness" to mean "timing" as well. "Like in football," he explains, "being able to hit the hole at just the right time, cut back, cut out, in one or two strides I can make my cut."

From the moment Fibber became a Carp, according to veteran second baseman Jiro Kanayama, he "took charge." Kanayama recalls his astonishment at the discovery, returning to the dugout between innings, that Fibber, after running in from the outfield, was already sitting on the bench. Thereupon Kanayama too began to run. Contrary to Japanese custom, Fibber also runs swiftly to first base in spite of the depressing effects of a ground ball weakly hit to the infield. In Japan, as in America, he has betrayed a dangerous but somehow inspiring tendency to crash into outfield fences in pursuit of fly balls, a form of behavior which resulted last year in a painful rib injury but which has contributed to the Carp in that magical way in which the contagious passion of a lone player often uplifts an entire team.

The Carp have openly emulated him, especially at those points at which his deportment afield is imaginative rather than theoretical. He sometimes scores from first base on a single, or from second base on an infield out. He has introduced to the Carp the bumptious but perfectly legitimate Occidental custom of foiling a double play by sliding into the relay man. The unhappy Carp tendency to miss a signal because it was not anticipated is fading in an atmosphere conditioned by Fibber's conviction that strategy ceases to be strategy when it is reduced to ritual. And some Carp, immobilized in former days by edifying visions of their own dexterity at one-handed fielding, have observed that the truest esthetic calls for Fibber's practical habit of speedily throwing the ball to the appropriate base.

It is natural enough that members of the Carp, being Japanese, have learned to play baseball as it has traditionally been played in Japan. This is not quite equivalent to playing baseball like baseball, although to the casual eye an afternoon's transaction at the Hiroshima Citizens' Ball Place looks like baseball. The diamond lies below in its American dimensions. The ball itself is the American ball in every essential stitch. The teams perform in American whites and grays, their names written in English across their shirts, their nicknames borrowed, as in America, from the kingdoms of beasts and demons—Giants, Tigers, Dragons, Lions, Whales, Hawks. It is the American stadium, complete with vendors, flags, fenceboard advertising, scoreboard, peanuts, soda pop and a raincheck—everything except, for some inscrutable reason, the seventh-inning stretch. Now and then it is Ladies' Day. On Sunday there's a "dubburuhedduru." There's a Most Valuable Player. The Central League opposes the Pacific League in an annual All-Star competition in July and in a Nippon Series in October. The "peetcha" (he may be a "souspaw") throws "carvus" and "droppus," perhaps a "nukkuruboru," or in temper a "binbol," the "battah" runs to "farst-o" on a "hit-o." "Get two," the players sometimes call, and when they do the umpires cry "Out-o." The "catchah" wears the protective equipment designed in America, and the players jogging in from "left-o," "right-o," "second-o," "short-o" and "sardo" now carry their gloves with them as they saw the touring San Francisco Seals do in 1949.

INTO THIS perfectly persuasive Ball Place the Japanese player carries not only his bat and glove but his culture. And Japanese culture has inhibited the free growth of baseball in a variety of subtle ways. For example, the Hiroshima Carp, whom Fibber Hirayama joined, were committed as truly as any group of Japanese workers, whether in industry, the professions or education, to the firm tradition of *senpai* and *kohai*. A *senpai* (superior) is bound in honor to advance the interests of some younger men (his *kohai*, inferior) with whom he is identified by virtue of their having attended the same high school, or because they originate from the same town. In turn, the *kohai*'s first loyalty is to his *senpai*. It is a paternalism whose beneficence is apparent in many areas of Japanese life, but to a baseball team it is crippling. It results not in unity but in fragmentation, and it hampers a learning process especially important in Japanese baseball, where that Harvard and Yale of American ballplayers—the minor league farm club—does not exist. The young *kohai* shortstop whose native place is Yamaguchi will disastrously offend his *senpai* (a catcher whose native place is likewise Yamaguchi) by seeking tips on shortstopping from another shortstop whose native place is unfortunately Sendai. The free interchange of criticism and information among players, which circulates upward and downward and across all lines of age and place in America, may travel only within sensitive limits in Japan.

   An outsider, untrained in America to honor a *senpai* or shelter a *kohai*, Fibber Hirayama, in the intimacy of railroad cars, baths and hotels, has behaved for three years as if all Carp were created equal. Response to this novel conduct has been especially quick among those younger Carp of a postwar generation already hopeful of loosening *senpai* ties, which control even the choice of a wife. Now that Fibber himself has assumed a senior status (he is the sixth-oldest player on the youngest roster in the Japanese major leagues), the cultural impulse has been diverted in his direction. But since he will be nobody's *senpai*, the impulse dissolves, and the team as a whole moves toward a unity unprecedented among Japanese baseball clubs.

When the atomic bomb burst over Hiroshima, at a point almost directly above the dome of the Industrial Promotion Building (which alone survives today as a monument to the blast), Fibber was playing baseball in Arizona sunshine at Poston Relocation Center Two. "There really wasn't too much else to do. The nearest town was 20 miles away, and we weren't allowed to go."

He was 15. Three years earlier he had been evicted from Exeter, Calif., by an anxious U.S. Government, which had somehow mistaken Fibber, pedaling his bicycle over the highways of Tulare County, for a potential enemy. With his father and two brothers (it was the year his mother died), their home and other possessions sold, he entrained to take up life in a single barracks room at Poston Two. And when, a few days after the dropping of the bomb—the "catastrophe," as Hiroshimans call it—the Hirayamas were permitted to return home, there actually wasn't, as Fibber now perceives, "too much to go back to."

But if the prospect was dark, he hadn't noticed. Or possibly he said, in the Japanese mood, "*Shikataganai*." In the home where Japanese foods had sometimes been prepared, where he had heard the language spoken by his mother and where he had bathed all his life in a woodburning bath modeled upon the magnificent tubs of the old country, it was inevitable that he should have been a little bit shaped by the philosophy of *Shikataganai*: "It cannot be helped . . . it is Nature." A household word in Japan, *Shikataganai* describes the ancient Japanese habit of submitting to fate, blending with the landscape: The Japanese mountain road winds its way not over nor through but around. If it was the nature of the U.S. Government or the citizens of California to view Fibber Hirayama with suspicion or mistrust, very well, *Shikataganai*. But at Exeter High, where he was the only Oriental boy, he discovered that it was also the nature of Americans to admire athletic skill. Devoting himself with all earnestness and all joy to games, he proceeded toward redemption, and on the playing fields of America, as afterward in Japan, he soon won not only acceptance but distinction.

AT FRESNO State College, with a tuition scholarship and $50 a month as wages for "art work" and other exhausting duties, he studied physical education and health education (he hopes to coach high school athletics in California), intellectual disciplines embodying tumbling, boxing, wrestling and hygiene. He played football in the autumn and baseball in the spring.

Weighing 150 pounds fully armored (18.13 Japanese *kan*), acclaimed by the Fresno press as "pound for pound" the best halfback on the Coast, he threw passes, ran the ends and squirmed and squirted through holes in the line which a larger man could never have maneuvered. On defense he was notably adept at intercepting passes, but his principal charm from the spectators' point of view perhaps was his finesse in upending competitors whose relative bulk might have awed him had he paused to calculate the risk.

The Fresno State College baseball teams of 1950–52, twice captained by centerfielder Fibber Hirayama, were among the strongest in the nation. The 1951 team won 36 games in 40 starts, 10 more in a 13-game postseason tour of Hawaii where, in addition to his memorable throw, Fibber typically distinguished himself by being twice hit by the opposing pitcher in a single game (once in the head), each time rising, trotting to first base and subsequently scoring. In 1952, against such major college competition as the University of California, USC, Stanford, UCLA and Oregon State, the Fresno team won 31 games and lost nine.

Perhaps of even more significance than his ability to master the nature of baseball was the singular fact of Fibber's personality, which seduces people, wherever he goes, to accord him honors he never seeks. As he was twice captain of the Fresno Bulldogs, so was he also twice voted most popular player at National Baseball Congress tournaments in Wichita. Voted in 1951 Nisei Player of the Year, admitted to the 1951–52 edition of *Who's Who Among Students in American Colleges and Universities*, he was also elected Campus King (Queen Norma Morrison was slightly taller), in which capacity he proclaimed a holiday, reigned over a carnival and led a grand march down a dance floor dominated by plaster figures of a prince and princess 18 feet tall.

If ever a man had rejoined his community, Fibber Hirayama had done so. The U.S. Government, which had exiled him from his home a decade before, now reclaimed him, and he found himself, in January 1953, once again in a barracks, this time at Fort Ord, Calif. Here, in addition to military duties, he batted .300 for the Fort Ord Warriors, 1954 All-Service champions. Discharged from the Army in October 1954, into a world in which, from the point of view of American baseball, he lacked *shaku* and *kan*, Fibber was fearful, at this time, that his race disqualified him for coaching jobs on the West Coast.

It was then that he was encouraged by his good friend Kenichiro Zenimura of Fresno to hire out to the faraway Carp. Kenichiro played for the Carp for varying periods between 1953 and 1956. "I realized that I wouldn't be able to go anywhere as far as pro ball in the States is concerned," Fibber says, "and there's no place to go unless you can play in the big time. I decided to take a chance."

Lured, too, by the opportunity to visit Kumamoto, where generations of Hirayamas have raised rice and green tea, he was supported in his intention by Jean Doi, whom he had first pursued in aggressive American fashion down a corridor of the Administration Building at the campus in Fresno, and to whom he was married on February 12, 1955 in the First Congregational Church. ("I like whatever country my husband is in," she was afterward to say.)

On a wedding trip to Nevada and a visit to relatives in Los Angeles they spent a portion of their savings in American dollars, and on March 7, with tickets purchased in yen by the Hiroshima Carp Limited Companies, they departed San Francisco by Japan Air Lines. Two evenings later they dined at a Chinese-style restaurant in Tokyo, where Fibber was alarmed to discover a coeducational lavatory. On March 11 they arrived at Hiroshima Station.

The poet-reformer Shiki Masaoka, explaining baseball to the Japanese as long ago as 1896, stressed that the game continues for nine innings, after which "the total number of points are compared, and those who have more points are considered to be the winners. For example, 8–23." But Japanese baseball players have been accustomed to capitulating in early innings to the nature of a losing day. Moreover, when they do so they smile, since to reveal one's own humiliation is considered un-Japanese.

Fibber Hirayama, who smiles easily, has nevertheless been unable to take a long, philosophical view of a bad day. Fresno State College baseball coach Pete Beiden recalls that during a period when Fibber went hitless in 42 attempts "he lost his sense of humor in the situation." He does not conceal emotions of disgust when he errs nor emotions of humiliation when he is outwitted by an opposing pitcher, nor has it ever occurred to him to consent to defeat until nine full innings have been played.

WAS THE smile better? The surrender to Nature? Deference to authority? Does Hiroshima need baseball at the expense of its mellow code? But it is a city whose recent convulsive history forces it to choose with unnatural haste a symbol of its intention. It must choose between the bombed dome and the Ball Place.

Significantly, its initial reception for Fibber Hirayama, followed by a 50-car parade, has recently been equaled by its reception for only two other individuals: India's Nehru, whom the city views as a principal spokesman for world peace, and Helen Keller, the American woman who has defied nature in her conquest of physical handicap. *Shikataganai* no longer serves.

In their support of their baseball team, the citizens of Hiroshima have enjoyed their first sustained opportunity to condemn a past which brought them to the edge of extinction. Never have citizens representing every economic level and every social distinction shared so clear a stake in a common endeavor. The Hiroshima Carp, organized nine years ago on a shareholding basis, is the only Japanese big-league team popularly bearing not the name of an industrial sponsor but the name of its city: Of the other 11 teams, six are owned by transportation companies, two by newspapers, one by a motion picture company, one by a fishery and one jointly by a newspaper and a motion picture company. This is a point of pride to Hiroshimans, who wish the world to know not only that their city fell but that it picked itself up again.

Last year Carp fans recorded a home attendance of 746,000, although the new 31,000-seat Ball Place was not put into use until late August. This year an attendance of 850,000—more than twice the city's population—is assured, a rate which will be nowhere approached in Japan and exceeded in the U.S. only by Milwaukee. In 1958 the Carp will show its first profit. Long before opening day, interest was high: in mid-February 20,000 people attended an exhibition double-header, while on March 2 an equal number viewed games in cold which turned to snow before the afternoon was over.

The carp, in Japanese lore, is a fish which swims upstream, even over waterfalls. The Carp, in Japanese baseball, must struggle upstream against the formidable Central League empires of Tokyo (three teams), Osaka and Nagoya, whose millions in population provide a financial basis unavailable to Hiroshima and whose teams recruit the outstanding college players. The Carp cannot pay, as the Yomiuri Giants recently did, a bonus of 25 million yen for a rookie third baseman.

Basically, if the Carp are to win, they can do so only by playing baseball like baseball, avoiding the mistake of confusing form with function: For baseball is more than a form. It is a spirit made in America and therefore, for better or for worse, the antithesis of *Shikataganai*. At the Hiroshima Citizens' Ball Place, accelerated by history and with an assist by Fibber Hirayama, the secret of that spirit is in the process of revelation.

Yet Fibber did not come to Hiroshima to instruct. He came as a workman, hired out to the Carp, as counterpart workmen in the U.S. hire out to the Red Sox or the Dodgers. On his new job he troubled himself to learn the language of his fellow workers; which he speaks in a frontal style, lopping from his speech that great variety of polite attachments of which Japanese is capable. He sacrificed meat and milk when necessary for rice and fish, although he deplores fish, especially raw, and once became morbidly ill on sardines. He has consistently rejected the special treatment Japanese hospitality daily offers the foreigner. He has asked neither privilege nor favor. He has given all he knows.

Although "a real good book reader," he has not yet encountered Fielding's *Joseph Andrews*, but he has somehow known—his name, after all, is Satoshi, wisdom—"that examples work more forcibly on the mind than precepts."

For his pains he has been rewarded. In the night, traveling through the sleeping countryside, a fellow player calls: "Hirayama, California farmer, look out the window," and Fibber, peering into the darkness, sees swiftly receding the lonely lights of a desolate rural station. "That," say the Carp, "is Fresno."

Less than profound, it is the baseball player's universal method of asserting affection. It is an affection earned. For his team, and for the city in which he has chosen to live his life so long as he can play baseball like baseball, Fibber has been an example working forcibly on the mind. It is much to have accomplished for a young man whom nature gave short supply in *shaku* and *kan*.

Dream of Glory
On the Mound

BY GEORGE PLIMPTON

*The author, in one of his early sports adventures, decided to find out what
it was like to pitch in Yankee Stadium against the best hitters in baseball. In a
postseason meeting between two all-star teams, he found out.*

IT WAS OBVIOUS SOMETHING WAS IN THE WIND. THE PLAYERS WERE off the field, the reporters and photographers gone, the batting cage wheeled away and the groundskeepers sprucing up the pitcher's mound and the area around home plate. Each team was standing by its dugout. Some of the players seemed puzzled by the change in the pregame schedule. I saw a few fingers pointing, and also little quick gestures of the head in my direction to indicate that it was "that guy over there—the guy with the blue cap," and the eyes looking, and I felt the sweat start to seep in my palms, my fielder's mitt suddenly uncomfortably clammy and hot.

Then, when the distant clock hands on the scoreboard stood at 1:30, one of the promoters walked me out across the foul lines and signaled the American League team to join us by the pitcher's mound. They constituted, in the vernacular, a pretty fair country ball club: Mickey Vernon, Nelson Fox, Billy Martin and Frank Malzone in the infield, and in the outfield Bob Cerv, Mickey Mantle and Harvey Kuenn. Elston Howard was my catcher. He looked puzzled. I don't believe anyone had had the chance to tell him why he was to put on his catching tools half an hour before the scheduled game.

The promoter checked to see that we were all present. Then he shuffled some papers on a clipboard. "Well, boys," he started to say.

At this point the recorded music which had been drifting in from centerfield stopped abruptly, in mid-chorus of *Tea for Two*. A stentorian cough came over the public-address system and we heard as follows:

"Your attention, please. George P . . . P . . . P . . . ," then a pause, the announcer apparently working over a name scribbled on a pad. "Prufrock," he said, and repeated with immeasurable confidence that boomed through the Stadium: "George Prufrock of SPORTS ILLUSTRATED will now pitch against the entire National League team, and the entire American League team . . . that team which collects the most hits to be awarded a prize of $1,000 by SPORTS ILLUSTRATED."

"Well, there you are, boys," said the promoter. They were all looking at me. "That's the idea," he continued. "Four points awarded for the four-bagger, three for the triple, two for the double—you field first through their first eight batters, and then you get your licks."

"You let 'em hit, kid," said Billy Martin. "And right at us, *pul-lease*, on the ground and in big, quick hops."

A few of the players laughed and someone said, "That's right, kid—you're out here to do the work; we're along for the ride," and around the circle they smiled again, trying to impart confidence, and as we stood together, waiting for something to happen to release us, I felt a sudden kinship with them. It was an entirely unexpected emotion, since I was so obviously an outsider, but it came: that warm sense of camaraderie one gets, if briefly, as a team member, or in a platoon, or just sitting around a café with friends— never mentioned, but there nonetheless, almost tangible, and very strong before, abruptly, it was dissipated. Someone said, "O.K., let's go," and the huddle broke up.

Surrounded by the players, I had felt protected and grateful for my obscurity among them. But when they withdrew and headed for their positions, leaving me standing alone just off the mound, it was like being unveiled. One sensed the slow massive gaze of the spectators—by then almost 20,000 of them—wheel and concentrate, and almost physically felt the weight of it. My hands were slick with sweat. I walked up on the pitcher's mound to find the rosin bag. There wasn't one there. A new ball was lying just off the pitcher's rubber. I picked it up but I didn't turn for the plate.

I kept looking out at my infielders, trying to recapture the confidence I'd felt fleetingly in their company. They seemed very far away; they were busy scooping up grounders Vernon was lobbing to them from first base. Out beyond the base paths, the outfielders had reached their positions. They were so far away I didn't feel we were identified with the same project. Deep back in the bleachers I could see a man, sitting up there alone, removing his coat to enjoy the afternoon sun.

I finally faced the plate. Howard was there waiting, his big dust-gray mitt up for the warmup pitches. I threw him a couple. Then I wasn't conscious of the crowd. I had forgotten that a pitcher, whatever his stature, concentrates on the strike zone to the exclusion of everything else. The crowd becomes a blur in the background. The noise it makes has a crisp quality, a sharp babble, since everybody is facing you, but it is impossible to distinguish its separate parts. Of course, if you listen for it, you can hear the vendors' "*Hot* franks," "Hey, *ice*-cream heah," but it isn't like sitting in the stands, where you can hang on to four or five conversations at the same time. Mostly you hear your own voice—chattering away, keeping you company in the loneliness, cajoling and threatening if things begin to go badly, heavy in praise at times, much of everything being said half aloud, the lips moving, because although you know you're being watched no one can hear you and the sound of your voice has a truly steady influence—the one familiar verity in those strange circumstances. I recall the first sentence I spoke to myself was, "O.K., bo, you're goin' to be O.K. Nothin' at all to worry about, nothin', nothin'," and at that moment, like a crack lawyer springing to rebut, the public-address system announced the arrival at the plate of the National League's leadoff batter, Richie Ashburn.

HE STEPPED into the batter's box wearing the bright candy-red-pinstriped uniform of the Phillies. A lefthanded batter, he punches at the ball, slapping it for a multitude of singles. The outfielders deploy for him like softball players. He chokes so far up on the bat that as he waited I could see his fingers flexing two or three inches up on the bat handle. He presented a surprisingly small target—indeed, all the batters seemed smaller than imagined. Half-consciously I had expected them to rear high over the plate, threatening portraits of power—but in fact their physical presence at the plate was not as overpowering as recognizing them; to look in and see under the batter's helmet a face which, jarringly familiar even from the pitcher's mound, I had only associated previously with the photographs of the sports sections.

Behind the plate Howard had settled in his crouch, his big mitt up for the target. Concentrating on it, barely aware then of Ashburn, I toed the rubber with my spikes, and, with an almost physical jolt of will I swung into a slow windup. Under the pressure of the moment I half expected to exhibit a pitching form as spastic as the cartwheeling fall of a man from a high tree. But conditioned reflexes took over, and I was surprised at the ease with which I got the pitch off.

I was not prepared, however, for what then happened: that, rather than speeding for Howard's catcher's mitt, the ball, flung with abandon and propelled by a violent mixture of panic and pent-up anxiety let loose, headed straight for Ashburn's head. Down he went, flat on his back, the bat flung away, and an explosion of sound—a sharp gasp from the crowd—sailed out of the stands as I hurried off the mound calling out, "Sorry! Sorry!"

I ran halfway to the plate. Ashburn picked himself up, collected his bat and looked out at me calmly, his face imperturbable. I could think of nothing to say to him. So I shrugged an inadvertent gesture that under the circumstances could only have indicated to Ashburn, and to Howard, standing peering at me through the bars of his mask, that I had no control whatsoever over my pitches. Then I wheeled for the mound to try again.

I threw three more pitches to Ashburn, finding myself growing in confidence as I pitched. I threw him another ball, then a pitch that he chopped foul. On the next delivery he punched under the ball and lifted a high fly between third and home. Howard threw off his mask with a violence that rolled it almost to the backstop, and with shin guards clattering went after the ball, got under it and stomped around with his face upturned like a Piute praying for rain until finally the ball came down to be smothered in his big glove.

It took a few seconds, while the ball was being thrown around the infield, before there was any sense of accomplishment—it came haltingly because, after all, one had expected devastation, not a harmless foul ball glinting in the sun. But finally it did come, and I lurched happily in a tight circle around the pitcher's mound, digging and scraping at the dirt with my spikes, pretending preoccupation. If there had been a rosin bag I would have picked it up and fussed with it. What had seemed an inhospitable place, a steep uneven hill of dirt on which I moved gingerly and awkwardly, suddenly became something of a natural habitat—all around everything was familiar, neat and orderly. But just as I began to admire the unmarked base paths, the bases unoccupied, with the fielders relaxed in their positions, there came a mounting roar from the stands, and a player with an established reputation for creating disorder in the pitcher's domain trotted up out of the National League dugout—San Francisco's Willie Mays.

He gets set quickly at the plate, hopping eagerly into the batter's box, where he nervously jiggles and stamps his feet in the dust, twisting on his rear foot to get it solidly placed, staring down at the plate in concentration to sense when his legs feel set, and when they do he reaches out and taps the plate, twice, three times, with the bat before he sweeps it back over his right shoulder and cocks it. Then for the first time he looks out at the pitcher.

Most batters tuck their chins down and glower out at the pitcher from under the brims of their batting helmets—which makes them look properly sinister and threatening. Mays, on the other hand, has a pleasant face to start with, and he looks out at the pitcher with a full, honest regard, his chin out, his eyes wide as if slightly myopic. He seems to inspect the pitcher as if he were a harmless but puzzling object recently deposited on the mound by the groundskeeper. Furthermore, when Mays's face is set in determination, his eyebrows arch up so that under the batter's helmet his expression is that of a lingering look of astonishment. But the deception is mild; you see the coiled power of his stance as he waits, and the chances are that you'll turn away to look at something else.

I threw Mays three pitches. The motion felt easy and the first two pitches were low and didn't miss by much. With the third pitch, though, I was aware that the ball, almost as it left my hand, was heading accurately for the plate and that Mays, flexing his bat back to increase the purchase of his swing, was going to go for it. As his bat came through into the pitch, I could sense the explosive power generated and I flinched. But from this flurry of power the ball rose straight—a foul ball like Ashburn's, I thought at first, but then I saw it carrying out over the infield. I had a glimpse of it high above me, small but astonishingly bright in the sunlight, and, remembering that a pitcher leaves the fielding to his infielders, I ran head down toward first to vacate the mound for them.

I misjudged the ball badly. Actually, it came down back of the shortstop's position. Billy Martin was there to catch it, and as I walked back to the mound he threw the ball to Malzone, and it began to go from infielder to infielder in that fine ritual of speeding the ball "around the Horn" which gives the pitcher a moment to peek modestly out from his cap and savor what he's just done. It was fine.

I stood absorbing that October instant so that it would be forever available for recall; seeing again and feeling the sudden terror of Mays uncoiling his bat, but then watching in surprise the ball rise clean and harmless, Billy Martin circling under it, catching it then and removing it from his glove to peer at it as if he'd never seen a baseball before.

I felt coming on a maniac grin of achievement which I had to control, knowing that pitchers don't grin after getting a man out, and so I solemnly stomped around the mound, tidying it up, watching with sidelong glances the ball whip from infielder to infielder. Finally Nelson Fox, the big orange-size chaw pushing out the side of his face, trotted onto the mound, looking at the ball in his hand, jiggling it, then popping it in the air at me and saying, "Come on, kid, easy, easy, easy."

THAT IS all of that day that I really would like to remember. Perhaps a bit more: that when I got the ball from Fox it felt familiar to the hand, a weapon suddenly adaptable, an instrument perfectly suited to my design. Of course, I should have known better. Polishing the ball, the glove slung on the wrist, I turned on the mound and saw Frank Robinson, the great Cincinnati slugger, standing in the batter's box. I knew then that the pitcher's pleasure is a fragmentary thing, that the dugouts, like sausage machines, eject an unending succession of hitters to destroy any momentary complacency a pitcher may feel during an afternoon of work.

Regardless, as I looked in at Robinson, with Howard behind him adjusting his mask, I thought: Well, why not, I've done pretty well so far—now's the time to unleash my curve ball, the hook. After all, I'd promised myself to throw that lazy roundhouse curve of mine just to see what would happen to it. And perhaps if the hook worked, I'd chance the change-of-pace and maybe even the knuckler. Given the opportunity, I knew it would be unforgivable not to try all the pitches in my repertoire; and so, swallowing hard, nervous again after the heady triumph of retiring the first two batters, I worked my fingers around the seams until I had the ball held properly for the curve. Robinson, the victim, was standing easily in the batter's box; Howard had settled into his position, his glove raised as a target. I didn't see how I could tell Howard a curve was coming up without tipping off Robinson. My catcher would have to fend for himself as best he could, I thought, and I pumped my arm twice and swung into the windup.

As I came through the delivery of my curve I failed to snap my wrist sufficiently and my hook got away from me in majestic style—sailing far over both Robinson's and Howard's heads to the wire screen behind home plate.

It was such an extraordinary wild pitch that I felt that I had to make some comment; what I'd done was too undignified to pass unnoticed. And so once again I hurried off the mound calling out, "Sorry! Sorry!" Howard and Robinson gazed out at me, both startled, I think, perhaps even awed by the strange trajectory of my pitch. The embarrassment was intense, and it took me a few pitches to steady down. Finally I threw a pitch Robinson found to his liking. He brought his hands around and the ball soared out between Mantle and Cerv in deep left centerfield, dropped between them and rolled for the Babe Ruth memorial out by the flagpole. By the time it was back in the infield Robinson was standing on second.

The public-address system announced "two points for the National League," and Robinson, his job done, trotted in from second base. I didn't have to worry about a man jiggling up and down the base paths. But there was something else bothering me as I watched Ernie Banks, the home run king of the National League, step out of the on-deck circle and head for the plate. Of the six pitches I'd thrown to Robinson one or two had seemed to me to catch the strike zone. He hadn't gone for them, and there was no umpire to contradict his choice. I hadn't arranged for an umpire for the simple reason that I didn't trust my control. I didn't consider, however, the possibility that the batters—and quite properly, since money was at stake— might get finicky about the pitches and wait for one they felt they could get "aholt" of.

I HAD a grand opportunity to study Banks. Or, rather, Banks was up at the plate for such a long time that for days afterward a slight and regretted tug at the memory would disclose him clearly in my mind's eye: a right-handed batter, slender, standing very quietly back in the farthest recesses of the batter's box. He had none of the nervous fidgeting of a Mays or a Ted Williams, his bat steady and cocked up vertically behind his right ear, rarely leveled out in a practice swing as he waited with his eyes peering out calmly from beneath the Cubs' outsized cap. His whole attitude was one of such detachment that I found it unnerving to pitch to him. Once in a while he'd step out of the batter's box and, resting his bat against his knees, he'd slowly pour dust from one palm to the other before settling back in with an attitude of faint disdain, as if in his opinion the pitcher's stature was that of a minor functionary whose sole duty was to serve up a fat pitch.

I threw Banks a total of 23 pitches. There may not have been an umpire to judge their quality, but it was certain that Banks found very few to his lik-ing. Sometimes he would lean over and watch the ball right into Howard's glove, then look up with a small encouraging smile, as if to indicate that it was close—that if the pitch had been a shade nearer the center of the plate, why, he would have whipped his bat around. Occasionally he would foul a pitch off into the stands, and from the first-base dugout someone would roll a new ball out to the mound; I'd pick it up, stalk back onto the mound, gaze mournfully at Banks, concentrate then on the bulk of Howard's catch-er's mitt, crank up and let fly.

As I worked away, my control began to vanish under the pressure. My sense of well-being, not bothered by Robinson's double, began to deterio-rate. I started to talk to myself loudly; the mound, the pitching rubber, pre-viously so familiar, quickly became alien ground that I stumbled over and couldn't get the feel of with my spikes; the baseball itself seemed noticeably heavier, the seams awry; the whole process of throwing a ball with accuracy became an absurdly hard task, and as I pitched, Banks seemed to recede into the distance, along with Howard, until the two of them looked like figures viewed through the wrong end of a telescope.

The gravity of my situation with Ernie Banks was compounded by not having anyone I could turn to. Elston Howard, my catcher, cared so little for the business at hand—having a full game to catch later on—that often if my pitches were out of the strike zone, or in the dust, he'd let them skip by without budging for them and balls would thud ignominiously against the backstop. Naturally there wasn't anyone in either dugout I could com-plain to—neither teammates nor even a manager. The only encouragement I had was the faint, apologetic smile of Banks himself. A quick, embar-rassed look around my infield was no help. Their faces were averted: Mick-ey Vernon was looking solemnly into his first baseman's glove; the others were either preoccupied with their shoetops or scratching with their spikes in the dirt of the base paths. In the outfield I caught one awful glimpse of Mickey Mantle turned toward one of the other outfielders and patting his mouth in an ostentatious yawn to show his boredom.

Finally, on pitch No. 23, Banks lifted a high fly ball out to Mantle in right centerfield, who was not so busy yawning that he didn't see the ball arch out toward him, and standing on the mound I saw he was going to catch it. I heaved a big shuddering sigh of relief to think that no longer did I have to look in to see Banks standing there with those redstriped blue socks high on his legs, his small head leaning over the plate, the thin smile. . . . And when he came up after the game and we joked about it I told him that one of the lasting impressions of that afternoon would be the relief I felt watching him trudge back to the dugout, trailing his bat along behind him as if it had become heavy during that long stay at the plate.

Ernie Banks was followed in the batter's box by Frank Thomas, then playing for the Pittsburgh Pirates. He was the only batter I faced who loomed over the plate. Despite a large, homely, friendly face over which his blue plastic helmet perched like a birthday paper hat, Thomas's size made him look dangerous; he had an upright batting stance which made him easier to pitch to than Banks, but the bat looked small and limber in his hands, and when he swung and missed one of my first pitches I imagined I heard the bat sing in the air like a willow switch. Thomas whacked the seventh pitch I threw him in a long high arc, deep into the upper deck in leftfield. The ball looped in at the downward end of its trajectory, and above the swelling roar of the crowd I could hear it smack against the slats of an empty seat. The upper deck was deserted, and it was a long time before a scampering boy, leaping the empty rows like a chamois, found the ball and held it aloft, triumphant, the white of it just barely visible at that great distance. The ball was hit well over 400 feet, and after the roar that had accompanied its flight had died down you could still hear the crowd buzzing.

MY OWN reaction, as I stood on the mound, was not one of shame, or outrage. Perhaps it should have been, particularly following my difficulties with Banks, but actually my reaction was one of wonderment at the power necessary to propel a ball out of a major league park. I could hardly believe a ball could be hit so far. Every time I return to Yankee Stadium I automatically look up into the section where the ball hit—it was section 34—remembering then that I enjoyed a strong feeling of identification with Thomas's feat, as if I were his partner rather than his opposition, and that between us we'd connived to arrange what had happened. It was as if I'd wheeled to watch the ball climb that long way for the upper deck and called out, "Look, look what I've helped engineer!"

Gil Hodges, the Dodger first baseman, followed Thomas in the batter's box, stepping in, hitching up his baseball pants, reaching out then and rubbing up the fat part of his bat as he set himself, picking again at those pants as if about to wade into a shallow pond. They call him Moon, and I remember how he looked, the rather beefy pleasant face under the blue helmet, and the blue piping of the Dodger uniform, and I remember the line-drive single he hit, how easy and calculated his swing, and how sharply that hit of his was going out. But mainly I remember something else.

It was while Hodges was at the plate that the inner voice, which had been mumbling inaudibly at first, and calmly, began to get out of control. On the pitcher's mound I was conscious not of the hum of the crowd or even, closer at hand, the encouragement of the infielders. What I remembered was this voice chattering away within my head, offering comfort, encouragement, advice. I was acutely aware of this separation of mind and body: the mind seemed situated in a sort of observation booth high above the physical self; looking down, like a skeptical foreman, and offering a steady commentary.

During the first moments on the pitcher's mound, as Ashburn set himself at the plate, the voice occupied itself with the general urging to "calm down and take it easy," but I felt the hypocrisy nonetheless, the hysteria lurking close at the edge of the voice, like a hyena beyond the firelight, and my mouth was very dry.

After the astonishing success with Ashburn and Mays, their high flies both caught in the infield, the voice became almost uncontrollable with delight. In its pleasure at the machine under observation it cried out to it "How t'go, bébé!" and "Boy, you kid!" and also there bounced around within my head such strange, effusive exclamations as "Gol-ding it!" and "Geezuz!" and when the grin tried to spread across my face it was in reaction to this close harmony between body and spirit.

But during Banks's tenure the inner voice refused to stay contained within my head. The lips began to move, and my mumbled voice, for some reason with a southern inflection which I have never used before or since, became increasingly audible on that lonely hill, moaning and squeaking like the fluttery breath of a tuckered hound.

"Lookit that thing go out theah!" it gasped when Banks had finally departed, and Frank Thomas's long home run started for the depths of the upper deck. "Lawd almighty!"

What caused the voice to crack utterly was a string of seven balls I threw to Gil Hodges before he hit three fouls in a row and then his single, none of these first pitches close enough to the plate to get him to so much as twitch the bat off his shoulder. At first the voice offered its usual counsel not to push the ball and to take things easy. Presently, however, it got exasperated—"Hey, come on now, bear down, Ah say" like a short-tempered farmer training a pup to come to heel. Then finally, as my control continued to flag, the panic surged in not by degrees but quickly, like a prowler's bulk suddenly filling a doorway, and it came in and throttled the voice so that all that came out was a thin high squeak.

And then this curious thing happened. The voice turned traitor. It went defeatist on me. It escaped and ran off, washing its hands of the whole miserable business. But it didn't desert me completely. Much worse, it capered around out there on the periphery, jeering and catcalling. "You po' fat fool, y'think y'all pretty fat and smart standing out theah pitching, hey? Well, lemme tell yo' sumpin. Y'all can't pitch yo' way out of a paper bag, that's what. Jes' try. Jes' le's see yo' try putting the ball ovah the plate."

So I would try—and when the ball missed the strike zone under Hodges's watchful eye, the voice would cackle gleefully, "Y'all see that? Oh my! Y'all see that ball roll in the dust? Ladies an' gen'men, d'y'all observe that ball drop down theah in the dirt? Haw! Haw! Haw!" it would roar gustily in my head. "Haw! Haw! Haw!"

My physical disintegration started in at the same time and it progressed quickly. For 20 minutes I had been burning every pitch in, feeling that if I let up and tried to guide the ball across the plate my control would vanish. I hadn't bothered to pace myself, and by the time Hodges stood in at the plate I was exhausted. I felt the numbness of it seep through my system like a sea mist. Acutely conscious of my physical self, I fancied I could see the engine straining and laboring—the heart crashing and thundering in the rib cage like an overworked pump, the lungs billowing in and out as they whistled heavy warm gouts of air up the long shaft of the throat and, below, the stomach churning and ambulating and wondering why breakfast hadn't been sent down to it that day, or lunch, for that matter, and peeved about it. And then this whole oscillating edifice would tip and sway in the delivery of a pitch, the muscles convoluting and squeaking as off the pitch would go, and then as everything came to a shuddering and wheezing pause down would drift that jeering inner voice of mine: "You nut! You fat fool nut! Y'all missed the plate *again!*"

When I finally got the ball over and Hodges lined out his hit, I felt like lying down. My interest in the proceedings was strongly affected now by an oncoming dizziness, a dizziness with a high ringing sound like the hum of a tiny bug caught deep back in the confines of the ear. While the ball was being fired in by Mantle in center, I was bent over, puffing hard, and trying to clear my head of its sounds and mists. I could feel the October sun pressing on my neck. When I looked up, Stan Lopata, the Phillies' catcher, was settling himself in the batter's box. He has a pronounced crouch as he awaits the pitch, hunched over as if he'd been seized by a sudden stomach cramp. Naturally, his stance diminishes his strike zone considerably, despite the fact that he's a big man, and I looked down at him in dismay.

I threw him 15 pitches. He seemed as permanent a fixture at the plate as a cast-iron garden sculpture. My mouth was ajar with fatigue, and I was swept by the numbing despair that must grip English bowlers who often have to work the same pair of batsmen for two or three hours, often more. Lopata and I were a sturdy pair, joined together by the umbilical cord of my wildness—and also by his propensity for hitting fouls. He hit six of them, lashing out like a cobra from his coil, and the ball would flee in big hops down past the coaching boxes or loft into the stands.

AT THIS point Elston Howard, my long-suffering catcher, took a sudden, almost proprietary interest in the proceedings. I think that crouching there in the dust behind home plate he'd counted on his fingers and realized that if we could get Lopata out, there was only one more batter to go. Previously, his reluctance to enter the spirit of things was such that he could barely persuade himself to lift his glove for a target. Now he began to rise from his crouch after every pitch and fire the ball back with increasing speed—steaming it back, trying to snap me out of my wildness. He threw the ball with an accuracy that mocked my control, harder than I was pitching it to him, and finally at such velocity into my weakly padded glove that I suffered a deep bone bruise which discolored my left hand for over a week. "Come on, kid, lay it in," I heard him call out once, making a fist of his right hand and pumping it at me, as if by sheer determination he could will my pitches into the strike zone. But the pitch always seemed to tail off, missing by an inch, or perhaps a foot—a moan escaping me as it did— and then I had to face the agony of Howard's return slapping hard enough in the glove to force a sharp intake of breath.

Suddenly the inner voice burst loudly upon my senses. It had been saying nothing of importance—just the usual raillery, still calling me a "fat fool" and an "aggressive nut," but from a distance, hardly distinguishable at times from the high whine of dizziness humming in my ears. But then my hand drifted up and touched my brow, finding it as wet and cold as the belly of a trout. It was a disclosure which sent the voice spinning off in a Cracker Cassandra's wail of doom. "Mah God!" it cried out, "y'all gonna faint out heah. Lawd Almahty! Y'gonna faint!"

I'd just caught the ball from Howard, grimacing as it whacked into the glove, and as I felt the lurch of nausea and that piercing disclosure echo in the brain I dropped the ball. My fingers began bumping gently against each other in a disembodied fashion, suggesting that they too had joined the voice in revolt. I stared at the fingers, fascinated. When I bent for the ball, the head cleared slightly, and the fingers came back under control. But I knew then that it was only a matter of time, and not too much of it, before that prescient wail would be proved accurate. I tried to persuade myself that you don't collapse out on the pitcher's mound in front of 20,000 people. But I knew, as I stood there in that momentary calm of self-appraisal, that the energy was draining from me like meal from a punctured burlap sack, and that presently I would stumble and go down.

Of course, I could have walked off the field. But calling off the whole thing—just stopping—seemed too complicated. What would happen then? There was no one to finish the job. The American League couldn't bat. What would Mickey Mantle say? How would the $1,000 be divided? Anything seemed infinitely more complicated than staying. So I became absolutely resigned to continuing, even if it meant falling in a heap, as limp and pale on the mound as a massive rosin bag.

There remained one small hope. If I could last through Lopata and Bill Mazeroski of the Pittsburgh Pirates, the last batter in the National League lineup, I might get a chance while the teams changed sides to puff a bit in the cool of the dugout, to put a wet towel around the back of the neck, and perhaps find a second wind to get through Fox and Mantle and Kuenn and the others in the American League batting order. It was a forlorn hope, and not one to look forward to with eagerness.

As soon as I started throwing to Lopata again, the weight of the previous 20 minutes of hard throwing—by then I'd thrown a few pitches short of 70—pressed down hard like a stifling tropic heat. The field seemed as limitless under that blazing sun as a desert, spreading out forever on all sides, unreal, and the players stiff and distant as obelisks in a surrealist landscape. The whine in my ears increased, the nausea fulminating, the knees rubbery, so shaky that the desert's fixity was disturbed, and the ground itself began to undulate softly and thickly, like a bog, and there were times when the motion became violent and the pitcher's mound hunched up under me so that I teetered on its summit, on the cone of a vast anthill whose slopes beat with that insect hum. At times its physical aspect would be inverted, and I would find myself at the bottom of a murky hollow, the air heavy and clammy, and I would twist and convolute and hurl a baseball as heavy and malleable as a ripe mango, throwing it toward Lopata, perched on that distant rim as implacable in the distance as a squatting Sphinx.

I don't remember Lopata grounding out, but he did, finally, hitting a big, hopping ground ball toward the shortstop position, where I was told afterwards Martin first gave a little startled jump as if in surprise to hear the whack of the ball being hit, then moved for it on legs that were described as "stiff from disuse" (after all, he'd been standing in his position for some time), and promptly fumbled it. I don't remember that at all.

I don't remember Bill Mazeroski either. I only know I pitched to him that afternoon—about four pitches. But when I look at his photographs in the sports magazines I feel no association, no sense of recognition.

THE FIRST definable face that emerged from the thick mist that descended on me when Mazeroski came to the plate was that of Ralph Houk— the tough, confident, chaw-chewing Yankee coach who is now Casey Stengel's successor as the Yankee manager. I was first aware of him when I sensed a movement on the first-base foul line and turned to see him coming toward me. I glowered at him. Whatever his reputation, as he came out over the base line I looked upon him as an intruder. He came on in a slow, nonchalant amble, looking off into the outfield, then down in front of his feet, never at me, and there was no apparent purpose in mind—just a man strolling across the infield—and then he came within the dirt circumference of the pitcher's mound, climbing stiff-legged up toward me, and he put his hand out for the ball.

"Needle-lily-eh?" he said.

"What!" I cried.

"Need a little help, hey?"

I stared furiously at him.

"Kid, you look a little tired out," he said patiently. "Don't you want some help?" He kept his hand out for the ball.

"No, no, no," I said. My voice came out in a croak. "Gotta finish. Lemme pitch just a li'l more." But Houk didn't turn for the dugout; he smiled, very broadly this time, and kept his hand out.

Finally I took a step forward, dropped the ball in his hand and stumbled off the mound.

I walked slowly toward the first-base dugout. Most of the players in the dugout were standing up, watching me come in, and many of them were grinning. Just as I reached the base line, Ralph Houk behind me threw a single pitch to Mazeroski, which, in a sort of final irony, he hit high and lazy to Bob Cerv in leftfield. Since my back was to the diamond I didn't see the ball caught, but when it was, the players in the field ran for the dugout, streaming by me without a word and clambering down the steps, most of them headed for the water cooler. I was bewildered by that rush of movement past me; I didn't know what was going on until Martin fell into slow step beside me. "Man," he said smiling broadly, "it's O.K. It's over," and I said weakly, "Sure," and went with him into the dugout, where I turned and sagged down on the bench.

Whitey Ford, the Yankee pitcher, came over and sat down.

"Know something?" he said. "We've been making book here in the dugout as to when you'd keel over."

"No kidding," I said weakly.

"Yup. He was sure sweating out there, wasn't he, Billy?" He leaned across and grinned at Martin. "Leaking out of him like it was sawdust."

"Sawdust? That was blood, man. First time," said Martin, "I ever thought I'd be running in for a mound conference to find out what was going on was a funeral service," and he and Ford leaned off the bench and bellowed with laughter that turned heads down the length of the dugout. They wanted to know what Martin had said, and so he said it again, and from down the line they were all looking and grinning. They called up the questions: "Hey, kid, what'ja think of it, hey? How'd ja like it out there? Pretty rough, hey?"—their joshing friendly, but you could tell they were pleased their profession had treated me as roughly as it had.

"Really sumpin'," I said.

"What'd he say?" someone called out.

"Really sumpin' out there," I repeated and slid off the bench and headed for the showers.

ᴥ

12 Reasons Why the Triple Is the Most Exciting 12 Seconds In Sports

BY ROY BLOUNT JR.

Singles are mere base hits, doubles are for the timid, and home runs are over too quickly. The discerning fan knows that nothing gets the adrenaline pumping like that mad dash for third.

BOMBS AND BASES ON BALLS: STATE-OF-THE-ART BASEBALL offense today. ¶ Barry Bonds. If the ball is not where he wants it (as every pitcher prays), he sneers. If it is where he wants it—Lord have mercy—he makes it disappear. Either way, he's the god of get-that-thing-away-from-me. Unlike most things called awesome these days, Barry Bonds batting is. But wouldn't it be nice if, when Bonds steps into the box, you could expect some fielding and running?

And Billy Beane. General manager of the Oakland A's, protagonist of Michael Lewis's crackerjack bestseller *Moneyball*. Having determined by computer analysis that on-base percentage is the single most significant offensive indicator, Beane devotes himself to the pursuit of men who are fat (so nobody else will want them) and who walk a lot. O.K. But who wants to watch fat men walking?

Isn't there something missing in baseball today? In *The Great American Novel*, by Philip Roth, the wealthy seductress Angela Whittling Trust tries to make the illiterate slugger Luke Gofannon love her more than anything else. She succeeds in making him love her more than a shoestring catch. Or a stolen base. Or even a home run. But she never. . . .

"Don't get me wrong, Angela, I ain't bad-mouthin' the home run. . . . But smack a home run, and that's it, it's all over."

"And a triple?". . .

"Well. . . smackin' it, first off. Off the wall, up the alley, down the line, however it goes, it goes with that there crack. Then runnin' like blazes. . . . Two hunerd and seventy feet of runnin' behind ya, and with all that there momentum. . . . Over he goes. Legs. Arms. Dust. Hell, ya might be in a tornado, Angela. Then ya hear the ump, 'Safe!'. . . Only that ain't all. . . . The best part, in a way. Standin' up. Dustin' off y'r breeches and standin' up there on that bag."

She never makes him love her more than a triple. The triple has been called the most exciting 12 seconds in sports. Hard to think of another generic 12 seconds in sports to compare it with, other than a furlong, but never mind that. A triple is absolutely the most exciting 12 seconds in sports, and here's why it still is, though it seems to be fading away.

I. The Triple, Once a Staple, Now Is Rare

It is like an unenhanced breast in Hollywood, service at a service station, a soda fountain in a drugstore, a free-range neighborhood dog. In on-base percentage a triple counts the same as a walk, although only an idiot would love a walk more than Angela Whittling Trust. In slugging percentage a triple counts 25% less than a home run, although it is 560% rarer. That's like valuing all minerals solely by weight. In the early days of baseball, when the game was played almost exclusively on the field as opposed to over the fences, a home run was appropriately the rarest hit, the triple next rarest, and so on. Today triples represent only 2.1% of hits, home runs 11.8%.

Some more numbers:

In 1921, 16 major league teams, each playing a 154-game schedule (a total of 1,229 games), hit 1,364 triples, more than one per game. In 1950 the number of triples was down to 793, or one per 1.56 games. In 1960 it was 658, one per 1.88 games. Last season 30 teams playing a 162-game schedule (2,425 games) hit 921, or one triple for every 2.63 games. Last year one triple was hit for every 202.61 plate appearances. This year there may be a few more; through Sunday, the ratio was one for every 201.69.

The triple is now the least common single box-score-statistic occurrence, except for its defensive cousin the triple play, which is so scarce as to be almost negligible, and the balk, which doesn't deserve to be mentioned in the same breath as the triple. (The inside-the-park home run doesn't show up separately in the box score, and at any rate should be properly regarded as an extra-base triple.) Even the somewhat lamented, widely disdained sacrifice bunt crops up more frequently now than the triple.

Ballparks have gotten smaller over the years, so hitting a home run is easier and hitting a triple is like building a ship in a bottle. Many of the new parks of the 1970s had artificial turf, which gave a ball in the gap enough scoot to enhance a triple's chances, but inorganic grass is finally going the way of the leisure suit. And as we know, the most powerful hitters hit the ball farther these days, for whatever reasons, so it's harder to keep in the park.

But the triple's decline is not entirely a matter of architecture and physics. From the player's point of view, there is little incentive to stretch a double into a triple. Offenses are so formidable these days that it generally makes more sense to stop at second and expect to be driven in from there than to risk making an out. It has long been gospel that you should never make the first or the third out of an inning at third base. Third base coaches protect themselves by interpreting this dictum conservatively, very seldom waving a runner to third on a close play—the runner can ignore the stop sign, but if he's out, it's his mistake.

Triples are not much of a bargaining chip in contract negotiations. When Jim Palmer and Davey Johnson were Baltimore Orioles teammates, Palmer recalls, Johnson hit what should have been an easy triple, in the late innings of a tie game with one out, but pulled up at second. The Baltimore bench was mystified. "We said, 'Why didn't you go for the triple?' He said, 'I've got a doubles clause.' We said, 'Don't you think they'd give you credit for a double on a triple?' He said, 'I've got a doubles clause.' He went on to make a pretty good manager," says Palmer, "but we called him Dum-dum."

It used to be that serious home run hitters—Lou Gehrig, Joe DiMaggio, Stan Musial, Willie Mays, Mickey Mantle—also sometimes led the league in triples. Doesn't happen anymore. Mark McGwire, who did so much to make the home run what it is in the 21st century, hit four triples as an A's rookie in 1987 and exactly two for the rest of his career. In one stretch he went 4,618 at bats between triples.

You don't have to be a bulked-up, walk-conscious slugger to get by without three-base hits. In 2002 Oakland shortstop Miguel Tejada, a slashing, free-swinging speedster, set an alltime single-season record for at bats (662) without a single triple. He was the American League Most Valuable Player that year. (The previous record was set by the Chicago

Cubs' Sammy Sosa, in 1998. He was the National League MVP that year.)

There is a traditionalist explanation for the triple's decline. Broadcaster Tim McCarver, who as a St. Louis Cardinals catcher led the National League with 13 triples in 1966, told the *New York Post*, "Players, through the years, have been in the habit of standing around, looking at the ball. The triple mostly comes from running hard right out of the box." In McCarver's day the hitter was past first when the ball went off the wall or cleared it. "You'd never see the first base coach congratulate a hitter [for a home run]; the hitter was long gone. Now you see it a lot."

Blame it on Deion Sanders, maybe. In 1992 Sanders, playing for the Atlanta Braves, led the majors with 14 triples, in only 303 at bats. Perhaps the triple ceased to strike him as enough of a challenge after that, for his triples production slacked off, but what remained distinctive about his triples was the way he produced them. "He'd kind of just cruise to first base," recalls Mark Grace, then with the Cubs and now with the Arizona Diamondbacks, "and once he saw it was in the gap, he could get from first to third faster than anybody I've ever seen. Deion was a guy who could actually outrun the baseball. There were a few I saw him hit in the gap, and I was just, like, I can't believe he's trying for third. He'd round second base and the ball would already be in the cutoff man's hand and he'd still get third base. It was almost like in football, how he would be way off his man, in pass coverage, and just goad the quarterback—he could close so fast. Same way in baseball, he'd goad guys into trying to throw him out at third."

It will be recalled that Sanders threw ice water all over McCarver, three times, in the Atlanta locker room after a 1992 National League Championship Series game, because McCarver had criticized him from an old school point of view. McCarver came by that attitude honestly, as a Cardinals teammate of the quintessential hard-nosed pitcher, Bob Gibson. Gibson was black and McCarver white, and this was back in the '60s, when racial integration was still aborning in the South, where McCarver came from. For years Gibson kept McCarver at arm's length and off-balance, testing him with racial jokes. But after McCarver hit a triple one day, Gibson said to him, "Hey, you like to hit triples," and the way he said it, it struck McCarver as a magic moment. The two went on to become close friends.

2. Here's Something Really Rare: A Walk-Off Triple

Ozzie Guillen, the Florida Marlins' amiable third base coach, is one of the few people who will say that his goal as a player was to hit as many triples as possible—he wound up with 69 in 16 years. Guillen points out that a walk-off triple hardly ever happens "because there's going to be a play at the plate, and most guys stay at second to let the winning run score." But Guillen has seen it done, by Lance Johnson, his teammate on the Chicago White Sox. (Johnson led the American League in triples four years in a row, from 1991 through '94, was beaten out by the Cleveland Indians' Kenny Lofton on the last day of the season in '95, then signed with the New York Mets and led the National League in '96.) Once in a sudden-death situation with Tim Raines, a fast man in his own right, on first base, "Lance hit a triple down the line and made it. He was sliding into third base when Raines was scoring." Of course, it could have been a smart play to reach third, if Raines had been thrown out at home for just the first out. But then it wouldn't have been a walk-off triple.

3. There Is Something about the Number Three
Heaven forbid we should slop over into mysticism here. In the computer-based, rigorously unsentimental, cost-effective baseball thinking of today, rationality rules. Let us just mention three outs; three strikes; Babe Ruth wore number 3; the red, white and blue (sorry, strike that); beginning, middle and end; Moe, Larry and Curly; and the eternal triangle. And consider this observation by science writer Jim Holt (not the same Jim Holt who hit 10 triples for the Minnesota Twins and A's between 1968 and '76) in *The New York Review of Books*: "Why does our everyday world have three dimensions? . . . In a space of more than three dimensions, it can be shown, there are no stable orbits, either for planets or for electrons. Therefore, there could be no chemistry, and hence no chemically based life forms."

4. The Junior Felix Factor
So named, not so much because the career of Junior Felix is such a clear-cut example as because *junior felix*, in Latin, means "younger happy."

There are, of course, many exceptions to the rule that triples tend to reflect youthful ebullience. If the Diamondbacks' Steve Finley, who at week's end had nine triples, placing him only one behind the Braves' Rafael Furcal for the National League lead, should wind up first in the category this year—as he did a decade ago with the Houston Astros—he will become the oldest player, at 38, ever to top either league in that department. So far that distinction is held by Jake Daubert, who led the National League at age 38 in 1922 with 22. But only 29% of league leaders in triples, going back to 1900, have been as old as 30. Home run prowess tends to build as a player matures, but triples are largely a phenomenon of the early years.

People slow down and muscle up as they get older, of course, but not as rapidly as their triple totals tend to decline. Consider the numbers of Junior Francisco (Sanchez) Felix, of Laguna Salada, Dominican Republic, in a career that stretched from 1989 through '94, with the Toronto Blue Jays, California Angels, Marlins and Detroit Tigers.

Rookie year: eight triples, one every 52 at bats. Second year: seven triples, one per 66 at bats. Third year: two triples, one per 115. Fourth year: five triples, one per 102. Fifth year: one triple, in 214 at bats. Sixth year: one, in 301. Then retirement. No doubt there were injuries along the way, but nobody slows down that progressively between the ages of 21 and 27. Conceivably the devil was in the home runs. As a rookie Felix hit just one more dinger than he did triples; in his second year, more than twice as many. In his last season Felix hit 13 home runs to the one triple. (After the second year, when Toronto traded Felix to California, Bill James wrote of a computer program that projected Felix to be a possible superstar, with 237 more home runs in his future; he had hit nine in '89, 15 in '90. His lifetime total was 55.)

He had lost zest. It tends to happen. In his first three full seasons Garry Templeton led the National League with 18, 13 and 19 triples, but then at age 24 he became alienated, told his manager he was tired and made an obscene gesture to a fan on Ladies' Day. In 11 more seasons he never again reached double figures in triples. In Pistol Pete Reiser's first season as a regular, at the age of 22, he hit 17 triples for the Brooklyn Dodgers to lead the National League. The almost mythical Reiser, who kept running full tilt into the concrete walls of Ebbets Field in the act of trying to kill opponents' triples, had several other productive campaigns, but all his dislocations and concussions took their toll: He never again hit more than five triples in a season. (Once, when Leo Durocher inserted Reiser into the lineup too soon after a hospitalization, he hit a shot that had triple all over it, then fainted dead away while rounding first.)

Ted Williams hit 25 triples in his first two seasons, when he was the Kid, and 46 in the next 17, as he became a more professional and irritable collector of walks and home runs. Ryne Sandberg, who hit a league-leading 19 triples in his third full season, when he was 24, never had another double-digit triples year in his 12 remaining seasons. Junior Gilliam's only year hitting more than eight triples was his rookie year, when he led the league with 17. Kirby Puckett's only double-figure season was his second one, when he hit 13. Paul Waner led the league in triples twice, his first two years. Willie Mc-Covey hit two triples in his first game, and 44 in his next 2,587.

Consider catchers. We do not associate them with triples, because they squat so much, but when it comes to the Junior Felix factor they are like most people. McCarver is one of only two catchers to lead his league in triples (Carlton Fisk, who hit nine for the Boston Red Sox in 1972, is the other), which he did at age 24. In his 20 other seasons he averaged 2.2. Yogi Berra hit 10 triples at the age of 23 and only 39 in his 18 other seasons. Mickey Cochrane, Bill Dickey, Wally Schang, Bill Freehan, Manny San-guillen, Andy Etchebarren, John Bateman, John Roseboro—each of these had one quite respectable triples season in his tenderest years, then crouched down into workaday reality. Ernie Lombardi, the most famously lumber-ing base runner of all time, who stole eight bases in 17 years, and about whom it was said, "A triple for an ordinary batter is a double for Lombar-di," managed in his first full season, 1932, to leg out nine triples—a third of his career total.

Consider large first basemen called Moose. Walt Dropo hit eight triples as a rookie and 14 over his other 12 seasons. Bill Skowron hit nine triples in only 215 at bats during his first year, an average of three in his other 13. Other large, unspeedy sluggers who played first base and had similar triples records include Vic Wertz, Dale Long and Harmon Killebrew.

It's as if every major league hitter wants to establish once, before he grows up entirely, that he can breathe the heady air of the game's most stimulating statistical category. Rich Rollins of the Twins hit half of his 10-year total in 1964, when at age 26 he led the American League with 10. Here are just a few of the one-time league leaders in triples: Gino Cimoli, Delino DeShields, Mike Kreevich, Del Unser, Buddy Lewis, Jim Rivera, Walt Wilmot, Buttercup Dickerson, Hoot Evers, Barney McCoskey, Tom McCreery, Jeff Heath, Ray (Rabbit) Powell, Gene Richards, Stan Spence, Luis Olmo, Hank Edwards, Wally Pipp, Jake Wood, Mitch Webster, Mari-ano Duncan, Darren Lewis, David Dellucci and Neifi Perez.

The triple's magic wears off as a player matures. Johnny Damon, the Red Sox' wide-ranging centerfielder, led two minor leagues in triples as a youth and last year led the American League with 11. At week's end he had six in 2003. Asked how hitting a triple makes him feel now at the age of 29, he says, "Exhausted. It used to be so easy."

David Halberstam, in his book *Summer of '49*, mentions that Tommy Henrich said early in 1950, when the New York Yankees outfielder was 37, "I think I can play the whole season as long as I don't hit too many triples. They're just too hard on my knees."

5. The Triple Is Not Too Retro for Your Consideration

The alltime record for triples by one player in one season is an incredible 36. It is one baseball record that will probably never be broken. It was set by a Pittsburgh Pirate in 1912—O.K., O.K., but consider this: The Pirate in question was named Owen Wilson. Name another record, in all of sports, that is held by a person with the same name as someone who costars in action movies with Jackie Chan.

6. To See a Triple, You Have to Be There

Home runs are telegenic: The ball that leaves the yard fits the box, visually, and a basic grasp of what a home run entails requires no more reflection than, say, Fox News does. (Perhaps there should be a home run channel, called HR!, though I don't mean to imply that home runs ought to be lumped in with everything that works on television, like people competitively eating bowls of caterpillars or one spouse being sandbagged into revealing to another that he or she has been carrying on with his or her teenage niece or nephew, who shows up, heavily tattooed, to declare that love is never wrong.) There is room in a segment of *Baseball Tonight* for lots of homers. Or jacks, or taters, or dingers. Home runs have always had catchy nicknames—who knows, we may see a revival of "circuit clout." (*Triples* don't require synonyms. Threebie? No thanks. Triple comes off the tongue trippingly enough in its own right, with *rip* and ripple in it.)

And there is no TV screen big or splittable enough to show all the things going on at once in a multifarious event like the triple: a man with the requisite pop and speed shooting the ball out there and the ball getting off into some kind of crazy limbo, and the man who has the best arm on the field chasing the ball down and firing it back with his cannon as the aspiring tripler cuts the second base corner just right ("Baseball is not statistics," wrote Jimmy Breslin, "it's DiMaggio rounding second") and. . . .

In Fenway Park a few weeks ago, during a big game against the Yankees, 6' 4", 230-pound David Ortiz of the Red Sox slashed a drive into the right-field corner that came off the wall so crazily that it hopped up off the ground and back over the head of Raul Mondesi, the Yankees' rightfielder at the time, who—clearly and understandably uncertain how to play the ball—waved at it as he slid feet-first into the wall. On the ESPN telecast we saw Ortiz's swing and his first two steps toward first. . . cut to Mondesi skidding into the wall and jumping back up after the ball ("It's rolling around out there," said play-by-play man Jon Miller with due enthusiasm). . . cut to a runner scoring. . . cut to the cutoff man receiving Mondesi's throw. . . cut to another runner scoring. . . cut to Ortiz standing on third grinning almost sheepishly with his first triple of the season.

Then the color man, Rick Sutcliffe, pointed out, "Lots of guys his size don't hit many triples because they don't want to. They don't want to have to run that far and that hard. But Ortiz will gladly take it—he appreciates the opportunity to stay in the game and hit against a lefthander."

There's a TV triple: several unavoidably disjointed flashes followed, aptly enough, by insider commentary that almost obliterates the achievement.

7. Triples Acquaint You with the Real Estate

Nooks and crannies are good for triples. Fenway is still a good park for triples, which is one reason Boston's Nomar Garciaparra, the opposite of a fat man walking—he is, in fact, so energetically fidgety at the plate that he looks like a rawboned, long-legged Little Leaguer who has to go to the bathroom—at week's end had 13 triples, one behind the major league leader, the Twins' Cristian Guzman. There's a big V-shaped recession in Fenway's right centerfield stands where a ball that gets past the centerfielder can roll and roll. And a visiting fielder who misjudges the rebound off the Green Monster in left can see a drive go over his head twice; Garciaparra got a big triple that way in June when the Cardinals came to town. In the right-field corner, says Trot Nixon, who patrols that garden for the Red Sox, "sometimes the ball takes on a life of its own." On its way to the corner it can tick off a little protuberance near where the ball girl sits, or it can come into the wall at the 302-foot point and hug its way around the barrier as it rapidly deepens to 380. Below where the wall is padded there's a concrete bit off which the ball can come back at the fielder like a rocket.

That sort of thing is to be expected in a park as quirky and venerable as Fenway, but even many of the newer fields are surprisingly varied in their conduciveness to triples. In San Diego's Qualcomm Stadium, for instance, balls can get up under the benches in the bullpen in the rightfield corner. And there's that flagpole hill out in centerfield at Houston's Minute Maid Park. On the other hand, when Yankee Stadium was remodeled in 1976, it changed from a great triples park possessing many odd and fascinating depths to something blander, tighter—well, let's not call it a bad face-lift, let's just say it wasn't good for triples.

8. When a Triple Is Over, It Isn't Over

You hit a home run, there's a big explosion of noise like one that ends a movie that nobody can think of any other way to resolve, and you trot around the bases and disappear. You hit a triple, and you're still a presence, basking in hurrahs or boos, dusting off, taking a lead, jigging around 90 feet away from pay dirt.

Or you're rolling around in the dirt with the third baseman. In the first inning of the deciding game of the 1977 American League Championship Series, the Kansas City Royals' George Brett (sixth among living triplers, with 137) drew first blood with a two-run triple, slid hard into third and without missing a beat began whaling away at the Yankees' fully reciprocating Graig Nettles, all in one continuous motion, as if this were a big-game triple's natural blowback. The Yankees won the game, though.

Shoeless Joe Jackson had a great triple-aftermath back in the early days. His triples inspired poetry, for instance:

> *Jackson, Joe, was a dashing young beau,*
> *And a slashing young beau was he:*
> *He larruped to left, and he hammered to right,*
> *Both of them good for three.*

Jackson inspired another scribe to write, "His triple was a pippin, and his two-bagger was a peach."

Jackson himself was illiterate. Once (there are other, ruder versions of this story, but this is the most mellifluous) he was being ragged by a fat lady in the seats near third base: "Hey, Jackson! Can you spell Mississippi? Hey, Jackson! Can you spell Mississippi?" Jackson smote a mighty blow, came steaming into third, dusted himself off, and hollered, "Hey, fat lady. Can you spell triple?"

9. Triples Trivia? Yes!

Which set of twins hit the most triples, lifetime? Off the top of your head you'd say Jose and Ozzie Canseco. But you'd be wrong. Jose hit 14, Ozzie none. Better answer: Ray and Roy (Bummer) Grimes, in the 1920s: Ray hit 25 triples for the Cubs, 12 in '22 alone. Roy (note nickname) had zero for the New York Giants. If, however, you want a set of twins, each of whom contributed at least one triple to the total, then the second pair you no doubt thought of was right: Johnny (five triples) and Eddie (four) O'Brien, the college basketball stars who were such versatile disappointments—at the plate, in the infield and on the mound—for the Pirates in the '50s. Runners-up: Mike and Marshall Edwards, who hit four and three triples, respectively, between '77 and '83.

There have been, perhaps blessedly, no big league triplets. Except, of course, for Coaker Triplett, who tripled 14 times in six years between 1938 and '45 for three National League teams. Interestingly, Jimmy Ripple hit exactly the same number of triples for four teams between 1936 and '43. Whether these two ever both hit a triple in the same game, inspiring headlines such as RIPPLE TRIPLE TRUMPS TRIPLETT'S, or what the odds are of that happening, remains unknown. When it comes to non-multiple-birth fraternal trios, the best three of the five Delahanty brothers, Ed, Frank and Jim, amassed more triples (266) than the three DiMaggios (212) or the three Alous (125), but you knew that.

Who hit the most triples (11) in a year during which he pulled off an unassisted triple play? Since 1920 the answer to that question has been Bill Wambsganss. But with two more triples this year Furcal would change all that. And if Furcal ends up atop the National League triples heap this year, he will become the first person to claim an unassisted triple play and a triples championship. Furcal, however, homered in his first two at bats in another game this year—his first-ever two-homer game, going back to his childhood in the Dominican Republic. This may also be the year that Furcal outgrows triples.

10. Who? Wahoo, That's Who

The greatest triples hitter of all time, Sam Crawford of the Tigers, who led the American League in triples six times and wound up with 312 in 19 years, was one of the most popular players of his day (1899–1917) and had one of the best nicknames ever: Wahoo Sam. He was from Wahoo, Neb.

11. Triplers Commit Triple-Robbery

In many cases the best hitters of triples have been the outfielders most noted for taking them away from people. Finley and Ichiro Suzuki come to mind today. The late Jim Murray wrote, "Willie Mays's glove is where triples go to die." The great catch Mays made of Wertz's drive in the 1954 World Series, some 460 feet from the plate, presumably snuffed out a triple. (Wertz had hit one earlier in the game.)

As maybe the fastest centerfielder ever, Willie Wilson probably robbed or cut off as many triples as he hit, and he led the American League in hitting them at the ages of 25, 27, 30, 32 and 33. Roberto Clemente, who hit three triples in one day in the middle of the 1958 pennant race, had the arm, the range and the flash in rightfield to make triples defense as exciting as triples offense.

Many of today's leading triples-hitters are shortstops, but they can help prevent triples in the role of cutoff man. Or . . . well, in the second game of the 1916 World Series, Boston's Chester (Pinch) Thomas hit a long blast to left center that was ticketed for three bases. Between second and third, however, Brooklyn shortstop Ivy Olson tripped him. Instead of getting up and running on toward third, Thomas elected to stay and fight. The two were wrestling on the ground when the home plate umpire came out, separated them and awarded Thomas third base. Well, it was worth a try. And forget about the most exciting 12 seconds, that may have been a 12-minute triple.

12. Triples Are Not a Result of Corporate Management Policy

TV is not the only box that has transformed baseball. There is also the computer. The hotshots who run the Oakland A's, according to *Moneyball*, don't seem to relish watching the game, as such. They regard the players as fungible rather than fun. They patch together lineups from chunks of data. Triples are not about data.

Triples-related information tends to be anecdotal and character-driven. For instance, one player who never hit a triple was Ron Herbel, baseball's alltime worst hitter with at least 200 at bats. In nine years, 1963 through '71, he got six hits for a lifetime average of .029. One of his two doubles was off the leftfield wall in the Astrodome. As Herbel blew into second base, flushed with success, he saw the third base coach signaling him to stop. He didn't. "As I ran past the shortstop, Bob Aspromonte was standing on third, holding the ball. I was out by 40 feet. But I slid, and I slid hard. I could always slide. They had this red infield in Houston, and I got dirt all over Aspro, and he goes ass-end over a teakettle. He gets up and is just livid. I got his uniform dirty. He hated that. He said, 'Ron, what the hell are you doing?' I got up and said, 'I don't know. I've never been this far.' "

Incidentally, one of the first things we learn in *Moneyball* is that Billy Beane hit three triples in a high school game, still a California schoolboy record. The outfielders kept moving back, and he kept hitting the ball over their heads. The last time he did it, the crowd actually laughed. But in six underachieving seasons as a big league player, the enormously talented Billy Beane achieved a handful of doubles and home runs, even a few—a very few—bases on balls. He never hit a single big league triple. Maybe he never got past the Junior Felix factor.

And do you know what the last thing that happens in *Moneyball* is? In the Arizona instructional league we see minor leaguer Jeremy Brown, the epitome of fat-man-walking, hit a deep drive to left, and Brown sees the left-fielder getting out of position to play it correctly off the wall, and he thinks, I'm gonna get a triple.

"It's a new thought for him," writes Michael Lewis. "He isn't built for triples. He hasn't hit a triple in years. He thrills to the new idea: Jeremy Brown, hitter of triples."

But then Brown slips and falls between first and second. He retreats to first and sees his teammates in the dugout "falling all over each other, laughing." His drive didn't go off the wall but over it. It's not a triple after all, just an old home run.

TOWERING
SHOTS

The Year, The Moment And Johnny Podres

BY ROBERT CREAMER

There were many worthy candidates for SI's second Sportsman of the Year award, but none more deserving than the man who led the Brooklyn Dodgers to the promised land by beating the Yankees in the World Series.

T*HE NINTH WAS JOHNNY PODRES'S INNING. THE anticipation of the victory rode on every pitch. The first batter tapped the ball back to the pitcher's mound and Johnny, plucking the ball from the netting of his glove, threw him out. In Yankee Stadium 62,000 people leaned forward to watch Johnny Podres face the next man. He raised an easy fly to leftfield and was out. (Fifty million or so TV watchers were holding their breath now too.) The third man took a called strike (the stadium crowd exploded with noise), took a ball, swung and missed (an explosion from coast to coast), took a second ball high, fouled one, fouled another. The Brooklyn Dodger infield moved restlessly, fidgeting. Podres threw again, a big, fat, arrogant changeup that the batter topped on the ground. After a half century of waiting the Brooklyn Dodgers were champions of the world.*

THE GRANDFATHER of Johnny Podres climbed out of the mines of czarist Russia and came to America in 1904, the year after Cy Young and the Boston Red Sox beat Honus Wagner and the Pittsburgh Pirates in the first World Series. The chances are excellent that Barney Podres had never heard of Cy Young or Honus Wagner, or of the Boston Red Sox or the Pittsburgh

Pirates, or of the World Series, or even, for that matter, of baseball. He was 24, and he had been working in the mines for 10 years.

In America he found his way to an iron-mining community in upstate New York in the rough foothills of the Adirondacks near Lake Champlain, married a Lithuanian girl and took his broad back and big hands down into the mines again. Forty-six years, two wives and eight children later he came out of the mines for the last time.

Now he sits in his weather-beaten house in the company village of Witherbee, N.Y., ailing from "the silica," the miner's disease, his great hands folded. His story is neither rare nor extraordinary; it has been repeated in one form or another in millions of American families. But it has a close relationship to the reasons why SPORTS ILLUSTRATED this week salutes the old man's grandson as its second Sportsman of the Year, to succeed Roger Bannister as the one person—of the millions active in sports all over the world in 1955—who was most significant of the year past.

For in the old man's lifetime sports has grown from a minor diversion for a leisurely handful of people to a preoccupying influence in almost every country on earth.

Consider Joe Podres, son of old Barney and father of Johnny, the Sportsman of the Year. Like his father, he went down into the mines in his youth. But working conditions in the mines have improved, like working conditions almost everywhere, and a man has more time that is his own. Joe Podres spent a good deal of his free time playing baseball. He worked all week and played ball on Sundays, or whenever the local team could schedule a game. He was a topflight semiprofessional pitcher for 25 years, until he reluctantly retired three years ago at the age of 43. Sports earned him no money to speak of ("Eight dollars in eight years," is one family joke about it), but the competition and the pride of victory over a quarter century did a great deal to offset the exacting drudgery that goes with simply digging iron ore. And it provided the key that opened the way for his son to make come true a modern version of one of those old legends of beggars and kings and gold pots in the cabbage patch that were told for centuries by miners, farmers, peasants and other wishful Old World dreamers.

Today, even the dream is different. It does not deal with beggar boys becoming kings, or knights on white chargers. The boy kicks a football along Gorky Street and imagines himself booting the winning goal for Spartak in Dynamo Stadi-

*um in Moscow. He belts a hurley ball along the rich turf with
a stick of Irish ash and thinks how grand it would be in Croke
Park in Dublin saving the All-Ireland title for Cork. He stands
on the edge of a street in a village in Provence as the Tour de
France wheels by and sees himself pedaling into Parc des
Princes Stadium in Paris, miles ahead of Louison Bobet. He
throws a ball against the battered side of a house and dreams
of pitching Brooklyn to victory in the World Series.*

JOHNNY PODRES, with three other high school boys, drove out of Witherbee in August 1949, and 265 miles south to New York City to see the
Brooklyn Dodgers play a baseball game with the Boston Braves. It was the
first major league game Johnny Podres had ever seen.

"We sat way up in the upper-leftfield stands," Podres recalls. "Newcombe
was pitching. The Dodgers had the same guys they have now: Robinson,
Reese, Campy, Hodges, Furillo, Snider. I've always been a Brooklyn fan,
and that day I made up my mind, I'm going to pitch for Brooklyn."

Johnny planned to see the Dodgers play again the next day but it rained,
and the day after that when the Dodgers were playing again, some other
youngster was sitting in the upper-leftfield stands daydreaming of playing in the majors. John Podres was back in Witherbee, still a high school kid
rooting for Brooklyn. While the Dodgers went on playing, winning and
losing pennants, John Podres went on to become captain of his high school
basketball team, to pitch his high school team to its league championship,
to date, to dance, to hunt deer in the hills outside of town, to fish through
the ice of Lake Champlain in the winter.

Then the major league scouts came around and the dream began to come
true for John Joseph Podres. Two or three clubs were interested in him for
their minor league farm clubs, but for one reason or another John did not
sign. His father says, "I think he was just waiting for Brooklyn to come
along." Come along they did, and Johnny signed a contract and, in 1951,
went off to the Dodgers' farm system. He won 21 and lost five in his first
year, later caught the eye of Dodger manager Charley Dressen and in 1953
was indeed pitching for Brooklyn in a World Series. That, however, was
far from being the magic moment, because young Podres was driven from
the mound by the New York Yankees, who were beating Brooklyn again, for
the fifth time in five World Series meetings.

John Podres is on good terms with luck, however, despite a chronic bad back and a midseason appendectomy. Last fall, as most of the world knows, he got a second try at immortality. Fittingly enough, it was on his 23rd birthday. Brooklyn had lost the first two games of the World Series—and Johnny himself had not finished a game since early summer—but he was the right man in the right place that day. The Yankees could not rattle him, nor could they connect solidly against his arrogant blend of fastballs and lazy-looking slow ones. The Dodgers not only won that game but the next two to take the lead in the Series and approach the brink of incredible victory.

Then they lost the sixth game, woefully. People in Brooklyn were saying, "those bums," and not in tones of rough affection. Rather it was an expression of heartbroken anger and frustration, that they should have come so close only to lose again. They had always lost to the Yankees in the World Series. They had always lost to everybody in the World Series. They were losing now. They would always lose.

At this propitious moment the grandson of old Barney Podres stepped forward, bowed to the audience and promptly became the hero of the year. It was the setting of the dream of glory, and Johnny Podres knew exactly what to do. He beat the Yankees for a second time, shut them out without a run in that old graveyard of Brooklyn hopes, Yankee Stadium itself. Johnny Podres pitched with his ears shut. The explosive noise of the crowd, the taunts of the Yankee bench never got through to him. "I guess I didn't really hear the noise," says Johnny, "until I came up to bat in the ninth." By that time the noise was for Johnny Podres, pitcher, and it was time for him to hear it.

In winning—and this was, in retrospect, the most exciting and fascinating thing about the Series—Johnny became the personification, the living realization of the forgotten ambitions of thousands and even millions of onlookers who had pitched curves against the sides of their own houses and evoked similar visions of glory, only to end up at the wheel of a truck or behind a desk in an office. What was happening transcended any game, or any sport. . . .

> . . . *The Russian more often than not ends up in a factory turning out heavy machinery for the state; he keeps his emotions under control until he can get to his seat high up on the side of Dynamo Stadium where he can yell his heart out for Spartak. The Irishman puts his hurley stick away and tends*

*dutifully to the farm, except when he can get down to Cork
City to shout for Cork against Tip or Limerick. The French-
man uses his cycle only to ride back and forth from home to
shop to cafe; but the day the Tour goes through his village
he's back on the curb again, watching, watching, as the wheels
fly by. Dreams die hard.*

And so, when the country boy from the small mining village stands alone
on the mound in Yankee Stadium in the most demanding moment of one
of the world's few truly epic sports events, and courageously, skillfully
pitches his way to a success as complete, melodramatic and extravagant
as that ever dreamed by any boy, the American chapter of the International
Order of Frustrated Dreamers rises as one man and roars its recognition.

There were others in the world of sport eminently fitted for the robes of
Sportsman of the Year. Sandor Iharos set five world records in 1955, astounding records that left track and field aghast. Rocky Marciano broadened
his omnipotent rule over heavyweight boxing. Paul Anderson performed
Bunyanesque feats of weightlifting that evoked admiration and applause
even in Russia. Aging Jackie Robinson retained the fiery spirit of the competitor sufficiently to light an exciting spark of success under his Brooklyn teammates during the pennant race and again in the World Series. Mil-
dred (Babe) Didrikson Zaharias brought great credit to sport by the courage,
serenity and bright good humor she displayed in the face of a terrifying
attack of cancer. Juan Fangio combined magnificent skill and cold, practical courage to drive racing cars faster than anyone else in the world. Otto
Graham came out of the ease of retirement to lead the desperate Cleveland Browns to yet another magnificent season. Eddie Arcaro rode a horse
as well as ever a horse can be ridden. Ray Robinson wrote a brilliant chapter of climax to the most dramatic comeback in the history of boxing. And
dozens of others, with names like Cassady, Tabori, Alston, Russell, Sow-
ell, Stengel . . . the list is endless if you listen to the sincere arguments from
every part of the world of sport.

But nowhere else in that vast, heterogeneous and wonderful world did
such a moment exist in 1955 as that of the seventh game of the World Series. Nowhere else did a man do what he had to do so well as Johnny Podres
did that day. Nowhere else in all the world did sports mean as much to so
many people as it did the day John Podres beat the Yankees.

❧

The Importance
Of Being Barry

BY RICHARD HOFFER

The Giants' Barry Bonds is the best player in the game today.
If you don't believe that, just ask him.

T HE PLAYERS CLUSTER CHILDLIKE ABOUT THEIR CUBICLES.
They brag or they sulk, depending on whether they've won
or lost, whether it's before a game or after, or whether
Jupiter's moons are in alignment or not. "You should see my
house," Barry Bonds is saying to Mike Jackson. This occurs in the San Francisco Giants' clubhouse before a game, the moons just so. "Major cribbage," Bonds continues. "Ceiling 40 feet high! Bring you a videotape." Jackson nods in appreciation.

This clubhouse is like any other, an enclave of protracted adolescence
where the players needn't mask their pride, or even their confusion, over
fame and fortune. A little later the same two players confer over pay stubs
that have just been distributed. They are two teens comparing report cards.
This invites talk of contracts.

"What's yours?" Bonds asks Jackson, a middle reliever.

"Two. What's yours?"

"Four," says Bonds, who is somewhat more than twice the ballplayer
Jackson is but still good-natured about the discrepancy.

"But soon it'll be eight." They are talking in millions of dollars.

But brag turns to sulk, just like that. "What is this $30,000 for?" Bonds suddenly asks, examining a deduction, and the moons are jolted out of orbit. An interview, so incidental to life in the clubhouse that it has been put off six days running and is a source of comedy among the players, is once more deferred. "Dude," Bonds says, waving the writer away, "later." And he vanishes. The clubhouse is otherworldly. The players are empowered by vast contracts, based on unusual, delicate, hard-won—and, in any other world, useless—skills. It seems they cannot ask for, or receive, enough. For them life is oddly generous. For example: Shoe salesmen—shoe givers, actually—come and go, delivering all manner of athletic equipment to the players, from gloves to golf clubs.

"I'd like some of those T-shirts too," a player reminds the shoe giver.

"How about a driver with a jumbo head?" the shoe giver asks.

This clubhouse, like any clubhouse, is redolent of the perfume of entitlement. A player uses the clubhouse phone to arrange for repairs to his BMW. "This is Robby Thompson," he says, adding, "of the Giants."

They have learned they are beyond normal citizenship. Why else would 40,000 people in Candlestick Park clamor to get close to them, to touch them? Why would the shoe givers grovel to have them wear their brands? Why would writers wait six days to be granted interviews?

In a corner of the clubhouse, Willie Mays, so far beyond citizenship as to be baseball royalty, practices golf swings with an invisible jumbo-headed driver while schmoozing with some shoe givers. Mays, the greatest Giant there ever was, is a special assistant to the club's president and general manager and is an all-purpose reminder of its past glory. Sometimes he's also a reminder of the Giants' past churlishness. Just this morning, in the *San Francisco Chronicle*, columnist Glenn Dickey compared Mays with Bonds—both great players, of course, but both mercurial characters. "Both men," Dickey wrote, "can be a royal pain in the rear."

"Glenn Dickey," says Mays, lifting a magnificent drive onto the fairway, "is an a------." Mays is especially upset about a passage in the column in which he reportedly said to another player, "F--- the fans."

"I never said that," Mays is saying to the shoe givers. "And anyway, that was 40 years ago." The shoe givers agree that even if he had said that, it was probably with reason.

Suddenly Mays seems determined to obliterate that column with a single public-relations act. "You still waiting to see Barry?" he asks the writer, whom Mays himself had blown off just five minutes earlier ("Gotta work, gotta work, gotta work," he'd said). Bonds is his godson. Mays played with Bobby Bonds, who had a record five seasons with at least 30 homers and 30 stolen bases and is Barry's father, but Mays's ties to Barry go beyond that. "Knew the boy's mother," he says. Now Mays seems friendly, as if to say, "Is this a royal pain in the rear? I don't think so." He volunteers to retrieve Bonds and set things straight. "I'll go get him," he says. "He's not as bad as you think."

Mays walks off to the trainer's room to get this job done. After a minute he returns, hacking at his hamstring. He is pantomiming treatment. "Ice," he whispers. "He's getting ice." And no more is said about Bonds, who snoozes undisturbed in the trainer's room. Mays and the shoe givers go back to their golf swings.

ONCE THIS spring, or so the story goes, Bonds hit an impressive home run, then turned in the batting cage to face his teammates and said, "Am I not a special f-----' person, or what?" Bonds claims it wasn't that way at all. He says he made a boastful comment, but that it was meant to be playful and not to be mistaken for arrogance. When Bonds is arrogant, there is no mistaking it. Yet the incident articulates two important facts: Bonds is quite special, and he knows it. You cannot deny his performance. Why should *he*?

In the last three seasons, during which he won two MVP awards and narrowly missed a third, he averaged 111 RBIs, more than 30 home runs and nearly 45 stolen bases a season, and he won three Gold Gloves in leftfield. And he's only 28. He began this season, his eighth in the big leagues and first with the Giants after seven years with the Pittsburgh Pirates, as if he were just hitting his stride. In April he batted .431 with seven home runs and 25 RBIs and won the National League Player of the Month award. And his torrid pace continued right into this month; at the end of last week Bonds was hitting .419 and ranked either first, second or third in seven offensive categories. After he hit two home runs (one of them one-armed) in a game against the New York Mets, Jeff Torborg, the Mets' manager, said, "Bonds belongs in a higher league."

He is so complete a player that it's almost infuriating. "Let's think of the things he can't do," said Ted Simmons, the Pirates' general manager. He is joking; there's nothing Bonds can't do. The day before Simmons said this, Bonds had climbed the leftfield wall to rob a Pirate of a homer.

Giant shortstop Royce Clayton is just as admiring. "I've never seen anyone like him," he says of Bonds. "Barry is like Magic Johnson—he makes everyone around him better."

How good is Bonds? Good enough to make you suspicious. The day he hit that one-armed homer against the Mets, it happened that teammate Matt Williams had just gone ahead of him for the league's home run lead. Can Bonds just turn it on and off? Well, Syd Thrift remembers watching Bonds in Triple A back in 1986, when Thrift was Pittsburgh's general manager. During batting practice before a game in Phoenix, Thrift saw Bonds pull five or six balls over the rightfield fence. "I told him any good hitter can do that," Thrift says, "but I'd like to see him hit a few over the leftfield fence. He hit five in a row and said, 'Is that good enough for you?' I said it was fine. I had the manager take him out of the game in the fifth inning, and I took him back to Pittsburgh that night."

Thrift, who used to make sure to talk to Bonds for at least five minutes every day to reassure him that he was appreciated, remembers one other thing: "The first five home runs he hit in Pittsburgh—they were over the left-field fence."

In Bonds's return to Pittsburgh, on April 9, he was hailed with boos and buckets of fake dollar bills to deride his free-agent defection to San Francisco, but he went 2 for 4 with a double, a triple and three runs scored. In the Giants' home opener he homered in his first at bat. If Bonds hadn't failed to produce in each of the last three National League Championship Series—he averaged .191 for the Pirates in those playoffs, all of which Pittsburgh lost—it would be reasonable to suspect that he was toying with the game. Even with his poor postseason record ("Call me Mr. July," he says), Bonds has become the richest player in a very rich sport. However, the money seems incidental to his story. With the kind of numbers Bonds has put up and continues to put up, nobody seems to mind how many numbers the Giants have put up. In fact, nobody makes a peep about Bonds's contract anymore. Who, besides Reggie Jackson, ever produced the way Bonds has during the first year after a big free-agent signing? San Francisco, which had an opportunity to sign him for $75,000 out of high school in 1982 (it lost him to Arizona State when it refused to offer more than $70,000), finally got him last December for $43.75 million over six years. In two or three seasons, if salaries continue to escalate and if Bonds continues to perform at anything like his present level, he'll seem like a blue-light special.

What the Giants may not get for their money is goodwill. Bonds does not create it. And it's not because of his enormous and highly visible self-confidence, which is expected and forgiven in great athletes. If Bonds makes a basket catch or struts around the bases after a home run and then faces the fans and asks, "Am I not a special f-----' person, or what?" he will still be loved. Nobody minds swagger at his level. Many people pay to see that. But his complaining, his rudeness, his insensitivity to teammates can wear a franchise out.

His return to Pittsburgh may serve as a cautionary tale for the Giants. In his seven years with Pittsburgh, Bonds couldn't have played much better or harder. Still, it seemed the Three Rivers Stadium fans would have welcomed a flu epidemic more warmly than they did Bonds. They went well beyond the usual free-agent-leaves-Pittsburgh booing.

It wasn't just the fans, either. When Bonds entered the Pirate clubhouse for what he may have imagined would be a joyous homecoming, the players didn't even look up from their card games. There was just too much history between Bonds and the Pirates. There was the 1990 playoff game in Cincinnati after which Bonds blasted teammate Jeff King. King had been scratched from the game after aggravating a lower-back injury the day before. (The injury would cause him to miss much of the next season.) "When we play Friday, Bobby Bonilla will be playing third, and Jeff King will be sitting there getting his back healthy. He'll be getting ready for spring training," Bonds said to reporters. On the trip back to Pittsburgh, R.J. Reynolds grew tired of Bonds's beefing—Reynolds and other Pirates had been outraged at his attack on King—and told him to grow up. Their argument on the team plane reached a climax when Bonds shoved a slice of pizza in Reynolds's face.

Then there was spring training of 1991, when Bonds, sulking over the Pirates' victory in his off-season arbitration hearing, got into a yelling match with Jim Lachimia, a club p.r. man. He then exchanged words with Jim Leyland, the Pittsburgh manager. This episode grew out of Bonds's decision to freeze out the press that spring; the argument began over whether two photographers could snap pictures of him. But the enduring moment was when Leyland yelled, "I've kissed your butt for three years! If you don't want to be here, then get your butt off the field!"

When the Pirates did not keep his close friend Bonilla from defecting to the Mets, Bonds wondered aloud if racism was at work. He wondered if Pirate centerfielder Andy Van Slyke, whom he called the Great White Hope, would have been treated the same way. It was no wonder that a Pittsburgh player was once quoted as saying, "I'd rather lose without Barry Bonds than win with him."

Van Slyke, for one, has often wondered why Bonds didn't own Pittsburgh. All he had to do was perform with the professionalism of a Mario Lemieux or a Willie Stargell. Just keep his foot out of his mouth. "If Barry is guilty of anything," says Van Slyke, "it's of not attaching meaning to his words."

The press certainly did not help Bonds in his relationship with the city. Most of the local writers, who had often been rebuffed by Bonds, disliked him by the time he left. Although Bonds was often a hot quote, he was also combative and moody. Or unavailable. Or just rude. Several times he explained his relationship with the media this way: "I thrive off you guys because I love to make you come back to my locker begging."

Such arrogance can be tough to swallow, especially when it seems calculated. The Pittsburgh writers still tell the story of one of their brethren who penetrated Bonds's inner circle just long enough to be invited for a round of golf. The next day Bonds passed the writer without speaking. The writer insisted it was nothing personal—"That's just Barry," he said, invoking the all-purpose explanation of Bonds's behavior. But to judge by the vitriol that greeted Bonds's return to Pittsburgh this spring, plenty of writers took his behavior personally.

It's likely none of this mattered to Bonds. He professes to be thick-skinned. "None of you know me, anyway," he likes to say, brushing aside his bad press; anything written, he insists, is irrelevant. He told one player last year that Bonilla made a big mistake in going to New York. "I can handle New York because I don't get my feelings hurt the way Bobby does," Bonds said.

At least on the subject of Bonds, Bonilla agrees: "He doesn't care what people say. Barry hears it, but he pays it no mind." Says Van Slyke: "I know Barry doesn't care what people think. It can't matter to him whether he's beloved here or not. It just can't, not the way he has behaved. All he's ever wanted—it's like his religion—is to be judged by what he's done on the field." Van Slyke holds no grudge. After all, look what Bonds did on the field for the Pirates. After the final game last year, when it was obvious that Bonds would no longer play for Pittsburgh, Van Slyke told Bonds that he wished Bonds could stay for five more years. "He is," Van Slyke says, "the greatest player I ever played with, or will ever play with." Still, the day Bonds returned to the Pirate clubhouse, Van Slyke didn't budge from his card game.

BONDS HAS always been insulated from his peers. He grew up in a privileged neighborhood in San Carlos, Calif., the son of a famous Bay Area
athlete. He had friends; to this day, one of his best friends is Bob McKercher,
who works for a recycling company in San Francisco. McKercher has known
Bonds since they were both six-year-olds. By his account Bonds was, and
remains, a fun guy. He remembers Barry making fun of his dancing ability and then setting about with Barry's mother, Pat, to give this "Italian-
Irish kid some soul." He remembers sleepovers with Barry that degenerated
into all-night gigglefests. "And we'd go to each other's Thanksgiving dinners,
like a revolving door, back and forth, and tape them on a video recorder,"
says McKercher. "I think people would pay to see Barry in his Afro."

But Barry could be aloof. The athletic director at Serra High, an all-boys
Catholic school of 700 that Barry attended, remembers that other students
tended to see Barry as "moody—basically keeping to himself." Kevin Donahue, who coached Barry in basketball at Serra ("He loved the limelight,
loved to take over the game with two minutes to go"), says, "He was not
cold, but if you weren't in his inner group, it might seem he was just keeping to himself. He might not say hi to everybody."

But in a pattern of behavior that continues to this day, Barry won attention from his elders. Donahue, who admits to having had minibattles with
Barry (a pattern of behavior that also continues to this day), says that Barry
demanded a lot of time and that Donahue was glad to give it. "You had to
take time to get to know him, and I did that," Donahue says. "We'd talk
often, about the jealousy in high school and how to handle it. It hurt him;
we'd talk about it a lot."

When Bonds returned to the Bay Area this spring, one of the first things
he did was to address the student body at Serra High. Donahue was not
surprised by the gesture, not surprised to be remembered. Bonds walked up
to him, first thing, and gave him a big hug. "That's Barry," Donahue says.

But another part of being Barry is to invite misunderstanding. This may
be genetic. His father certainly invited it during his playing days, and he
doesn't seem to have taught his son any of the social skills necessary to
avoid misunderstandings. "Important to be popular?" Bobby huffs, his jaw
muscles revealing the strain produced by any relations with the press. "All
the superstars I've met, popularity wasn't important to them. Barry just
wants to play baseball. He's not pushing ballots for popularity."

It's hard to say what Bobby's indifference to popularity or his independent
streak has cost him; his peers have granted him the utmost respect as an

athlete and as a hitting coach, the position he now holds with the Giants. However, until his close friend Dusty Baker got the San Francisco manager's job in December, Bobby was in baseball limbo, out of work for five years. And no one can say why. As a kid Barry had much less attitude, and even now he can't manage the surliness of his father. Even so, he could be a handful at times. Donahue once had to cajole Barry into doing weight training, for example. "But it was a game I won," Donahue says. "I would not call him rebellious or argumentative. He was a fairly typical, if highly gifted, high school kid."

Yet he came out of high school with something of a dubious reputation. Before offering Barry a baseball scholarship, Arizona State coach Jim Brock even went so far as to quiz a long-ago baby-sitter of Barry's. Brock was suspicious after Bonds, for all his talent, was left off one of California's most important high school all-star teams. "It was not totally clear to me why," Brock says. According to McKercher it was because tryouts for the northern California team were held the morning after Serra's senior prom. Bonds nodded off during the workout, and a coach—who perhaps was envious on behalf of the less-gifted and less-privileged kids trying out—left him off the team.

Brock was pleasantly surprised by Bonds once he arrived at Arizona State. He remembers a kid with a "twinkle in his eye, never malicious, but a kid who might say silly things at any time." Like every one of Bonds's coaches before him, Brock was somehow drawn into Bonds's world, even though few of his teammates were.

"There are some players who come and go here," Brock says, "and you never get to know them. Who is Bob Horner? He came here, he went. Now, Barry, I got to know him a lot better. It was attention I wanted to give him. I really liked the hell out of him. In fact, you know what the other kids called him? Barry Brock."

But Brock admits there were difficulties and that Bonds got special handling. "There was an inherent jealousy among the other players," he says. "Of course, he did roll in here with that big black Trans Am, he did have more money, he did have a bigger name. And he wasn't real interested in living any of that down." Brock's memory is that the team—"half white, with a redneck factor"—simply froze Bonds out.

"I had to talk to him a lot," Brock says. "He wanted to be liked, tried so damn hard to have people like him. Tried too hard. But then he'd say things he didn't mean, wild statements. I tried to tell him that these guys, 20 years from now, would be electricians and plumbers, but he'd be making millions. I didn't know how many millions, of course. Still, he'd be hurt. People don't realize he can be hurt—and is, fairly often."

Brock has a harder time getting through to Bonds these days; there are layers of agents and secretaries who screen all calls. And Brock says, laughing, that Barry still holds a grudge against him for not recruiting his brothers, Ricky and Bobby Jr. "Those Bonds people are awfully loyal," Brock says. But Bonds did return to Arizona State this spring for an awards ceremony. "Nobody hugs me," Brock says, "but Barry walked right up and hugged me. Kind of embarrassing. But that's Barry."

AS FAR as anyone can remember, nobody who has really wanted to interview Bonds has failed to get his man. But negotiations for his time are not for the fainthearted or deadline-driven. A writer might spend the first three days just trying to establish the possibility of an interview. Bonds might fail to look up or register any recognition during conversations with the would-be interviewer, might pick at imaginary scabs on his arm and repeat "Whatever, dude" over and over. The next phase might be a series of decreasingly vague promises by Bonds as he warms to the idea of the interview. This part of the process also includes actual recognition of the interviewer. The third, most tantalizing phase includes specific appointments, at first broken and later delayed. For Bonds it's a kind of social aerobics. Day Seven: "Aw, dude! I forgot about stretching!" he says, slapping dude on shoulder as he breaks yet another appointment and heads out to the field. Teammate Willie McGee, who is passing by, is not so much amazed by the excuse—Bonds, alone among his teammates, does not stretch—as by the sheer determination of the interviewer. "Man," he says under his breath, admiringly, "dude's been here a week."

But later on Day Seven and on Day Eight, Bonds finally sits down, as he promised so long ago.

"He has made his point," a club official explains. And that point would be. . . ? The club official shrugs.

"Why talk about things?" Bonds says, explaining his aversion to interviews. "When you talk about stuff too much, you overkill it. You get your glory when the people are happy. That's the glory of it all—when your team wins, you got that big hit, made that big play. That says enough. Why talk about it?"

He is mystified by the amount of attention he gets and mildly depressed by its nature. "You can look and look into the life of Barry Bonds," he says, "and the worst thing you'll find is about four traffic tickets, and all of them before I came to the majors."

Certainly he is mystified by the demands that fans make on him. He believes that he discharges all of his obligations to the public on the field. He prepares well (whatever you do, don't ever try to talk to him before a game), and he plays hard. He does not let the game down, ever. The elder Bonds, whose own career was damned by the word *potential,* says Barry is never satisfied at the end of the season: "He tells me, 'I've got to throw, got to get better.' "

As if all that weren't enough, Bonds performs with a flamboyance that hovers between annoying and spectacular, but is good value however you see it. "Why can't people just enjoy the show?" he wonders. "And then let the entertainer go home and get his rest, so he can put on another show? But in baseball, you get to see us, touch us, trade our cards, buy and sell jerseys. To me, that dilutes the excitement. Autograph seekers! When I go to a movie, after the final credits roll, I get up and leave. It's *the end*! But (at a ball game) I'm supposed to stand out there for three hours and *then* sign autographs?

"If fans pay $10 to see *Batman,* they don't expect to get Jack Nicholson's autograph."

In fact, Bonds does sign autographs from time to time. But otherwise he doesn't feel he needs to share his life off the field—with anybody. That house of his? The major cribbage, where he lives with his wife, Sun, and their two children, Nikolai, 3, and Shikari, 2? You ask the style. "Mediterranean," he says. You ask the setting. "Oh, no you don't. I don't want you finding my house." It's hard work being *this* private.

But he has had practice. Says his father: "When he was a kid and all the other kids were out playing, he'd stay in and entertain himself. He didn't need a lot of people. He didn't even like sharing a bedroom with his brothers, that's how private he was."

Anyway, why go public? Barry dismisses his celebrity; he says he's like everybody else. "The other day, I mowed the lawn with my cousin," he says. "I eat at McDonald's, I eat at Denny's. People want to know what Barry Bonds eats in the morning, where I go at night. And I don't do anything different from anybody else. Off the field, I'm an average guy."

This average guy has had bit parts in two movies, *Rookie of the Year* and *Jane's House*—"The usual, act like a stupid ballplayer," he says—and he clearly enjoyed rubbing shoulders with actor James Woods. And then, of all the people he might have chosen to present his second MVP award—his father, his manager—he chose Mays and singer Michael Bolton. It was an odd scene at Candlestick Park before this year's home opener: Mays hand-ed the trophy to Bolton, who handed it to Bonds. What was wrong with this picture? It was as if Bonds, who had met Bolton when he played in one of the singer's charity softball games, were saying that his personality could no longer be contained by baseball. He would henceforth like to be identified with entertainment supernovas.

Obviously Bonds doesn't fight fame with all his heart. "Well, it's nobody's fault but my own," he says. "It's like my dad said, I didn't have to go out there and do all those things, draw all this attention to myself. Could have been an average player."

What can you do? Cursed with greatness. Still, it's a shame that a game of such purity has to be complicated by all this attention, and so much of it negative. "The only time in my life I feel free is when I'm on the field," Bonds says. "No one can bother you, no one can talk to you. You can do whatever you want, be whoever you want."

The sanctuary of leftfield also becomes a stage for him, and he is often sur-prised by how much he enjoys it. "It's my showtime," he says. He once watched a tape of one of his home run trots and was amazed to see himself pointing a finger as he rounded first base. "It was something that just hap-pened," he says.

Does that make him a jerk, or does it make him interesting?

Thrift, one of the father figures in Bonds's high-maintenance career, thinks it only makes Bonds unique. "*The Little Drummer Boy* wasn't writ-ten for Barry," Thrift says. "Just because he doesn't grin when everybody wants him to . . . well, that's Barry." Thrift is told that hardly anybody can speak of Bonds without concluding "that's Barry." He laughs. "Now, isn't that nice?" Thrift says. "To be just Barry?"

Mostly it is, certainly while playing baseball. But the game is not held as sacred as Bonds would like it to be. "Why can't you just do your best and walk away from it?" he wonders. "Why can't you just make it as good as you can for as long as it's going to last? Dude, the one thing I know: When it's over, it's just over. I know it's not going to last forever." So why can't he be left alone to enjoy it?

But nobody leaves him alone. And the attention and expectations grind at him. The reflection he sees in people's eyes—a rich and spoiled brat—

disappoints him. He once popped a foul ball that struck a child on the head. A reporter, noting that Bonds had shown his concern by giving the kid a bat, asked Bonds if he had done it to curry the fans' favor. Bonds tells you that and quickly reminds you, "But I don't care what they think."

He does, of course. Doesn't everybody? For some reason Bonds is reminded of his childhood, of a play in which he performed in elementary school. He had to go onto the stage and introduce each new act, each time wearing a different costume. He remembers that for one introduction, he was supposed to wear a wet suit, but he didn't have time to don it and, instead, went out bare-chested. It wasn't much of a gaffe; maybe there haven't been many of those in his nearly perfect life. But what he most remembers is that nobody booed. "Kids never get booed, no matter how they mess up," he says. "You never see a five-year-old get booed. Always applauded, because they're trying. Always getting encouragement or praise. Because that little boy is trying."

It's an odd thought for a rich superstar, years and MVPs removed from grade school. But then Bonds says something even odder. More that little boy than anyone might believe, he says, "That's the way it should always be."

⁊

End of the
Glorious Ordeal

BY RON FIMRITE

*Henry Aaron gracefully endured the pressure of the chase for Babe Ruth's home
run record, and then put an end to it with one lash of his bat.*

H ENRY AARON'S ORDEAL ENDED AT 9:07 P.M. MONDAY.
It ended in a carnival atmosphere that would have
been more congenial to the man he surpassed as
baseball's alltime home-run champion. But it ended.
And for that, as Aaron advised the 53,775 Atlanta fans who came to en-
shrine him in the games pantheon, "Thank God."

Aaron's 715th home run came in the fourth inning of the Braves' home
opener with Los Angeles, off the Dodgers' Al Downing, a lefthander who
had insisted doggedly before the game that for him this night would be "no
different from any other." He was wrong, for now he joins a company of victims that includes Tom Zachary (Babe Ruth's 60th home run in 1927), Tracy
Stallard (Roger Maris's 61st in 1961) and Guy Bush (Ruth's 714th in 1935).
They are destined to ride in tandem through history with their assailants.

Downing's momentous mistake was a high fastball into Aaron's considerable strike zone. Aaron's whip of a bat lashed out at it and snapped it in
a high arc toward the 385-foot sign in left centerfield. Dodger centerfielder Jimmy Wynn and leftfielder Bill Buckner gave futile chase, Buckner
going all the way to the six-foot fence for it. But the ball dropped over the

fence in the midst of a clutch of Braves' relief pitchers who scrambled out of the bullpen in pursuit. Buckner started to go over the fence after the ball himself, but gave up after he realized he was outnumbered. It was finally retrieved by reliever Tom House, who even as Aaron triumphantly rounded the bases ran hysterically toward home plate holding the ball aloft. It was, after all, one more ball than Babe Ruth ever hit over a fence, and House is a man with a sense of history.

House arrived in time to join a riotous spectacle at the plate. Aaron, his normally placid features exploding in a smile, was hoisted by his teammates as Downing and the Dodger infielders moved politely to one side. Aaron shook hands with his father Herbert, and embraced his mother Estella. He graciously accepted encomiums from his boss, Braves board chairman Bill Bartholomay, and Monte Irvin, representing Commissioner Bowie Kuhn, who was unaccountably in Cleveland this eventful night. Kuhn is no favorite of Atlanta fans and when his name was mentioned by Irvin, the largest crowd ever to see a baseball game in Atlanta booed lustily.

"I just thank God it's all over," said Aaron, giving credit where it is not entirely due.

No, this was Henry Aaron's evening, and if the Braves' management overdid it a bit with the balloons, the fireworks, the speeches and all-round hoopla, who is to quibble? There have not been many big baseball nights in this football-oriented community and those few have been supplied by Aaron.

Before the game that great man did look a trifle uncomfortable while being escorted through lines of majorettes as balloons rose in the air above him. There were signs everywhere—MOVE OVER BABE—and the electronic scoreboard blinked HANK. Much of centerfield was occupied by a massive map of the United States painted on the grass as an American flag. This map-flag was the site of a pregame *This Is Your Life* show, featuring Aaron's relatives, friends and employers. Sammy Davis Jr. was there, and Pearl Bailey, singing the national anthem in Broadway soul, and Atlanta's black mayor, Maynard Jackson, and Governor Jimmy Carter, and the Jonesboro High School band, and the Morris Brown College choir, and Chief Noc-A-Homa, the Braves' mascot, who danced with a fiery hoop.

This is not the sort of party one gives for Henry Aaron, who through the long weeks of on-field pressure and mass media harassment had expressed no more agitation than a man brushing aside a housefly. Aaron had labored for most of his 21-year career in shadows cast by more flamboyant superstars, and if he was enjoying his newfound celebrity, he gave no hint of it. He seemed to be nothing more than a man trying to do his job and live a normal life in the presence of incessant chaos.

Before this most important game of his career he joked at the batting cage with teammate Dusty Baker, a frequent foil, while hordes of newsmen scrambled around him, hanging on every banality. When a young red-haired boy impudently shouted, "Hey, Hank Aaron, come here, I want you to sign this," Aaron looked incredulous, then laughed easily. The poor youngster was very nearly mobbed by sycophants for approaching the dignitary so cavalierly.

Downing, too, seemed unaware that he was soon to be a party to history. "I will pitch to Aaron no differently tonight," he said, as the band massed in rightfield. "I'll mix my pitches up, move the locations. If I make a mistake, it's no disgrace. I don't think the pitcher should take the glory for number 715. He won't deserve any accolades. I think people will remember the pitcher who throws the last one he ever hits, not the 715th."

Downing's "mistake" was made with nobody out in the fourth inning and with Darrell Evans, the man proceeding Aaron in the Braves' batting order, on first base following an error by Dodger shortstop Bill Russell. Downing had walked Aaron leading off the second inning to the accompaniment of continuous booing by the multitudes. Aaron then scored on a Dodger error, the run breaking Willie Mays' alltime National League record for runs scored (after the home run, Aaron had 2,064).

This time, with a man on base, Downing elected to confront him *mano-a-mano*. His first pitch, however, hit the dirt in front of the plate. The next hit the turf beyond the fence in leftfield.

"It was a fastball down the middle of the upper part of the plate," Downing lamented afterward. "I was trying to get it down to him, but I didn't. He's a great hitter. When he picks his pitch, he's pretty certain that's the pitch he's looking for. Chances are he's gonna hit it pretty good. When he did hit it, I didn't think it was going out because I was watching Wynn and Buckner. But the ball just kept carrying and carrying."

It was Aaron's first swing of the game—and perhaps the most significant in the history of baseball. It was also typical of Aaron's sense of economy. On Opening Day in Cincinnati, against the Reds' Jack Billingham, he tied Ruth with his first swing of the new season. But this event, noteworthy though it may have been, was merely a prelude, and Aaron recognized it as such.

"Seven-fourteen only ties the record," he advised well-wishers at the time. And in yet another ceremony at home plate, he reminded everyone, "It's almost over."

Aaron's innate dignity had been jarred in that opening three-game series by the seemingly irresolvable haggling between his employers Bartholomay and manager Eddie Mathews, and commissioner Kuhn. Bartholomay
and Mathews had hoped to keep Aaron out of the lineup for the entire series so that he might entertain the home fans with his immortal swats.
When Kuhn suggested forcefully that it was the obligation of every team to
put its best lineup on the field at all times and that any violation of this
obligation would be regarded by him as sinful, Mathews and Bartholomay
relented—but only partially. After Aaron tied the Babe, Mathews announced
that he would bench him for the remaining games of the Reds' series, saving him for the adoring home folks.

This brought an iron rebuke from the commissioner: Aaron would play
or Mathews and the Braves must face "serious consequences." This message
was delivered after the Saturday game, in which Aaron did not play. Aaron
was in the lineup for 6½ innings on Sunday, striking out twice and grounding weakly to third in three at bats. The stage—and a stage it seemed—
was set for Monday night.

It rained in Atlanta during the day, violently on occasions, but it was warm
and cloudy by game time. It began raining again just before Aaron's first
inconsequential time at bat, as if Ruth's phantom were up there puncturing
the drifting clouds. Brightly-colored umbrellas sprouted throughout the
ball park, a brilliant display that seemed to be merely part of the show. The
rain had subsided by Aaron's next time up, the air filled now only with tension. Henry wasted little time relieving that tension. It is his way. Throughout his long career Aaron had been faulted for lacking a sense of drama,
for failing to rise to critical occasions, as Mays, say, or Ted Williams had.
He quietly endured such spurious criticism, then in two memorable games
dispelled it for all time. And yet, after it was over, he was Henry Aaron again.

"Right now," he said without a trace of irony, "it feels like just another
home run. I felt all along if I got a strike I could hit it out. I just wanted to
touch all the bases on this one."

He smiled slightly, conscious perhaps that his words were not sufficient to
the occasion. Then he said what he had been wanting to say since it became
apparent that he would eventually pass Ruth and achieve immortality. "I feel
I can relax now. I feel my teammates can relax. I feel I can have a great season."

It is not that he had ever behaved like anyone but Henry Aaron. For this
generation of baseball fans and now for generations to come, that will be
quite enough.

Williams
Does It!

BY RICHARD HOFFER

*The author imagines a return to 1941 in order to recall one
of the greatest feats in baseball history.*

PHILADELPHIA, SEPT. 28, 1941—
You can say this about the Kid: He does some damage. He
hit a shot here today in Shibe Park that punched a hole in
one of Connie Mack's loudspeaker horns way out there in
right center. You add that bit of destruction to all the lights he took out in
Fenway last year while he was taking target practice with a .22 on the 400-
foot sign, and you've got to admit that Ted Williams is a player who brings
a lot of overhead to the ballpark. If the Kid continues to dismantle American League stadiums piece by piece, well, the boys in the press box will
have to come up with another nickname for him—maybe the Splendid
Splinter or some such. (Hey, you heard it here first.)

Of course, if the Kid turns in a couple more .400 seasons like this one
for Boston, Mr. Tom Yawkey will gladly pay Mr. Mack for the horn, even on
top of the $18,000 salary he pays Williams. And don't be surprised to see
the Red Sox owner give his young slugger a raise. It's well known that Mr.
Yawkey thinks the world of the Kid—just last year the two spent a couple
afternoons together shooting pigeons inside Fenway with 20-gauge shot-
guns. But on Sunday against the last-place Athletics in Philadelphia, in a

season-ending doubleheader, Williams worked alone and used no fire-power other than his Louisville Slugger. Including that bolt off the speak-er on the right-center wall (after the game, Williams said it was the hard-est he'd ever hit a ball), he was 6 for 8 in the twin bill and—*whew!*—finished the season with a .406 average. Keep in mind, it's been 11 years since any-one topped that magic mark; the last was Bill Terry, who batted .401 back in 1930 for the New York Giants.

Williams, who's just 23 and looks like he has a few more .400 seasons ahead of him, provided more drama in getting this .400 than he would have liked. He was hitting as high as .438 in June and .414 in mid-August, and people were wondering if he'd break Hugh Duffy's record of .440, set before the turn of the century. That was the big question.

When all was said and done today, Williams broke no records and made little news—not like Joe DiMaggio did with his 56-game hitting streak ear-lier this season. But we've been watching the Kid three years now, and the boys knew Williams would hit .400 before DiMaggio. Hey, even during the Yankee Clipper's great streak, Williams outhit him .412 to .408.

But the Kid cooled with the weather, and in a recent 10-day stretch he dropped nearly a point a day. With only the final three games in Philadel-phia left to play, he stood at .401. That meant he'd need to go 5 for 12 to finish at .400. Trust us. Some of the boys figured it out.

The two off days before the last series gave all of us too much time to think. Some of the writers played with the numbers, and within a day one of them had discovered that Williams would dip below .400 as soon as he went 0 for 2. Decimal points were being carried out so many places that the sports page looked like a science journal. Even Joe Cronin, the Red Sox manager, was agonizing. The pennant race, of course, ended weeks ago as the Yankees ran away with it, and Boston had already clinched second. So Cronin thought about not playing Williams at all in Philly. In fact, he ap-proached the Kid on Friday and offered to sit him out, to protect that .401. But Williams told Cronin to pass the word that he wouldn't take any mollycoddling.

Still, the skipper was in a dither. Cronin gathered some of us in the lobby before Saturday's game and announced his plans. He said, "You've got to admire the kid for being so courageous, but if he gets his hits, I may yank him in the second game Sunday."

On Friday, Williams went with a catcher and a coach to Shibe Park and took extra batting practice, experimenting with the placement of his right foot, pointing the toe toward second base one time and more toward third another. A Philly writer thought that was a sign of desperation and wrote, "He's worried, though you can't get him to say so. He must be a little on the panic side."

But the rest of us knew: That's just Ted. He's always been nuts for batting practice, and he told us recently that one of the keys to his hitting this season was Boston's trade for Joe Dobson last December. Dobson hasn't pitched much for the team, but he's become Williams's personal BP pitcher. This season, if you got to the park early, you'd see the two of them out there, Williams saying, "O.K., Joe, ninth inning in Detroit, bases loaded, two out." Williams is never casual about his hitting.

Anyway, what the Philly writer forgot to write was that the Kid was ripping shot after shot off the rightfield wall (probably trying to locate some stadium accessory he could destroy, come to think of it). "I want to hit over .400," Williams told some of the boys afterward. "But I'm going to play all three games here even if I don't hit a ball out of the infield. The record's no good unless it's made in all the games." Some of the boys, knowing the skipper's plans, had to stifle smiles.

Down the stretch, most people have been rooting for the Kid. In Yankee Stadium three weeks ago, the fans booed Yank pitcher Lefty Gomez when he walked Williams with the bases loaded. In Detroit in late August, Harry Heilmann (who hit .403 for the Tigers in 1923) came down on the field from the Tiger radio booth, took Williams aside and said, "Now, forget about that short fence. Just hit the ball where you want it." In Philadelphia there was at least one guy rooting against Williams: A's coach Al Simmons. Simmons hit .390 one year with the A's, and that apparently was as high as he felt anyone should bat. "How much do you want to bet you don't hit .400?" he groused to Williams before Saturday's game.

Sure enough, the Kid got only one hit in four at bats Saturday, and his average fell—we were back to doing high-level arithmetic again—to .39955. A lot of people might be inclined to round that off to .400, and maybe with any other average you would. But the papers had it right on Sunday morning: WILLIAMS DROPS BELOW .400. There was no getting around that. You could stretch .3995555 all the way under the masthead, and it still wouldn't amount to .400. All the same, the boys ganged up on Cronin, wondering whether he'd bench Williams and try to save the day on a technicality. But everybody knew—and Cronin did too—that it was too late now.

Saturday night Williams walked the streets of Philly with the clubhouse boy, Johnny Orlando. Williams loves to walk, and he tends to take his strolls with unlikely folks. His best friends are policemen, theater managers and, of course, Johnny. According to Johnny, the two of them walked about 10 miles; every now and then Johnny would slip into a tavern for a quick Scotch while the Kid would stop in a malt shop for a milk shake. You knew something was up because Ted didn't get back to the hotel until 10:30. He's usually in bed by 10.

So it all came down to the last day. Never mind the Kid's terrific year; never mind his game-winning homer in the All-Star Game in Detroit or even the 374-pound tuna he caught on an off day earlier this summer. If he missed .400, it was going to feel like a failed season.

Williams was scheduled to face one of Mr. Mack's rookies, Dick Fowler, and Ted says that facing a rookie is always at least one lost at bat until you figure him out. Williams was greeted at the plate by A's catcher Frankie Hayes, who told him, "Mr. Mack says we have to go right after you and pitch to you." That was good news: In earlier games this season Mr. Mack's particular idea of putting the shift on Williams was to relocate the strike zone to Delaware County. In their last eight games with Boston, the A's pitchers had walked Williams 14 times.

So his first time up against Fowler, Williams greeted a strike like a gift and rifled a drive in the hole between first and second for a single. Almost before we could calculate his average, the Kid homered and then singled two more times. In the ninth inning he reached first on an error.

It was a wild game, with the Red Sox winning 12–11, but the only numbers anyone paid attention to were 4 for 5. Williams was up to .404. He'd have to go hitless in his next five at bats to drop below .400. Anyway, in the Kid's first at bat in the second game, against another rookie, Fred Caligiuri, he singled to right. And then, in the fourth inning, he locked on that loudspeaker at the top of the wall and had to settle for a double, while Mr. Mack tallied the damage in his notebook. Williams finally popped up in the seventh inning, the first time all day he made an out, just before the game was called on account of darkness. Final: Athletics 7, Red Sox 1, Williams .4057.

"Can you imagine that kid?" Cronin said after the game. "Four singles, a double and a homer when the chips were down." Cronin wasn't the only happy fellow. The boys breathed their own sigh of relief at not having to figure any more decimal places.

Afterward one of the writers congratulated Williams on the feat and mentioned the Most Valuable Player Award to him. "Do you think there's a chance I could win it?" Williams asked. But even he knows there is none, not with what the Clipper has done. "Even if I don't," the Kid said, "I'll be satisfied with this. What a thrill! I wasn't saying much about it before the game, but I never wanted anything harder in my life."

Some of us who were wise to the 10:30 milk shake nodded to each other. The thing is, we all know we're going to be down this pike again. The Kid is just 23, getting to know the pitchers, approaching his prime. Mark these words: By the time Ted Williams is done, .400 won't be such a magic number.

Heady
Stuff

BY TOM VERDUCCI

*As remarkable as it is to win 300 games, Greg Maddux's most amazing
feat was to thrive as a finesse pitcher in a power era.*

THE MASTER LEARNED TO PITCH WITH A VOICE IN HIS EAR. IT
was the voice of a man who would be dead inside of two
years. That would be enough time—this brief intersection
of skinny kid and wise old muse—to engender what may be
the most highly evolved pitching ever witnessed.

"First pitch, fastball in," the voice said.

Greg Maddux was 15 years old when he heard it. The batter was Marty
Barrett, a 23-year-old minor leaguer headed for a 10-year career in the
bigs. The voice belonged to Ralph Medar, a former scout who assembled
pickup baseball games every Sunday at nine in the morning in Maddux's
hometown of Las Vegas. The good ballplayers somehow always knew about
the games, the same way basketball players know when and on which court
to find the best neighborhood run. See you at Medar's, they'd say. Medar
would stand behind the pitchers and give instruction. Maddux listened to
the voice. The kid threw a fastball in. Barrett pounced upon it, sending a
double screaming to leftfield.

The next inning Barrett stepped in again. (The games almost never drew
enough players for nine to a side.)

"First pitch, breaking ball," came the voice.

The kid broke a decent curve over the plate. The pro took it for a strike.

"O.K. Now, fastball in."

Maddux threw. This time the barrel of Barrett's bat was not so quick. He connected, only not as solidly. The same pitch, but this time cleverly set up by slow stuff, produced a lazy fly ball to centerfield.

Oh, O.K., the kid said to himself. Now I get it.

VAN GOGH had the south of France, Hemingway the battlefields and bullrings of Europe. Maddux had Medar's. The genius of the 22nd, and perhaps last, 300-game winner in the major leagues was inspired by the old man's voice. "Kid," the sage said, "you throw hard enough to get drafted. But movement is more important than velocity."

"I believed it," says Maddux, now 38 years old and in his 19th big league season. "I don't know why. I just did."

How do you explain it? The kid heard it, and he believed it, the way a seminarian hears with clarity the call of God in a noisy, profane world. He was born to this calling. The other kids, muscles growing and hormones flowing, wanted to throw baseballs through brick walls, and the other coaches kept imploring, "Throw strikes!" But the old man would say, "Bounce a curveball in the dirt here," and the kid would understand the intended subterfuge. It didn't hurt, either, that when the kid threw a baseball with his right index and middle fingers each atop the seams, the ball darted and sank with preternatural movement.

"God gave it to him, I guess," says Chicago Cubs bench coach Dick Pole, who worked with Maddux as far back as 1987, when the Cubs righthander was in his first stint with the team. "It's always moved like that."

Maddux is sitting in the visitors' dugout at Miller Park in Milwaukee the day after career victory 299, a 7–1 win over the Brewers in which he'd given up four hits and one run in six innings. Only three 300-game winners have ever had better control, as measured by walks per nine innings, than Maddux (1.90): Cy Young (1.49), Christy Mathewson (1.59) and Grover Cleveland Alexander (1.65). All of them were done by 1930. Only two pitchers, Lefty Grove and Walter Johnson, ever won this many games with a relative ERA (that is, ERA measured against his contemporaries') better than Maddux's 28.2% differential. Grove's ERA was 33.2% better than his peers', and Johnson's was 30.8% better. Both of those pitchers were finished by 1941. Maddux is, to most of us, unlike anyone else we've ever seen.

Once Maddux nails down number 300, only he and Roger Clemens will have survived maple bats, billiard-hard baseballs, steroid-juiced lineups, a construction boom of hitter-friendly ballparks and a laser-guided tightening of the strike zone—in short, the greatest extended run of slugging the game has known—to reach that milestone. Clemens did so with the sledgehammer of a mid-to upper-90s fastball. Maddux has needed stealth and intellect. A beautiful mind, but with a killer changeup.

So expertly has Maddux mastered the subtleties of pitching that he has become an iconic presence. What Ripken is to durability and Ruth is to power, Maddux is to finesse, forever the measuring stick for the few who might follow in his path. "It's amazing," Pole says of the Maddux-Medar relationship, "to think what came about when two people collided. Right time, right place."

Maddux still hears the voice of the old man when he pitches, only the voice long ago became so familiar that it now sounds the same as his own. These are the commandments of pitching that he hears:

1) Make the balls look like strikes and the strikes look like balls.

2) Movement and location trump velocity every time.

3) When you're in trouble, think softer. Don't throw harder; locate better.

4) Have fun.

His physical gifts fading, Maddux must work harder than ever to obey those commandments. All except the last one, anyway.

MADDUX'S OLDER brother Mike, now the pitching coach for the Brewers, pitched with modest success for 15 seasons, the last in 2000. "I remember my brother telling me in his last year or two, 'You don't know how good I have to pitch just to get out of an inning,'" Greg says. "I'm thinking, What's he talking about? I'm starting to understand more and more what he meant by that."

At his very best, Maddux won four consecutive Cy Young Awards (1992 to '95) and had the lowest ERA (2.14) in any six-year span since World War II (1992 to '97), lower than the sublime six-year prime of Sandy Koufax (2.19) in a pitcher's era. Such was Maddux's sleight of hand with a baseball that future Hall of Fame third baseman Wade Boggs called him "the David Copperfield of pitchers" after he shut out the New York Yankees over eight innings in Game 2 of the 1996 World Series.

Maddux, however, never did get enough credit for just how nasty his stuff was. He threw his fastball 90 or 91 mph with the sudden movement of a jackrabbit flushed from the brush. The ball naturally sank and ran away from lefthanders. A slight twist of the wrist, and it cut toward their hands. "I pulled out tapes from 10 years ago, back when I was throwing up those really good years," Maddux says. "I made more mistakes then than I do now! It's just that I got away with them. My movement was better because my velocity was better."

Maddux typically throws at about 85 mph now. "I may not have the same success as I did earlier when I was doing it at faster speeds, but I can still have success," he says. "My bad games may be worse, though. I think I have to pitch better now than 10 years ago. I have to locate better because my stuff is not as good. It's still good enough to win, but not good enough to make mistakes. I don't throw hard enough for the ball to break as much as it used to."

Brewers outfielder Geoff Jenkins says of Maddux, "He still keeps the ball down in the zone. I try to be aggressive against him and attack early in the count because the deeper you get in the count against him the more he seems to mess with you and outthink you. It just seems like he hits his spots and all of a sudden it's the end of the night and you have a comfortable 0-fer."

The more Maddux's physical skills decline, the deeper he must tap his mental well to stay sharp—and at that he is unrivaled. He is, for instance, a voracious observer. He often can tell what a hitter is thinking by where he stands in the batter's box, how he takes practice swings, how he fouls off a pitch or takes a pitch.

"It's like kids at school—some pay more attention than others," Pole says. "He's on a different level from everybody else when it comes to attention."

Says New York Mets lefthander Tom Glavine, Maddux's rotation mate with the Atlanta Braves for 10 years, "That's the biggest part of what sets him apart. It helped me. I never really paid attention to any of that stuff until Greg came to Atlanta [in 1993]. It opened up a whole new world I had never seen before. He was way ahead of everybody else in that regard."

Once while seated in the Braves' dugout as third baseman Jose Hernandez batted for the Los Angeles Dodgers, Maddux blurted out, "Watch this. The first base coach may be going to the hospital." On the next pitch Hernandez drilled a line drive off the chest of the first base coach.

Another time Atlanta manager Bobby Cox visited Maddux on the mound with runners on second and third and two outs. Cox suggested an intentional walk.

"Don't worry," said Maddux, who then spelled out to Cox the sequence of his next three pitches: "And on the last pitch I'm going to get him to pop up foul to third base." Maddux proceeded to escape the jam on his third pitch—getting a pop-up to third base that was a foot or two from being foul.

Cubs ace Mark Prior, a 23-year-old power pitcher, says he likes to sit next to Maddux in the dugout on days when neither is pitching. "He's helped me tremendously," Prior says. "I've always gone harder whenever I've been in trouble. He's got me thinking, Go softer when I'm in trouble. I never thought that way before, and it's helped me develop confidence in my changeup. As we watch games, he'll talk about what I might throw in certain situations."

Maddux prefers to downplay his reputation as a mound savant. He has told teammates, "People think I'm smart? You know what makes you smart? Locate that fastball down and away. That's what makes you smart.

"I don't surprise anybody with what I throw anymore," Maddux says. "You just have to mix your pitches up. And even if the hitter is guessing right, if you locate it, you won't get hurt. You might give up a single or a double, but it's not the end of the world. Yeah, the hitters are stronger, the balls are harder, some parks are smaller and the strike zone's smaller. Still, for me, it's all about movement and location. If you have those, you're going to have success."

Episodes of Maddux's clairvoyance, however, still abound. Last week before his start in Milwaukee, he shouted to Pole in the clubhouse, "Hey, what's Brady Clark hitting with runners in scoring position?"

"How the hell do I know?" Pole replied.

"Well, find out for me, will you?" Maddux said.

Pole tracked down and passed along the information: The outfielder was hitting .226 with runners in scoring position. That night Maddux pitched around slugging first baseman Lyle Overbay with a runner on second and Clark on deck, then whiffed Clark on a changeup. "He knew which hitter he wanted to face if that very situation came up," Cubs lefthander Kent Mercker said afterward. "He doesn't miss anything."

Maddux lives for such moments, like a chess grandmaster who has specific killer moves cataloged in his head and finds utter joy when the board suddenly presents the perfect opening to employ one. Three hundred wins? It is just a number to him right now. That is not why he pitches. He pitches for the intellectual and physical challenges, the small moments that go unseen by most.

Asked to explain the best part of pitching, Maddux says, "I enjoy watching the other guys, talking on Monday [about a game plan] and trying to do it on Tuesday. Guys who just show up on Tuesday and pitch, I don't understand that.

"The best part? The best part is knowing on Monday you're going to do something and then actually doing it on Tuesday. You know what? It might be just a strike. It might be a foul ball, [telling yourself,] If I throw this guy this pitch, he's going to hit it foul right over there. And then to go out there and do it, that's pretty cool. To me, that's fun.

"You're only talking about 10 pitches a game where that may happen. The other 80 or 90 pitches you're trusting what you see and what you feel. It's still just fun playing the game."

It's still so much fun that he cannot yet imagine it ending. "Who knows?" he says, when asked how long he will pitch. "As long as I can do it. I don't want to embarrass myself, by any means. But I'd rather pitch bad than not pitch at all."

"THERE'S ONE thing I've learned about Greg Maddux," Cubs manager Dusty Baker says. "He shags better than anybody I've ever seen. I don't see him out there running foul poles, but I see him out there getting his running in shagging."

It's not uncommon for a pitcher, especially a veteran, to loathe workouts, but two or three times on his off days between starts Maddux chases fly balls during batting practice like an eager teenager hauled out of the stands. "I like to stay in shape, baseball shape, by playing baseball," Maddux says. "And it's fun. It's a lot more fun running around the outfield pretending you're Andruw Jones than running on a treadmill watching *Jerry Springer* reruns. To me, even the four days in between starts are fun."

Maddux makes certain that every throw he makes, even when shagging flies, is delivered from the same arm angle as one of his pitches, and never off-balance. He lifts light weights for his arm and shoulders from December through April, then, he says simply, "I trust my arm." At week's end he had thrown 4,110⅓ innings in his career and had never been placed on the disabled list with an arm injury of any sort.

There are model Rockets all around baseball, tall power pitchers in the mold of Clemens with here-it-comes fastballs. The next Maddux, however, may be a long time coming. "Now," says Maddux, who stands six feet tall and weighs 185 pounds, "if you don't throw 95, you're a wimp. If you're not 6' 4" with a 90-plus fastball, you'll never get drafted."

Says Glavine, "It's such a game of power pitching and power hitting now. Every pitcher throws flat-out gas with maximum effort. I don't know if we'll ever see anyone like Greg."

Here is the next Maddux. He is throwing a baseball against a dugout fence at Miller Park. Chase Maddux, Greg's son, is seven years old. He throws a pitch submarine-style. "Like the guy from Oakland," he says, referring to reliever Chad Bradford.

"Stay on top, kid. Stay on top," Greg says.

The father raises his right arm in a classic L shape, his elbow slightly above the height of his shoulder. "Look," he says. "Like this."

That voice is a familiar one. Medar, who died in 1983 at age 69, never lived to see one of Maddux's 300 wins, never lived even to see him selected by the Cubs in the second round of the 1984 draft.

Chase winds up and, with a still head and properly raised elbow, lets fly a perfect strike.

"That's better," the sage says. "That's much better."

୧୬

You Had to See It to Believe It

BY RICK REILLY

In his pursuit of Roger Maris and the mystical 61, Mark McGwire took baseball—and America—back to a better, simpler time.

TO MY GRANDDAUGHTER,

I write this now, 40 years after the fact, because I want you to know how it really was, not through some yellowed video you play on your contact lenses.

I've seen a few things. I saw a 46-year-old Jack Nicklaus win a Masters with tears in his eyes. I saw North Carolina State win an NCAA basketball title with eight nobodies. I saw a heavyweight title fight turn into a human buffet. But I've never seen anything like Mark McGwire chasing Roger Maris's home run record.

People stood on seats through every one of his at bats. Fans held up MARK, HIT IT HERE signs at *football* games. So many flashes would go off as he swung, Busch Stadium looked like a giant bowl of blinking Christmas lights.

That was such an odd time in this country. Washington seemed to be filled with liars, cheats and scumbags, yet our games were as pure and shiny as I'd ever seen them. I still think that year in sports, 1998, was the best of my lifetime. A bow-legged magician named John Elway finally won a Super Bowl. Michael Jordan became the first person in history to steal an NBA title in 42 seconds. Pete Sampras's serve was only a rumor.

But the best of all was this simple, joyful home run chase that didn't involve salary caps or parole boards or even Don King. Around laptops logged on to the Internet, nightly TV highlight shows and morning sports sections, the whole nation was brought together by a giant playing a kid's game. One day as McGwire was coming up on 60, an older couple was making their way through the airport in St. Louis, he limping along with his polio-damaged leg, she holding his hand. Suddenly from every cocktail lounge came this huge roar. It could only mean one thing. The couple turned and hugged. Their son had hit another.

You're the 14-year-old MVP of your Mark McGwire League and you always have your chocolatey McGwire after the game and all your buddies' parents are named McGwire This and McGwire That, but back then we knew him as a person.

I can still see his face. He had this withering glare at the plate, like a bouncer with bunions, but he was as quick to laugh as any man I've known. He would sign for all the kids, but he could spot a collector at a hundred rows. He would pick a piece of spinach out of his teeth and it would make the 11 o'clock news, yet he stayed decent and next-door through it all.

And then the strangest thing started happening. People started acting decent and next-door, too. Nearly every time he'd hit a home run, fans would give the ball back to him, walking straight past collectors offering tens of thousands of dollars. Opposing pitchers talked about how "cool" it would be to give up number 62.

The home run race was as American as a Corvette. The day McGwire tied Babe Ruth at 60, for instance, began with the St. Louis Cardinals unveiling a statue of Stan (the Man) Musial, who then went out and stood at home plate and played *Take Me Out to the Ball Game* on his harmonica in a red sport coat and red shoes at high noon on Labor Day weekend in the middle of the nation.

Sometimes you were sure the whole thing was a DreamWorks production. When McGwire hit his 61st, he hit it in front of his father, John, who turned 61 that day. He hit it in front of his 10-year-old Cardinals batboy son, Matt, whom he scooped up and hugged. He hit it in front of the sons of Maris, the man who had been so tortured by the number, and now, thanks to McGwire, redeemed by it. McGwire saluted them, touched his heart and threw a kiss to the sky in Maris's memory. And in the chaos John said quietly to himself, "What a wonderful gift."

Earlier, after another cloudscraper, McGwire sat down in a cavern under the stands and started answering questions from 600 reporters in his own square-as-fudge way. Two seconds after each answer, he'd hear this great cheer coming from the field. He couldn't figure it out until somebody explained that the press conference was being piped outside to the thousands of fans who had waited, in the wilting Missouri heat, an hour after the game to hear him.

Well, that was just too much for McGwire. He took his big waffle-sized hands and pulled his hat over his head and leaned back in his chair and giggled. "They're still here?" he said.

Some of us never left.

Hand It
To Cal

BY RICHARD HOFFER

While honoring athletes dedicated to their craft and respectful of their games, SI *signaled out one man who surpassed the rest in diligence and generosity of spirit, and named him Sportsman of the Year.*

THIS HAS BEEN AN ERA OF DIMINISHED EXPECTATIONS, OF lowered standards in sports. Today's fan, disappointed by his heroes and his pastimes, watches his games with more resignation than anticipation. It seems eccentricity has taken the place of performance, celebrity the place of character. A funny-looking guy with orange hair reclines on a basketball floor, pouting, pointedly ignoring the play of his teammates. It's entertainment, all right, but it's not what the fan remembers as sport.

And there's hardly anything to root for anymore. There are no home teams, few reliable citizens, and there's not always a World Series. This is a sad time when neither virtue nor achievement can be taken for granted. One episode after another breeds cynicism, conspires against the fan's pleasure, deadens his joy. He settles for the sullen competence that is allowed to qualify as stardom these days.

Then there comes a year like this, a year in which sports were brightened by athletes whose skill and effort and energy and personality answered the fan's yearning for true heroes.

There was a black teenager, poised to overtake a white man's game, deflecting angles of race in a race-weary year as smoothly as he swung an eight-iron. A Spaniard whose fifth consecutive Tour de France victory established a once unthinkable dominance. An unbeatable horse. A seven-foot native Nigerian whose play in the NBA postseason raised the threshold for basketball greatness. A 76-year-old football coach, 55 years on the job, the same job, who reached the 400-win milestone. And there was a pitcher who quietly revealed his preeminence, irrefutable after four straight Cy Young Awards.

Any one of them could be Sportsman of the Year. There were so many, and they were so diverse. Yet there was something about all of them that the fan recognizes, something decidedly retro and refreshing. It's hard to say what it is. Let's think about it for a minute. There's a man, close-cropped gray hair, looks older than 35, standing in the partial glow of stadium lights, standing along the railing of an empty field, signing autographs hours after a game. He doesn't really have any place to go, his family is asleep, so it's no big deal. He signs away, not to rekindle a country's love affair with its national pastime (that kind of calculation is beyond him) but because somebody wants something and it's easy to give. A teammate offers him a big leaguer's diagnosis: "You're sick."

The man shrugs. He has played in more games consecutively than any other man, dead or alive. Punched in, punched out. It's not so much a record, not a reward for greatness, as it is a by-product of sustained adolescence and, of course, unusual good health. A milestone is all it is. He knows it, too. The man shrugs, signing away beneath the stadium lights. "If you could play baseball every day," he says, "wouldn't you?"

CAL RIPKEN Jr., though he'll surely go into the Hall of Fame as a power-hitting shortstop, is not the greatest baseball player ever, or even of his day. But how could he not be our Sportsman of the Year? He's dedicated to his craft, respectful of his game and proud enough of his abilities to continue their refinement well into his 30s. As you read this (maybe the snow is drifting against your door and encouraging a couch-bound indolence), he is taking grounders in his home gym, rotating groups of five into his athletic compound for daily basketball games, lifting weights.

Ripken and the 11 others we celebrate here along with him are all kind of old-fashioned, all seem to be playing for something other than money. Oh, they'll do a shoe commercial (well, Cigar won't), but when it's over, they'll all be better remembered for careers than ad campaigns. Whatever they're doing, they're doing for the love of their game. Almost to a man and a woman, they've had grind-it-out careers, athletic lifetimes in which the usual perks, if there are any, are incidental. Do you believe that Eddie Robinson has been thinking about moving up to the NFL during all these years he has been coaching football at Grambling? For that matter, do you doubt that Pete Sampras, despite his advertising duel with that other tennis player, believes that substance shall prevail over style? And amateur golfer Tiger Woods, the cub of this group: Don't you think he might be designed for the long haul? They're all a little different in their particulars, but each gives off that whiff of doggedness, stoicism, a gladiator's spirit in which everything is sacrificed for performance. They assure the fan, in this grim time, that he need not settle for just anything, anymore.

The athletes we've assembled in this supporting cast can all look up to Ripken, at least this year, after the way he almost single-handedly restored the once loyal fan's faith in baseball, single-handedly turned attention to a pioneer work ethic. His "assault" on Lou Gehrig's record of 2,130 consecutive games played was surely the least dramatic record run of all time. We knew for years that, barring an injury to Ripken, Gehrig's record was going to fall. Nobody had to wonder whether some Baltimore Oriole manager was going to yank Ripken from the lineup to rest him, or whether Ripken himself was going to beg out of the second half of a doubleheader to nurture some mysterious ache. And assuming the fan could read a baseball schedule, he knew months in advance exactly when (Sept. 6) and where (Camden Yards) the record-breaking would happen. There was nothing conditional about this record except Ripken's attendance. He didn't have to hit in his 57th straight game, pitch a seventh no-hitter, clout his 62nd home run. No record, before or since, has been set with less pressure. All Ripken had to do to set it was be there.

Yet it turned out to be one of the great feel-good events in sports—ever— and if there wasn't a lump in your throat when Ripken circled the field in a reluctant victory lap, you weren't paying attention. It released a pent-up emotion after two strike-shortened seasons, a missed World Series and a general surliness had destroyed a hundred-plus years' worth of fan loyalty. The fan had long ago learned to cope with the huge salaries and the sordid commerce that had infected his game. But the owners' and players' indifference to tradition was stunning. They would sacrifice a World Series for . . . what? Can anybody remember? A fan who was no stranger to nostalgia was used to wondering, Can't anybody play this game? It was an old argument, an inviting complaint, harmless. But now he had to ask the far more discouraging question: *Won't* anybody play this game?

Ripken would. He would play all the games he could, as hard as he could. In a sport accustomed to celebrating freaks of different and unique abilities, Ripken was instead a freak of disposition. He just liked to play baseball. You can't play 14 seasons through and through if you don't like it. Why Ripken liked baseball this much is anyone's guess, though there surely is a genetic component to it.

For him, family life was the residue of baseball; it was whatever was left over from the game. Cal Sr. was a longtime manager and coach in the Oriole organization, making stops in places like Elmira and Rochester, dragging the family along. And Cal Jr. took to the game, understanding his childhood to be privileged—taking infield practice with future major leaguers or just listening to his father detail the Oriole cutoff play. As a 12-year-old he was developing resource material.

Still, heredity doesn't account for the sense of obligation and appreciation he has for baseball. Nor does his entry into pro ball, when scouts placed him on the slow track, to the extent they put him on any track at all. Remember that Ripken was not encouraged to believe he had any special talents back in 1978, when eight shortstops were picked ahead of him in the baseball draft.

Sixteen years later he has outlasted those eight and plenty more. His endurance has become the new standard of sport, and his run for the record couldn't have been more timely. In an era of slouching gods, this devotion to duty was a curative. Here was Ripken, looking somewhat old in his gray-stubble buzz cut, coming to the park every day. It helped that he didn't bounce around, didn't exaggerate his love of the game, didn't act like some caricatured goof from a Norman Rockwell painting. He just kept coming to work because . . . why wouldn't you? "Look," he says, wholly ignorant of the heavenly glow he might attach to his myth with this statement, "the season's long, 162 games, and a pennant could be decided in any one of them. You never know which one. But do you want to take a chance? Is that the game you'd want to sit out?"

Of course, this being the era it is, not everybody respected the purity of his motives. Since everything seems to have merchandising possibilities these days, it was natural that Ripken's march on the great Gehrig, who had died so dramatically, would be suspect for some. It was a gimmick, a staged attack. He could have and should have taken himself out plenty of

times by now. In fact, it was suggested last July by columnist Robert Lip-
syte (playfully, we assume) in *The New York Times* that Ripken might better honor his own name by honoring Gehrig's. He should take a day off
before Sept. 5 and then resume playing. "The idea wasn't all that fresh,"
says Ripken. "It actually was put to me about three years ago, by I won't say
who. 'Think of the marketing possibilities,' I was told. Well, I wasn't doing
this for a record in the first place, so I wasn't going to *not* do it for the
record either. It never entered my mind."

Most people lauded his effort, however. A happy side effect of the Streak
was encountered in newspapers throughout the country, demonstrating
anew that positive values can leak from sports into the greater parts of our
culture. Usually some horrible issue like domestic violence or drug use
among athletes would spill out of the sports pages and into the news sections, as if lifestyles of the rich and spoiled might be instructive to the
general populace. But this time Ripken's example prompted a hurried
search for people with unusual work records. Think about it: Did your
hometown newspaper or your local TV station fail to come up with a
nurse who hadn't missed a day in 37 years, a warehouseman who hadn't
been sick in 25? Going to work every day was, generally, a good idea, or
used to be thought so. It seemed to suggest something adult, like responsibility. And by the way, did anyone ever tell that teacher in your
town, that assembly-line worker, to knock off that crazy consecutive-
workday stunt and take a day off?

Of course, no country, not even one as abashedly sentimental as ours,
would reward an athlete with affection based on attendance. Ripken did
more than just show up every day; he was and is a good player. Maybe his
offensive numbers don't stack up with Gehrig's, but they'll do for a shortstop of any generation. No other shortstop has hit so many home runs—at
least 20 in each of his first 10 full seasons and 327 in all. Few have fielded
so flawlessly for so long: highest fielding percentage for a shortstop (.996)
in a season, only 75 errors in the last seven seasons combined. Just in case
you thought the Streak was the product of some Baltimore hype, remember that he was chosen by fans across the nation to start in 13 straight All-
Star Games.

Ripken deserved to play all 2,153 consecutive games, his total at the end
of the season. Oh, there were whispers in 1990, when Ripken endured a
prolonged slump. After hitting .257 the year before, he was getting extra
scrutiny for a sub-.220 batting average in mid-June. Ripken says now that

it was during that time that he came the closest to interrupting the Streak; he was willing to sit, but teammate Rick Sutcliffe cautioned him that rest might not be the cure-all he was looking for. "Just fix what's broken," Sutcliffe told him. In 1991 Ripken was the American League MVP—he hit .323 with 34 home runs and 114 RBIs in one of the best years ever by a shortstop—and then the Streak didn't seem like such a bad thing. "The word *stubborn* does come to mind," says Ripken.

Actually, *stubborn* is the perfect word. A devotion to principle, whether that principle makes much sense to the rest of us, is usually something to marvel at. And Ripken's devotion to his principle—to play well and at every opportunity—knows no season. His conditioning program goes well beyond what makes sense. His vast home gym is an altar to physical fitness. And Ripken believes he has only so many hours of concentration available to him on any given day, and he likes to save them for the game. As available as he may seem to the public, signing autographs into the wee hours, he is actually extremely protective of his private time with his wife, Kelly (a sometime basketball opponent), and their children, Rachel and Ryan. A photographer on a recent PEOPLE magazine shoot discovered this when his session spilled over into Ripken's personal schedule. Cal had to pick up Rachel at school, and that was that. The photographer was left mouth agape, holding his light meters as Ripken defiantly drove away.

It is no doubt infuriating to today's athletes that our expectations of them are contradictory. We want them to behave as adults, even though we want them to play with the enthusiasm of children. We want them to act modestly, even though we shower them with attention. We want them to treat their job like work, even though we consider it a game. Not many athletes of any generation can deal gracefully with our antithetical yearnings; Ripken is one of the few.

Even in the gray light of November in Baltimore, he was still trying to understand all the fuss. "Emotionally, I feel it," he said, "but intellectually, I don't get it." The emotion, he admitted, was overwhelming. When the number hanging from the warehouse beyond rightfield at Camden Yards changed to 2,131—well, he knew something larger than any streak was at work. He wonders how he ever got through his little speech that night, although there is no mystery to us. (He went over it 10 times in his office, until he no longer choked up upon references to his wife and mother.) He wonders how he ever got through any of it. Of course, another season approaches. And the time he thought he would be given to understand the events of last summer has flown. A tape of *The Pride of the Yankees*, which he is curious about ("I hear that the movie speech is different from the real one," he says) is still on a coffee table. So is the video of his own milestone night. He'll get to it all someday. But November is already disappearing, and spring training is beginning to loom, and it seems as if there are more games to play. He has to work out.

HOW LONG has it been since the fan has had to acknowledge the athlete's give instead of his take? Since he was forced to recognize an athlete's diligence, stability, effort? It feels as if it has been ages, doesn't it, since sports was something other than a playful preamble to an advertising career? But at least the fan had this year to arrest his growing cynicism. And it could happen again. Maybe the fan just needs to know where to look: down the first base line, where in the half glow of stadium lights a gray-haired guy signs autographs into the wee hours.

ONE OF
A KIND

❧

Heaven Help Marge Schott

BY RICK REILLY

The Reds' owner, long since reduced to a life of loneliness, needed six men in fire-retardant suits to clean up her messes.

ALONE IN HER BEDROOM, ALONE IN A 40-ROOM mansion, alone on a 70-acre estate, Marge Schott finishes off a vodka-and-water (no lime, no lemon), stubs out another Carlton 120, takes to her two aching knees and prays to the Men. To Charlie, the husband who made her life and then ruined it. He taught her never to trust. To Daddy, the unsmiling father who turned her into his only son. He taught her never to be soft. To Dad Schott, the calculating father-in-law, whom she may have loved most of all. He taught her never to let herself be cheated.

"I pray to them every night, honey," she says. "How many owners do that, huh? Hit their knees every night?"

Hard to say. For that matter, how many baseball owners keep in their kitchen drawer plastic bags containing hair from a dog that died five years ago? Or are worth millions but haven't shopped for clothes in nine years? Schott just wears the stuff people send her. "If it fits, honey," she says in her No. 4 sandpaper voice, "I wear it."

Honey is what Schott calls everybody, unless you're *baby* or *sweetheart*. It's what she does instead of remembering your name. "This guy is from

SportsChannel, honey. He's here doing a big story on me."

"SPORTS ILLUSTRATED, Mrs. Schott."

"Right, honey."

Schott does not really have to remember anyone's name, because she's 67 years old, as rich as Oman, and she answers to nobody. She owns 43% of the Cincinnati Reds, but she hasn't had time to actually learn the game yet. After all, it has only been 12 years since that Christmas when she "saved the team for Cincinnati," as she has said over the years. (Why ruin the story by mentioning that the previous owners insisted that they never would have sold the Reds to anyone but a Cincinnatian, and there were no offers on the table from any other city. None of the men in Cincinnati were stepping up to buy the team, she says now.)

It is not unusual, for instance, for Schott not to know the names of her players. Oh, she knows a few—Eric Davis, Barry Larkin, Chris Sabo—but the rest are just uniforms that she steers her current St. Bernard, Schottzie 02, around before games, hoping to spy a familiar face.

"Who's that, honey?"

"George Grande, Mrs. Schott."

"Oh."

Grande has been the Reds' TV broadcaster for four years.

Marge sees Sabo. "Hi, honey."

"Hi, Mrs. Schott."

"Tell Schottzie you're going to win for her tonight."

Sabo looks around uncomfortably, then mutters at the ground, "Uh, we're going to win for you tonight . . . Schottzie."

In a recent game against the Philadelphia Phillies, there was a hot smash to Reds first baseman Hal Morris, who shouldn't have meant anything to Schott except that he has played on her team since 1990 and was leading the club in hitting at the time. Morris bobbled the ball. "Oh, you stupid guy!" Schott screamed.

Morris recovered and flipped the ball to the pitcher, who covered first.

"Who was that, honey?"

"Who was who?"

"Who ran over?"

"The pitcher?"

"Oh, good."

Schott is not big on baseball history, either. There is not a single banner commemorating the Big Red Machine years in Riverfront Stadium, not a single retired number on display to honor Pete Rose, Johnny Bench, Joe Morgan or Tony Perez. Not a single reminder of Rose's record 4,192 hits. That kind of thing sounds expensive, and Schott is much bigger on saving money than memories. Besides, who can remember all that stuff? During a rain delay in the game against Philadelphia, the JumboTron was showing highlights of the classic 1970 World Series between the Reds and the Baltimore Orioles, in which Orioles third baseman Brooks Robinson was merely Superman.

"Who's that, baby?"

"Brooks Robinson."

"Brooks Robinson? I thought he was one of the first black players."

"That was Jackie Robinson."

"No. . . ."

Of course, having Aunt Bee as your team's owner has its advantages. For instance, Schott doesn't raise her ticket prices every season, as a lot of other owners do. You don't do that to family members, which is what Reds fans are to her. Riverfront's most expensive seat is $11.50, cheapest in the majors. Schott still charges only $1 for a hot dog. (A jumbo frank costs three times as much at Shea Stadium in New York.) She does not often meddle in player deals, mostly because she has no real interest in baseball. Night after night she sits alone in her vast luxury box with just her telephone and Schottzie, not paying much attention to the game, waiting for some high-ranking employee to show up at the door and take Schottzie for a walk. Afterward there's always a report.

"Tinkle or poo?" she will ask.

"Just tinkle," the director of marketing or some other front-office-type will answer sheepishly.

In the sixth inning Schott moves down to her box seats behind the Reds' dugout to chain-sign autographs, hardly looking up except after loud cracks of the bat. She hates it when the bats break, but she does not lose money on them. She has an employee take them to the gift shop at a downtown Cincinnati hotel and sell them. (To show their undying love for her, some Cincinnati players smash their cracked bats into two pieces so they're in no condition to be sold.)

After the game Schott drives the 20 minutes to her mansion in suburban Indian Hill, where she is even more alone: no husband, no kids, no grandchildren, no live-in help, precious few friends, a tiny television sitting cold in the kitchen, the newspaper lying unread, books untouched.

She doesn't sleep much at night, despite all the Unisom she takes, not to mention the vodkas (Kamchatka, the cheap stuff). She sits in bed making picture frames to match her furniture and falls asleep, only to wake up in half an hour to smoke another cigarette. Finally she rises, fresh from a good night's nicotining, ready to seize the day.

Because she's set apart from the world like that, it's no wonder Schott's political and social views have not really changed since the Edsel. Over the years she has insulted homosexuals ("Only fruits wear earrings"), blacks ("Dave is my million-dollar nigger," she said of Dave Parker, a Reds outfielder from 1984 to '87) and Jews ("He's a beady-eyed Jew," she said of Cincinnati marketing director Cal Levy, according to *Unleashed*, the exhaustive biography of Schott written by Mike Bass in 1993). As for Adolf Hitler, she takes a compassionate view. "He was O.K. at the beginning," she says. "He rebuilt all the roads, honey. You know that, right? He just went too far." Two weeks ago she repeated that opinion in an interview with ESPN, setting off a storm of protest, including outrage from the Anti-Defamation League and other Jewish organizations, and casting baseball in an embarrassing light yet again. Two days later she issued a written apology, which was accepted by the Jewish Community Relations Council of Cincinnati.

Schott is a proud third-generation German-American. Her mother's sister had five sons who fought for Germany in World War II. "She used to send us little Nazi soldier dolls with the swastikas and everything, honey. We used to play with them," says Schott. She even has a Nazi armband she keeps in a bureau drawer in the hallway leading to her living room. She forgot about the armband until a Christmas party in 1987, when Levy happened to find it and asked her about it. "Figures a Jewish guy would find it, huh, honey?" Schott whispers, which she does when a matter under discussion is a little sticky. "What's a Jewish guy looking through my drawers for anyway? Right, honey?" (Levy, who is no longer with the club, says Schott had sent him in search of a dinner bell.)

She says she's not really a Nazi sympathizer, although she once told ABC's Diane Sawyer that the armband "is not a symbol of evil to me." Mostly it's a case of Schott not throwing anything away. If a bag lady had a trust fund, her house might look like Schott's: crammed with junk. There's a room full of stuff she received on two baseball goodwill visits to Japan. There are closets full of mementos and stuffed Saint Bernards and clocks with miniature baseball bats for hands, most of which were given to her. Charlie's suits still hang in his closet, right where he left them, and he has been dead, what, 28 years?

MargeVision is set on the 1950s, and she sees it clear as a bell. She often feels like speaking out for what she believes, and it hasn't hurt her much. While Al Campanis, Jimmy the Greek and Ben Wright lost their jobs for saying one-fiftieth of what Schott has said, she got only a one-year suspension from baseball in 1993 for making racial and ethnic slurs. A sensitivity-training course was thrown in for good measure. The course didn't really take. Sending Schott to sensitivity training is like sending a pickpocket to a Rolex convention.

Take a recent night, when Schott was leaving the Montgomery Inn restaurant in suburban Cincinnati after actually tearing up over the all-American vitality and clean-cut looks of a girl who had asked her for an autograph. As Schott was piling into her junk-strewn Riviera, she saw a group of high school-aged Asian-Americans walking down the street, laughing and talking.

"Look at that," she said.

"What?"

"That's not right, honey."

"What isn't?"

"Those Asian kids."

"It's not?"

(Whisper) "Well, I don't like when they come here, honey, and stay so long and then outdo our kids. That's not right."

If you were her public relations adviser, you would have her followed by six men in flame-retardant suits with a fire hose. In 1989 at Riverfront Stadium, as *60 Minutes* cameras rolled on her and Bart Giamatti, who was then the baseball commissioner, Schott saw something she didn't like.

Schott: "Is this a girl batboy or a boy that needs a goddamn haircut?"

Giamatti: "Well, Marge, that's a question you ought to take up with the young person after the game."

Schott: "Is that a boy or a girl?"

Giamatti: "It's a young man with a modern haircut."

Schott: "Well, he'll never be out here again with long hair like that. . . . "

Giamatti: "Marge, you're killing me here!"

Even in trying to say something nice about someone, Schott gets it all wrong. In boasting recently of her meeting with Japanese prime minister Kiichi Miyazawa on one of her baseball goodwill visits, in 1991, she recalled what he had said to her, using a cartoonish Japanese accent: "He says to me, honey, he says, 'No want Cadirrac, no want Rincoln, want Mosh Shott Boo-ick.'"

In the first six weeks of the 1996 season, Schott rewrote the book on loafer-in-mouth disease.

Chapter 1: When umpire John McSherry died of a heart attack after collapsing at home plate on Opening Day at Riverfront, Schott objected to the cancellation of the game and complained about how McSherry's death put *her* out: "I don't believe it. First it snows, and now *this*!"

Chapter 2: The next day Schott took flowers somebody had sent her, ripped off the card, wrote a new one with heartfelt condolences and sent the flowers to the umpires' room at Riverfront.

Chapter 3: At the start of the season the Reds weren't providing fans with scores from other games on the Riverfront scoreboard. "Why do they care about one game when they're watching another?" argued Schott, who had stopped paying her bill for the service (it costs $350 a month) last season.

Chapter 4: Following the sixth home game, after being raked over the coals by the media for her stinginess, she reversed her scoreboard decision and blamed it on her employees, saying in front of a roomful of reporters, "I've got to have the worst public relations staff in America!" Now those employees have to track the scores by calling to other ballparks and listening to the radio.

Chapter 5: On April 14 she tried to apologize for her McSherry gaffe minutes before the first pitch against the Houston Astros by approaching the umpires working the game—none of whom were at Riverfront on Opening Day and all of whom resented her publicity-minded opportunism. One, Harry Wendelstedt, turned his back on her.

Not that sheer Jell-O-headedness is always behind Schott's troubles. Many of her idiocies are clearly thought out in advance. For years she has made it known that she would prefer that the Reds not hire women of childbearing age. Women in the workplace is not a cause Schott champions, despite the fact that she is one herself. (Besides the Reds, she owns two car dealerships, at least three vehicle-leasing firms, a concrete company and several other businesses in various states, not to mention a large chunk of General Motors stock, most of it under the control of her Cincinnati-based holding company, Schottco.) "I'll tell you something, honey," she says. "Some of the biggest problems in this city come from women wanting to leave the home to work." And: "Why do these girl reporters have to come into the locker room? Why can't they wait outside?" And: "I don't really think baseball is a woman's place, honey. I really don't. I think it should be left to the boys."

She despises the city ordinance that prohibits smoking at Riverfront, the one that keeps her sitting alone in her 20-chair luxury box instead of behind the dugout with the fans, whom she loves. Besides, MargeVision doesn't see cigarettes as being all that bad. "I'll tell you something, honey," she says in her smoker's rasp. "They had a jazz festival here awhile ago, and we walked around, and they were doing nothing but crack!"

Schott detests facial hair, too, and forbids it on any player or employee. The close, comfortable shave, she feels, is her lasting contribution to the game, even though it was a long-standing club policy that Cincinnati players not grow facial hair when she bought the team. "If nothing else, the thing I'm most proud of [about the Reds] is the no-facial hair and earrings," she said recently to Chip Baker, her one-man marketing department (by comparison, the Atlanta Braves' marketing department has 10 employees), even as she looked at a photo of the 1896 Reds, all of them bewhiskered.

"Don't you think, Chip?"

"Yes, ma'am."

"Did Jesus have a beard, Chip?"

"I think so, Mrs. Schott."

"Oh." Pause. "Have you met our friend from Sports America here, honey?"

"SPORTS ILLUSTRATED, Mrs. Schott."

"Right, honey."

It is not just baseball Schott is a little behind on. She seems to have been on Neptune for much of the 20th century. Once, she showed up very early for a meeting in a Chicago hotel and then was overheard growling into a pay phone, "Hey, why didn't you tell me there was an hour difference between Cincinnati and Chicago?"

Schott and computers don't see eye to eye, either. At her car dealerships and other local businesses, which she usually visits in the mornings before going to the ballpark, some employees have taped signs to their computers begging her not to turn them off. She does that to save electricity, even though, she admits, it makes a computer "lose all those thingies on the screen."

Schott doesn't read much anymore, either. "I don't like the words so much, honey. I like the pictures. Pictures mean so much more to me than words, honey."

She is always ready with her stack of photos. Here's a shot of Marge as a baby, one of five daughters of Edward Unnewehr, who made a fortune in the lumber business (mostly from plywood and veneer). Five daughters, and all Daddy ever wanted was a boy.

"Well, what'd you have, Ed?" people would ask him.

"A baby," he would snarl.

Daddy was strict. "Very *achtung*!" as Schott says. When Daddy wanted Mother, he would ring a bell. Daddy did not eat meals with his children until they were over the messy age—about four. And you had better be tough. "You didn't get sick in Daddy's family, honey," Schott says. "We coughed into our pillows."

Since Daddy couldn't have a boy, he treated Marge like one. He called her Butch. She grew up the wisecracking girl Daddy took to work whenever he could, the circle-skirted jokester who would bring cigars to slumber parties and smoke them. She was less comfortable around women than men, whom she was learning to love and hate all at once.

And here's a photo of Butch marrying Charles Schott, son of a wealthy society family in Cincinnati. Here's Daddy, sulking throughout the wedding. "He wanted me to run his business, honey," she says, "and now he was losing me." Here's Marge with Charlie's father, Walter, who took her on the road with him, took her to make the boys in the board meetings laugh at all her one-liners. Once the meeting started, though, she had better stay quiet.

Still Marge learned a lot at the feet of Dad Schott, who in 1938 had become the largest auto dealer in Ohio. Today she knows where every penny goes, how every tax shelter works, how wide every loophole can be made. Schott may come off as having sniffed too much epoxy, but she knows her way around a financial statement and the county courthouse. "I hate lawyers, honey," she often says, "but I keep 'em busy."

The Men ran her life, enriched it and, ultimately, ruined it. According to *Unleashed*, Charles was a hopeless alcoholic, who left her alone on their wedding night to play cards and left her alone hundreds of nights after that.

Yeah, she learned lots about men. Like when she found out years after the fact that it had been two male members of her family who, shortly after she was married in 1952, had sneaked one of her Saint Bernards out and had it killed because they didn't like it. You don't think that hurt? Men, honey.

Here's one last picture of her with the chubby, grinning Charlie. When he died in 1968 of a heart attack, he was rumored to have been found in the bathtub of his mistress, Lois Kenning. It is a subject Schott does not like to discuss but has not quite figured a way to lie about.

"Where did your husband die, Mrs. Schott?"

"I don't know, honey."

Since then she has waged a one-woman war for fidelity. Her goal is to rid baseball of "cutesy-poos," as she calls them: the groupies who end up in ballplayers' hotel rooms. She says she has hired private investigators to videotape her players getting on and off buses and going in and out of hotels, to make sure there is no cutesy-pooing going on. Reds general manager Jim Bowden confirms only a little of this. "A couple of years ago we videotaped our players getting off a couple of charter flights, just to make sure our rules and regulations were being followed," he says. "At no time were rules being violated."

The last two seasons Reds players have complained that their mail has been opened and taped shut again. "Ray [Knight, the team's rookie manager] thought some of the boxes that came in the mail looked like they'd been opened," says Bowden. "He told Mrs. Schott, and she said she would look into it." Some of the players suspect Schott did the opening. Schott says she doesn't know a thing about it.

Then there are the phone calls. "I tape every call in and out of the clubhouse," Schott boasts. "These players are not going to pull any cutesy-poo stuff on me."

"But isn't that illegal, Mrs. Schott?"

"Oh. Oh, no. Not tape, honey. I just mean I have the operator log every call to the clubhouse. That's all, honey."

Schott is tighter than shrink-wrap, but whatever price she has to pay to protect the Great American Family, she will pay it. This is because she never had children herself. It is her single greatest sorrow. "I just don't think I did my job," she lamented recently in her Riverfront office. "In my day girls were raised to raise kids, and I didn't do it. My life would've been completely different with kids. I wouldn't be here, honey, I can tell you that."

It did not help that her sister Lottie had 10 kids, the way Marge thinks good Catholic girls should. And it was not because Marge didn't try. She hired the best doctors, up to and including one who she says had treated the shah of Iran. "And he about killed me, honey, giving me all these drugs," she says. "About killed me." She says she tried to adopt twins once, "but the nuns wouldn't let us, honey. Wouldn't let us." She whispers: " 'They're interbreds,' they told us. 'They'd only be a frustration to you.' I told 'em, 'No, we'll educate 'em,' but they wouldn't let us have 'em.'" In *Unleashed*, Bass reported that Charlie's mother attempted to arrange adoptions, but Marge and Charlie refused to follow through because they didn't know the children's backgrounds.

When Charlie died, Marge was only 39. She could have tried for kids again, but all the men who seemed attracted to her were already married. "I never knew so many guys' wives didn't understand them, honey," she cracks. She was going to marry Harold Schott, Charlie's uncle. She says he called her six times one day to tell her he was flying back from Florida to ask for her hand, but he died that same day. "First the family said it was a heart attack," Marge explains. "Then they said he drowned. The best swimmer in the family. Something funny going on there."

And so she was left alone to raise other things: 22 Saint Bernards, a baseball team and even cattle, though she refused to let anybody slaughter the calves. She let them live. She looks out on the calves in the distance from her yard and grabs your elbow and says, "Look at them. Isn't it beautiful seeing the families out in the field?"

Adults, especially ballplayers and newspaper people, she's not so big on, but she is nuts for animals and children. Once a week or so she will get to the ballpark early, gather up 20 or so small kids and let them run out to the rightfield wall and back before a game. Once she went to the opening day of a little league for disabled children and spent most of an hour crying like a baby.

On April 3, Reds second baseman Bret Boone flew to Birmingham to have elbow surgery just hours after his wife, Suzi, gave birth in Cincinnati to their first child, Savannah. Immediately after the operation he flew home to be with her and their hours-old baby. Schott went to the hospital that night to check on them. She took gifts and stayed with Suzi for a couple of hours while Bret, still groggy from his surgery, slept on a couch. "It was weird," says one former marketing employee. "She was great to our families. Absolutely terrific. But she treated us like s---."

Whatever generous spirit there is inside Schott flickers out when she sits behind that owner's desk. "I think she is the single worst person I've ever known," says one longtime Reds employee. "Spiteful, mean-spirited and evil."

Says a former top-level employee, "She's the most cold, calculating person I've ever known. To feel sorry for her is ridiculous."

Schott believes she must be bottom-line tough, like the Men, coughing into her pillow all the way. Drink hard, work hard, feel hard. And this is how you get the dimly lit discount hell that is the Reds today. There is not a drop of sweetness left in the organization, possibly because Schott watches even the candy. In a stadium storeroom there are boxes and boxes of leftover donations from a Leaf candy promotion tied to the Celebrity Bat Girl and Bat Boy nights at Riverfront. But Schott did not hand it out. She did not give it away to charities. She hoarded it for special occasions. One was last January, when she indicated to her shrinking, pitifully paid front-office staff (Exhibit A: Former public relations assistant Joe Kelley more than doubled his salary by taking a similar job with the city's minor league hockey franchise) that there would be no holiday bonus again by throwing some Leaf candy on each person's desk. How old was it? On the outside of some of the wrappers was an ad for a contest. It said, "Win a trip to the 1991 Grammy Awards!"

Schott has a front-office staff of only 41 people, fewest in the league. Almost every other team has twice as many employees. The New York Mets have 120, the Colorado Rockies 111, the San Diego Padres 104. This does not include scouts, on whom Schott has never been big. "All they do is sit around and watch ball games," she once said. The Reds have 25 scouts. The Los Angeles Dodgers have 57.

Schott is paranoid about being cheated. Reds policy is that she must sign any check over $50, and any purchase over that amount requires three bids before she'll agree to it. "That means even if you're reordering paper clips," says a former publicity employee, "you have to call around and get two more bids, even though you know exactly what you want already."

During the 1994–95 baseball strike Schott stopped having the Reds office bathrooms professionally cleaned, so some employees did the job themselves. She has been known to rummage through the trash barrels to make sure scrap paper is written on both sides. She eliminated free tissues for employees. She keeps the lights off whenever possible, extinguishing them when you leave your office just to walk down the hall. The hallway carpeting is so old and tattered that the seams are held together with duct tape. Schott wants the heat turned down to 55° at five o'clock, so some employees have been known to bring in their own space heaters. She does all of this at every place she owns.

No wonder, according to Bass, that male employees of Schott's occasionally ask her to sign a publicity shot for a "niece," then take it into the men's room, place it in the urinal and fire away.

Schott has eliminated the Reds' customer-service and community relations departments. Her private secretary became fed up with Schott and quit last spring, and for a year Schott answered her own calls rather than hire a replacement. The *New York Post* called last season to request head shots of the Reds' players, and after the playoffs Schott had a member of her staff call the newspaper and ask for them back.

"It's so crazy," she says. "You're spending millions and millions out on the field for these players, honey, and you find yourself arguing about envelopes and paper clips in the office. You try to cut on silly stuff. It's like Disneyland on the field and the real world in here."

"No," says one employee. "It's like Disneyland on the field and Bosnia in here."

Schott does have one of the major leagues' highest player payrolls— "They [Bowden and her other baseball advisers] con me into spending money on the players, honey," she says—though she has cut back this year and plans to make serious cuts next year. But just because she has had to purchase a Rolls-Royce doesn't mean she won't use the drive-thru window. Schott won't pop for video equipment to let players check past performances against certain pitchers and hitters. She won't pop for Cybex machines. She won't even pop for extra hats or sweatshirts. "Anything extra," says outfielder Davis, "we pay for ourselves."

Even when the glory comes, Schott does not seem to be able to pry open her pocketbook. When the Reds won the World Series in 1990, she didn't throw a party for them. Some of the players finally went out and brought back hamburgers.

To Schott, most of the players are just empty uniforms into which she pours money, and it sticks in her craw. One game in April, Cincinnati pitcher Mark Portugal gave up a line drive base hit. Watching from her front-row seat in the stands, Schott shook her head. "Three million dollars," she grumbled, apparently unaware that Portugal is earning $4.33 million this year, "and he's just not worth a damn."

Then there was this exchange during the same home stand in April, as she sat looking at the program in her luxury box, waiting for the coat-and-tied security director to come back from his walk with Schottzie.

"There's what's-his-name, honey."

"Who?"

"The guy I'm paying $3 million a year to sit on his butt."

"Jose Rijo?"

"Yeah. Three million, sweetheart. For crying out loud."

Rijo, the 1990 World Series MVP, who actually is making $6.15 million this season, hasn't pitched for the Reds since July 18, 1995, because of a serious elbow injury.

"It's kind of a circus atmosphere, but you do your job," says Larkin, the 1995 National League MVP. "The only thing I don't like is when the dog takes a crap at shortstop, because I might have to dive into that s---."

Even though Cincinnati won the 1990 World Series and was the NL Central champion last year, anybody in baseball will tell you privately that the Reds are leaking oil three lanes wide. They routinely lose their best scouts to better-paying clubs. Attendance is down for the second straight year. In the playoffs last year there were more than 12,000 unsold seats for one game at Riverfront and more than 8,000 for another. For some reason, aside from Bowden, who is considered one of the best young executives in the game, top-notch baseball minds aren't inclined to come to work in an office chilled to 55 degrees for substantially less than what other teams are paying, bringing their own tissues to the office and wondering who else is listening to their phone messages.

The Reds don't often bid for high-priced free agents, which is fine with Schott, who prefers to bring in players from her farm teams. But Cincinnati's minor league system is unraveling. *Baseball America* recently listed the top 100 teenage prospects, and no one in the Reds' organization was listed in the top 50. No problem. One day recently Schott returned from seeing a thrilling trapeze act and had a great idea. "We need to start checking that circus for ballplayers," she reportedly told a member of her staff. "There are some real athletes there."

Another of her ideas is to have a woman playing on her team. "I've got my scouts looking for a great girl," Schott says. "Wouldn't that be something? Her coming in and striking all these boys out, honey?"

Incredibly, the county plans to build new stadiums for both the Reds and the NFL Bengals, and town leaders are petrified about the influence Schott might have over the new ballpark. Pay toilets? Bugging devices in every showerhead? A dog run in left center? "I just wish she'd get out," says one source high in the Reds' ownership structure. "We all wish she'd get out. She's a despicable person."

Baseball would not miss her, to say the least. She is on none of the owners' committees and has shown no interest in helping to resolve the issues that plague the game. Wouldn't baseball be better off without her? "There is no appropriate answer to that question," says Bud Selig, acting baseball commissioner and owner of the Milwaukee Brewers. But one owner did say that Schott is "truly embarrassing. Worse than embarrassing."

Wait your turn. People want Schott out of more than baseball. General Motors has tried twice over the last eight years to take her Chevrolet dealership from her. The reason, says Chevrolet, is the franchise's poor sales performance. Schott twice hauled Chevrolet before the Ohio Motor Vehicle Dealers Board, which regulates auto manufacturers and dealers throughout the state, and on both occasions she managed to retain her franchise. But there may be questions still. According to documents obtained by SI, a former Reds employee has received ownership notices and a service reminder for a 1996 vehicle he does not own and says he has never seen. In fact, last weekend the car the former employee supposedly bought was on one of Schott's lots. Schott says that if these facts are correct, they are the result of an innocent mix-up, and she denies that her dealership is falsifying records to inflate sales figures in order to meet quotas set by Chevrolet. Chevrolet says it will look into the matter.

So, you've got to ask, why doesn't Schott just take the $30 million profit she stands to make if she cashes in her stake in the Reds, go ahead with her plans to build a new elephant wing for the Cincinnati Zoo ("Elephants never ask you for any raises, honey," she says), sell the car dealerships, the concrete company and the holding company and just find a good canasta game somewhere?

"I don't know, honey," she says, sitting all alone in that luxury box, the lights off, the thick windows keeping her from the cheers and the sun and the joy of the baseball game that is being mimed below. "As long as the little guy out there still thinks I'm doing a good job, that's all that matters. I don't give a damn what the stupid press thinks."

Actually, the little guy may have had it up to here. Schott has fallen drastically in popularity polls in Cincinnati. Last summer a *Cincinnati Post*-WCPO-TV poll found that approximately 47% of the public had a positive impression of Schott, compared to only 34% for Cincinnati Bengals owner Mike Brown. The most recent poll, though, gave Brown a 49% favorable rating, compared to only 37% for Schott. But she has an explanation: "I think somebody's trying to get me out, honey, somebody that wants to buy the team. It's a kind of vendetta against me, honey. It's kind of like a woman thing." She asks herself all the time, would the Men have given up?

"Nah," she says, "I don't wanna cave, baby. I've been through bad times before. Besides, I'm always best when I'm battling."

Right about then, an employee in a full-length dress and pearls comes back from walking Schottzie.

"Poo or tinkle?"

"Tinkle."

"Hey, have you met this guy from Sports Thingy?"

The Guiding Light

BY STEVE WULF

*Buck O'Neil bears witness to the glory of the Negro leagues,
not just to the shame of segregation.*

*There's nothing greater for a human being than to get his body to react to all the
things one does on a ball field. It's as good as sex; it's as good as music. It fills
you up. Waste no tears for me. I didn't come along too early. I was right on time.*
                                                                    —Buck O'Neil

BUCK STUCK, but he was Foots first. He has also been
called Country and Cap and just plain Jay, and while
Satchel Paige was alive, he was a man called Nancy.

John Jordan O'Neil, born Nov. 13, 1911, in Carrabelle,
Fla., has collected almost as many nicknames during his seven decades in
the game as all of the current major leaguers combined. But then he has led
so many different baseball lives, and with the exception of that month back
in 1937 when he played in a straw skirt for the Zulu Cannibal Giants, all of
them have been distinguished.

As a smooth-fielding first baseman for the Kansas City Monarchs from
1938 to '54, O'Neil won a Negro American League batting title (hitting
.350 in '46) and played in three Negro League East-West All-Star Games and

three Negro World Series. As the manager of the Monarchs from '48 until '55, he won five half-season pennants and shepherded 14 of his players, including Ernie Banks and Elston Howard, into the majors. As a scout for the Chicago Cubs he signed four elected or near-certain Hall of Famers: Banks, Lou Brock, Lee Smith and Joe Carter. In 1962 the Cubs made him the first black coach in the major leagues.

At 82, the still-graceful, still-handsome O'Neil still scouts for the Kansas City Royals. When he's not doing that, or shooting his age over 18 holes, he champions the players and memories of the Negro leagues. But O'Neil is most impressive not for what he does or what he did, but for what he is. Banks, who knew O'Neil when, says, "He is a role model, a father, a mentor, a teacher, a *sensei*, a hero, a gentleman, a man. Who do you think I got my let's-play-two attitude from? From Buck O'Neil, that's who."

Hal McRae, the Royals' manager, says, "Buck just makes you feel good. You might be blue, you might be in a slump, but a few minutes with Buck and the world is a wonderful place. Do you know what he is? He's the guiding light."

It's a light that shines on the past as well as the present. The Negro leagues were born because organized baseball wanted nothing to do with integration, and O'Neil and his teammates encountered prejudice daily. But the Negro leagues were also a glorious enterprise well worth celebrating, and that's where O'Neil comes in. He takes particular pride in the Monarchs, and he harbors no bitterness over the fact that he was past his prime when Jackie Robinson finally broke the color line, in 1947. "Buck never curses his fate," says Banks. "He knows that what he did as a player and manager paved the way for the rest of us."

And O'Neil's light shines often in *Baseball*, a documentary by Ken Burns, of Civil War renown, that presents a sweeping panorama of the national pastime. While *Baseball* has much to recommend it, its best moments come while O'Neil is on the screen.

He is at the heart of *Baseball*'s "Fifth Inning," subtitled "Shadow Ball." On one level, shadow ball was the amazingly realistic pantomime of baseball without the ball—often performed by Negro leaguers before their games. But it is also a metaphor for the black baseball that shadowed the segregated major leagues. O'Neil illuminates those shadows, bringing the Negro leagues to life in all their glory and pain, jazz and blues.

As an eyewitness he links Babe Ruth to Josh Gibson to Bo Jackson. As a confidant of Paige's he reveals a new side to the great pitcher. As a singer

. . . well, if you can't watch all 18½ hours of *Baseball*, be sure to catch O'Neil during the "Seventh Inning Stretch." He'll take you out to the game.

FOOTS

"How old is this ballpark?" someone asks Jordan Kobritz, the principal owner of the Daytona Cubs.

"As near as anyone can document," says Kobritz, "it's 55 years old."

"Sixty," says Buck O'Neil. "It's at least 60 years old. I played here in 1934 for the Miami Giants, on our way up to face the Jacksonville Red Caps, a *good* team made up of railroad porters. Over there, that's where the Jim Crow section of the bleachers was."

The field in question is now known as Jackie Robinson Ballpark because this is where Robinson played his first integrated game in organized ball, as a member of the 1946 Montreal Royals. O'Neil has come to Daytona to rekindle some memories and visit his niece, Sally Griffin.

There's nobody on the field on this June afternoon, but O'Neil can still see the Giants: "That's me over there on first base, 22-year-old Foots O'Neil from Sarasota [Fla.]. On second, Winky James from Key West. Our shortstop is Bill Riggins, who played for the New York Black Yankees, and at third base is Oliver Marcelle. Ollie was a Creole from New Orleans, a fine-looking man. But he got part of his nose bit off in a fight in Cuba, and he had to play with a piece of tape on the nose. He'd been so proud of his looks, so he was never the same after that."

Griffin has brought along some mementos, one a 70-year-old report card from a school in Sarasota for sixth-grader John O'Neil. He earned excellent grades, including an A in personal hygiene, which will come as no surprise to people who know how meticulously he dresses.

Back then he was known as Foots because he had size-11 feet, pretty big dogs for a 12-year-old. He was also a pretty good first baseman, and one day the manager of the semipro Sarasota Tigers asked Emma Booker, the principal at Foots's small school, if he could borrow the kid for a game. She said yes, and soon Foots, not yet in his teens, was traveling all over the state playing baseball. He also got to see a lot of the white man's game during spring training: John McGraw's New York Giants trained in Sarasota, Babe Ruth and Lou Gehrig were based in Tampa, and Connie Mack's Philadelphia Athletics were in Fort Myers.

But there was work to be done, and because his father, John Sr., was a foreman in the celery fields, Foots became a box boy, carrying the crates of celery. "I was considered a good box boy because, while most of the box boys could only carry two crates at a time, I was big and strong enough to carry four," O'Neil says. "I did that for about three years, at $1.25 a day. One day I was having lunch by myself next to a big stack of boxes, and it was so hot, I said out loud, '*Damn*, there has got to be something better than this.'

"It turns out my father and some of the older men were on the other side of the stack having their lunch. That night my father told me, 'I heard what you said today.' I thought he was going to reprimand me for swearing, but he said, 'You're right. There is something better than this. But you can't find it here. You're going to have to go out and get it.'

"In those days there were no high schools for blacks in Sarasota, but thanks to the eighth-grade education Booker gave him, Foots was able to get an athletic scholarship to Edward Waters College, a Methodist school in Jacksonville. There they called him Country, and they made him the first baseman on the baseball team and a lineman on the football team. The baseball coach, Ox Clemons, schooled O'Neil so well that the Miami Giants, a Negro semipro team, stole him away in 1934, by which time O'Neil had earned his high school diploma but was still two years short of a college degree. It just so happened that one of the owners of the Giants was a man named Buck O'Neal, although it would be a while before Country became Buck.

In 1935 Marcelle, the third baseman with the taped-up nose, invited O'Neil to join him on a team he played for called the New York Tigers. "We started out in Sarasota, mind you, and we had nothing to do with New York," says O'Neil. "That was just a way to get the people to come to the games. Out where we were headed, nobody was going to know the difference." They were also headed into the Depression, and the Tigers spent the summer and fall chasing after ball games in Louisiana, Texas, Kansas and Colorado, living hand to mouth, hopping freight trains, sometimes relying on O'Neil's pool-playing abilities for money.

O'Neil and Doby Major, another player from Sarasota, decided to go home from Wichita, Kans., that October, and O'Neil's father wired them train tickets. But they had only 75 cents between them for the three-day trip, and used it to buy day-old bread in Chattanooga. By the time they got home, O'Neil says, "our day-old bread was two days gone. When I got home I ate so much, my mama cried."

Up in the stands at Jackie Robinson Ballpark, O'Neil recalls another adventure from that summer of '35: "One night we had to sneak out of a boardinghouse in Shreveport without paying our bills. But a few months after that, I sent the landlady a check for what we owed her, which wasn't much, maybe $50.

"Many years later I'm passing through Shreveport on my way to scout a player, and I decide to stay at this same boardinghouse. I inquire after the landlady, and a woman says, 'That was my mother. She passed away a few years ago. Did you know her?' I tell the woman my name, and she smiles and leads me into one of the rooms. There on the wall, framed like a picture, is my check. I guess I had restored her mother's faith in us."

BUCK
A hand comes down hard on the shoulder of Ken Burns. "Can we have Buck back now?"

Burns, who is sitting in the press dining room at Kauffman Stadium on the night of Aug. 3, turns around to see that the hand belongs to the Kansas City vice president for baseball operations, George Brett. "Actually," says Brett, "we don't need him now that we've won 11 in a row. It's when we start losing that we'll need him."

The Royals have given O'Neil time off this summer to help promote *Baseball*, but don't think for a moment that his role with the club is ceremonial. "I depend on him," says McRae. "Whether it be for advice or for information, he's a big help around here." Indeed, when O'Neil walks into the Royals' clubhouse, the room gets a little warmer. He'll do ball tricks with one of the kids, swap stories with K.C. first base coach Lee May or quietly advise a player in a slump.

This night also happens to be Monarchs Night, and the Royals are about to play the Oakland A's while wearing replica uniforms of the 1924 Kansas City Monarchs, who were the first "world champions" of the Negro leagues. This unprecedented homage to a Negro league team by a major league team is a wonderful—albeit overdue—gesture that bridges time, culture, race and spirit.

On the mound to throw the ceremonial first pitch is Burns, dressed in a Monarch jersey. But as he goes into his windup, his catcher, every inch a Monarch, every inch a ballplayer, waves him off. Much to the delight of the crowd, O'Neil takes off his glasses and puts them on Bob Motley, a former Negro league umpire standing behind him. Only then does O'Neil signal for his batterymate to throw the ball.

O'Neil didn't actually become a Monarch until 1938, when he was 26. He had played the '36 season with the Shreveport Acme Giants and most of the '37 season with the Memphis Red Sox. He did spend one month in '37 playing in that straw skirt for the barnstorming Zulu Cannibal Giants. "I was making $100 a month with the Red Sox, and the Giants offered me a lot more, so I jumped," says O'Neil. "Abe Saperstein owned the team, and we didn't think that much about wearing the costume. This was *show* business. At least I didn't have to put on the war paint like some of the guys. Besides, we had trunks on underneath our skirts. A first baseman in a stretch would have been pretty vulnerable without those trunks."

His stay with the Cannibal Giants was memorable for another reason. The promoter for the team, Syd Pollock, had also worked for the Miami Giants when O'Neil played for them, and Pollock somehow confused this O'Neil with that club's co-owner, Buck O'Neal. So he started billing the Giants' first baseman as Buck O'Neil, and the name stuck.

The next year, J. Leslie Wilkinson brought O'Neil to Kansas City. Wilkie, who was the only white owner in the Negro leagues, had had his eye on O'Neil for quite some time, and O'Neil immediately became the Monarchs' starting first baseman and number six hitter. "It hit me my first week with the Monarchs," says O'Neil. "I caught a routine throw from the second baseman, and as I was trotting off the field, I thought, Damn! I just caught a throw from Newt Allen. Newt was one of the greatest players in the Negro leagues back when I was a child."

From 1939 to '42 the Monarchs won four straight Negro American League pennants. They had a number of stars: pitcher Hilton Smith; shortstop and rightfielder Ted Strong, who also starred for the Harlem Globetrotters; and outfielder Turkey Stearnes, a peculiar man who liked to talk to his bats. And in '39 Paige joined them, but that's another two dozen stories.

"We were like the New York Yankees," says O'Neil. "We had that winning tradition, and we were *proud*. We had a strict dress code—coat and tie, no baseball jackets. We stayed in the best hotels in the world. They just *happened* to be owned by black people. We ate in the best restaurants in the world. They just *happened* to be run by blacks. And when we were in Kansas City, well, 18th and Vine was the center of the universe. We'd come to breakfast at Street's Hotel, and there might be Count Basie or Joe Louis or Billie Holiday or Lionel Hampton."

World War II broke up the Monarchs' dynasty, at least temporarily. One of

O'Neil's few regrets is that he didn't get to play for Kansas City in 1945, the year Jackie Robinson was a Monarch. O'Neil was then in the Navy, stationed with a black stevedore battalion at Subic Bay in the Philippines. Recalls O'Neil, "We loaded and unloaded ships. I was a bosun with 18 or so men under me. One night at about 11 o'clock the commanding officer gets on the horn and says, 'John O'Neil, please report to my office immediately.'

"I didn't know what he could want. But when I got to his office, this white man said to me, 'I just thought you should know that the Brooklyn Dodgers have just signed Jackie Robinson to a minor league contract.' Well, I got on the horn and said, 'Now hear this! Now hear this! The Dodgers have signed Jackie Robinson.' You should have heard the celebration. Halfway around the world from Brooklyn, we were hollering and firing our guns into the air."

After the war O'Neil returned home to Kansas City and married Ora Lee Owen, a schoolteacher from Memphis whom he had met a few years before.

As she did then, Ora is waiting patiently on this Aug. 3 night for John— as she calls him—to return. She is sitting in a private box at Kauffman Stadium while Buck and some of the other Monarch alumni sign autographs outside the stands. The demand for the signatures of these once-forgotten players has been so great that they are still signing an hour and a half after the first pitch of the game.

Finally, after about six innings, the men come back from their grueling autograph session. Rather than looking tired, however, the Monarchs, in their uniforms, actually seem younger than they did a few hours earlier. Is it possible, O'Neil is asked, that a little time spent in a baseball uniform can take years off your age?

"You got *that* right."

NANCY

Standin' in a corner, 18th and Vine.

Those aren't exactly the lyrics to *Kansas City*, but on the morning of Aug. 4 they're close enough. Standing in a corner of the Negro Leagues Museum at 18th and Vine are the now familiar team of Buck and Burns. In their own ways they are eloquent preachers, and they are here to address the audience at a benefit breakfast for the museum. Burns introduces O'Neil as the most remarkable man he has ever interviewed and then adds, "Buck is 82. I'm 41. I guess that makes me half a Buck."

O'Neil tells a story about his 80th-birthday celebration at his church:

"There was all this babbling about Buck O'Neil *this* and Buck O'Neil *that*. Just in case any of it went to my head, a young boy I knew came up and introduced his friend to me. He said, 'I want you to meet Buck O'Neil. He's an old *relic* from the Negro leagues.' I said, 'Son, you are *so* right.' "

As he almost always does before such an audience, O'Neil tells a Satchel Paige story. He has a lot of them, always making sure that the absent Paige addresses him as Nancy. There was the time Paige heard an opposing player in Denver call him an "overrated darkie." He told Nancy to bring in the infielders and outfielders and had the seven of them kneel around him as he struck out the side on nine pitches.

But as O'Neil points out in the "Fifth Inning" of *Baseball*, Paige was more than a clown, more than a great pitcher. "A part of Satchel that no one ever hears about," says O'Neil, "is this part of Satchel. We're going up to Charleston, but the rooms weren't ready yet. So he says, 'Nancy, c'mon with me. We're gonna take a ride. . . .' We went to Drum Island (S.C.). Drum Island was where they had auctioned off the slaves. . . . We stood there, he and I, maybe 10 minutes, not saying a word, just thinking.

" 'You know what, Nancy?' he says.

" 'What's that, Satchel?'"

" 'Seems like I been here before.'

"I said, 'Me, too.' "

At the breakfast at 18th and Vine, someone in the audience asks the question everybody wants O'Neil to be asked: "Why did Satchel call you Nancy?" O'Neil smiles the way he must have smiled at a hanging curveball in 1946.

"We were playing near an Indian reservation in Sioux Falls, South Dakota, on our way to Chicago to play the Chicago American Giants," he says. "Satchel met a beautiful Indian maiden named Nancy, and he asked her if she'd like to visit him in Chicago, and she said sure, so Satchel gave her the name of our hotel. Well, now we're in Chicago, and I'm sitting in the coffee shop of the hotel when I see a cab pull up, and out steps Nancy. I greet her and tell her that Satchel is upstairs, and the bellhop carries her bags to his room.

"A few minutes pass, and another cab pulls up, and out steps Satchel's fiancée, Lahoma. I jump up and say, 'Lahoma, so good to see you. Satchel's not here right now, but he should be along shortly. Why don't you sit here with me, and I'll have the bellman take your bags up.' I go over to the bellman, explain the situation to him and tell him to move Nancy's bags into the room next to mine, which is next door to Satchel's. A few minutes later he comes down and gives me the sign that everything is O.K. In the meantime, Satchel has climbed down the fire escape, and lo and behold, here he comes walking down the street. I say, 'Look, Lahoma, here's old Satch now,' and Satchel gives her a big greeting and takes her upstairs.

"That should've ended the trouble, but when we were turning in that night I heard Satchel's door open and close. Then I heard him knock on Nancy's door. I know he wanted to give her some money and apologize. But while he's whispering kind of loud, 'Nancy! Nancy!' I hear his door open again, and I knew it was Lahoma coming out to see what was going on. I jumped out of bed, opened my door and said, 'Yeah, Satch. What do you want?' And he said, 'Oh, Nancy. There you are. I was looking for you.'

"And from that day on, Satchel called me Nancy."

CAP
"Hello, Cap," says the former first base coach for the Monarchs.

"Hello, Hamp," says O'Neil.

At a New York screening of the "Seventh Inning" of *Baseball*, the two octogenarians greet each other like long-lost friends. It has been a while since O'Neil has seen Lionel Hampton. "I loved to watch the Monarchs play," says Hampton, the great bandleader and vibraphonist. "One day in 1948 Cap—that's what the players called Buck—said to me, 'You're around here so much, I might as well put you to work.' So Cap let me coach first base for one game, and then he gave me the jersey. It was one of the great thrills of my life."

As strong as jazz and black baseball were in Kansas City in the 1930s and '40s, by the early '50s they had begun to diminish. Nightclubs closed, and the Monarchs, like all the other Negro league franchises, began to suffer because of the integration of the big leagues. O'Neil's job as manager was no longer to win but rather to prepare young black players for their chance at the majors: Banks, Howard, Gene Baker, Pancho Herrera, Sweet Lou Johnson, Hank Thompson.

Before the day-old bread was two days gone again, O'Neil quit the Monarchs after the 1955 season to scout for the Cubs. His job was to find black players in the South, and he put 40,000 miles a year on his car. He discovered Brock when he was a skinny outfielder at Southern University. He tracked down 17-year-old Oscar Gamble in Montgomery, Ala. He also found trouble one night in Jackson, Miss.

O'Neil and Piper Davis, the black scout who signed Lee May, were in Jackson looking for a high school game. They saw the lights of a ballpark, pulled into the parking lot and asked the two men at the entrance if this was where the game was. "Oh, yeah, this is where it is, all right," said one. O'Neil and Davis got out of their car and walked to the field. On the mound, though, was not a pitcher but a member of the Ku Klux Klan. The ballpark was filled with men in sheets, and the two scouts made a hasty exit.

In May 1962 the Cubs made O'Neil the first black coach in the major leagues. Although *Ebony* did a big feature on him, the predominantly white media largely ignored his appointment. (SPORTS ILLUSTRATED did O'Neil as a FACE IN THE CROWD.) At the time, the Cubs were in their College of Coaches stage, rotating several different coaches as the head coach (i.e., manager), and John Holland, the Chicago general manager, paid lip service to the idea that O'Neil might one day be the manager.

But the Cubs were never serious about that; they didn't even want him on the coaching lines. Perhaps the one man in this world for whom O'Neil holds any animosity is Charlie (Jolly Cholly) Grimm, the old Chicago first baseman and manager who occupied a front-office position while the college was in session. During a 1962 game with the Houston Colt .45s, both head coach Charlie Metro and third base coach El Tappe were ejected. O'Neil was the logical choice to take over third base, but Fred Martin, the pitching coach, was brought in from the bullpen to man the box. "After 40 years in baseball and 10 years of managing, I was pretty sure I knew when to wave somebody home and when to have him put on the brakes," says O'Neil. "Later I found out that Grimm had ordered the other coaches never to let me coach on the lines."

It wasn't until 1975 that the Cleveland Indians made Frank Robinson the first black manager. In the meantime, O'Neil returned to scouting, signing Smith and Carter, among others. It's no coincidence that O'Neil's four Hall of Fame–quality players—Banks, Brock, Smith, Carter—all share his positive outlook on life. "The measure of a man," says Banks, "is in the lives he's touched."

And, in O'Neil's case, the lives he has preserved. "Sometimes," he says, "I think the Lord has kept me on this earth as long as He has so I can bear witness to the Negro leagues." As a member of the Baseball Hall of Fame veterans committee, O'Neil fulfills that responsibility. He says there are still 10 Negro Leaguers worthy of the Hall. For now, he will settle for just one: Leon Day, an outstanding pitcher and outfielder for the Newark Eagles who's still alive and well at 78 in Baltimore. O'Neil also wants to correct the impression of the Negro leagues left by the movie *The Bingo Long Traveling All-Stars & Motor Kings*. "We weren't a minstrel show," he says. "We didn't just pile into a Cadillac and pick up a game here and there. We had a schedule. Wc had spring training. We had an all-star game. Most years, we had a World Series. We were professional ballplayers."

Over the years, O'Neil has been a strong force behind many Negro league reunions. In fact, it was at such a reunion, in Ashland, Ky., in 1981, that he spoke those life-affirming, baseball-affirming words: *Waste no tears for me. I didn't come along too early. I was right on time.*

He has also been raising funds for an expanded Negro Leagues Museum, to be built across the street from the current one and next to a new Jazz Hall of Fame. "Wouldn't that be something?" hc says. "To see folks flocking to the corner of 18th and Vine again."

JOHN

O'Neil is leading a small caravan to Forest Hill Cemetery in South Kansas City. That's where Paige is buried. It's also where Confederate General John Shelby put up Shelby's Last Stand, and the irony certainly isn't lost on Burns, who visited the cemetery for his Civil War research: "One of the reasons I decided to do *Baseball* after *The Civil War* was that the first real progress in racial integration in this country after Reconstruction didn't come until the Dodgers signed Jackie Robinson."

Paige's gravesite, which he shares with Lahoma, whom he married in 1947, is extraordinary. For one thing, it's on an island of grass in the middle of the cemetery's main road. "Satchel was buried someplace else in the cemetery, but they moved him here so that more people could find him," says O'Neil. "Even after he died, Satchel was on the run."

For another thing, there are portraits of Satchel, who died on June 8, 1982, and Lahoma, who passed away four years later. And on the tombstone are inscribed his famous Rules for Longevity: AVOID FRIED MEATS WHICH ANGRY UP THE BLOOD, etc.

We have to know: "Did Lahoma know why Satchel called you Nancy?"

"Oh, yes," says O'Neil. "She loved the story. She knew Satchel. I never would have told the story if she hadn't heard it from him first."

When Paige was buried, O'Neil delivered the eulogy. "People say it's a shame he never pitched against the best," O'Neil said at the time. "But who's to say he didn't?"

It's funny that John Jordan O'Neil is only now being discovered, at the age of 82. But in an age when the racial divide seems to be widening, at a time when baseball is being torn apart, along comes this man to repair some of the damage.

Yes, Buck O'Neil is right on time.

❧

The Transistor Kid

BY ROBERT CREAMER

When Vin Scully came to Los Angeles with the transplanted
Brooklyn Dodgers, he was a stranger in alien corn. But he soon became
as much a part of Southern California as the freeways.

G IVE A WORD-ASSOCIATION TEST TO A BASEBALL FAN
from Omaha or Memphis or Philadelphia and suddenly
throw in the phrase "Los Angeles Dodgers" and almost
certainly the answer will be "Sandy Koufax" or "Maury
Wills" or "Don Drysdale" or even "Walter O'Malley" or "Chavez Ravine."

Give the same test to a fan from Los Angeles and the odds are good that
the answer will be "Vin Scully."

Scully is the tall, slim, red-haired native of New York City who has been
broadcasting Los Angeles Dodger games ever since there has been a team
called the Los Angeles Dodgers and who, for eight seasons before that, did
the play-by-play of Dodger games back in Brooklyn. This year, at 36, he is
in his 15th season of broadcasting major league games, a statistic that is
bound to startle anyone who ever heard Red Barber turn the mike over to
Scully in the old Ebbets Field days with a cheery, "O.K., young fella. It's
all yours."

In the six years that he has been in California, Scully has become as much
a part of the Los Angeles scene as the freeways and the smog. His voice
reporting the play-by-play action of the 162 games the Dodgers play dur-

ing the regular season, plus the few dozen extra in spring training, plus playoff games (the Dodgers have been in two postseason playoffs in six years), plus World Series games, floods Southern California from March until October. He is on television a few times a year (the Dodgers usually telecast only the nine games the team plays against the Giants in San Francisco). "Everybody" probably is not a mathematically precise description of the number of people who listen to Scully's broadcasts, but it is close enough. When a game is on the air the physical presence of his voice is overwhelming. His pleasantly nasal baritone comes out of radios on the back counters of orange juice stands, from transistors held by people sitting under trees, in barber shops and bars, and from cars everywhere—parked cars, cars waiting for red lights to turn green, cars passing you at 65 on the freeways, cars edging along next to you in rush-hour traffic jams.

Vin Scully's voice is better known to most Los Angelenos than their next-door neighbor's is. He has become a celebrity. He is stared at in the street. Kids hound him for autographs. Out-of-town visitors at ball games in Dodger Stadium have Scully pointed out to them—as though he were the Empire State Building—as he sits in his broadcasting booth describing a game, his left hand lightly touching his temple in a characteristic pose that his followers dote on and which, for them, has come to be his trademark.

Baseball broadcasts are popular in all major league cities, but in Los Angeles they are as vital as orange juice. For one thing, the Dodgers have been an eminently successful and colorful club in their six seasons in Los Angeles (two pennants and a tie for a third, two world championships, a Maury Wills stealing 104 bases, a Sandy Koufax winning 25 games). For a second, the Los Angeles metropolitan area is huge (six million people in the 1960 census, the biggest in the country after New York). For a third, because of a minimum of efficient public transportation, practically everybody drives to and from work and, for that matter, to and from everywhere, and in almost every car there is a radio, and every radio is always on. When a home-rushing driver bogs down in a classic freeway traffic jam, he finds that nothing else is as soothing as Vin Scully's voice describing the opening innings of a Dodger night game just getting under way a few thousand miles and three time zones to the east. This time difference has been a key factor in the growth of Scully's audience. A man who drives home from work listening to an exciting game is not about to abandon it when he reaches his house. As a result, millions of Southern Californians have Vin Scully with their supper.

But it is not just the happy timing of road games that endears Scully to his audience. He appeals to them when the Dodgers are home, too. In fact, he holds his listeners when they come to the ballpark to see games with their own eyes. When the Dodgers are playing at home and Dodger Stadium is packed to the top row of the fifth tier with spectators, it seems sometimes as though every member of the crowd is carrying a transistor radio and is listening to Scully tell him about the game he is watching. Taking radios to ballparks to listen to the game as you watch it is a fairly common practice, but nowhere is it so pronounced a characteristic as it is in Los Angeles, and has been since 1958, the year the Dodgers left Ebbets Field and moved west. Los Angeles was hungry for major league ball, and though the Dodgers had a dreadful season that first year (they finished seventh), the crowds jammed into Memorial Coliseum, where the team played until Dodger Stadium in Chavez Ravine opened in 1962. Perhaps their unfamiliarity with major leaguers prompted so many fans to bring transistors along at first in order to establish instant identification of the players. But a large percentage brought radios not just to identify players but to learn what they were doing. Scully was talking to an audience that had not been watching baseball. The old minor league teams that Los Angeles and Hollywood had in the Pacific Coast League seldom drew more than a few hundred thousand spectators in their best years. Now a million and a half, two million, two million and a half were pouring into the ball parks. Through Vin Scully they learned the fine points, the subtleties, the language of the game.

Scully was an instant success, and his hold on his near and remote audiences became extraordinary. The thousands of transistor radios in the stadium add up to substantial volume, and Scully, sitting in the broadcasting booth, can hear his voice coming back at him from the crowd around him. The engineers have to keep close watch on field microphones (the ones designed to pick up the background noise of the crowd) to screen out the feedback. Scully says, "It keeps you on your toes. When you know that just about everybody in that ball park is listening to you describe a play that they're watching, you'd better call it right. You can't get lazy and catch up with a pitch that you've missed. You can't fake a play that you've called wrong. I guess the thing I'm proudest of is the fact that in six seasons I have never gotten a letter from a fan who had seen a game at the ball park and listened to it at the same time on a transistor telling me that I'd been wrong on a play. I've gotten a few letters telling me to go soak my head, but none that said I described a play inaccurately."

ONE DAY in 1960 Scully did something on the spur of the moment that
provided extraordinary evidence of his impact on his audience. It was a
fairly drab game, and Scully, as is his habit, was filling in the duller moments with stories and anecdotes and revealing flashes of information. He
began talking about the umpiring team, one of whom was Frank Secory.
Scully leafed through the record books and cited a few things about Secory. He mentioned his age and then did a double-take when he noticed the
date of Secory's birth. Over the microphone he said, "Well, what do you
know about that? Today is Frank Secory's birthday." And because it was a
dull game and because he was acutely aware, as always, that most of the
people at the game were listening to him on transistors, he said, "Let's
have some fun. As soon as the inning is over I'll count to three, and on
three everybody yell, 'Happy birthday, Frank!' "

The inning ended. Scully said, "Ready? One, two, three!" And the crowd
roared, "Happy birthday, Frank!" Secory looked up, astounded, and the
crowd sat back, bubbling with self-satisfaction.

Early last season a similar incident revealed that Scully had not lost his
grip on his listeners. The National League had told its umpires to strictly enforce the balk rule, which provided that with men on base a pitcher had
to stop for one full second in the course of his windup before throwing the
ball to the plate. Many pitchers were violating the rule unintentionally, and
the umpires soon made so many balk calls that they sounded like a flock of
crows in a cornfield. The league office eventually backed down and everything became serene again, but before that happened one of the real crises
of the Great Balk War occurred at Los Angeles during a game between the
Dodgers and the Cincinnati Reds. The Reds, the Dodgers and the umpires
became embroiled in a loud, long discussion on the question of whether
or not a pitcher had stopped for one full second. The argument went on
and on, and up in the broadcasting booth Scully was obliged to keep talking. He reviewed the balk rule, the National League's effort to enforce it, the
numbers of balks that had been called thus far in league play compared
to the number of balks called in previous seasons, and so on. Finally, with
the argument still dragging on down below, Scully brought up the obvious but intriguing fact that one second is a surprisingly difficult length of
time to judge. He asked his audience if they had ever tried to gauge a second precisely. He said, "Hey, let's try something. I'll get a stopwatch from
our engineer. . . . " And with thousands of spectators watching him as he sat
in the broadcasting booth, he reached up and back and took a watch from

the engineer. " . . . I'll push the stopwatch and say, 'One!' and when you think one full second has elapsed you yell, 'Two!' Ready? One!"

There was a momentary pause and then 19,000 voices yelled, "*Two*." The managers, the umpires, the players, the batboys, the ball boys all stopped and looked around, startled. Scully said into the microphone, "I'm sorry. Only one of you had it right. Let's try it again. One!" And again, a great "*Two*" roared across Dodger Stadium and out into Chavez Ravine. The ballplayers were staring up at the broadcasting booth, and one of them got on the dugout phone, called the press box and asked, "What the hell is going on?" The crowd, immensely pleased with itself, waited patiently for the argument on the field to end.

The loyalty of Scully's listeners, who seem to feel very close to him, and the accuracy with which he reports a game can be traced to his training under Red Barber, the first great baseball announcer and the man who broke Scully into sports broadcasting. In the late 1930s Barber moved from Cincinnati, where he had been doing the Reds' games, to Brooklyn. At Cincinnati, Barber had a relatively small radio audience. At Brooklyn he had the biggest one in America. He created thousands and thousands of new baseball fans in the years when the Dodgers, under Larry MacPhail and Leo Durocher, climbed from the second division to the top of the National League. Barber's homely country expressions, like "rhubarb" and "tearing up the pea patch" and "the catbird seat," entered the language. His influence on metropolitan New York (and despite legends to the contrary, there were more Brooklyn Dodger fans outside that colorful borough than there were in it) was profound. He had the pitchman's gift of getting people on the outskirts of the crowd to come closer. One of his converts in those days was a pleasant middle-aged lady whose interest in baseball before Barber's voice began to sound regularly in her home had been about as intense as her feeling for the problems of Patagonian sheepherders. One Sunday afternoon her two teen-age sons were sprawled in the living room listening to a Dodger game. The other team got a man to first base, but the next batter hit a ground ball to deep short. The ball was thrown to second base in time for the forceout, but the relay on to first was not in time and the batter was safe. As Barber was describing the play, the mother hurried in from the kitchen, carrying a mixing bowl and a spoon and wearing a concerned expression. She cocked her head, heard the end of the play, shrugged and said, "Oh, well. We got the front man."

BARBER LATER developed a tendency to preach to his listeners about certain aspects of the game—his scathing comments on people who would cheer when an umpire got clipped by a foul ball were refined fire and brimstone—but even so he could make the complications of baseball fascinatingly clear to the tyro without irritating the knowledgeable fan. Scully, more relaxed on the air than Barber, is even more successful at doing this. His knowledge of the game is very broad. Counting World Series, playoffs, spring training and regular seasons, he has watched at least 2,500 major league games over the past 14 seasons. That is more than most players ever see, and it is more than a sportswriter would have seen in the same period (since sportswriters get a day or two off each week, whereas announcers do not). Too, Scully devotes a good deal of his spare time to conversation with players and managers, and most of that is spent listening and learning.

Despite his long association with the Dodgers, he never roots on the air. A Scully admirer has said, "If I tune in a game in the middle I can never tell from the tone of Vin's voice whether the Dodgers are ahead or behind. Oh, sometimes I can figure it out from the situation he describes—if the Dodgers have a pinch hitter going up for the pitcher in the fourth inning, say—but I can't tell from his voice. It doesn't get gleeful, it doesn't get dull and flat. I like baseball, and I think he does, too. He tells me what is going on, he tells me things about the game that I want to know."

The fact that Scully does not root for the Dodgers in his broadcasts stems from a decision he made in his first winter in Los Angeles. There was considerable discussion among club officials about the attitude that the play-by-play broadcasts should take. Although the broadcasts are sponsored— Union Oil Company holds the rights and usually sells half the commercial time to another advertiser—Scully is an employee of the Dodgers. He is paid about $50,000 a year and is responsible primarily to the club. In 1958 some of the Dodger officials thought that Scully might be wise to adopt an all-out pro-Dodger tone over the air. Such an approach had been considered impossible back in Brooklyn because New York City at that time had three major league teams (Yankees, Giants and Dodgers) and those tuned in to any game always comprised a mixture of adherents to all three clubs. An announcer openly rooting for one team would have quickly alienated a substantial part of his listening audience. But in Los Angeles, the pro-rooting faction contended, the city was all ours! (And would be until the American League Angels came into being in 1961.)

Scully spent weeks pondering the suggestion and finally came to the conclusion that he would be better off following the style he was used to—that
is, to be as objective and factual as possible. "It turned out to be one of the
luckiest things that ever happened to me," he said recently. "When Los Angeles had minor league baseball the games were broadcast on a frankly
partisan basis. The announcer rooted for the teams. But when major league
baseball came to Los Angeles and Jerry Doggett and I did the games straight,
without rooting, it had a very favorable impact. It was as if the city, without knowing it, had been waiting for this kind of announcing. People were
seeing major league baseball for the first time. It was different, and they
liked it. When they heard us they assumed that this was the way major
league games were broadcast, and they liked that, too. I think they appreciated the compliment—that what they wanted was a factual report, and
they didn't have to be told how to root. Another thing: There are a lot of
people living here in Los Angeles who come from back East, from the Mid-
west, from New York, from all over. They were looking forward to seeing the
teams they used to follow back home, and they would have resented it if we
had knocked those teams in favor of the Dodgers.

"Besides, I had been brought up in that school of announcing. Brooklyn and the Dodgers meant more to Red Barber than to almost anyone,
but on the mike he was always objective, always fair. Barber has been the
big influence in my life."

Scully was born in New York City and grew up in Washington Heights,
at the narrow northern end of Manhattan Island. He went to Fordham
Prep, entered Fordham University, took time out for two years in the Navy,
returned to Fordham and graduated in 1949. He played some baseball
there (he was a good-field, no-hit outfielder), but by his senior year Fordham's campus radio station had become Scully's consuming interest. "I
remember when I was in grammar school in the 1930s," he says, "when
there couldn't have been more than a couple of sports announcers around.
I wrote a composition about what I wanted to be when I grew up. I wanted to be an announcer."

He studied speech. (When he was a small boy he and his mother made
a long visit to Ireland after his father died, and when they returned Vin
had a thick Irish brogue. Yet despite that and despite his New York background, Scully's voice today has no noticeable accent or regional inflec-
tions.) Before his graduation from Fordham in 1949 he wrote dozens of
letters to radio stations up and down the East Coast, applying for a job. To

his surprise he landed a summer spot as an announcer with a station in Washington. That position ended when the summer did, and Scully returned to New York. One day he walked into the Columbia Broadcasting System office and asked to speak to Red Barber, who at that time was also sports director of the CBS network. Scully managed to see Barber and they had a pleasant, if brief, chat, but there was no job available and, in fact, Scully did not even fill out an application.

That fall CBS had a Saturday afternoon college football program, which Barber ran, that utilized a roundup broadcast of several games from around the country. Barber, on the air, would contact the announcer at one of the games, get a quick report from him and perhaps a few minutes of play-by-play and then switch to another game. One week the announcer who was supposed to handle the Notre Dame-North Carolina game in Yankee Stadium fell ill at the last minute. Ernie Harwell, who had broadcast Dodger games with Barber, was scheduled to do the Boston University-Maryland game in Boston, but Barber switched him to New York for the Notre Dame game, which was supposed to be the big game of the week. Then Red looked around for someone to take over the game in Boston. No one was available. Every experienced announcer was busy. Barber thought for a while and then said, "Who was that redheaded kid who came in here that day looking for a job? Anybody remember his name? Where was he from? Fordham, wasn't it?"

Barber knew Jack Coffey, director of athletics at Fordham, and phoned him. Coffey instantly recognized the "redheaded kid" as Scully, and put Barber in touch with him. Vin, of course, leaped at the chance, and the next day, Saturday, he was on a train for Boston. It was a cold day, and Scully had packed long underwear and extra sweaters, but on the train he ran into some Fordham men he knew who were on their way to Boston for a game between Fordham and Boston College. They told Scully that there was going to be a party after the game and they invited him to join them when he finished his broadcast. Scully checked into his hotel, decided not to bother with the long johns and the sweaters so that he would not have to go back to the hotel to change before going on to the party, and went off to his first job wearing a light topcoat.

The BU-Maryland game was played at Fenway Park. Scully was directed to the roof of the stadium. There he met his engineer, who had rigged up a table for his equipment and had strung a 60-watt bulb, on a pole for illumination, in case light was needed later on. Scully was given a head set, a microphone, a program, 50 yards of cable and the run of the roof.

"Boy, it was cold," Scully said recently, remembering. "There I was with my warm clothes back in the hotel and the wind blowing across that roof. I have never felt so cold in my life. I had assumed that I'd be in a booth—not a heated booth, but anyway a booth. But no, sir. And it turned out to be a terrific game. Harry Agganis was playing for BU, and Maryland had come up with one of those good teams they had, with Ed Modzelewski and those guys. I didn't have any spotters, and I had to identify the players from the program. I'd hear Red Barber's voice say, 'And now up to Vince Scully in Boston. Give us a quick 15-second rundown, Vinny.' I learned radio discipline fast that day. You had to have your facts clear and ready to say anything in 15 seconds; there wasn't time for any floss about the clouds scudding across the cold New England sky or anything like that. I had to say something like, 'Maryland scored in the middle of the first period after a 70-yard drive, mostly on the ground, and leads 7–0, but here in the second period, after an exchange of punts, Boston University has marched across midfield and down to Maryland's 42, where it is now first and 10. Back to Red Barber in New York.'

"What happened then was that all the other games on the roundup that day turned out flat. Notre Dame beat North Carolina 42–7, or something like that, and the other games were just as one-sided, while the game I was doing was getting better and better. I'd finish a 60-second report and say, 'Now back to Red Barber in New York,' and he would say, 'Right back to you, Vinny. I think we'll stay with you for awhile up there.' So I was doing more and more play-by-play. Whenever Red took it back for a few minutes I'd go over to the engineer's table and cup my hands around the electric light bulb to get them warm. The game ended with Maryland leading 14–13 and Boston on their eight-yard line, I think. It was really a tremendous game. But, oh, I was cold.

"Yet the cold and everything else turned out to be another lucky break. I didn't say anything to Red during the game about the conditions we were working in. I didn't have time, for one thing, but for another I thought it was routine and that I hadn't known about things like roofs because I was inexperienced. And when I got back to New York I was so excited about having had the chance to do the game that I didn't say anything about it then, either. But the Boston University officials wrote a note to CBS apologizing for not having a booth for us and for having to stick us up on the roof. Well, now, this impressed Red—not so much the fact that the conditions were bad but that I hadn't said anything about it, that I hadn't complained, and that I had gotten the job done. He was very pleased. A couple of weeks later be called me up again and said, 'Want to do another game for us? I said, 'Yes, sir.' He gave me the Yale-Harvard game.

"That winter Ernie Harwell shifted from the Dodgers to the Giants. Ernie had come up to the Dodgers in the first place when Red had gotten ill suddenly in Pittsburgh during a road trip, and when Red got better there were three of them broadcasting, Red, Ernie and Connie Desmond, who had been with Red for years. When Red came back, Ernie more or less made a job for himself but when he got the chance to go over to the Giants he took it. Now the Dodgers needed someone to take his place. But they didn't want anyone with a great deal of experience. They wanted someone who could handle commercials and fill in for an inning or two now and then. Red suggested me. The agency that handled the advertising had some doubts, but Red got the ball club to let me go to spring training on a trial basis. Then Red called me and asked me if I'd be interested. Oh, boy! Here I was, 22, single, just out of college, and I'm asked if I'd like to go to spring training with the Dodgers!

"I had to go over and be interviewed by Branch Rickey, who was president of the Dodgers then. I spent three hours with him; I remember that because he had lunch brought in. He did most of the talking. He talked about the pitfalls a young man faced. He asked me, 'You married?' I said, 'No, sir.' He said, 'Engaged?' I said, 'No, sir.' He said, 'Go steady?' I said, 'No, sir.' He said, 'Got a girl? I said, 'Well, no.' He chewed that cigar of his for a minute and then he snapped, 'Get a girl, go steady, get engaged, get married. Best thing in the world for a young man.' "

Scully worked with Barber and Connie Desmond for four seasons. He says, "I don't think anyone has ever been better than Red when he was doing play-by-play every day. He was so thorough. He taught me to get out to the ball park early, to talk to the players and to the managers, to find out why someone was not starting and why somebody else was, to learn as much as you could about the club and the visiting club so that you weren't surprised at anything when it happened. He sometimes treated me like a little boy—the first day I went into the Ebbets Field press box he announced, kiddingly, that they had hired me to carry the bags—but he certainly was good to me."

A significant turning point in Scully's career came at the end of the 1953 season. The Dodgers had won the pennant and would meet the New York Yankees in the World Series, but Red Barber turned down the job of announcing the Series with Mel Allen because of a disagreement with the sponsors concerning his fee. The Dodgers' No. 2 announcer was ill, and the sponsors went to Walter O'Malley, who had succeeded Rickey as president of the Dodgers, to discuss the situation. O'Malley said, "I have nothing to do with how much you pay whom, but I'll tell you this—there better be a Brooklyn announcer on that Series broadcast." The sponsors turned to the youthful Scully and, as Vin likes to put it, they said, "Hey, kid. You want to get into the game for nuttin'?"

Then, that winter, Barber switched from the Dodgers to the Yankees in a move that startled New Yorkers only slightly less than Leo Durocher's managerial transfer from the Dodgers to the Giants five years earlier. Desmond was ill and in semiretirement, and Scully was de facto the No. 1 Dodger announcer. He was 26 years old.

After the 1957 season came the move to California, the crowds, the transistors, the overwhelming acceptance, the establishment of Scully as a fixture in the Los Angeles scene. "There are some drawbacks," he admits. "The travel is difficult. You're away from home for two and three weeks at a stretch half a dozen times a year. And we have no short trips, except San Francisco, and that's 400 miles away. There are days when I'm sitting in a hotel room in a city 2,000 miles away from my wife and my kids, and I say to myself, What am I doing here? What kind of life is this? I guess everybody does that once in a while."

Scully lives in a house that is a strikingly successful blend of eastern clapboard and California glass, on the side of a hill on a dead-end street ("In Los Angeles we say *cul-de-sac*," Scully tells his New York friends) in the Brentwood hills. He lives in Brentwood, one of the most attractive sections of Los Angeles, because of another instance of his feeling for luck and opportunity. "When I was in the Navy I was stationed in San Francisco for a time," he says, "and I came down to Los Angeles on liberty to meet a friend of mine who was a marine at Camp Pendleton. We were wandering around Hollywood one Sunday morning when a girl stopped in a car and asked us if we'd like to come to her parents' house for Sunday dinner. We said sure. Can you imagine that? Inviting a couple of strangers off the street for dinner? It was great—nice dinner, nice family, a very nice house. That evening the girl drove us back to Hollywood and dropped us off where she had found us. But I asked her, 'Where were we today? What's it called?' And she said, 'Brentwood.' Well, when we came out here in 1958, Joan and I had been married only a few months. [Scully's wife is a beautiful dark-

haired Massachusetts girl who was a model in New York when they met
and whose maiden name was Joan Crawford. They have two sons, Mike, 4,
and Kevin, who was born last autumn.] We had never had a home. Went to
the West Indies on our honeymoon and then on to Vero Beach for spring
training. When we reached Los Angeles we started looking for an apartment, the real estate man said, 'Do you have any idea where you want to
live?' We looked at each other and then I remembered the Sunday dinner
in Brentwood. I said, 'How about Brentwood?' He said fine and he found
us a nice apartment and we lived there until Mike came along and then
we bought our house. As far as I'm concerned, that's where we're staying
from now on. It's only 25 minutes from Dodger Stadium and about the
same from the broadcasting studios." He laughed. "We had a pitcher on
the Dodgers a few years ago named Danny McDevitt, a little lefthander
from New York. He used to shake his head and say, 'Everything in Los Angeles is just 25 minutes away.'

"People from New York ask me if I miss the East. I really don't. I like Los
Angeles. When I was in my 20s we moved from Manhattan out to a town
in New Jersey, a very pretty town. But the people there sort of resented all
the New Yorkers moving out and cluttering up their nice roomy suburb,
and I couldn't blame them. Well, that's the way I feel about Los Angeles
now. When my New York friends say, 'I don't see how you can live out
there,' I nod my head and say, 'You're right, it's terrible, don't move out.' I
don't want things to change."

✑

He Does It by The Numbers

BY DANIEL OKRENT

With esoteric equations and uncommon sense, a statistician named Bill James began to challenge much of baseball's conventional wisdom.

ALL RIGHT, IT'S QUIZ TIME, BASEBALL 101. TRUE OR FALSE: 1) One big reason why Billy Martin has had such remarkable managerial success in reviving listless teams in Minnesota, Detroit, Texas, New York and now Oakland is his genius for inspiring young ballplayers.

2) Another reason for Martin's repeated success is his insistence on having a team that steals bases.

3) O.K., Nolan Ryan loses nearly as many games as he wins, but give him a lead in the late innings and he is incomparable, almost unbeatable.

4) And even though Ryan is paid an enormous salary, he more than earns it as a big gate attraction.

5) Montreal had better watch out for September. The Expos blew their chances of winning the NL East the last two seasons by cooling off in that month.

6) Any analyst who picked the champion Phillies to finish fifth last year ought to turn in his statistics.

There you have it. Easy quiz, isn't it? Every real fan within earshot of Joe Garagiola knows that all these statements are true, right?

Sorry. They're all false:

1) Of Billy Martin's teams, only Oakland and Texas could be called young. By the time of the All-Star break, his first Minnesota squad had only one nonpitching starter under the age of 27. His first Detroit team had only one under 28. His first Yankee team had two under 27, but one, age 26, was replaced by a 31-year-old the next year. The secret must lie elsewhere.

2) Speed? The Twins were third in steals in the American League the season before Martin took over, but fell to fourth with him. His division champion Tigers stole only 17 bases all season. The Rangers barely improved their league ranking under Martin, moving from sixth to fifth. The Yankees did jump from sixth to third in steals during Martin's first year as their manager, but fell to seventh the next season, when he won his world championship in New York.

3) When Nolan Ryan shifted from the California Angels to the Houston Astros after the 1979 season, the experts produced an amazing statistic that keeps cropping up: In games he started in which he held a lead in the eighth inning, Ryan had won 109 times and lost only twice, a startling .982 career percentage: Wow! However, *all* American League starters in 1979 who held a lead in the eighth inning won 586 times and lost 18, a percentage of .970, or 12/1000 worse than Ryan's. That means that the average starting pitcher performs worse than Nolan in the late innings about once every 80 or 90 starts, or not quite twice in four seasons.

4) Although Ryan led the staff in per-game attendance on the road, more folks came to the Astrodome last year when Joe Niekro pitched—or, for that matter, Vern Ruhle—than when Ryan started, which is nothing new. In California in 1976 Nolan was outdrawn in per-start attendance by such Angel stalwarts as Don Kirkwood and Gary Ross. In 1978 he was the fourth-most-watched pitcher per start on the Angel staff.

5) The Expos may finally win the NL East, but September hasn't been the problem in the past. The Pirates in 1979 and the Phils in 1980 did edge ahead of them near the wire to win the division, but in those two seasons the Expos had an admirable 44–22 (.667) record beginning Sept. 1. In fact, only once since 1973 have the Expos failed to play better down the stretch than their seasonlong percentage.

6) The man who picked the Phils to finish fifth last year is also responsible for the iconoclastic information detailed in the answers to 1), 2), 3), 4) and 5). His name is Bill James, and he lives in Lawrence, Kans., where he digs through mountains of baseball statistics and comes up with out-of-

the-ordinary conclusions. Some of these he prints in magazine articles, but most of them are saved for an annual he calls *Baseball Abstract*, of which he is owner, publisher, editor, statistician and staff. Sometimes James gets carried away and makes extravagant statements, even errors, but he ought to be forgiven them because most of the baseball tidbits he comes up with—some speculative, some factual—are fun to chew on (lefthanded pitchers throw more double-play balls than righthanders do; power pitchers tend to have longer careers than control pitchers; base stealing, even when it's successful two-thirds of the time, doesn't add much to a team's run total; managers who get close to their players and exhort them may have early success, but they often aren't as successful in the long run as those who don't get emotionally involved; contrary to accepted belief, it's not essential that a relief pitcher be able "to come in there and throw strikes"). As with Babe Ruth, when James hits one it's a beauty, and even when he strikes out it's worth watching.

Like this Phillies business for instance. James ordinarily doesn't care to make flat-out predictions. "I have never told anybody, any time, any place, that I could predict who was going to win a pennant race," he says. "The reason I *sometimes* make predictions is that people who run what I write insist that I do, or they won't pay me."

Still, the world champions *fifth*? James says he had good reasons for denigrating the Phillies before last season began. As he wrote then, "The starting eight of the Phils has nearly 100 years of professional experience, which would be wonderful if they were in the real estate business. There is a tunnel at the end of the light, and it is not far off." In short, the Phils were a very old ball club, and very old ball clubs tend to fall abruptly.

What happened? James, entranced by numbers even when they're not at all what he anticipated they would be, sifted through the stats to find out: "You hear baseball people say every winter that this player is going to make us 10, 15, 20 games better. No player in the history of the game has ever been 20 games better than the average player at his position, not Babe Ruth, not Ty Cobb. The difference between a Most Valuable Player and an average player at the same position is as little as three games in some seasons, usually five to eight, maybe once in a decade 10. But what happened in Philadelphia in 1980 was unprecedented. Three players— Mike Schmidt, Steve Carlton and Tug McGraw—made up virtually the entire difference between the world championship team and a contender for last place.

"The Phillies had only one player, Schmidt, who was able to combine the accomplishments of batting as high as .260 and hitting as many as 10 home runs. Schmidt batted .286 and hit 48 home runs, or 41% of his team's total. Only one other time since 1950 has anyone on a world championship team had more than 30% (Willie Stargell nosed past that figure 10 years ago with 31% of the 1971 Pirates' homers). Yet Schmidt had 41%! It's so out of line, it's off the chart.

"Now Carlton. The Phils were 91–71 in the regular season, or 20 games over .500. Only three Phillie pitchers were able to win more than seven games, but Carlton was 24–9, or 15 games over .500 by himself.

"Finally, McGraw. I certainly didn't expect Carlton and Schmidt to have the seasons they did, but I knew they were capable of it. But Tug McGraw? At 35? Coming off a 5.14 ERA in 1979? He had a 1.47 ERA in 1980, a better than 5-to-1 strikeout-to-walk ratio, excepting intentional walks, and gave up only 6.07 hits per nine innings. Astonishing. Considering everything, what I wrote the Phillies a year ago doesn't look bad at all."

Babe Ruth never apologized for striking out with the bases loaded either.

James is 31, with a B.A. in English and economics, graduate credits in psychology, a passion for William Faulkner and an abiding interest in the French Revolution—all more or less standard attributes for a resident of a college town like Lawrence, site of the University of Kansas. But James spends less time analyzing Faulkner's prose or Robespierre's motives than he does calculating the average time of games worked by various umpiring teams, or figuring statistically which pitchers are really best at holding runners on first base. His father, George, 74, who still lives in Mayetta, Kans. (pop. 246), where Bill was raised, says of his son's boyhood. "Mostly Bill had his nose in books, but he was a baseball nut, too, like a lot of other people. He was just nuttier than most." And a lot smarter, too. Unfortunately a statistician's mythology is not like that of a fastball pitcher; we have no mental picture of young Bill hurling stats at the side of a barn, sharpening his nominal curve.

In any case, in 1975, when he was a graduate student at Kansas, a professor told him it would take five to eight years for him to get the Ph.D. he was working toward, and that even after he had it there probably wouldn't be many jobs available. "What am I doing?" James remembers asking himself. "Why should I invest all this time in a degree I don't really want and won't be able to sell?" He decided to pack it in and try instead to become a writer. What would he write about? Something he knew. What did he know? Baseball. He'd turn his lifetime obsession with the game into a professional endeavor. Easy.

It turned out to be not so easy. His early baseball articles usually ended up in publications that paid him "with free copies and misspelled bylines," and a living obviously had to be made, even though James says he has learned from his wife, Susan McCarthy, an artist, "how to live on nothing." In 1976 he became a high school English teacher and earned $9,500, still the most he's made in a year. Later, he worked for a time as a boiler attendant—a watchman of sorts—in a food-packing plant in Lawrence, which turned out to be an ideal job for James. "I'd spend five minutes an hour making sure the furnaces didn't blow up," he says, "and 55 minutes working on my numbers."

The numbers were baseball statistics, which fascinate James as much as they do most baseball fans. The difference is that he finds things in them that most people don't know are there. "A baseball field," he says, "is so covered with statistics that nothing can happen there without leaving its tracks in the records. There may well be no other facet of American life, the activities of laboratory rats excepted, which is so extensively categorized, counted and recorded." James distinguishes himself from most other stat men by adding, "I love numbers; but not for themselves. I don't care for them as conclusions. I start with the game, with the things I see there or the things people say are there. And I ask, 'Is it true? Can you validate it? Can you measure it?' For instance, why do people argue about which shortstop has the best range or which catcher has the best arm? Why not figure it out? You can get a pretty good idea by abstracting information from the available data."

In 1977 James produced his first *Baseball Abstract* and has come out with a new edition each year since. At first glance, it's a simple, straightforward-looking publication, with lists of numbers, detailed charts and blocks of copy presented in orderly fashion, all of it reproduced on a photocopying machine. The book has four main sections, one for each of major league baseball's divisions, and these are subdivided into team-by-team analyses. There might be four or five pages for each team, with detailed information on its top 10 or 12 hitters and top five or six pitchers, as well as a commentary (sometimes quite pungent) on some aspect of the team, or its stars, or its manager. Here and there through the *Abstract* are other, more generalized, lists and two or three longer essays bearing such titles as "Trade Value" or "De Facto Standards for the Hall of Fame" or "Pythagoras and the Logarithms."

James softens the heaviness of such titles, as well as the relentless march of statistics, with his writing, which is spry and graceful. Disparaging the distinction made in baseball between all runs allowed by a pitcher and just "earned runs," he says, "It seems pointless to hold the pitcher responsible if the catcher can't throw, the second baseman can't pivot, the leftfielder can't move and the centerfielder thinks that the cutoff man is a plastic surgeon, but to excuse him for responsibility if a ball bounces off someone's glove." Discussing Mickey Rivers's reputation for having a bad throwing arm, James says, "Rivers is famous for his throwing not because his throws are so bad but because he looks so funny making them. A lot of his throws are bad, but if he didn't throw like a chicken, people wouldn't notice it."

Some observations are more matter-of-fact. On base stealing: "The common wisdom, which is to say that most often quoted by the announcers, is that you don't steal on the catcher, you steal on the pitcher. I suspect that the repetition this little acorn receives is largely an attempt to overcompensate for the audience's natural disposition to think of stolen bases coming against the catcher; whatever, it is clear that bases are stolen against both the pitcher and the catcher, and a serious inadequacy on the part of either will surely cost both."

After the 1978 season, quite a few people argued that Ron Guidry should have won the American League's Most Valuable Player award instead of Jim Rice because Guidry's 25–3, 1.74-ERA season was far more remarkable than Rice's 46 homers, 139 RBIs and .315 batting average. James wrote a thoughtful, detailed analysis that convinced at least one reader (this one, who had felt otherwise) that Rice did indeed merit the award. James wrote, "The argument that what Guidry did is more unusual than what Rice did is specious. . . . It's an award for the most valuable performance, not the most unusual. The most unusual performance was turned in by Bob Stinson of Seattle, who reached base six times on catcher's interference."

And some of James's remarks are almost poetic. Musing on the appeal that statistics have for the baseball fan, he asks, "How is it that a chart of numbers that would put an actuary to sleep can be made to dance if you put it on one side of a card, and Bombo Rivera's picture on the other?"

Along with the fun of reading him and of relishing his odd discoveries, you'll find in James a pleasant antidote to the statistical precision that baseball holds to be sacred. In a note to his readers, he cautions, "If you check my work against the spotty statistics available in other guides and the league stats, I'm sure you'll find some discrepancies. It seems fair to assume that, in the majority of these cases, I'm wrong. I make mistakes but I'm certainly not trying to kid anybody that, doing all the things I do, I can maintain the same levels of accuracy that the Elias Sports Bureau or *The Sporting News* does; I figure that I sell two things, a novel way of looking at the statistics which brings out insights you can't get otherwise and the general truths which emerge from that. The general truth, for example, is that Fred Lynn hit vastly better at Fenway Park last year than on the road. If it is important to you that the difference is .342/.273 rather than .345/.270, or that games started by a certain pitcher may have had only 49 doubles rather than 50, then I suggest you do two things: Ask for your money back, and count them yourself. And have fun."

James does most of the work on the *Abstract* in a tiny bedroom in one of the tiniest houses in Lawrence, squeezing his substantial frame (he's 6' 4" and weighs 199) into the limited space bounded by bed, desk and filing cabinet. "I write the *Abstract*," he says, "because selling it helps pay the cost of work I'm going to do anyway." The "work" is merely James's own variety of mental gymnastics: he mines information from data. And he is almost always delighted with what he discovers. Driving home one night with a friend from a Royals game in Kansas City, James stopped for a lonesome red light while delivering a brilliant soliloquy on the statistical evidence of shortstop Freddie Patek's decay as an effective player. The traffic light changed to green, and then it changed back to red. It changed to green again, back to red and back to green again before James's disquisition ran its course and he returned to earth. "Oh, the light's changed," he said, and proceeded calmly down the road.

The first *Abstract*, in 1977, sold 75 copies, at $4 apiece. In 1978 sales edged up to all of 325 copies. Undaunted, James slogged ahead, checking the boilers, working on his numbers and producing new editions of the *Abstract*. Sales passed 600 copies in 1979 and 750 last year, but the readership, while small, is enthusiastic, and James has become something of a cult figure. *Esquire* magazine assigned him to do season previews, and he even received an order for the *Abstract* from Norman Mailer, which left James, a literary hero-worshiper, feeling both honored and abashed. He sent Mailer a copy but returned the writer's check. Mailer sent it right back with a note saying, "If ever an author earned his five dollars, you have." The price has climbed since then (to $13 for the 1981 edition), but James has yet to break the $10,000 income barrier. "It's been discouraging," he says, "but not as discouraging as having to get out of bed in the morning and go off to work."

ALTHOUGH JAMES says, "Statistics exist primarily so people can argue about them" and "Information is not to be held accountable for every misleading claim that somebody can derive from it," he has developed at least one analytic procedure that has resolved an age-old baseball problem. He can evaluate fielding statistically, something that hitherto seemed impossible, because, as all fans know, traditional fielding averages are almost meaningless. "Everybody senses what a .312 hitter is," James says, "but no one knows what a .965 fielding average means. Brooks Robinson is known as a great fielding third baseman, not because of the number of plays he made but because he looked so good making them. Hitters are judged on results; fielders on form."

A fan knows that a .300 hitter is a good hitter, a .275 hitter a mediocre one, but James defies anyone to tell the difference by watching both men hit. He points out that the actual, measurable difference between the two over the course of a season is about one hit every two weeks. How then, he asks, can you possibly judge fielders by just looking at them? The traditional fielding average (total chances fielded divided into total chances handled without error) is "an excellent measure of a player's ability to get out of the way of a potential error." On the other hand what James calls Range Factor, or the total errorless chances per game that a fielder handles, is a more accurate measure of his true ability. After the Phillies acquired Pete Rose two seasons ago, they briefly talked of keeping him at third base, where he had played in Cincinnati, and moving Schmidt to second. James noted that in 1978 Rose had cleanly handled 2.39 chances per game at third base, Schmidt 3.01. Over, say, 150 games, that .62 difference translates to 93 balls Schmidt would handle that Rose wouldn't.

Frequently, our visual sense of the great fielders is surprisingly accurate: Brooks Robinson, Graig Nettles and Schmidt all have had high Range Factors. But the eye can deceive, too. The balloon James most enjoys bursting is that of shortstop Larry Bowa, who has, he says, "the range of the Birdman of Alcatraz." During the past few seasons, according to James's figures, Bowa has gotten to and fielded cleanly substantially fewer batted balls than fellow National League shortstops Garry Templeton, Ozzie Smith,

Ivan DeJesus, Dave Concepcion and Tim Foli. Bowa is a fielder "who looks good," James says, "on the balls he reaches." During the 1980 World Series, James charted every batted ball hit by the Phillies and Royals and found the locale of base hits by both sides to be virtually identical, except for balls hit through the middle. The Phils had six base hits between U.L. Washington and Frank White, the Kansas City shortstop and second baseman, while the Royals had twice as many (13) between Bowa and Phils second baseman Manny Trillo. The sample—six games—is small, but the result seems significant.

James has also produced a team fielding statistic that he calls Defensive Efficiency Record, which reveals what proportion of fair balls hit against a team are converted into outs and what proportion fall in for hits. Before the 1980 season began, he noted that Atlanta had acquired new players who, he said, would significantly improve the Braves' Defensive Efficiency rating. "The improved defense will cause the Braves to allow markedly fewer runs than they allowed in 1979," James wrote, "but the pitching will get the credit for it." The 1980 Braves in fact allowed 103 fewer runs than the 1979 club did and—yes—the pitching was praised.

As for pitching, James investigated the old adage that it is "75% of the game" and claims it's meaningless. If pitching in fact determines most of what happens, which would be the case if it were three-quarters of the game, then why, he asks, don't pitchers impose *their* tendencies on the situation and create extreme totals? "Yet," he says, "no pitcher allows home runs as often as Mike Schmidt hits them, or as rarely as Duane Kuiper. No pitcher allows opposition batters an average as high as George Brett's, or as low as the league's lowest average." In short, he argues, "the offense sets the extremes and is the dominant force, not pitching." James is exaggerating a bit here—he admits there could be exceptions—but his point is inescapable: the attempt to measure pitching's part of the game is futile, because baseball is many things interacting simultaneously. To say pitching or defense is more important than offense, or vice versa, is like saying the head of a coin is more important than the tail.

Not all of James's analyses are lucid. He has come up with a system for grading a player's offensive ability that he feels is a good yardstick for measuring the relative contributions of the speedster who walks and steals a lot, the high-average singles hitter and the low-average slugger. More or less on a pragmatic basis (it works, he argues), he devised a rating called Runs Created, the formula for which is:

$$\frac{RC = (H + W - CS) \times (TB + .7SB)}{AB + W + CS}$$

Got that? Translated, it means that Runs Created equals hits plus walks minus times caught stealing multiplied by total bases added to seven-tenths of bases stolen divided by the sum of at bats plus walks plus times caught stealing. The formula's elements—why .7 stolen bases, and why is caught stealing both above and below the line?—seem hopelessly arbitrary, but James says that if you apply the formula to any team's season statistics for the last 20 years your answer will likely be within 3% and virtually always within 4% of the actual number of runs the team scored that season. It didn't work with the 1980 Red Sox, who were 7% below the number of runs the formula said they should have scored, but James blames that on the Red Sox. ("No lefties, no speed, what's a bunt?")

Otherwise, Runs Created seems to work. Apply the formula to the records of individual batters and you can evaluate a player's true offensive worth to his team. James is proud of Runs Created, and his devotees love it. They also like his VI-RBI, or Victory Important Runs Batted In, his VAM, or Value Approximation Method, his EV, or Established Value, and his HOFPS, or Hall of Fame Prediction System.

Less technical-minded readers get their kicks from James's judgments. On ball parks, for instance. Everyone knows that some stadiums are said to be "hitters' parks" and others "pitchers' parks." James goes a step further and says the differences between parks are so important that "unless you play for Boston, Minnesota, Kansas City or Detroit, you have very little chance of leading the American League in hitting; unless you pitch in Baltimore, New York, California or Oakland, you have very little chance of leading the league in ERA." What surprises him is that club managements don't seem to catch on to such things. "Shea Stadium is a horrible hitters' park," he says. "All new hitters in Shea see their averages drop. Yet the Mets trade off promising youngsters because they don't hit as well as they were expected to." Invariably, the youngsters live up to their earlier expectations after they depart Shea (Amos Otis and Ken Singleton are two notable examples). And it isn't just Shea. In 1978 when Ron Fairly, coming off a .279 year in Toronto, was traded to the Angels, James wrote that Fairly would be lucky to bat .220 in Anaheim He hit .217.

He made a similar remarkable projection last year for pitcher Tom Underwood, acquired by the Yankees from Toronto. The lefthanded Underwood had been only 9–16 with the Blue Jays in 1979, but the Yankee front office was hoping he might blossom into a star in Yankee Stadium. James surmised that the combination of Yankee Stadium and Yankee defense, coupled with the better run support, would improve Underwood's record to 15–11, four games over .500. Underwood finished with a 13–9 record, four games over .500.

This season James relishes the textbook cases he expects will develop from the big Boston-California switches of the past winter, when players shuttled between the best hitters' park in the league (Fenway) and the third-worst (Anaheim). "One is tempted to say," he writes, "that when you put Carney Lansford in Fenway he will inherit Fred Lynn's statistics, and when you put Lynn in the Big A, he will pick up those left behind. That could very possibly happen, and I've hung myself on cruder scaffolds."

Says James: "It's not important to me that people agree with what I have to say, just as long as they understand why I've said it." A couple of years ago, after he had noted that Bobby Murcer, then with the Cubs, had an embarrassingly low Range Factor, James received a letter from an outraged Murcer fan who declared that Bobby was "acknowledged to be one of the best rightfielders in baseball."

If you say so, James replied; still, he pointed out, the fact couldn't be disputed that Murcer got to fewer batted balls per game than any other rightfielder in the majors.

It's all there in the numbers.

The Bird
Fell to Earth

BY GARY SMITH

For one fairy-tale year, Mark Fidrych was king of baseball,
but the reign ended far too soon.

T 5:50 A.M. THE ALARM CLOCK RINGS, AND THE DREAM
he has started having recently—the one in which he
keeps throwing strike after strike after strike; no crowd,
no cameras, no reporters, just he and his body back in
that sweet sweaty rut—comes to an end. Sasha, his ancient black mutt,
lifts her grizzled face from the single bed they share and blinks.

He pulls on his long johns, tattered jeans, boots, red flannel jacket and the
blue denim jacket with four rips in the right sleeve, then plops an old brown
hat on his head of tangled hair. There are three puncture marks on his
right shoulder, a little wariness in his brown eyes and the frailest footprints
of crow around his eyes, but the face is still young and the dirty blond curls
still fall around it.

Yella, the half-St. Bernard, half-collie evicted from the single bed because
of overcrowding, shakes himself down and falls into line behind his master and Sasha. They shuffle quietly past the room of his sleeping parents.
"You stay," he orders Sasha. It is too cold for the old mutt, and she doesn't
fight the order.

Out the kitchen door they walk into the flat gray dawn, his boots crunching old snow, the late February chill sneaking in through each hole in his sleeve. Ten years ago, almost to this very day, on a sunny morning in Lakeland, Fla., Mark Fidrych entered the dream year. Today he enters his beat-up blue Chevy pickup with Yella, pulls up to the back door of a restaurant called The Grille and muscles two garbage cans full of pig slop onto the truck bed.

He drives the scraps back to his farm, where there are 20 pigs, 12 cows, three sheep, two goats, six chickens and six geese. One of the baby pigs is dead, smothered perhaps in the litter's crush for their mother's milk. Mark Fidrych lifts it by the back legs and stretches it out on a steel barrel. "It's no skin off my butt," he says. "I just haven't buried it yet."

Pigs and pitching arms die young. Sometimes, when a man grows weary of trying to understand why, his only alternative is indifference. Fidrych pours the slop into a feeding box, flecks of tomato sauce spattering his boots, and watches the pigs bite and shove each other to get to the food. "They're wee-uhd," he says in his New England accent.

Some mornings it almost seems to him as if that dream year never happened. Other times, taking long crunching steps across a minefield of frozen manure on a shivering morning, the question of who he is seems hopelessly clouded by who he was. "No, I'm not a farmer," he says. "You don't make any money doing this. You do it because it's something to do. You do it because it keeps you going."

He pauses. "I'm in love with my land. I got it all from playing ball. It gives me prestige. Someone says, 'What you got?' I say, 'One hundred and twenty-one acres of nice land.' "

BY 8 A.M. Fidrych has the sure thing in his hands, the surest thing since a baseball and glove. "When you have a chain saw in your hands, there's nothin' that can hurt you," he says. "A chain saw goes through anything."

After baseball deserted him for good, in June 1983, his friends would often find him sitting on a woodpile on his farm, staring deep into nothing. "It's over, it's over, it's over" kept rolling in his head. "Why me? Why me?" Sometimes that question rose in his throat as rage, rage against something too large for a man's bare hands. So he would yank the starter on the chain saw and press its angry teeth into the closest and tallest piece of life he could find, leaning into the cut until he felt the wicked satisfaction of the tree's groan and crash. "I'd say to myself, 'See ya. Chop it down. Next tree. See ya. Chop it down. . . . ' "

Once a tree was felled, he would reduce it to 16-inch logs and then, still working frantically, drive the splitting maul through the core. But it wasn't enough. "Why me?" is a question of being, and he lived in a country that had no time for that. "What do you do now?"—the question of *doing*—is the one Americans always ask, and he didn't know how to answer that. "He refuses to tell people he's a farmer," says a friend.

Two years ago Fidrych and two buddies formed a three-man team for a wood-chopping contest in their little town of Northboro, Mass., and Fidrych got to splitting so frenetically he drove the wedge through his friend's arm, chipping a piece off the bone near the elbow, and then split two more logs before he realized what he had done. The competition was canceled.

Some days Fidrych would leave his chain saw and splitting wedge behind, walk into the woods and scream. Just after the dream year, he had looked down at his hands and told a reporter, "I've got a trade now. These hands are vital. I can't pour cement with these hands." Since he left baseball, those hands have poured cement for swimming pools, cleared lots for new houses, fed pigs and chopped wood. He has sold a pig or cow now and then, or a piece of land that he had bought when he was playing ball. A few times a year, someone pays him to speak at a banquet. For six months last year he was a traveling liquor salesman, but the money and the necktie were no good, so he quit. He doesn't need much, just enough to pay the $6,000 in taxes on his mostly wooded farm, with a little left over for hamburger and beer money—and to have an answer for "What do you do?"

So he sips his beer and talks of plans to buy a bulldozer, a car mechanic's garage, a gas station, a car wash, a limousine service, a trucking company, or maybe he would become a truck driver, a real estate developer. . . . "A hundred and fifty ideas going on at once," says Mark Philbin, a friend. "I'll say, 'Slow down, *Mahk*. What are you talking about?' "

Fidrych was a country boy and maybe chopping wood and pouring pig slop on his own 121-acre farm was more than he ever would have asked for if a dump truck full of fame hadn't pulled up to his life, buried him in it and then left, letting the wind blow it all away. But the dilemma won't go away. "Why do I need big money?" he asks. "I make 18 to 20 thousand a year. You got a thousand dollars, you got a thousand problems. I've always been small. I just want to stay small."

Then a Miller commercial flickers across the TV screen and he flings the back of his hand at the set and growls, "I could be doing one of those goddamn things, too."

This morning he has two big scratches on his neck from hacking at the brush on his land, clearing it for the house he plans to build. He is 31 and it is time he no longer lived with his parents.

TEN A.M. "Maybe the dream is a vibration that I should try to pitch again. There weren't no outside things in the dream, no score, no outcome. Just me, pitching. Just me, playing." He's back in the truck now, heading to Mike's Donut Shoppe in Northboro to get coffee for the three men helping him clear his land; Sasha and Yella are panting in the back. In the truck his mind wanders. Hell, ever since the doc opened up the right shoulder last summer, sewed up the two tears in the rotator cuff and chiseled down the end of the bone sticking up under his armpit, the wing has felt good again. Once more he can open car doors and drink beer with his right hand. He no longer tosses and turns Sasha awake at three in the morning from the pain. "I know I could get a major league hitter out now," he says. "I know it."

Damn, maybe it could be 1976 all over again. Remember that?

On an April day in Oakland, Ralph Houk, then manager of the Tigers, signaled to the bullpen. On the run, still half-zippered, shoving his shirt and cup into place came a gangly kid with curly blond hair bouncing over his ears, entering his first major league game.

He dropped to his knees and smoothed out all the little holes the other pitcher had left on the mound, like a little kid in his sandbox, lost in an imaginary world. When his infielders or outfielders made a good play, he ran to them to shake their hands in the middle of an inning. He did knee bends and squats on the mound, and when he set himself to pitch, he held the ball in front of him and appeared to talk to it. Of course, he was actually talking to himself, focusing on his task, but in 1976, when a children's game was becoming overrun with attaché-carrying shortstops and talk of holdouts and strikes and agents' percentages, who cared about details like that?

"Never in my 37 years of baseball have I seen a player like him, and never will I again," says the Tigers' president, Jim Campbell. "My gosh, I don't know why we don't see more people like Mark Fidrych. He was what he was. All natural. So hyper, so uninhibited. A minute after he came into my office he'd have one cheek of his butt on the corner of my desk. Before you knew it, he'd be *lying* on my desk, his head resting in one hand, the other hand gesturing in the air."

"The best young pitcher I've ever had in my career," says Houk.

A 10th-round pick by the Tigers in the '74 draft, Fidrych had stayed in a tent his first few days of Rookie League ball until management talked him into a motel. His fastball and slider were as naturally hyper as he; his control, for a wild kid, was confounding. A minor league manager, assessing Fidrych's tall, gawky body, his plume of hair and free spirit, nicknamed him the Bird after the *Sesame Street* character Big Bird. The night the Tigers told him he was going north with the big team in '76, he smuggled a girl over the fence of their Lakeland complex, lay down on the mound with her and celebrated.

His salary was $16,500, he didn't have an agent, and the guy in the upper deck didn't need four beers to gaze down at Fidrych and imagine he saw himself. On June 28, before 50,000 fans at Tiger Stadium and a *Monday Night Baseball* national audience, Fidrych pitched a seven-hit, 5–1 victory over the Yankees. The camera hopped from him apparently talking to the ball to a fan in a yellow bird costume frolicking through the stands, and twice after the game, Fidrych had to make curtain calls for the mob that chanted "Bird! Bird! Bird!" and wouldn't leave.

"Our family, the whole town, felt part of it," says his sister, Carol Ann. Her eyes look off. "We had the best times going to his games. Ahhhh, the best times. About once a month I still go back and look at a video of highlights of him pitching that year. He was the happiest I've ever seen him. On the video you can see it—his face *glowed*."

He became the second rookie in history to start an All-Star Game, went 19–9 on a next-to-last-place team, led all major league starters in ERA (2.34), was voted Man of the Year by the National Association of Professional Baseball Leagues, and singlehandedly boosted Tiger attendance by more than 400,000 over the year before. Bird T-shirts, buttons and records appeared; helicopters bearing greetings to the Bird circled the stadium. A man named his baby after him, and a resolution was introduced in the Michigan state legislature demanding that the Tigers raise his pay. The Twins delayed a game for nearly half an hour to funnel the huge crowd into one of his games. The Angels, afraid to disappoint a packed house when Fidrych missed a start, put him in a cage in their stadium concourse to sign autographs. Men who had spent their lives trying to become polished and sophisticated fought for position to get the signature and shake the hand of a man who had remained spontaneous and natural.

Maybe if he could have kept it small, if he could have risen off his knees from the dirt, thrown the hyper fastball by the batter and gone home, it could have lasted longer than a year. Maybe in a country that had become obsessed with building and dismantling celebrities, and expert at turning the natural into the stale, it was better that it didn't. The day after the Monday night game, a man from the William Morris Agency in Manhattan called and soon was lining up commercials and appearances. After a while Fidrych would hide in the stadium until near midnight, then dash for his car, zigzagging to avoid fans leaping onto the hood. The parking lot and hallway of his apartment became so jammed with people that he had to move to a complex in the suburbs with a 24-hour security patrol. "He'd call me and tell me reporters were calling his hotel room at midnight the night before he had to pitch, that people were banging on his hotel door all day," recalls Stephen Pinkus, the William Morris agent. "'They're driving me nuts,' he'd say. 'Why?' I'd say. 'Because you're a star and that's what happens.' He didn't understand. He was completely out of his league. All he wanted to do was drink beer and listen to rock music and have fun."

Fidrych taped an appearance for Bill Cosby's children's show, during which the director screamed at him when he had trouble reading the cue cards. "Hey, man," Fidrych screamed back, "this isn't my field. I'm a baseball pitcher."

The Tigers asked him to get rid of his two motorcycles. When he accepted a Thunderbird from the Ford Motor Company, a Detroit columnist wrote that Fidrych had lost his innocence. *Rolling Stone* published a story chronicling his sex life. Every day, no matter whether he pitched or not, a troop of reporters asked him for every detail of things that he had done unconsciously, gnawed on each particular until it stopped seeming natural at all. "I never thought all that would be part of it," Fidrych says. "As soon as people started writing about it, talking about it so much, you *think* about it."

The daydream in the truck has lasted too long. He pulls onto his farm, surveys the growing piles of cut brush with pleasure and calls the workers to come drink their coffee. "Hey," one of them, asks through the steam from his cup, "we were wondering, Mahk, back when you played, how fast could you throw a ball?"

"In the 90s."

"Nineties, huh?"

Fidrych's eyes shift. "How much more you think you'll get to today?"

LUNCHTIME. CHET'S DINER. Thank God the blowhard isn't here, the one who can blow an entire lunch away talking about how he wants to make Mahk a pitchah again. Because if the blowhard had been here Mahk would have had to disappear inside himself or out the door, suddenly remembering an appointment, as if Mahk was the kind of guy who made *appointments*. Then he couldn't have sat and watched that pretty little black-haired bundle of laughter and efficiency, the waitress at Chet's, the Greek man's daughter, Ann, whom he is going to marry in October.

"Need a Chetbuhgah, a Supah Deluxe with no tomatoes and a bread setup, sweetie," she calls to her mother at the grill. "Need a bowl o' chowdah, Dad. How ya doin', guys? Watcha want today? Onion ring-a-lings and a rootin'-tootin' beer? . . . Dad, I said chowdah, not chili. Quick, quick, like a bunny. No, Mothah, no tomatoes on that buhgah. I know, sweetie, isn't life hahd?"

A biochemistry major who graduated from Fairfield University and then decided she'd rather get up at 4:30 every morning and work the diner with her folks, a 30-year-old woman, smart and strong, who went to Algonquin High in Northboro with him but barely even knew him then and never saw him throw a baseball—that's the kind of girl Mark Fidrych needed. For three months, in a little town rampant with gossip peddlers, where everyone knew Mark and everyone knew Ann, no one in town knew about Mark and Ann. Fidrych cloaked their relationship in secrecy, as if afraid of the effect other eyes might have upon something he considered sacred. "It's my thrill, just her and me," he says. "People don't understand. It's better when it's a secret, when no one knows. If baseball could have been that way. . . . "

There was another reason for the secret, too. As soon as everyone knew, it became a commitment. Commitments scare Fidrych. He could sit on a woodpile for weeks, but when he decided to chop, he chopped every bloody limb, human or hickory, that got in his way. He gave so much of himself he couldn't shrug and walk away if the commitment splintered. So he sat on a barstool or the back of the truck and talked about 150 jobs he *might* do, or, before Ann, ogled the three girls in tight sweaters he *might* ask out. The first girl he'd ever fallen for had left him, then a 2½-year relationship in Detroit had ended when the woman wouldn't go with him to the minor leagues, or to Northboro. That left the women who recognized him at the bars. "Of course I felt women only liked me because of baseball," he says. "It made me wonder if it was worth giving myself to any woman again.

It's hard to be confident about showing feelings. "Ann doesn't *know* me, that's probably why we get along so well. You don't understand. I committed myself once. I committed to baseball. . . . "

ONE-THIRTY p.m. Fidrych is honking and helloing to the guys in the duckbill caps, waving and joking with the old women coming out of the shops. "What's up, Joe? How ya doin', Steve?" Driving past Pierce's Sunoco, where he used to pump gas, past Murray's Package Store, where they still have the picture of him in his Tiger uniform, past the empty lot where the Cut Off bar used to be before it was condemned, where he and the boys locked themselves into the little bathroom for wrestling matches or had competitions to see who could slide the farthest down the bar on his backside. Little town. Good town. Quiet and simple.

He arrives back at his land and finds the two surveyors, the ones he's paying to plot a road to the site where he will build his new house, taking a break to find batteries for their headsets. "So we can communicate through the forest," explains one.

"Hell, what's wrong with yellin' and screamin?" retorts Fidrych.

What a world. He had wanted to be a car mechanic, back in the days when if you heard a car cough, you knew it was either the plugs or points or carburetor. But now the engines are computerized and the mechanics hook up blinking machines to them as if they're coronary patients, and Fidrych doesn't have the heart for it anymore. He had dreamed of owning land, and suddenly, at 22, he had enough to buy a piece you could fit a couple dozen ballfields on, cash on the barrelhead—no loans, man, no interest payments. He wanted to keep life simple. Then came tax time and the accountant looked at him as if he was a lost little boy: 121 acres of pine and birch and not a single stick of *shelter*.

Pinball used to be good, too. "Five balls for a quahtuh, and it didn't take that many points to win a free game," Fidrych says. "Then it became three balls for a quahtah and you needed a million points. Then came Pac-Man and all that crap. Do good and you only get to put your initials next to your score. It ain't what it used to be. Nothin' in life matches up to anything."

God knows, he tried to keep it simple. He turned down the back-slapping jobs he could have had in Detroit and returned to the little town to stay near the dirt and wear torn jeans that showed his underwear. People marveled at the way he still rolled on the ground with dogs and kids. But then he had to shake himself off and get vertical, and the only place verticality had ever meant simplicity was on a hill of dirt, 60' 6" from a batter. "Base-ball stayed the same," he says. "Three outs an inning, nine innings and the game's over. I remember Alleycat Johnson, a guy who was my teammate in the minor leagues, telling me, 'You know, Mahk, when you're on that mound, you're a master, a scientist. But when you walk off it, you're crazy; no one knows what you'll do. You've got a million-dollar arm and a 10-cent mind." Fidrych laughs, then pauses. "He was right. I've never found another place as comfortable as a mound. *Never.*"

The simple life was gone, and every time he returned to Detroit and the baggage handlers ran for his luggage and the Avis folks tried harder, he wondered if he should surrender to it, exploit it. He did promotional work for an auto-parts company long enough to get a bellyful of small talk and a pocketful of business cards, then moved on. He interviewed with a Detroit TV station last summer to do sports commentaries but lost interest when he realized he would have to move there. He did some color commentary for the Tigers' cable TV network in 1984 and received no offer to continue working there. "He'd say *anything* on the air," recalls Bill Freehan, the ex-Tiger catcher who also did commentary for the network. "He'd yell, 'That pitch was a hooo-rah!' and the guy on the air with him would say, 'Huh?' He'd be talking when it was time to cut to a commercial, and the director would be tapping him on the shoulder, and Mark wouldn't understand what he wanted. But I love the guy. He's flat-out genuine."

Fidrych considered becoming a pitching coach. "I've got to be honest," says Campbell. "Mark isn't cut from that bolt of cloth." Bob Woolf, the Boston attorney who began to represent him in 1982, arranged a non-speaking role for Fidrych as a pitcher in a movie called *The Slugger's Wife* and an interview with the Hyatt Regency in Cambridge, Mass., to do pro-motional work. The movie bombed, and Hyatt never called back. Fidrych went to New York three times in 1984 to do casting tapes for Miller Lite, au-ditioning for a commercial in which he talked to a ball at a bar, and froze when the camera rolled and he had to read the cue card. Reading has always been difficult for him. "I've boycotted books," he says. Finally, after 80 takes, he was told the commercial would run during the '84 World Series. It never aired, and no one else called. The reason corporate America loved him when he pitched—he was natural, unsophisticated, *real*—was the same reason they shunned him when he couldn't pitch.

"Maybe if he'd lasted a few more years. . . . " says Woolf. "I've been able to do a lot of things for a lot of athletes, but I've never come up with an answer for one when the people start asking 'Who did you *used* to be?' "

"Hey, let's take a plane ride to Michigan," says Fidrych, kicking his boot at the snow. "They recognize you like it was yesterday. That's a plus in my atmosphere, right? It wasn't just one year of publicity. Even when I was sent to the minors, every town I went to, there was my picture in the paper and a story about me. Why didn't they just tell me I'm not good enough to do a commercial? It's obvious I didn't fit in. So I'm not pitching anymore. What in hell's wrong with showing me cutting wood and drinking a Miller Lite or a Coke?"

He remembers that he doesn't want that anyway, that he opted for the simple, uncluttered life. "Look, if it doesn't come, fine," he says. "It's no skin off my butt."

Pinkus, Fidrych's agent at the height of his popularity, estimates that the dream year grossed his former client $125,000 in off-the-field money, mostly from Florida Citrus and Aqua Velva TV ads, some speaking engagements and a book. Ten years later, when the American marketing machine was greased and waxed, another country boy with a nickname, another natural, burst into prominence on a Monday-night nationally televised game. Before his dream year ends, William Perry will make well over a million dollars off the field.

"If Mark had that year in 1986?" says Pinkus. "Oh *God*. I'd sign him to a five-year with the Tigers at one to one-point-five million per, with an MVP bonus and a 20-win bonus. That's close to two million. *Easy.* I'd sign him to represent a chicken frankfurter company, which we had contracts all written up for when he got hurt—the Bird Frankfurter line—with a guarantee of $100,000 the first year, $150,000 the second, plus a percentage of the company's profits. That would have made him another million, easy. I'd get him a sporting goods line. He'd probably be a regular on his own TV series, 10 grand an episode. He'd be a national spokesman for something—an airline, a car, a major insurance company. That's at least a quarter million a pop. Do four—it's a million. Personal appearances— $15,000 per. *Easy.* Kissinger and Ford get $15,000—that shows where America's at. He'd have made 10 to 15 million in the last five years, if he'd maintained who he was. *Easy.* He'd have been a *giant*.

"You say he's not working a regular job now? Maybe I could make him a sports announcer or something, pull some strings. Honey, bring me Fidrych's phone number—excuse me, I was talking to my secretary. I have the most extensive Rolodex in the country, got Ronald Reagan's number when he was president of the Screen Actors Guild. What do you mean, it's not there? How could you not have Fidrych in my Rolodex?"

Dusk. Work is done. Fidrych enters through the kitchen door, past the unused living room where the furniture is covered with sheets and all the plaques and trophies from his career rest in darkness. In the attic and cellar are cardboard boxes full of the stuffed birds that fans besieged him with in '76. "I'll put everything out when I move into my new house," he says.

This house is the one Fidrych bought for his parents in '77. He always thought first of family. On a promotional tour with the Tigers that year, he kept running to the phone to see if the oldest of his three sisters had delivered her baby. "When she finally did," recalls Campbell, "he was so excited you'd have sworn *he* was the father."

Fidrych doesn't eat dinner at home much anymore, now that he's got a girlfriend. Sometimes his dad, Paul, an assistant principal of an elementary school in Worcester who is a year and a half from retirement, intercepts him just after he's showered off the farm dirt, just before he bolts out the door. "What did you do today, Mahk?"

"Nothin'."

"Where you goin'?"

"Out."

"I'll ask him what he's going to do with his life, and he'll say, 'Don't worry about it,' but I do," says his father. "If I mention to him, 'Spring training opened today,' he'll just say, 'Yep.' He doesn't want to hear it from me. He keeps saying that part of his life's over."

It all started with Paul Fidrych, a superb athlete whose dream and thigh bone snapped one day when he was playing football in high school. Rather than talk of what he was or could have been, Paul spent hours hitting ground balls and pop-ups, squatting like a catcher for his only son, quietly feeding the dream to him. He coached Mark's team in Little League and Babe Ruth, and during the hush when his son stood at the foul line in a high school basketball game, you could hear Paul Fidrych holler, "Concentrate, Mahk, concentrate!"

With a baseball in his hand, or a snowball or a rock, Mark could. In a classroom his mind roamed, his fingers and feet fidgeted, the words on the page in front of him danced themselves into a blur. He flunked first grade, then flunked second. A few friends taunted him, but most of them just moved onto the next grade and forgot him. Tall for his age, he towered over classmates two years younger, and when he dominated them at recess, it only made things worse. Patiently his dad tried to tutor him, but the words kept dancing and the boy knew he was disappointing everyone. "I stopped raising my hand in class," he says. "I wanted to disappear. I still have an inferiority complex about it today. I remember my Aunt Nel telling me that you should go into the woods and scream if you felt real bad. I thought she was crazy back then."

Ten or 15 people might show up at his high school baseball games—played when the outfield snow had melted—and sometimes almost that many ground balls skipped by his fielders' gloves. His father urged him not to quit. Says the younger Fidrych, "He'd say, 'Mahk, you're not the smartest kid in the world, and there's money to be made in sports.' Your dad tells you something when you're a kid, you believe him, right?"

Everyone in town thought Mark was just a wild, fun-loving, floppy-haired hyper kid, quick to do 360s in his sister's car on the frozen pond or lie on his back on a barroom dance floor and wriggle to the music. (Why, don't you know, that's *The Worm*.) Underneath, he often didn't feel that way at all. "Sometimes," he says, "I'd think, 'Why live?' "

His father wanted him to go to college, Mark wanted to do oil changes at Pierce's Sunoco. For his dad, he would do almost anything. His first Scholastic Aptitude Test score was too low for college entrance, so he gave his ID card to a smart buddy who had offered to pinch-hit for the second. The difference was so dramatic that the SAT board officially notified him he was a cheater.

Suddenly, miraculously, came the call from the Detroit Tigers, and Fidrych didn't need the car on the pond to feel himself spin. "All of a sudden I had guys behind me who could field; I just threw strikes and let the other team hit ground balls," he says. "All of a sudden people actually wanted to hear what I had to say!"

After two years in the minors, the dream year came. His father, his shirt buttons straining to accommodate his pride, shuttled to and from Detroit to watch his boy pitch.

By the end of the year, Mark was asking a doctor for something to calm his nerves. "Next year I hope a kid comes along that does better than me," he said then. "Then they'll leave me alone."

A few months later, in March of '77, a fly bail arced toward him and Rusty Staub in the Lakeland outfield.

"You want this one, Rusty?"

"No, kid. You take it."

Exuberantly, as he did everything on a ball field, he streaked beneath the towering fly ball. His left knee popped, tearing cartilage. SPORTS ILLUSTRATED decided not to run his picture on the cover of its baseball issue that year. "What kinda horsebleep's that?" he said. "So I got hurt. I ain't dead. Ill never talk to those bastards again. People using me, man. I'm sick of people using me."

He cried in his hospital bed, as security guards kept the anxious, overwrought fans away. "I've *gotta* fight back," he said. "Baseball is my whole life. It's the only thing I know."

Ten days after he returned from the disabled list, his right shoulder popped. He went 6–4 that season, plagued by arm pain, and the dream was gone. In his rage he broke the washer and dryer in the Tiger laundry room, then, stricken with remorse, fell to his knees and fixed them.

Nobody knew what caused the crippling pain, but many suspected it was Fidrych's overeagerness to be a superstar pitcher again, that he'd begun throwing too hard too soon after he had injured the knee. "Maybe it was my stupidity," he says. "I kept throwing. I didn't want to give up. If you can't perform, you're gone, so you fool them as much as you can. I *had* to. I saw what was going on in my life."

Most of the next six years were spent in the minors—the last year and a half with Boston's Triple A team in Pawtucket, R.I. He tried doctors, osteopaths; chiropractors, hypnotists and psychologists, long rests and no rests. He gulped aspirin and anti-inflammation pills by the handful and rubbed all sorts of strange substances on his arm. Fans wrote in with miracle cures, suggesting that he stick the troubled arm into a swarm of bees, that he pack it in red Florida clay. An old man with arthritis-swollen knuckles drove to Northboro from New Jersey to give him some red gook that smelled like kerosene. All the old guy wanted was for Fidrych to sign a contract guaranteeing him 10% of his salary once Mark was healed. Fidrych signed the contract, but the stuff only made the shoulder stink as well as hurt.

One night in June 1983, a lonely man with a 2–5 record and a 9.68 ERA called his father from Norfolk. "I'd always wanted to give him a feeling of accomplishment," says Fidrych. "I said to him, 'I'm done, Dad. They've let me go. Thanks for everything you've taught me, but I've got to get out of this game. I did it for you.' "

"I still think you've got it in you, Mahk," said his dad.

"No, Dad."

"Don't give up this easy. You've got to look in the mirror."

"Dad, I've been looking in the mirror for the last six years."

Sometimes, when Paul Fidrych is watching a ball game these days, he still feels the emotion rising up into his larynx. "I wish he would try it again," he says. "I find myself wondering how far he could have gone. I don't want that question in his mind, the way it's always been in mine since I broke my leg. I think he could do it; he has the desire. Did you see him cut wood today?"

"Once in a while he'll be sitting here watching a game and he'll say, 'I had 29 major league victories, that's not too bad,' and I'll say, 'Yeah, Mahk, that's not too bad.' But you know something? Jim Palmer stole the Cy Young Award from Mahk that year. He stole it. The Gold Glove, too—Mahk had *no* errors. I don't understand why he doesn't get any commercial with him sipping a Coke and not saying a word.

"Listen, I'm going to give you a name: *Charles Grogan.* He's got the same determination Mahk used to have, never gets tired of practicing. He's big and strong, same way Mahk used to be. He's only eight years old. He's my grandson."

EIGHT P.M. A deep quiet grips the little town. Ten years ago, Mark Fidrych lived with an urge to roll down the window and pierce the quiet, but he is 31 now, engaged, and his soul howls less and less. "Get a few beers in him and you can still get him going," says his farming partner, Wayne Hey. "He'll wrestle with the pigs and cows when they won't go where he wants them to. He'll go to a few ball games in Boston a year and yell at the ump just like any fan. Last July 4 he started a Roman candle-throwing battle with a friend.

"Deep down, I think he's been completely lost without baseball. A lot of people wouldn't know it, because he's got something to say to almost everyone. Ann is very good for him—she's giving his life some direction."

"He has to be totally honest with himself now," Ann says. "I just ask him direct questions: Are you facing facts or are you avoiding the issue, Mahk?"

Fidrych walks into a Northboro bar and begins methodically drinking beer. Memories come tumbling from him. The child comes back into his voice. "I got Yaz's bat, I got Pete Rose's bat, I got Fred Lynn's bat, I got George Scott's bat—know how I got that? I told Bill Freehan, 'Ask George Scott when he comes to the plate to give me one of his bats, and if he says yes, tell him to look over at me in the dugout and tip his hat." Fidrych's eyes widen. "He did! I remember pitching in my third or fourth game against Yaz and Rico Petrocelli. Wow! Those guys were my heroes growin' up: And strikin' out Rico on a 3–2 pitch that was a ball. I said, 'Wow!' And. . . . "

He is reminded of the media people who haunted him and of the fans who mercilessly stalked him. Don't complicate it, his voice begs. "It wasn't the fan who hung all over me," he protests. "The fan had to go home after the game, go to bed and get up for work. The people who did that, they were another person."

No matter how hard he tries, the complications remain. His life has been forever set apart from the others in the town. No matter how many times he enters the forest with his chain saw and splitting wedge, his woodpile will never be cut and stacked the same neat way as those of his friends, the house painter and oil-truck driver and cable TV serviceman.

Maybe settling down and getting married will help. "This commitment will last," he says. "You can be married and have a sore arm, right? But what if the Kansas City Royals call tomorrow and say they need a pitching coach? I still got it in my blood."

Maybe Mark should try to pitch again. "My arm has felt fine since the surgery. The doc finding all those things wrong inside was the best relief of my life. Now I know my problems weren't in my head. I haven't thrown a baseball since, only a snowball. Maybe that dream means I should just play in the Stan Musial League around here and see how it, feels. I won't count baseball out. I won't."

Maybe Mark shouldn't try to pitch again. "I'd lose a full five months of my life getting in shape. I don't want to be that dedicated again. What if I say I'll play in the Musial league, and I can't make it to a game or enough guys don't show up to play? I can't screw around in life anymore."

Maybe he should have children. "The best thing I loved about playing ball was seeing a little kid's happy face. Yeah, I want kids. But sometimes I feel I wouldn't want to bring a kid into this world. The poor kid. . . . It was so hard for me."

Surely, with the family and fiancée and two dogs who care and the little town that accepts him, he would come through this. After all, it was only one year. . . .

He stands up. It is 11 p.m., early for a 21-year-old idol, late for a 31-year-old pig farmer.

"Ten years," he says. "It's hard to believe. I got no regrets. I'd do it like that all again. I got memories, I'll always keep them alive. I'd tell William Perry to have fun, grab it while you can, 'cause you never know when it's gonna disappear. You can't think about it; you gotta just go until something happens."

He lingers. "You know, I still get fan mail. I wait a week before I answer it, so it builds up. It sounds crazy but it makes me feel more important. Please, just end this story by saying thank you to the people. Thank you to our society."

Master of the Joyful Illusion

BY WILLIAM BARRY FURLONG

*Bill Veeck was a baseball visionary and the game's
master showman—a major league owner who believed he owed fans not just
a good team but all the pleasures a ballpark had to offer.*

I N THE SECRET REACHES OF HIS PRIVATE UNIVERSE, THERE IS little that the dreamer in Bill Veeck says can't be done. His success, his failures, his joys, his sorrows have created an extravagant legend that even for him tends to obscure reality. To the public, Bill Veeck, president of the Chicago White Sox baseball club, is a brashly clamorous individual who has fashioned a brilliant career out of defying the customs, conventions and crustaceans of baseball. It is an authentic yet one-dimensional view. For Veeck is also an intelligent, impetuous, whimsical, stubborn, tough-fibered, tireless individual with a vast capacity for living and a deep appreciation for humanity. He is full of the humor that springs from the unsuppressed human being. To Veeck, baseball is not an ultraconstitutional mission, a crusade, a holy jousting for men's minds, souls and pocketbooks, but simply an exhilarating way to make a living. His approach to the game is seasoned with an almost visceral irreverence, a wit that is sometimes droll, sometimes raffish, sometimes wry or macabre, and sometimes abusive. A few months after emerging from the hospital where his right leg had been amputated, he threw a "coming-out" party. The high point of the party was achieved when Veeck ripped off his artificial leg and flourished it before the startled eyes of his guests. "It itches," he said.

He has the wit and the grace to make fun of what Veeck hath wrought. When he took over the St. Louis Browns in 1951, he warned the fans to "stay away unless you have a strong stomach." Naturally, many fans rushed out to the ballpark to see what he was talking about. "They came out to see if the ball club was as bad as I said," he says, "and it was." Later on, while making a public appearance in New York, he apologized for his nervousness. "As operator of the St. Louis Browns," he explained, "I am not used to people." He outlined his strategy for making the Browns a pennant contender, "We've sold half of our ballplayers and hope to sell the rest," he said. "Our secret weapon is to get a couple of Brownies on every other team and louse up the league."

Behind this façade is a man with a highly perceptive vision of baseball's appeal. "This is an illusionary business," Veeck said not long ago. "The fan comes away from the ballpark with nothing more to show for it than what's in his mind, an ephemeral feeling of having been entertained. You've got to heighten and preserve that illusion. You have to give him more vivid pictures to carry away in his head." The most exalted illusion of all is satisfaction about the game ("The only guarantee of prosperity in baseball is a winner"), but that illusion, says Veeck, must be augmented by a feeling that it was fun to be at the ballgame. In support of this conviction, Veeck has given fans live lobsters, sway-back horses, 30,000 orchids, a pair of uncrated pigeons and 200 pounds of ice. He has staged circuses and brought in tightrope walkers and flagpole sitters and jugglers and the Harlem Globetrotters to perform between games of a double-header. He has shot off several kilotons of fireworks after night games. ("If you win, it's a bonus for the fans on top of the flush of victory; if you lose, they go away talking about the fireworks, not the lousy ballgame.")

At the age of 46, Veeck retains many of the elfin enthusiasms of his youth, though the years have thinned his once-bushy, pinkish-blond hair to a pair of tracks and a tuft of straw, and his face has assumed the rutted dignity of a mask done in clay by a slightly arthritic sculptor. But there has been a quickening of the currents and contradictions that make up the man. He is an omnivorous reader who likes to talk out his thoughts. He is a gregarious companion with an introspective streak. He is an undisciplined spirit of spontaneous inspirations, yet he is hard-working—he rises at 4 or 5 o'clock virtually every morning and works 16 to 20 hours a day. He is intensely competitive. Even though he has only one leg, he continues to play tennis and paddleball. "Does a man stop smiling because he wears false teeth?" he asks. He is painstakingly unpretentious. He works in a onetime reception room in Comiskey Park, answers all his mail himself (writing in longhand on the margins of the letters) and takes phone calls at all hours of the day and night.

Unlike most larger-than-life personalities, Veeck exhibits in public a self-deprecatory air and in private a remarkable sense of charity of heart and purse.

At times he is as insistent and impetuous in his charities as in his business dealings. When one friend refused to allow Veeck to buy him a much-needed automobile, Veeck phoned a children's home in which the friend was interested and announced he would buy anything it needed. "Take a little time to think it over," he said. "Take six hours."

Veeck has studied—*studied*, not browsed in—accounting, architecture and "at law." (He discovered a few years ago that some states still offer admission to the bar to persons who study, as Abraham Lincoln did, under a lawyer's guidance and tutoring.) He reads four books a week, has written a novel ("50,000 words and now they want me to put in dialogue!") and played a role in an allegedly professional production of *The Man Who Came to Dinner*. "Putting me on the stage was like putting Sarah Bernhardt on second base," he said at the time. "The theater people would think she was out of place and the baseball people would know it." His conversation ranges restlessly over a seemingly limitless mental horizon, from baseball to philosophy and back again.

It was this restlessness that touched off, some 11 years ago, the intellectual revolution that led to his becoming a convert to Roman Catholicism. "I'd studied everything from Buddhism to Magna Mater," he says. "In fact, I gave quite a bit of thought to Judaism." He approached Catholicism with a healthy skepticism, challenging and even dropping instruction when it did not respond to his intellectual need. "He had the toughest mind I've ever encountered," says the Rev. George Halpin of Chicago, the priest who ultimately brought Veeck into the Church. "He was a great student of comparative religions. He never asked an ordinary question." When Veeck voiced doubts about a single footnote in a 600-page volume on Catholicism, Father Halpin spent three days and probed through 13 books with him in an effort to establish its intellectual validity. "It was a most interesting three months," says Father Halpin of the period of Veeck's instruction.

All this mental activity takes place on a sort of subterranean level, the generative but not always visible level of Veeck's nature. On the surface, he remains invincibly the Clown and the Irritant. His volcanic relations with the other owners in baseball stem not so much from his picaresque approach to the game as to his unsheathed candor. His feud with the New York Yankees started years ago as a professional matter and quickly became a personal one. "George Weiss is a sensitive man and I am an outspoken one," he says. "I'm sure that when I say George is a fugitive from the human race he does not think it is funny." Many owners profess to find Veeck's Midas touch distasteful. "He is nothing but a capital-gains gypsy," says one whose own disaffection for money is not pronounced.

That Veeck has a gypsy nature is indisputable. "I've had seven children and no two of them have been born in the same state," he says. That his ball clubs make money is also indisputable. In Cleveland, by Veeck's own testimony, his backers got back $20 for every $1 they put into the club. At St. Louis, Veeck bought stock at $7 a share and sold it 2½ years later for $12 a share; even when the huge operating losses are included, the transaction netted Veeck and his backers a 38% profit. In Chicago the appraised value of the White Sox rose from $195 a share to $450 a share in the first year of Veeck's management. But that he shuffles franchises for profit motive alone is disputable. Veeck sold the Milwaukee Brewers in 1945 because he thought he might restore health to his ailing legs and ailing marriage by dropping out of baseball. He sold the Cleveland Indians in 1949 to raise enough cash to provide trust funds for his three older children and for a final settlement on his divorce. He sold the St. Louis Browns in 1953 at the insistence of an American League cabal led, he claims, by the Yankees.

None of this negates the alienation of Veeck from the community of owners or the real reasons for that alienation: that Veeck is a person of greater dimensions and grander vision than his contemporaries. All this would be tolerable if Veeck fitted the baseball men's image of such an individual—i.e., a failure. But his success offers a suggestion of their own inadequacy and threatens some of the longtime institutions of baseball, such as the domination of the American League by the Yankees. For if other clubs in the league continue to find Veeck's club a better draw than the Yankees, they may undergo a polar shift from domination by the Yankees—who, through the years, have offered them so much money that they couldn't defy Yankee wishes in league councils—to domination by Veeck.

The hostility of the owners is not shared by their players. Veeck is probably the most popular "players' owner" in history. He speaks the players' language without condescension and tends their needs without personal or financial reserve. Once in Milwaukee, Harry (Peanuts) Lowrey, an outfielder demoted to the Brewers by the Chicago Cubs, explained that his poor performance in Milwaukee was due to the fact that he and his family couldn't find a home there. "Move into my place," said Veeck—and promptly moved his own family out so Lowrey's could move in. Another time, Veeck spent $10,000 arranging for the birth and adoption of illegitimate children sired by three of his ballplayers. "I'd handled about 15 cases like this before but never three in one season!" he says—and then spent $100,000 of his own money fighting various legal actions just to keep the players' names secret. "We were trying to keep their families from breaking up," he says, "and we did."

Historically, Veeck is perhaps the most notable mutation in baseball. He developed his bizarre techniques out of a sturdy tradition of conservative training and heritage. The only employer he ever knew was Philip K. Wrigley, the correct, conservative owner of the Chicago Cubs. Of him Veeck says: "A very bright man, more about things than about people, but very bright nevertheless." Veeck's father, for 15 years president of the Cubs, was a dignified person who, says Veeck, "was basically in favor of many of the same things I stand for—a clean ballpark, a happy atmosphere. The kidding part I do—well, you must remember we operate in different eras. When my daddy started with the Cubs [as a vice president in 1917] baseball was just about the only mass sport there was. This meant that your competition was a lot less and of an entirely different nature from today. You didn't have much golfing. You didn't have the huge race tracks and legalized betting of today. You didn't have hunting and fishing in reach of everybody, or sailing and boating. You didn't have radios that you can carry around on a golf course so you can listen to the games but never have to go to one. You didn't have television. It's true, certain things I do would be completely foreign to my father's nature. But he was indoctrinated in a different era and he reacted to it in a different way."

The elder Veeck was a sportswriter working under the name Bill Bailey on the Chicago *American* when Bill was born on Feb. 9, 1914. Bill had an older brother, Maurice, who was killed in a childhood shooting accident playing cops and robbers. He still has an older sister, Peggy Krehbiel, who lives in Downers Grove, a suburb near Chicago. In his sportswriting days, the senior Veeck was a trenchant critic of the Cubs. "My infant son can throw his bottle farther than this team can hit," he said of one Cub team.

Thus needled, the Cubs took Veeck into the organization as a vice president and, after the 1918 season, raised him to president.

It was in these years that young Bill became attuned to the hidden tempos and secret life that make a ballpark pulse with personality. When he was 11, he was helping mail out tickets for ladies' day, a novelty brought to Chicago by his father. In his teens he worked in the stockroom, in the concession stands, in the grandstand hawking popcorn and programs, with the grounds crew, any place where his exceptional energies could be harnessed. (In 1929 he lost $10,000 worth of tickets to the World Series and didn't find them until two months after the season was over.) After hours he went rollicking with many of the players, a raucous, hard-drinking crew. From them he learned all the facts of life and the childlike enthusiasm with which ballplayers explore them. "One thing I tell our sons," says Veeck's wife, Mary Frances, "is that there is nothing they need to keep from their father. There isn't any kind of trouble they can get into that he hasn't seen."

His own father did not approve of all this. When Mr. Veeck took his wife and daughter partying, Peggy would have to rush into the speakeasy and flush the teen-age Bill and his friends out the back way before the elder Veeck walked in. "Bill could never understand why, if it was illegal for his father to be there, it was *more* illegal for *him* to be there," says Peggy.

In September 1933 the elder Veeck became ill with leukemia and on October 5, he died. Bill dropped out of Kenyon College and went to work as an office boy for the Cubs at $17 a week. Eight years later, still in his 20s, he was treasurer of the Cubs and earning $17,000 a year. He was also a husband and father; in 1935 he had married Eleanor Raymond, a childhood friend from Hinsdale whose horsemanship won her a role as a bareback rider in the Ringling Brothers Circus. "I thought when I married Bill I was leaving the circus," she was quoted as saying some years later. She was wrong. Ideas were burgeoning in Veeck's mind, ideas that won no welcome from the Cubs. "It got," Veeck has said, "so that when Mr. Wrigley saw me coming, he automatically said, 'No.' "

IN 1939, when he was only 25 years old, Veeck had tried unsuccessfully to buy the White Sox. Two years later, on June 21, 1941, with nothing but $11 and a ticket to Milwaukee in his pocket, Veeck quit the Cubs. In Milwaukee he blew $10 partying with newspapermen to celebrate his liberation and imminent purchase of the Milwaukee Brewers of the American Association. At the time the Brewers were, if possible, in worse financial shape than

Veeck. They were close to bankruptcy, the league had taken over the franchise, and the bank was about to foreclose. Veeck hurried to the bank to buy the club and get an extension on the loan. He persuaded the bankers that all he really wanted to borrow was time, and he got it. On the strength of this he talked some more and asked for $50,000. He got that too.

On the night that Veeck took over the Brewers, they drew a total of 22 fans. "They were all people who liked to attend hangings," says Veeck. Within 24 hours he had brought in Charlie Grimm as manager and started building the Legend of Bill Veeck. He shuttled players in and out on almost daily schedules. He cleaned up the ballpark. He rocked staid Milwaukee with his zany stunts. He began throwing money around as if he were the last of the great spenders. "Fortunately, in Milwaukee it didn't take an awful lot of money," he says. The ball club remained an indomitable last in 1941, but the next year it shot to within a game of first place. Veeck wiped out all but $17 of the club's $135,000 debt, then started earning large profits as the Brewers won three straight American Association pennants and began setting minor-league attendance records. In October 1945, after spending 22 months in the Marines ("I was a four-time buck private"), Veeck sold the Brewers at a personal profit of $275,000. With this, he temporarily retired from baseball, bought a ranch in southern Arizona and moved there with Eleanor and their three children.

While Veeck had been fighting with the Marines on Bougainville during World War II, both his legs were attacked by a jungle rot that threatened to dissolve the bones. In addition, his right leg was injured in the recoil of an antiaircraft gun. Veeck underwent 10 operations, had bone grafts taken for both legs ("I now have very little bone in my right hip"), and suffered as many as 24 penicillin shots a day for five months while lying in traction. Ultimately his left leg was saved but his right leg was amputated about six inches below the knee in November 1946. Since then, Veeck has had seven more operations to pare off more and more of the bone—the last only a week ago. This time the knee itself was sacrificed, and Veeck may virtually have to learn to walk again.

If Arizona partially saved his legs, it could not save his marriage. Eleanor was an intelligent young woman who, as it developed, was considerably more introverted than her husband. "Eleanor just didn't understand Bill's moods," says one of Veeck's close friends. After a period of separation, the couple was divorced in 1949. At about that time Bill met Mary Frances Ackerman, a onetime drama student who was a press agent for the Ice Capades. They dated almost daily for two weeks, then Bill asked her to marry him. The proposal was enormously complicated by the fact that Mary Frances was a Catholic and Bill a divorced man. Ultimately, the Church made a thorough investigation of Veeck's first marriage and found that a civil but not a sacramental union had taken place: Neither Bill nor his first wife had been baptized nor had they been married in a church, so he was granted the Pauline Privilege to rewed. In the meantime, as a test of his faith and his love, Veeck refrained from seeing Mary Frances for six months. They finally were married by Father Halpin in the Cathedral at Albuquerque in the spring of 1950.

LONG BEFORE that he had returned to baseball. In June 1946, less than a year after selling the Brewers, he acquired the Cleveland Indians for $1,750,000. "The team looked hopeless," he says, "so I bought it." Within 2½ years the Indians had won their first pennant in 28 years, won the World Series and set an alltime attendance record of 2,620,627. Because of his need for cash, Veeck sold the Indians for $2.2 million in 1949 and then, almost as if he had a drive for self-immolation, bought the cellar-bound St. Louis Browns for $1.5 million in mid-1951. "They were the worst-looking collection of ballplayers I've ever seen," he said. "It hurt to look at them." Very few people did.

By the end of 1952, however, attendance was up 60%, and the Browns were outdrawing the Detroit Tigers, Chicago White Sox and Philadelphia Athletics on the road. Veeck, meanwhile, was learning some harsh facts of economic life. He was, in fact, engaged in a fight for survival. In February 1953, Fred Saigh, who was about to go to prison on an income tax evasion charge, sold his St. Louis Cardinals to the Anheuser-Busch Brewery. That altered the balance of power in St. Louis. Veeck felt he could compete against the limited resources of Saigh, but he knew that he could not compete against the virtually unlimited resources of the brewery. His only alternative was to move the Browns out of town. In March 1953 he asked permission of the American League to move to Baltimore and saw a unanimous agreement turned into a 5–3 vote against him. He traced the switch to the Yankees. "Let's put it nicely," he has said. "They figured they could beat my brains out—and they did."

The technique was simple: By forcing Veeck to remain in St. Louis, where he was now unpopular because of his plans to move, they could force him to near bankruptcy. They were right. Within a few weeks Veeck found he was getting three cancellations for season tickets for every new one be sold. He had to sell some of his players, then he had to sell his ballpark to the St. Louis Cardinals for $900,000 and rent it back for $175,000 a year. He sold his stocks and bonds, his ranch in Arizona, his annuities and much of his personal property. Rudie Schaffer, long his closest aide, mortgaged his own home to help meet payrolls. Unable to raise more than 10% of the $30,000 asking price for a likely-looking shortstop in the Negro league, Veeck told the Cubs about Ernie Banks "to keep him out of the American League." By June, attendance had dropped 87%, Veeck had lost $400,000 of his own money in the club and he was being hanged in effigy regularly at the Browns' ball games. "It was the most difficult year of my life," he says.

At length, their sense of duty only half-fulfilled, the Yankees relented. They allowed the American League to allow the Browns to move to Baltimore if Veeck did not move with them. He and his backers agreed to sell out for $2.5 million.

It was a cankerous personal defeat for Veeck, but within two weeks he was back in baseball as a $1,000-a-month special assistant to Phil Wrigley, seeking ways of getting major-league baseball to the West Coast. Veeck spent 14 months and $75,000 of his own money on the project. At one point, in the hope that American League owners loved money more than they hated him, Veeck teamed up with hotel man Conrad Hilton and construction man Henry Crown to try to buy the foundering Philadelphia Athletics and move them to Los Angeles. But the league blocked him and arranged for the club to be sold instead to the late Yankee landlord, Arnold Johnson, who moved the Athletics to Kansas City.

Subsequently Veeck failed in a bid to buy the Cleveland Indians again ("We were really setting a price so that Hank Greenberg could sell his stock"), saw his high bid for the Detroit Tigers ($5.5 million cash or $6 million "on time") turned down for a lower bid ("Sometimes you run into riverboat gamblers," he said bitterly) and failed to buy the Ringling Brothers Circus for $21.1 million.

Not until Dorothy Comiskey Rigney tired of her bitter legal battle with her brother Charles over control of the White Sox did Veeck get his chance to acquire a club again. In the winter of 1958–59 he moved in swiftly and with half a dozen backers bought the 54% of the club controlled by Dorothy for $2.7 million.

The fiery illusions of fun he built around the game in Chicago—notably the exploding scoreboard, which fires off $60 worth of skyrockets and aerial bombs every time a White Sox player hits a home run—are now part of the durable Veeck legend. But some others of Veeck's changes were quite subtle. "Anything that happens in a ballpark, from the moment a fan arrives to the moment he leaves, can ruin the impression of fun that you're trying to build," he says. "This requires an attention to detail." He offers, as an example, the metamorphosis of the dun-colored roach pit that was Comiskey Park. "If you remember, it was dark and dank when you came in; it was like going into a dungeon," he said. "So we painted everything under the grandstand white, tore down a few useless pillars and ripped out everything that hung overhead, that loomed over you. We wanted to get away from that dungeonlike atmosphere to one of cleanliness and airiness." Other details he labored over ranged from putting cloth towels in the washrooms instead of paper towels (cost: $500 a month just "to get a little extra class") to establishing contact with the radar screen around Chicago in order to get early warning of approaching rainstorms so ushers could hand out plastic rain capes to fans in rain-exposed areas. "The important thing is to give them the capes before it starts raining, not after they've got wet," he says. "The intrinsic value of the capes [they cost 4½ cents apiece] is nothing. But the fact that you went out of your way to protect people is important to the fans."

The impact of his methods was demonstrated in an important area; banishing the historic dislike women had for Comiskey Park. To overcome this attitude, Veeck worked on a variety of details. He stationed ushers just inside the gates to look for women who appeared confused and to escort them personally to their seats. He cleaned up and redecorated the once-nauseating powder rooms. He installed lighting in them that was subtly flattering ("A woman likes to think she's looking her best when she goes back into the world") full-length mirrors ("so she can check her seams") and different levels of vanity tables. He gave away orchids and roses, let mothers in free on Mother's Day, gave away green stamps (instead of cigars or beer) on certain Sundays. The result was that the number of women attending games at Comiskey Park tripled (to about 420,000) and the proportionate number went up from less than 20% to more than 30%.

By far the most vivid part of the illusion which Veeck built up, however, was the bravura defiance of destiny by the 1959 White Sox. Employing an anachronistic philosophy of speed, pitching and defense, the White Sox won their first pennant in 10 years and drew 1,423,144 fans to Comiskey Park, double the attendance of 1958.

Ever since moving to Chicago in March 1959, the Veecks have lived in a three-bedroom apartment on the ninth floor of a lake-front hotel on Chicago's South Side. They have four children, ranging from 21 months to 9 years old. At home, as in baseball, the impact of Veeck's personality is electric ("All of our children learned to say 'Daddy' first," says Mary Frances) but, in her own way, Mary Frances exercises the tyranny of the weak over the strong with great subtlety. She does all the personal buying for her husband, from toothbrushes to the 50 white sport shirts and the half dozen identical blue sports coats and slacks that Bill needs every year. ("I haven't bought anything in 10 years," says Bill. "Not even a razor blade.") But she has never insisted that Bill wear a tie, not even at their nuptial Mass. She has achieved only one change: She succeeded in switching Bill from tan sports clothes to navy blue because navy blue was simply more practical for handling by the wife in this family.

The only routine that Veeck follows is early in the morning. Usually he spends 60 to 90 minutes bathing the shrunken stump of his right leg. This is the time when he gets a chance to read and reflect, when the reality of Bill Veeck—the substance behind and beyond the legend—becomes apparent and the far reaches of his private universe are explored. "I'm for the dreamer," he said not long ago. "The only really important things in history have been started by the dreamers. They never know what can't be done."

༄

The Spirit of St. Louis

BY RICK REILLY

*Cardinals play-by-play maestro Jack Buck didn't let a little thing
like Parkinson's shake him.*

PROMISE ME ONE THING. PROMISE THAT AT THE END OF THIS
you won't feel sorry for Jack Buck.

As square as a pan of corn bread, as American as a red
Corvette, Buck has been doing what he loves in the St. Louis
Cardinals' radio booth for 47 years, which makes him just about the exact
center of this country. The last thing he wants is sympathy.

Yeah, Buck has Parkinson's disease, which makes his hands tremble and
his arms flail. He also has diabetes, which means poking needles into himself twice a day. He also has a pacemaker. And cataracts. And vertigo. And
excruciatingly painful sciatica. And a box of pills the size of a toaster. But
all that only gives him more material to work with.

"I wish I'd get Alzheimer's," he cracks. "Then I could forget I've got all the
other stuff."

Luckily, you can still find the 76-year-old Buck at the mike during every
St. Louis home game, broadcasting to the Cardinal Nation over more than
100 radio stations in 11 states. Herking and jerking in his seat, his face
contorting this way and that, he still sends out the most wonderful descriptions of games you've ever heard.

"I've given the Cardinals the best years of my life," Buck says. "Now I'm giving them the worst."

That's a lie. Despite enough diseases to kill a moose, Buck has gotten even better lately. "I have no idea how," says his son and radio partner, Joe, "but his voice has been stronger lately. It's like he's pouring every ounce of energy God can give him into those three hours of the broadcast."

Yet Buck makes it all sound effortless, like talking baseball with the guy across the backyard fence. He's natural, simple and unforgettable. When Kirk Gibson hit his dramatic home run for the Los Angeles Dodgers and limped around the bases in the 1988 World Series, Buck, calling the game for CBS Radio, said, "I don't believe what I just saw!" When St. Louis's Ozzie Smith hit a rare lefthanded home run in Game 5 of the 1985 playoffs, Buck said, "Go crazy, folks! Go crazy!" When Mark McGwire hit No. 61 in 1998, Buck said, "Pardon me while I stand and applaud!"

Like thousands of other eight-year-old boys in Middle America in 1966, all I had of baseball most nights was Buck. If I fiddled enough with my mom's old radio in our kitchen in Boulder, Colo., I could pick up Buck doing the Cardinals' games on KMOX. Bob Gibson. Tim McCarver. Curt Flood. I worshiped Buck then. I respect him now.

He was a kid whose family couldn't afford toothpaste; who didn't go to the dentist until he was 15 (and immediately had five teeth pulled); who worked as a soda jerk, a newspaper hawk, a boat painter, a waiter, a factory hand; who was the first person in his family to own a car; who took shrapnel in an arm and a leg from the Germans in World War II; who danced in Paris on V-E Day.

This is a man who is coming up on his 10,000th game broadcast; who was in the stands the day that Joe DiMaggio's 56-game hitting streak ended; who called Stan Musial's five-home-run doubleheader; who ate dinner with Rocky Marciano in Havana; whom Jesse Owens called friend; who survived the Ice Bowl—and 16 years in the booth with Harry Caray.

I would eat a bathtub full of rubber chicken just to hear him emcee a banquet. He has more lines than the DMV. If an Italian woman wins the door prize, Buck says, "You know, I've always had a fondness for Italian women. In fact, during World War II an Italian woman hid me in her basement for three months. [Pause.] Of course, this was in Cleveland."

If anything, Parkinson's has given Buck more banquet material. "I shook hands with Muhammad Ali recently," he says. "It took them 30 minutes to get us untangled."

This may be Buck's last year behind the mike, so he's savoring every inning. So should we. "This is his victory lap," says Joe. "This is him circling the outfield."

That lousy day is coming, of course, when he opens his mouth and the Parkinson's won't let anything come out. But don't feel sorry for him. "Hell, I've touched so many bases," says Buck, "I've got no quarrel with these last few."

So, on the day he quits, he'll have to pardon us while we stand and applaud.

Max

BY STEVE WULF

After more than 40 years, the Clown Prince of Baseball,
Max Patkin, could still leave 'em laughing

I know that you hate me and laugh in derision,
For what is the Clown? He plays but a part.
Yet he has his dream, and his hope and his vision,
The Clown has a heart.
And ah when you pass me, uncaring, unseeing,
You know not my sorrow, so cruel and sweet.
I give you my spirit, my life, and my being, I die at your feet.
                                             —I Pagliacci

MAX PATKIN IS DYING. NO, HE HAS NOT BEEN PLACED ON IRREVOCABLE waivers or anything like that. On this particular summer night, he is dying in the comedic sense. It is warm and drizzly in Gastonia, N.C., and nothing is working for the Clown Prince of Baseball. Not the imitation of a chicken, not the shadowing of the first baseman, not even the countless (actually 24) geysers he sends into the air from his five-toothed mouth. "What a crowd!" Max tells the crowd. "I had more people in my bed last night."

This is a slight exaggeration, not because Max had company the night before, but because there are 47 people in the stands at Sims Park. It seems that the owner of the Gastonia Rangers in the Class A Sally League, a gracious man named Jack Farnsworth, had forgotten that Max was coming and so neglected to promote his appearance. Farnsworth, who made a fortune selling Bibles and who operates one of the few dry ballparks in all of baseball, had recently undergone brain surgery, so you could hardly blame him.

There are a few people laughing at Max's gyrations on this night, but too few for him to hear. So when the public-address announcer, who is about half the age of Max's uniform (the one with the question mark on the back), blows the introduction to the *Rock Around the Clock* number, Max stalks off the field in a huff. Ever the trouper, he returns to finish off his act and squeezes out a few more chuckles. One of the people laughing hardest is a man who is taking notes behind home plate and who looks like a schoolteacher. He is Joe Frisina, a scout for the Montreal Expos and, in fact, a former schoolteacher. Frisina says, "I've seen Maxie 50 times over the years, and I still laugh."

Everybody in baseball knows Max Patkin. Some of them may try to hide when they see him coming, but there are probably only a handful of major leaguers in uniform who haven't seen the Clown Prince of Baseball at one time or another. And if they haven't laughed, they're not human. The funny thing about Maxie's act is that it is still funny. It's the same corny shtick that he has done for 40 years in 400 ballparks on 4,000 different days or nights over the course of four million miles. "If it was a class act, I would have been out of business a long time ago," he says.

Max is 68 now, and suffering from glaucoma, bad knees and a herniated disk in his back, but he's strong as a horse and has every intention of taking his act into the '90s, which would be its sixth decade. In all that time, and over all those miles, he has never missed a performance. He has jumped out of a burning plane, dodged tornadoes and been mistaken for a fugitive from justice—"I feel sorry for the guy if he looked like me," says Max. He nearly bought the farm 30 years ago in Gastonia, of all places, when he wrecked the De Soto he was driving. Still, the only time he ever had to cancel a booking (as opposed to missing a scheduled performance) was when, in a scene worthy of *I Pagliacci*, his wife at the time hit him over the head with a hammer. "True story," says Max, who always says that.

It's safe to guess that nobody has given more of himself to the game than Max. He has certainly poured more sweat on the diamond than anyone else ever has. He has taken thousands upon thousands of showers in minor league ballparks in all 50 states and several countries, and almost all of them were lonely showers, since he is usually finished by the sixth inning. His only companion under the nozzle is the tired, dirt-encrusted baseball cap he washes after every performance.

Consider this chunk of his 1987 schedule: Burlington, N.C.; Winston-Salem, N.C.; Wichita, Kans.; San Antonio; Salem, Ore.; Albuquerque; Tucson; Honolulu; Nashville; Charleston, W.Va.; Richmond; Norfolk, Va.; Anchorage, Alaska; Fairbanks, Alaska; Vancouver; Portland, Ore.; Las Vegas. That, ladies and germs, was what Max did in the month of *July*, returning home to King of Prussia, Pa., on weekends. He doesn't even bother redeeming his frequent-flier miles. "What would I do with a free airplane ticket?" he asks. "Travel?"

What does baseball give Max in return? He gets anywhere from $900 to $1,500 a performance, depending on the size of the ballpark, or $200 if the game is rained out. The Chicken, his main competition for minor league yuks, gets $5,500—guaranteed, rain or shine—for a Class A game, $7,500 for Triple A. "Don't get me wrong, I like the Chicken," says Maxie. "But he's a little thief."

Max is not especially interested in making a lot more money. He drives a Cadillac of recent vintage, and he lives comfortably with his brother Eddie, and close by his daughter, Joy. But he could use a little more recognition. He's not necessarily talking Hall of Fame, although there are a few unofficial clowns there already. What the Clown Prince of Baseball would like to be, one time only, is the King of Baseball. At baseball's annual winter meetings, you see, the National Association, which is the governing body of the minor leagues, honors someone as the King of Baseball at its big banquet. In a sappy little ceremony, the honoree is led to the dais, placed on a throne and given a crown, a robe and a scepter. Just once you would think they would put the jester on the throne. Oh well, says Max, "screw 'em if they can't take a joke."

On May 29, he embarked on his 43rd season of one-night stands. First stop, West Palm Beach; last stop, Vancouver; with 70 stops in between. He will also appear in a baseball movie, *Bull Durham*. In the movie, Max plays a clown coach, and he gets to dance with the leading lady.

That night last summer in Gastonia wasn't the first time Max died before an audience, and it won't be the last. But every once in a while, when the mood hits him and the crowd is really into his act, Max feels like he's 24 again and chasing Joe DiMaggio around the bases, which is how the whole thing got started. On a really good night, he can look into the stands and see Connie Mack laughing. Sometimes he can stand in the first base coaching box in Butte or Birmingham or Buffalo and see Eddie Gaedel take ball four and scamper down to first.

The day that Max Patkin stops kissing base runners or crawling through catchers' legs or covering himself with dirt or getting the heave-hohoho from umpires, chances are that's the day he takes the Big Pratfall. And if Maxie has his way, that still wouldn't be the end of his act. "When I die," he says, "I want to be buried in the first base coaching box in some bush league ballpark, and I want my nose sticking out of the ground. That way, every once in a while, some poor guy will trip over me and yell, 'It's that sono-fabitch Patkin again!' "

A song of tender memories deep in his listening heart

An hour or so before an Appalachian League game between the Johnson City (Tenn.) Cardinals and the visiting Kingsport (Tenn.) Mets, Max walks onto the field and gets a familiar greeting. "I can't believe you're still doing this, you sonofabitch," Chuck Hiller, a Mets instructor, tells him.

"Forty-two years, haven't missed a performance yet," says Max.

"When did you first catch Max?" Hiller asks another Mets coach, Joel Horlen.

"Lincoln, Nebraska, 1959," says Horlen.

"Remember the tornado?" asks Max, and Horlen nods. "I first saw you in Cocoa, 1957," says Hiller.

Don Blasingame, a Cards instructor, walks by, shakes Max's hand and says, "Winston-Salem, 1953, my first year."

This is one of the nicer parts of Max's job: the pregame reunion with the old guard. The camaraderie usually doesn't last very long, because he has to brief both teams and the P.A. announcer on his routine. But a ferocious storm turns this night in Johnson City into a rainout for Max, which leaves him without a lot of money but with lots of time for stories.

A long, long time ago Max was a wild righthanded pitcher. He grew up around Philadelphia, the son of a Russian immigrant. "Sam Patkin from Minsk," he says. "He would come out to see me pitch, and yell, 'Strike 'em out, Maxie!' Once when I was playing third base and another pitcher wasn't doing so well, my father stopped the game, walked onto the field, took the ball from the other pitcher and gave it to me." Playing on a semipro team with Elmer Valo, Max was 6' 3", 150 pounds, and, he says, "I looked like a nose on the end of a lollipop stick."

Max got a tryout with the Chicago White Sox in 1940, and they sent him to spring training with their Waterloo, Iowa, farm. But the general manager of the Waterloo club, Joe L. Brown, didn't like his looks, which is sort of funny because Max was often mistaken for Brown's father, the comedian Joe E. Brown. Anyway, Max was sold for $100 to the Wisconsin Rapids, where in 1941 he won 10, lost 8, struck out close to 200 batters and nearly killed one sportswriter. "The press box there was real low," he says, "and one day a pitch got away from me, sailed into the press box, bounced off the wall and hit this guy in the back of the head, knocking him out cold. True story."

He had 32 wild pitches that season, but the world was also out of control, and the following year he joined the Navy. He was assigned to former heavyweight champ Gene Tunney's unit in Honolulu as a physical instructor. Bobby Riggs was also there, attached to a special entertainment troop, and one day he challenged Max to a little Ping-Pong match. Unbeknownst to Riggs, Max was a pretty fair table tennis player, so when Riggs gave him 14 points a game, the hustler lost $100. And kept losing, even though the handicap was eventually reduced to 10 points a game. "We played day and night for three days until he got shipped out," says Max. "He ended up owing me $2,000, and the other guys wouldn't let him out of there until he paid up. He paid me $500, and every time I saw him after that, he bought me dinner, although not $1,500 worth of dinners. True story."

His career took a comedic turn in the Army-Navy baseball game in Honolulu during the war. Playing on the Navy team, Max had to pitch against none other than Joe DiMaggio. Struck him out the first time. But the second time up, DiMaggio hit the longest home run anybody had ever seen. "I don't know why I did it," says Max, "but as he was running around the bases, I fell in behind him, imitating that lope of his. When we got to home plate, his whole team came out of the dugout to shake my hand and walk me back to the mound. True story."

Max got the hint. He began to expand his comic repertoire: He turned his cap sideways, developed a loose-limbed dance, imitated a dying fish when working in the coaching box. He still harbored a dream of pitching in the majors, but when the war ended and he was with the Wilkes-Barre (Pa.) Barons, Max came down with tendinitis of the shoulder. Released by Wilkes-Barre in 1946, he caught on with Harrisburg, Pa., and during an exhibition game with the Philadelphia Athletics, old Cornelius McGillicuddy himself, stiff collar and all, cracked up at Max's antics in the coaching box. "That's when I knew I was funny, when I made Connie Mack laugh," says Max.

The Cleveland Indians also came into Harrisburg, and Max was so laughable that player-manager Lou Boudreau recommended to his owner, Bill Veeck, that he hire the clown as a coach. The $1 contract he signed to coach the Indians began the most meaningful association of his life, because Veeck became a friend as well as a frequent employer. Of Max, Veeck said, "He looks like he was put together by somebody who forgot to read the instructions." But Veeck accorded him as much respect as anyone Max has ever known. "He never made fun of me, and always treated me as a human being," he says. "You know, it's a helluva thing when someone comes up to you and says, 'Be funny, Max; make a funny face.' I may be a clown, but I have my dignity."

Max remembers his major league debut in 1946: "They had 80,000 people in Municipal Stadium for my first game. Of course, it may have had something to do with the fact that they were honoring Babe Ruth, Ty Cobb and Tris Speaker that day. I was scared to death. The thing I remember most about that day is this: Al Schacht, who was the original Clown Prince of Baseball, performed before the game. Now, most everybody in baseball disliked Schacht, even his partner. Well, Schacht is out there on the field, and Ruth, who's watching from the dugout, says to Mel Harder, one of our old pitchers, 'I hate that sonofabitch. Go out and throw some to me.' Now, this is in the middle of Schacht's act. But, of course, when Ruth walks out, the fans just rise as one, and Schacht has to disappear. Babe knew what he was doing.

"Anyway, Ruth goes up to the plate, rolls up his trouser legs and damn if he doesn't hit a single off Harder. Babe is two years from dying, but he takes about 15 swings, each one weaker and weaker until he quits, a tired old man. Honest to God, it was the most tender scene. There were 80,000 people with tears streaming down their faces. True story. That's what I remember about my first game in the majors. God, I hope people don't dislike me as much as they hated Schacht."

It may seem odd now that the Indians would employ a clown coach, but back then baseball and vaudeville had a sort of partnership. At one time, there were about a dozen baseball clowns. And in the wintertime, players like Lefty Gomez would hit the boards. Besides, the Indians were so bad then that they employed not one, but two clowns. The other one was Jackie Price, who was the cleverest of them all, according to Max. Price used to hang upside down from the batting screen and hit pitches; he would shoot baseballs up in the air with a bazooka, jump in a Jeep and catch them.

Price and Patkin didn't last very long with the Indians—not because they weren't funny, but because the team was getting serious. In 1947 the Indians had the makings of the team that would win the world championship a year later. The clowns' departure was also accelerated during a train ride that spring from Los Angeles to San Diego for an exhibition game when Price let his pet snake loose in a car full of women bowlers. As the women screamed and scrambled through the train, Boudreau decided this was no way to run a ball club.

So Veeck sent Max into the hinterlands to perform. His next major league stop was with the St. Louis Browns in 1951. Veeck, who had just purchased the Brownies, decided to put together a fun show for an Aug. 19 double-header with the Detroit Tigers; the Browns were 36 games behind the Yankees at the time. Between games the fans were treated to jugglers, acrobats, fireworks, a band led by Satchel Paige and a routine by Max. There was a huge cake on the pitcher's mound, and out of it popped a 26-year-old midget named Eddie Gaedel. The rest, of course, is history. In the second game, bottom of the first, the announcer intoned: "For the Browns, number one-eighth, Eddie Gaedel, batting for Frank Saucier." Says Max, "Imagine getting upstaged by someone who didn't weigh as much as my nose."

Max didn't stick with the Browns for long; Veeck's new manager, Rogers Hornsby, figured he had enough clowns on the field. So Max continued working the minor league parks. And his act wasn't restricted to the baseball field. He toured with the Harlem Globetrotters, performed with Vaughn Monroe and his orchestra, traveled overseas for the State Department, made 'em laugh on the pro tennis circuit and did ice shows, changing costumes to fit the occasion. In the early '50s, he was on the sports trade-show circuit with Jim Thorpe, who bequeathed Max the baseball glove he still uses in his act. Max worked with Jack Benny, Bob Hope, Groucho Marx, Ed Sullivan, Dick Van Dyke, Bob Newhart and even ZaSu Pitts. Once, in the middle of his routine with the Harlem Globetrotters, in St. Louis, he inadvertently mooned the audience and brought down the house. "I shoulda kept it in my act," he says.

In the meantime, all the other baseball clowns were dying off like dinosaurs. Max kept going because 1) he was strong, 2) he gambled away a lot of his money and clowning was what he knew how to do, and 3) he had a good act. The road was a lot rougher in the old days—trains and buses instead of planes, hotel rooms without air-conditioning and with bed bugs, occasional bouts with anti-Semitism. But still Max did his one-night stands.

From time to time Patkin would pop up in the majors. When Veeck owned the White Sox, he brought Max to Chicago a few times, and Toronto booked him in the early days of the Blue Jays. In 1973, George Steinbrenner, of all people, had him perform with the team he had just bought, the Yankees. When he was a kid in Cleveland, Steinbrenner had loved watching Max. Unfortunately, the Boss did not clear Max with the Major, Ralph Houk, who was managing the team. Max says, "Houk sees me and says, 'Get out of here. We're fighting for a pennant, and we don't need your crummy act.' This is in May, mind you. Once they get him to calm down, they make him rub my nose for luck. The Yankees then win four straight. They pay me $600 for four performances, the cheapskates, and this is right after they signed Catfish Hunter. True story." Actually, Max gets his facts mixed up sometimes. The Yanks didn't sign Hunter until 1975. But what the heck.

One of the reasons his act is so good is that it's a game act. He does it in the middle of the ball game, so there's an inherent sacrilege and an element of danger that can be very appealing. When he stands in the first or third base box, yelling, sleeping, blowing kisses, spraying water, there is an actual baseball game going on, and some managers—Gene Mauch and the late Paul Richards, for instance—tried at various times to keep Max from taking the field. Over the years, he has worked through at least 10 no-hitters. Although Max says he has never really affected the outcome of a game, he has been accused of doing so. Once when he was coaching third for the baby Blue Jays and Jim Palmer of the Orioles was pitching to John Mayberry, Max shouted "Fastball!" just as Palmer was about to throw. Sure enough, it was a fastball, and Mayberry walloped it over the fence. "I'm standing in the box, and Palmer is staring at me with those penetrating blue eyes of his," says Max. "He didn't say anything. He just stared until I felt about as big as Eddie Gaedel. True story."

> *This evening at seven of the clock I invite you*
> *To see our performance, I know 'twill delight you.*

"So be sure to watch for Max in the third inning." The public-address announcer for the Columbia (S.C.) Mets has just finished his introduction before a Sally League game with the Macon (Ga.) Pirates. At first glance, you might think that the well-groomed man in the stands along the first base line had just come off the golf course. If not exactly handsome, he is at least presentable. But then he walks over to a group of teenage girls, extends his neck and makes a funny face out of what Jim Murray once described as "the world's biggest hunk of bubble gum." The girls giggle, and Max says, "What'd you expect, Robert Redford? I may not be good-lookin', but I'm tall."

Having put his game face on, Max retires to the clubhouse to don the rest of his uniform. He naturally likes to work games in which the home team is winning, but the Mets are not cooperating on this night. By the time Max slinks into their dugout in the top of the third, they trail 5–1. Luckily, though, he finds a willing and savvy assistant for his act, a young outfielder named Cliff Gonzalez, who puts him in a good mood. "You were a pitcher?" Gonzalez asks Max, who then proudly recounts some of his early exploits.

Singing, "Make 'em laugh, make 'em laugh," under his breath, Max goes over behind the Macon first baseman and does his shadow routine. He perfectly mimics the first baseman as he warms up the other infielders, even when the Pirate fakes a throw. Then Max hits him over the head with his glove—the one Jim Thorpe gave him. Max, of course, has briefed the kid before the game. And the crowd can't tell that he is whispering instructions to the first baseman. But it's still one of the funnier parts of his act. (At one time or another, Max has aped almost all the great first sackers, as well as a former first baseman for Yale named George Bush.)

After that routine is over, he throws aside his glove and takes his position in the coach's box. He flashes an incredibly elaborate, ridiculous series of signs. He takes a handful of dirt and sprinkles it all over himself. "What I'll do for a lousy $5,000," he says in a stage whisper. When a Mets runner reaches first base, Max kisses him on the mouth and says, "Did that the other night, and the kid followed me home." He keeps up a running commentary on the game, shouting things like "All we need is a touchdown!" and "Don't take too long a lead—you don't get on base that often." And, sure enough, he tells the crowd, "What a crowd! I had more people in my bed last night." When the Macon catcher goes out to talk to the pitcher, Max walks over to eavesdrop. As the last Mets batter of the inning runs past first base, Max kicks his leg over him. All that in the bottom of the third.

Before the fourth inning starts, Max does his imitation of a chicken. This has nothing to do with the San Diego Chicken; Max was doing this comic prance long before Ted Giannoulas was even an egg. And he does it so well on this night that the Columbia fans give him a hand. He recedes into the Mets dugout for the top of the inning but then reemerges to do his *Rock Around the Clock* bit, in which he goes through all sorts of silly baseball gyrations to the tune of Bill Haley's 1955 hit.

In the bottom of the fourth, Max goes over to the third base box and does a few cute, throwaway gags like falling asleep on the bag and playing hopscotch in the box. The bottom of the fourth is basically a rest period for

Max, especially if there isn't much traffic at third.

In the top of the fifth, he throws a soda can to Gonzalez and tells him, "Go fill this up with water." Gonzalez takes him aback by saying, "Yessir, Mr. Durante," then hustles over to the water cooler. The water comes into play in the bottom of the fifth, and this is the most amazing part of Max's act, the thing that makes people say, "How does he *do* that?" He goes out to the first base box and knocks back the can of water. (A few times, practical jokers have filled the can with urine, and Max did the act anyway. "Tastes like weak beer," he says.) Then in the course of the next three outs, he sprays geysers of mist into the air. He'll pat his body progressively upward, as if squeezing a tube of toothpaste, then lets go. Once, twice . . . 20 times. He has never kept count, but on a really good night he can do 30. "There's no real trick, and it's the easiest part of the act," he says. "I just hold all the water up in my mouth and let it out a little at a time."

On this night, Max does it 25 times. Meanwhile, the Mets rally and score two runs. So there's a wonderful energy in the air, a combination of excitement that the home team is back in the ballgame and amazement over Max's Old Faithful routine. "If you think this is good," he says to the fans, "you should have seen me when I was alive." (In fact, over the years Max has had to drop about 25% of his act because of the physical toll. "I used to do a bit where I took off my shoe, smelled it and fell over backward. Sounds simple, but my back just couldn't take it anymore.")

And now, the finale. Max announces to the crowd that he is going to show the Mets how to hit. He hoists a huge load of bats over his shoulder, walks toward the plate and takes a pratfall. Then he comes up behind the opposing catcher and crawls through his legs. It's staggering to consider that Max has done that to almost every catcher from Yogi Berra to Johnny Bench to Benito Santiago.

The opposing pitcher, who has been briefed, throws the ball high and tight, and Max falls over backward, then rows himself back into the box, using the bat as an oar. He gets up, knees shaking, and watches nervously as the next pitch plops into the catcher's mitt. Then he knocks the catcher over, and the catcher bounces up and raises the ball at Max, as though angered. Max is supposed to hit the third pitch, but he has been in a slump for several years, so it may take him a few more cuts than that to get a solid hit. On this night, he hits the fifth pitch and runs to third. When he gets there, he points up in the air, the third baseman takes the fake, and Max slides headfirst into the bag. But the umpire calls him out. Max argues, the umpire gives him an exaggerated thumb, and that's usually the end of the act, but there have occasionally been one or two wrinkles to the finale. Many years ago, when Max was working a game in the Pacific Coast League, umpire Bruce Froemming, who's now in the National League, gave a starter's pistol to the third base ump, who shot Max while he was arguing. Ad-libbing, Max keeled over backward.

As Max walks off the field, he gets a very nice ovation. "He's funnier than Pee-wee Herman," Blake Derrick, 7, tells his friend Michael Vande Kamp, 7½. High praise indeed. Even though the Mets eventually lose, the fans go away happy. But Max still isn't satisfied. "On a scale of one to 10, I'd give that a six," he says. "Honestly, you should see the crowds I get in Latin America. They love me down there. *El Max*. I once got off an airplane in Cuba, and they had a red carpet rolled out for me. True story."

> *Laugh, Punchinello! The world will cry "Bravo!"*
> *Go hide with laughter thy tears and thy sorrow,*
> *Sing and be merry, playing thy part,*
> *Laugh, Punchinello, for the love that is ended,*
> *Laugh for the sorrow that is eating thy heart.*

True stories. Maxie has a million of 'em. There's one true story that's a heartbreaker, though.

In 1953 Max started dating a cigarette girl in a Philadelphia nightclub. She was some 15 years younger than Max, and they went together for seven years before they got married. They adopted a baby girl in 1963.

"We had some good times together," he recalls one afternoon before a performance. "God, she was a good-looking blonde. But she was leading a double life while I was on the road. I was blind. Look, I was probably no picnic to live with, but all the time I was on the road, she was fooling around.

"I didn't catch on till she told me she wanted a divorce. Then I caught her with the 19-year-old caretaker at our home. I chased that sonofabitch out of the house into the garage. I cornered him behind the freezer. There are my golf clubs. I took out my three-iron. I swung and I missed. I swung and I missed. I swung and I missed. I like to tell people I bogeyed that hole." Max is telling a joke here, but his eyes are sad.

"Things got so bad, I was sleeping alone in a room in my own house. One day I came out of my room, and she hit me over the head with a hammer. She laughed. My daughter saved me. She picked up the bloody hammer. I stumbled out onto the lawn with a slightly fractured skull. Fortunately, my neighbor, who was an FBI man, took me to the hospital.

"Two weeks I spent in the hospital. I got out just so I could attend this banquet in Norristown (Pa.) for Tommy Lasorda. So there I am with my head all bandaged. Joe Garagiola is the emcee. Don't get me wrong, Joe has been beautiful to me over the years. But when he introduces me, he says, 'There's Max Patkin. His head is bandaged because his wife hit him with a hammer.' Got a big laugh, too. True story.

"We finally got divorced after 17 years. You know what? She married that caretaker. What really hurt, though, was that in all the years I knew her, she never once saw me perform. Not once. For all she knew, I was an airline pilot. She moved to Phoenix a year or so ago, then committed suicide on her 50th birthday. She must have been a very sad woman.

"God, I thought of committing suicide myself sometimes. My life was so lonely. Once, I stuck my head in an oven for 20 seconds. I tell people, 'I didn't like the smell,' to get a laugh. I almost had a couple of nervous breakdowns. I still get a little edgy, but way back when, I'd really get the shakes before a performance. It's hard to be funny when you're so sad, when you think your life is falling apart.

"Things are better for me now. The loneliness still gets to me sometimes, but I've got Joy and Eddie to go home to on weekends. She's a good girl, and Eddie's a prince."

In *I Pagliacci* (which is based on a true story), Canio, who is Punchinello in the play within the play, discovers his much younger wife's infidelity and kills her and her lover. The last line of the opera, spoken by Canio, is "The comedy is ended."

But for Max the comedy goes on and on, night after night, flight after flight, ballpark after ballpark, Holiday Inn after Days Inn after Rodeway Inn after International House of Pancakes. His is a life of *Addams Family* reruns at 6 a.m. when he can't get back to sleep. He could do something else for a living—he used to sell janitorial supplies and shoes in the off-season. He could even retire. Why does he go on being the Clown Prince of Baseball? He can't really explain it, any more than he can explain why he always kisses the motel Bible 14 times before he leaves for the park.

Hail, Punchinello!
Long live the merry king,
Who keeps us mellow! He is the blithest fellow!
Long life to him we sing,
Hail, Punchinello!

This night, it's Burlington, N.C., where the Burlington Indians will be playing an Appalachian League game. The Indians are only a couple of years old,
so Max doesn't know quite what to expect when he gets to the ballpark.
Tom Chandler, the former Texas A & M coach, is managing the Indians,
and he gives Max a warm welcome: "Max Patkin, you old sonofagun. I
can't believe you're still doing this."

"Tom Chandler. I can't believe you're still in this game. Where was it we
first met?" asks Max.

"Alpine, Texas, 30 years ago. The millionaire who built that ballpark out
in the middle of nowhere. Remember?"

"I sure do."

The Indians average 2,100 a game, which is excellent for A ball, but with
a well-promoted appearance by the Clown Prince of Baseball, 3,500 fans
stream through the gates. The weather is fine, the P.A. announcer is professional, and the field at Burlington Stadium is close to the stands. In
short, Max has the perfect setting.

And the crowd loves him. A group of senior citizens laughs as hard as a
neighboring group of Little Leaguers. When he mocks the first baseman,
giggles fill the air. The fans *ooh* and *aah* when he does his leg kick over the
Indian base runner, and they eat up his chicken imitation. During *Rock
Around the Clock*, they clap in rhythm. Adding to the excitement, the Burlington pitcher has a no-hitter going through four innings.

In the bottom of the fifth, the spray routine goes over very big. "How
does he do that?" people ask one another, and he does it 27 times. In the finale, he actually nails the third pitch to him and lines a clean single. The fans
bring him back for a curtain call, or in this case, a backstop call. "I'd give that
a nine," Max says later.

He lingers a while after the game to kibitz with Chandler and Miles Wolff,
the owner of the Indians. When he walks out to the parking lot, it is almost empty. Suddenly, out of the darkness, comes a rough-hewn man in
a John Deere baseball cap. Max stiffens, thinking it might be a holdup.

"I just wanted to shake your hand," the man says. "God bless you. You
made the kids laugh. You made me laugh."

"Thank you very much," says Max Patkin. His eyes say, "This is what I live
for."

True story, by the way.

GIANTS

Aches and Pains and Three Batting Titles

BY MYRON COPE

*How good was Roberto Clemente? Though the Pirates outfielder
suffered countless real and imagined ailments, Sandy Koufax said that the
only way to pitch him was to roll the ball up to the plate.*

THE BATTING CHAMPION OF THE MAJOR LEAGUES
lowered himself to the pea-green carpet of his 48-foot living room and sprawled on his right side, flinging his left
leg over his right leg. He wore gold Oriental pajama tops,
tan slacks, battered bedroom slippers and—for purposes of the demonstration he was conducting—a tortured grimace. "Like dis!" he cried, and
then dug his fingers into his flesh, just above his upraised left hip. Roberto Clemente, the Pittsburgh Pirates' marvelous rightfielder and their stead-
iest customer of the medical profession, was showing how he must greet
each new day in his life. He has a disk in his back that insists on wandering, so when he awakens he must cross those legs, dig at the flesh and listen for the sound of the disk popping back where it belongs.

Around the room necks were craned and ears alerted for the successful
conclusion of the demonstration. Clemente's wife—the tall, beautiful Vera—
sat solemnly in a gold wing chair a few feet away. Way out in the rightfield
seats, ensconced on a $1,000 velvet sofa in what may be called the Italian
Provincial division of Clemente's vast living room, were his 18-year-old
nephew, Pablo, and Pablo's buddy, Wilson. They sat fascinated, or at least

they seemed fascinated, for it may have been that Wilson, who says his hobby is girls, was wishing that minute that Roberto would lend them his Cadillac.

"No, you cannot hear the disk now," shouted Roberto. "It is in place now. But every morning you can hear it from here to there, in the whole room. *Boop!*"

Boop? Certainly, Boop. Not only one boop but two, for there is another disk running around up in the vicinity of Roberto's neck. For that one he must have someone manipulate his neck muscles until the boop is heard.

All this herding of disks, mind you, is but a nub on the staggering list of medical attentions that Clemente has undergone during his 11 years as a Pirate. Relatively small at 5' 10" and 180 pounds when able to take nourishment, the chronic invalid has smooth skin, glistening muscles and perfect facial contours that suggest the sturdy mahogany sculpture peddled in the souvenir shops of his native Puerto Rico. His countrymen regard him as the most superb all-round big-leaguer to emerge from this island, while many Pittsburghers have concluded that the only thing that can keep Clemente from making them forget Paul Waner is a sudden attack of good health.

Now 31, Clemente over the past five pain-filled years has won three National League batting championships (to say nothing of leading *both* leagues for the past two years) and has averaged .330, a level of consistency that no other big-leaguer has equaled during this half decade. In strength and accuracy his throwing arm has surpassed that of the old Brooklyn cannon, Carl Furillo, and if Roberto's genes are any indication, his arm is not about to weaken. "My mother is 75," he says. "Last year she threw out the first pitch of the season. She put something on it, too." Because Roberto smolders with an intense belief in himself, some ballplayers argue that his only real malady is a serious puffing of the head, but the clicking of the X-ray machines, the scraping of scalpels, the trickle of intravenous feeding and the scratching of pens upon prescription pads have mounted to such a fortissimo that Roberto would seem to be a fit subject for graduate research. The moment when Roberto first set eyes on his wife is the story of his life: He spied her in a drugstore, where he had gone to buy medication for an ailing leg.

"I played only two innings in the winter league this year," sighed Roberto, having picked himself off the carpet and dumped himself into a chair. "I was having headaches, headaches, headaches, so I had to quit." He had hoped to rest at his split-level Spanish-style house atop a hill in Rio Piedras, a suburb of San Juan. To the left of the living room an open-air tropical garden flourishes in the sun and rain that descend through overhead beams, and along the front of the living room a sunken parlor looks out on a veranda that by night offers a glittering view of all San Juan, clear down to the bay. Roberto had the house built a year ago at a cost of $65,000 and, because of galloping real-estate values, it is worth at least $100,000 today. But now his voice rose and swept out across the veranda and transported down the Puerto Rican hillside all the heartfelt melancholy that has ever been sounded in sad Spanish song and story.

"My head still hurts. The pain splits my head. The doctors say it's tension. They say I worry too much. I've tried tranquilizers, but they don't work. My foot is killing me. I got this tendon in my left heel that rubs against the bone, and I cannot run on it at all. I'm weary, I tell you. All the time it's go here, speak there, do dis, do dat. Always, always, always. When I go to spring training, that's when I take my rest."

On days when Puerto Ricans did not require him to address luncheons and cut ribbons, Roberto lay abed from midnight till noon, then arose for breakfast and returned to bed till 4:30 p.m. He usually got about two hours' sleep in all that time. He is one of the world's great insomniacs because, he explained earnestly, he lies awake worrying that he will not be able to fall asleep.

"When I don't sleep I don't feel like eating and I lose weight," Roberto said.

Has he tried sleeping pills? Yes, he answered, but they kept him awake all night.

Opera companies have performed *Parsifal* in scarcely more time than it takes Roberto to get ready for bed. When the Pirates are on the road he memorizes every aspect of his hotel room. Where is the door? To the right? Is the window to the left? Four paces or five? "Suppose I have a nightmare and jump up. 'Hoo!' I'm screaming, and I rush through the window and my room is on the 13th floor."

Does he have nightmares? "No," said Roberto.

But the point is, he *might* have a nightmare sometime and, besides, when he is memorizing that room he is carefully noting the exact position of the telephone, which is vital. Suppose the phone rings. Roberto is able to pick up the receiver without opening his eyes. When he is forced to open his eyes, he explained, it frequently happens that tears well up in them and then he finds it perfectly impossible to fall asleep. Earlier in his career Roberto roomed with Gene Baker, but Baker snored. Roman Mejias and Alvin McBean, two others with whom he tried rooming, came in too late and awoke him by rattling hangers. So now, management having granted him privacy, he is able at least to hope for a little sleep before it is time to boop his back.

Surely the Lord cannot be punishing Roberto. A generous man and the devoted father of an infant son, he has been the sole support—since age 17—of his parents, a niece and nephew Pablo, to whom he recently gave an 18-foot cruiser. Before that he built a house for his parents. When pitcher Diomedes Olivo joined the Pirates at age 40, too late to make a pile, Roberto gave him half of all his banquet fees.

"I always try to lead the clean life," says Roberto. He does not smoke and rarely drinks, indulging himself only in his original milkshake recipes. His fruit cocktail milkshake consists of milk, fruit cocktail, the yolks of eggs, banana ice cream sugar, orange juice and crushed ice. "As much as you want of each," he says. "If I want a peach milkshake, I put a peach in it. If I want a pear milkshake, I put a pear in it."

Sighing and limping through his clean life, Roberto has acquired a reputation as baseball's champion hypochondriac, but his personal physician, Dr. Roberto Busó of San Juan, says, "I wouldn't call him a true hypochondriac, because he doesn't go to the extreme of just sitting down and brooding." Far from it. Roberto gallops across the outfield making acrobatic catches; with a bat in his hands he is all over the batter's box, spinning like a top when he swings. "I'm convinced of his weakness," says Dodger vice president Fresco Thompson. "Throw the best ball you've got right down the middle. If you pitch him high and outside, he'll rap a shot into rightfield. If you pitch him high and outside, he'll rap a shot into rightfield. If you throw one to him on one hop, he'll bounce it back through the mound and it'll probably take your pitcher and second baseman with it." In the past few years, alas, Roberto has become relatively orthodox. "If I have to jump three feet over my head to hit the ball, now I don't do it," he points out, deadly serious.

For all his exertions, Roberto *is* perpetually unfit, because, as Dr. Busó goes on to explain, he has a low threshold of pain, which causes him to take minor ailments for crippling debilitations. "If his back hurts he worries," says Dr. Busó, "and then it becomes a vicious circle, leading to more things. If he has a little diarrhea, he worries that he has a serious stomach difficulty." Roberto is endowed with an exceptionally supple musculature that enables him to race full speed into a base and then stop cold on it—which he likes to do instead of rounding it. But even he pulls muscles, twists ligaments and generally raises hell with his supple musculature that way. "It's his natural style," sighs Dr. Busó.

Still, ballplayers wink and giggle whenever Roberto announces that something or other is killing him; his problem is that he is seldom able to come up with a good, visible injury—say, a nice compound fracture with the bone sticking through the flesh. He spent four of his first five big-league years complaining of an agonizing back ailment that a battery of Pirate specialists could not track down. When a chiropractor, whom Roberto consulted in defiance of front-office warnings, told him he had a curved spine, a pair of legs that did not weigh the same and a couple of wayward disks, Roberto immediately saw why the physicians had overlooked such a mess. "They always X-rayed me lying down," he says. "They never X-rayed me standing up."

Then, a little later, there were chips floating in his elbow. Nobody doubted they were there, because Dr. George Bennett of Johns Hopkins said so, and promised he'd remove them at the end of the season. But when the time came—great Scott!—the chips had floated off somewhere. Dr. Bennett could not find them.

By all odds, Roberto's most exotic infirmity struck him after the 1964 season, when he fell desperately ill in Puerto Rico. Dr. Busó is not certain to this day whether Roberto had contracted autumnal malaria barnstorming in Santo Domingo or had picked up a systemic paratyphoid infection from the hogs on a small farm he owns, but Roberto himself knows what he had. "Both," he says.

His condition alternated daily between delirium and stupor, says Dr. Busó, and he lost 23 pounds. Alas, none of the Pirates had been in Puerto Rico and been an eyewitness. When Roberto reported to spring camp and began cracking line drives, all hands agreed that if he'd had malaria, they wanted some.

Clemente bridles at the suggestion that perhaps he only thought he had malaria. "If a Latin player or even an American Negro is sick," Roberto protests, "they say it is all in the head. Felípe Alou once went to his team doctor and the doctor said, 'You don't have anything.' So he went to a private doctor and the doctor said, 'You have a broken foot.' "

For Roberto, life in the big leagues has been a series of outrages. He is by no means anti-gringo—in fact, his relationship with Pittsburgh fans is one of the unwavering love stories of the national pastime—but, as a Latin, he feels persecuted. He is vociferously resentful of the fact that he is the least known, least sung superstar in baseball. "With my eyes blind I can throw to the base," he snaps. "I *know* that. If Mantle have the arm I have, you will put it in headlines 'cause he is an American. You never give me credit. How many players in history win three battling titles?" Not including Roberto, only 11 since 1876. "The sportswriters don't mention that. They ask me, 'What you think about dis, what you think about dat?' "

Refusing to underestimate himself, Roberto repeatedly has declared, "For me, I am the best ballplayer in the world." His words provide indignation on all sides, and his efforts to explain them merely stiffen the indignation. "I say, 'For *me*, for *myself!*'" he shouts. The Stateside listener, taking him literally, can only conclude that in Roberto's mind he does think he is better than Mays or Aaron or anyone else in the business, and the impression remains fixed until one happens across a man named Libertario Avilés, a worldly San Juan engineer who built Roberto's house and is one of his good friends. Says Avilés, "You have to understand that the Latin is touchy. If you say to me, 'Who is the best engineer in town?' I will say, 'For me, I am the best.' It is a Spanish saying, an expression of self-respect. You are not to underestimate yourself, but that does not mean you are to underestimate anyone else's ability."

Though Roberto's imperfect command of English has prevented him from explaining himself as clearly as Avilés does, he bristles that no amount of fluency would spare him from being portrayed in the American press as a stupid greenhorn. "I'm gonna tell you dis—it's one of the things that kill me most in the States," he says. "I know I don't speak as bad as they say I speak. I know that I don't have the good English pronunciation, because my tongue belong to Spanish, but I know where the verb, the article, the pronoun, whatever it is, go. I never in my life start a sentence with 'me,' but if I start it with 'I' the sportswriters say 'me'. 'Me Tarzan, you Jane.' "

For a fact, Roberto is typed, even by ballplayers who dress alongside him daily. Says one Pirate, "Just before he goes out and wears the ball out he'll say, 'Me no feel good today. Maybe me no play.' " During Roberto's one season of minor league ball, at Montreal in 1954, he understood practically no English. A player whom he had robbed of an extra-base hit called him an s.o.b., whereupon Roberto, assuming he was being complimented on the catch, replied, "Sank you." But he worked hard at his English. He still garbles an occasional phrase, says dis and dat somewhat more often than *this* and *that* and sometimes is stumped for the word he seeks, yet his conversation is perfectly intelligible. He resents coming off in print like an M-G-M Sioux chief, almost as much as he resented the Pittsburgh woman who once asked him if he wears a loincloth when home in Puerto Rico.

Clemente probably is wrong to think the Stateside press has neglected his talent because he's a Latin, but his batting averages of the past six years—.314, .351, .312, .320, .339 and .329—make it seem incredible that his name has not entered the elite Mays-Mantle-Aaron circle.

In the outfield he has done it all. Although not exceptionally swift, he is the master of the shoestring catch. ("I can run very fast bending down," he explains.) Only last season Roberto fielded a bunt—that's right, a bunt—that had rolled to shortstop. Shortstop Gene Alley had gone to cover third base but, as if from nowhere, Roberto dived headlong at the ball and, with his face in the dirt, threw out Houston base runner Walter Bond at third.

Scarcely credible? Nevertheless, the description suits Clemente's throwing arm, too. From Forbes Field's right-centerfield gate, a distance of about 420 feet, he once threw out Harvey Haddix at the plate, on one bounce. "I tear a ligament," he of course recalls.

Roberto's value, so far as Braves manager Bobby Bragan is concerned, is on a par with that of Hall of Fame players. "The best way to describe Roberto Clemente," says Bragan, "is to say, if he were playing in New York they'd be comparing him to DiMaggio. I would say his greatness is limited only by the fact that he does not hit the long ball consistently and by the fact that he is not playing in New York, or even Chicago or Los Angeles."

In an age of power, the fact that Clemente has never hit more than 23 home runs (and has never driven in more than 94 runs) weighs heavily against his prestige. There is no doubting that his muscular arms and outsize hands are capable of power, for one of his home runs—a shot over Wrigley Field's left-center bleachers—stands as one of the longest smashes ever hit out of the Cub ballpark. Yet because he plays half the schedule in spacious Forbes Field, where the man who guns for home runs undergoes traumatic revelations of inadequacy, Roberto wisely has tailored his style to the line drive and the hard ground ball hit through a hole. Thus he hit only 10 home runs last year, but he is certain he can hit 20 any season he pleases, Forbes Field notwithstanding.

"If I made up my mind I'm going to hit 20 homers this year," he bellows with indignation, "I bet you any amount of money I can hit 20." A change of style would do the trick, he claims. But what sort of change? Roberto becomes tight-lipped. He is one of baseball's most sinister practitioners of intrigue.

"Nothing," he replies. "A little change in the hands, that's all. I don't want to tell you what it is."

In baseball any player who obviously exaggerates simple moves is labeled a hot dog, and on two counts Clemente seems to fall within this definition. First, he not only favors the basket catch made famous by Mays but lends to it an added element of risk by allowing fly balls to drop below his waist before catching them. Second, when fielding routine singles he often underhands the ball to second base in a great, looping arc instead of pegging it on a line.

Hotly defending himself, Clemente points out that both the low basket catch and the underhand throw are nothing more than natural habits carried over from his youth, for until he was 17 he was a softball player, not a baseball player. Not until a softball coach named Roberto Marin persuaded Clemente that he might earn big money in baseball did he turn to the sport. From the outset he was a natural wonder, and yet a problem.

The Dodgers signed him for a $10,000 bonus but were not quite sure what to do with him. At the time, if a first-year player who received more than $4,000 was sent to the minors, he not only had to stay there for a full season but would be eligible to be drafted by another club in November. The Dodgers could have protected Clemente from the draft by making room for him on their own roster, but they were gunning for a third straight pennant and felt that an untested 19-year-old would be dead weight on their backs. In the end Walter O'Malley's brain trust assigned Roberto to Montreal but told the Montreal manager, Max Macon, to hide him—that is, play him sparingly lest enemy bird dogs take a fancy to him.

Roberto recalls that '54 season with a shudder. "If I struck out, I stay in the lineup," he says. "If I played well, I'm benched. One day I hit three triples and the next day I was benched. Another time they took me out for a pinch hitter with the bases loaded in the first inning. Much of the time I was used only as a pinch runner or for defense. I didn't know what was going on, and I was confused and almost mad enough to go home. That's what they wanted me to do. That way nobody could draft me."

By religiously discomposing him, Max Macon held Roberto's batting average to .257, but a Pirate scout named Clyde Sukeforth was onto Macon's act. One day in Richmond, before a Montreal-Richmond game, Sukeforth had seen Clemente cut loose with a couple of eye-popping practice throws. He stayed in Richmond four days. Macon countered by keeping Clemente on the bench except for two pinch-hitting appearances, but Sukeforth saw enough of Clemente in batting and fielding practice to be satisfied.

"Take care of our boy," he said to Macon as he prepared to leave town. "You're kidding," Macon said, trying a last-ditch con. "You don't want that kid." Sukeforth smiled and said, "Now, Max, I've known you for a good many years. We're a cinch to finish last and get first draft choice, so don't let our boy get into any trouble."

At $4,000 Sukeforth had the steal of the century.

FROM THE Dodger viewpoint, such setbacks are all part of the game, but for reasons the Dodgers had no knowledge of, Roberto has regarded their failure to protect him from the draft as a betrayal of trust. The Dodgers had been his boyhood favorites. Right after he had made a gentleman's agreement to accept their $10,000 bonus the Braves offered him $30,000, he says, but he turned it down. "It was hard," Roberto says, "but I said I gave the Dodgers my word." As he sees it, the Dodgers took a faithful servant and gambled with him in the draft pool as they would with a handful of casino chips. Teaching the Dodger front office the importance of ethics, Roberto in the past five seasons has hit .375 against the pitching staff of Koufax, Drysdale, Osteen, Podres and company. The only way to pitch him, guesses Koufax hyperbolically, is to roll him the ball.

By now one thing should be clear to Pittsburgh's opponents. For their own good, they ought to warm the cockles of Clemente's heart with praise, commiserate with him when he has a hangnail, elect him to the All-Star team with a landslide vote, punch any sportswriter who does not quote him as if he were Churchill on the floor of Parliament and campaign for him to receive his first Most Valuable Player award. "If I would be happy I would be a very bad player," Roberto says. "With me, when I get mad it puts energy in my body."

This business of failing to elect him to the All-Star team (as was the case last year when the malaria and/or paratyphoid caused Roberto to get off to a poor start) only assured that he would win another batting championship. Moreover, he cannot forget that in 1960, when he batted .314 and the Pirates won the pennant, he finished a shabby eighth in the voting for MVP. Dick Groat hit .325 for the Pirates that year, leading the league and winning the MVP trophy, but Clemente drove in 94 runs to Groat's 50, and demands to know why, if he was not Pittsburgh's most valuable player, he was the one the pitchers most often knocked down? When told that Groat sparked the team, Roberto proves that his American idiom is on the upgrade by retorting, "Sparked, my foot!" The point is, however, that he hit .351 that following year. Lest he ever simmer down and acquire a happy disposition, his teammates call him No Votes.

Ignored and rebuffed by baseball's In crowd, Clemente nevertheless leads all popularity polls where it counts—with the paying customers in Pittsburgh. They seem to grasp that if he is a man who covets recognition, he would rather have it from Joe Doaks than from all the members of the Baseball Writers Association of America. "Winning the World Series in 1960 was not the biggest thrill I ever have in my life," he said not long ago, looking out on the lights of San Juan from his veranda. "The biggest thrill was when I come out of the clubhouse after the last Series game and saw all those thousands of fans in the streets. It was something you cannot describe. I did not feel like a player at the time. I feel like one of those persons, and I walked the streets among them."

Such utterances by Clemente are not a pose for public consumption. Behind closed doors he urged his teammates to set their sights high, for the novel reason that "we owe these people another pennant." Says Pitcher Bob Friend, a Pirate until traded to the Yankees in December: "He gets pretty windy on the subject, and you wonder how to turn him off. A lot of players leave the game feeling the world owes them a living, but Clemente's an exception to that rule. He knows what baseball's done for him, and he expresses his appreciation."

Puerto Ricans, meanwhile, hold Clemente in an esteem they otherwise tender only to cellist Pablo Casals and elder statesman Luis Muñoz Marin. "He is a glory to the island," says a nightclub guitarist named Frankie Ramirez, whose sentiments are echoed from San Juan to Mayagüez. One recent morning Roberto and his engineer friend, Libertario Avilés, drove into the countryside east of San Juan. Avilés steered his Wildcat convertible past the old sugarcane fields that were now being bulldozed for factory sites. Roberto's father had owned a few acres once and at the same time had worked as a foreman of a great plantation and with his wife had run a grocery and meat market for the workers. "My mother and father, they worked like racehorses for me," said Roberto. He has the mid-Victorian morality of the old Spanish families, and his sense of obligation runs strong. "Anybody who have the opportunity to serve their country or their island

and don't, God should punish them. If you can be good, why you should be bad?"

The Wildcat coursed through the seaside village of Fajardo and, not far beyond, turned up a dirt road where lay a dream that had possessed Roberto's emotions all winter. He was negotiating with the government to lease a lush 20 acres on which he plans to construct a sports camp for boys, plowing the profits into camp scholarships for the underprivileged. He will call the camp Sports City. Tramping through the seaside forest where Sports City will rise, Roberto explained his ambition: "We are known as a good sportsmanship people, and I'm proud to be part of that recognition. But today life is moving too fast for these kids. You see 15-year-old boys and girls holding hands. They hang out on street corners. Maybe if I can keep them interested in sports they will not always be talking about stealing and about gangster movies. I'm proud to do good for my island."

As Roberto spoke of his dreams, he seemed no longer the worrier on whose lips are complaints of headaches, backaches, sore feet, sore arms and tired blood. "I like to work with kids," he said. But then he added with a frown, "I'd like to work with kids all the time, if I live long enough."

ॐ

The Mick Always Swung From the Heels

BY RICHARD HOFFER

Upon Mickey Mantle's passing in 1995, SI contemplated the legacy of the greatest player on the last great team.

ICKEY MANTLE, WITH HIS DEATH SUNDAY AT 63, passes from these pages forever and becomes the property of anthropologists, people who can more properly put the calipers to celebrity, who can more accurately track the force of personality. We can't do it anymore, couldn't really do it to begin with. He batted this, hit that. You can look it up. Hell, we do all the time. But there's nothing in our library, in all those numbers, that explains how Mantle moves so smoothly from baseball history into national legend, a country's touchstone, the lopsided grin on our society.

He wasn't the greatest player who ever lived, not even of his time perhaps. He was a centerfielder of surprising swiftness, a switch-hitter of heart-stopping power, and he was given to spectacle: huge home runs (his team, the New York Yankees, invented the tape-measure home run for him); huge seasons (.353, 52 HRs, 130 RBIs to win the Triple Crown in 1956); one World Series after another (12 in his first 14 seasons). Yet, for one reason or another, he never became Babe Ruth or Joe DiMaggio—or, arguably, even Willie Mays, his exact contemporary.

But for generations of men, he's the guy, has been the guy, will always be the guy. And what does that mean exactly? A woman beseeches Mantle, who survived beyond his baseball career as a kind of corporate greeter, to make an appearance, to surprise her husband. Mantle materializes at some cocktail party, introductions are made, and the husband weeps in the presence of such fantasy made flesh. It means that, exactly.

It's easy to account, at least partly, for the durability and depth of his fame: He played on baseball's most famous team during the game's final dominant era. From Mantle's rookie season in 1951—the lead miner's son signed out of Commerce, Okla., for $1,100—to his injury-racked final year in 1968, baseball was still the preeminent game in the country. This was baseball B.C. (Before Cable), and a nation's attention was not scattered come World Series time. Year in, year out, men and boys in every corner of the country were given to understand during this autumnal rite that there really was only one baseball team and that there really was only one player: No. 7, talked with a twang, knocked the ball a country mile. But it was more than circumstance that fixed Mantle in the national psyche; he did hit 18 World Series home runs, a record, over the course of 65 of the most watched games of our lives.

Even knowing that, acknowledging the pin-striped pedigree, the fascination still doesn't add up. If he was a pure talent, he was not, as we found out, a pure spirit. But to look upon his youthful mug today, three decades after he played, is to realize how uncluttered our memories of him are. Yes, he was a confessed drunk; yes, he shorted his potential—he himself said so. And still, looking at the slightly uplifted square jaw, all we see is America's romance with boldness, its celebration of muscle, a continent's comfort in power during a time when might did make right. Mantle was the last great player on the last great team in the last great country, a postwar civilization that was booming and confident, not a trouble in the world.

Of course, even had he not reflected the times, Mantle would have been walking Americana. His career was storybook stuff, hewing more to our ideas of myth than any player's since Ruth. Spotted playing shortstop on the Baxter Springs Whiz Kids, he was delivered from a rural obscurity into America's distilled essence of glamour. One year Mantle is dropping 400 feet into the earth, very deep into Oklahoma, to mine lead on his father's crew, another he's spilling drinks with Whitey Ford and Billy Martin at the Copa.

A lesson reaffirmed: Anything can happen to anybody in this country, so long as they're daring in their defeats and outsized in victory. Failure is forgiven of the big swingers, in whom even foolishness is flamboyant. Do you remember Mantle in Pittsburgh in the 1960 Series, twice whiffing in Game 1 and then, the next day, crushing two? Generations of men still do. The world will always belong to those who swing from the heels.

Still, Mantle's grace was mostly between the lines; he developed no particular bonds beyond his teammates, and he established no popularity outside of baseball. As he was dying from liver cancer, none of the pre-tributes remarked much on his charm. And, as he was dying from a disease that many have presumed was drinking-related, there was a revisionist cast to the remembrances. Maybe he wasn't so much fun after all.

But, back then, he most certainly was. Drunkenness had a kind of high-life cachet in the '50s: It was manly, inasmuch as you were a stand-up guy who could be counted on to perform the next afternoon, and it was glamorous. Down the road, as Mantle would later confess from the other side of rehabilitation, it was merely stupid. But palling around with Billy and Whitey—just boys, really, they all had little boys' names—it amounted to low-grade mischief. Whatever harm was being done to families and friends, it was a small price to pay for the excitement conferred upon a workaday nation.

In any event, we don't mind our heroes flawed, or even doomed. Actually, our interest in Mantle was probably piqued by his obvious destiny, the ruin he often foretold. As a Yankee he was never a whole person, having torn up his knee for the first time in his first World Series in '51. Thereafter, increasingly, he played in gauze and pain, his prodigal blasts heroically back-lit by chronic injury. But more: At the hospital after that '51 incident, Mantle learned that his father, Mutt, admitted to the same hospital that same day, was dying of Hodgkin's disease. It was a genetic devastation that had claimed every Mantle male before the age of 40. The black knowledge of this looming end informed everything Mickey did; there was little time, and every event had to be performed on a grand scale, damn the consequences. Everything was excused.

As we all know, it didn't end with that kind of drama. It was Billy, the third of Mantle's four sons, who came down with Hodgkin's, and who later died of a heart attack at 36. Mickey lived much longer, prospering in an era of nostalgia, directionless in golf and drinking, coasting on a fame that confounded him. (Why was this man, just introduced to him, weeping?)

Then Mantle, who might forever have been embedded in a certain culture, square-jawed and unchanged, did a strange thing. Having failed to die in a way that might have satisfied the mythmakers, he awoke with a start and

262   *The Mick Always Swung from the Heels*

checked himself into the Betty Ford Center. This was only a year and a half ago, and, of course, it was way too late almost any way you figure it. Still, his remorse seemed genuine. The waste seemed to gall him, and his anger shook the rest of us.

The generations of men who watched him play baseball, flipped for his cards or examined every box score must now puzzle out the attraction he held. The day he died there was the usual rush for perspective and the expected sweep through the Yankee organization. They said the usual things. But former teammate Bobby Murcer reported that he had talked to the Mick before he had gone into the hospital the final time—neither a liver transplant nor chemotherapy could arrest the cancer or stop his pain— and Mantle, first thing, asked how a fund-raiser for children affected by the Oklahoma City bombing was going, something he and Murcer, also from Oklahoma, were involved in. It was odd, like the sudden decision to enter rehab and rescue his and his family's life, and it didn't really square with our idea of Mantle.

But let's just say you were of this generation of men: that you once had been a kid growing up in the '50s, on some baseball team in Indiana, and you remember stitching a No. 7 on the back of your KIRCHNER'S PHARMACY T-shirt, using red thread and having no way of finishing off a stitch, meaning your hero's number would unravel indefinitely and you would have to do it over and over, stupid and unreformed in your idolatry. And today here's this distant demigod, in his death, taking human shape. What would you think now?

The Left Arm
Of God

BY TOM VERDUCCI

*He was a consummate artist on the mound, the most dominant
player of his time, yet he shunned fame and always put team above self.
On the field or off, Sandy Koufax was pitcher perfect.*

H E SAT IN THE SAME BOOTH EVERY TIME. IT WAS
always the one in back, farthest from the door. The
trim, darkly handsome man would come alone, without his wife, nearly every morning at six o'clock for
breakfast at Dick's Diner in Ellsworth, Maine, about 14 miles from their
home. He often wore one of those red-and-black-checkered shirts you expect to see in Maine, though he wasn't a hunter. He might not have shaved
that morning. He would walk past the long counter up front, the one with
the swivel stools that, good Lord, gave complete strangers license to strike
up a conversation. He preferred the clearly delineated no-trespassing zone
of a booth. He would rest those famously large hands on the Formica table-
top, one of those mini-jukeboxes to his left and give his order to Annette, the
waitress, in a voice as soft and smooth as honey.

He came so often that the family who ran the diner quickly stopped
thinking of him as Sandy Koufax, one of the greatest pitchers who ever
lived. They thought of him the way Koufax strived all his life to be thought
of, as something better even than a famous athlete: He was a regular.

Dick Anderson and his son Richard, better known as Bub, might glance up from their chores when Koufax walked in, but that was usually all. One time Bub got him to autograph a napkin but never talked baseball with him. Annette, Bub's sister, always worked the section with that back booth. For three years Koufax came to the diner and not once did he volunteer information to her about his life or his career. It was always polite small talk. Neighborly. Regular.

Koufax was 35, five years since his last pitch, in 1966, when he came eagerly, even dreamily, to Maine, the back booth of America. He had seen a photo spread in *Look* magazine about the Down East country homestead of a man named Blakely Babcock, a 350-pound Burpee Seed salesman, gentleman farmer and gadfly whom everybody called Tiny. Tiny would invite neighbors and friends over for cookouts and dinner parties, during which he liked to consume great quantities of food and then, laughing, rub his huge belly and bellow to his wife, "So, what's for dinner, Alberta?" Tiny's North Ellsworth farmhouse caught Koufax's fancy at just about the same time one of his wife's friends was renovating her farmhouse in Maine. Wouldn't it be perfect, Koufax thought, to live quietly, almost anonymously, in an old farmhouse just like Tiny's?

Alberta Babcock was pulling a hot tin of sweet-smelling blueberry muffins from the oven when Koufax first saw the place in person, and the old Cape-style house was filled with so many flowers that it looked like a watercolor come to life. Koufax was sold, and on Oct. 4, 1971, Sanford and Anne Koufax of Los Angeles, as they signed the deed, took out a 15-year, $15,000 mortgage from Penobscot Savings Bank and bought what was known as Winkumpaugh Farm from Blakely and Alberta Babcock for about $30,000. A cord was cut. The rest of Sandy Koufax's life had begun.

The Babcocks had lived in the farmhouse since 1962, but no one was exactly sure how old the place was. Property records were lost to a fire at Ellsworth City Hall in 1933, and records from 1944 list the farmhouse's age even then only as "old." Nestled on the side of a small mountain off a dusty dirt road called Happytown Road and around the corner from another called Winkumpaugh Road, the farmhouse was the perfect setting for a man hoping to drop out of sight, even if that man was a beloved American icon who mastered the art of pitching as well as anyone who ever threw a baseball. A man so fiercely modest and private that while at the University of Cincinnati on a basketball scholarship, he didn't tell his parents back in Brooklyn that he was also on the baseball team. The man whose mother requested one of the first copies of his 1966 autobiography,

Koufax, so she could find out something about her son. ("You never told me anything," she said to him.) The man who in 1968, two years after retiring with three Cy Young Awards, four no-hitters and five ERA titles, mentioned nothing of his baseball career upon meeting a pretty young woman named Anne who was redecorating her parents' Malibu beach house. Koufax did offer to help her paint, though. It wasn't until several days later that she learned his identity—and he learned hers: She was the daughter of actor Richard Widmark. They were married six months later in her father's West Los Angeles home in front of about a dozen people.

The last two years that Anne and Sandy Koufax lived at Winkumpaugh Farm were the first in his life when he was bound by neither school nor work. After commuting from Maine during the summer of 1972 for his sixth season as a television commentator for NBC, he quit with four years left on his contract. He loathed the work. He could tell you every pitch thrown by every pitcher in a game without having written anything down, but there was a problem: He didn't like to talk about himself. At a meeting before Game 5 of the 1970 World Series, fellow announcer Joe Garagiola noted that Cincinnati's starting pitcher, Jim Merritt, had an injured arm. "I said, 'Sandy, what a perfect thing to talk about. That's what you had, too.'" Garagiola says. "But he said he didn't want to talk about himself. He wouldn't do it."

"Every time he had to leave Maine to work one of those games, it broke his heart," says MaJo Keleshian, a friend and former neighbor who attended Sarah Lawrence College with Anne. She still lives without a television on land she and her husband bought from Koufax. "He was very happy here. He came here to be left alone."

Since then only his address has changed—and many times, at that. Joe DiMaggio, baseball's other legendary protector of privacy, was practically Rodmanesque compared with Koufax. DiMaggio was regal, having acquired even the stiff-handed wave of royalty. We watched the graying of DiMaggio as he played TV pitchman and public icon. Koufax is a living James Dean, the aura of his youth frozen in time; he has grayed without our even knowing it. He is a sphinx, except that he doesn't want anyone to try to solve his riddle.

Koufax was the kind of man boys idolized, men envied, women swooned over and rabbis thanked, especially when he refused to pitch Game 1 of the 1965 World Series because it fell on Yom Kippur. And when he was suddenly, tragically, done with baseball, he slipped into a life nearly monastic in its privacy.

One question comes to mind: Why? Why did he turn his back on Fame and Fortune, the twin sirens of celebrity? Why did the most beloved athlete of his time carve out a quiet life—the very antithesis of the American dream at the close of the century? For the answer I will go searching for the soul of Sandy Koufax, which seems as mysterious as the deepest Maine woods on a moonless night.

BOB BALLARD is a retiree in Vero Beach, Fla., who works part time as a security guard at Dodgertown, the sleepiest spring training site in all of baseball. Sometime around 1987 he told the secretary who worked for Peter O'Malley, then the owner of the Dodgers, how much he would enjoy getting an autograph from Koufax for his birthday. A few days later Koufax, working for the Dodgers as a roving pitching instructor, handed Ballard an autographed ball and said, "Happy birthday."

Every year since then, on or about Ballard's birthday, Koufax has brought the old man an autographed ball. Koufax delivered on schedule this year for Ballard's 79th birthday. "He's a super, super guy," says Ballard. "Very courteous. A real gentleman. A lot nicer than these players today."

It is a lovely day for golf. I am standing in the tiny pro shop of the Bucksport (Maine) Golf Club, a rustic, nine-hole track. The parking lot is gravel. Even the rates are quaint: $15 to play nine holes, $22 for 18, and you are instructed to play the white tees as the front nine, then the blue tees as the back nine. There is no valet parking, no tiny pyramids of Titleists on the scrubby range, no MEMBERS ONLY signs, no attitude. This is Koufax's kind of place. I am standing in the imprint of his golf spikes, a quarter-century removed. He was a member of the Bucksport Golf Club, one of its more enthusiastic members.

It wasn't enough that he play golf, he wanted to be good enough to win amateur tournaments. Koufax was working on the engine of a tractor one day when a thought came to him about a certain kind of grip for a golf club. He dropped his tools, dashed into his machine shop, fiddled with a club and then raced off to the Bucksport range. He was still wearing dungaree shorts and a grease-splattered shirt when he arrived. "That's how dedicated to the game he was," says Gene Bowden, one of his old playing partners.

Koufax diligently whittled his handicap to a six and entered the 1973 Maine State Amateur. He advanced to the championship flights by draining a 30-foot putt on the 18th hole. He missed the next cut, though, losing on the last hole of a playoff.

Koufax is exacting in every pursuit. Ron Fairly, one of his Dodgers roommates, would watch with exasperation as Koufax, dressed suavely for dinner in glossy alligator shoes, crisply pressed slacks and a fruit-colored alpaca sweater, would fuss over each hair in his sideburns. "Reservation's in 15 minutes, and it's a 20-minute ride," Fairly would announce, and Koufax would go right on trimming until his sideburns were in perfect alignment.

He brought that same meticulousness to Maine. It wasn't enough to dabble in carpentry and home electronics—he built and installed a sound system throughout the house. It wasn't enough to cook—he became a gourmet cook, whipping up dishes not by following recipes but by substituting ingredients and improvising by feel. Later in life it wasn't enough to jog; he ran a marathon. He didn't just take up fishing, he moved to Idaho for some of the best salmon fishing in the world. He defines himself by the fullness of his life and the excellence he seeks in every corner of it, not the way the rest of the word defines him: through the narrow prism of his career as a pitcher. "I think he pitched for the excellence of it," Keleshian says. "He didn't set out to beat someone or make anyone look bad. He used himself as his only measure of excellence. And he was that way in everything he did. He was a fabulous cook, but he was almost never quite satisfied. He'd say, Ah, it needs a little salt or a little oregano, or something. Once in a great while he'd say, Ah-ha! That's it!"

Walt Disney, John Wayne, Kirk Douglas, Daryl Zanuck and all the other Hollywood stars who held Dodgers season tickets when Koufax was the biggest star in America never came to Winkumpaugh Farm. The fans never came, either, though a fat sack of fan mail arrived every week, even seven years after he last threw a pitch. The place was perfect, all right. He could move about without fuss, without having to talk about his least favorite subject: himself. "He did say once that he'd rather not talk baseball and his career," Bowden says. "And we never did."

"WHEN HIDEO NOMO was getting really, really big, Sandy told me, 'He'd better learn to like room service,'" O'Malley says. "That's how Sandy handled the attention." Koufax almost never left his hotel room in his final two seasons for the Dodgers. It wasn't enough that he move to a creaky, charmingly flawed farmhouse in Maine with a leaky basement, he quickly bought up almost 300 acres adjacent to it.

Not even the serenity of Maine, though, could quell Koufax's wanderlust. After three years he decided the winters were too long and too cold. The farmhouse needed constant work. His stepfather took ill in California. Koufax sold Winkumpaugh Farm on July 22, 1974, leaving for the warmer but still rural setting of Templeton, Calif., in San Luis Obispo County.

Koufax is 63, in terrific shape and, thanks to shoulder surgery a few years back, probably still able to get hitters out. (In his 50s Koufax was pitching in a fantasy camp when a camper scoffed after one of his pitches, "Is that all you've got?" Koufax's lips tightened and his eyes narrowed—just about all the emotion he would ever show on the mound—and he unleashed a heater that flew damn near 90 mph.)

The romance with Anne ended with a divorce in the early '80s. He remarried a few years later, this time to a fitness enthusiast who, like Anne, had a passion for the arts. That marriage ended in divorce last winter. Friends say Koufax is delighted to be on his own again. Says Lou Johnson, a former Dodgers teammate, "He has an inner peace that's really deep-rooted. I wish I had that."

He is the child of a broken marriage who rejected everything associated with his father, including his name. Sanford Braun was three years old when Jack and Evelyn Braun divorced, and his contact with Jack all but ended about six years later when Jack remarried and stopped sending alimony payments. Evelyn, an accountant, married Irving Koufax, an attorney, a short time later. "When I speak of my father," he wrote in his autobiography, "I speak of Irving Koufax, for he has been to me everything a father could be." Koufax rarely spoke to Jack Braun, and not at all during his playing days. When the Dodgers played at Shea Stadium, Jack would sit a few rows behind the visitors' dugout and cheer for the son who neither knew nor cared that he was there.

Now there is but one Koufax bearing that name. He has no children, no immediate family—both his mother and stepfather are deceased. The death of his only sibling, a sister, in 1997, had a profound impact on a man who has struggled to deal with the deaths of friends and other players from his era. "People react to death differently," O'Malley says. "Sandy takes a death very, very, very hard."

He has a small circle of close friends, and many other buddies who always seem to be one or two phone numbers behind him. "It sounds odd, but he's very home-oriented," Keleshian says, "yet very nomadic."

His list of home addresses since he stopped playing baseball reads like a KOA campground directory: North Ellsworth, Maine; Templeton and Santa Barbara, Calif.; Idaho; Oregon (where his second wife ran a gallery); North Carolina (where he and his second wife kept horses); and Vero Beach—not to mention extensive trips to Hawaii, New Zealand and Europe. This spring he was looking for a new place to spend the summer and once again had his eye on rural New England. "He doesn't say much about what he's up to," says Bobby McCarthy, a friend who owns a Vero Beach restaurant that Koufax prefers to frequent when it's closed. "We'll be sitting in the restaurant in the morning, and that night I'll see he's at a Mets game in New York. And he hadn't said anything that morning about going there. But that's Sandy."

At 8:30 on a lovely Sunday morning in March, I attend a chapel service in the Sandy Koufax Room at Dodgertown. Players and coaches in their fabulously white Dodgers uniforms are there, but not Koufax. The Dodgers give glory to Jesus Christ every Sunday in a conference room named for the greatest Jewish ballplayer who ever lived. Outside the room is a picture of a young Koufax, smiling, as if he is in on the joke.

DON SUTTON is a native of Clio, Ala., who reached the big leagues at age 21 in 1966, which is to say he got there just in time. His first season in the majors was Koufax's last. Says Sutton, "I saw how he dressed, how he tipped, how he carried himself and knew that's how a big leaguer was supposed to act. He was a star who didn't feel he was a star. That's a gift not many people have."

Tommy Hutton, who grew up in Los Angeles, also made his big league debut for the Dodgers in '66, entering the ninth inning at first base as Koufax finished off the Pirates 5–1 on Sept. 16. Says Hutton, now a broadcaster for the Marlins, "I'll never forget this. After the game he came up to me and said, 'Congratulations.' Ever since then, I've always made it a point to congratulate a guy when he gets into his first game."

I AM STANDING in a tunnel under the stands behind home plate at Dodger Stadium on a clear summer night in 1998. Koufax is about 75 feet in front of me, seated on a folding chair on the infield while the Dodgers honor Sutton with the retirement of his number before a game against the Braves. When the program ends, Sutton and all his guests—former Dodgers Ron Cey and Steve Garvey among them—march past me toward an elevator that will take them to a stadium suite. All except Koufax. He is gone. Vanished. I find out later that as soon as the ceremony was over, he arose from his chair, walked briskly into the Dodgers dugout and kept right on going into the team parking lot and off into the night. "That's Sandy," said one team official. "We call him the Ghost."

I am searching for an apparition. I never saw Koufax pitch, never felt the spell he held over America. I had just turned six when Koufax walked into the Sansui room of the Regent Beverly Wilshire Hotel on Nov. 18, 1966, to announce his retirement from baseball. To have missed his brilliance heightens the fascination. For me he is black-and-white newsreel footage shot from high behind home plate, and an inexhaustible supply of statistics that border on the absurd. A favorite: Every time he took the mound, Koufax was twice as likely to throw a shutout as he was to hit a batter.

Koufax was 30 years old when he quit. Women at the press conference cried. Reporters applauded him, then lined up for his autograph. The world, including his teammates, was shocked. In the last 26 days of his career, including a loss in the 1966 World Series, Koufax started seven times, threw five complete-game wins and had a 1.07 ERA. He clinched the pennant for Los Angeles for the second straight year with a complete game on two days rest. Everyone knew he was pitching with traumatic arthritis in his left elbow, but how bad could it be when he pitched like that?

It was this bad: Koufax couldn't straighten his left arm—it was curved like a parenthesis. He had to have a tailor shorten the left sleeve on all his coats. Use of his left arm was severely limited when he wasn't pitching. On bad days he'd have to bend his neck to get his face closer to his left hand so that he could shave. And on the worst days he had to shave with his right hand. He still held his fork in his left hand, but sometimes he had to bend closer to the plate to get the food into his mouth.

His elbow was shot full of cortisone several times a season. His stomach was always queasy from the cocktail of anti-inflammatories he swallowed before and after games, which he once said made him "half-high on the mound." He soaked his elbow in an ice bath for 30 minutes after each game, his arm encased in an inner tube to protect against frostbite. And even then his arm would swell an inch. He couldn't go on like this, not when his doctors could not rule out the possibility that he was risking permanent damage to his arm.

Not everyone was shocked when Koufax quit. In August 1965 he told Phil Collier, a writer for *The San Diego Union-Tribune* to meet him in a room off the Dodgers' clubhouse. Koufax and Collier often sat next to each other on the team's charter flights, yapping about politics, the economy or literature. "Next year's going to be my last year," Koufax told Collier. "The damn thing's all swelled up. And I hate taking the pills. They slow my reactions. I'm afraid someone's going to hit a line drive that hits me in the head."

Koufax didn't tell anyone else, and he made Collier promise not to write the story. So they shared that little secret throughout the 1966 season. When the Dodgers went to Atlanta, Collier whispered to Koufax, "Last time here for you." And that is exactly how Koufax pitched that season, as if he would never pass this way again. He won a career-high 27 games, pushing his record in his final six seasons to 129–47. He was 11–3 in his career in 1–0 games. In 1965 and '66 he was 53–17 for the club that scored fewer runs than all but two National League teams.

"He's the greatest pitcher I ever saw," says Hall of Famer Ernie Banks. "I can still see that big curveball. It had a great arc on it, and he never bounced it in the dirt. Sandy's curve had a lot more spin than anybody else's—it spun like a fastball coming out of his hand—and he had the fastball of a pure strikeout pitcher. It jumped up at the end. The batter would swing half a foot under it. Most of the time we knew what was coming, because he held his hands closer to his head when he threw a curveball, but it didn't matter. Even though he was tipping off his pitches, you still couldn't hit him."

Koufax was so good, he once taped a postgame radio show with Vin Scully before the game. He was so good, the relief pitchers treated the night before his starts the way a sailor treats shore leave. On one rare occasion in which Koufax struggled to go his usual nine innings—he averaged 7.64 per start from '61 to '66—manager Walter Alston visited his pitcher while a hungover Bob Miller warmed in the bullpen.

"How do you feel, Sandy?" Alston asked.

"I'll be honest with you, Skip," Koufax said. "I feel a hell of a lot better than the guy you've got warming up."

On Nov. 17, 1966, Collier came home from watching the Ice Capades and was greeted with this message from his babysitter: "Mr. Koufax has been trying to call you for a couple of hours." Collier knew exactly what it was about. He called Koufax.

"I'm calling the wire services in the morning," Koufax told him. "Is there anything you need from me now?"

"Sandy," Collier said, "I wrote that story months ago. It's in my desk drawer. All I have to do is make a call and tell them to run it."

Says Collier, "It was the biggest story I'll ever write. They ran it across the top of Page One with a big headline like it was the end of World War II."

I HAVE GOTTEN ahold of Koufax's home telephone number in Vero Beach, but I do not dare dial it. Even from afar I can feel the strength of this force field he has put around himself. To puncture it with a surprise phone call means certain disaster. I have read that Koufax so hated the intrusions of the telephone during his playing days that he once took to stashing it in his oven. Buzzie Bavasi, the Dodgers' general manager, would have to send telegrams to his house saying, "Please call."

I don't call. I am an archeologist—dig I must, but with the delicate touch of brushes and hand tools. I enlist the help of Koufax's friends. Now I understand why people I talk to about Koufax are apprehensive. They ask, Does Sandy know you're doing this story? (Yes.) It's as if speaking about him is itself a violation of his code of honor.

There is a 58-year-old health-care worker in Portchester, N.Y., named David Saks who attended Camp Chi-Wan-Da in Kingston, N.Y., in the summer of 1954. Koufax, who is from Brooklyn, was his counselor. "He was this handsome, strapping guy, a great athlete who had professional scouts trying to sign him," Saks says. "I was 13. He was 18. We all were in awe of him. But even then there were signs that he wanted people to avoid fussing about him to the nth degree."

Saks needed a day to think before agreeing to share two photographs he has from Camp Chi-Wan-Da that include the teenage Koufax. "Knowing how he is . . . ," Saks explains. Saks has neither seen nor spoken to Koufax in 45 years. He does, however, have recurring dreams about happy reunions with him.

In Vero Beach, where Koufax spends much of his time now, the townsfolk choose not to speak his name when they come upon him in public. They will say, "Hello, Mr. K.," when they run into him at the post office or, "Hello, my good friend," rather than tip off a tourist and risk creating one of those moments Koufax detests.

"Sandy has a quiet, productive way about him," says Garagiola, president of the Baseball Assistance Team (BAT), a charity that helps former players in medical or financial straits. Garagiola sometimes calls Koufax to ask him to speak with former players who are particularly hurting. "He can't really understand that," Garagiola says. "He's got a great streak of modesty. He'll say, 'What do they want to talk to me for?' He is a Hall of Famer in every way. He'll make an impact. You won't know it and I won't know it, but the guy he's helping will know it. Above anything else, I'll remember him for his feelings for fellow players."

There was an outfielder named Jim Barbieri who joined the Dodgers during the 1966 pennant race. He was so nervous that he would talk to himself in the shower, and the pressure so knotted his stomach that he once threw up in the locker room. One day Koufax motioned toward Barbieri in the dugout and said to Fairly, "I have a responsibility to guys like him. If I pitch well from here on out, I can double that man's income." Koufax, who was referring to World Series bonus money, went 8–2 the rest of the season. From 1963 to '66 he was 14–2 in September, with a 1.55 ERA.

Earlier in that 1966 season a television network offered Koufax $25,000 to allow their cameras to trail him on and off the field. Koufax said he would do it for $35,000, and only if that money was divided so that every Dodgers player, coach and trainer received $1,000.

Koufax attends Garagiola's BAT dinner in New York City every winter, and always draws the biggest crowd among the many Hall of Famers who sign autographs during the cocktail hour. "I grew up in Brooklyn," says Lester Marks of Ernst and Young, which secured the Koufax table this year. "I went to Ebbets Field all the time. I'm 52. I thought seeing Sandy Koufax pitch was the thrill of a lifetime, but meeting him as an adult was an even bigger thrill. My guests were shocked at what a down-to-earth gentleman he is."

After this year's dinner I walked through the crowded ballroom toward Koufax's table, only to see him hustle to a secured area on the dais. He posed for pictures with the Toms River, N.J., Little League world champions. Then he was gone, this time for a night of refreshments in Manhattan with New York Mets pitcher Al Leiter, as close to a protégé as Koufax has in baseball.

I should mention that I did meet Sandy Koufax a few years ago, before I embarked on this quest to find out what makes him run. I was at Dodgertown, standing next to the row of six pitching mounds adjacent to the Dodgers' clubhouse. "Sacred ground," as former Dodgers pitcher Claude Osteen calls it, seeing as it was here that Branch Rickey hung his famous strings, forming the borders of a strike zone at which every Dodgers pitcher from Newcombe to Koufax to Sutton to Hershiser took aim. (Koufax was so wild as a rookie that pitching coach Joe Becker took him to a mound behind the clubhouse so he would not embarrass himself in front of teammates and fans.) Tan and lean, Koufax looked as if he had just come in from the boardwalk to watch the Los Angeles pitchers throw. He was dressed in sandals, a short pair of shorts and a polo shirt. I said something to him about the extinction of the high strike. Koufax said that he hadn't needed to have that pitch called a strike in order to get batters to swing at his high heater. When I followed up with a question about whether baseball should enforce the high strike in today's strike zone, Koufax's face tightened. I could almost hear the alarms sounding in his head, his warning system announcing, This is an interview! He smiled in a polite but pained way and said in almost a whisper, "I'd rather not," and walked away.

When chatty reporters aren't around, that lonely pedestal called a pitching mound still gives Koufax great pleasure. He is the James Bond of pitching coaches. His work is quick, clean, stylish in its understatement and usually done in top-secret fashion. He has tutored Cleveland's Dwight Gooden and L.A.'s Chan Ho Park on their curveballs and Houston's Mike Hampton on his confidence; convinced L.A.'s Kevin Brown that it was O.K. to lead his delivery with his butt; and taught former Dodger Orel Hershiser to push off the rubber with the ball of his foot on the dirt and the heel of his foot on the rubber. Hershiser removed some spikes from the back of his right shoe so that he could be more comfortable with Koufax's style of pushing off.

Koufax has tried since 1982 to teach his curveball technique to Mets closer John Franco. "I can't do it," Franco says. "My fingers aren't big enough to get that kind of snap." Koufax was God's template for a pitcher: a prizefighter's back muscles for strength, long arms for leverage and long fingers for extra spin on his fastball and curveball. The baseball was as low as the top of his left ankle when he reached back to throw in that last calm moment of his delivery—like a freight train cresting a hill—just before he flung the weight and force of his body toward the plate.

His overhand curveball was vicious because his long fingers allowed him to spin the ball faster than anybody else. Most pitchers use their thumb to generate spin, pushing with it from the bottom of the ball and up the back side. Koufax could place his thumb on the top of the ball, as a guide—similar to the way a basketball player shooting a jumper uses his off-hand on the side of the ball—because his long fingers did all the work, pulling down on the baseball with a wicked snap. On the days he wasn't pitching Koufax liked to hold a ball with his fastball and curveball grips because he believed it would strengthen the muscles and tendons in his left hand by just the tiniest bit.

Koufax may be the best pitching coach alive, though he wants no part of that job's high visibility or demands on his time. He cannot be pinned down any easier than a tuft of a dandelion blown free by the wind. After quitting NBC in February 1973, Koufax didn't take another job until 1979, when he explained that his return to the Dodgers as a roving minor league pitching coach was partly due to financial concerns. Koufax pitched 12 years in the majors and made only $430,500 in salary. He has steadfastly rejected endorsement offers and supplements his income with perhaps two card shows a year.

In the '80s Koufax enjoyed staying under the big league radar by doing his coaching for the Dodgers at the minor league level, in places such as San Antonio, Albuquerque and Great Falls, Mont., where he liked to stay up late talking pitching with the players and staff. He likes helping young players. In Great Falls he saw the potential of a righthander the organization was down on for being too hot-tempered. "He's got the best arm on the staff," Koufax said. "Stay with this guy." He was right about John Wetteland, the Texas Rangers' closer, now in his 11th season as one of the most reliable short relievers in baseball.

Koufax abruptly quit the Dodgers in February 1990. O'Malley had thought he was doing Koufax a favor by ordering the farm director to cut back on Koufax's assignments in 1989, but Koufax told O'Malley, "I just don't think I'm earning what you're paying me." He also was ticked off when one of the Dodgers bean counters bounced back an expense report to him over a trivial matter. Since then Koufax has worked on an ad hoc basis, ready to help his friends. Fox baseball analyst Kevin Kennedy, who carries a hand-written note from Koufax in his wallet, invited him to spring training in 1993 when Kennedy was managing the Texas Rangers. Koufax stayed one week, insisting that he wear an unmarked jersey with a plain blue cap rather than the team's official uniform. "He really enjoyed it," says Osteen, who was Kennedy's pitching coach. "Every night we'd go out to dinner and just talk baseball deep into the night. At the end of the week he said, 'You know, I've really had a good time.' I was floored. For him to acknowledge how he felt was a major, major thing. Believe me. I could tell he had missed the game. But at the same time, after a week of it he was ready to go back to his own private life. One week was enough."

Last year Koufax visited the Mets' camp in Port St. Lucie, Fla., as a favor to owner Fred Wilpon, a former teammate at Lafayette High School in Brooklyn, and Dave Wallace, the Mets' pitching coach who befriended Koufax when Wallace was working in the Dodgers' minor league system. Koufax sat in front of the row of lockers assigned to the Mets' pitchers and began talking. A crowd grew, pulling into a tight circle like Boy Scouts around a campfire. Koufax looked at Leiter—also a lefthander—and said, "Al, you've had a nice career. Pitched in the World Series. But you can be better."

"I know," Leiter said. "Can you help me?"

Koufax liked that. He showed Leiter how he used to push off the rubber. He asked Leiter about where he aimed a certain pitch, and when Leiter said, "I'm thinking outer half—" Koufax cut him off. "Stop!" he said. "You never think outer half. You think a spot on the outside corner. Think about throwing the ball through the back corner of the plate, not to it."

What Koufax stressed most was that Leiter needed to pitch away more to righthanded hitters. Koufax lived on fastballs on the outside corner. Leiter, who says that many hitters today dive into the ball, prefers to pound cut fastballs on their fists. But Koufax showed Leiter how to make the ball run away from righthanders by changing the landing spot of his right foot by one inch and by letting his fingers come off slightly to the inside half of the ball. And Koufax shared the lesson that saved his career, the lesson it took him six years in the big leagues to learn: A fastball will behave better, with just as much life and better control, if you throttle back a little. "Taking the grunt out of it," is how Koufax put it.

In 1961 Koufax was a career 36–40 pitcher with awful control problems. He was scheduled to throw five innings in the Dodgers spring training B game against the Twins in Orlando, but the other pitcher missed the flight, and Koufax said he'd try to go seven. His catcher and roommate, Norm Sherry, urged him to ease up slightly on his fastball, throw his curve and hit his spots. Koufax had nothing to lose; manager Walter Alston and the front office were at the A game. Cue the chorus of angels and dramatic lighting. Koufax got it. He threw seven no-hit innings and, as he wrote in his book, "I came home a different pitcher from the one who had left."

A few weeks after Koufax spoke to the Mets' staff, an excited Wilpon approached Leiter in the clubhouse and said, "I don't know what you did with Sandy, but he wants you to have his home number. I've never known him to do this before with any player. If you ever want to talk with him, just give him a call."

Leiter says he rang the dial-a-legend line three or four times. "I wasn't sure what to do," he says. "I didn't want to call so much where he would think I was taking advantage of our friendship. On the other hand, I didn't want to not call, and he'd think, 'That guy is blowing me off.' It's kind of delicate, you know what I mean? But Sandy's cool. Real cool." At 32, Leiter had the best season of his career (17–6, 2.47). "I accepted the idea of throwing outside more," he says. "The times when I did it fairly often were the three or four most dominating games I had all year."

Koufax likes to slip into Dodgertown during spring training unnoticed, parking his Saab convertible or his Jeep Wagoneer in a back lot, visiting with O'Malley if he sees the shades open to Villa 162 and watching pitchers throw on the sacred ground of the practice mounds. He has noticed that there are a lot more microphones and cameras at Dodgertown since Rupert Murdoch bought the team last year. He is not happy about that.

I am chatting with Bobby McCarthy, Koufax's friend from Vero Beach, during an exhibition game at Dodgertown when Dave Stewart, a former Koufax pupil (who himself coached the pennant-winning San Diego Padres pitching staff last year), stops by. "We were talking about Sandy," McCarthy says.

"Oh, yeah?" Stewart says. "I just saw him in the clubhouse."

I bolt, but when I get to the clubhouse, the Ghost has vanished. I can practically smell the ethereal contrails.

A few days later I get the official word from a member of Koufax's inner circle: "He doesn't want to talk. He's at the point where he doesn't care what people write; he just doesn't want to say anything. Sorry."

I fire my last bullet. The home phone number. I haven't needed to muster this kind of courage to dial a telephone since I asked my date to our high school prom. The phone rings. I remember the code: The answering machine is on if he's in town, off if he's not. The phone just keeps ringing.

IT IS Opening Day of the 1999 season. I am standing before the house at Winkumpaugh Farm. Or what is left of it. It burned to the ground 22 days ago.

I am staring at a cement hole in the ground filled with ash and garbage and the stump of a chimney. Standing with me is Dean Harrison, a 45-year-old intensive-care nurse who grew up in West Orange, N.J., rooting for Koufax. He bought the property last year and lives in a house farther up the hill. When his power goes out during a winter storm, he calls the utility company and says, "The Koufax line is out." And they know exactly where the problem is. He knows the history of the place.

Koufax sold Winkumpaugh Farm to Herbert Haynes of Winn, Maine, who sold it three months later to John and Kay Cox of Mare Island, Calif. Cox was an absentee landlord, renting it when he could. Young people used it as a party house. Necessary repairs were left undone. By the time Henderson bought it last fall, Winkumpaugh Farm was in awful shape. "I wanted to save it," he says. "I was about 30 years too late." He finally decided to donate the farmhouse to the Ellsworth Fire Department.

When the fire company went out to the house on March 14, patches of ground were showing through what was left of winter's last snowfall. The first thing the firemen did was grab pieces of Sandy Koufax's life for themselves. They pulled up floorboards and planks of clapboard siding. A policeman, Tommy Jordan, tossed some switch plates, two faucet handles and a small pile of bricks into the back of his squad car.

After this bit of scavenging, the firefighters practiced a few rescues with a controlled fire, then they scattered hay on Winkumpaugh Farm's old wood floors and torched it. The old place went up quick as kindling, gone before a tear could fall to the snow.

After the fire burned out, Keleshian reached into the smoldering ruin and took some ancient square-headed nails. She also took some of the farmhouse's charcoaled remains, with which she plans to sketch from memory two drawings of Winkumpaugh Farm—one for Anne and one for Sandy.

The early spring sun holds me in its warmth as it begins to sink behind the mountain beyond the valley. The quiet of North Ellsworth is profound, disturbed only by the gentle whisper of the wind through the pines and the bare branches of the oak, beech, birch and apple trees.

The farmhouse is gone, and yet I see it clearly. I see the weather vane atop the tiny cupola, the second-floor dormers, the screened-in porch and the white sign under the eaves that says WINKUMPAUGH FARM in black letters. I can hear classical music playing through homemade speakers. I can smell dinner wafting through the cozy house. Without the recipe in front of him, Sandy is making his grandmother's stuffed cabbage. He is surrounded by friends, laughter, the glow of a wood-burning stove and the warmth of walls lined with hardbound books. He is home.

Koufax always hated it when people described him as a recluse, and I have come to understand how wrong that label is. A recluse doesn't touch so many people with lifelong lessons of generosity, humility and the Zen of the curveball.

I have rebuilt his farmhouse in my mind, and it is sturdier and more beautiful this way. Why shouldn't I do the same when taking the measure of the man who once lived there? Must every blank be filled in, leaving us no room to construct parts of him as we wish? What we don't see can help us keep him forever young, unflinchingly true to himself, forever an inspiration.

Looking at the ruins of Winkumpaugh Farm at my feet, I realize that I no longer need that Vero Beach phone number. I have found Sandy Koufax.

The Quiet Warrior

BY ESMERALDA SANTIAGO

*He's called the most talented player in baseball, but Vladimir Guerrero
didn't want to discuss that during his first MVP season. He wanted to talk,
instead, about his family and his mom's home cooking.*

VLADIMIR. IT IS A NAME THAT CONJURES UP IMAGES OF caviar, shots of vodka, bitterly cold winters and perhaps even a feisty Cossack horse. So when you see Vladimir attached to a Guerrero, one born and raised in the Dominican Republic, you begin to wonder about the creative impulse that pushed those two names together. "My children's names are all from the Bible, or saints," Doña Altagracia Guerrero says. Vladimir, Eliezer, María Isabel, Julio César and Wilton. Wilton? Well, *almost* all of her children. . .

Vladimir the Great, prince of Kiev (956–1015), was a savage warrior with a sword, a barbarian who converted to Christianity, then gave away his fortune, spread the gospel to his countrymen and was later made a saint. Doña Altagracia's Vladimir, born and raised in Nizao Baní, a small town less than an hour southwest of Santo Domingo, is both a Guerrero and a *guerrero*, a warrior with a bat. "They were raised Christian," Doña Altagracia says of her children, "and while they sometimes stray, they still believe, and do the best they can."

The best that Vladimir Guerrero—now, officially, an Angel—could do against major league pitching through Sunday was a .323 batting average with 27 home runs, 94 RBIs (including nine in a game on June 2) and a slugging percentage of .564. Not that any of that should come as a surprise. "He's the best player in the league," says onetime Montreal Expos teammate Rondell White. "He's Superman, and there's not too much kryptonite in the league."

"I'm the same person I always was," Vladimir Guerrero insists when asked how his life has changed since he signed with the Anaheim Angels last winter after eight seasons with the Expos. A quiet, thoughtful man, he's not comfortable talking about who he is or what he does. That discomfort is partly due to his unsteady English, but even when speaking Spanish, he is modest and shy, and he subtly deflects questions he deems too personal by using the distancing Spanish pronoun for "one" instead of "I." When asked about his impressive statistics this year, he brushes away the compliment. "One wants to do a good job and do one's best for the team," he says. His agent, who has been monitoring the conversation, jumps in, eager to sell his client just a little harder. "Vladimir's come a long way," he says. "As a boy he played barefoot, with a stick for a bat."

Guerrero's smile fades, and his eyes grow wary. He knows the media loves a rags-to-riches story, and that the trajectory of his life could easily be trivialized into the cliché of poverty-racked Dominican boys being discovered by major league scouts and made into stars. "One is grateful for the opportunity to play baseball at the professional level," Guerrero says. "There are many more who don't make it this far."

He takes nothing for granted, but he clearly doesn't want to focus on his story. Nor does he want to examine the mechanics of what he does. In fact, he would rather not talk about any of this, especially to reporters. He would like nothing more than to be allowed to play baseball and, afterward, spend as much time as possible with his family and friends. But it's precisely because he has done so spectacularly well and so rarely talks about it that he's asked again and again to do just that. His ability has awed people in both leagues. "He's just one of those special hitters," says Braves manager Bobby Cox. "I don't know that anyone ever worked with him. I'll bet he's had that same swing since he was six years old."

Guerrero views every day he plays as a gift. Last year he felt something snap in his back. He played in pain for a month before aggravating his back further on a slide. Doctors then found a herniated disk, and he was ordered to rest and undergo physical therapy. He missed 39 games.

Before the injury many teams were eagerly anticipating his impending free agency. Some of that interest was tempered by his bad back. Mets doctors examined his medical records in January, and he was offered a three-year contract with caveats that told Guerrero the Mets had no faith in him. "After I came back from the disabled list, I hit 14 more home runs," he says. "They didn't respect that."

Guerrero is a proud man and knows his value. When the Angels offered him a five-year contract, he signed. He has rewarded them for their confidence by helping to keep the Angels in the thick of the tightest divisional race in baseball.

AS A BOY Vladimir wanted to be a singer-dancer. His mother remembers her four boys putting on shows for the family in which they imitated the popular *merengueros* Los Kenton. Their sister, María Isabel, was the backup dancer. They concocted costumes that vaguely approximated the spiffy outfits the band wore, and they perfected the acrobatic moves Los Kenton performed in concerts and on television.

Doña Altagracia says Wilton, an infielder for the Kansas City Royals, is the only one of her sons who still sings in public. "His band plays in our church," she says.

Vladimir is still fond of merengue music, though, which he listens to at ear-splitting volume, but it was his ability to play baseball that distinguished him early from other boys. This was not baseball as it is played in Little Leagues across America. Vladimir and his friends sometimes had to play with sticks for bats and lemons wrapped in rags for balls. They played on cobblestoned streets, in cleared pastures and sandy lots. "Whenever the kids got together to play," his mother says, "they always chose him for their team because he could hit."

Vladimir tries to deflect even this compliment. "I didn't run fast, though," he says, "because I was fat."

"But you were strong," says his mother, "and you could hit."

He says his strength came from his work in the fields. "I had to bring in the cattle," he says. "The bulls were stubborn, and I had to pull them until they did what they were supposed to." He points to his arms: "That's what made me strong up here."

"My mother," Doña Altagracia adds, "once told me, 'All your boys play baseball well, but this one—Vladimir—someday will be a famous *pelotero*. I won't live to see it, but the ants will come and tell me in my grave.' "

The Guerreros' first home was a sod dwelling with a palm-frond roof built by Don Damián, Vladimir's father, and Doña Altagracia while she was pregnant with Eliezer, her first child. They built it, she says, because she was determined that her children would be born in their own home—not in a rental, not in a relative's house. "Little by little, we improved it," she says, "first with wood, then concrete walls with a tin roof. That roof blew away in a hurricane, but we fixed it."

She pulls out pictures of the new dwelling the family is building near their first home. Vladimir watches proudly as his mother describes what is depicted in the photographs. "Over here will be the gym," she says, "and the pool will go right there."

The sprawling house sits in a valley surrounded by mountains. "Everyone has already claimed a room," Vladimir says laughing. "The house is not finished yet, but the rooms are all spoken for."

"The whole family will be together," Doña Altagracia says, pleased.

During the season Guerrero's house, 15 minutes from Angel Stadium, is filled with relatives, whom he flies to California because he likes having them near. "My nieces and nephews are my children," he says. "I don't distinguish between my kids and those of my sisters or brothers. I love them all as if they were my own and treat them all as if I were their father."

He sits down on a roomy leather sofa in the den of his home, and within seconds there is a child on his lap, and then another is leaning on him as she watches a big-screen TV. "It makes me happy to have my family here," he says, smiling as he looks around the room to take it all in. He is clearly happy with what he has accomplished as a man, as a son, and as a father.

THE FAMILY comes to every game Guerrero plays at home. It occupies a suite high above rightfield. Tonight the box holds Guerrero's mother and father; his five-year-old son, Vladimir Jr.; Eliezer's wife, Raquel; eight nieces and nephews visiting this week from New York City and the Dominican Republic; and a few friends.

A table is strewn with half-eaten pizzas, hot dogs, popcorn and empty soda cans. A television on one wall of the suite is tuned to *telenovelas*, the soaps that dominate Spanish television. But no matter what vicissitudes her favorite characters endure, Doña Altagracia's eyes are trained on her son when he's at the plate or playing defense, as he is now. She anxiously follows the arc of a deep fly ball off the bat of a Seattle Mariner, heading toward Vladimir in rightfield. Her hands clutched to her chest, she mutters under her breath, "Catch it, son. Catch it. . . . " He leaps at the wall and comes down with the ball, and over 43,000 fans are on their feet chanting "Vlady!"

Everyone in the suite, and everyone in the stadium, is on alert when Guerrero comes to the plate. They know that anything can happen when he has a bat in his hands. He's an aggressive hitter who frequently lunges at first pitches as if he's not going to get another chance. Opponents and teammates marvel at Guerrero's indifference to the strike zone. "He's *so* aggressive," says Angels DH Tim Salmon. "He'll hit a pitch six inches off the ground for a homer."

"If it's coming forward, he's pretty much going to swing at it," says Angels pitcher John Lackey. "Back in June he hit a slider about 800 feet. He came back to the dugout and said, 'I like slider.' I said, 'Yeah, I can tell.' "

He's one of the most dangerous hitters in baseball and certainly the most entertaining. "I believe Vladimir Guerrero and [Colorado's] Todd Helton are more dangerous [than Barry Bonds]," says Toronto pitcher Miguel Batista, "because Barry will take a walk, but with those guys there's nothing too high or too low." Guerrero is also a terror on the bases—a threat to steal (he swiped 40 bases in 2002) or to stretch a base hit. His long gait eats up ground at a rate that sometimes startles fielders. And it sometimes gets him in trouble. He was caught stealing 20 times in 2002.

"MY SONS could not get the education they wanted," Doña Altagracia says, "because we had to work so hard just to survive." Her husband nods. He's a tall, quiet man with a regal bearing. When his children were growing up, Don Damián, now 54, drove a shuttle. The competition was fierce, and he had to navigate over potholed roads from before dawn until there were no more people on the street looking for a ride.

To supplement Don Damián's income, Doña Altagracia opened a small food stand, selling the Caribbean version of fast food: fried or roasted chunks of pork, fried plantain, fish, rice and beans. When business was slow, she sent her boys to the center of town with pots of freshly prepared food for sale. But even that did not produce enough income to raise five children, so when Vladimir was 12, Doña Altagracia went to Venezuela to work as a maid for a wealthy family. What she earned was sent back to Nizao. She called home once a month; because there were no phones in the town, Don Damián drove the children to a public phone in Santo Domingo so that they could speak to their mother. She came home every other year, during Christmas, and spent a month with them.

Wilton and Vladimir were signed by major league scouts while their mother was in Venezuela—Wilton with the Los Angeles Dodgers, at 16; Vladimir with the Expos when he was 17. "It was hard. We were scattered all over the place," she remembers. When Vladimir was called up by the Expos, Doña Altagracia left her job in Venezuela and moved to Canada during the baseball season. Vladimir rented three apartments in the same building so that his family could be together again.

Now 51, Doña Altagracia is a proud, straight-backed woman with the strong hands and facial lines of someone who has worked hard all her life, and she thanks God frequently for the blessings bestowed upon her and her children.

VLADIMIR GUERRERO knows baseball English. The other kind, the kind you need to speak to sportswriters with confidence, does not come as easily. When a reporter speaks to him in Spanish, relief washes across his face, his whole body relaxes, and he flashes the charming smile that all the Guerreros have. "He's a great teammate," says Lackey. "He's a superstar who doesn't act like one."

He has made many friends on the Angels, but he spends most of his time with the ones who speak Spanish. They hang out at one another's homes playing billiards and video games, swimming in large, immaculate pools. He's also friends with many of the Dominican players on other teams—Pedro Martinez, Manny Ramirez, Alfonso Soriano. He grew up with San Francisco Giants shortstop Deivi Cruz, playing in the fields of Nizao; Baltimore Orioles shortstop Miguel Tejada, who grew up in nearby Baní, is also a close friend. When Guerrero's friends from other teams come to Anaheim, he brings them home-cooked food prepared by his mother.

"How many dinners do I send today?" Doña Altagracia asks as he gets ready to leave for the ballpark.

Guerrero closes his eyes and makes a quick tally. "Four," he says, and names the players. She packs four meals and puts them in individual shopping bags. If her son has a day game, she also cooks a big postgame meal, and he will bring some friends home.

"It pleases me that they like my food," she says. "And I know that when Vlady goes to their cities, their families will take care of my son, like I take care of theirs."

AT ANGEL Stadium one July afternoon before a night game, Vlady and An-gels infielder Alfredo Amezaga are playing catch with one of the little boys in the extended Guerrero family. The five-year-old wears a man's outfield-er's glove, comically big for his hand, but he grips it fiercely and runs with great determination for grounders or jumps for balls lobbed his way.

Guerrero challenges him. He makes the boy run and jump to catch the ball.

"You're throwing too hard," Amezaga says as the boy runs for a ball that has flown over his head.

"He has to learn," Guerrero says. "He doesn't learn if it's too easy."

Amezaga laughs. "He's only five!"

Guerrero smiles but doesn't let up, and the child doesn't seem to mind. He chases the ball, jumps, lunges, tries his best not to let it get past him. When Guerrero has to leave to take batting practice, the boy hugs him tightly around the thighs, and Guerrero bends down, strokes the top of his head.

"Good job," he says, and the boy saunters away grinning as if he's just received the biggest gift of his life. Guerrero, too, grins as he jogs toward the batting cage, a long way from the fields of his boyhood and his grand-mother's prediction. Somewhere in the Dominican Republic, the ants are talking about him.

⌘

'Everyone Is Helpless And in Awe'

BY ROY BLOUNT JR.

That, says Reggie Jackson, is the reaction after one of his majestic drives, and it was becoming commonplace as the Oakland slugger raced on to a higher stardom, unfettered in life as he was at the plate.

Perfect speed, my son, is being there."

—Jonathan Livingston Seagull

THE NEARLY EMPTY CLUBHOUSE OF THE WORLD CHAMPIONSHIP Oakland A's looks like the men's room of an old, disreputable movie theater, except that Reginald Martinez Jackson, a superstar advancing toward superduperstar status, is naked in it, taking his naturally beautiful lefthanded stance and swinging a 35-inch, 37-ounce flame-treated bat, intensely, reflectively. *Whupp. Whupp.* Even though he is cutting through thin air he seems to be making good contact. Last year, after seven big-league seasons of ups, downs, moping and controversy, he was the American League's home-run leader, RBI leader and Most Valuable Player. This year he might win the Triple Crown, and he has already—nobody else could have—one-upped Henry Aaron's 715th and subsequent home runs.

Whupp. "My strongest point is my strength," he says. "Shoulders to fin-

gertips." Indeed, he has 17-inch biceps, as Sonny Liston had, and he is one
of the top raw-power men in the league, along with Chicago's Dick Allen and
Detroit's Willie Horton (who once broke a bat in two by abruptly checking his swing). But mighty isn't all he is.

By birth Afro-Latin-American, by faith an Arizona Methodist, Jackson
is a man who grew up in a Jewish neighborhood outside Philadelphia,
roomed in the majors with a WASP named Chuck, currently pals around
with two Portuguese motor sportsmen—one weighing 250 pounds, the
other 305—wears around his neck a string of wampum beads and a gold
crucifix he bought from a Cuban pitcher and is built like a Greek god. On
paper he is a millionaire in land development.

Whupp. Facially, thanks in part to his mustache, beard and fullish Afro,
he resembles the charismatic civil-rights leader Jesse Jackson, with overtones
of sprightly pop-off Pirate pitcher Dock Ellis. He has the eagerly concerned,
unsettled, open-eyed look of a man who will never be cynical, boring or
fully aware (or unaware) of how he affects people. He is a half-inch over six
feet tall and weights 207 pounds, and aside from an arthritic spine, near-
sightedness and astigmatism, there is only one thing wrong with him.

"Feel that," Jackson says, indicating the back of his right thigh, which
is as big around as a good-sized woman's waist. Though unflexed, it feels
like an only slightly deflated football. "Hard, isn't it?" he says. His thighs are
overdeveloped. That is why he is prone to pull a hamstring when he turns
on his 9.6-in-the-100 speed. This day in Oakland he is out of the lineup
and nearly alone in the dressing room because of such a pull, rashly in-
curred. But he is keeping in touch with his stroke. *Whupp. Whupp.*

"Richie Allen told me once, 'Don't speak with this [he points to his
mouth], speak with this.' " With a flowing gesture he indicates his body,
and the bat. " 'Through this [he holds the bat up like a torch] you can speak
to the *world.*' "

But even though Jackson may be on his way to one of the best years anybody ever had with a bat—after two months of the season he is hitting
close to .400 with 42 RBIs and a league-leading 15 home runs—it was
orally that he faded the man who recently passed Babe Ruth. A reporter
asked Jackson, who is 28, what he thought of his chances of breaking
Aaron's lifetime home-run record. Jackson replied, "No way. They couldn't
afford to pay me to play that long."

Now that was a partly humorous remark. Please do not consider it over-
proud, because Reggie is loath to come on as a braggart. He even feels dubious

about all the bare-chested pictures of himself that have been appearing lately. "My peers may not like it," he says. "And I am one of my peers."

To be sure, White Sox pitcher Stan Bahnsen says of Jackson, "he's a hel-
luva ballplayer, but I'm not one of his fans. I don't like him. I think he's a
prima donna. That whole team seems to think they're spokesmen for the
game." And the aforementioned Allen, whose own thighs are lean and flowing, the way he likes a racehorse's to be, says, "I look in the record book
and I see Reggie has never hit .300. And I wonder how he can do all that
talking." But other players commend him roundly. He is established. Whatever his flaws and rough edges, Jackson has put together a package of
power, speed, science, flash, funk, outspoken quotability, popularity, fun-
lovingness, social and economic independence, responsibility, diversifica-
tion and winningness that is unique among ballplayers. And Reggie knows
and loves it. *Whupp.*

NOW, AS the rest of the team grapples on the field with the Kansas City
Royals, Jackson is in the whirlpool discussing his assets. "I've got seven
people I can call my friends. That makes me an awful rich man. People
who would hurt themselves to help me." One of these is Gary Walker, an intense white 35-year-old who tried to sell Jackson a $10,000 life-insurance
policy nine years ago when Reggie was at Arizona State. "I turned him
down, I stood him up," Jackson says. "But he kept after me. And now my
life's insured for one million eight!" When Jackson signed on with the A's
for an $85,000 bonus and began making contacts among professional ath-
letes, he and Walker formed the Tempe, Ariz.–based United Development,
Inc., which puts together syndicates of investors to speculate in land.

"He was making $5,000, $6,000 a year then," says Jackson, "and our
office was in his extra bedroom. Now he's making over $100,000 a year,
and we've got an office that costs $2,500 a month. He's my best friend in
the world." Reggie lends his fame to the business and also rounds up
investors—some 300 athletes so far, including a number of the pitchers
he faces.

Not only has United Development achieved its goal of "proving that
black and white could equal green," it is trying to hasten the greening of
America, or at least of Arizona. The company's 61-employee office features
a piano for impromptu community sings, an art gallery complete with resident artist, a crafts room and encounter-group sessions in which Jackson
takes an active part during the off-season. There will be company plays,

too, in which Reggie will probably act, and United is setting up two homes for delinquent boys and even plans to found a college—"an alternative to the four-year rip-off most of us went to without learning anything," in Walker's words. When UCLA's Bill Walton was looking for a relevant pro basketball team, United Development went to him with a proposal that would have built around him a new ABA franchise with, among other things, subsidized seating for poor fans, freedom for all players to sign with other teams after a year and a woman psychological coordinator who would have set up programs on the road so that players could, says Walker, "go to the ghettos and work with kids instead of trying to see how many broads they could chase and how much trash they could smoke." For signing, Walton would have received such bonuses as a 10-speed bicycle, a mountain house (provided he designed and built it himself with the help of experts and boys from the homes for delinquents) and a $1-million loan (on condition that he spend 20 hours a month working with the delinquent boys). "I think it freaked Walton out," Walker says.

Jackson has not been freaked out by anything in the last couple of years. Other friends he cites are the bulky Portuguese brothers, Wayne and Tony Del Rio, at whose garage in San Leandro he works on the four show and racing cars he owns. After Jackson received a death threat involving a "voodoo curse" during last year's World Series, Tony Del Rio served as his bodyguard.

"How did the death threats make you feel?"

"Like a star," Jackson says with a sort of radiance from the whirlpool, but quickly his expression becomes more discreet. "Naw," he says. "It scared me." But not enough to deter him from driving in six runs, making superb catches in rightfield and being named MVP.

"A lousy MVP," said A's Owner Charles Finley, speaking of Jackson's regular-season honor, when contract arbitration time came around. "They had to give it to somebody." Finley is an innovative businessman himself, but not in the spirit of United Development. The people of Oakland come out in very small numbers to see the A's, and accordingly Finley has made economies: getting rid of the ballgirls (one of whom Jackson was dating), ceasing to furnish stamps for the players' answers to fan mail, keeping the clubhouse seedy and fighting as hard as ever to hold down salaries. He is the only owner in baseball whose leading players—with Jackson in the forefront—regularly denounce him for quotation. The A's don't mind faulting their manager, either. Last year, when it was Dick Williams, Jackson criticized him for being too critical of players. This year it is Alvin Dark, and the A's criticize him for not being critical enough. Dark takes stoical-ly the kind of interference and abuse Finley has always handed out to his managers. One night recently after a loss, Finley went into Dark's office and chewed him out loudly enough for everyone in the dressing room to hear. "If you'd lose 25 pounds off that fat ass of yours, you could think bet-ter" was one of the things Finley yelled at Dark.

This is the way Jackson is currently managed: Dark crosses his path in the dressing room, wordlessly pats him on the behind and goes on by. Jack-son shrugs. After being lifted from a game when he was still going strong, lefthander Ken Holtzman told Ron Bergman of the Oakland *Tribune*, the only reporter who travels with the team, "Dark is [expletive] and so is Fin-ley, and print that."

"Finley is so cold-blooded," Jackson says, "he ought to make antifreeze commercials. But actually he's *very* sensitive. When the players voice their opinions about him he is really hurt. If he would just quit thinking that people are trying to take advantage of him. He wants to be the dominating party."

So does Jackson. The newly instituted arbitration procedure this past off-season gave him real financial leverage against Finley for the first time, and with such documentation as a telegram from California's Frank Robin-son calling him the best player in the league he won a $60,000 raise to his current $135,000. That and his half interest in United Development add up to an annual haul of $250,000.

So what was he doing in the whirlpool? Well, the score was 4–0 in the bottom of the 4th against the Twins the Saturday before Mother's Day, and Jackson was on second with none out. In that situation, according to all baseball wisdom and a consensus of his teammates, a power hitter has no business risking injury by trying to steal. But Jackson was interested in doing what Bobby Bonds of the Giants had won acclaim for doing: hitting 30 home runs and stealing 30 bases in the same year. "I know one way to play," he says. "That's *hard*-ball. If I don't steal a base when I can, I'm short-changing myself, my family, my peers, the owner and the fans—and the man upstairs, God." So he lit out for third and about halfway there his right hamstring went *sproing*. "You know how a pulled hamstring feels?" He reaches out and digs deep into the back of the interviewer's leg with hard fingers, producing a sensation of grave fundamental insult, like a poker up the nose. The injury will cause Jackson to miss six games and consign him to designated hitting for 12 games after that. "I guess I'm going to have to cut down on running," he concedes.

His primary job, after all, is getting the big hit, and that is what thrills him most. When asked to explain what hitting feels like, he grimaces fiercely, clenches his fists and caused the whirlpool water to slosh dramatically as he searches for words. He finds plenty of them: "Being in complete control. *You* have been the dominant force—not the ball, not the pitcher. You have taken over and *lined* it somewhere. Right on the *sweet* part of the bat. And you can look back and smile, 'cause you have done it. You have dominated. You have won for that particular moment."

And when you jump on a heater, or fastball, and hit a long dinger, or home run, it is an overwhelming sensation. Jackson's two most famous drives are the ball he hit off the beer-bottle cap on a sign in right centerfield 517 feet from the plate in Minnesota and the one he hit off a light tower atop the right centerfield stands in the 1971 All-Star Game in Detroit "I have never seen a ball jump off the bat like that one," says Royals veteran Cookie Rojas. "The guys in the dugout and everybody in the stands—it just brought us all to our feet. The ball hit the thing way up there and bounced back to the ground before he had time to leave the plate."

When you hit a terrific shot, says Jackson, "all the baseball players come to rest at that moment and watch you. Everyone is helpless and in awe. You charge people up. And when you're a good hitter, you do that every day. You're the center of confidence. The man can hit—they say that. And you *know* it. You're a master. *Dealing*. The man who can do it is a dominating force when he walks out of the dugout. There's no feeling like that."

But Jackson wants to be more than an astounding hitter. "I started thinking about playing ball when I found out who Willie Mays was," he says. "Guy who could beat you the most ways. He could go 0 for 4 and beat you."

Jackson acknowledges that the A's call him Buck, which is what the Giants called Mays. "Yeah, Chuck Dobson gave me that name because he knew how much I admired Mays," he says. "I wouldn't. . . . It wouldn't sound right coming from anybody but them." *Buck* from his teammates means a lot to him, but there are other, fancier tags he aims to earn.

"Star is a tarnished word. And superstar. . . . I want to maintain some consistency of greatness. Win five world championships in a row. There are guys better than superstars."

Superduperstars?

"Yeah. Tom Seaver. Pete Rose. Frank Robinson. Henry Aaron. Jim Palmer. Pete Rose is a living morale. A living philosophy. These guys are living human definitions of the word *determination*. They walk on the field and you sense it. They buy an ice-cream cone and you sense it. They can go to a movie and stand out in the crowd with the lights out." Jackson wants to be such a complete ballplayer, so "you can *feel* guys looking at you when you pass their dugout."

He subsides into the vortical bath to read a collection of quotes about him from ballplayers around the league. Most of the comments are glowing, for example, "I'd pay to see him play"—Ralph Houk. There are what might be taken as criticisms, too.

"Jesus. Nolan Ryan says I could be better! 'If he ever plays up to his potential he's going to be something else.' That's a compliment. Nolan Ryan throws harder than anybody since 1 B.C. And *he* could be better." A little potential right back at you, Ryan! Jackson sloshes happily, thinking of being better.

THE NEXT evening he is still sidelined but that doesn't mean he is inactive. He has plenty to do in his capacity as the league's foremost fraternizer. Players caught talking to opponents on the field before a game are subject to a $50 fine. Jackson disapproves of this rule and flouts it expansively. "What's $50 to a man like you?" he says to Kansas City slugger John Mayberry as the A's and Royals warm up.

"See where Texas pitched to you with first open," Mayberry says. This is a dig because dominating forces are supposed to be walked in such a situation. But then again it is not a dig, because there were two outs in the eighth, and the A's were behind 2–1, and what Jackson did, feeling challenged by such a lack of deference, was foul off seven of Steve Harman's pitches until he got the one he wanted and then hit that one out of the park—"left the yard with it" is the current expression—for a game-winning three-run job. That is what you call bat control.

"Understand you're not hitting the deep ones anymore," says Mayberry, chortling. "Getting consistent and losing that good depth."

"Yeah," Jackson says, "I'm staying down around 400 feet. Here. . . . " He hands Mayberry one of his own bats, a 288 RJ. "No, you better not swing that timber," he adds. "Might sprain your wrist."

Then he exchanges a few words with the fans. There are so few of them, he says, he almost feels he knows them all personally. "You enjoying that hot dog?" he asks one. "Where'd you get that watch?" he asks another. A boy in the stands wants a ball. "No, son, I don't give anything away, except

a hard time. Especially if you're 60 feet away with a ball in your hand."
But the boy is six feet away without a ball in his hand, and he persists.
"You're here every day," Jackson objects. "How many balls you got at home?"

"I ain't got no balls at home. I swear to God, Reggie, I sell every one of
'em before I leave the park." Unable to resist such candor, Jackson tosses the
boy one of Finley's strictly-rationed spheroids. "I was going to steal that
one for myself," he grumbles.

Then he goes back to the dressing room, hits the whirlpool again and
returns to watch the game in civilian clothes from a vantage along the
walkway to the dugout, between the stands and the screen behind home
plate. He yells at everybody—A's, Royals, umpires, fans who yell at him.

The A's are having trouble with Lindy McDaniel's forkball, and Jackson
keeps admonishing them to *look* for it: "He got to come in with that pitch.
And it's always the same speed. You got to wait for it." Jackson used to have
trouble with off-speed pitching, but now he looks forward to facing junk-
throwers like Wilbur Wood and Mike Cuellar. He is a guess hitter—"I call
it calculated anticipation"—which means he goes up to the plate looking for
a certain pitch (not a ball inside or outside, which is what Allen and other
area-guessers lay for, but a curve, say, or a fastball, anywhere) and waits
until he gets it. If a two-strike pitch is not the one he is set up to rip he will
just try to get his bat on it, either fouling it off, as against Hargan, or perhaps slapping it for a hit. He can generate such last-instant momentum
that he may power a ball out by just flicking at it this way.

"Hey, Nietzsche! he yells to teammate Jesus Alou, or so it sounds. "Let's
see something! Look for the forkball!"

What is this! Can Jesus Alou's nickname possibly be Nietzsche?

"No, I called him *Niché*. It's Spanish for soul brother." Jackson has a half-
Latin father and a full Chicano ex-wife, he holds the modern Puerto Rican
home run record and, what with one thing and another, he is the rare mainland U.S.-born player who can converse in down-home terms with peers
who are Latin. He is also fluent in unvarnished soul talk ("With all the nig-
gers on this team, how come this dressing room got no pick?" he will cry,
demanding an Afro-comb) and most of his best friends are white. But his
pan-racialism, like most of his other characteristics, tends to make him
more of an anomaly than one of the boys. When he started rooming with
Chuck Dobson both of them got heat from teammates black and white.

One of the black A's Jackson wishes he communicated better with, he
says, is Vida Blue, who is so disenchanted with the A's organization this

year that he has announced his desire to change sports and play in the World Football League. In high school Blue was an ambidextrous quarterback. "I see a lot of me in Vida," Jackson says. "Finley hurt him. He took the little boy out of him. He did that to me, too, but I got it back. I *love* to play. I love to hit *bullets*. I mean I love to hit *peas*."

As player rep, big bat, the loudest voice in the clubhouse, Jackson stays in the thick of his team's turbulent affairs. But in speaking of his life he often comes to estrangement, to being alone.

There was the time early in 1970, his third full year with the A's, when after a big 47-homer season he held out for $50,000, incurred Finley's wrath, started slow, was benched by Finley and even was threatened with being sent to the minors. One night, after 13 games on the bench, he pinch-hit and delivered a grand-slam homer. As he crossed the plate he raised his fist in defiance toward Finley in his box.

Finley called a meeting in his office: Jackson surrounded by the owner, the coaches, the manager and the team captain, Sal Bando, who looks like Alan Arkin and is now noted for keeping things loose around the A's, for bringing Jackson down to earth with deft, good-natured kidding. But there was no kidding in that meeting.

"Finley had a public apology drawn up for me to sign," Jackson recalls. "I told him ain't no way. It was right what I did; I'd do it again. He said we were going to sit there till I signed it. Or I'd suffer the consequences. The commissioner was involved, he said. Nobody spoke up for me. I'd never been so alone, so alienated from people who I thought were my friends. I was so lost from companionship I cried. I was supposed to eat dinner with some people at nine o'clock, and I couldn't get out of there to meet them until two a.m. I never actually signed the apology, but I said I would. I'll never forget that. I'll never forgive."

And then there was the time in the '72 division-championship playoff with Detroit, when in the process of stealing home successfully, he felt something give in his left thigh. "I pulled a hamstring. Ran further and tore it. Little further and ruptured it. Little further and it was like someone went in there and ripped some muscle off the bone.

"Finley was the first one inside to see me. He was emotionally hurt. I think he gained a lot of respect for me that day as a ballplayer. But here I was in a World Series—the *World Series*. Everybody's watching. Every pitch is money. And I couldn't play. I couldn't put my underwear on. Had to lay 'em down on the floor and stand in 'em and pull 'em on."

Catcher Dave Duncan, who was traded after that series for telling off Finley on the plane home, was a close friend of Jackson's. "After I was hurt, he cried. He said, "You got to play, for me!" And I started crying. That night he put me to bed. And the next day he and Joe Rudi came over and fed me.

"But then when they won the last Series game, it was the worst feeling I ever had. When they jumped, and tumbled over each other I couldn't run onto the field. They all ran past me into the clubhouse. I hobbled. My leg hurt. I felt so dejected, so disgusted. I remember the next spring, last spring, I said to everybody, 'I'm going to the World Series this year. You going with me?' "

A LOT goes on in Reggie Jackson's life. At home there is night life—the A's, like the Yankee teams of the '50s, have no curfew—with Playboy Club bunnies and steadier girl friends. There is a tastefully-decorated penthouse apartment in Oakland, which he gets rent-free, with closets full of good clothes, including a couple of dozen leather jackets, which he also gets free. Over Jackson's bed there is a painting of a lone seagull flying in darkness. He sees himself in Jonathan Livingston Seagull, the fictional gull that breaks away from the crowd to transcend itself and then returns to help others toward limitlessness in flying.

Twice a year he trades in his free Pontiac Grand Prix on a new one. He has thriving houseplants that he waters vigorously and urges on. "Look at that boy," he exclaims, regarding a split-leaf philodendron. "He's *dealing*, isn't he?" He shares his big-league clothes and apartment (from which he will soon move to an $85,000 condominium in Oakland Hills) with John Summers, a white rookie. In the morning he may drive by to see his friend Ed Dohnt, the distinguished-looking white businessman who provides him his cars, and his friend Everett Moss, who is black and a handyman, and then drive on and have breakfast at Lois the Pie Queen, a pork chops-biscuits-grits-and-eggs place, where he calls Lois "Mom" and kids around with a black man wearing two gold dollar-sign pinkie rings and an Evil-Eye Fleegle hat.

And on the road he cuts a wide swath, as in downtown Minneapolis one fine afternoon, checking out high-heel shoes and leather coats, grading every girl he sees on a scale from one to 10 and rapping with all the eights and above. He even offers conversation to a girl who turns out to be plain and uninterested in talking to him, which offends him greatly. "She was a *one* and didn't want to talk! A *one* and she's got no time!" To a blonde eight in a department store he walks right up and says, "You're the best-looking lady we've seen so far. You're a superstar," and gets a date. To another blonde eight, a receptionist in a health club who remains businesslike, he says no, he doesn't need to sign up for some exercise: "I was born this way." And he runs into Bando in a department store and is delighted when Bando greets him by checking out his white shirt and red-and-white jacket and saying, "White on white went out with Sh-Boom."

In Chicago he dislikes the ribs served to him in the Playboy Club and describes them as follows to the bunny: "They were 0 for 4. With a couple of strikeouts thrown in. And a weak pop-up to the pitcher."

He gets his interviewer lodging in the booked-up hotel where the A's are staying by telling the desk clerk he needs a room for his parents. The interviewer points out all the reasons why it will be difficult for him to pose as Reggie's mom and dad: He is one person, white, not named Jackson and only four years older than Reggie. "I could've been adopted, couldn't I?" Jackson replied.

At breakfast in Chicago, Jackson talks about being a fan, a devourer of box scores: "Stargell hasn't started to pump yet. Ralph Garr started out 0 for 13, he's hitting .350 now. Willie McCovey just got his first home run after 79 at bats. Scotty was 3 for 4 yesterday." And he does his imitation of his friend the slugger, George Scott of the Brewers, saying on the phone, "I-i-i is y' got good weatha theyah?" Reggie loves George Scott, likes to call him up to discuss slugging, does him imitation of him over and over, savoring it.

Then he talks about his father, Martinez Jackson, the Philadelphia tailor who played semipro ball and raised Reggie in the suburb of Wyncote. "He was a hustler. Sold anything—from numbers to baloney. I know two things I can do: play ball and make money. That's what my old man could do.

"Everybody in my family is high-strung. My father told me, go about things hard. If he sent me to the store for some ice cream he expected me to get it. He didn't want to know if it was raining or I had to hitch a ride or walk or wire Western Union—he wanted that ice cream. He had a phrase—he didn't want to hear any 'ar ray boo.' Any bull, in other words. I believe that now, in baseball. If the man's got to be moved to third base, you do it. Don't care how you do it, do it. Dick Williams felt the same way about it.

"My father was divorced from my mother when I was six. He was father to us three boys by day and mother by night. I didn't get close to my mother until I was 17, 18. My father didn't do things by the law every day, but he had food on the table, and we had shoes and socks and hats on. He was a good old dude.

"I had trouble adjusting socially in high school. I was suspended three times. In part of my junior and part of my senior year my father was away for six months. He never hurt anybody, but he sold numbers and bootleg whiskey. I'd go to school for a week without saying a word. I was mean and bitter. 'Cause I was alone. Nobody took any care of me. I was a hell of a football player 'cause I was mean and nasty. I ran through the center of the line and a guy hit me in the mouth and busted my front tooth. I said, 'Run that play again.' They blocked him down, and I ran over his chest and face. Right over his face mask with my feet.

"Being mad helped me in football, but not in anything else. When I was in high school, I needed a psychiatrist. One day I'd bought me a box of pretzels for lunch. I came into class about 10 minutes late and set my pretzels down on my desk and turned away to give the teacher my pass. When I turned back, one of the boys had busted open my pretzels and taken them.

" 'Now you know I live in a bad mood,' I said. 'Who took my pretzels?' Nobody said anything. 'Whoever took my pretzels, give me a nickel.' Nothing. I turned to the teacher: 'Tell these guys to do something, 'cause they done messed up my food.' Somebody threw a nickel and it rolled around on the floor. I turned around and caught one guy smiling and I grabbed him and set him up against the window and said, 'Boy, don't you know I'll kill you?' He got nervous. Said, 'Man, don't do that.'

" 'You know you're not supposed to do that to me,' I said. 'You know I'm crazy.' And my girlfriend was all crying in the back. She was a Jewish girl. And they used to tease her. In her home-ec class the teacher said, 'I heard Reggie went on another tantrum today.' I went over to the home-ec class and cussed her out.

"Me and my buddies all had '55 Chevys. We'd sit up in the church lot, four of us, drink six quarts of beer and eat potato chips. Then go crash parties. Beat up on rich kids. Take their coats. 'Cause it was cold and we didn't have no coats. And we'd wear 'em to school the next day. And these rich kids better not say nothing. We'd whip 'em."

Through the window of the Chicago coffee shop Jackson waves at John Summers, walking by on the sidewalk wearing one of Reggie's coats.

"Me and my friend Irwin would take our bicycles and go stealing on Saturdays. Magazines, candy, yo-yos. One time I went into a store with my father and I stole a candy bar. He made me go back in and tell the cashier

I stole it. I never stole anything again in my life. I was so ashamed."

Was he ashamed when his father was away?

"I *missed* him. It was sad 'cause I couldn't get near him."

EVER SINCE that painful separation Mr. Jackson has kept in close touch with his son, writing him to hang in there against lefthanders, to be quick with the bat, to have respect for his coaches and managers. Reggie also now enjoys warm relations with his mother, who lives in Baltimore—he bought her a new house—and with a lot of other relatives. "I play ball for my *family*." He was divorced two years ago—"I was too wrapped up in being a good ballplayer. I had no conception of being a husband"—and says he misses the steady companionship of one woman, as opposed to several. He has no children, but he lavishes gifts on his young nieces and also on a poor Indian-Mexican-black community in Arizona.

Finley likes to call his ballplayers "Son." Jackson, of course, doesn't go for that, but he can deal with his owner coolly now, and thanks to psychotherapy and the avuncular or big-brotherly counseling of Dick Williams and Frank Robinson, who managed him in Puerto Rico in the winter of '70, he says he is over his rage and "meanness." He says, "I had to learn that R-E-G-G-I-E didn't spell J-E-S-U-S. I've got good linear thinking now."

But in the Chicago airport, after having some beers with teammates, discussing how to hit and how to deal with Finley and accommodating yet another kid pestering for an autograph ("I'd like to slap him in the head," he says, but he signs), he strides down the concourse restlessly and says, "I hate airports. I hate airplanes. I'm callused. I'm in a cage now. I like to be *left alone* by people snatching at me, grabbing at me. I don't go out all that much with that many people on the team. I just float until the game. When I get that bat in my hands people are paying *attention*. I'm alone then. I'm out of my cage. I'm free to move, to run, to go. I'm like an animal running through the woods."

He seems to be fascinated with the calluses on his hands, from hitting. "Feel those," he says, and indeed they are formidable. "Jesus Alou shook my hand the other day and said it was like shaking the damn *road*, it was so hard." Women are often amazed to touch those calluses, he says. "He's hard all over," Summers says. "He's one big callus. Skin's *tight*."

HE COMES into the dressing room in Minnesota after the rest of the team one evening and sees his interviewer talking to centerfielder Bill North. North has refused to speak to Jackson every since Reggie chewed him out in front of everybody for not running out a ground ball hard. (And last week the two traded punches in the Detroit locker room.) Dark will not upbraid people, so Jackson takes it upon himself. "Who does he think he is?" teammates complained after Reggie criticized North.

It bothers Jackson that North, who is black, formerly his friend, a fine base runner, a very cool and intelligent talker, won't make up with him. "I see a lot of me in him," he says of North. He feels eager to help teammates (and opponents, too, for that matter). Before he has a chance to ask the interviewer what North said, Jackson is pleased that an occasion arises for him to show how he can deal as player rep. Finley has called up minor-leaguer Phil Garner, but now threatens to send Garner back down right away if he won't sign a big-league contract on Finley's terms. Jackson takes over. He gets Finley on the phone and reasons with him, tells him that sending Garner back down will only reflect badly on the club. Finley listens—everyone is amazed. Garner gets the contract he wants.

"Is it true you have to have a law degree to be player rep on this team?" reporter Bergman kids Jackson.

"That, or be indispensable," says Reggie. But he is worried about something. "What did North say?" he asks the interviewer.

"That you were a great player, but off the field he didn't have any use for you."

Jackson suppresses agitation. "But nobody else on the team said that, did they?"

On the field he watches his teammates hit, has good words for the ones like Bando and Rudi who use their top hands effectively, who have a *theory* of hitting, grumbles about the ones whose bats are lazy, who could be good hitters but won't work at it. He hits with the regulars and also with the reserves, tries to coach Summers, who is appreciative but says he just can't apply those fine points yet, he has to get his own feel for his stroke first. Jackson is impatient. He takes several cuts with the 50-ounce leaded bat, eliciting admiration, but also a hoot from Bando: "Reggie! If the lead flies out of that and hits me, I'm suing."

"You saw me," Jackson tells the interviewer. "I tried to talk to North again. He wouldn't talk to me." He turns on Garner, whose big-league career he may have saved half an hour before, and snaps, "Why don't you take batting practice with your helmet on! You have to wear it when you hit in a game don't you?" Garner gulps. First baseman Pat Bourque, who knows the big man better, reaches over and touches Jackson's cheek, as if to remove a speck of dirt.

Jackson holds out his freshly bat-chafed hand to the interviewer. "Feel those calluses. They're rough. They're red. They're *ready*." But is he feeling too much of that old meanness maybe, to think linearly tonight and hit peas?

No. What Jackson does tonight is hit a 400-foot home run and a single to drive in five runs in a 7–4 last-inning victory. The A's are leading the league, leading it, as usual, by no more games than necessary, winning the ones that count, showing the class—conceivably the overconfidence—of the best team in baseball.

Teammates are coming up to their big gun in the dressing room after the game, calling him Buck in admiration.

"One thing you haven't asked me," Jackson says to the interviewer. "About my teammates." He goes on for 10 minutes, naked, skin tight, bursting, about how pitchers like Catfish Hunter and fielders and runners like Campy Campaneris and hitters like Gene Tenace keep games close for him, enable him to be great. He mentions nearly every man on the squad, North prominently. His portable tape recorder is playing the Jazz Crusaders' *Scratch*, easy postgame music to relax him. It is a great team he is on, he says. He feels it at the park. He feels it in the *hotel*. He is playing for a *champion*. And yes, he thinks he could bat .400 for a season if he tried to go for average, and if everything went right some season he could hit 65, 70 home runs. Earlier he had carried a Baby Ruth bar and an Oh Henry! bar, representing the Babe and Aaron, around the clubhouse soliciting opinions as to what the candy bar that will doubtless be named after him out to be called. The responses tended to be unprintable and he loved them.

And Bando spoke of what a highly developed hot dog Reggie was, how he'd gotten his antics refined now to the point that they were a part of him, no longer obnoxious, and maybe therefore he ought to pose for the cover of SPORTS ILLUSTRATED next to a huge hot dog dressed in a full Oakland uniform. The interviewer noted that players polled around the league tended to say of his antics, "That's just Reggie."

Hearing that, Jackson allowed a flash of nonlinear bemusement to cross his face. "Yeah," he said, looking proud still, but somewhat troubled. "I wonder what they meant by that?"

AUGUST 21, 1967

Going Fishing With the Kid

BY JOHN UNDERWOOD

*No longer a splinter, Ted Williams was still just as
splendid—and brash as ever when he turned his skill against another
worthy opponent: the leaping tarpon of the Florida Keys.*

THE KID SAID IT WAS ABOUT TIME WE SHOWED UP. IT WAS 5:15 in the morning. The sun had not yet begun its assault on the Florida Keys. By 10 o'clock it would be 85 degrees, and Charley Trainor, the photographer, would have his freckles double-coated with a petroleum compound made for World War II aviators marooned at sea. The Kid had bacon—a good two pounds of bacon—bubbling and spitting in twin skillets on the stove, and the coffee was hot. "All right," he said, "get the hell out of the road."

We were standing there like children who have awakened to strange events. "Just sit your behind down and stay out of the road. We're making history here. How do you like your eggs?"

There was some ponderous shuffling as the three of us who were now his subjects found seats at the large dinette table. There were Charley the photographer and Edwin Pope, the writer from Miami, and myself, and however improbable our status as fishermen, we were there to go for tarpon with The Kid, who is an expert at it, who may be, in fact, the best at it, the way he used to be the best at putting a bat on a ball. He had invited us to breakfast because he said he didn't trust us to find our own at that hour and he wanted to be at the fishing spot no later than seven. He had it scouted.

The Kid said his cooking would not win prizes, but as a man alone after two aborted marriages, he knew some of the mysteries of steaks, chops, broiled chicken and roast beef. "I do a pretty fair job with them," he said. "I do not make pies," he said, raising his eyebrows and the side of his mouth.

He had on the red Bermuda shorts I have come to think of as his home uniform in Islamorada, and a faded red shirt that had a few character holes in it. He wore Sears, Roebuck tennis shoes without socks, and his copper-brown calves stuck out prominently from the tails of the Bermudas. In 1938, when he was 19 years old and a pitcher-outfielder in San Diego, just starting as a professional ballplayer, he was 6' 3" and weighed 168 pounds. Eventually, when he had been exposed to major league regimens, he got up to 200 pounds, but it was still appropriate to call him The Splinter. The Splendid Splinter, to be sure, because there was more to him than attenuation. His own particular preference for a nickname was always The Kid. Occasionally in conversation he still refers to himself as The Kid. It is a pleasing way of taking the edge off the first person singular.

The exposed calves were a giveaway to his enormous natural power. He had never appeared terribly strong in a baseball uniform, but baseball players do not audition in Bermuda shorts. The power had to be there somewhere. There were always the wrists and hands, of course, and the eyes. Everybody talks about the wrists and eyes. People used to say he could read the label on a revolving record with those eyes, but he says that was fiction. The wrists and eyes look ordinary enough. His legs give him away.

He decided that the way we wanted our eggs was soft-boiled. He brought them to the table hot and distributed them unopened in little egg holders and was back at the stove when we began fumbling with them, trying to get inside without burning our fingers. "Will you look at that?" he said, mocking us in a loud voice. "Isn't that something? *Isn't that something?* What an exhibition." He fixed a particular scorn on Pope, whose attempts must have been spectacular. I do not know, because at the time I was trying desperately to be nonchalant with my egg. "The great Edwin Pope. *The great Edwin Pope can't even open an egg.* Here," he said, circling the table with a knife and spoon, deftly opening all our eggs. "Isn't that funny?" he said. "Boy."

Pope had been itching for two days to tell of an episode involving his 16-

year-old son, Eddie. When told that his daddy was going fishing with Ted Williams, Eddie had replied, "Gee, Ted Williams. That's great. That's the guy who designs all that terrific fishing equipment for Sears!" Pope said he pointedly informed his son that Williams had also appeared in a few major league box scores in days gone by. Eddie said, "Oh, does he play ball, too?" Pope was apprehensive that Williams might take the episode as a knock on his baseball skills and the historical position they deserve. The Kid had always guarded that reputation zealously, kicking and spitting his way through the stormy years in Boston, baring his teeth to sportswriters and tipping his hat to no man.

Once Williams said all he wanted in life was to walk down the street and have people say, "There goes the greatest hitter who ever lived." Those of us who think he made it and would gladly so testify may not represent the majority opinion, but if he did not make it, there were certainly mitigating circumstances. He was interfered with by two wars, each one drawing him uncomplaining into the cockpits of fighter planes, each extracting precious time—4½ years—from the peak of his young man's physiology. He hit .406 one year (1941) before he went to World War II, and when he came back from Korea, he had a season in which he hit .388. That was 1957, when, like Williams, who was then 39 years old, baseball was passing from its golden age. None of the alleged great hitters of today have come close to either of those figures.

Williams had been a fisherman almost before he was a ballplayer, and he said that when he could no longer hit .300 he would just quit and go fishing, but he never proved he could not hit .300. At 42 he batted .316. Three-sixteen is what Frank Robinson hit to win the American League batting championship last year ('66).

Pope told of his son's sacrilege anyway, risking it, and Williams laughed the loudest. He has an almost limitless enthusiasm for spontaneity, for getting the most out of a moment. He reacts. Getting the most sometimes means to ignite his famously combustible temper, to engage his iridescent vocabulary. If, however, he ever had the egotist's inability to laugh at himself, he surely does not have it now.

"Hell, it's been almost seven years," he said to Pope. "Your boy is a new generation. Listen, *listen*, I'm a grandfather. Isn't that something? Isn't that *funny*? A *grandfather*." He said he could tell he must be getting old by the way he was getting so critical of young hitters. "I remember when Cobb criticized me for not trying to punch the ball to leftfield away from

Boudreau's shift. Boy, I thought Cobb was an old crab, and here I am getting older, and I find I'm more critical." He did that little thing with his mouth and eyes, denoting scandalous behavior. "I try not to knock anybody," he said, "but some of these guys just aren't hitting what they should be. Listen, you know I have a lot of respect for hitters like Mays and Kaline and Clemente, and I like some of these young kids—Rico Petrocelli of our club (the Red Sox) and that kid in Houston—Rusty Staub—I'm impressed with him. But they all could be better.

"So many of them get up there just to swing. You see them all the time, hopping after that first pitch. Dammit, take a strike. See what the guy's got. I bet if you checked you'd find the guys who swing at that first strike hit about .050 on that pitch. Do they learn? No, hell, no. They keep swinging at it. You sure as hell ought to be able to remember what you learn. I think, *I know* I can tell you the exact pitch and pitcher I hit every one of my first 250 home runs off of."

Jack Brothers arrived almost simultaneously with a little black cat that began to mew at the back door in response to the aroma of Williams's cooking. "Where the hell you been, Bush?" said Williams to Brothers. "We're trying to make history, and you're sleeping. Pour yourself some coffee."

Brothers said Ted would be pleased to know he had already eaten and was ready to go, but he took a cup anyway. More often than not Williams fishes alone; he just gets into his custom-made 17½-foot open boat with its 100 horses and goes out and finds his own. But he also likes to patronize the guides and has firm friendships with many of them, and there were too many of us for one boat. Brothers has been an Islamorada fishing guide for 15 years. He is from Brooklyn. Williams had known Brothers a long time but had not fished with him prior to the day before, when we had also chartered young Billy Grace's boat. Today Grace would meet us at the fishing spot.

The little cat was now mewing in earnest at the back door. "Damn cat," said The Kid. "I hate cats. Been trying to run him off for weeks. I've thrown things at him—for crissakes, I've done everything but drown him." He began to gather up the leftover bacon. There was enough to feed 10 cats. He opened the screen door and fended off the cat gently with his foot. "Get the hell out of the road," he said. He laid the platter of bacon down on the concrete floor of the *porte cochère*, and the cat went to it hungrily. "No sense letting it go to waste," said The Kid.

"All right, let's go," he said. "Let's get serious. It's time to start thinking about fishing. Bear down, Bush. *Let's start bearing down.*"

ISLAMORADA IS the jewel inset of a two-mile key called Upper Mate-cumbe, 68 miles south of Miami and 82 miles north of Key West. Until the word got around about the fishing, it was mostly inhabited by a tribe of big-hearted, hardheaded, industrious white natives called Conchs who years ago had infiltrated from the Bahamas after first having fled the American Revolution as supporters of the Crown.

The Gulf Stream runs by, five miles offshore to the east, a playground for sailfish, dolphin, marlin, wahoo and kingfish. On the coral reefs there are snapper, jack, barracuda and grouper; on the flats of the Gulf side, or Florida Bay side, there are snook, bonefish, permit, redfish and the champion fighter from prehistoric days, *tarpon atlanticus*, the silver-king tarpon.

Bonefish drew Ted Williams to Islamorada years ago, and the Conchs have helped keep him there. The best thing about Conchs, Williams found, was that they did not make a fuss over him. They took him for granted. He was just "Hi, Ted" to them. He could bonefish in peace. As the years went by, he ran his box score to more than a thousand bonefish. Satiated, the thrill fading, he switched to tarpon as the principal quarry. He became hooked on tarpon. In 1964 he needled the Islamorada Fishing Guides Association into putting together a highly selective invitational tarpon tournament called the Gold Cup, which he won in 1965. The guides say it is the best fishing tournament in the world, and one of the most heavily gambled on. The Kid was using our trip to get himself tuned up for the tournament.

Williams had left his boat at the Coral Shores Marina on Long Key, where he has a standing 50-cent bet with the proprietor that every time he goes out he will get a tarpon. It would be quicker by car to Long Key and, from there, quicker by boat to the spot. We piled into Williams's Ford and he drove.

The Kid drives much the way he used to get ready to hit a baseball. When he was waiting in the on-deck circle or standing at the plate, he could not be still. He moved his arms and jerked his shoulders, pumped his bat, squeezing the handle as if to wring out the reluctant base hits. When he drives a car, he is no less convulsive. He is a highly animated conversationalist and sometimes finds it necessary to take both hands off the wheel to make a point. He drives with his knees. He does not drive slowly.

To fish with Williams and emerge with your sensitivities intact is to undertake the voyage between Scylla and Charybdis. It is delicate work, but it can be done, and it can be enjoyable. It most certainly will be educational. An open boat with The Kid just does not happen to be the place for one with the heart of a fawn or the ear of a rabbit. There are four things to remember: 1) He is a perfectionist; 2) he is better at it than you are; 3) he is a consummate needler; and 4) he is in charge. He brings to fishing the same hard-eyed intensity, the same unbounded capacity for scientific inquiry he brought to hitting a baseball.

Fishing guides are, by tradition, bullies, but the guides do not bully Williams. Jimmie Albright, who has fished with him for almost 18 years and is more or less his regular companion the six months a year Williams lives in Islamorada, says that this is because Williams knows more about fishing than they do.

Williams encourages a constant ebb and flow of ideas, theories, critiques, digs, approvals and opprobriums. His favorite appellation is Bush, short for bush leaguer, but with Williams a mark of accreditation. If he calls you Bush, you're in. Often he confers it on the guides.

That first day we had gone with the falling tide to a spot a mile east of Long Key. Most of the time was spent situating the boat in the prospective line of the tarpon run at the edge of a channel. Naturally, Williams questioned Brothers's choice of position. Brothers asked him if he had brought his fly rod, just in case. "I think you'll find spinning gear better by two to one," said The Kid. "I think you will also find I'm prepared, that *I'm very well prepared.*" He began to switch the color of his lure from red and yellow to pink. The lures he makes himself from dyed bucktail. Brothers joked that the color of the lure was to satisfy the fishermen, not the fish; that it was a matter of "proper presentation." Williams's fingers moved nimbly, tying the knots and biting off the ends with his teeth. He winked at me. "Boy, the guides would like to know how to tie *that* knot," he said. "That's one knot I'll never show them." He said it was a 100% knot. Brothers said there was no such thing. They argued about that for a while.

The Kid put a shapeless white hat on his head and an extra layer of grease on his lips and assumed his waiting stance on top of a tackle box, looking out across the water, his left hand on his hip, his right holding a weapon: a Ted Williams reel with 15-pound monofilament line and a Ted Williams seven-foot rod. Sears puts the Williams name on its top line of equipment, *after* Williams himself approves it. He grants Sears about 60 days a year of his time, attending clinics, making films, doing promotional work. It takes another 45 days to fulfill his obligation as a Red Sox vice president, which consists mainly of trying, in the spring, to pound into the heads of young hitters the recipe for becoming the greatest hitter who ever lived.

Another 60 days are spent at his boys' camp in Lakeville, Mass. From August to October he retires to a little cabin on the Miramichi River in New Brunswick and fishes for Atlantic salmon.

From the tackle box Williams could make conversation and watch for the coming of the tarpon. In this stance The Kid allowed his stomach to take its course uninhibited, letting it stick out. Sometimes he rolled on the sides of his feet as he kibitzed with the rest of us. His stomach is no longer a splinter's stomach, but otherwise he appears in excellent condition. He is 48 now but looks 35. As a young man he had been shocked to see the hair on his chest turning silver, but only a little of the silver ever got to his head. His great curly thatch is still brown. He weighs 230 pounds. Late in his baseball career, when he was harassed by injuries, he hit pinch home runs in four straight at bats, and I suggested that he looked like he could go up there right now and make a living pinch-hitting. He said that prospect never appealed to him at all. Nor had he ever wanted to be a manager. He said it had something to do with the "knights of the keyboard," his antagonists in the press box.

Standing there, he gave the impression he did not have to talk at all to enjoy himself; that he could stand there, perfectly silent, by the hour waiting for fish, a demonstration of patience he had never exhibited waiting to bat.

"Bear down, just bear down, Bush," said The Kid.

When the fish came, his demeanor abruptly changed. He went into a slight crouch, like a cornerback anticipating a charge; where before only his eyes were alert, the prospect of action seemed to galvanize and bring to attention the rest of his body, and when he made his cast, it was quick and sure.

It is The Kid's opinion that he will average one score for every five tarpon that strike. The average for lesser tarpon fishermen is much lower, maybe one for 10. That first day he had four fish on the line. One was down at Long Key. When we switched across to the Florida Bay side, seven miles southwest of Islamorada on the edge of Buchanan Bank, to catch the falling tide there, he had three more. On this side, especially in June, Brothers said, the tarpon seem more eager to cooperate.

The first one jumped and spit out Ted's bucktail. The second rolled and spit it out. Finally the third took it firm. The fish exploded into the air. *Sawhack-whack-whack.* The tarpon jumped seven times, swooshing spectacularly into the air as Williams played it, worked it, reeled, kept the pressure on. All the time he was instructing us, telling us what he was doing, advising Charley when to shoot and what lens opening he might use, cautioning Jack about getting too eager with the gaff.

"It's a medium-size fish . . . about 50, 60 pounds. . . . When he rolls, that's the time to put on the pressure. If you can turn him there, it takes a lot out of him. If he jumps, get on him again. . . . See how I lighten the drag when it's under the boat? Watch, now, he'll jump. When I say, 'Now,' be ready to shoot. Now!" and the fish was up again, just feet away from the boat. The fish tired rapidly, and then when he had it next to the boat and Brothers stood waiting with the gaff, the silver monster slipped the hook, as if at that critical moment it decided the entire episode was distasteful, and it was gone.

I have heard of the carnage when the Williams temper stirs. The fractured golf clubs. The snapped fishing rods. The busted watercoolers. He does not have much sympathy, either, for another man's errors when the man is represented to be something he is not. Once on this same Buchanan Bank, when he was going through his paces for a movie photographer he had hired to get footage for Sears, a tarpon he was playing actually jumped into the boat. He predicted aloud that it was about to happen, sensing the line of the jump, and when he discovered the photographer had missed this wildest of scenes, he paid him off on the spot and told him to just get the hell back to shore. But with himself he is especially severe. So I expected him to blow.

But he did not. "That's all right, it happens," he said calmly. "It happens."

In the meantime I had found time to make a few tentative tries myself at getting in the way of a tarpon. I had made up my mind I would not attempt to carry out a fiction that I knew the ins and outs of tarpon fishing. I was very careful to point out that I had never fished for tarpon, had never used a rod that required two hands for casting. I did this as insulation against the inevitable embarrassment. Things not done out of habit usually feel awkward, and awkwardness is the mother of error.

In short order I had proved to their satisfaction that if I was no tarpon fisherman, I was also no liar. Williams began to refer to my casts as "Chinese," as in Chinese homers, or bloopers. He tried to advise me. "Here," he said, grabbing the rod. "Now, keep the line here, just off the fingertip, and wait longer before you let it go." He shot one out about 60 feet. "Yes," I said, "I got it. Right." I popped another straight up into the air. "Damn," I said. "Beautiful Chinese cast," he said, but shortly after the cast a fish hit my lure in spite of myself. It jumped once, a silver blur in my face, and broke the line. "Wow," I said. Williams was paternally comforting. "It wasn't your fault," he said. "It must have been one of Jack's knots." He grinned as Jack tried to make a comeback. "It wasn't my knot, it was. . . ."

SO NOW, with the sun just rising on our second day and Trainor busily lathering up with his World War II marooned-aviator's suntan lotion, we were heading back out to Buchanan. "Bet you $100 I get one today," said The Kid. Over the roar of his 100 horses he and Jack began a discussion on the amount of drag necessary for tarpon. They differed sharply. Jack likes a heavier drag. About seven pounds. Ted said *that* heavy a drag will pop your line when you get a real hot fish, and he brought up my miss as an example. The argument carried us to Buchanan Bank.

Brothers got us situated, and in the quiet moments as we waited, the sun getting higher, The Kid opened up for discussion one subject after another, sampling them as if they were unlabeled canned goods, each offering something worth considering. There is a difference between knowing and knowing it all. Williams has a keen, honest intellectual curiosity. The things he knows and feels sure of he is adamant on (baseball, the size of a hook, the value of his time); the things he does not know, he wants to know. He wants to know what you think, right now, here in the car, in the living room, in the boat. From Charley he wanted to know about cameras, and he demonstrated an exceptional knowledge himself by the questions he asked. Listen, Edwin, tell me about this Frazier guy. Is he much of a fighter? Is Shoemaker better than Hartack? Why is that? What do you think about Vietnam? Why did SPORTS ILLUSTRATED pick Jim Ryun as its Sportsman of the Year? What's he got that Frank Robinson doesn't have?

He carted out some of his stronger thoughts about baseball, his game; how it would better serve a faster generation to limit the season to 140 games and play seven-inning second games in doubleheaders. He said too much leisure was keeping talented kids off the diamond. He said he still felt it took more individual talent than any other sport, more individual work, the work of a loner. He said Joe McCarthy was the only real manager he ever played for, that the others were just guys in the dugout. He said he would be less than honest if he expressed surprise over being elected to the Hall of Fame. "I felt I had the record for it, but"—a big grin—"I thought a couple of the knights of the keyboard might try to keep me dangling awhile."

It was just after 11 o'clock when the tarpon hit. Actually, it hit The Kid's second cast; it passed by his first, spooking slightly, and he had to put the second one out 80 feet. The tarpon jumped, exposing its great body, the scales jingling like castanets. It was obviously bigger than the one he had lost the day before. Swiftly Williams joined the battle, planting the hook with those three quick bursts. He moved with the action, leaning, sitting down, knees bent, knees straight, talking, checking the drag, getting Jack to maneuver the boat. A mixture of suntan oil and sweat got into his eyes, and he wiped at it with his left hand. We were a quarter of a mile from the spot where the tarpon hit when he got it up to the boat and then had to frantically pass the rod under the boat and grab it on the other side as the tarpon desperately maneuvered. "I hope it isn't this tough in the tournament," said Jack. "It will be," said The Kid, holding firm.

The nose of the tarpon thudded into the stern of the boat, and it moved off; Jack wanted to gaff it. "I'll tell you when I'm ready, Bush," The Kid said. "I'm going to put him right there at the side. I'll tell you right where he'll be. Don't try to do anything unless he's ready." He yelled to Billy Grace in the other boat, where Trainor was clicking off pictures. "Get closer, Billy, bring it closer so he can get this. I'll lead him right up now"—Jack had the gaff poised—"don't scare him, don't scare him. All right, c'mon up, Billy, dammit. All right," and the gaff was home. They hoisted the fish up in the air. "Ninety-five pounds," said Brothers. It had taken 35 minutes. "The guide's dream," said Jack Brothers. "All you do is pole the boat and gaff the fish when he says gaff it."

"Here, look at this," said Ted, displaying the broken head of the red-and-yellow bucktail lure that he took from the fish's mouth. "Isn't that something?" He split it in half. They lowered the stricken tarpon into the water, and Jack began to work it around, washing water through the gills, and gradually it began to revive. "He's going to make it," said Ted. "He's all right, he'll make it. He'll make it unless some shark comes along and bites his tail.

"All right," he said. "Lunchtime."

THE KID'S house is easy to find once you have found it the first time, which we had the day before. There are a couple of faded signs, one tacked to a telephone pole, that mark the intersection—Madero and List roads—near his home, but they are not to be taken seriously. If you ask a native where Ted Williams lives, he will tell you by landmarks instead of street names. He has five acres. The two-story, two-bedroom white stucco house is backed up to a small lagoon, where he has a dock. Coconut trees hang over the water. One day when I was there he was sitting with a friend, watching out the rear window through binoculars as a white crane dived for fish in the lagoon; he marveled at the skill with which the bird made its kill.

The front of the house is camouflaged by a grove of rubber trees and gumbo-limbos and lignum vitaes and sea grapes, all tucked in by a high chain-link fence, with a NO TRESPASSING sign for emphasis and a burglar alarm for protection. Separated from the main house is a small shed where he keeps his large supply of fishing equipment and tools and where he devotes hours to tinkering around and making lures. He holds one up, fresh off the workbench: "Now, *that* is a well-tied fly."

WILLIAMS is in small script on the front screen door, but except for in the den upstairs, there is little on display to associate the name with baseball. The book of photographs in the living room is mostly of fishing triumphs; there are mounted fish on the walls and two beautiful salmon flies suspended in glass on top of the TV set. On the cypress-paneled den walls there are pictures that go back. There is a skinny kid with curly hair and a smile, standing at the train station in Boston in a double-breasted suit and brown-and-white wingtip shoes. There is an autographed picture of Cardinal Cushing. There is one of The Kid and Casey Stengel at Cooperstown, and one of The Kid swinging a bat. There are some of his prize catches: a 1,235-pound marlin he got in Peru; a 500-pound thresher shark in New Zealand. There is a picture of the 20-pound salmon he got the day after he beat out teammate Pete Runnels for the American League batting championship on the last day of the 1958 season, when he had to travel all night to make it to the Miramichi before the fishing season closed.

All through the house, the prevalent face is that of his daughter and only child, Barbara, called Bobbie Jo. In the pattern of the compulsive snapshot photographer, they show her metamorphosis from stringy-cute, when they were fishing buddies, to rounded-winsome, when she made him a grandfather. She is everywhere—under glass on tabletops, on walls, standing partially upright on bureaus. He had wanted a boy.

There is a large collection of books, but no trophies. He says his trophies are up north. He reminds himself that he will have to get them down here one day. He reads a lot, and he will not leave a page unturned if it pertains to something he is interested in or would like to absorb. He has, for example, a library of how-to books on golf. He says he prefers Middlecoff's to Hogan's among the better ones, because Hogan's is too technical. Williams says that his practical application, however, was rotten. "Jeez, I sliced everything, you know? I had no control over my long shots." His golf was a series of broken club heads and bent shafts. He has developed a theory on that, too. Like Ty Cobb, he was a natural righthander who just happened to pick up a bat one day and started batting lefthanded. As a result his real power hand, his right, was always farther away from the ball at contact. He believes this diminished power and direction. He believes he would have been an even better hitter had he started righthanded. And that he might have been able to hit a golf ball straight.

His celebrated appetite for privacy has not been diminished by the years. His phone is unlisted. It is not even printed on the receiver. When it gets to be too well-known, he changes it. To get in touch with him requires liaison with his secretary. Then *he* calls *you*. And when he says he will call at 7:30, he calls at 7:30, on the dot. Presumably, close friends and fishing guides are the only ones who know how to make direct contact, and Conchs don't snitch. In turn he seeks out their company. Often in the mornings, at daybreak, he materializes at Islamorada Tackle and Marine, where the guides congregate, and he hangs around ribbing and needling. He has been especially close to Albright. He was visiting Albright when word came that he had been called back into the service for the Korean War in 1952, and when an AP guy came around to seek him out, The Kid jumped into one of Albright's closets. Albright invited the reporter in, and deliberately small-talked for an hour as Williams silently melted in the closet.

Once or twice a week he forgoes the pleasure of his own cooking to patronize a Cuban-style restaurant called Manny and Isa's, just on the other side of the Over-Sea Highway on the crusty little road that used to be the highway. He prefers it there, because recognition is less likely and he can wear his fishing uniform, and because the food is excellent. Manny was the cook at the more fashionable Green Turtle Inn before he struck out on his own with blackeyed Isa, his wife, who knows how to make a Key lime pie. Isa is Ted's pet. He does not spare her the needle.

"Veal," he says loudly, and patrons at other tables look up knowingly. "People tell me there are a lot of restaurants on the Keys selling veal and saying it's turtle steak. This tastes like veal to me, Isa." "Oh, no, Ted," says Isa with a Spanish accent, pouting and shaking her finger at him. She runs off to the kitchen and returns with a great slab of meat, which is unmistakably turtle. "You see?" says Isa. "Well, I don't know," says Ted, making that wry face. "Oh, Ted, you are fooling me," says Isa, jabbing him on the shoulder.

It was here, at Manny and Isa's, that we went for lunch: Cuban sandwiches all around, recommended strongly by The Kid. "How about a beer?" he said. "A beer's good with Cuban sandwiches." Drinking beer is one of his more recent diversions. When he was younger he traveled strictly on nonalcohol. He still bridles when downwind from a cigarette smoker. At the table I asked if in view of the obvious effort he puts into fishing, he got as much satisfaction from it as baseball gave him. He said no, that to become a success at baseball required more hours of practice, more competition, more everything, so he could not say that. But he said he had concluded that the two most enjoyable fish to fish for in the world were the tarpon and the Atlantic salmon. He crossed his legs, pushing back his chair, and launched into a soliloquy.

"The tarpon is dynamic, eager, tackle-busting—well, he's just a sensational, lively, spectacular fish. He jumps better than any of them. He'll take any kind of lure, artificial or live. He requires you to have the ability to handle tackle, probably more than any fish I know of. First place, you're playing the fish with basically freshwater equipment, which means you don't have the best drags or the fastest retrieves, and you're also using fairly light line. As a result, your knots have to be right—I want to show you that 100% knot, I can show you real quick, *before you leave I want to show it to you*—and everything has to be right. They don't know a whole lot about its life cycle, and you can't eat it, but it has more attributes as far as the gameness of the fish itself is concerned.

"Now, *now*, the Atlantic salmon. They are caught in beautiful streams. They are wonderful eating. Extremely game. They jump. They're sometimes so hard to catch, you think they're smart, then the next time they're easy. Sometimes you cast for two hours in the same arc, here, then here, here, and all the time you're seeing fish, but you think you're never going to get one, and then you change the angle a foot and it drifts right over him and, boom, you've got one. On the average, I would say it takes 400 casts per salmon, 400 to 600 casts per salmon. But on every cast you have the expectation that it's going to happen.

"Gee, it's a romantic fish. The life cycle is so damn romantic. They know specifically that certain salmon will be hatched in this area, will stay in the river for three years, go out, nobody really knows where, except to sea, and that they grow an awful lot at sea, and then two of them, male and female, come back as adults to the exact same area to spawn. Two of them, five years later, coming back upstream out of maybe 10,000 eggs. I guess if I had to spend the rest of my life fishing for just one fish, it would have to be the Atlantic salmon."

THE NEXT week, with Albright as his guide, The Kid won the Gold Cup tarpon tournament for the second time. He won it on the last day of the tournament. On the morning of that day he was in 11th place. By midafternoon he had caught five tarpon.

Before the tournament the betting got lively, and the two of them, Jimmie and The Kid, wound up with $1,100 riding on the outcome. Every time Jimmie would venture into a group of anglers and guides, Ted would say, "I don't know what you have in mind, Bush, but you better bring your checkbook Friday night when this is over."

When the bets were collected, he gave the entire $1,100 to Albright, plus an extra $200 he claimed he won. Jimmie doubts it. He also gave Jimmie the gold tiepin with the leaping tarpon that goes to the winner. The Kid does not wear ties. He has a couple of clip-ons he calls "phony-baloney ties," but they stay in the drawer. Jimmie compared it to the time in 1946 when The Kid played in his only World Series. He gave his Series check to the Boston clubhouse boy.

Jimmie said that every morning before they went out during the week of the tournament, Ted stopped to feed the little black cat. "The cat was so determined," said Albright. "He just kept hanging in there. And Ted hates cats, you know."

600 and Counting

BY TOM VERDUCCI

When Barry Bonds passed another milestone in his run at Hammerin' Hank,
SI took stock of his unprecedented late-blooming power.

O N A PLEASANT SUMMER NIGHT IN SAN FRANCISCO LAST Friday, Barry Bonds did something the rest of us should try. No, hitting the 600th home run of a major league career is beyond the general populace, not to mention all but three other ballplayers in history. What's instructive is what Bonds did *after* he connected with a fastball from Pittsburgh Pirates righthander Kip Wells. Like De Kooning before a drying canvas, Bonds took a step back and admired the majesty and magnitude of his work.

A Bonds home run typically leaves nothing to doubt from the violent, noisy moment of contact. This one screamed for 421 feet before landing among the centerfield loonies of Pacific Bell Park. They clawed, pummeled and bloodied one another at the chance to own the five-ounce piece of history, at least until it could be sold to the highest bidder. And just as Bonds took a long, steady view of the moment when he joined Hank Aaron, Babe Ruth and Willie Mays in an exclusive fraternity, so do we need to take a long view of his career.

We need to pause because Bonds is not only a late boomer, but also a mostly unembraceable presence. He has, despite his unsurpassed skills, engendered no simpatico emotions or even a nickname. After blasting 73 home runs last year in one of the greatest seasons of all time, Bonds finished third—*third!*—among outfielders in fan balloting for the All-Star Game this year, drawing less support than Ichiro or Sammy Sosa.

"People don't appreciate him," says teammate Shawon Dunston, an 18-year veteran. "We're playing with arguably the best ever, but he won't get that recognition because people say he's not nice. He's going to break [Aaron's] record. He's going to hit 800."

So step back and behold. On Friday night Bonds was again at that jewel of a ballpark beside the shimmering waters of McCovey Cove. He hit No. 500 there. He hit 71 there. He hit 600 there, as if joining Hammerin' Hank, the Babe and the Say Hey Kid was another return engagement on the tour, like Sinatra at the Mirage or Springsteen at the Garden. You half expected the crowd not only to cheer but also to flick cigarette lighters. "To be in that select group is great," Bonds said after the game, "but nothing's more satisfying than doing it in front of 40,000 fans in San Francisco."

Perspective? Bonds is the only player who broke into the big leagues in the past 47 years to hit 600 homers. If he plays another four seasons with a modest decrease in production, the 38-year-old leftfielder might retire as the alltime leader in home runs, extra-base hits, runs, walks and intentional walks (a mark he already has). Explaining how he arrived at 600 is a lesson in spontaneous combustion.

The alltime greats announce themselves early, like youthful princes born to the throne. Ruth, Ted Williams, Mays, Mickey Mantle all glowed with an unmistakable destiny from their first moments as big leaguers. Outside this regal procession is Bonds, the only man to sneak up on one of baseball's numeric Mount Everests. Ever defiant, Bonds has overturned the game's actuarial tables.

Bonds began his career as a lithe leadoff hitter for the Pittsburgh Pirates in 1986. In determining Bonds's statistical twin after each of his first eight seasons, the comprehensive website Baseball-Reference.com found him to be most similar, in career production by age, to this mixed bag of hitters from throughout major league history: Bob Coluccio, Tom Brunansky (twice), Jack Clark (thrice), Bobby Bonds and, as recently as '93, Greg Luzinski. Two years ago Bonds wasn't even among the 10 outfielders named to major league baseball's All-Century team.

Today he ranks not only among the greatest players of all time, but also as perhaps the most feared hitter ever. Never before have pitchers avoided a batter as much as they do the lefty-swinging Bonds, who, like a super-sized Danny Almonte, seems too good for his league. In 2001 pitchers walked Bonds a record 177 times, or 26.7% of his plate appearances. They have been even more careful this year, walking him 31.6% of the time. The respect Bonds gets is most extraordinary with runners in scoring position (47.3%), and with runners on and first base open (67.2%).

That fear factor is a late-career development. Entering this season Bonds had almost the same number of plate appearances as Williams (14 more, or 9,805 to be precise), but he had made 13% more outs and struck out 82% more often. Bonds trailed Williams by wide margins in batting average (.344 to .292), on-base percentage (.483 to .419) and slugging percentage (.634 to .585). Ruth and Williams were feared throughout their careers—they walked in 20% or more of their plate appearances in nine and 10 seasons, respectively. Bonds has done so only four times.

"When he was younger, you were more concerned about him hitting a line drive in the gap or stealing a base than you were about him hitting a home run," says Atlanta Braves veteran lefthander Tom Glavine, against whom Bonds, at week's end, was 24 for 75 (.320) for his career. "He's a different hitter now. In fact he's a different hitter over the last five years than he was, say, when he first went to San Francisco [in 1993]. He went from a guy who would occasionally hit the mistake pitch for a home run to somebody who hits mistakes out all the time."

No batter ever has made himself this good this late in his career. How did it happen? Most evident, the 6' 2", 228-pound Bonds filled out physically without losing any of the snap to one of the quickest batting strokes in the game. (He has repeatedly denied that he uses steroids and says his growth is attributable to his workout routine and nutritional supplements.) More subtly, Bonds's development as a power hitter accelerated when baseball entered this post-Camden Yards age of long-ball worship and he learned to lift the ball.

His career can be delineated into three stages. In Stage 1, from 1986 through '89, Bonds was a slasher who hit as many ground balls as he did fly balls. In Stage 2, from '90 through '97, Bonds was a consistent run producer who became a better home run hitter by getting the ball in the air more often. In those eight seasons his ground-ball-to-fly-ball ratio fluctuated between 71:100 and 87:100. Not coincidentally, Stage 3 began in '98, an expansion year best remembered for the McGwire-Sosa home run race, when an even bigger, smarter Bonds moved into the company of the alltime power hitters. Over this last stage his ground ball-to-fly ball ratio has decreased every full year: 63:100 (in '98), 62:100, 57:100, 56:100 (56:100 in 2002, through Sunday). In other words, he now hits almost two flies for every grounder. This transformation would not be possible without Bonds's putting more arc in his swing—he's *looking* to go deep. With his added strength, many of those fly balls are sailing far beyond the fences of today's cozy retroparks.

Further, in Stage 3 Bonds has crept closer to home plate, enabling him to pull pitches on the outside half of the plate with power rather than hitting line drives to the leftfield gap. The defensive shift most teams employ against him is also a Stage 3 development. "He's so close to the plate, he can take a pitch away and turn on it," Glavine says. "If you hit him on the hands, it's almost a strike. Yet he's so quick that he kills the inside pitch. You have to pitch him inside to keep him honest, but you'd better bury it way in because if you miss [over the plate], it's gone."

In Stage 1 Bonds hit 21 home runs per season; in Stage 2, 36. Through Sunday he was on pace to slug 48 homers this year—his average during Stage 3—which would give him 615 for his career at season's end. With another 48-homer season next year he would pass Mays, who finished with 660. If he continues to maintain his Stage 3 rate, Bonds will pass Ruth (714) and Aaron (755) in 2005, the year he turns 41.

Is it possible for Bonds to maintain this production at such an advanced age? In his final season (1960) Williams, at 41, hit 29 homers—sixth in the American League—in a much less homer-friendly, much less muscular time. In '72 Mays, at 41, hit eight homers and followed that with six the next year, his last. In '75 Aaron, at 41, hit 12 homers and bowed out the next year with 10.

If Bonds has taught us anything, it's that the arc of his career is like no other's—especially not like Bob Coluccio's.

GOD'S
SQUADS

Motley Crew

BY STEVE RUSHIN

*The world champion 1974 A's—a rainbow coalition of brawlers,
boozers and malcontents—were truly America's team, although most of us
were too square to realize it.*

H E STANDS UNSTEADILY AT THE FOOT OF A BEAUTIFUL staircase. Its pine handrails are supported by 78 posts, each post a Louisville Slugger, each Slugger game-used by a Hall of Famer. The staircase ascends to a small attic that is floor to shoulder with baseball memorabilia, but from where he stands, gazing up, it resembles a stairway to heaven.

"I go up there every once in a while and look at old pictures," says Jim (Catfish) Hunter, who now lacks the energy to climb these stairs off the living room of his small brick home in Hertford, N.C., unassisted. "The ballplayers, some of 'em, I don't even know who they are anymore. But I'll look and look and say to myself, Oh, yeah, that's so-and-so. . . . " And the boys in his attic begin to stir.

Twenty years ago to the day, Hunter's friend and batterymate with the New York Yankees, Thurman Munson, was killed in a plane crash. "It's today?" Hunter says, coldcocked by the anniversary. "God." The air goes out of him, and he falls silent. Then a smile fissures out from beneath his white mustache. "I got the last picture of Thurman in uniform," he says. "It was the day before he got killed. He fouled a ball off his foot. I was jumpin' up and down in the dugout, screamin' like a dawg, imitatin' him, and a photographer took a picture: It's Thurman lookin' at me like, You stupid son of a bitch."

Catfish Hunter, who was once thrown *into* a bar in Chicago (the police wanted him off the street) and then thrown out of the bar he'd been thrown into—"Damn, we couldn't go *anywhere*," he says of himself and his Oakland A's teammates—thinks today's ballplayers are just slightly duller than tournament Scrabble. "We went out and raised hell," he says. "Five or six of us always went out together: Me, Lindblad, Sal, Gene, Dave Hamilton, Glenn Abbott. Geno always ordered the same thing Sal did, and Sal would always say it was because Geno couldn't read the menu."

Munson is gone. Paul Lindblad, 58, Hunter's roommate for 10 years in Kansas City and Oakland, moved to the Peach Tree Place nursing home in Weatherford, Texas, two years ago, his memories taken by Alzheimer's disease. Hunter himself can't raise his hands, much less hell: He has amyotrophic lateral sclerosis—Lou Gehrig's disease—diagnosed only 10 months ago but swiftly rendering his muscles useless. Hunter, a Hall of Famer, says he receives less mail today than he did before the diagnosis became public last November, " 'cause people know that I can't sign anymore."

His arms hang like empty coat sleeves, both palms splayed backward, as if he has concealed a coin in one of them and is asking you to guess which hand it's in. "My arms and legs don't work like I want them to," he had said hours ago, after descending his concrete front stoop to greet me in the driveway, where I extended a hand he couldn't shake.

ON THIS 100-degree day he repairs to a wooden swing beneath a large shade tree on the property he purchased in 1969 with a $150,000 loan from A's owner Charlie O. Finley. The Finley A's, who won three world championships from 1972 to '74, remain the last baseball team to three-peat and the only club other than the New York Yankees to do so. "The '74 team was our best," says Hunter, who won 25 games and the American League Cy Young award that season, after which he became baseball's first de facto free agent and its first instant millionaire.

He's wearing shorts, and a spider is slowly scaling his right leg. "Would you get him for me?" Hunter asks. I carefully flick the spider off his thigh and apologize, disingenuously, for putting him through this, for imposing, for strip-mining him of his memories. But Hunter won't hear of it. "I don't get tired of this," he says in a thick east Carolina drawl that turns *tired* into *tarred*. " 'Cause it brings back good memories, all the good times we had together, my teammates and me."

So where was he? Oh, yes. "The '74 Oakland A's," he says, "was one of the better teams that ever played baseball. . . . "

And just like that, the boys in the attic come to life.

There was a time when all the world was young and shag-carpeted, kitchen appliances were avocado-colored and neckties resembled kites. "There was a time," says Sal Bando, third baseman and captain of the A's dynasty, "when men carried little purses. Reggie carried one. It was fashionable. I'll never forget, Mike Epstein got on the bus one day wearing saddlebags. It was hilarious."

There was a time, 25 years ago, when women were women and men were . . . well, they were women too, sometimes. The A's wore so many different uniforms, in such sundry color combinations, that confused players often had to change two or three times before taking the field. "Our favorites," says Hunter, grinning sardonically, "were what we called the wedding-gown whites."

Perhaps to compensate for all this femininity, most of the A's grew big porn-star mustaches, for which Finley paid them $300 each. "We broke the mold in baseball," says Bando. "The mold was short hair and black shoes and no mustaches. We brought color to the game and loosened people up. People thought we were radicals from Berkeley. In fact, most of us were politically conservative, but we enjoyed ourselves."

They enjoyed themselves and, on rare occasions, one another. "We were like a family of four boys," says reliever John (Blue Moon) Odom, who gave fellow Oakland pitcher Rollie Fingers five stitches in the Dodger Stadium visitors' clubhouse before Game 1 of the 1974 World Series. The A's fought with each other but wouldn't countenance assaults from the outside. "Try that," says Moon, "and you were messing with the family." Try that, he says, "and we'd rock your clocks."

After one long day of clock-rocking, in which Reggie Jackson drove in seven runs against the Texas Rangers, he swaggered through the Dallas/Fort Worth Airport carrying, on a string, a helium-filled balloon in the shape of a hot dog.

The Gothic, Hester Prynne A on their chests stood for Arrogance. Says Bando, "We were arrogant enough to always think we were the better team." That certainty came from years united in indentured servitude. Bando and Jackson had been teammates at Arizona State and—like most of the A's lineup—played in Finley's farm system. The players' confidence had to come from within: In 1974 the A's drew fewer than 850,000 fans to the Oakland Mausoleum. "Is that *right*?" says the manager, Alvin Dark, now 77 and enjoying his grandchildren in Easley, S.C. "Man, that's amazing."

America, too, paid scant attention. The Cincinnati Reds, with their sensible black shoes and strict no-facial-hair policy, were far more popular than the A's. So were the Dodgers, squarer than Steve Garvey's jaw. "To this day, everyone talks about Cincinnati's dynasty," says Bando, "and we beat them [in the 1972 World Series] without Reggie and [ace reliever] Darold Knowles! I don't think we've ever gotten the credit we deserve."

"We were just a matter-of-fact great team," Jackson says. "Seventy-four was the last year in which, if we had a two-game lead in the division, it was pretty much over."

Jackson was 28 years old in 1974, living rent-free in a penthouse apartment paid for by the team, with a painting of Jonathan Livingston Seagull over the bed, before he decided midseason to splurge on an $85,000 condo in the Oakland Hills. And why not? Salary arbitration was instituted in the winter of 1973–74, following the A's second straight World Series victory. For the first time the players knew what everyone else in baseball was making. Until then the champs didn't know how underpaid they were. An arbitrator ordered Finley to give Jackson, the '73 American League MVP, a raise from $75,000 to $135,000. "He was a lousy MVP," Finley protested to reporters. "They had to give it to someone."

Finley threw around compliments as if they were manhole covers. With money, he could sometimes be generous—lending Hunter the six figures for his farm, paying Odom a $75,000 signing bonus at age 19, investing second baseman Dick Green's money in the stock market to great profit. More often, though, he was tighter than the A's double knits. When Reggie hustled through DFW with that hot dog on a string, it was to catch a commercial flight, where he, world champion and MVP, sat in 4B, in front of some salesman from Topeka. Finley was too cheap to charter regularly, even though some teams had begun to do so. That season, Finley also cut off the players' franking privilege: The club would no longer pay the postage on their responses to fan mail.

In spring training for the '74 season, the '73 World Series rings were presented to the players—not in an elaborate ring ceremony, but by traveling secretary Jim Bank on a practice field in Mesa, Ariz. Fingers said the rings looked "like something out of a Cracker Jack box." Ron Bergman of the *Oakland Tribune,* the only beat writer to travel with the A's, speculated in print that the green glass in the ring's centerpiece was cut from 7-Up bottles. Hunter, who to this day thinks Finley didn't spend even the small subsidy the league office pays any World Series champion toward its ring costs, told reporters that his owner was "a cheap son of a bitch."

When Finley read that quote, he called Hunter from his insurance office at 310 South Michigan Avenue in Chicago, where he worked during most of the baseball season. "Tell me you didn't say that," said Finley, who had suffered two heart attacks in the past two years. "Tell me you didn't call me a cheap son of a bitch."

"Mr. Finley," replied Hunter, "you *are* a cheap son of a bitch."

Hunter heard what sounded like a telephone falling to a desk and then Finley calling for his secretary: "Roberta! Bring me my pill! I think I'm having the big one!"

"Cat could get away with that," says Bando. "Cat had a special relationship with Finley going back to the day he signed."

On the day in 1964 that the 18-year-old Jim Hunter became a Kansas City Athletic, Finley asked him if he had a nickname. Hunter told him that he did not. "Well, you've got to have one," said Finley. "What do you like to do?"

"I hunt and fish," replied Hunter.

"Mr. Finley kind of hesitated on the phone," recalls Hunter. "Then he said, 'You were six years old when you ran away from home. You went fishing. Your mom and dad looked for you all day. About three o'clock your mom and dad found you. You had caught two catfish and were bringing in a third, and from that day on you were Catfish. Now repeat the story to me.' " When Hunter did, Finley said, "Anybody ever asks you anything, that's how you tell it."

When Finley died in 1996, Hunter and Jackson were the only players at his funeral. Then-acting commissioner Bud Selig came, but no other team owners came. "That surprised me," says Hunter. "I know Mr. Finley was different, but he was still the owner. He had his own ways, but everybody's taken up his ways now. He was the one that brought night baseball to the World Series, the buyin' and sellin' of ballplayers, the different-colored uniforms that all the teams wear today, different-colored shoes, different-colored bats, everything. Only thing is, he never got his different-colored ball."

Catfish shakes his head at the terrible injustice of it all: "Never got that."

HEAVEN KNOWS Finley tried. He even had his team play some spring training exhibition games with the orange balls. "The pitchers couldn't grip the orange ball," Dark remembers. "If Finley could have found a hide that wasn't so slippery—or if another owner had thought of it first—the orange ball would be in today, I guarantee it. You could definitely see it a lot better. It really stuck out. But the other owners just didn't like Finley."

The other owners could ignore Finley, but Dark had to listen to him. A week before spring training for the '74 season began, Finley hired Dark to replace Dick Williams, who'd had enough of Charlie O.'s meddling. So Dark suddenly found himself in Mesa, managing the world champions. "The owner makes the rules," says Dark. "He's got the money." One of Finley's epiphanies that spring was to sign former Michigan State sprinter Herb Washington as a designated runner.

Dark says he was never ordered to play Washington or anybody else. "Charlie would try to influence you," he says. "If you were strong in your opinion, he'd say go ahead and do it your way. If you weren't strong, you did it his way. He didn't demand. He was just very . . . vocal." Washington would appear in 92 games in 1974, steal 29 bases in 45 attempts and never once appear at the plate. In Game 2 of the World Series, he would pinch-run for Joe Rudi and, before a single pitch was thrown, get picked off first base. No matter. It's remarkable enough that he appeared in a World Series, one more Finley first.

Finley's Cracker Jack rings lit a fire under the A's even before they left Arizona. "I predict a third world championship," Jackson said after receiving his 7-Up souvenir. "We got the turmoil going already."

Turmoil was their oxygen, and most of the A's produced it like trees. "There were a lot of guys on our team who talked a lot of smack," says Billy North, the Oakland centerfielder. "And sometimes somebody would talk it at what somebody else considered the wrong time, and there would be a flare-up or two. There's always somebody in a locker room who has the gift of gab. Sometimes I didn't know whether it was a gift or not."

Hunter had the gift. He could talk smack like Mozart could play piano. Still can. Hunter remembers a game in which Bando walked to the pitcher's mound bearing a ball he'd just fielded that had three broken stitches. Bando handed the ball to Fingers, called his attention to the damage and said, "You can throw at least two good sinkers with this before the ump checks the ball."

"So Rollie takes the ball," says Hunter, laughing preemptively, "looks in for the sign and then straightens up and says, 'Oh! Time out, Mr. Ump! There's somethin' wrong with this ball!' Man, he was the dumbest damn pitcher I ever seen in my life."

"Those guys had some truly vicious tongues," says North, a quiet, studious player who's now a financial planner in Kirkland, Wash. "When they'd start talking about each other, it was something to behold."

"Dick Williams always let us get on each other," says Hunter. "He called it corrective criticism. Bando and I'd get on 'em on the bus rides, and we'd get on 'em good. Every once in a while it would almost come to a fight. Sal and I would always get on each other just to get things goin'. Campaneris [Bert, the A's great bantamweight shortstop] would go to the front of the bus and tell Williams, 'You better get back there—Sal and Catfish are gonna fight!' And Williams would always tell Campy, 'Aw, let 'em fight.' "

North wasn't speaking to Jackson for most of the '74 season, not since early May, when Reggie had chewed him out in front of the team for not running out a ground ball hard enough. On June 5 the two fought in the visitors' clubhouse at Tiger Stadium in Detroit, and catcher Ray Fosse ruptured a cervical disk attempting to break it up. Fosse spent 12 weeks on the disabled list, while Jackson and North played on. By then the A's were notorious for their bare-knuckle brawling. It was expected of them. "Maybe we were playing to the crowd," says North.

In May, Dark fined pitcher Vida Blue $250 for contemptuously flipping the ball to him while being removed from a game. (Blue would pay the fine with a shower of small coins dumped on Dark's desk.) In another game Dark ordered Fingers to pitch to Munson, with a man on second and first base open. Fingers, who walked only 29 men all season, walked the Yankees catcher on four pitches and said afterward, "I lost my control momentarily."

In August, Richard Nixon resigned the Presidency, and some A's sensed that their own profane regime was in its final days. Hunter, for the only time in his career, asked each of his teammates for an autographed photo. Those teammates, many of whom he had played with as Kansas City Athletics, had become stars—a June SI cover billing coined a new noun for Jackson: *SUPERDUPERSTAR*—but oftentimes they themselves were scarcely aware of the fact because Finley frequently treated them like children. "We sometimes played Saturday-afternoon games when we were in Chicago," says Bando, "so the whole team would have to go out to Finley's farm in La-Porte, Indiana, on Saturday night for a picnic with all his friends and neighbors. God, the guys hated that."

On the field the A's seemed to toy with opponents. "What a great bunch of talented ballplayers," says Dark, reverently reciting the A's lineup: catcher Fosse, first baseman Gene Tenace, second baseman Green, whom teammates called Bass Jaws for his odd but infectious laugh. Campaneris was the leadoff hitter and shortstop. "Campy was very underrated," says Bando. "He was our offensive igniter. He could hit home runs and steal bases, and played excellent defense."

You want underrated? The Oakland leftfielder, Joe Rudi, was "the most overrated underrated player in baseball," according to Jackson. "I'm getting more ink about not getting ink than most people do who always get ink," Rudi said in 1974, when he was en route to hitting .293 and driving in 99 runs for the season. "Rudi was outstanding," says Dark. "He wasn't the fastest, but he always got a great break on the ball." Indeed, the A's were remarkably disciplined on the field. "We played the game generally without making mistakes," says North.

"We never had a real good bench," says Dark. "Had a great bullpen—Lindblad and a few other guys would get us to Fingers." The four-man starting rotation was the best in baseball, and balanced like a bookkeeper's ledger: righthanders Hunter and Abbott, lefthanders Blue and Ken Holtzman.

The nougat holding all these nuts together was Bando. "Everybody respected him as a leader," says Dark. "Just a class fella."

Far from subverting American ideals, as so many squares (and Dodgers fans) thought at the time, the A's exemplified *E pluribus unum*. They were 25 men of wildly divergent backgrounds—Jackson is a black Latin Methodist raised in a Jewish neighborhood—who stopped swinging their handbags at each other long enough to play a complicated game brilliantly. Out of many, one. "We had a 25-man team, and everybody had a job," says North, "right down to the designated runner."

The Kansas City Royals and the Texas Rangers were Oakland's closest pursuers in the American League West, but the A's never acknowledged them. Before the first game of their last series of the season, with the A's leading the West by five games, Jackson shouted at Royals outfielder Amos Otis during batting practice, "Otis, got that new TV yet?" Otis, who wasn't in the market for a new television and couldn't fathom what Jackson was talking about, replied against his better judgment: "What TV?"

"The *new* TV!" said Jackson. "You're gonna wanna watch the Fall Classic!"

The A's won the division by five games over Texas.

As the Baltimore Orioles arrived in Oakland for Game 1 of the playoffs, Hunter was meeting with Finley and baseball officials. Hunter claimed, through his attorney, that Finley had paid him only half of his $100,000 salary in 1974, and that his contract, therefore, was voided. In the meeting the owner grandly produced a check and said, "Jim, here's your money."

"No," replied Hunter. "You pay it like the contract is written—not to me, to the insurance annuity."

"See, Mr. Commissioner, Mr. League President," said Finley, who addressed everyone as Mister. "I tried to pay him and he won't take it." Finley dismissed the commissioner and the other suits and then told Hunter, "Go beat Baltimore. We got to get in the World Series."

"And that was it," recalls Hunter. "He never said another word about my contract. Ain't *never* said a word. To this day, I wish I had asked him if he meant for me to be the first free agent. I believe he did. He always wanted to be the first in everything."

Almost bored, the A's steamrollered the Orioles in the playoffs. "Mike Cuellar and Ross Grimsley pitched a one-hitter in the final game," says Jackson, "and we beat 'em 2–1. We won the American League pennant, and we didn't even celebrate. We just went to L.A. to beat the Dodgers."

THEY LITERALLY couldn't wait to rock some clocks: Fingers and Odom attacked each other in the visitors' clubhouse at Dodger Stadium before the team's workout the day before Game 1. "That fight was my fault," says Hunter. "In Baltimore during the playoffs, Rollie got a phone call that his wife was in Oakland, and her boyfriend and her was packin' up all the furniture and movin' outta the house. Her boyfriend was drivin' Rollie's car. And so Rollie flew home, we beat Baltimore, went to L.A. and there's Rollie and his wife, arm-in-arm. And I told the guys, 'S---, Rollie and his wife was stayin' in the room next to me and they fought all night long, throwin' s--- at each other, bouncin' off the walls. I can't believe this s---. Only thing she's here for is the damn World Series money.' Blue Moon heard all this. And then Rollie comes walkin' into the clubhouse."

"I can barely remember what happened," demurs Blue Moon. Hunter can. He remembers Odom greeting Fingers thusly: "Who's leavin' tickets for your wife's boyfriend tonight? You?"

"The clubhouse attendant at Dodger Stadium had been telling me how nervous he was," recalls Bando. "He had heard so much about this team fighting, and I told him, 'Believe me, it's completely blown out of proportion.' At that second, Blue Moon and Rollie go after each other."

"Oh, s---!" says Hunter, seeing it all vividly a quarter-century later. "There they go! Rollie falls down and hits the corner of a locker and splits his head wide open."

"Fingers shoved a shopping cart," says Odom, his recollection refreshed, "and it hit my ankle and turned it."

"I was in the training room," says Dark. "Fosse, who had been injured breaking up that fight in June, came running in and said, 'Skip! Fingers and Odom are fighting, and I'm not getting involved!' "

"I played bridge through the fight," recalls Green. "It didn't matter one single bit."

This was the A's in all their splendor. Finley's seatmate for Game 1 of the World Series was the incumbent Miss California, Lucianne Buchanan. He had asked Richard Nixon, nine weeks removed from office, to throw out the first pitch for Game 4 in Oakland, but the disgraced President "regretfully declined because of health reasons." Hunter's lawyer, Jerry Kapstein, was on the field during batting practice the day before the opener, declaring his client a free agent because Finley had not made those payments to Hunter's insurance annuity—he was free to pitch for the Dodgers in this Series, if he chose to do so. Jackson led off the second inning with a home run, Fingers pitched 4⅓ innings in relief and laughed off the five stitches in his head. "The team record is 15," he told reporters, "held by many."

With the A's leading by a run with two out in the ninth, Dark called on a surprised Hunter—in his first relief appearance that season—to pitch to Dodgers catcher Joe Ferguson. "This man can't hit a curveball with a paddle," Dark said when Hunter reached the mound from the bullpen. "What are you gonna throw him?"

"Fastball," replied Hunter.

Splat! Dark spat on the mound and said, "This man can't hit a curveball with a paddle! What you gonna throw him?"

"Fastball," said Hunter.

Splat! The pair repeated the exchange one more time, then Dark, exasperated, finally said, "*Why* are you gonna throw him a fastball?"

" 'Cause I ain't got a curveball today," said Hunter, who struck out Ferguson on five straight heaters. The A's won 3–2 and destroyed the Dodgers in the Series, four games to one. By the fifth game, in Oakland, the A's had finally won a hometown following: Dodgers' leftfielder Bill Buckner, who had dissed the A's to reporters after Game 3, was pelted with Frisbees, garbage and whiskey bottles. The World Series, as an institution, would not be kind to this man.

Indeed, Game 5 would provide another indignity for Buckner and a coda to the A's greatness. Leading off the eighth, he singled to center and, when the ball got past North, took second base and headed for third. Jackson, backing up North, fielded the ball and fired to Green on the edge of the outfield grass. Green threw a perfect relay to Bando, who applied the tag. Buckner was out. "The play that epitomized the Oakland A's dynasty," Jackson calls it today. "We had played so long together as a unit that we knew where everybody would be without looking. It was all instinct with us."

Jackson and Hunter would go on to win two more world championships—with the Yankees. In December 1974, an arbitrator ruled that Finley's failure to make payments to Hunter's insurance annuity in a timely manner voided his contract with the A's, and Hunter was free to sign with any team. He chose the Yankees, on New Year's Eve, for $3 million over five years. Thus ensued one of the longest and most diabolical wars in baseball history.

In the winter following the 1974 season, Bando purchased a new overstuffed leather chair to put in front of his locker. The first time the Yankees played in Oakland in '75, Hunter slipped into the A's clubhouse very early one afternoon and cut the chair to tatters.

Bando said nothing for two years, during which time he signed as a free agent with the Milwaukee Brewers after the 1976 season. Hunter pitched in Milwaukee one afternoon in 1977 and then retreated to the visitors' clubhouse. "I took a shower and put my pants on, and they felt kinda loose," Catfish says. "I go get my wallet out of the valuables locker, try to put it in my back pocket and it falls out on the floor. I walk to the mirror, take a look: I don't have the ass-end of my pants! I start yellin' for the clubhouse guy: Big Jim! Has Sal been in here? Big Jim says, 'Mmm-hmm. Sal *has* been in here.' So I have to wear my jacket around my ass to get to the bus. When I get there, Sal and his wife are waitin' in their car. He says, 'I've been waitin' two years, Cat.' "

Bando used to wear a beautiful white fedora. Once, when the Brewers were playing in New York, he returned to his locker after a game to find the crown autographed, in bold black Magic Marker: JIM "CATFISH" HUNTER.

"HIS PERSONALITY has not changed one bit since 1965," says Bando. "From the time Cat signed his first contract through stardom in New York, he has remained the same, down-to-earth, good person. If you didn't know who he was, you would never guess he was a famous athlete."

Hunter lives in a small ranch-style house in Hertford, two miles from the house he grew up in. His wife of 33 years, Helen, is his former high school sweetheart. When Hunter's illness became public last November, Bando telephoned immediately. "Most of the guys didn't know if it was O.K. to call," says Hunter, "but then word got out"—he was the same old Catfish—"and a lot of people started callin'."

"It kind of brought guys together," says Bando.

People send him quack medications in the mail—"hoaxes," Hunter calls them—followed, two weeks later, by a bill. But he has also received cards and letters that have touched him beyond measure: Hank Aaron, Sandy Koufax and Harmon Killebrew are among those who have written. He received a donation for ALS research from the final batter of the perfect game he pitched in May 1968. Former Minnesota Twin Rich Reese wrote on the memo line of his check, "The Last Out."

There are two 1,000-yen notes on Hunter's kitchen table. They're not charitable donations. A Japanese man sent him baseballs to sign, and Hunter mailed them back unsigned. "Cost me $22 in postage," he mock-complains. "He sent me back Japan money."

Though flying is difficult for ALS sufferers, Hunter flew to Oakland in June for Catfish Hunter Day. Many of his '74 teammates were there. A current member of the A's, a young reliever named T.J. Matthews, introduced himself before the game, but his name meant nothing to Hunter. "My father," said T.J., "is Nelson Matthews."

"Nelly Matthews," replied Hunter. "Centerfielder. Did he ever tell you about the time in Cleveland?"

"I thought he made that up," said T.J.

"Oh, no," said Hunter, who then told the story. On an idle afternoon in Cleveland, Cat and Nelly decided to kill a few hours at the train station. The pair had their portraits taken from the front and side in one of those four-a-sheet photo booths. Then Hunter, wearing a trench coat and flashing a plastic badge, asked an old lady if she had seen this man in the photo, this unspeakable monster, this Nelson Matthews. She shrieked and pointed to the felon, standing nearby, and Hunter began chasing Matthews around the depot. "God, we were laughing," says Hunter, laughing all over again at the recollection. "Just runnin' around that train station while the lady screamed. . . . "

If there's one photograph of Hunter and his A's to keep forever in your attic, to conjure to life at your leisure, it's this image: Catfish, running through a train station in a trench coat, flashing a plastic badge, chasing a teammate and laughing like a little boy.

The Worst Baseball Team Ever

BY JIMMY BRESLIN

The newborn Mets and their matchless manager, Casey Stengel, were
testing the limits of futility when New York's favorite columnist chronicled for SI
the team's ineptitude and the city's affection for its lovable losers.

IT WAS LONG AFTER MIDNIGHT. THE BARTENDER WAS falling asleep, and the only sound in the hotel was the whine of a vacuum cleaner in the lobby. Casey Stengel banged his last empty glass of the evening on the red-tiled bartop and then walked out of this place the Chase Hotel in St. Louis calls the Lido Room.

In the lobby the guy working the vacuum cleaner was on his big job, the rug leading into a ballroom, when Mr. Stengel stopped to light a cigarette and reflect on life. For Stengel this summer, life consists of managing a team called the New York Mets, which is not very good at playing baseball.

"I'm shell-shocked," Casey addressed the cleaner. "I'm not used to gettin' any of these shocks at all, and now they come every three innings. How do you like that?" The cleaner had no answer. "This is a disaster," Stengel continued. "Do you know who my player of the year is? My player of the year is Choo Choo Coleman and I have him for only two days. He runs very good."

This accomplished, Stengel headed for bed. The cleaner went back to his rug. He was a bit puzzled, although not as much as Stengel was later in the day when the Mets played the St. Louis Cardinals in a doubleheader.

Casey was standing on the top step of the dugout at Busch Stadium and he could see the whole thing clearly. That was the trouble.

In front of him the Mets had Ken Boyer of the Cardinals in a rundown between first and second. Marvin Throneberry, the marvelous first baseman, had the ball. Boyer started to run away from him. Nobody runs away from Marvin Throneberry. He took after Boyer with purpose. Marv lowered his head a little and produced wonderful running action with his legs. This amazed Stengel. It also amazed Stan Musial of the Cardinals, who was on third. Stanley's mouth opened. Then he broke for the plate and ran across it and into the dugout with the run that cost the Mets the game. (Throneberry, incidentally, never did get Boyer. Charlie Neal finally made the putout.) It was an incredible play. It also was loss No. 75 of the season for the Mets. In the second game Roger Craig, the Mets' starter, gave up so many runs so quickly in the seventh inning that Casey didn't have time to get one of his great relief pitchers ready. The Mets went on to lose No. 76.

Following this, the team flew to New York, where some highly disloyal people were starting to talk about them. There seems to be some sort of suspicion around that the New York Mets not only are playing baseball poorly this season but are playing it worse than any team in the modern history of the sport. As this week began, the Mets had a record of 28 won and 79 lost and seemed certain to break the modern record for losses in one season. This was set by the 1916 Philadelphia Athletics, who lost 117 games—an achievement that was challenged by the Boston Braves of 1935, who lost 115 games and were known as The World's Worst Team. But, by using one of the more expensive Keuffel & Esser slide rules, you discover that the Mets, if they cling to their present pace, will lose 120 games. You cannot ask for more than that.

Figures, of course, are notorious liars, which is why accountants have more fun than people think. Therefore, you just do not use a record book to say the Mets are the worst team of all time. You have to investigate the matter thoroughly. Then you can say the Mets are the worst team of all time.

"I never thought I would have an argument," Bill Veeck says. "I was always secure in the knowledge that when I owned the St. Louis Browns, I had the worst. Now it's different. You can say anything you want, but don't you dare say my Brownies were this bad. I'll prove it to you. There are still a few Browns in the major leagues and this is nine years later. How many Mets do you think are going to be around even two years from now? I'm being soft here. I haven't even mentioned my midget, Eddie Gaedel."

Reporting from Philadelphia is Pat Hastings, proprietor of the Brown Jug bar and a man who has sat through more bad baseball than anybody in America. For consistency, Philadelphia baseball always has been the worst. On nine occasions during Pat's tenure at the old Baker Bowl and Shibe Park, both the Phillies and A's finished in last place.

But Pat, who has viewed the Mets on several occasions this season, refuses to put any team in a class with them. "The 1916 Athletics had Stuffy McInnins, you got to remember that," he says. "And some of them Phillies teams could hurt you with the bat pretty good. There was players like Chuck Klein, Virgil Davis, Don Hurst—I seen 'em all. Why, we used to make jokes about Buzz Arlett. He played rightfield for the Phillies in 1931. People used to go out and get drunk if they seen him catch a fly ball. I feel like writing the fellow a letter of apology now. Why he done more fielding standing still than some of these Mets I seen do at full speed."

In Brooklyn there is Joseph (Babe) Hamberger, who once associated with the old Dodgers and vehemently denies he ever saw a Brooklyn club as bad as the Mets. "When Uncle Robbie [Wilbert Robinson] was managing, he didn't even know the names of the players," Babe says. "But he won two pennants and was in the first division a couple of times. Casey was over here, too. Ask him. He'll tell you. It got rough, but never like now."

Now all this is not being pointed out as an act of gratuitous cruelty. Quite the opposite. The Mets are so bad, you've got to love them. Name one true American who could do anything but root for a team that has had over 135 home runs hit against it. In New York a lot of people root for the Mets. They are mainly old Brooklyn Dodger fans and their offspring, who are called the "New Breed" in the newspapers. They are the kind of people who, as San Francisco Giant publicist Garry Schumacher once observed, never would have tolerated Joe DiMaggio on their team at Ebbets Field. "Too perfect," Garry said.

The Mets are bad for many reasons, one of which is that they do not have good players. The team was formed last year when the National League expanded to 10 teams. ("We are damn lucky they didn't expand to 12 teams," manager Stengel says.) The other new team, the Houston Colt .45s, has done a bit better than the Mets. It's in eighth place, 11½ games ahead of New York. For players, the Mets were given a list of men made available to them by the other eight National League teams. The list was carefully prepared and checked and rechecked by the club owners. This was to make certain that no bona-fide ballplayers were on it.

"It was so thoughtful of them," Stengel says. "I want to thank all of them owners who loved us to have those men and picked them for us. It was very generous of them."

Actually, the Mets did wind up with a ballplayer or two. First baseman Gil Hodges was fielding as well as ever before a kidney ailment put him in the hospital. Centerfielder Richie Ashburn, at 35, is a fine leadoff hitter, although he seems to be on his way to getting some sort of a record for being thrown out while trying to take an extra base. If Jim Hickman, an outfielder, ever learns to swing at good pitches he might make it big. Here and there Al Jackson and Roger Craig produce a well-pitched game. And Frank Thomas can hit. But all this does is force the Mets to go out of their way to lose.

And once past these people, the Mets present an array of talent that is startling. Most of those shocks Casey talks about come when his pitchers throw to batters. There was a recent day in St. Louis when Ray Daviault threw a low fastball to Charley James of the Cards. James likes low fastballs. He hit this one eight rows deep into leftfield for the ballgame.

"It was bad luck," Daviault told the manager after the game. "I threw him a perfect pitch."

"It couldn't have been a perfect pitch," Casey said. "Perfect pitches don't travel that far."

One of Casey's coaches is the fabled Rogers Hornsby. Rajah was a batting coach during spring training and for the early part of the season. But all of his work now is done with prospects out on the farms. Which is good, because Hornsby hates to lose. Oh, how he hates to lose. One day he was sitting in the dugout at the Polo Grounds before a game and you could see him seething. The Mets had been losing. So was Hornsby. He couldn't get a thing home and he was in action at three or four different major tracks around the country.

"You can't trust them old Kentucky bastard trainers," he confided.

The general manager of the Mets is George Weiss, who was let go by the Yankees after the 1960 season because of his age. He is 68 now. George spent all of last year at his home in Greenwich, Conn. As Red Smith reported, this caused his wife, Hazel, to announce, "I married George for better or for worse, but not for lunch." She was pleased when George took over the Mets this year and resumed his 12-hour working day away from home.

The Mets also have many big-name sports reporters who write about them. This may be the hardest job of all. As Barney Kremenko of the *New*

York Journal-American observes, "I've covered losing teams before. But for me to be with a non-winner!"

There are some people, of course, who will not stand still for any raps at the team. They say the Mets have a poor record because they lose so many one-run games. They point out that the Mets have lost 28 games by one run so far. However, this figure also means the Mets lost 51 other games by more than one run.

One who advances the one-run theory is Donald Grant, the Wall Street stockbroker who handles ownership details for Mrs. Joan Payson, the class lady who put up the money for the Mets. It is Mr. Grant's job to write letters to Mrs. Payson, explaining to her just what is happening with the Mets.

"It is annoying to lose by one run, but Mrs. Payson and I are pleased with the team's progress," Grant says. "She is perfectly understanding about it. After all, you do not breed a Thoroughbred horse overnight." Grant obviously doesn't know much about horse racing.

Whether the Mets lose by a run or by 14 runs (and they have done this, too), it doesn't matter. They still lose. They lose at night and in the daytime and they lose so much that the only charge you can't make against them is that their pitchers throw spitters.

"Spitters?" Stengel says. "I can't get them to throw regular pitches good."

Basically, the trouble with the Mets is the way they play baseball. It is an unchanging style of walks, passed balls, balks, missed signs, errors, overrun bases and bad throws. You see it every time. It doesn't matter what day you watch the Mets play or if they win or lose. With this team, nothing changes. Only the days.

On July 22, for example, the Mets were in Cincinnati for a doubleheader. They not only lost both games, but they also had four runners thrown out at home plate in the course of the day. Nobody could remember when this had happened before—probably because it hadn't. What made it frightening was the ease with which the Mets brought the feat off. You got the idea that they could get four runners thrown out at the plate any day they wanted to.

In the first game Choo Choo Coleman was out trying to score from second on a single to left. In the second game Stengel jauntily ordered a double steal in the second inning. He had Cannizzaro on first and Hot Rod Kanehl at third. Cannizzaro took off and drew a throw. Kanehl broke for the plate. The Cincinnati shortstop, Cardenas, cut it off, throw home, and that took care of Kanehl. In the fourth inning Elio Chacon tried to score from first when the Reds messed up a fly in the outfield. But Vada Pinson finally got to the ball, and his throw home beat Chacon by a couple of steps. In the fifth inning Jim Hickman was on third. He broke for the plate as Rod Kanehl hit the ball. Kanehl hit the ball square at third. The throw had Hickman by a yard.

The day before that, Roger Craig, the team's version of a big pitcher, had gone over to Stengel and volunteered for relief pitching in the double-header, if he were needed. Stengel nodded. It was nice of Craig to say he would work between starts. And the next day the Mets certainly did need Craig. Going into the ninth inning with a 3–3 tie against the Reds, Stengel called on Roger to save the day. Roger took his eight warmup pitches. Then he threw two regular pitches to Marty Keough of the Reds. Keough hit the second one eight miles, and the Reds won 4–3.

Two days later in the first inning of a game in Milwaukee, the Braves had runners on first and second. Henry Aaron hit the ball hard, but Chacon at shortstop made a fine backhanded stop. As Chacon regained balance, he saw Roy McMillan of the Braves running for third. Chacon yelled to Felix Mantilla, the Mets' third baseman. He was going to get McMillan at third on a sensational play. Mantilla backed up for the throw. Then he backed up some more. By the time Chacon threw, Mantilla had backed up three yards past the base and when he caught the throw all he could do was listen to the crowd laugh. McMillan had his foot on third.

The Mets fought back, however, and had the game tied 4–4 in the 12th. Casey called on a new pitcher to face the Braves in this inning. He was R.G. Miller, making his first appearance as a Met. At the start of the season, R.G. was managing a car agency and had no intention of playing baseball. Then Wid Matthews, the Mets' talent scout, came around to talk to him. Miller, Matthews had found, needed only 18 days in the major leagues to qualify as a five-year man under the baseball players' pension. R.G. had spent a couple of years with Detroit before deciding to quit.

"Go to Syracuse for us," Matthews said, "and if you show anything at all we'll bring you up. Then you can put in your 18 days. When you reach 50, you'll get about $125 every month until they put you in a box."

Miller went out front and spoke to the boss. The job would be waiting for him after the season, Miller was told. So Miller went to Syracuse. He pitched well enough to be brought up. Now he came out of the Mets' bullpen to take on the Milwaukee Braves.

Miller loosened up easily, scuffed the dirt, looked down and got the sign and glared at Del Crandall, the Milwaukee batter. Then Miller threw a slider, and Crandall hit a home run. Miller, with his first pitch of the year, had lost a game.

"He makes the club," everybody on the Mets was saying.

Marvin Throneberry, the fast-running first baseman, has had his share of travail this year, too. In fact, anytime you meet some old-timer who tries to bore you with colorful stories, you can shut him up quickly with two Marv Throneberry stories for every one he has about players like Babe Herman or Dizzy Dean. Throneberry is a balding 28-year-old who comes out of Memphis. He was up with the Yankees and once even opened the season as a first baseman for them. After that, he was with the Kansas City A's and the Orioles. Throneberry is a serious baseball player. He tries, and he has some ability. It's just that things happen when he plays.

Take the doubleheader against the Cubs at the Polo Grounds early in the season. In the first inning of the first game Don Landrum of Chicago was caught in a rundown between first and second. Rundowns are not Throneberry's strong point. In the middle of the posse of Mets chasing the Cub, Throneberry found himself face to face with Landrum. The only trouble was Marvin did not have the ball. During a rundown the cardinal rule is to get out of the way if you do not have the ball. If you stand around, the runner will deliberately bang into you, claim interference and the umpire will give it to him.

Which is exactly what happened to Marv. Landrum jumped into his arms and the umpire waved him safely to first. Instead of an out, the Mets now had to contend with a runner on base—and that opened the gates for a four-run Chicago rally.

Marv had a big chance to make good when the Mets came to bat. With two runners on, Marv drove a long shot to the bullpen in right-centerfield. It looked to be a sure triple. Marv flew past first. Well past it. He didn't come within two steps of touching the bag. Then he raced toward second and careened toward third. While all this violent motion was taking place, Ernie Banks, the Cubs' first baseman, casually strolled over to umpire Dusty Boggess.

"Didn't touch the bag, you know, Dusty," Banks said. Boggess nodded. Banks then called for the ball. The relay came and he stepped on first base. Across the infield Throneberry was standing on third. He was taking a deep breath and was proudly hitching up his belt when he saw the umpire calling him out at first.

It was suggested to Throneberry on a recent evening that his troubles, and those of the entire Mets team, come from unfamiliarity. A year of playing together might help the team considerably, Throneberry was told. Marv took this under consideration.

"I don't know about that," he allowed. "They's teams been established for 30, 40 years and they's still in last place."

Marv has been rankled only once all year. It involved Ed Bouchee, whom Stengel put on first for a couple of games. In San Francisco, Roger Craig, who has a fine pickoff motion for a righthander, fired to first and had Orlando Cepeda of the Giants clearly nailed. But Bouchee dropped the throw. Two windups later, Craig again fired to first. He had Cepeda off the bag, with all his weight leaning toward second. It was an easy pickoff. The ball again bounced out of Bouchee's glove.

Back in New York, when Bouchee stepped out on the field at the Polo Grounds, the fans gave him a good going-over.

"What are you trying to do, steal my fans?" Throneberry complained.

It is a long summer, but the man who is probably finding it longest is Weiss. He is a pale-eyed, bulky, conservative old baseball business man who, as he was saying a couple of weeks ago, is not used to losing.

"I've been in baseball since 1919," George said, "and this is only the second time I have had a second-division team. My first year in baseball I had the New Haven club and we finished seventh. That was in the Eastern League. This year is, I must say, a bit of an experience with me. No, it is certainly not a funny thing to me. But you could say I am not doing things halfway. When I finally get in the second division, I really get there.

"The job this year was simply to get a club started, Why, we couldn't even hire office personnel at first because we didn't have an office. Now we have what I think is the finest office in the majors. Of course we don't want to confine ourselves to leading the league in office space. The future depends on how hard we work now. The main thing is to build up our scouting staff. We had great scouts with the Yankees. Kritchell, Devine, Greenwade. We have Wid Matthews now, but we have to wait until contract time and some of the other good scouts become dissatisfied with their organizations. Then we can make moves. But right now all we can do is hope the players come along and it gets a little better. Anyway the manager is doing a fine job, isn't he?"

The manager certainly is. This is, everybody agrees, Casey Stengel's finest year. When he was running the Yankees and winning 10 pennants and becoming a legend, Casey never really struck you as the one they wrote of in the newspapers. His doubletalk was pleasant, but it had a bit of show business lacquer to it. And he could be rough on young players. Norman Siebern, at one time a tremendous outfield prospect, never really got over a couple of tongue-lashings from Casey. And Bobby Richardson and Clete Boyer were not the most relaxed players in the world under Stengel.

But here with the Mets, at age 73, Stengel is everything you ever read or heard about him. The man has compassion, humor and, above all, class. There is no grousing, and no screaming that players are letting him down. Mr. Stengel came to baseball this year ready to stand up no matter how rough it became. Well, it has become awful rough and he is standing up as nobody ever has. And trying. He talks to the players and he makes all the moves he knows. When they do not work out, he simply takes off his cap, wipes his forehead, then jams it back over his eyes and takes it from there.

In the rare instances when he does have the material to work with in a situation, that old, amazing Stengel magic is still there. Two weeks ago in St. Louis, the Mets won two of a five-game series against the Cards and one of the games was a result of Stengel's moves.

Curt Simmons, a lefthander, was pitching for the Cards, and Stengel sent up Gene Woodling, a lefthanded hitter, to pinch hit. Normally, this is not protocol. But Simmons had been coming in with a screwball as his best pitch. In a left-against-left situation, a screwball breaks toward the hitter and is easy to follow. Simmons had to go with a fastball. Woodling hit it on top of the roof in right and the Mets had two runs and a ballgame.

"I remembered another thing," Casey said after the game. "Once when I had Ford goin' for 20 games over with the Yankees, Woodling beats him with a home run down in Baltimore. What the hell, don't tell me he can't hit a lefthander. I remember him doin' it, and that's why I put him in there."

A few lockers down, Woodling was talking about the manager.

"I was with him for five championships with the Yankees," he was saying, "and he and I had our differences. It's nothing new. Everybody knew that. But I've never seen anybody like him this year. This is a real professional.'"

You could see it a day later, when Casey and his Mets came into the dressing room after losing a doubleheader to the Cards. The manager had a wax container of beer in his hand and he was growling about a call that he said cost him the first game.

"The man don't even know the rules," Casey was saying. "My man was in a rundown between third and home and when he tries to go to home the catcher trips him right on the baseline. You could see the chalk was all erased. The umpire don't call it. Costs me a game. It was an awful thing."

He kept talking about this one play, as if nothing else had happened during the long afternoon. He was going to give "my writers," as he calls newspapermen, something to put in the paper the next day. And maybe it would give these 25 beaten players getting dressed in the room with him something to get mad about. Maybe it would help a little.

When he stopped rasping about the play for a moment, he was asked about a couple of particularly costly plays by Throneberry and Charlie Neal. "Aaahhh!" Casey said. "Bonehead. They was bonehead plays. Damn bonehead plays." His eyes flashed.

Then he leaned back and spoke in a soft voice. "Look," he said, "I can't change a man's life. I got four or five guys who are going to make it up here. The rest of them, we just got to get along with. I'm not goin' to start breakin' furniture because of them. It's the man and I got him and I can't change his life."

Then he got dressed and a guy named Freddie picked up his suitcase and led him out of the dressing room. They had a taxicab waiting across the street, in front of an old, one-story brick-front place named Gus & Marge's Tavern. Casey pushed through the crowd and got into the taxi. He was carrying on a running conversation with the crowd as he shut the door and the taxi started to pull away.

It was, you figured, the way it should be. For over 50 years now, Casey Stengel has been getting into taxis in front of old saloons across the street from a ballpark. He has done this with great teams and with bad teams. Now he has the worst outfit anybody ever saw. But even if the players don't belong, Stengel does. He'll be back next year.

God help him.

Lost
In History

BY WILLIAM NACK

From 1929 to 1931, the Philadelphia A's were the best team in baseball, with four future Hall of Famers and a lineup that dominated Babe Ruth's legendary Yankees. So why hasn't anyone heard of them?

IN HIS BOX FESTOONED WITH BUNTING ALONG THE THIRD BASE line, President Herbert Hoover had just quietly flashed the sign that the fifth game of the 1929 World Series was over. The President had buttoned up his overcoat. At his side, his wife, Lou, had taken the cue and pulled on her brown suede gloves. Around them Secret Service men were arranging a hasty presidential exit from Philadelphia's Shibe Park. Yogi Berra had not yet illuminated the world with his brilliant epiphany—"It ain't over till it's over"—so how on earth were the Hoovers to know?

It was nearing 3:15 p.m. on Monday, Oct. 14, and the Chicago Cubs were beating the Philadelphia Athletics 2–0 behind the elegant two-hit pitching of starter Pat Malone. For eight innings, bunching a potpourri of off-speed pitches around a snapping fastball, Malone had benumbed one of the most feared batting orders in the history of baseball. At its heart were Al Simmons, who batted .334 and hit 307 home runs over his major league career; Jimmie Foxx, who once hit a home run with such force that it shattered a wooden seat three rows from the top of the upper deck at Yankee Stadium; and Mickey Cochrane, who batted .331 in the '29 regular season and is widely regarded as one of the finest hitting catchers ever to play the game.

Now it was the last of the ninth in a game Chicago had to win to stay alive in the Series. The Cubs were down three games to one, and all they needed to return the Series to Chicago was one more painless inning from Malone. Out at shortstop, scuffing the dirt, a 22-year-old Ohio country boy named Woody English had been watching Malone cut down the A's one by one. Only Simmons and Bing Miller, Philadelphia's rightfielder, had been able to rap out hits, a measly pair of singles.

Of the 50 players who suited up that day, only English survives, and the 89-year-old former All-Star remembers savoring the prospect of returning to Wrigley Field for Game 6. "Malone could throw real hard, and he was throwing very well," English recalls. "All we needed was three more outs and we were back in Chicago for the last two games. It looked like we had it salted away."

As things would turn out, only the peanuts were salted. For this was the '29 Series, which had already been one of the wildest, most twisting, most dramatic Fall Classics of all time. By the bottom of the ninth inning of Game 5, 24 Series records had been either broken or tied. The Cubs had struck out 50 times, and their surpassing second baseman, Rogers Hornsby, had fanned eight times.

This was the Series in which A's manager and part owner Connie Mack had stunned everyone in baseball by reaching around his pitching rotation—the strongest of its era, anchored by the sensational southpaw Robert (Lefty) Grove—and handing the ball in the opener to an aging, sore-armed righthander named Howard Ehmke. This was the Series in which Philadelphia, losing 8–0 in the seventh inning of Game 4, had come back swinging in what is still the most prolific inning of scoring in more than 90 years of Series history. Finally, this was the Classic that crowned a regular season in which the A's had won 104 American League games and finished 18 ahead of the second-place New York Yankees, the vaunted pinstripes of Babe Ruth, Lou Gehrig, Tony Lazzeri and Bill Dickey.

The 1927 Yankees, who won 110 games and finished 19 ahead of second-place Philadelphia, are venerated as the finest team ever assembled. In fact, according to most old-timers who played in that era, the 1927 and '28 Yankees and the 1929 and '30 Athletics were nearly equal, with the A's given the nod in fielding and pitching and the Yankees in hitting.

"I pitched against both of them, and you could flip a coin," recalls Willis

Hudlin, 90, who won 157 games for the Cleveland Indians between 1926 and 1940. "They both had power and pitching. A game would be decided on who was pitching and what kind of a day he had. You could throw a dart between 'em."

In truth, the chief difference between the two teams had less to do with how they played in any given game than with where they played their home games. Many veteran baseball observers believe that the Yankees' far more exalted status in history is due largely to the fact that they played in New York, in media heaven, where the manufacture of myth and hype is a light industry. "Those A's never got the credit they deserved," says Shirley Povich, 91, the retired sports editor of *The Washington Post*, who covered both teams. "The A's were victims of the Yankee mystique. Perhaps the 1927 Yankees were the greatest team of all time. But if there was a close second, perhaps an equal, it was those A's. They are the most overlooked team in baseball."

Indeed, from 1929 to '31 the A's were a juggernaut quite as formidable as the Yankees had been between '26 and '28. Both teams won three consecutive pennants and two of three World Series; both teams lost a seven-game Series to the St. Louis Cardinals (the Yanks in '26 and the A's in '31). Statistically the New York and Philadelphia mini-dynasties were remarkably even: The A's had a record of 313–143 (.686) between 1929 and '31; the Yanks, 302–160 (.654) between 1926 and '28. And while Philadelphia scored six fewer runs than the Yankees—2,710 to 2,716—the A's had five fewer runs scored against them: 1,992 to 1,997. That represents a difference between the two teams, in net scoring, of *one run*.

The Yankees had the best single year at the plate, hitting .307 and scoring 975 runs in 1927. The Athletics' strongest offensive showings came in '29, when they batted .296, and '30, when they scored 951 runs. On defense the A's were clearly superior; over their three-year reign they committed only 432 errors, 167 fewer than the Yankees made during their period of hegemony.

Old-timers assert that if there was any position where those forgotten '29 A's had the edge over the '27 Yankees, it was behind the plate. The Yankees platooned two mediocre catchers, Pat Collins and Johnny Grabowski. In contrast, the A's started Cochrane, a lifetime .320 hitter who competed with the kind of fiery abandon that would one day characterize Pete Rose. On top of all that, Cochrane played his pitchers like violins.

The finest of them was the sullen, hard-assed Grove—"the greatest left-

handed pitcher I ever saw," says Chief Hogsett, 92, who won 63 games for
three American League teams between 1929 and '38. Grove was the premier
stopper of his era. "He could shut you out any day," Hudlin says. "The Yankees didn't have any pitcher that overpowering."

The Athletics had no compromising weakness. "They had it all," says
Ray Hayworth, 92, who caught for the Detroit Tigers from 1926 to '38.
"Great pitching and great hitting and exceptional defense. And they first
proved themselves to be a great baseball team in the '29 Series."

IN THE bottom of the ninth that Oct. 14 at Shibe, Malone quickly fanned
Walter French, the pinch hitter who led off for the A's, and English again
sensed that Game 5 belonged to the Cubs. He was not alone. Hundreds of
people in the crowd of nearly 30,000 began watching the game over their
shoulders as they made for the exits. Then it all began to unravel. The
pitcher had two strikes on Max Bishop, the A's second baseman, when
Bishop slashed a single past Chicago third baseman Norm McMillan and
down the line in left. At once the departing crowds stopped in the aisles
and at the exits and turned around. Even President Hoover decided not to
forsake his seat.

Next up was Philadelphia centerfielder George Haas. His sad eyes and
long, tapered face had inspired his nickname, Mule, but there was nothing
plodding about his baseball. Haas was a fluid, quick-jump fielder and,
when the screws were tightening, a ferociously intense all-fields hitter. He
had batted .313 during the regular season. In fact he was one of six A's—
along with Simmons (.365), Foxx (.354), Miller (.335), Cochrane (.331)
and Jimmy Dykes (.327)—who had hit over .310 with more than 400 at
bats that year. Haas was heard muttering an oath as he went into the box.
The curse, according to *Chicago Tribune* columnist Westbrook Pegler, was
"a noise which the baseball players bandy back and forth from bench to
bench during the season and the intent is strictly contumelious."

Malone studied the signs from catcher Zack Taylor and fired his first
pitch into Haas's wheelhouse, and the Mule struck the ball flush, lifting it
in a high arc past rightfielder Kiki Cuyler and toward the row houses on
North 20th Street, where hundreds of people sitting on makeshift rooftop
bleachers and leaning out windows saw the ball bounce on the pavement.
For eight innings, according to one writer, Shibe had been as solemn as "a
convention of morticians." Suddenly it erupted. "The place went up in a
roar," English recalls.

Bishop skipped over second base and then slowed down, waiting for Haas to catch up to him, and shook Mule's hand before trotting on toward home. From the presidential box the mayor of Philadelphia, Harry Mackey, sitting two seats to the left of Hoover, vaulted over the railing and embraced Haas as he swam into the arms of teammates gathered at the dugout.

Up in the press box the rhapsodies began. Cy Peterman, writing for *The Evening Bulletin* of Philadelphia, penned this ode: "They sing of joy when long lost sons come home. They prate of happiness when wars are done. But did you ever see a homer in the ninth that tied the score? There, ladies and gentlemen, is joy."

Standing at short, English could feel the game slipping away. In front of him Malone stepped off the mound toward home and stuck out his jaw at his catcher, yelling angrily, "You asked for that one!"

Taylor walked forward and tried to calm Malone. "How was I to know?" the catcher asked. "Bear down now and win it back in the 10th. You're the one to do it."

Just then, up to the plate went the menacing Cochrane, who was hitting .429 in the Series. Malone settled down at once and got the A's catcher to bounce a ground ball to Hornsby for the second out. The pitcher was now one out away from extra innings, but his woes were far from over. The Philadelphia leftfielder, Simmons, with his weak ankles and heavy thighs, went lumbering to the batter's box like Br'er Bear in the Uncle Remus tales, carrying on his shoulder his 38-inch-long club. At times like this nobody, except perhaps Foxx, could stir the crowds at Shibe the way the former Aloysius Harry Szymanski, the son of a Polish immigrant from Milwaukee, could.

Simmons was known as Bucketfoot Al for his unorthodox hitting stroke: Instead of stepping toward the pitcher when he swung, he stepped toward third base, into the bucket. As awkward as the maneuver looked, however, Simmons unfailingly leaned into pitches, driving through them with his left shoulder. Most pitchers were terrified of him because he could drive the ball to all parts of the park. "He had the best power to the opposite field of any hitter I saw," says Hayworth. "He used to hit the ball over the rightfield scoreboard like a lefthanded hitter."

Indeed, for years Simmons's line drives beat like distant drums off the right-centerfield fence at Shibe. On the eve of the '29 Series, in *The Evening Bulletin*, Ty Cobb had called Simmons "the gamest man in baseball with two strikes on him." Whenever the A's were compared to the Yankees, Simmons was Gehrig to Foxx's Ruth.

For kids who haunted the perimeters of Shibe, Simmons was the grist of legend. This was a time when players often lived in private homes near the ballparks where they played. Simmons lived across the street from Shibe's rightfield fence, in a second-floor bedroom in the home of Mr. and Mrs. A.C. Conwell. Simmons was a notoriously late sleeper, and the discreet Mrs. Conwell would ask neighborhood boys to awaken the star so he would not miss batting practice. One of the lads was Jerry Rooney, whose family lived three doors away, and at age four, he recalls, he entered Simmons's room and whispered, "It's time to wake up, Al. You're in a slump, and it's time to go to batting practice."

He was in no slump now. Simmons had an oft-expressed contempt for pitchers. "They're trying to take bread and butter out of my mouth," he used to say. Going to bat against Malone, Simmons treated the pitcher as if he were throwing batting practice. On the second pitch Simmons stepped in the bucket and lofted a drive to right center that looked like a home run. It fell just short, but by the time centerfielder Hack Wilson played the ricochet off the scoreboard, the crowd was on its feet, singing, and Simmons was pulling up at second.

Malone walked Foxx intentionally, setting up a force at three bases, and then Miller stepped into the box, looking for a curve that never came.

SHIBE PARK, which had opened in 1909, occupied a single city block of North Philly. The stadium, bounded by streets on all four sides, was at the center of a predominantly Irish neighborhood of row houses and small factories. Like a ballpark in a Norman Rockwell painting, Shibe had knotholes in the wooden fence in rightfield where dozens of smudge-nosed boys lined up daily to peer in, as if looking into a giant magic egg. To hear old-timers in Philadelphia remember it, Shibe had a stunning shag rug of deepest green, its paths and boxes and pitcher's mound immaculately manicured, in the middle of a city blackened by factory chimneys and coal-burning locomotives. "Shibe was this perfect place," says Walt Garvin, a 76-year-old Philadelphia native. "Everything was green. No advertisements on the fences. Neat and clean and perfectly kept."

The Phillies played in the dilapidated Baker Bowl, six blocks east of Shibe on Lehigh Avenue, and attending one of their games in those days was tantamount to slumming. From the first year a Philadelphia team played in the World Series—back in 1905, when the New York Giants defeated the A's four games to one—until the Whiz Kids won the pennant for the Phillies in 1950, this was an American League city, a town whose heart belonged to the A's.

That first Athletics-Giants Series, not incidentally, had powerful social overtones. It set the tall, reserved, lace-curtain Irishman from Massachusetts, Cornelius McGillicuddy, against the scrappy shanty Irishman from New York, John McGraw. But the 1905 Series represented something broader than the class divisions among the immigrant Irish on the Eastern seaboard. It symbolized the historic struggle for primacy between the two largest and most prosperous cities in the U.S.: New York and Philadelphia.

In Colonial days Boston had been the first U.S. city in size and importance. But by the end of the 18th century Philadelphia had become ascendant, and so it remained until the mid-1800s, when New York took over as the economic and cultural mecca of the New World. In the early days of the 20th century Philadelphia was the nation's second city, and its teams' most memorable clashes on baseball diamonds—first against the Giants and later against the Yankees—expressed the city's aspiration to reclaim its place as the nation's center.

"The battle between New York and Philadelphia in baseball was symbolic of that battle for urban supremacy," says Bruce Kuklick, Nichols Professor of American History at Penn and author of *To Every Thing a Season: Shibe Park and Urban Philadelphia*. And at the center of the battle, always, was Mack.

It was he who pieced together the powerful A's team that whipped Chicago in the 1910 World Series, four games to one, and then twice crushed the Giants, 4–2 in 1911 and 4–1 in 1913. And it was Mack who, after selling the stars of those teams to avoid a bidding war with the emerging Federal League, ultimately retooled the A's into an even better team through a series of remarkably sage moves in 1923, the year he bought a curveball artist named Rube Walberg; in '24, the year he took rookies Simmons and Bishop to spring training; and in '25, the year he obtained Cochrane and Grove from minor league clubs and, at the urging of one of his retired sluggers, Frank (Home Run) Baker, picked up a grinning, moonfaced farm boy from the Eastern Shore of Maryland: Foxx.

Thus the A's acquired four future Hall of Famers—Simmons, Grove, Cochrane and Foxx—in two remarkable years. By 1928, still fishing, Mack had plucked Haas out of the minors and added a strapping 6' 4" graduate of Swarthmore College, George Earnshaw, who threw a blazing heater and a nasty snake. By then Mack was also recycling through Shibe some of the greatest has-beens in the game, including Cobb and fellow outfielder Tris Speaker. John Rooney, Jerry's brother, recalls the day in 1928, when he was five, that his father took him to the roof of their row house at 2739 North 20th Street. Pointing to the A's outfielders, the elder Rooney said, "See those three men? I want you to remember them. They are Ty Cobb, Tris Speaker and Al Simmons. Three of the greatest ballplayers of all time."

The Yankees won successive World Series in 1927 and '28, but the latter year it took all they had to keep the salty A's from stealing the pennant. New York finished 2½ games in front of Philadelphia, but what hurt Athletics fans was not so much losing but losing to the Yankees. "They were terribly disliked in Philadelphia," says Allen Lewis, who in 1928 was an 11-year-old A's fan and who later would become a baseball writer for the *Philadelphia Inquirer* and a member of the Veterans Committee of the Baseball Hall of Fame. "The papers used to write 'Noo Yawk Yankees.' It was ridiculous, but they did."

All of which made '29 the sweeter for the waiting. The A's clinched the pennant on Sept. 14. They had become the new irresistible force in baseball. And while Mack had a superb pitching rotation—Grove finished 20–6 and Earnshaw 24–8—it was he, the manager, who threw the most sweeping curve in World Series history. Two weeks before the season's end, Mack secretly decided to start the Series with Ehmke, a 35-year-old journeyman who had pitched fewer than 55 innings during the year. Mack confided his decision to Ehmke, sending him to scout the Cubs, but told no one else.

The press speculated that Earnshaw or Grove would pitch in the opening game, and not even Ehmke believed that Mack would allow him to fulfill his dream of starting in a World Series. As the players warmed up at Wrigley Field, Mack refused to name his starter. At one point Ehmke sat down on the bench next to his manager. "Is it still me, Mr. Mack?" he asked.

"It's still you," Mack said.

Fifteen minutes before game time, Ehmke took off his jacket and started to warm up. Jaws dropped in both dugouts. Grove and Earnshaw stared at each other in disbelief. Ehmke hadn't pitched in weeks. Simmons was sitting next to Mack, and he could not restrain himself. "Are you gonna pitch him?" Simmons asked.

"You have any objections to that?" Mack answered. Simmons shook his head. "If you say so, it's all right with me," he replied.

Over the next three hours, in one of the most dazzling performances in World Series history, Ehmke struck out 13 batters, then a Series record, with a bewildering array of sneaky-quick fastballs and off-speed curves. Looking loose-jointed and nonchalant, Ehmke at times seemed half asleep. "He looked like he didn't give a damn what happened," English recalls. "He threw that big, slow curveball that came in and broke away from righthanders." All but one Cubs starter, first baseman Charlie Grimm, hit from the right side, and Ehmke twice struck out Chicago's toughest batters— Hornsby, Wilson and Cuyler—throwing junk. "Ehmke was a change from the guys we were used to, who threw hard," English says. "Not many pitchers used that stuff against us."

Ehmke went all nine innings and won the game 3–1. Mack would relish that victory the rest of his days. "It was beautiful to watch," he would recall years later.

"That was the surprise of the century," says Hudlin. "Nobody would have done that but Connie Mack. I don't know how Connie figured it. A hunch, I guess. Then Howard went out and made monkeys out of the Cubs."

Ehmke's memorable pitching aside, the Series of '29 showed why that year's Athletics, if overshadowed by the '27 Yankees, have been admired by baseball insiders as one of the best teams in history. Foxx, the first baseman who was known as both Double X and the Beast, hit 33 home runs and batted in 117 runs during the season, and twice he hit prodigious homers in the World Series to put the A's in front to stay: a 400-foot solo shot in Game 1 and a three-run line drive that helped propel Philadelphia to a 9–3 victory in Game 2, in which Grove and Earnshaw fanned 13 Cubs between them.

Foxx retired after the 1945 season with 534 home runs, 1,921 RBIs and a lifetime batting average of .325, but numbers hardly express the high and delicious drama he brought to the plate. He used to cut off the sleeves of his uniform to show off his picnic-roast arms, and he could drive balls 500 feet on a line with a whip of his powerful wrists. "I think he had more power than Ruth or Gehrig," says Mel Harder, who won 223 games for the Indians between 1928 and '47.

It was Lefty Gomez, the Hall of Fame pitcher for the Yankees, who threw the ball that Foxx drove into the upper deck in Yankee Stadium, splintering the back of that seat. Many years later Gomez was sitting at home with his wife watching U.S. astronauts on television as they walked the surface of the moon collecting rocks in a sack. At one point an astronaut picked up what appeared to be a white object.

"I wonder what that is," said Gomez's wife.

"That's the ball Foxx hit off me in New York," Gomez replied.

After winning the first two games of the '29 Series at Wrigley, the A's went home to Shibe looking for a sweep. The Cubs won the third game 3–1 behind the pitching of Guy Bush, but that merely set up the most spectacular game of the Series—one that drew upon the resources of Philadelphia's most formidable pitcher and all the power of its batting order.

By the middle of the seventh inning of Game 4, the Cubs were winning 8–0, and they were riding the A's mercilessly. In the dugout Bush had been celebrating each run by donning a blanket as if it were a headdress and doing what one writer described as "a mock Indian war dance" along the Cubs' bench.

Mack was at the point of surrendering the game when a frustrated Simmons, who earlier had swung so hard on a third strike that he had fallen down, took a cut at Charlie Root's third pitch in the bottom of the seventh and struck a thunderous home run that bounced on the roof of the pavilion in left, making the score 8–1. Four successive A's batters then hit singles: Foxx to right; Miller to center; Dykes to left, scoring Foxx; and shortstop Joe Boley to right center, scoring Miller. With the score 8–3, George Burns, hitting for pitcher Ed Rommel, popped up to English for the first out.

After Bishop singled to center, scoring Dykes, Cubs manager Joe McCarthy called on Art Nehf to relieve Root, who was booed as he walked off the field. "They ought to have cheered him," English says.

On every afternoon of the '29 Series thousands of people jammed City Hall Plaza in downtown Philly to hear the play-by-play piped through speakers and to follow the movement of steel figures on a large magnetic scoreboard. Hundreds watched from open windows at City Hall and nearby office buildings. On other city corners thousands more gathered around P.A. systems that blared the play-by-play. During Game 4 the crowd's voices rose each time the A's scored in the seventh.

Haas went to the plate to face Nehf. The Mule stroked a low liner to center. English turned and saw Wilson lose the ball in the sun. "It went over his head," English says, "and he turned and ran for it." Boley scored. Bishop chased him home. The ball rolled to the wall. Haas rounded third and raced to the plate for an inside-the-park home run. In the A's dugout Dykes pounded on the man standing next to him. "We're back in the game!" Dykes shouted. Reeling under Dykes's blows, the man fell against the bats and spilled them. It was the spindly Mack. Never once had Dykes seen his manager leave the bench. Mack usually just sat there, dressed in a dark suit, like an undertaker, and moved his fielders around with a wave of his scorecard. But he left his seat that day. "I'm sorry," said Dykes.

The 67-year-old skipper just smiled. "That's all right, Jimmy," he said. "Wasn't it wonderful?"

At Mason's Dance Hall in Philly, in a crowd gathered around a radio set on a table, 12-year-old Carmen Cangelosi leaped to his feet, screaming, as the announcer described Haas galloping home: "They're gonna win now! They're gonna win now!" City Hall Plaza erupted in howls.

The score was 8–7. Nehf walked Cochrane and was relieved by Sheriff Blake. Simmons met Blake with a single to left. Foxx then singled through the box, scoring Cochrane and tying the game up. At Philadelphia's Franklin Field, where Allen Lewis was in a football crowd of 30,000 watching Penn play Virginia Poly, the makeshift baseball scoreboard in the west stands had shown the Cubs leading 8–0. "And then the crowd erupted," says Lewis. "In the bottom of the seventh, they put '8' up on the board. Play on the field stopped, and the players all turned around and looked up. I can still see that today."

Malone was brought in to face Miller. Trying to brush the batter back, Malone grazed him with the first pitch, loading the bases. All that English remembers of the waning moments of that historic seventh was the ball cracking off Dykes's bat and flying into deep left, and Riggs Stephenson going back and reaching up but fumbling the ball. "He should have made the catch," English says. The ball bounced off the wall. Simmons and Foxx scored.

The A's led 10–8. Malone then fanned Boley and Burns to end the inning.

When Mack called on Grove to pitch the last two innings, not a boy in all of Philly doubted the game's outcome. Grove was a lanky 6' 3", and in his windup he looked like an oil rig: His head and hands and torso rose and dipped rhythmically—once, twice, three times—until they rose a final time and he fired. "I can still hear Grove's fastball popping into Cochrane's glove," says former A's fan John McLaughlin, 77. No one in Grove's day threw harder, and there are those who believe he threw the hardest of all time.

The Washington Post's Povich remembers a day in the mid-1930s when Bob Feller was the phenom of the hour and was to pitch at Washington's Griffith Stadium against the Senators. The retired Walter Johnson, an old friend of Povich's, was living in Maryland, and Povich invited him out to Griffith to see the kid with the heater, once clocked at 103 mph. "Walter was the most modest man you would ever know," Povich says. "And he's looking at Feller for a couple of innings and saying, 'Oh, he's fast!' Then a little while later he says, 'Oh, my! He's fast!' And then I popped the question: 'Does he throw as fast as you did?' And Walter said, 'No. And I don't think he's as fast as Lefty Grove.' "

Grove's best fastball came in at the letters and rose out of the strike zone. "If you took it, it would be a ball," English says. "But if you had two strikes on you, you couldn't take it. It was that close, and he had great control."

Tales of Grove's exploits abound. One afternoon while leading the Yankees 1–0 in the ninth inning, Grove gave up a triple to the leadoff hitter, shortstop Mark Koenig. Throwing nothing but darts, Grove then struck out Ruth, Gehrig and Bob Meusel. On nine pitches.

Grove had a Vesuvian temper that was quite as famous as his fastball, and he left behind him a trail of wrecked watercoolers and ruined lockers. There were many days when players, particularly skittish rookies, dared not speak to him as he observed the world from the long shadows of his bony scowl. One day in 1931, against the woeful St. Louis Browns, Grove was trying to win his 17th straight game without a loss—and thereby set an American League record—when a young outfielder named Jim Moore, substituting for the ailing Simmons, misjudged an easy fly ball and cost Grove the game, 1–0. Grove swept into the clubhouse like the Creature from the Black Lagoon. He picked up a wooden chair and smashed it into splinters. He then tried to rip off his locker door and settled for kicking it in. His rage unappeased, he tore off his uniform, sending buttons flipping like tiddlywinks, and shredded it like a rag. He bellowed, "Where is Simmons? He could have caught that ball in his back pocket!" Grove refused to speak to anyone for a week, and it was years before he forgave Simmons for staying out sick that day.

After his team stormed back to take the lead in Game 4 of the '29 Series, Grove took to the mound for the final two innings. He faced six batters and blew the ball past four of them. Hornsby, swinging late, flied to Miller to end the game.

There were celebrations in the streets of Philadelphia that night. The A's miraculous victory was the biggest story of the day. No wonder Hoover and his wife went north behind the locomotive *President Washington* to be on hand for Game 5.

PROHIBITION WAS still the law, and as Hoover walked across the field to Shibe's presidential box at 1 p.m., the crowd chanted, "Beer! Beer! We want beer!" What the crowd ended up with was something headier: Simmons standing on second with the score tied in the bottom of the ninth, and Bing Miller, known as Old Reliable, at the plate. Miller was looking for his favorite pitch—"He was the best curveball hitter in the league," Hayworth says—so Malone whipped two fastballs past him for strikes.

"I thought, It will be another fast one," Miller would later recall. So he shortened his grip and moved closer to the plate. Malone threw another fastball, and Miller swung. To this day English can see the ball flying over Hornsby's head, dropping in right center and rolling toward the fence. Simmons charged home to win the game 3–2. The Series was over.

Mack always said that the 1929 World Series was the greatest he ever saw, and that a diorama of that final moment should be built and set in a special corner at Cooperstown: Here is Wilson chasing Miller's double to the fence. Over there is Simmons plowing toward home, his spikes chopping up dirt on the path. In the middle is Malone, standing on the mound with his head down. And there is Hoover on his feet, applauding, and Mayor Mackey leaping from the box again, this time tossing his hat in the air, while all the A's charge out of the dugout onto a perfectly manicured patch of green.

It was the last World Series game that America would watch in innocence. Fifteen days later, on Black Tuesday—Oct. 29, 1929—the stock market would crash, and the country would begin to slide into the Great Depression. While the A's would win the World Series again in 1930 and a third straight pennant in '31, their fate would mirror the desperate nature of the times. By the end of 1932, scrambling to stay afloat financially, Mack had sold Simmons, Dykes and Haas to the Chicago White Sox for $100,000. In December '33 Mack sent Grove, Walberg and Bishop to the Boston Red Sox for $125,000 and two nobodies, and Cochrane to the Tigers for $100,000 and one nobody. Foxx hit 58 home runs in 1932 and 128 in the three years after that, but following the '35 season, Mack sold him to the Red Sox for $150,000 and two players. Through the 1930s and '40s the A's never got near another pennant and often had the worst team in baseball.

Of course, New York won the battle for urban supremacy. The A's were Philadelphia's last illusion of ascendancy. The poignant aftermath to all this was that the Yankees led the lobby that drove the A's out of Philadelphia and into Kansas City for the 1955 season. Like conquered warriors, the Kansas City A's became a sort of farm team for the Yankees, and over the years they fed New York players such as Roger Maris and Clete Boyer. The A's moved to Oakland in 1968 and won three straight World Series, from 1972 to '74. Then, when owner Charles Finley began feeling financial pressures, much as Mack had years before, the Yankees fed on Oakland's remains. Two of the A's best players, Jim (Catfish) Hunter and Reggie Jackson, figured prominently on the Yankees' 1977 and '78 championship teams.

The A's of '29 to '31 left a generation of Philadelphians with memories of what it was like to have a team that ate the great Yankees for dinner, with Cubs on the side. Today, most fans who recall the A's of that era are in or nearing their 80's. What they all remember most vividly is that '29 World Series—the day Ehmke whipped the Cubs, the day the A's scored 10 in the seventh and the day Simmons scored from second to win the final game.

Carmen Cangelosi still remembers sitting in Mason's Dance Hall and listening to that seventh inning of Game 4 on the radio. "That inning made me a baseball fan for life," says Cangelosi, 78, a retired graphic artist. "I was an Athletics fan for life. I still know all the players. I know where they played. I know their nicknames: Bucketfoot Al. Double X. Old Reliable. Lefty. Mule. I know that 10-run inning and who scored and how they score, just like it was yesterday at Mason's. I remember when they won the World Series. There was a buzz in the air. An energy. You felt good about yourself, about your city, about everybody around you.

"It broke my heart when they moved. They're long gone, but I remember everything. I sometimes go to sleep thinking about them. What a team!"

APRIL 7, 2003

❧

Hey, Chicago, Wait Till This Year

BY RICK TELANDER

As another season dawned, long-suffering Cubs and White Sox fans got their hopes up again (sort of).

A S I STAND HERE ON THE WOODEN "L" PLATFORM AT Addison Street, peering between a pair of three-story buildings at empty Wrigley Field, this is what I think: If a fired-up Sammy Sosa batted lefthanded with a stiff breeze out of the Iowa cornfields, in the heat of midsummer, he could launch a ball that would soar over the rightfield wall and Sheffield Avenue and the bleachered roofs of these brownstones and land at my feet.

Why not? Once, in a breeze, Cubbies slugger Dave Kingman smacked a home run ball that cleared the ivy-leafed leftfield wall, crossed Waveland Avenue and hit the first house on Kenmore Street, perpendicular to Waveland.

Lefty-hitting Billy Williams routinely broke apartment windows along Sheffield. His righty pal Ernie Banks broke them on Waveland. It's just a few more feet to hit the train stop where I stand. O.K., maybe a hundred feet. Maybe 150.

But Sammy—the god of rightfield-bleacher worshipers, the chest-thump, finger-kiss, point-to-the-fans ambassador of happy—what couldn't Sammy do?

Ah, Chicago baseball. It is like a drink that makes you laugh, then cry, then babble. Hope springs eternal in Chicago. It springs insane. This same train line that can carry me south 13 stops to 35th Street and the home of the White Sox, Comiskey Park—excuse me, U.S. Cellular Field—ties together those two pockets of hope like a bungee cord. WHAT DO SOX FANS AND CUBS FANS HAVE IN COMMON? asks the placard inside each car. THE RED LINE.

But they have so much more than that. Start with the hope. A lot of knowledgeable baseball people have picked the White Sox to win their division this year. This is a team that finished .500 last season. This is a team that hasn't won a playoff series since 1917. The *Chicago Tribune*'s Phil Rogers has the Sox going all the way to the World Series. "There," Rogers gasped in his March 27 column. "I actually wrote the sentence and haven't yet turned to stone."

And the Cubs. Dear God, this is the team that hasn't won the World Series since 1908, the longest stretch of futility for any continuously active pro team in any sports league in the history of North America. And yet Cubs fans are fired up. There's a new manager in town, toothpick-twirling Dusty Baker, direct from the San Francisco Giants and their 2002 Series appearance. Baker hasn't managed a losing team since 1996, and he has a kid, four-year-old Darren, who looks so sweet in his miniature Cubs uniform that he could be replicated as a good-luck dashboard ornament. Yes, the Cubs finished 67–95 last year, 30 games out of first, but they've got Sammy, who through Monday was one homer short of 500 (and didn't he almost destroy the Miller Field scoreboard at last year's All-Star home run derby?), and a young rotation that is headed by 25-year-old fireballer Kerry Wood and includes three other twentysomethings—Mark Prior, Matt Clement and Carlos Zambrano. The bullpen may be suspect and the defense dubious, but what does that matter if you're a Cubs fan feeling macho in your WE'VE GOT WOOD T-shirt?

"I was looking for a team that could be this year's Angels," says ESPN.com baseball analyst Jayson Stark of his assessment of which formerly bad team could turn it all around, the way the '02 Series champs did. "The Angels finished 41 games out of first in 2001, you know." So Stark eliminated teams based on various criteria and private theories and, as he says, "there I was with the Cubs and the White Sox." After further review, he eliminated the Sox, and voilà! He was left with the Cubs going to the World Series.

"I recognize how much money I could have lost on the Cubs over 80 years," he says. "Nevertheless, starting pitching, Dusty, the fact that Sammy will be good, Moises Alou can't be worse, the NL Central's nothing special, so. . . . " He seems to be recalculating, like a mathematician stunned by his own equation. "Why not?"

By such ringing endorsements are Chicago hearts inflamed.

Think of it: There are experts who say (if you condense their many thoughts and select the ones you like) that the Cubs and the White Sox will meet this October in a subway series. Then there is reality. Deep down, Chicagoans know—history has proved—that their baseball dreams are just bubbles. New York can have its Bronx-Queens classics with the Yankees and the Mets. But the odds against the Cubs going 95 years without a World Series crown are huge. And the odds against the Cubs and the Sox giving one city 180 years of combined futility are, according to Elias Sports Bureau, 10,000 to 1. Which is to say, statistically implausible. Yet true.

"Maybe there's somebody up there not looking after us," says former star White Sox pitcher Billy Pierce.

What all that losing has done is unite the teams' fans in an unacknowledged bond of self-contempt. The hope is there—Chicago is a hardworking, extreme-weather town that handles even February with optimism—but not the deep-seated belief that either team will amount to anything. The Cubs had the metal removed from their spines in the storied collapse of 1969—up by 9½ games in August, they finished eight behind the Mets. The Sox had a giddy pennant drive in 1959 and then were slapped aside by the Dodgers in the World Series. That, of course, was 44 years ago, the last time either Chicago team would play for it all.

But the Sox also had 1983, when they won their division by 20 games and were promptly thrashed by the Baltimore Orioles in the American League Championship Series. Worst bummer of all, though, was 1994, the strike year. The Sox had their best team in decades—led by guitar-playing pitcher Jack McDowell and young slugger Frank Thomas, they were 21 games over .500 when baseball shut down—only to see it neutered by the strike, with management's biggest nut-cutter being the Sox' chairman, Jerry Reinsdorf.

"Oh, poor Chicago," says Pierce, who played on that '59 team, never dreaming it would be a pinnacle that would erode like a spring ice chunk in Lake Michigan. "That's a long time ago. You think about a big city like this, and you think there's something wrong. The Cubs in 1984—you couldn't believe that could happen."

Oh, right. The '84 Cubs of Ryne Sandberg and Rick Sutcliffe fame were up two-zip on the San Diego Padres in the five-game National League

Championship Series, then lost three straight. And let's not forget 1998, when the Cubs and their fans celebrated wildly after the club won a wild-card playoff game against the Giants. The reward? A 3–0 divisional spank-fest on the Atlanta Braves' knee.

Bill Peterson, the Chicago-born star of the TV show *CSI: Crime Scene Investigation*, is a Chicago sports fan of such intensity that he once left a film set in Atlanta and took a commercial flight to Washington, D.C., for a few hours just so he could watch the Bears play on TV. He is a Cubs fan and is on the April cover of *Men's Journal*, sitting at a bar with other rabid Cubs nuts.

"It's all about Fergie Jenkins and Ernie and Ron Santo," Peterson says. "A tie to your childhood." And, of course, dislocation makes the tie grow stronger. "I sit here in Los Angeles," says Peterson, "and it's just a wasteland. In Chicago you have elements to contend with. Here it's 76 degrees, it's perfect. And you know what? It sucks."

That's a Chicago sentiment. That's where the empathy for the '69 Cubs comes from. Hey, folks, we know how scrawny Don Kessinger suffered in that September heat. Hey, I once lost my car in a snowdrift. Kessinger was nearly a skeleton by Labor Day. Peterson says he would root for the White Sox if there were no Cubs, and at any rate, "I don't root against them." But the Sox have what he describes as "bad dynamics." Many Cubs fans agree. "Man, they used to have exciting guys like Luis Aparicio and Nellie Fox. Now, Frank Thomas, Mark Buehrle, Bartolo Colon? Like I could care? There are heroes on the North Side. Thomas is a mope. Snap out of it! Plus, I hate the park."

U.S. Cellular Field is the new name of the park that will host this year's All-Star Game, but it may be years before anyone refers to the place as anything other than Comiskey, or New Comiskey, which came into vogue after the original ballpark was demolished, in 1991. The newly renamed park—fans will appreciate the improvements we're making with the signage money, says Reinsdorf—is not exactly sterile, but it has roughly the charm of a clean utensil drawer.

Wrigley, on the other hand, is a quaint little relic from the days when elevators and parking lots weren't on ballpark architects' radar. Wrigley is so nestled into its yuppified neighborhood that its outside wall at one point is only 7½ feet from the gutter of Addison Street. "A lot of the Sox fans' problems with the Cubs is jealousy," admits former White Sox home run champ Bill Melton, himself a diehard Sox man. Melton means the Wrigley attendance—which is huge regardless of the Cubs' performance. (The past five seasons were among the Cubs' six best attendance years ever at Wrigley, despite the team's having finished a combined 107½ games out of first place over that span.) He also means the festive atmosphere in a ballyard surrounded by dozens of bars, restaurants and million-dollar condos. "But Wrigley is a dump," Melton says. "I'd love to hit there. But it's a dump."

A dump can be beautiful and rare in its way, which is why the city of Chicago is trying to designate Wrigley a historic landmark. Naturally, Cubs ownership, the Tribune Company, doesn't want such a distinction. You can't build more skyboxes in a landmark or add giant bleachers to it. That's another thing: Chicago mayor Richard M. Daley is a born-and-raised South Side Sox fan, like his dad, former mayor Richard J. (Boss) Daley, and you always wonder if Junior wouldn't like to stick it to the Cubs somehow. But the North Side Cubs have a unique quality that seems to be tamper-proof. Let's let Bill Jauss, the veteran *Tribune* sportswriter and a North Sider through and through—and, of course, the son of a Cubs fan—explain. "I have interviewed literally hundreds of Cubs fans around the park, made it a point to talk to them after excruciating losses," says Jauss. "I ask them, 'Did you have fun?' And about 90 percent say yes. I ask them why. *Well, we saw the girls fall out of their halter tops. The beer was cold. The breeze was off the lake. What's better on a summer afternoon?*

"The answers imply that the Cubs are not in the baseball business but the entertainment business. And the biggest entertainer in the troupe is Sosa. You can see it in the kids' faces. [Former White Sox manager] Jeff Torborg told me last year that when he sees Sammy run out before the first pitch—with his right hand up and his finger pointed to the sky, his head down, sprinting as fast as he possibly can, circling in front of the rightfield bleachers in a counterclockwise fashion toward centerfield and back—he gets goose bumps.

"Santo wore his emotions on his sleeve. Hank Sauer before him. The fans loved Rod Beck. The Cubs don't have to win to entertain. And the '69 Cubs epitomized that. When else has a loser been so glorified? Sox fans are more discriminating. They think they know more baseball than Cubs fans. They think they're all Tony La Russas. In the meantime the Cubs fans are having more fun."

That wasn't always the case, because the sly and effervescent charlatan Bill Veeck once ran the White Sox, bringing in midgets and spaceships and all manner of nonsense to amuse folks and deflect awareness that he had almost no money to invest in players. Veeck was once an executive with the Cubs, too—it was he who planted the first ivy at Wrigley—but his heart was on the South Side, where he could work with the common man who would happily come to his baseball sideshow. "Listen to me carefully now," Veeck wrote in *The Hustler's Handbook*, "because if you are a hustler, you are going to start out with a bad team. A bad ball club is generally the available one, the cheaper one, and the one you can best bring your talents to bear upon."

"Hoyt Wilhelm one time was pitching [for the Orioles] at Comiskey, and he was attacked by furious clouds of gnats," recalls Jauss. "He just smiled. He suspected Bill Veeck."

One of Veeck's friends, 81-year-old Chicago sportswriting legend Bill Gleason, retired these past two years, points out that there are other divisions in Sox-Cubs fandom besides geography or even economic class. "It's religious," the Irish Catholic South Sider says. "The Cubs started with Protestants on the West Side. Comiskey came in with the newer American League club, and the Irish Catholics were down here on the South Side. My grandfather, who came from Tipperary, was a Sox fan, and my father, who was born in Joliet, came up on the Inter-urban to old White Sox Park at 39th and Wentworth. I'm a Sox fan. I have two brothers who are Sox fans and one sister who is. Another sister became a heretic, a Cubs fan. My father said, 'I'd rather she left the church.'

"In 1959 Mayor Daley and his pals set off the air-raid sirens after the Sox clinched the pennant, and it scared a lot of little old ladies on the South Side—they thought we were being attacked by the Russkies." Gleason pauses to reflect. He sighs. "It was so typical of the Sox, to get all excited and do the wrong thing. I'm convinced the White Sox are cursed. The Black Sox scandal is proof of that. Ray Schalk was the catcher on that team, and if you ever used the words *Black Sox* or *scandal* in his presence, you would hear a stream of curse words. He referred to it only as '1919.' But it destroyed the Sox. They lost eight players. Schalk told me, 'There never would have been any f----- Yankees if it weren't for 1919!'"

The lint of truth therein lingers sadly. Of the first 15 World Series, 10 were won by teams from Chicago or Boston. Since 1919 the Yankees and the Mets have won a total of 31 titles, and of course the Sox and the Cubs have won none. The Red Sox haven't won a Series since 1918, and they gave Babe Ruth to the Yankees way back then. But we'll let Red Sox fans tell their story another time.

There is one other factor in determining the Cubs' and the Sox' fan bases. "Yes, it's north and south," says Chicago native Michael Wilbon, a sports columnist for *The Washington Post* and cohost of ESPN's *Pardon the Interruption.* "But it's also racial." Wilbon, who grew up on the South Side, remembers that black Sox players and even black Cubs players lived near him because they couldn't get housing on the North Side. "My dad tried to go see Jackie Robinson at Wrigley in 1948, and he was turned away, and he vowed he would never go see the Cubs again. Walt (No Neck) Williams of the Sox lived near us, and Ernie Banks lived just east. We'd all take the "L" to Comiskey, like, 20 times a year. But Wrigley, that might as well have been in Minneapolis."

Still, Wilbon is now a fan of the Cubs as well as the Sox, sensing their common ineptitude and linked striving. He has a satellite dish and a baseball package at his home in Maryland just so he can watch his hometown clubs. "Michael Jordan and the Bulls relieved pressure on Chicago baseball," says Wilbon. "Ditka and McMahon and the Bears of the '80s took a lot of summertime depression out of it.

"But I don't expect to see the Cubs or Sox win a World Series in my lifetime. I stopped daydreaming about it. I let it go."

All the bad trades and dumb deals by both clubs are enough to make most fans exhale like Wilbon. The Cubs' 1964 trade of leftfielder Lou Brock to the Cardinals for sore-armed pitcher Ernie Broglio, who won all of seven games for the Cubs while Brock became a Hall of Famer, is generally considered the worst in team history. But letting Greg Maddux go to Atlanta also ranks right up there, or down there.

The White Sox' signing of human virus Albert Belle for tons of money was bad. As was bringing in goofball pitcher David Wells, pre-diet. But canning singular manager La Russa in 1986, three years after he won the division and was named Manager of the Year, might win the dunce cap.

And what of on-field blunders? How about Sox manager Terry Bevington going to the mound and calling for a righty out of the bullpen, only to discover nobody of either arm was warming up? The White Sox' red uniforms and their honest-to-god game shorts would make even Elton John blush. But let's also recall Cubs eccentric Joe Pepitone, who once, after reaching first, got a wink sign from first base coach Joey Amalfitano confirming a hit-and-run play. Pepitone, who spent great lengths of time grooming his toupee, winked back at Amalfitano, blew him a kiss—and was promptly picked off.

Hack Wilson, who holds the major league single-season RBI record, with

191, was such a drunk in the 1930s that an enlargement of a newspaper story titled HACK'S LAST WARNING is posted in the Cubs' training room. "Talent isn't enough," Wilson says in the old interview, when he was near death. "You need common sense and good advice. . . . I spent all of my money, most of it in barrooms."

Wrigley Field itself has been compared to an outdoor barroom, and former Cubs manager Lee Elia's tirade against the Wrigley daytime habitues in 1983 was half-inspired, half-deranged. "The f---ers don't even work!" Elia ranted. "That's why they're out at the f------ game! Tell 'em to go out and get a f------ job and find out what it's like to earn a f------ living! Eighty-five percent of the f------ world works, the other 15 come here!"

Well, not all of them. A fellow like me is wandering around the outside of the park, marveling again that the only statue at Wrigley is not of Hack or Tinker or Evers or Chance—Cubs all—but of bloated, grinning announcer Harry Caray, holding out a microphone to an invisible crowd, singing silently in the seventh inning. LET ME HEAR YA. . . . the legend chiseled on the base reads. A ONE. . . . A TWO. . . . A THREE. . . . It's perfect, really, just like Disco Demolition at Comiskey years ago, the blow-up-the-albums riot that canceled a game and destroyed the turf as well as the sanity of the place. Deejay Steve Dahl, who concocted the event and wore a military helmet during the detonation, says now that Sox fans and Cubs fans can accept the endless losing because "we're happy just to be outside for a few months."

There's truth there. But I think also of the bond among all the finger-pointing Chicago baseball fans, the loop of yearning and hope and wistfulness and suffering that ropes them all together like a herd. "All the baseball infighting in this city, and it means nothing," says veteran WMVP-AM 1000 radio producer Tom Serritella. "It's like the slug calling the worm a crawler."

And so I return to the "L" and climb aboard for the 25-minute ride south to the place called U.S. Cellular Field, thinking that this would be the preferred mode of transportation for fans in the event of a Chicago subway series. But what am I thinking? Even hope has its limits. A train can chug, but it can't fly.

✌

At the End of the Curse, A Blessing

BY TOM VERDUCCI

The 2004 Boston Red Sox staged the most improbable comeback in baseball history and liberated their long-suffering nation of fans.

THE CANCER WOULD HAVE KILLED MOST MEN LONG AGO, but not George Sumner. The Waltham, Mass., native had served three years aboard the USS *Arkansas* in World War II, raised six kids with a hell of a lot more love than the money that came from fixing oil burners, and watched from his favorite leather chair in front of the television—except for the handful of times he had the money to buy bleacher seats at Fenway—his Boston Red Sox, who had found a way not to win the World Series in every one of the 79 years of his life. George Sumner knew something about persistence.

The doctors and his family thought they had lost George last Christmas Day, more than two years after the diagnosis. Somehow George pulled through. And soon, though still sick and racked by the chemo, the radiation and the trips in and out of hospitals for weeks at a time, George was saying, "You know what? With Pedro and Schilling we've got a pretty good staff this year. Please let this be the year."

On the night of Oct. 13, 2004, George Sumner knew he was running out of persistence. The TV in his room at Newton-Wellesley Hospital was showing Pedro Martinez and the Red Sox losing to the New York Yankees in

Game 2 of the American League Championship Series—this after Boston had lost Game 1 behind Curt Schilling. During commercial breaks Sumner talked with his daughter Leah about what to do with his personal possessions. Only a few days earlier his wife, Jeanne, had told him, "If the pain is too much, George, it's O.K. if you want to go."

But Leah knew how much George loved the Red Sox, saw how closely he still watched their games and understood that her father, ever quick with a smile or a joke, was up to something.

"Dad, you're waiting around to see if they go to the World Series, aren't you?" she said. "You really want to see them win it, right?"

A sparkle flickered in the sick man's eyes and a smile creased his lips.

"Don't tell your mother," he whispered.

At that moment, 30 miles away in Weymouth, Mass., Jaime Andrews stewed about the Red Sox' losing again but found some relief in knowing that he might be spared the conflict he had feared for almost nine months. His wife, Alice, was due to give birth on Oct. 27. Game 4 of the World Series was scheduled for that night. Jamie was the kind of tortured fan who could not watch when the Red Sox were protecting a lead late in the game, because of a chronic, aching certainty that his team would blow it again.

Alice was not happy that Jaime worried at all about the possible conflict between the birth and the Sox. She threatened to bar him from the delivery room if Boston was playing that night. "Pathetic," she called his obsession with his team.

"It's not my fault," Jaime would plead and fall on the DNA defense. "It was passed down through generations, from my grandfather to my mother to me."

Oh, well, James thought as he watched the Red Sox lose Game 2, at least now I won't have to worry about my team in the World Series when my baby is born.

Dear Red Sox:
My boyfriend is a lifelong Red Sox fan. He told me we'll get married when the Red Sox win the World Series. . . . I watched every pitch of the playoffs.

— SIGNED BY A BRIDE-TO-BE

THE MOST emotionally powerful words in the English language are monosyllabic: love, hate, born, live, die, sex, kill, laugh, cry, want, need, give, take, Sawx.

The Boston Red Sox are, of course, a civic religion in New England. As grounds crew workers tended to the Fenway Park field last summer after a night game, one of them found a white plastic bottle of holy water in the outfield grass. There was a handwritten message on the side: GO SOX. The team's 2003 highlight film, punctuated by the crescendo of the walk-off home run by the Yankees' Aaron Boone in ALCS Game 7, was christened, *Still, We Believe*.

"We took the wording straight out of the Catholic canon," club president Larry Lucchino says. "It's not *We Still Believe*. Our working slogan for next year is *It's More than Baseball. It's the Red Sox*."

Rooting for the Red Sox is, as evident daily in the obituary pages, a life's definitive calling. Every day all over New England, and sometimes beyond, death notices include age, occupation, parish and allegiance to the Sox. Charles F. Brazeau, born in North Adams, Mass., and an Army vet who was awarded a Purple Heart in World War II, lived his entire 85 years without seeing the Red Sox win a world championship, though barely so. When he passed on in Amarillo, Texas, just two days before Boston won the 2004 World Series, the *Amarillo Globe News* eulogized him as a man who "loved the Red Sox and cheap beer."

Rest in peace.

What the Red Sox mean to their faithful—and larger still, what sport at its best means to American culture—never was more evident than at precisely 11:40 EDT on the night of Oct. 27. At that moment in St. Louis, Red Sox closer Keith Foulke, upon fielding a ground ball, threw to first baseman Doug Mientkiewicz for the final out of the World Series—and the first Red Sox world championship since 1918. And then all hell didn't just break loose. It pretty much froze over.

All over New England, church bells clanged. Grown men wept. Poets whooped. Convicts cheered. Children rushed into the streets. Horns honked. Champagne corks popped. Strangers hugged.

Virginia Muise, 111, and Fred Hale, 113, smiled. Both Virginia, who kept a Red Sox cap beside her nightstand in New Hampshire, and Fred, who lived in Maine until moving to Syracuse, N.Y., at 109, were Red Sox fans who, curse be damned, were *born before Babe Ruth himself*. Virginia was the oldest person in New England. Fred was the oldest man in the world. Within three weeks after they had watched the Sox win the Series, both of them passed away.

They died happy.

Dear Red Sox:
Can you get married on the mound in, say, November at Fenway?

ON ITS most basic level, sport satisfies man's urge to challenge his physical being. And sometimes, if performed well enough, it inspires others in their own pursuits. And then, very rarely, it changes the social and cultural history of America; it changes *lives*. The 2004 Boston Red Sox are such a perfect storm.

The Red Sox are SI's Sportsmen of the Year, an honor they may have won even if the magnitude of their unprecedented athletic achievement was all that had been considered. Three outs from being swept in the ALCS, they won eight consecutive games, the last six without ever trailing. Their place in the sporting pantheon is fixed; the St. Jude of sports, patron saint of lost athletic causes, their spirit will be summoned at the bleakest of moments.

"It is the story of hope and faith rewarded," says Red Sox executive vice president Charles Steinberg. "You really believe that this is the story they're going to teach seven-year-olds 50 years from now. When they say, 'Naw, I can't do this,' you can say, 'Ah, yes you can. The obstacle was much greater for these 25 men, and they overcame. So can you.' "

What makes them undeniably, unforgettably Sportsmen, however, is that their achievement transcended the ballpark like that of no other professional sports team. The 1955 Brooklyn Dodgers were the coda to a sweet, special time and place in Americana. The 1968 Detroit Tigers gave needed joy to a city teeming with anger and strife. The 2001 Yankees provided a gathering place, even as a diversion, for a grieving, wounded city. The 2004 Red Sox made an even deeper impact because this championship was lifetimes in the making.

This Boston team connected generations, for the first time, with joy instead of disappointment as the emotional mortar. This team changed the way a people, raised to expect the worst, would think of themselves and the future. And the impact, like all things in that great, wide community called Red Sox Nation, resounded from cradle to grave.

On the morning after the Red Sox won the World Series, Sgt. Paul Barnicle, a detective with the Boston police and brother of *Boston Herald* columnist Mike Barnicle, left his shift at six, purchased a single red rose at the city's flower market, drove 42 miles to a cemetery in Fitchburg, Mass., and placed the rose on the headstone of his mother and father, among the many who had not lived long enough to see it.

Five days later, Roger Altman, former deputy treasury secretary in the Clinton Administration, who was born and raised in Brookline, Mass., flew from New York City to Boston carrying a laminated front page of the Oct. 28 *New York Times* (headline: RED SOX ERASE 86 YEARS OF FUTILITY IN FOUR GAMES). He drove to the gravesite of his mother, who had died in November 2003 at age 95, dug a shallow trench and buried the front page there.

Such pilgrimages to the deceased, common after the Red Sox conquered the Yankees in the ALCS, were repeated throughout the graveyards of New England. The totems changed, but the sentiments remained the same. At Mount Auburn Cemetery in Cambridge, for instance, gravestones were decorated with Red Sox pennants, hats, jerseys, baseballs, license plates and a hand-painted pumpkin.

So widespread was the remembrance of the deceased that several people, including Neil Van Zile Jr. of Westmoreland, N.H., beseeched the ball club to issue a permanent, weatherproof official Red Sox grave marker for dearly departed fans, similar to the metal markers the federal government provides for veterans. (Team president Lucchino says he's going to look into it, though Major League Baseball Properties would have to license it.) Van Zile's mother, Helen, a Sox fan who kept score during games and took her son to Game 2 of the 1967 World Series, died in 1995 at 72.

"There are thousands of people who would want it," Van Zile says. "My mom didn't get to see it. There isn't anything else I can do for her."

One day last year Van Zile was walking through a cemetery in Chesterfield, N.H., when the inscription on a grave stopped him. BLOUIN was the family name chiseled into the marble. Beneath that it said NAPOLEON A. 1926–1986. At the bottom, nearest to the ground, was the kicker of a lifetime. DARN THOSE RED SOX.

Dear Red Sox:
Thanks for the motivation.
    —JOSUE RODAS, MARINE, 6TH MOTOR TRANSPORT COMPANY, IRAQ

LIKE SNOWFLAKES in a blizzard came the e-mails. More than 10,000 of them flew into the Red Sox' server in the first 10 days after Boston won the World Series. No two exactly alike. They came from New England, but they also came from Japan, Italy, Pakistan and at least 11 other countries. The New England town hall of the 21st century was electronic.

There were thank-you letters. There were love letters. The letters were worded as if they were written to family members, and indeed the Red Sox were, in their own unkempt, scruffy, irreverent way, a likable, familial bunch. How could the faithful not love a band of characters self-deprecatingly self-dubbed the "idiots"?

DH David Ortiz, who slammed three walk-off postseason hits, was the Big Papi of the lineup and the clubhouse, with his outsized grin as much a signature of this team as his bat. Leftfielder Manny Ramirez hit like a machine but played the game with a sandlot smile plastered on his mug, even when taking pratfalls in the outfield. Long-locked centerfielder Johnny Damon made women swoon and men cheer and, with his Nazarene look, prompted a T-shirt and bumper sticker bonanza (WWJD: WHAT WOULD JOHNNY DAMON DO? and HONK IF YOU LOVE JOHNNY).

First baseman Kevin Millar, with his Honest Abe beard and goofball personality, had the discipline to draw the walk off Yankees closer Mariano Rivera that began Boston's comeback in the ninth inning of ALCS Game 4. Righthander Derek Lowe, another shaggy eccentric, became the first pitcher to win the clinching game of three postseason series in one October. Foulke, third baseman Bill Mueller, catcher Jason Varitek and rightfielder Trot Nixon—the club's longest-tenured player, known for his pine-tar-encrusted batting helmet—provided gritty ballast.

The love came in e-mails that brought word from soldiers in Iraq with Red Sox patches on their uniforms or Red Sox camouflage hats, the symbols of a nation within a nation. The cannon cockers of the 3rd Battalion 11th Marine Regiment built a mini Fenway Park at Camp Ramadi. Soldiers awoke at 3 a.m. to watch the Sox on a conference-room TV at Camp Liberty in Baghdad, the games ending just in time for the troops to fall in and receive their daily battle briefing.

A woman wrote of visiting an ancient temple in Tokyo and finding this message inscribed on a prayer block: MAY THE RED SOX PLAY ALWAYS AT FENWAY PARK, AND MAY THEY WIN THE WORLD SERIES IN MY LIFETIME.

Besides the e-mails there were boxes upon boxes of letters, photographs, postcards, school projects and drawings that continue to cover what little floor space is left in the Red Sox' offices. Mostly the missives convey profound gratitude.

"Thank you," wrote Maryam Farzeneh, a Boston University graduate student from Iran, "for being another reason for me and my boyfriend to connect and love each other. He is a Red Sox fan and moved to Ohio two years ago. There were countless nights that I kept the phone next to the radio so that we could listen to the game together."

Maryam had never seen a baseball game before 1998. She knew how obsessed people back home were about soccer teams. "Although I should admit," she wrote, "that is nothing like the relationship between the Red Sox and the fans in New England."

Dear Red Sox:
Your first round of drinks is free.
                    —THE LOOSE MOOSE SALOON, GRAY, MAINE

NIGHTFALL, AND the little girl lies on her back in the rear seat of a sedan as it chugs homeward to Hartford. She watches the stars twinkle in between the wooden telephone poles that rhythmically interrupt her view of the summer sky. And there is the familiar company of a gravelly voice on the car radio providing play-by-play of Red Sox baseball. The great Ted Williams, her mother's favorite, is batting.

Roberta Rogers closes her eyes, and she is that little girl again, and the world is just as perfect and as full of wonder and possibilities as it was on those warm summer nights growing up in postwar New England.

"I laugh when I think about it," she says. "There is nothing wrong with the memory. Nothing."

Once every summer her parents took her and her brother, Nathaniel, to Boston to stay at the Kenmore Hotel and watch the Red Sox at Fenway. Nathaniel liked to operate the safety gates of the hotel elevator, often letting on and off the visiting ballplayers who stayed at the Kenmore.

"Look," Kathryn Stoddard, their mother, said quietly one day as a well-dressed gentleman stepped off the lift. "That's Joe DiMaggio."

Kathryn, of course, so despised the Yankees that she never called them just the *Yankees.* They were always the *Damnyankees,* as if it were one word.

"We didn't have much money," Roberta says. "We didn't take vacations, didn't go to the beach. That was it. We went to the Kenmore, and we watched the Red Sox at Fenway. I still have the images . . . the crowds, the stadium, the sounds, the feel of the cement under my feet, passing hot dogs down the row, the big green wall, the Citgo sign—it was green back then—coming into view as we drove into Boston, telling us we were almost there. . . . "

Roberta now lives in New Market, Va., her mother nearby in a retirement facility. Kathryn is 95 years old and still takes the measure of people by their rooting interest in baseball.

"Acceptable if they root for the Sox, suspect if they don't, and if a Damnyankee fan, hardly worth mentioning," Roberta says.

On Oct. 27, two outs in the bottom of the ninth, Boston winning 3–0, Roberta paced in her living room, her eyes turned away from the TV.

"Oh, Bill," she said to her husband, "they can still be the Red Sox! They can still lose this game!"

It was not without good reason that her mother had called them the *Red Flops* all these years.

"And then I heard the roar," Roberta says.

This time they really did it. They really won. She called her children and called "everybody I could think of." It was too late to ring Kathryn, she figured. Kathryn's eyesight and hearing are failing, and she was surely sleeping at such a late hour.

So Roberta went to see Kathryn first thing the next morning.

"Mom, guess what? I've got the best news!" Roberta said. "They won! The Red Sox won!"

Kathryn's face lit up with a big smile, and she lifted both fists in triumph. And then the mother and daughter laughed and laughed. Just like little girls.

Dear Red Sox:
I really want to surprise my whole school and the principal.
—MAINE HIGH SCHOOL STUDENT, ASKING THAT THE ENTIRE TEAM VISIT HIS SCHOOL

"IS THAT what I think it is?"

The conductor on the 11:15 a.m. Acela out of Boston to New York, Larry Solomon, had recognized Charles Steinberg and noted the size of the case he was carrying.

"Yes," the Red Sox VP replied. "Would you like to see it?"

Steinberg opened the case and revealed the gleaming gold Commissioner's Trophy, the Red Sox' world championship trophy. Solomon, who had survived leukemia and rooting for the Sox, fought back tears.

The Red Sox are taking the trophy on tour to their fans. On this day it was off to New York City and a convocation of the Benevolent Loyal Order of the Honorable Ancient Redsox Diehard Sufferers, a.k.a. the BLOHARDS.

"I've only cried twice in my life," Richard Welch, 64 and a BLOHARD, said that night. "Once when the Vietnam War ended. And two weeks ago when the Red Sox won the World Series."

Everywhere the trophy goes someone weeps at the sight of it. Everyone wants to touch it, like Thomas probing the wounds of the risen Jesus. Touching is encouraged.

"Their emotional buckets have filled all these years," Steinberg says, "and the trophy overflows them. It's an intense, cathartic experience."

Why? Why should the bond between a people and their baseball team be so intense? Fenway Park is a part of it, offering a physical continuum to the bond, not only because Papi can stand in the same batter's box as Teddy Ballgame, but also because a son might sit in the same wooden-slat seat as his father.

"We do have our tragic history," says the poet Donald Hall, a Vermonter who lives in the house where his great-grandfather once lived.

The Sox specialized not, like the Chicago Cubs, in woebegone, hopeless baseball, but in an agonizing, painful kind. Indeed, hope was at the very breakable heart of their cruelty. From the 1967 Impossible Dream team until last season, the Red Sox had fielded 31 winning teams in 37 years, nine of which reached the postseason. They were good enough to make it hurt.

"It's probably the desperately cruel winters we endure in New England," Mike Barnicle offers as an explanation. "When the Red Sox reappear, that's the season when the sun is back and warmth returns and we associate them with that.

"Also, a lot has to do with how the area is more stable in terms of demographics than most places. People don't move from New England. They stay here. And others come to college here and get infected with Red Sox fever. They get it at the age of 18 and carry it with them when they go out into the world."

If you are born north of Hartford, there is no other big league baseball team for which to root, just as it has been since the Braves left Boston for Milwaukee in 1953. It is a birthright to which you quickly learn the oral history. The Babe, Denny Galehouse, Johnny Pesky, Bucky Dent, Bill Buckner and Aaron Boone are beads on a string, an antirosary committed to memory by every son and daughter of the Nation.

"I've known nothing different in my life," says David Nathan, 34, who, like his brother Marc, 37, learned at the hand of his father, Leslie, 68, who learned at the hand of his father, Morris, 96. "It's so hard to put into words. I was 16 in 1986 sitting in the living room when the ball went through Buckner's legs. We all had champagne ready, and you just sit back and watch it in disbelief.

"I was at Game 7 last year and brought my wife. I said, 'You need to experience it.' The Sox were up 5–2, and my wife said to me, 'They've got this in the bag.' I said, 'No, they don't. I'm telling you, they don't until the last out.'

"I used to look at my dad and not understand why he cried when they lost or cried when they won. Now I understand."

At 11:40 on the night of Oct. 27, David Nathan held a bottle of champagne in one hand and a telephone in the other, his father on the other end of the line. David screamed so loud that he woke up his four-year-old son, Jack, the fourth generation Nathan who, along with Marc's four-year-old daughter, Jessica, will know a whole new world of Sox fandom. The string of beads is broken.

David's wife recorded the moment with a video camera. Two weeks later David would sit and write it all down in a long e-mail, expressing his thanks to Red Sox owner John Henry.

"As my father said to me the next day," David wrote, "he felt like a burden was finally lifted off of his shoulders after all these years."

He read the e-mail to his father over the telephone. It ended, "Thanks again and long live Red Sox Nation." David could hear his father sobbing on the other end.

"It's nice to know after all these years," Leslie said, "something of mine has rubbed off on you."

Dear Red Sox:
I obviously didn't know what I was talking about.
—FAN APOLOGIZING FOR HIS MANY PREVIOUS E-MAILS, ESPECIALLY THE ONE AFTER GAME 3 OF THE ALCS, IN WHICH HE VERY COLORFULLY EXPRESSED HIS DISGUST FOR THE TEAM AND THE PEOPLE RUNNING IT

IT WAS one minute after midnight on Oct. 20, and Jared Dolphin, 30, had just assumed his guard post on the overnight shift at the Corrigan-Radgowski correctional facility in Montville, Conn., a Level IV security prison, one level below the maximum. The inmate in the cell nearest him was 10 years into a 180-year sentence for killing his girlfriend's entire family, including the dog.

Some of the inmates wore makeshift Red Sox "caps"—a commissary bandanna or handkerchief festooned with a hand-drawn iconic "B." Technically they were considered contraband, but the rules were bent when it came to rooting for the Red Sox in October. A few inmates watched ALCS Game 7 on 12-inch portable televisions they had purchased in the prison for $200. Most leaned their faces against the little window of their cell door to catch the game on the cell block television. Others saw only the reflection of the TV on the window of another cell door.

A Sox fan himself, Dolphin watched as Alan Embree retired the Yankees' Ruben Sierra on a ground ball to end the greatest comeback in sports history. Dolphin started to cry.

"Suddenly the block erupted," Dolphin wrote in an e-mail. "I bristled immediately and instinctively my hand reached for my flashlight. It was pandemonium—whistling, shouting, pounding on sinks, doors, bunks, anything cons could find. This was against every housing rule in the book, so I jumped up, ready to lay down the law.

"But as I stood there looking around the block I felt something else. I felt hope. Here I was, less than 10 feet away from guys that will never see the outside of prison ever again in their lives. The guy in the cell to my immediate left had 180 years. He wasn't going anywhere anytime soon. But as I watched him scream, holler and pound on the door I realized he and I had something in common. That night hope beamed into his life as well. As Red Sox fans we had watched the impossible happen, and if that dream could come true why couldn't others.

"Instead of marching around the block trying to restore order I put my flashlight down and clapped. My applause joined the ruckus they were making and for five minutes it didn't stop. I applauded until my hands hurt. I was applauding the possibilities for the future."

Dear Red Sox:
Any player who speaks Latin.
—REQUEST FOR A RED SOX PLAYER TO VISIT THE LATIN CLASS
AT A MIDDLE SCHOOL IN NEWTON, MASS.

ON THE day after Christmas 2003, Gregory Miller, 38, of Foxboro, Mass., an enthusiastic sports fan, especially when it came to the Sox, dropped dead of an aneurysm. He left behind a wife, Sharon, six-year-old twin boys and an 18-month-old daughter. Sharon fell into unspeakable sadness and loneliness.

And then came October and the Red Sox.

Sharon, not much more than a casual fan before then, grew enthralled with the team's playoff run. She called her mother, Carolyn Bailey, in Walpole, as many as 15 times during the course of a game to complain, exult, worry, commiserate and celebrate. She even made jokes.

"My eyes need toothpicks to stay open," Sharon would say during the run of late games. "More Visine. I need more Visine."

Carolyn laughed, and her heart leaped to see her daughter joyful again. She had not seen or heard her like this since Gregory died.

"It was the first time she started to smile and laugh again," Carolyn says. "The Red Sox gave her something to look forward to every day. They became like part of the family."

The day after the Red Sox won the World Series, Carolyn wrote a letter to the team. In it she said of her daughter, "The Red Sox became her medicine on the road back from this tragedy. On behalf of my entire family—thank you from the bottom of our hearts."

Leah Storey of Tilton, N.H., composed her own letter of thanks to the Red Sox. Her father had died exactly one year before the Red Sox won the World Series. Then her 26-year-old brother, Ethan, died of an accidental drug overdose only hours after enthusiastically watching the Red Sox win ALCS Game 5. When the Red Sox won the World Series, Ethan's friends and family rushed outside the Storey house, yelled for joy, popped open a bottle of Dom Perignon and gazed up in wonder at a lunar eclipse, and beyond.

"To us, with the memory of Ethan's happy night fresh in our minds, those games took on new meaning," Leah wrote of Boston's run to the championship. "Almost as if they were being played in his honor. Thank you for not letting him down. I can't express enough the comfort we derived from watching you play night after night. It didn't erase the pain, but it helped."

Dear Red Sox:
I would even volunteer my time to clean up, do the dishes, whatever.
—FAN ASKING THAT THE SOX HOST AN EVENT WHERE PLAYERS GREET FANS 80 AND OLDER

ON OCT. 25 the Sox were two victories away from winning the World Series when doctors sent George Sumner home to his Waltham house to die.

There was nothing more they could do for him. At home, though, George's stomach began to fill with fluid, and he was rushed back to the hospital. The doctors did what they could. They said he was in such bad shape that they were uncertain if he could survive the ride back home.

Suddenly, his eyes still closed, George pointed to a corner of the room, as if someone was there, and said, "Nope, not yet."

And then George went back home to Waltham. Leah knew that every day and every game were precious. She prayed hard for a sweep.

On the morning of Game 4, which stood to be the highlight of Jaime Andrews's life as a "pathetic," obsessed Red Sox fan, his wife, Alice, went into labor. Here it was: the conflict Jaime had feared all summer. At 2:30 p.m. he took her into South Shore Hospital, where they were greeted by nurses wearing Red Sox jerseys over their scrubs.

At 8:25 p.m., Alice was in the delivery room. There was a TV in the room. The game in St. Louis was about to begin.

"Turn on the game."

It was Alice who wanted the TV on. Damon, the leadoff hitter, stepped into the batter's box.

"Johnny Damon!" Alice exclaimed. "He'll hit a home run."

And Damon, his long brown locks flowing out the back of his batting helmet, did just that.

The Red Sox led, 3–0, in the bottom of the fifth inning when the Cardinals put a runner on third base with one out. Jaime could not stand the anxiety. His head hurt. He was having difficulty breathing. He broke out in hives. It was too much to take. He asked Alice to turn off the television. Alice insisted they watch until the end of the inning. They saw Lowe pitch out of the jam. Jaime nervously clicked off the TV.

At home in Waltham, George Sumner slipped in and out of sleep. His eyes were alert when the game was on, but when an inning ended he would say in a whisper, which was all he could muster, "Wake me up when the game comes back on." Each time no one could be certain if he would open his eyes again.

The Red Sox held their 3–0 lead, and the TV remained off in the delivery room of South Shore Hospital. At 11:27 p.m. Alice gave birth to a beautiful boy. Jaime noticed that the baby had unusually long hair down the back of his neck. The nurses cleaned and measured the boy. Jaime was still nervous.

"Can I check the TV for the final score?" he asked Alice.

"Sure," she said.

It was 11:40 p.m. The Red Sox were jumping upon one another in the middle of the diamond. They were world champions.

George Sumner had waited a lifetime to see this—79 years, to be exact, the last three while fighting cancer. He drew upon whatever strength was left in his body and in the loudest whisper that was possible he said, "Yippee!"

And then he closed his eyes and went to sleep.

"It was probably the last real conscious moment he ever had," Leah says.

George opened his eyes one last time the next day. When he did he saw that he was surrounded by his extended family. He said, "Hi," and went back to sleep for the final time.

George Sumner, avid Red Sox fan, passed away at 2:30 a.m. on Oct. 29. He was laid to rest with full military honors on Nov. 2.

On the day that George Sumner died, Alice and Jaime Andrews took home a healthy baby boy. They named him Damon.

Dear Red Sox:
Thank you, 2004 World Series Champs, Boston Red Sox. It was worth the wait.
—CLOSING LINES OF THE OBITUARY FOR CYNTHIA MARIE RILEY-RUBINO IN A HAMDEN, CONN., NEWSPAPER, SENT TO THE TEAM BY ANOTHER FAN

BALLPLAYERS ARE not social scientists or cultural historians. Quite to the contrary, they create an insular fortress in which all considerations beyond the game itself are feared to carry the poison of what are known generically as "distractions."

The Red Sox are not from Boston; they come from all corners of the U.S. and Latin America, and flew to their real homes immediately after a huge, cathartic parade on Oct. 30, during which normal life in New England was basically TiVoed for three hours. ("Three and a half million people there *and* a 33 rating on TV!" marveled Steinberg.)

There is an awful imbalance to our relationship with athletes, as if we are looking through a one-way mirror. We know them, love them, dress like them and somehow believe our actions, however trivial, alter the outcome of theirs, all while they know only that we are there but cannot really see us.

Howard Frank Mosher of Vermont was in northern Maine in the summer of '03 for a book-signing, during which he discussed his upcoming novel, *Waiting for Teddy Williams*, a fanciful tale in which the Red Sox (can you imagine?) win the Series; he heard a small group of people singing in the back of the bookstore. It sounded like, *Johnny Angel, how I love him....*

As Mosher drew closer he realized they were singing, *Johnny Damon, how I love him....* What was going on? he wondered.

"We're performing an incantation," one of the men said. "Damon has been in a slump. We think it's working. He was 4 for 5 last night."

Crazy. How could Damon know this? How could any Boston player know that the Reverend William Bourke, an avid Sox fan who died in his native Rhode Island before Game 2 of the World Series, was buried the day after Boston won it all, with a commemorative Sox baseball and that morning's paper tucked into his casket?

How could Pedro Martinez know that on the morning of World Series Game 2, Dianne Connolly, her three-year-old son, Patrick, and the rest of the congregation of St. Francis of Assisi parish in Litchfield, N.H., heard the choir sing a prayer for the Red Sox after the recessional? "Our Father, who art in Fenway," the singers began. They continued, "Give us this day our perfect Pedro; and forgive those, like Bill Buckner; and lead us not into depression...."

How could Curt Schilling know that Laura Deforge, 84, of Winooski, Vt., who watched every Red Sox game on TV—many of them *twice*—turned the ALCS around when she found a lucky, 30-year-old Red Sox hat in her closet after Game 3? Laura wore it everywhere for the next 11 days, including to bingo. (And she's still wearing it.)

"I've only been here a year," Schilling says, "and it's humbling to be a part of the relationship between Red Sox Nation and this team. I can't understand it all. I can't. All I can do is thank God that He blessed me with the skills that can have an impact on people's lives in some positive way."

The lives of these players are forever changed as professionals. Backup catcher Doug Mirabelli, for instance, will be a celebrity 30 years from now if he shows up anywhere from Woonsocket to Winooski. The '04 Red Sox have a sheen that will never fade or be surpassed.

The real resonance to this championship, however, is that it changed so many of the people on the other side of the one-way glass, poets and convicts, fathers and sons, mothers and daughters, the dying and the newborn.

The dawn that broke over New England on Oct. 28, the first in the life of little Damon Andrews, was unlike any other seen in three generations.

Here began the birth of a new Red Sox Nation, sons no longer bearing the scars and dread of their fathers and grandfathers. It felt as clean and fresh as New Year's Day.

Damon's first dawn also was the last in the fully lived life of George Sumner.

"I walked into work that day," Leah Sumner says, "and I had tears in my eyes. People were saying, 'Did he see it? Did he see it? Please tell me your dad saw it.' You don't understand how much comfort it gave my brothers and sisters. It would have been that much sadder if he didn't get to see it.

"It was like a blessing. One lady told me he lived and died by the hand of God. I'm not religious, but he was blessed. If he was sitting here, he would agree there was something stronger there.

"It was the best year, and it was the worst year. It was an unbelievable year. I will tell my children and make sure they tell their children."

The story they will tell is not just the story of George Sumner. It is not just the story of the 2004 Boston Red Sox. It is the story of the bond between a nation of fans and its beloved team.

"It's not even relief," Leah says. "No, it's like we were a part of it. It's not like they did it for themselves or for money or for fame, but like they did it for us.

"It's bigger than money. It's bigger than fame. It's who we are. It's like I tell people. There are three things you must know about me. I love my family. I love blues music. And I love baseball."

A Series
To Savor

BY STEVE RUSHIN

*In a World Series of delicious drama, the Minnesota Twins barely
bested the Atlanta Braves in what was truly a Fall Classic.*

THE TRUTH IS INELASTIC WHEN IT COMES TO THE 88TH
World Series. It is impossible to stretch. It isn't necessary
to appraise the nine days just past from some distant horizon of historical perspective. Let us call this Series what
it is, now, while its seven games still ring in our ears: the greatest that
was ever played.

Both the Minnesota Twins and the Atlanta Braves enlarged the game of
baseball, while reducing individual members of both teams to humble par-
ticipants in a Series with drama too huge to be hyperbolized. There were five
one-run duels, four of them won on the game's final play, three extended to
extra innings—all categories that apply to the ultimate, unfathomable game
played on Sunday night in Minneapolis, in which a 36-year-old man threw
10 innings of shutout baseball in the seventh game of the World Series.
Grown men were reduced to tears and professional athletes to ill health
in the aftermath of the Twins' winning their second world championship
in five seasons.

This was the *winners'* clubhouse: An hour after Jack Morris beat the
Braves 1–0 for the title, Twins pitcher Kevin Tapani broke out in a red rash.

"I'm surprised if I don't have ulcers," said infielder Al Newman, slouched lifelessly on a stool. "I think I'll get checked out."

Across the room, Morris lay propped against a television platform, pondering the events of the previous days. "I don't know if it will happen tomorrow or the next day," he said, "but somewhere down the road, they're going to look back on this Series and say. . . . "

Say what, exactly? Morris, like the scribes spread out before him, was overwhelmed by the thought of describing all that had transpired, and he allowed his words to trail off into a champagne bottle. The bubbly had been broken out by clubhouse attendants shortly after 11:00 p.m., when pinch hitter Gene Larkin slapped the first pitch he got from Alejandro Pena to left center, over the head of Brian Hunter, who, like the rest of the Atlanta outfield, was playing only 30 yards in back of the infield in an effort to prevent Minnesota's Dan Gladden from doing precisely what he did: bound home from third base in the bottom of the 10th, through a cross-current of crazed, dazed teammates, who were leaping from the third base dugout and onto the field.

Even Atlanta second baseman Mark Lemke, whose name had become familiar to the nation earlier in the week, was moved, in defeat, by the momentous nature of the game. "The only thing better," he said, "would have been if we'd stopped after nine innings and cut the trophy in half."

Impossibly, both the Braves and the Twins had loaded the bases with less than two outs in the eighth inning and failed to score. Improbably, both threats had been snuffed with mind-boggling suddenness by double plays. Atlanta was done in by a slick 3-2-3 job courtesy of Minnesota first baseman Kent Hrbek and catcher Brian Harper. The Twins were stymied by a crowd-jolting unassisted DP by Lemke, who grabbed a soft liner off the bat of Hrbek and stepped on second. So by the bottom of the 10th, when Harper, seeing Larkin make contact, threw his batting helmet high into the air in the on-deck circle and Gladden jumped onto home plate with both feet, the switch was thrown on a 30-minute burst of emotion in the Metrodome stands, an energy that, if somehow harnessed, would have lit the Twin Cities through a second consecutive sleepless night.

For it was only 24 hours earlier that Minnesota centerfielder Kirby Puckett had virtually single-handedly forced a seventh game by assembling what has to rank among the most outrageous all-around performances the World Series has ever seen. Puckett punctuated his night by hitting a home run in the bottom of the 11th inning off Atlanta's Charlie Leibrandt. The solo shot gave the Twins a 4–3 win and gave Puckett's teammates the same "chill-bump feeling" Braves manager Bobby Cox confessed to having had in Atlanta, where the Braves had swept Games 3, 4 and 5 earlier in the week to take a three games to two lead into Minneapolis.

Hrbek was reduced to a 10-year-old when the Series was tied last Saturday night; Sunday morning would be Christmas Day. "Guys will be staring at the ceiling tonight," he said following Game 6. "They won't even know if their wives are next to 'em. I know I won't. She won't want to hear that, but. . . ."

Minnesota hitting coach Terry Crowley was reduced to a doddering man in long underwear that same evening, pacing a small circle in the clubhouse, head down and muttering to no one, "It's unbelievable. Unbelievable."

And Twins manager Tom Kelly fairly shed his skin in the aftermath of that game, wriggling from the hard exterior he has worn throughout his career and revealing himself to be, like the rest of us, both awed and addled by all he had witnessed. "This is storybook," Kelly said. "Who's got the script? Who is writing this? Can you *imagine* this?"

Understand what Kelly and 55,155 paying customers had just seen Puckett do beneath the dome. In addition to his game-winning home run, he had singled, tripled, driven in a run on a sacrifice fly, stolen a base and scored a run of his own. In the third inning he had leapt high against a Plexiglas panel in centerfield, hanging there momentarily like one of those suction-cup Garfield dolls in a car window, to rob Ron Gant of extra bases and Atlanta of an almost certain run.

After the game had remained tied at three through the eighth, ninth and 10th innings, Cox brought in lefthander Leibrandt to face the righthanded-hitting Puckett, who was leading off in the bottom of the 11th. Why Leibrandt? He had won 15 games in the regular season, Cox pointed out later. But Cox may as well have said what was on everybody's mind—that it didn't matter whom he put on the mound to face Puckett. The man was going to hit a home run, no matter what. That was the only logical conclusion to his Saturday in the park. Puckett did just that, and the tortured Leibrandt walked off the field, his face buried in the crook of his right arm.

Afterward, teammates filed almost sheepishly past Puckett's locker, some shaking his hand, others embracing him, most of them without any words to say. This 5' 8" escapee of one of North America's worst slums—Who *is* writing this, anyway? Who *did* imagine this?—acknowledged he was having difficulty grasping the enormity of the evening. "Ten, 30, 50 years from now, when I look at it, it might be different," he said. "Right now? Unbelievable, man. Unbelievable."

Yes, this Series was baseball's most epic tale. It included twin props—the Minnesota fans' fluttering hankie and the Atlanta fans' chopping tomahawk—that grew equally tiresome as the Series grew increasingly enervating. And it was a tale that engaged two teams that, preposterously, had finished last in their divisions a year ago. Yet, similar as they were, the teams had two distinct followings for the Series: The nationally cabled Braves were America's Team, while the Twins became Native America's Team.

After the Twins put a stranglehold on the first two games of the Series, which had opened on Oct. 19 in Minneapolis, by producing game-winning dingers from two bottom-feeders in their batting order—Greg Gagne and Scott Leius? Who *is* writing this?—the Series went south in geography only. Before Game 3, Native Americans picketed Atlanta-Fulton County Stadium, protesting from behind police lines that the Braves' nickname and the team's tomahawk-chopping fans were disrespectful to their people. Ticket holders approaching turnstiles were implored by placard-bearers to, among other things, "Repatriate remains to ancestral burial grounds!"—which is a difficult thing to do between pitches. "No one," said Atlanta pitcher John Smoltz, "is going to stop this city from having fun right now."

Likewise, no gun-toting yahoo was going to stop Hrbek from having his usual hellacious good time in the ballyard. His mother, Tina, was telephoned at 3:30 a.m. on the eve of Game 3 by an anonymous moron, who told her that her son would "get one between the eyes" in Atlanta. Yet Hrbek, who in Game 2 had leg-wrestled Gant from first base to tag him out and kill a rally, came to Georgia wary of nothing more than . . . gingivitis. He tipped his cap to the bloodlusting crowd that booed him during introductions, tomahawk-chopped the fans from the top step of the Minnesota dugout and blithely flossed his teeth during live TV interviews. All the while he went one-for-Dixie and found the time to reconcile the joy of playing in the Series with the anguish of a death threat. "This game sucks," he said, "but it's a lot of fun."

Their villain already cast, 50,878 Braves fans showed up for Game 3, the first World Series game ever played within 500 miles of Atlanta. When it finally came time to play ball, y'all, and the first pitch was thrown by 21-year-old Braves starter Steve Avery at 8:38 p.m., flashbulbs popped throughout the park like bursts of white lightning. "I feel sorry for Dan Gladden," said Braves first baseman Sid Bream later of the Twins' leadoff hitter. "He was probably seeing 5,000 baseballs thrown at him."

For each flashbulb, there was photographic evidence for a fan that he or she was present the night the largest cast ever to appear in a World Series game put on the longest-running night show in Series history. When the curtain dropped four hours and four minutes later at 12:42 a.m. after a record 42 players had traversed the stage, Atlanta reserve catcher Jerry Willard would pronounce himself "exhausted." And he was one of two position players on either roster who *didn't* play.

When Chili Davis, pinch-hitting against Pena, squeezed off a two-run tracer bullet to leftfield in the eighth inning, the game was tied at four. It would go to extra frames and send scorekeepers into a hopelessly dizzying spiral of pinch hitters, double switches and defensive replacements, thus birthing the biggest box score the World Series has ever known.

Before the bottom of the 12th, Braves catcher Greg Olson told Lemke, a career .225 hitter with a dwarflike presence at the plate, that Lemke—a.k.a. Lumpy, a.k.a. the Lemmer—would get the game-winning hit that inning. Olson is a Minnesota native who spent 13 days with the Twins in 1989, during which time he was given the T-shirt, emblazoned with a caricature of Puckett, that Olson wears beneath his uniform to this day. Lemke, having no such talisman to draw upon for strength, pretended not to hear his teammate's prediction. "But I said to myself, 'Ehhhh, I don't *think* so,' " said the Lemmer later. This recollection came, of course, shortly after Lemke had singled to drive in rightfielder David Justice, who scored inches ahead of Gladden's throw and Harper's tag.

With Lemke's late game-winner, bedlam and then bedtime ensued in Atlanta. The Braves were 5–4 victors, and Lemke, at his locker, looked longingly at a bottle of Rolaids the size of a sweepstakes drum. "I get big-time heartburn," he said as just one of several cardiologically concerned members of the Braves. As Justice put it: "If we win the World Series now, I think you're going to see some guys have heart attacks in here. I really do."

Eighteen hours later, as baseball commissioner Fay Vincent settled into his special overstuffed, faux-leather easy chair along the first base line and prepared to take in Game 4, he needed only a reading lamp and a stand-up globe to look completely at home. And that was all an observer needed to do on this night: Look at home, to the thick and transfixing traffic at the plate. It was there, in the fifth inning, that Harper tagged out Lonnie Smith in a bone-rattling collision and, moments later, put the touch on Terry

Pendleton as Pendleton tried to score on a not-wild-enough pitch that bounded in front of home plate.

In the top of the seventh, Minnesota's Mike Pagliarulo hit a solo homer to break a 1–1 tie. In the bottom of the seventh, Smith did the same to retie things. Stomach linings could be heard eroding throughout the stadium before Lemke, who wears a PROPERTY OF UTICA COLLEGE INTRAMURALS T-shirt under his uniform, slugged a one-out triple in the bottom of the ninth. One batter later, Willard emerged from the dugout to pinch-hit.

Willard's parents, Faye and Jerry Sr., had arrived two days earlier from Port Hueneme, Calif. They had driven three straight days to Atlanta, only to see their son sit on the bench during the most populous World Series game ever played. *Coach Cox, why don't you play my son? You play all the other kids.* On this night, however, Willard would heroically fly out to shallow rightfield, just deep enough to allow Lemke to tag up from third and slide past Harper, who appeared to tag him out as the two made contact. In fact, Harper never laid the leather on the Lemmer, and another page in the epic was turned. "Same two teams here tomorrow," Skip Caray dryly told his radio audience as he signed off following Atlanta's 3–2 win.

Game 5 was a godsend for both teams, though Minnesota wouldn't acknowledge that at the time. The Braves' 14–5 tom-tom drumming of the Twins at last broke the skein of hypertense games that had endangered the central nervous systems of all those who had been watching them. On the Atlanta side, Smith tied a Series record by homering for the third consecutive game. On the Minnesota side, Kelly removed oh-fer rightfielder Shane Mack from his lineup and rendered him Mack the Knifeless as well. "We hid the razor blades," said Kelly of Mack, who was so disconsolate after the benching that "he was ready to cut his throat."

After the Twins had taken their Game 5 punishment, Atlanta fans stayed at the stadium to send off their team, and the players enthusiastically embraced the crowd in this love-in. The Braves were fully expected to return from Minneapolis with a world championship, what with Avery pitching on Saturday against Minnesota starter Scott Erickson. The former was so cool that when former President Jimmy Carter introduced himself in the Atlanta clubhouse following Game 5, Avery responded, "Howyadoin'?" The latter, meanwhile, had posted a lukewarm 5.19 ERA in the postseason. And yet. . . .

Erickson allowed only five hits in six innings in Game 6, though various Braves scorched balls right at Twins infielders or launched missiles that landed millimeters foul. But give the Twins credit. "If you got any pride at all, and your back's against the wall, you're going to fight your way out," said Puckett, who was raised in the crime-infected Robert Taylor Homes on Chicago's South Side and who fought his way out of Game 6 with two fists. Said the man afterward, "I'll get my rest when I'm dead."

Twins reliever Rick Aguilera picked up the win, just as he had in the dramatic sixth game of the 1986 Series as a member of the New York Mets, cannibalizing the Red Sox and Bill Buckner. What is it about Game 6? Boston's Carlton Fisk hit his unforgettable body-English home run off Cincinnati's Pat Darcy in the 12th inning of Game 6 in '75. And while the Red Sox went on to lose Game 7, they are as inextricably linked to that Series as are the Reds. The same unforgotten status would be bestowed upon Sunday's loser, no doubt. "Whatever happens tomorrow," Puckett said haltingly on Saturday, "it's been a great Series. I mean, I want to win. But if we don't, I'm just honored to be a part of this."

Morris would concede no such thing. "In the immortal words of the late, great Marvin Gaye," he said on the eve of Game 7, " 'Let's get it on.' " And that they did, the Braves and the Twins. Morris outlasted the 24-year-old Smoltz. On this night it appeared he would have outlasted Methuselah.

When the seventh game and the Series had finally been bled from the bodies on both sides, when the two teams had stopped their cartoon brawl, raising ridiculous lumps by alternately slugging each other over the head with a sledgehammer, when all of 60 minutes had passed after the last game, Pagliarulo stood wearily at his locker. "This was the greatest game," he said. "How could the TV guys describe it? They had a chance to win—but they didn't. We had a chance to win—but we didn't. Then we did. I kept thinking of the '75 Series tonight. This is why baseball is the greatest game there is."

The greatest game there is. The greatest games that ever were.

OPPOSITE FIELDERS

You Can Take the Boy Out of the Country

BY MARK KRAM

Dean Chance, a big, rangy farm boy from Ohio with all the ability and cocky confidence of a fictional busher, said he was good and then went out and proved that he was the best pitcher in the major leagues.

WILMER DEAN CHANCE SAT IN THIS LITTLE CAFETERIA filled with giggling office girls, the smell of sauerkraut and the mumbling of old men hiding from the cold rain, and destroyed a hill of mashed potatoes. His pants, white flannel, were cuffless and tight, and they hung about three inches above a pair of alligator shoes, which he said he should be saving for Los Angeles, where people are more accustomed to such flash. A white knit tie rested comically short on a white shirt, and his pale-blue summer sport coat seemed a size too small. The customers stared at him, not because of his costume or the ferocity with which he attacked his lunch, but because—next to producing the first Christmas tree and a small Presbyterian college—producing Dean Chance is the biggest claim to identity that Wooster, Ohio, has ever had. For better or—heaven forbid—for worse.

Chance, for those who may remember him only because of his widely chronicled nocturnal gambols with Bo Belinsky, his flamboyant teammate on the Los Angeles Angels for the past three seasons, was the best pitcher in the big leagues last year. After being only 5 and 5 in July at the All-Star Game break, he won 15 of his last 19 games to finish with a 20–9 record and a 1.65 earned run average. He shut out the Yankees three times, beat them four times and allowed them only one run in 50 innings—a home run by Mickey Mantle. In all, he pitched 11 shutouts during the season. "Walter Johnson," said Dean, "was the last in the league to get that many shutouts."

For these and all his other accomplishments ("I gave 100 less hits than innings pitched, and ain't nobody done that before") he won the Cy Young Award, presented annually to the outstanding pitcher in the major leagues. From the Angels, who finished in fifth place, largely through his efforts, Chance last week received a contract for $42,000, which would seem enough to help him support his wife, Judy, a Wisconsin farm girl he met when playing minor-league ball in Fox Cities, Wis., and his two-year-old son—plus 60 head of cattle and 100 pigs that lounge on the 80-acre farm near Wooster that he bought several years ago. All of this, the success, the money, the family, the farm and another year of age, will serve to bring about, the people of Wooster hope, a sharp change in Chance's character—from something near Frank Sinatra, say, to nothing more extreme than Henry Aldrich.

To many in his audience in Wooster, a slightly puritanical community in which pool is still considered by some to be a nefarious distraction, a new Chance would be welcomed with a sigh of relief. His past conduct, which to conservative Wooster people has been only a shade short of cut-purse, has been an embarrassment. People here ain't used to those sort of things. They ain't used to the way he's acted, always in a pool hail, always carrying a pool stick around everywhere he goes, always saying things he ought not to be saying, always getting in trouble with that Belinsky.

They seem to be asking whatever happened to the big kid who pitched on the sandlots wearing street shoes and street socks and bottle caps on his hat, the boy who used to walk home from 4-H competition with blue ribbons all the time. Other citizens of Wooster, more worldly, wonder why in his big-city travels he has never acquired sophistication and discretion, and why he remains a heedless clod (Chance has many advisers in Wooster) stumbling into one fuss after another.

Still, none of these views appeared to hurt the attendance at a Dean Chance testimonial dinner this winter in Wooster that Chance seemingly created and produced himself. Dean sold tickets and newspaper ads and arranged for the appearances of other stars (free) as well as for the distribution of baseballs, bats, Los Angeles Angel yearbooks, photos and 50 pounds of bubble gum. The *Wooster Daily Record* published a special section devoted to the dinner and the life of Dean Chance. Chance volunteered his profile for 23 ads ("No Need to Take a *Chance* when Buying Your Meat") and his thoughts to a number of interviewers, like Ernie Infield, who concluded: "There can't be too much wrong with a kid who prefers to spend the hours of his greatest triumph with his home folks—and for their benefit." A big crowd turned out "for their benefit." Tickets were $6, and all of the proceeds were contributed to the Northwestern High athletic fund. Chance was visibly elated by the town's response, and the town was pleased to see that there was a lot of the farm still left in the boy.

"Look, he's only 23," explained a sympathetic friend. "Who was any different at 23? Especially a farm boy loose on the town!"

"I just like to have a little fun now and then," Chance said. "I do what I want to do, and I pick my own friends. Belinsky is the best friend I've ever had. He's never tried to influence me."

Much of the criticism of Chance's personal conduct is provoked by his relationship with Belinsky, who this winter was traded away from Los Angeles and Chance to Philadelphia. The names Belinsky and Chance had a vaudeville ring, and Los Angeles was more than suitable for their act. With Bo as his sponsor, Chance plunged into the social swirl of the city. Parties and introductions to "big, important people" followed. It was a long way from Wooster, where the manager of the bowling alley might well be considered a celebrity. "Bo sure knows his way around," said Chance. Dean found fun with Bo—and trouble. Curfew infractions, absence from a spring training practice, a nebulous involvement with a woman who, sporting a black eye and cuts, railed about them to a policeman, and other activities not considered particularly uplifting to Little Leaguers caught the disapproving eye of Los Angeles general manager Fred Haney. For the episode with the woman, Chance, along with Belinsky, was fined $250, despite Dean's plea that he was being victimized for just being there. For missing the practice, Haney relieved him of $500. "Five Cs!" ranted Chance. "That's a lot of dough. I could buy five cows with that." And then he said, "I don't understand it. Other guys get in trouble, and they give 'em a small fine. But with Bo and me they gotta make a federal case out of it."

Naturally, Belinsky emerged from all this as Chance's Svengali. It was Bo, critics contended, who was responsible for Dean's behavior. Dean, they said, was just a dumb old farm boy who did not know any better, and Dean was just a caddie for Bo. Someone said Chance trailed behind lugging Belinsky's collapsible cue. Leon Wagner, the hip and outspoken outfielder who has since been traded from the Angels to the Cleveland Indians, disagreed. "Dean isn't any starry-eyed hanger-on," said Wagner. "Compared to Chance, Belinsky is a quiet guy. Dean knows his way around, and he can show Bo a few things."

There is partial truth in what Wagner said. For instance, Chance was not unoriented to the pool room before he met Belinsky; pool and cards have always been his favorite diversions. But though Chance is not the bumpkin so many think he is, he is still a big kid oscillating between two widely disparate environments—the austerity of life in small-town Wooster and the swinging world of a young man with a big name in a huge city.

Chance might be described as a blend of Brett Maverick—television's bungling and handsome gambler—and Cecil (Highpockets) McDade, a less glamorous character who appears in a book by John R. Tunis. Bo appealed to the Maverick in Chance, and Maverick, at times, is all that Chance would like to be—slick, picaresque and cavalier. Skip the bungling. Action! Gambling in Las Vegas, wheel and deal and let the good times roll. Suddenly all his friends were show people, the world's greatest pool players, the richest men in town. Maverick (Dean's son is named Brett) travels with the best. But more often than not Chance is only Highpockets—practical, plotting, egocentric, intractable, brutally candid and, after a while, a bore. It is Highpockets who is the baseball pitcher, and it is Highpockets who has got him into as much trouble as Maverick, and Highpockets who has been the dominant part of Chance from the beginning.

Chance was born in the little township of Wayne, just outside Wooster, on June 1, 1941. Until he entered Northwestern High in Wooster he had spent most of his young life helping his father Wilmer with the daily routine of their family farm. At that time it was farming first, and then baseball. In high school the two were reversed. At Northwestern High his coach was Roy Bates, and Chance never misses an opportunity to stress Bates's contribution to his development as a baseball pitcher. "He taught me how to win," Chance says, "and he gave me the desire to beat the other guy's brains out in competition." Bates, a little man with a crippled arm and an overwhelming sense of obligation to the boys in his charge, is a tough, dictatorial coach who brooks no bad deportment from his athletes. In fact, he has been known to make a boy practice in a dress if the boy has given a woman teacher a difficult time in class.

"Dean was in the fourth grade when I first ran into him," Bates said recently. "I'd come out of church, and he'd be outside waiting for me. He used to tell me about himself, and even then he told me he would be a star in the majors one day. 'Yes, sir, Mr. Bates,' he used to say, 'I have a snake ball and a super snake ball.' A few years later I saw him pitch a sandlot game. What a sight! He had bottle caps on his hat, and he was wearing street shoes and socks. He pitched a no-hitter, and he was quite the hero. I left to go to the car, and he came running up, saying, 'What'd ya think of that?' I told him, and he didn't like it. I told him he'd have to learn how to dress before he could pitch for me. When he came to me in high school, he showed up the first day of practice with those street shoes on again. He always claimed that spikes hurt his feet. I told him to take 25 laps after the workout, and then take the balls and bats in.

"Actually, he was never much trouble," Bates said. "Though there was one thing about him. If you said please, you'd never get anywhere with him; he'd run you right out of school if you gave him a chance. Once in a basketball game, after being held scoreless in the first half, he complained that his pants were too tight. I told him to go get dressed and let me know the next day if his pants were still too tight. He didn't, and he scored 20 points in the second half.

"The best things done to Chance as a player were the things that were not done. We never tampered with the way he threw—you know, the way he turns his back to the plate before he pitches? We never allowed him to fool with a curve or a slider. We just made him throw fastballs, and we told him to work on keeping the ball low. He always had great control. In his first year we only allowed him to relieve. In his second we started him in spots. As soon as he began to get hit, we pulled him. He was never humiliated in a game. And from his third year on he was unbeatable. Oh, he'd loaf now and then. He'd get ahead, and he'd take it easy. Once he did that, and I walked out to him in big, high steps. He said, 'What are you walking like that for?' I said, 'I just don't want to step on your guts.' Naturally, he was furious, but he bore down again.

"DEAN ALWAYS had a lot of confidence in himself. As far as he was concerned, nothing was impossible. One time a kid needled him about not being able to play anything but basketball and baseball. That was a mistake. Chance practiced for a week and then won the school table-tennis championship. Another time he bet a boy a milk shake that he could strike out nine men in a row, and he did. Another time, before we started in the first round of the state baseball tournament, he said flatly that we'd win it. 'How can we miss,' he said, 'if we don't give up any runs?' We weren't really that good, but Chance kept his promise. He gave up only two runs, and we won it. He was always like that. There never was anything modest about him. When the scouts came around, he said—after winning 51 games and losing one and pitching 18 no-hitters—'I'd have a better record if I'd have been with a better club.' When he graduated he could have taken his choice of 30 basketball scholarships: and there were over a dozen major league scouts waiting for him."

Chance says, "I was the greatest high school pitcher in the history of Ohio."

The Baltimore Orioles agreed, and they signed Dean for a $30,000 bonus. "The thing that impressed me about the boy," said farm director Harry Dalton, "was his attitude. There was never any doubt in his mind that he would be a top pitcher in the big leagues. You could see that the first time you met him." Chance was sent to Bluefield, W.Va., in the Appalachian League, and only occasionally did the manager have to caution him about late hours. "We knew," said Dalton, "he wasn't an average-type kid. He was a strong individual. We knew he liked to gamble and have a good time, but he didn't take too much handling." For Chance (he does not drink or smoke) a good time was simply meeting people, and if it required staying up past the curfew, he would do it. He loved to be around people.

At Bluefield, Chance became annoyed easily. After not being picked to start either the first or second game of the season, he went to see Dalton, who was traveling with the team. "Mr. Dalton," he said, "if I'm not going to pitch for this here club, I'd like to go with some other organization."

The Orioles had to part with Chance later, in 1961, when the American League expanded to 10 teams and the eight existing clubs were required to put players into an expansion draft pool, but they did so reluctantly. There are a number of opinions concerning the Orioles' decision. Some believe that the Orioles had been disappointed in Chance's "breaking stuff." Others claim that Paul Richards, who had been a dominant figure in the Baltimore organization, had been disturbed by Chance's attitude—his swagger and his boasting. At any rate, Chance was drafted by the brand-new Los Angeles Angels.

Chance spent the 1961 season in the minors at Dallas-Fort Worth and then joined the Angels in 1962. If the Angels were to be rankled later on by his Brett Maverick behavior, they were initially piqued by Highpockets. From the start, Chance was the prototype of every brash rookie who ever appeared in sports fiction. He was 14 and 10 in his first season. Manager Bill Rigney was impressed, but the players looked beyond his performance. "He should get a trophy for mouth-flapping," said one. Leon Wagner said, "You can't tell him anything. You say, 'Now, don't pitch high to this guy,' and he asks you why. He says, 'He can't hit my fastball.' I say, 'Man, this is the big league, and they hit everything.' So he throws high, and wham! So then he says, 'Oh, that was an accident, because nobody can really hit my fastball.' That boy is some stubborn."

In 1963 Chance had a 13–18 record, and he always seemed to be right smack in the middle of a controversy. When Chance is not winning ball games he is not exactly the stoic type; he does not see games being lost, he sees dollar bills falling out of his pocket. All during the season he irritated his teammates with cutting remarks. In one game he struck out 12 batters and later told the press: "I had to strike 'em out. I didn't dare let 'em hit the ball to anyone." In Washington he wailed because he was credited with a five-hitter instead of a four-hitter. "Don Lock should never have got a triple on that ball," he said. "Albie should have had it easy." Later in the season, a bad one all round for the Los Angeles club, he growled: "I'm getting the shaft. There's not a clutch hitter on this whole lousy team. I can't make a living this way." His teammates retaliated bluntly but effectively by filling his locker with garbage. Above it they put a sign that read: I'M NOT NATURALLY STUPID. I'M JUST PRACTICING.

A man who had never been so humiliated previously, Chance brooded and plotted during the winter. He was continually rumored to be involved in one trade or another, but the rumors were always started by Chance, and it was always Chance being traded for a star. General manager Fred Haney was not impressed by the rumors. Chance then shifted the campaign to the subject of money. In his rookie year he had made the minimum major league salary of $7,000, and he was raised to $15,000 for 1963. After Chance lost 18 games, Haney offered him the same salary for 1964. Chance balked, reeled off his other pitching statistics. Despite the losses, they were impressive. "I think they are fantastic," Chance said. Haney did not agree, but eventually he relented and offered a $3,000 raise.

Chance signed. "That's all right," he said. "If I pitch well and show a good attitude, Fred says he'll give me an extra $7,000." Chance had a poor start in 1964, and Rigney sent him to the bullpen for a while. After superb relief work he was again made a starter, and he pitched well—though without luck. The promised extra money was not forthcoming. "Haney's gone back on his word," Chance complained. "I want my $7,000, or I want to be traded." He showed up one day washing car windows at a service station. "My family has to eat," he said. Haney laughed—for a while, anyway. Skillfully using the press, Chance kept attacking Haney. "There's no room for me and Fred on this here club," he said finally. "I hate that man and I'll never speak to him again, not about salary or anything else."

At this point, Chance was invited to talk things over with the Angels' top officials, Gene Autry and Bob Reynolds. Dean was given his extra money and responded with brilliant pitching the rest of the season. Now, after receiving a $42,000 contract for 1965, Chance says he is extremely fond of Haney. "There's nothing in the world," he says, "that I wouldn't do for that man. He's a fair and generous man."

CHANCE WAS really not being inconsistent. Haney's generosity with the 1965 contract pleased him immensely; if there is one thing that fascinates him more than himself, it is money. The mere mention of money brings a glitter to his eyes and a pounding beat to his voice. Riding around Wooster with one of his many advisers, a lawyer named Henry Critchfield, the conversation, which Dean dominated, held fast to money.

"Look at that house, Hank," shouted Chance. "How much you think that cost?"

"Oh, about $60,000," said Hank.

"Hey, look at that bank," said Dean. "My, what a pretty bank."

"Yeah," said Hank, unimpressed.

"Hey, about that farm, Hank?" asked Chance. "How much you think he'll take for it? Four hundred acres. He'll probably want $150,000. You think he'll take $100,000, Hank?"

"Maybe," Hank said.

"Hey, look at that nice bank," yelled Chance, passing another monument to bland architecture.

"Just have another good year," Hank smiled. Chance had better, because there are plenty of people hoping he will be unable to back up his brag and bluster.

"If he doesn't keep making it big," says one friend, "I'm afraid he'll end up being just a bitter, big-mouth farmer."

Chance does not think so. "If I never have another good year, and if I'm out of the majors in two years, I'll feel bad, but it wouldn't be the end of the world. I'd just plunge into farming, and I wouldn't even look back. I might think of the money I missed, now and then. But I'm just a farmer. I belong on the farm because that's what I know best. I never want to live anywhere but on a farm here in Wooster. I like the people here, and you can depend on them. Some of the people here don't like me for the way I acted, but I'm a changed man after last season. No more cards. No more late hours. No more pool."

"No more criticism of other players, either?" he was asked.

"Look, sure I knocked 'em, but really they deserved it," he said. "And you'll never hear me knock a guy behind his back like the others do. Anyway, I only knock the guys that don't put out. Take last year. I can't say enough good things about Bobby Knoop and Jim Fregosi and Joe Adcock. They were a big help in my winning 20 games. In fact, the players named Knoop the most valuable player. I didn't even vote for myself."

"Did that bother you?"

"No," he said, "I'm not popular. I'm a bad loser."

"No, you're not," a friend protested. "You're just honest."

"Well, anyway," Chance said, "I'm gonna keep my big mouth shut this year. I really am a changed man."

"Where do you think the Angels will finish?" he was asked.

Chance paused a moment, and then he said, "Well, not too good. The only way they could move up is if they trade me."

"What could they get for you?"

"Five front-line players," he said.

Everybody laughed, but not Dean.

"Trouble is," he moaned, "nobody appreciates me for what I really am."

Ring Lardner would have.

❦

Son of
Ball Four

BY JIM BOUTON

On his way back to the bigs, the author of Ball Four *found
players who weren't like the ones he met his first time up. They were looser
and lazier and preferred pot to potables.*

I HAVE HAD MY SHARE OF THRILLS IN BASEBALL. I WON 21 GAMES
for the Yankees in 1963, pitched the pennant-clinching game and
made the All-Star team. Don Drysdale beat me 1–0 in the World
Series. In '64 I won 18—plus two in the World Series against the
Cardinals. In those days I could throw as hard as anybody. My hat used to
fly off my head, I threw so hard. I could "bring it," as they say. And I was
known as a tough competitor. Yankee catcher Elston Howard nicknamed
me the Bulldog. Then I hurt my arm in 1965, and I hung on for a few more
years; I resurrected an old knuckleball I had thrown as a kid and won a
few games—very few—for Seattle and Houston. After eight years in the
bigs, I retired in 1970. That's the year my book came out—*Ball Four*.

That's also when I got my new first name. Controversial, as in Controversial Jim Bouton, author of . . . or Controversial Jim Bouton, Sportscaster for. . . . *Ball Four* told a few truths about baseball, so naturally the baseball Establishment hated it. The owners were furious. The commissioner
wanted to ban the book. The housemen among the writers called me Judas
and Benedict Arnold and other names. My favorite was social leper. Dick
Young of the New York *Daily News* thought that one up. While I was on

the mound trying to pitch, players on the opposing team hollered obscenities at me from the dugout.

All that screaming and hollering sure sold books. *Ball Four* went for 200,000 in hardcover, is still going strong in paperback and just got translated into Japanese. It's the largest-selling sports book ever. I was so grateful, I dedicated my second book, *I'm Glad You Didn't Take It Personally*, to my detractors. They didn't appreciate the gesture. I think they're still mad at me.

One way I can tell is that I never get invited back to Oldtimers' Days. Understand, *everybody* gets invited back, no matter what kind of rotten person he was when he was playing. Muggers, drug addicts, rapists, child molesters, all are forgiven for Oldtimers' Day. Except a certain author. Just giving you a little background.

Because I am such a reprehensible character, I had a little difficulty getting back into professional baseball. In 1977 Bill Veeck gave me a chance with his Double A farm team in Knoxville, Tenn. I was released after six weeks, but I didn't take it personally; my pitching record was 0–6. Then I made a bunch of phone calls and ended up playing in Durango, Mexico. Only a foreign country would have me. After five weeks of 26-hour bus rides and galloping *turista*, I returned to the U.S. and finished the season with the Portland Mavericks (Northwest League, Class A), an independent team of players nobody wanted. My knuckleball was getting better. I won five, lost two.

At that point, all 26 major league teams refused to even let me try out for one of their 112 farm teams. The cellar-dwelling, expansionist, player-poor Seattle Mariners told me I couldn't even try out for their Class A team. They probably didn't want their players to get sick and die from whatever dread disease I have.

Even Charlie Finley told me on the phone he didn't want me. It may be the only thing he's ever had in common with the other owners.

It's not like they had anything to lose. I told them I'd pay all my expenses; I just wanted a uniform and a chance. And I was flexible on that. I would have brought my own uniform. I even promised I wouldn't write a book. Something told me they weren't dying to read *Son of Ball Four*. I never said I wouldn't write a magazine article.

Then I got lucky. During the winter of '77–'78, I was giving a talk to some businessmen, and one of them, Jeff Hammond, editor of *Motor Boating & Sailing* magazine, said he was a friend of the Atlanta Braves' owner, Ted

Turner. Hammond arranged for me to meet Ted when he came to New York to accept the Yachtsman of the Year award for winning the America's Cup.

Years ago an owner would not deign to speak to a common player. During my six years with the Yankees, I was only allowed to view Dan Topping and Del Webb from a distance. I was once permitted to speak with Dan Topping Jr., but only for a short while. He made me feel like I should've taken my shoes off before I came into his office. And I wasn't wearing spikes. I never did catch a glimpse of the Astro owner, Judge Roy Hofheinz. And I never even knew who owned the Seattle Pilots. Baseball owners used to be like the Wizard of Oz before anybody got wise. Things must've changed when players got to be free agents. Maybe the owners started talking to players so they could be closer to their money.

Ted said, "What the hell! Sure, why not?" He told me to come on down to Florida, and he'd give me a chance to make one of his minor league teams. So what if I was 39 years old? He said he was 39, and *he* wasn't washed up. Besides, he already had one 39-year-old knuckleballer—Phil Niekro—so why not one more? He also had a 5' 9" guard on his pro basketball team. Ted said he believed in the American way, that everyone should get his chance, and let the best man win in fair competition. I told him I believed in the same thing. Later on in the summer, a sportswriter said that Ted gave me a chance because he was hoping I would write a book. And mention Ted.

Why would a 39-year-old man with a good job in television even want to go back? It's hard to explain. I felt a certain restlessness. It seemed like I had to find something, but I didn't know what. Besides that, I love pitching a baseball. And I like a good challenge. A tiny voice in the back of my head said I could make it. The voice wouldn't shut up, so I had to try.

It was almost a decade since I played in the big leagues with the Astros. And it was 20 years ago that I started out in the Yankee farm system. I'll tell you one thing, baseball sure has changed a lot in that time.

Take the competition in spring training. It used to be much fiercer than it is today. That's because there were more players back then. Lots more. Now there are only four levels of minor league competition—Rookie, A, AA, AAA. Most organizations have just one team at each level. There used to be seven levels—D, C, B, along with the surviving four—and when I first signed, the Yankees had eight farm teams and also shipped players out to unaffiliated teams. That's a lot more bodies to climb over on your way to the top. I used to keep a list of pitchers who were above me on the ladder. My first year I wrote down 134 names. Guys were running around with numbers on their backs like 78 and 84. Football numbers. One spring my number was 68. I was a pulling guard. There were so many players, I once lockered in a broom closet. Make that half a closet. I shared it with an outfielder named Jim Pisoni. The coaches couldn't remember all the names, either. One year they kept calling me Mackenzie. I don't know what they called Mackenzie.

Last year at the Braves' minor league camp, no one called me Mackenzie. They called me other things. In my first exhibition game, I was in the middle of winding up for my first pitch when my shortstop hollered, "Come on, Mr. Bouton." I had to call time out to laugh. Actually, the players were very kind to me. They called me Dad. Or Oldtimer. "Take it easy, Oldtimer," they would say during wind sprints. "We don't want to have to give you mouth-to-mouth resuscitation."

Then they stopped kidding me about my age. That's because I was running them into the ground. I made their tongues hang out. On purpose. First, I wanted to prove that my advanced age didn't matter. Second, it was fun knowing I was in better shape than these kids.

I made it look easy, but it wasn't. I had worked out all winter at Fairleigh Dickinson University near my home in Englewood, N.J. I'd go to the gym from midnight till two in the morning, when nobody else was using it. I worked out four nights a week, even if there was a blizzard. I'd run and pitch to a friend, Johnny Belson, and when John couldn't make it, I'd throw against a wall. Some nights my knuckleball was really jumping. I was 14–0 against the wall.

I knew I had to look good in spring training. Real good. I had two chances of making it: slim and none. There's no margin for error when you're 39. Especially if you've been away for eight years and your first name is Controversial.

Also, I didn't exactly feel welcome. Early in the winter, before I met Ted Turner, general manager Bill Lucas had told me the Braves weren't interested. In spring training I had a hunch that they still didn't want me after farm director Hank Aaron told the press I was there only because Turner had invited me. And I was the only player who didn't have a locker with his name stenciled on. I found an empty one in a corner and wrote my name on top with a Magic Marker.

At least the players were nice to me. In the beginning I was a real curiosity. They would sneak glances at me and whisper a lot. But they seemed to respect me. Maybe that's because I was old enough to be their father. Also, they were minor-leaguers, and I had eight years in the big leagues or, as they call it, the Show. "At least you got some time in the Show," they would say. Because of my vast experience, they called me Rook.

They knew I was the guy who wrote *Ball Four*, but they didn't dislike me for it. In fact, they liked me because I wrote it. A few players came over the first day and said they'd always wanted to meet me. They brought dog-eared copies of my book for me to autograph. I loved it.

Most of the players had read *Ball Four* in high school or, as some of them enjoyed telling me, in junior high. They liked the book because it told them what big league ball would be like in case they ever got there. They enjoyed all those sexy anecdotes. A few players told me it sounded like so much fun, they were inspired to play harder so they would be sure to make it. Now *there's* a side effect I never get credit for—*Ball Four* improving the quality of baseball.

Guys were always coming over to ask me questions about the book. Did the Yankees really run around the roof of the Shoreham Hotel in Washington to look in windows? Did the Mick really hit a home run with a terrible hangover? I said I didn't want to topple their idols, but it was all true. They said the book didn't destroy heroes. No matter what the Mick did, he was still the greatest ballplayer ever. Everybody thought I was coming back to write another book. But these players weren't afraid of that. They figured it was a great idea. They all said I should be sure to spell their names right.

Ted had promised me a fair chance, and I believed him. Now all I had to do was be sensational. I was optimistic. In my entire career, I never failed to make the team I tried out for in spring training. One spring, 1962, I even made a team I wasn't trying out for—the Yankees. I was a minor-leaguer, invited to spring training just to pitch batting practice. I had won 14 games the year before in AA, and the plan was that on cutdown day I would get shipped out to AAA. Except I fooled them.

We were playing an exhibition game against the Cardinals at Al Lang Field in St. Petersburg. After pitching batting practice, I changed my sweat-shirt and sat in the bullpen to watch the game. At the end of nine innings, the game was tied, and we were out of pitchers, having brought only enough to play a regulation game. In spring training, guys who aren't going to be needed in games can work out, then leave early to play golf. Who could the Yankees get to pitch the 10th inning? The batting practice pitcher, who else? Neither team scored in the 10th, so I had to pitch the 11th. And the 12th. Then the 13th. In the 14th we lost on a blown double play, but the day was mine. Along the way I struck out a couple of guys.

If my teammates had anything to do with it, I wouldn't have struck out anybody. I could tell they weren't exactly rooting for me after what they told me on the bench between innings. Johnny Blanchard was playing rightfield, and he was steaming.

"Hey, Meat," said John. "Lay the damn ball in there, and let them hit it."

"What?" said I.

"Let them hit the damn ball for Chrissakes. It's hot. I want to get the hell out of here."

"But, John, I'm trying to make the club."

"Forget it, Meat. You're only pitching because we got nobody else."

John was a wonderful inspiration to young pitchers. I'm glad he wasn't catching that day. He might've told the hitters what was coming. Don't laugh. I've seen that happen in spring training when a game's gone on too long.

When a rookie does well, it fouls up the manager's plans. So he lets you pitch until you have a bad inning, which happens sooner or later. Then he can ship you out as planned. Trouble was, I never had a bad inning. I had about 35 good ones. When spring training was over, the Yankees had no choice. They had to keep me.

Last spring with the Braves, I felt just like I did in '62. I wasn't in their plans. One bad inning, and I'd be history. So what I did was pitch 13 scoreless innings. It didn't keep them from releasing me. The way they did it was typical baseball. It's almost comforting to know that in some ways the game will never change.

IT WAS the morning before our last workout, and we were standing around the clubhouse, waiting to go on the field. I remember looking down at my gray practice uniform, wondering whether I would exchange it for a Richmond (AAA) or Savannah (AA) uniform. Then something funny happened during roll call. They didn't mention my name. This was surprising since I was standing right up front, like I always did. "Hey, you missed me," I said brightly. Coach Ken Rowe stared intently at some microscopic dot on his clipboard. Everybody else's eyes were on me. "Didn't Hank tell you?" said Rowe. Tell me what, I wondered. Hank hadn't told me anything all spring, not even hello. "You better see Hank," said Rowe, still examining his clipboard. Then I knew. Everyone knew. The only thing Hank wanted to tell me was goodbye. It was like that old military joke where they break the news from home that someone's mother has died: "Now listen up. All those men with mothers take one step forward. Not so fast, Johnson."

It was the same years ago with the Yankees, who had subtle ways of letting you know your services were no longer needed. You'd come in after a day's workout, and everyone's equipment bag would be packed for the next day's road trip. Everyone's bag, that is, except those marked for extinction. "Hey, how come my bag isn't packed?" It's been nice knowing you.

I should have suspected something when Hank didn't watch me pitch even one inning. The other players told me not to feel bad about that because Hank hardly saw anyone play. He didn't like to watch ball games, probably because he'd played in so many himself. The players said Hank would come to a few of their games during the season and then leave early. Very early, like in the first or second inning. "As soon as he finished his beer." Once, they said, he'd left during the national anthem.

The players said I should be glad that at least Hank knew my name. As a running joke, they did instant replays of meetings with Hank that they swore actually took place.

"I'm sorry you've been released, Bob."

"My name is Pete."

"I'm sorry, Pete, but we've already got too many second basemen."

"But I'm an outfielder."

"Uh, we also have too many outfielders."

At 9 a.m. Hank told me what I already knew. At 2 p.m. I was sitting in Ted's office, 600 miles away in Atlanta. I didn't have an appointment. On the plane from Florida I had written a short speech. I knew Ted was a busy man. Building a communications empire can be time-consuming. I told him to listen for five minutes, and then I'd get the hell out. I started off by saying I was a lot like him. I was a winner, too. The great spring I had just had wasn't luck. What's more, the yachting establishment didn't like him either. They would sink his boat if they could. I told him that I'd won my preliminary trials just like he had, and now I deserved to stay in the race. I wanted my boat back.

I guess Ted liked my speech because he picked up the phone, with me sitting right there, and told Lucas to find a place for me. Lucas said I could pitch batting practice for the Richmond farm team. No salary, just expenses, and I could stay in shape and wait for some pitcher to get a sore arm.

My going to Richmond as batting-practice pitcher was like Br'er Rabbit getting thrown into the briar patch. The Richmond pitching coach was Johnny Sain. Johnny is not only the best coach in baseball, but he also happens to be my friend. He was the Yankee pitching coach the year I won 21. And he's famous for refurbishing sunken pitching derelicts. Jim Kaat, Mudcat Grant and Jim Perry come to mind. Maybe I could be refloated, too.

If you're wondering why the best coach in baseball is in the minors, it's simple. The system for selecting coaches hasn't changed since the days of Abner Doubleday. The manager picks the coaches. And managers always choose an old teammate, close friend, brother-in-law or next-door neighbor—anybody who will be loyal to the manager. Loyalty is more important than ability. The best qualification a coach can have is being the manager's drinking buddy. Johnny Sain drinks milk shakes and is loyal to pitchers.

Sain got credit for winning pennants in New York, Detroit and Minnesota. Ralph Houk, Mayo Smith and Sam Mele never won anywhere without him. And that's another thing. Managers don't like it when the pitching coach gets his name in the paper more than the manager. Which is too bad. If I owned a baseball team, I'd hire Sain as my pitching coach, and let *him* choose the manager.

So I went to Richmond, and for six weeks I pitched batting practice. At game time I'd get out of my uniform, buy some peanuts and sit in the stands. Then one day the patron saint of batting-practice pitchers handed me the ball. The Atlanta Braves were coming to town for an exhibition game against their top farm team. Ted said, let Bouton pitch for Richmond. Ted would umpire at third base.

To make a long—but fascinating—story short, in front of the second-largest crowd in the history of Parker Field, I did a job on the Atlanta Braves. I was removed to a standing ovation in the seventh inning with a 3–1 lead, having struck out seven of the big boys, including Jeff Burroughs, the National League's hottest hitter. I think I surprised a few people. It took them a week to figure out what the hell to do with me. Then they sent me down to Savannah to pitch in real games.

I joined the Savannah Braves on the road in Chattanooga. I walked into the clubhouse all smiles. But nobody smiled back. I soon found out why. It seems the guys liked me in spring training because they thought I was joking about a comeback. Now that I had replaced someone in the pitching rotation, I was a bad guy. The stiffest competition in the minors is never the opposing team. It's players on your own team. I had been to the big leagues once, so why didn't I stay home and give someone else a chance?

This kind of thinking was strange to me. These guys were clearly different from the players years ago. These kids believed someone owed them a chance. I grew up thinking you had to earn it. Do I sound like an old fogey?

The spring I made the Yankees, my competition was Robin Roberts, who was 35 years old, had 14 years in the big leagues and was a guaranteed Hall of Famer. It was down to me or him. At no time did the thought occur to me that he should step aside. Never entered my mind. If he beat me out, congratulations to him. I'd go work on my curve.

That's not the only thing about today's players. All summer long I saw hitters get called out on strikes with alarming frequency. There were more called strikeouts than swinging ones. Naturally, they said the umpires were blind, lazy, incompetent, retarded, without fathers or all of the above. What amazed me was, after a player would scream at an umpire, during his next at bat, with two strikes, he'd take a close pitch again and leave it up to that same ump.

Why, back when I played, boys and girls, hitters swung that bat. *Nobody* got called out on strikes. If a pitch was close, it got swung at.

I remember Ralph Terry protesting when he had to pitch spring training games against minor-leaguers. They always bombed him. He said borderline pitches meant nothing to those free-swinging kids. They wanted to hit their way to the big leagues. Today's player is content to walk there.

Or walk out. One of my teammates last summer, an infielder, quit baseball because he wasn't called up to AAA in midseason, as the Braves had promised him. He was batting .173. I couldn't believe it. What's more, other players sympathized with him. It's an epidemic.

Another thing. Players complained about the condition of the fields. A Southern League ground crew consists of one old man with a rake, so the diamonds are always in bad shape. Hitters went 0 for 4 because the batter's box had footholes bigger than the Grand Canyon. Runners were thrown out stealing because the base paths were about as easy to run on as a beach. Pebble Beach. Balls were always taking bad hops. Yet nobody ever did anything about it.

Years ago, I remember players coming out four hours early to pick up stones at their positions or level out the batter's box. My Savannah teammates thought I was nuts when I rebuilt the mound each time I pitched. At home or on the road, I'd go out the morning before a game with a shovel and rake, dig up fresh clay and build myself a big league mound. I didn't want to lose even one ball game because the mound wasn't right. I once asked the fastest man on our team why he didn't shovel some clay between first and second base, make a firm running track and steal an extra 10 bases. He just smiled at me and walked away.

Why are today's players like this? Maybe they learned it in college. A minor league team used to be a very diverse group. There were kids right off the farm, high school dropouts, ghetto dudes, a few older guys just out of service, and one or two college boys who always got nicknamed Professor or Harvard. Now it's *all* college guys except for a few imported Latins. Scouts won't sign anybody else. The minor leagues are being phased out for a simple reason. It's cheaper to let colleges develop players. And college kids with more experience are easier to evaluate and less of a gamble to sign. Plus, a college draft cuts down on bidding for players. Baseball owners learned these things from NFL and NBA owners. In college, the instruction is better, too. They have coaches running around with stopwatches and videotape machines. Lower minor league teams used to have no coaches. Just an old alcoholic manager who threw a bag of balls on the field and said play.

And baseball's got this new thing called central scouting. A lot of scouts don't work for just one team anymore. After they watch a kid play, they send their reports to a bureau that feeds them into a computer. All the teams subscribing to the service then get a look at the readout. There's very little incentive to be the scout who beat the bushes and found the next Babe Ruth. The legendary Yankee scout, Tom Greenwade, would have had to feed Mickey Mantle's stats into the computer. The St. Louis Browns would have drafted him. Mickey Mantle of the St. Louis Browns. Mickey would have had to get drunk with Ned Garver.

This is a wonderful new system, except for one thing. They tend to miss a certain kind of player. Guys like Whitey Ford. Whitey would never get a contract today. Scouts don't hang around as much at places like Aviation High in New York, where Whitey went to school. Maybe Whitey would have gone to college. Maybe not. Even so, his stats wouldn't look good enough on the printout. Today, a player has got to have "the tools"—great arm, size, speed, power, etc. Five-feet-nine isn't big enough to be a pitcher today. The speed gun doesn't clock a sneaky fastball. There's no little box on the IBM card for cleverness. Guts and brains are tough to gauge if you don't get to know a kid well.

Scouts used to do that. They would talk to you after games, take you out to dinner, get to know your parents, become your friend. I remember that lots of guys signed with certain teams because they were friends with some scout. Or friends with a bird dog.

Bird dogs were people who scouted for a scout. They were usually retired guys who roamed the most obscure ball fields, getting to know players. The bird dog who found me was an elderly gent named Mr. Fred. Mr. Fred would watch me pitch and then buy me a hot dog and a Coke after the game. A small investment for the future. He used to give me tips. He'd tell me to wear a jacket over my arm to keep it warm between innings, or not to drink cold water on a hot day, things like that. I liked Mr. Fred. He was a bird dog for Art Stewart, the Yankee scout who signed me.

If a kid signed, the scout sent the bird dog some wandering-around money. If the kid made it to the big leagues, the bird dog got money and a nice gift at Christmas as long as the kid stayed up there. You could always spot a bird dog in the stands by his uniform—wide-brim hat, binoculars, stopwatch, pad, pencil and cigar. But not anymore. With central scouting, there is not much need for bird dogs. Like an endangered species, they're becoming extinct.

Another baseball species already extinct is the suspect. That's what players called guys who weren't prospects anymore. A suspect was an older guy kept around to fill out a roster, or because he was a local hero in some minor league town. He was a real downer to have around the clubhouse. The suspects were continually bitching. They always complained that they should be playing in a higher league. I would ask a suspect what his batting average was in *this* league. Strangely enough, it was always low.

Today, there aren't enough teams to carry suspects. As soon as a kid ceases to be a prospect "he gets his No. 1 box punched," as my Savannah roommate, Stu Livingstone, used to say (Box No. 1 means "released unconditionally" on the standard form given to every player who gets released, transferred, sold or waived). Suspects weren't all bad. You could learn a few things from them. Like how to chew tobacco or pick up a cocktail waitress.

Players today don't pick up girls too often. They don't need to. Their regular girl friends come live with them, even on road trips. Of course, that's against the rules. It's a $200 fine if you get caught. Smart managers, like Bobby Dews at Savannah, never check on their players. Last summer we got a letter from Hank Aaron reminding us about the fine for having girl friends in our rooms. For college guys who had lived in coed dorms, it was the funniest item on the bulletin board.

Except for the all-night bus trips, life on the road in the minors is very different now. Years ago, we'd stay at some old downtown hotel. We'd spend the day walking around town, playing pool, going to the movies. Now, the teams stay at those budget motels located at highway interchanges 20 miles from town. I didn't like being stuck out there. The only things you can walk to are a waffle house, a gas station or another motel. I wanted to visit the towns. I never felt like I was playing in the Southern League. It was more like the Interstate League. The scenery was always the same. It's bad enough when you stay at a motel and wake up looking at the wall and not knowing what town you're in. In the Interstate league, you can look out the *window* and not know what town you're in. The only thing to do was sit around the pool—no swimming after noon—and play backgammon. Or read a book. Now that's different. If you read books 10 years ago, you were strange. Twenty years ago, you were downright weird.

In spite of the age difference, I felt more at home with the Savannah Braves than I ever did with the Yankees. I always liked minor league players better. Major-leaguers lose perspective about themselves. It was that way with the Yankees. They thought fans were a nuisance. They hated reporters. And it's even worse now. "The old Yankees just ignored us," says a friend who covers the team. "The new Yankees scream and holler at us from across the room." Too many big-leaguers think playing baseball is some great contribution to society. They used to think the world owed them a living. Now, it's a fortune. Bill Russell, the former basketball player, said they're like that because they've been on scholarship since the third grade. Today's gargantuan salaries reinforce those misperceptions.

LAST SUMMER was the time of my life. After the Savannah players got used to me, I became the team guru. I was the fountain of all wisdom on matters of pitching, careers, love lives, etc. We'd sit around my room at night. I'd make some popcorn on my hot plate, and we'd have a few beers and shoot the bull. Or one of the players would bring some grass, and we'd pass around a few joints.

This certainly is a new thing in baseball. Years ago, players just got drunk. It was O.K. with the manager because he got drunk, too. Some managers will tell the whole team to go out and get drunk to forget a bad loss. Players today still drink, but more often they get high. Except for being against the law, grass makes more sense than booze. It's not fattening, and you don't have to play with a hangover.

Managers never tell a team to go get high. They're against marijuana the way temperance ladies used to be against alcohol. In spring training they give a warning speech about drugs. Not the kind of dangerous drugs that are used to make an injury heal faster, but the "drug" marijuana. As one coach put it, "Boys, if you get caught with Mary Jane, you better be hitting four-bleepin'-eighty at the all-star break."

The drug speech wasn't very effective. I don't want to get anybody in trouble, or cause some big investigation, but from what I saw, about half the players on all teams, not just mine, smoked marijuana. One night, after he had downed about a six-pack, my Knoxville manager in '77, Jim Napier, asked me what he could do about players smoking grass. I told him he might as well try to hold back the tide with his fingers. Ballplayers reflect society, and that's what's happening. The law hasn't caught up yet. Napier asked why couldn't ballplayers just get drunk like they used to.

I had fun pitching in Savannah. I threw a one-hitter and a two-hitter and a 13-inning shutout, pitching in 100° heat after all-night bus rides and with two days' rest. I won 11, lost nine and pitched the league's most inexperienced team to a title. I won my division playoff game 4–1 and the Southern League's hustlingest-pitcher award. The Atlanta Braves had to call me up.

I knew I was getting called up because I read it in the newspaper. That's how players find out. It's an old baseball tradition. For the past two years I had fantasized about getting back to the big leagues. I always saw myself crying for joy. When I walked into Atlanta's Fulton-County Stadium, I was floating as if in a dream. How large it was, compared to little Grayson Stadium in Savannah. When I got into my uniform, with my old No. 56 on it, and went out to the field, my heart was jumping out of my shirt. But I didn't cry, because it wasn't a gift. I had earned it. In fact, I was thinking they should have called me up a month earlier.

What a feeling, standing on the mound, listening to the national anthem, waiting to pitch my first game. I thought, How lucky I am! This was better than my first time around in 1962. Then I was nervous and too young to appreciate it. This I would savor. I had flown my family down for the weekend, along with a few friends, like Johnny Belson, who caught all those knuckleballs at 2 a.m., and Steve Katz, the trainer for the Portland Mavericks, who taught me to eat real food instead of junk. And Rob Nelson, pitching coach for the Mavericks. Rob said I was his first pupil to make it to the majors.

Thousands of players had made it to the big leagues once; no one had ever done it twice—from scratch. I knew I was a long shot because my 14-year-old son had bet $5 I wouldn't make it. Now the early-morning work-outs, the batting practices, the bus trips and the Mexican bathrooms were paying off. I felt like I was standing on top of Mount Everest. This was the thrill of my life.

In the next 24 hours I got the shock of my life. My first pitch to Dodger second baseman Davey Lopes was a called strike. Four pitches later, with a full count, I struck Lopes out, swinging, on a dancing knuckleball. The crowd roared. I felt like Rocky. After I got the next two hitters on easy outs, I ran to the dugout and threw my arms up in a victory salute. In the fourth inning the Dodgers broke up my no-hitter. Also my ball game. They scored five runs. My son Mike, 15, wasn't surprised. "I figured you'd get clobbered, Dad," he said afterward. But the day was more important than the game. And it was extraordinary fun. I laughed a lot—until I read the papers the next day.

"He showed me nothing," said Lopes. "Nothing." "It was a circus," said Reggie Smith. "It was like batting against Bozo the Clown," said Rick Monday. "The commissioner should investigate this," said Cincinnati manager Sparky Anderson. "We're in a pennant race. Bouton should have to pitch against the Giants and Reds, too."

Incredible! Sparky was losing a pennant, so I understood about him, but why were the Dodgers angry? My phone was ringing off the hook. Reporters wanted to know what I thought. I didn't know what to say. I felt sorry for the Dodgers, who were obviously suffering from sunstroke.

In his next game, Bozo the Clown beat the San Francisco Giants 4–1. The pennant-contending San Francisco Giants. It should have been 4–0, but I threw a double-play ball into centerfield. After the game, reporters asked me if I had won because it was windy. I said that was it. The wind blew hot-dog wrappers around the field, and the batters couldn't see the ball. I had won my first major league game since July 11, 1970. I couldn't wait for the reviews.

"Next time I'm going to bring up my little boy to bat against him," said Bill Madlock, who was hitless in two at bats. "It was the most humiliating experience of my life," said Darrell Evans, who had a pop-fly double in three at bats. "Terrible," said Mike Ivie, who was hitless in three at bats. I almost forgot who won the game.

Johnny Sain told me later I had revolutionized the sport. I had invented a new way to judge baseball ability. Results in a game didn't count anymore. You just ask the opposition what they think.

Maybe the hitters were confused by how I got them out. Players today don't mind being outmuscled, but they hate being outsmarted. It looks foolish from the stands. Take Randy Jones of the Padres. When he was the Cy Young winner in 1976, some hitters said they "couldn't respect that" because he didn't throw hard enough. He didn't "challenge" the hitters. It's a macho thing. When Atlanta reliever Gene Garber ended Pete Rose's hitting streak last year by getting him out with a changeup, Rose got mad. He said Garber should have "challenged" him with a fastball. This is a recent phenomenon in baseball. I heard it all summer in Savannah, too. Whenever a pitcher got a hitter out with slow stuff, someone would holler, "Challenge the hitter, damn it!" I've got a question: Why? The last I heard, the object of the game for pitchers was to get hitters out.

I used to challenge the hitters. And win. When I won 21 for the Yankees in '63, every game was a battle. And I was heavily armed. But there's more than one way to skin a cat. Now I had no guns, no velocity, not even a great knuckleball, if you want to know the truth. Just a little slider, and a sinker that Sain taught me in Richmond, and a changeup. But I never felt so much in control on a pitcher's mound as I did last summer. Now I had something else going for me. A sense of being in control. What I brought to the game when I was 20 was strength and youth and bulldog determination. What I brought to the game at almost 40 was much more powerful. It was something I had found inside myself. It was what I had left home to look for.

When I first asked Ted Turner to give me a chance, I told him that Hoyt Wilhelm threw knuckleballs in the big leagues until he was 48. That meant I had almost 10 years left. Actually, I thought I'd play for five years. But it occurred to me that I wouldn't stay around that long right after I pitched that first game.

I was on the team flight from Atlanta to San Diego. It was a charter, and we had the whole plane to ourselves. I was sitting by myself in my own private row of six seats, the overhead lights were out, and most of the players either slept or played cards. And as I watched this scene, it suddenly hit me. This is boring. I had been on hundreds of flights like this years ago. It wasn't nearly as much fun as the bus rides in Savannah.

After I beat the Giants, I pitched a few more games. I went seven innings against the Astros. My pitching opponent, J. Rodney Richard, maybe the hardest thrower in baseball, chose the occasion to break the modern league strike-out record for righthanders. The flamethrower and the junkballer. We were both taken out with the score tied 2–2. A standoff. I loved the contrast. There was no criticism this time, just silence. Then Sparky Anderson of the Reds got his wish. I pitched against Cincinnati, and they beat me. But only 2–1. I allowed just five hits. Anderson said, "We didn't even hit the ball hard off him. We got two runs we shouldn't have gotten." Well, what do you know?

DURING MY second tour as a major-leaguer, I had my own room at the best hotels, ate at fancy restaurants and changed clothes in carpeted locker rooms. But I could not shake that feeling I had on the plane. This was all too familiar. And not nearly as much fun as the cheap motels, or the chili at 3 a.m., or the steamy cement box that was called a locker room by the Savannah Braves.

I waited a while before I called Ted to tell him I wasn't coming back for another season. My desire to play ball had been so strong that I didn't trust this new feeling. I declared myself a free agent so the Braves wouldn't waste a contract on me. I could always sign with them in the spring if the feeling went away. But it didn't. And I'm glad.

I knew for certain it was the right decision about two months after the season ended. I had signed a contract to report sports for WCBS-TV in New York. The station was doing a half-hour news special about me. As part of it, they wanted me to throw a baseball to reporter Jim Jensen. We went to the Fairleigh Dickinson gym. I was surprised when I walked in. It was cold and bare, not warm and cozy like it used to feel at two in the morning. And then I picked up a baseball. It felt strange to me. Uncomfortable in my hand. I gripped it again. And again. I tried my knuckleball grip and swung my arm around. I couldn't make it feel right. A baseball used to feel like part of my body, an extension of my arm. Now it felt like some strange object. In the past, I would have panicked. Now I was different. This time I simply smiled. Now I could release my grip on the baseball. It didn't matter anymore. Baseball had released its grip on me. And it was O.K.

The Hub Hails Its Hobbling Hero

BY PETER GAMMONS

Even though Bill Buckner let Game 6 slip through his injured legs, the fans in Boston admired his courageous play in the World Series.

H E AWAKENED ON THE MORNING AFTER THE MORNING after, knowing that he had two more rivers to cross. First, there was a parade in downtown Boston. Then he would drive 40 miles to Worcester, check into the University of Massachusetts Medical Center hospital and, after 10 years of ice, acupuncture, DMSO and holy water, have an operation to clean out his junkyard left ankle. As he started to get out of bed, he heard some mention of the Mets' parade on the radio. "More than two and a half million people honored the world champions yesterday in New York," said the announcer, "and the parade finished with the Mets' team bus going through Bill Buckner's legs."

"Here I just experienced the best year of my life with a team, and I feel rotten," Bill Buckner said to his wife, Jody, as they drove down Route 93 toward Boston last Wednesday. "This whole city hates me. Is this what I'm going to be remembered for? Is this what I've killed myself for all these years? Is a whole season ruined because of a bad hop? I've got to go through the humiliation of this parade, partly because I know I don't deserve it. Oh well, there'll only be two or three players and about 50 people who'll show up to boo us."

When Buckner got to the Red Sox clubhouse, he found at least 15 team-mates and coaches waiting for the parade. It was a crystal-clear autumn morning as the Red Sox climbed aboard the flatbed truck that would take them to the rally. When the truck turned onto Boylston Street, Buckner heard the bells of the Arlington Street Church pealing, *Take Me Out to the Ballgame,* and when the truck neared Copley Square, he saw that the street was lined with faces and banners as far as he could see. Buckner had asked not to speak at the rally at City Hall Plaza, and so he stood at the end of the stage. But when he heard the ringing one-minute ovation that followed his name, Buckner stepped forward and thanked the crowd.

"That was the most incredible experience of my career," he said to Jody as they drove to Worcester, past a THANKS, RED SOX sign on the Mass Pike and a HOMETOWN OF MARTY BARRETT sign at the city limits of Southborough. When the Buckners stopped at traffic lights in Worcester, people in other cars beeped their horns and waved at them.

While Buckner was checking into the hospital, the clubhouse kids were piling up his mail at Fenway Park. "He normally gets no more than one letter a week," said batboy Dean Lewis. "He's gotten almost twice as much World Series mail as anyone else." A New York City policeman told Buck-ner he was "a symbol of courage." A California polio victim called him "an inspiration," a New Jersey man said he was "a true model for all our chil-dren," and a 70-year-old lady in Illinois wrote, "because of you, I watched my first World Series." Among the hundreds of pieces of mail, the most negative was a letter from a Rhode Island doctor who chastised Buckner for risking permanent damage.

In an exhausting World Series that ended in New York with the Mets as world champions, the Red Sox became this generation's Brooklyn Dodgers. And former L.A. Dodger Bill Buckner, 36, with 2,464 hits and 16 major league seasons behind him, became baseball's Walter Brennan. He often looked as if he were running in galoshes, and after he staggered around third and belly-flopped across home plate in Game 5, he admitted, "I didn't slide—I died." He crawled like an alligator into one base. He went after a pop-up, fell down and did a backstroke trying to make a catch in Game 4. He scurried on hands and knees to tag the first base bag with his glove. He limped out for the national anthem, bat in hand, just in case he need-ed a cane. He wore a high-topped right shoe for the Achilles tendon he pulled in the seventh game of the playoffs, but it was the pain in two parts of his left ankle that had created the original limp and had necessitated nine cortisone shots since April. Little wonder Buckner ended up hitting .188 for the Series, finished 18 innings, stranded 31 runners and made the error on Mookie Wilson's ground ball that gave the Mets their dramatic 6–5 victory in the 10th inning of Game 6.

"I just want to tell you that you'll always be my inspiration," said a small boy who ducked into Buckner's hospital room Wednesday night. "Thanks for a great season." Then the boy disappeared.

"Today cleared a lot off my chest and my mind," said Buckner as he settled back in his hospital bed. "From my perspective, I didn't think the error was such a big deal. Letting them tie up the game was more important. There was no guarantee we would have won. Hell, there was no guarantee that Bob Stanley or I could have beaten Wilson to the bag if I had caught the ball. When Jody and I got back to the room that night, I watched the replay and I was right there, head down, glove down, completely relaxed. . . . It just took a funny sideways bounce between my legs. By the time I watched it, I wasn't bothered because I was completely geared towards the seventh game.

"Then Monday I agreed to do an interview for *The NBC Nightly News*, and all the guy kept asking me was, 'How can you look at yourself in the mirror? How can you face your teammates?' I went out for batting practice, and I thought one sign that said, 'Nice legs,' was funny, but when I got the standing ovation from the Mets' fans during the introductions, it wasn't so funny." Neither was the Mets' management's decision to replay the error on the Shea Stadium message board before the bottom of the fifth inning. Nor were the post-seventh-game questions from the press about manager John McNamara's decision not to pinch-hit or bring in a defensive replacement for Buckner in Game 6.

"I hadn't been pinch-hit for all season, and the only time (Dave) Stapleton had gone in for me on defense was when the Achilles was killing me back at the start of the Series," Buckner said in the hospital. "The one thing anyone has ever said about me defensively is that I have good hands. And, while my average stunk, [hitting instructor] Walt Hriniak figured out that I hit the ball hard for outs 11 times in 32 at bats. When I hit the line drive to deep left center with the bases loaded that ended the second inning of the final game, I thought I had knocked in three runs. Ron Darling was pitching me inside, and Lenny Dykstra always played me to right center, but for some reason Mookie played me to left center. Dykstra never would have caught the ball. That's when we should have won the damn thing. Right now, that hurts more than anything."

That, even more than the ankle. Buckner has won a batting title (1980), hit .300 or better seven times and knocked in 212 runs in the last two seasons. He has a good shot at 3,000 hits, which means the Hall of Fame, and he has always had a big and justified reputation as a clutch hitter. And people who know him wonder what he might have been were it not for the ankle. "He could get down to first base with anyone when he was young," says Tom Lasorda, who signed Buckner, took him to the Rookie League and had him in Triple A. "Dick Vermeil, who recruited him for Stanford, was once asked which recruit he most regretted not coaching," says Lasorda. "And he answered, 'Wide receiver Bill Buckner.' He could fly."

Buckner batted .314 and stole 31 bases for the Dodgers in 1974. Then on April 18, 1975, when they were playing the Giants in Dodger Stadium, he tried to steal. "I remember it as if it were yesterday," Buckner says. "John Montefusco was pitching, Marc Hill catching. I'd just been trying to learn to slide from Davey Lopes, the way he barely hit the ground. I never did hit the ground, my foot caught under the bag and I flipped right over." He struggled through the season, had a tendon removed in September and bone chips taken out in October. After a .301 average and 28 stolen bases in '76, he went back in for yet another operation that winter. That surgery resulted in a staph infection. Then came the preseason trade to the Cubs in 1977 for Rick Monday, and when Buckner reported to the Cubs' training camp hobbling on a cane, Chicago asked the National League to annul the deal on the grounds that he was damaged goods. "I was damaged goods," he says. "But I wanted to prove them wrong, so I played the first half of the season. It was a painful mistake. I never walked right again."

Says Buckner, "I always said that I'd wait until after I retired to have the cleanup operation because I learned to cope with it, and it didn't get any worse. This year it got worse." For the last eight seasons, Buckner has soaked his feet in ice for an hour before—and 30 minutes after—every game. In 1978, he began working in Chicago with bodybuilder Bob Gadja and chiropractor George Ruggerio, who created a series of machines and exercises for the ankle. "They saved me," Buckner says. Buckner has tried vitamins, acupuncture, DMSO and, before Game 5, holy water from a fan.

His diet helped. He is the same 185 pounds he was when Vermeil sought him for Stanford in 1968, and he and Jody are health food nuts. Buckner, who owns a 1,000-acre, 300-head cattle ranch in Star, Idaho—it's run by his brother, Bob—says, "I may be the only cattle rancher in America who doesn't eat red meat."

But then, as his closest baseball friend, Bobby Valentine, says, "Buck is unique, thank goodness. When we were freshmen at USC, he would challenge me to a race every day. Every day I beat him, and as soon as we had finished, he would swear that he'd beat me the next day." Says Buckner, with a laugh, "There are a lot of Bill Buckner stories."

His brother, Bob, says, "Bill gets his mind set on something, and won't accept that it doesn't work out the way he wants. One Christmas he thought he was going to get a shotgun. He didn't, and he stayed in the bathroom for five hours."

The Buckners grew up in a small California town called Rancho del Mar, halfway between Napa and Vallejo, where, Bob says, "All there was to do was play baseball and hunt." Bill was both an exceptional athlete and student whose college choices came down to USC and Stanford. When he went to visit Southern Cal, he met Valentine, who was another football-baseball recruit. A week later, Valentine was selected in the first round of the 1968 June draft by the Dodgers, who then made Buckner their second pick. Though Buckner attended USC, he never played sports there.

After the draft, Lasorda, who had scouted in the spring and was going to manage the Dodgers' Rookie League club in Ogden, Utah, went to sign the 17-year-old Buckner at a doubleheader in San Rafael. Buckner had seven hits in the two games, and afterward Lasorda asked him, "Do you like to fight?" Buckner nodded. "Then you're coming with me to Ogden, where we're going to fight and we're going to win."

"We fought," says Buckner, "and we won." Lasorda and his players developed a special camaraderie in Ogden. That was also the place where the legend of Bill Buckner, with an assist from Lasorda, was established. The manager wrote letters to then Dodgers Wes Parker, Willie Davis and Ron Fairly, promising to take those players' jobs away, and signed the names of Buckner, Valentine and Tom Paciorek, respectively. "I visited the clubhouse after the season," Buckner recalls, "and you should have seen the look I got from Parker."

"Buck was always getting thrown out of games," says Lasorda. "Throw helmets? He broke one a night. Finally I told him I'd fine him if he ever did it again. He made an out and I heard this banging. I look over and he was smashing his head against the wall so hard he was bleeding. One night in Triple A (1970), he and Valentine collided going for a pop fly. Buck broke his jaw, and the front office told me to sit him out for five weeks. Buckner missed only one game and wound up hitting .335 and learned to spit and swear with his jaw wired shut."

Buckner didn't stop battling all the way to Boston. He once fought Cubs manager Lee Elia on the top step of their dugout. His fight with Gary Carter is legend. Buckner got so mad at popping up in a 1980 game in Montreal that he smashed his bat down, accidentally breaking Carter's mask. The next week in Wrigley Field, after Buckner got a hit, Carter picked up Buckner's bat and broke it over home plate. So after Carter rounded the bag on a base hit, the two of them ended up rolling on the ground, swinging.

Buckner would never be accused of being California mellow. He still yells at the wind, the hitting background or line drives that get caught. But ever since his first winter in Boston in 1984–85 when Hriniak told him, "If you'll shift your weight, you can hit homers," his fire has been devoted to hitting. In his 14 seasons before 1985, Buckner never hit more than 16 homers and only once did he drive in more than 75 runs, but in the last two years, he has hit 16 and 18 homers and knocked in 110 and 102 runs. Last year, when his ankle didn't bother him as much, he stole 18 bases, played 162 games and amassed 201 hits.

In 1986, Buckner's body finally broke down, and after hitting in the low .200s for two months, he limped to a .267 average. It wasn't unusual to see him before games with ice taped to his ankle, Achilles tendon, lower back, elbow and shoulder. "This is weird," he said last Friday, 24 hours after the operation. "I hardly hurt. I won't know what it's like."

After Dr. Arthur Pappas removed a large chunk of bone from the top of the left foot and cleared bone chips and other debris from the ankle, he told Buckner that he should feel better than at any time since 1976. "I used to think, 'One year at a time,' " said Buckner, his left ankle in a cast and his right foot in a bandage. "Now I'm thinking three years and 3,000 hits. There's no reason I can't do it now if I'm healthy. Not only that, but I'll be wearing the high tops. Maybe they'll do for me what they did for Y.A. Tittle."

Maybe he can even get people to forget about a certain ground ball.

Love, Hate and Billy Martin

BY FRANK DEFORD

*He had a profound affection for the game and an uncanny knack
for turning losers into winners—and for getting fired anyway. As a player and
a manager, for good or ill, he was always a fighter.*

IT WAS A YEAR AGO THIS SPRING THAT THE YANKEES GOT RID of Billy Martin. He was a bad influence, they said. Nobody saw him land a punch at the Copacabana nightclub when a bunch of his teammates got involved in a scrap with some fellows celebrating the end of their bowling season, but it was Martin's birthday party, and since he had a record for brawling, much of the blame landed on him. Then, the next month, he was in the middle of a big scuffle with the White Sox at Comiskey Park, and was thrown out of the game. Three days later the Yankees sent him to Kansas City for Harry (Suitcase) Simpson. In the clubhouse Mickey Mantle cried. Casey Stengel told Martin, "Well, you're gone. You're the smartest little player I ever had."

In the cheerless cavalcade of the playing career that followed, Martin lasted no more than one season with any team: Detroit after K.C., then Cleveland, Cincinnati, Milwaukee and Minnesota. The late Jimmy Cannon wrote the foam about Martin that all the baseball people blew off their beers: "Now to Cincinnati in another league. And Billy Martin is positive he has come home at last. He always is."

A few years later, when Martin got a chance to manage, he won a division championship for the Twins and was fired, all in his first season. He won a division title with Detroit, but couldn't last out another year. Then Texas. He was Manager of the Year last season. This is his second full season with the Rangers. "It's been a truthful relationship here with everybody," says Martin, a man who prizes truth. "I have a real foundation here. I think I'll stay here for the rest of my career." So now Texas. And Billy Martin is positive he has come home at last. He always is.

The problem is not just that Billy Martin gets in fights and becomes a pugnacious embarrassment for more civil men. Were he merely truculent he would have long since been cut loose from baseball. The problem is that he is a terribly complicated personality—not necessarily sophisticated-complicated, more ironic-complicated. He is a kind of Sir Walter Scott knight errant cast loose into this strange modern world of compromise and convention, where duels are frowned upon and damsels in distress can be put on waivers. Despite all the donnybrooks, Martin is a man of sweet sentimentality. He believes in absolutes—some might say simplicities—and he is nurtured by the fundamental of chivalry, which he introduces into conversation as readily as he might order breakfast or argue with an umpire. Words such as loyalty, honor, truth, love, belief and pride surface regularly; and in his universe, where such absolutes rigorously figure, we should not be surprised that Martin also finds liars, back-stabbers, cowards, bullies and other blackguards lurking about, anxious to do him in. When in fact they do cross him, he does the only thing left for him to do in his well-defined world, which is to pop them in the chops or, where bosses are involved, to supply the lexical equivalent. Frank Lane, a man never known for being demure, admits that Martin is in a league all his own. "When I've talked like he does," Lane says, "I've always made sure I was talking on a five-year or seven-year contract."

Yet Martin also possess powerful qualities of organization, inspiration, evaluation and attention to detail that make him nearly peerless among managers. Counting a minor-league season managing Denver in 1968, he has taken four teams with losing records and turned them instantly into winners. This bespeaks more than a touch of genius. Since his abrasiveness draws attention, he also sells tickets, which managers and coaches almost never do, whatever the sport. The enraged citizenry of the Twin Cities and Detroit responded with classic organized American hysteria to his firings—printing up buttons and bumper stickers and indignantly registering their opinions on radio call-in shows. So we can be sure there will always be a home for Billy Martin.

Wherever he goes, Martin wants things his way, and he is not bashful. While it is politic for most baseball managers to utter platitudes about the managerial dependence upon the athletic talent at their disposal and to allow that they can really only do a little bit here and there—a suicide squeeze twice a season, that sort of thing—Martin believes that the manager should be the force about which the team revolves. Copernicus, you may recall, had similar public-relations difficulties with the Establishment over what revolves around what. "A manager can change the outcome in anywhere from 20 to 50 games," Martin proclaims heretically.

Twenty to 50? Why, you're talking about one out of almost every three games.

"Sure," says Martin. "That is, if he's the kind of guy I am, who handles everything himself. I'm not talking about the managers who just make out the lineup cards. *I call everything myself.* Infield in, halfway, back; all the pitchouts; whether to throw through or not. I call a lot of the pitches, too. There's someone out there looking at me before every pitch."

Charley Dressen failed to impress his players with a similar view of self-eminence: "Stay close, boys, and I'll think of something." But while Martin has quipped that the secret of his profession "is to keep the five players who hate you away from the four who are undecided," he has really been quite popular with his minions. What he did learn from studying Dressen—who once, furious and fully clothed, followed the naked Martin into a shower to get the last word—is that confidence need not be confused with majesty.

But if Martin picked up this or that from Dressen and some of the others he played for, Stengel, his patrons, is the lone Influence. Indeed, on the days when a breeze blows, so that Martin's dark blue Ranger jacket billows in back above where he jabs his right hand into the rear pocket, a man can take off his glasses, and it seems once more that it is the bandy-legged old man going out to lift Lopat for Page, not merely his favorite protégé about to lift Bibby for Foucault. *Lift*: that is precisely the word. Any hired hand can change pitchers, replace them, signal to the bullpen; but a man does not truly become a manager until he can *lift* a pitcher. Billy Martin lifts pitchers.

He juggles lineups as well, promiscuously, if not capriciously. He gambles, always forcing the action (as he played). "The manager who runs scared usually gets beat," he declares. He much regrets that the American League permits the designated hitter because that makes managing easier, and with his confidence and skills Martin would rather have everybody in with him a little deeper.

Baseball intelligence seems to have infiltrated Martin by osmosis. When he was 15, 16 years old he was 5' 5", 125, mostly ears and nose, playing sandlot ball in the off-season in Berkeley with major-leaguers. He roomed with Cookie Lavagetto while he was still in his teens. The first time Mantle saw Martin, the Kid was telling Frankie Crosetti, a sacred font of keystone wisdom, how it was you made the double play. From Stengel he may have most obtained the psychology of leadership.

"Stengel showed me how you don't even have to mention names to get discipline. That's good." Pause. "Stengel. . . . " Martin puts the name off by itself, rolling it in pleasant reverie over the taste buds of the mind. "Yeah, there was this time he called a team meeting. 'Now, first, you lovers,' he began, 'You single guys who are out chasing something all night and you married guys who are telling the girls you're single.' We thought he was gonna stop there. But he went on. 'And you drinkers'— Case was getting some guys more than once—'I'm the only one who is gonna stay up all night drinking.' Everybody was sure he was through then, but he went on. 'And you churchgoers and milk-shake drinkers. Now, it's fine to have some of you guys on a team, but if you don't start showing me some guts out there, if you don't play hard enough for me, I'm going to make every one of you go out and get a double Scotch and a woman.' Oh, he got everybody that time, Casey did. He didn't mention a name, and he got the whole team."

At the batting cage Jim Fregosi, a Ranger infielder, says, "You know, one of the things Billy can do, he can get his point across without naming names. I remember one time last year some pitcher forgot to cover first base. The next day he had the whole staff out there covering first base for a half hour or more. Billy never said a word. I don't think anybody messed up on that the rest of the season."

Finally, although they largely go unnoticed, are Martin's tutorial achievements. In a way they gratify him the most. "When I was a kid," he says, "I never understood what teachers got out of it. But now I know. Why, to see somebody do something you showed them—that's a wonderful feeling. You feel better than if you had done it yourself."

And yet there is always a frenetic atmosphere attending Martin, so that his players must constantly remain at psychological battle stations. "The team was always so tense," said coach Joe Schultz after Martin was axed at Detroit, "because we weren't sure what Billy was going to do next, personally or strategically." For one thing Martin usually fights a three-front war, battling his own front office while carrying on the traditional attack against other teams and The Men in Blue. The skids were greased for his firing at Minnesota after an argument over the farm system with a front-office subaltern. "If he'd been a younger guy, I'd have punched his lights out," Martin says now. He lets fly these declarations very casually, although one would never assume idly; he and the Twins' traveling secretary, had already, in fact, exchanged punches in a hotel lobby one 4 a.m. Martin's end at Detroit came about strictly because of his policy disputes with general manager Jim Campbell, who fired Martin despite advancing the opinion that "foul line to foul line," Billy had been exemplary.

It is not generally known, but Martin stood on the brink twice last year at Texas. In one instance he went to the front office and said that David Clyde, the local fireball sensation, should be sent out for seasoning. No doubt Martin was right; Clyde is in the middle minors now playing the title role in *The Von McDaniel Story*. But at that time Clyde was still attracting crowds and the accountants hated to see him go. So Martin said well then, if Clyde doesn't get farmed out I quit. The Rangers replied that they would be real sorry to see Billy leave. For once Martin backed down without resorting to either tongue or fists. But then, late in the season, in a perfectly asinine dispute over a players' wives' auxiliary, Martin slapped the team's traveling secretary, and his job was in serious jeopardy for a time.

Martin looks even more like a genuine desperado now, thanks to his big, looped mustache, which is certainly more appropriate than the pointed wise guy's face that he owned when he first came up and established his scrapper's reputation with a one-two knockdown of Jimmy Piersall. Before that, back in Berkeley, it had been Martin's jug ears and Naples nose, and the uncomplimentary remarks they occasioned, that had introduced him to fisticuffs. But now, helped by the mustache, he has settled into his looks, and it is neither his nose nor his ears, but his eyes—soulful and dark, brooding more than menacing—that hold one's attention.

The manager uses half glasses for reading, peering over them in a scholarly way, and he relaxes, if he can be said to relax, by drawing on those big U-shaped pipes that one associates with Swiss grandfathers. His desk is littered with pipe apparatus, and with tapes from his country-and-Western music collection, a taste he came to via Mantle. Martin was attracted to country songs by the lyrics—visceral, brutally hurting, soupy and troubled. *I'm So Lonesome I Could Cry* is his favorite.

Martin shares his office with Art Fowler, his pitching coach, who has been with him since the minor league year at Denver. The club was 8–22 when Martin arrived. Like King David sending Bathsheba's husband to battle, the Twins urged Martin to go out there in order to get rid of him; feeling guilty, a Twins' executive admitted this later in private. They figured Martin would louse up a bad team more, panic, get frustrated, get in trouble and give them an excuse to zap him. But Martin crossed up the organization by bringing the 8–22 team in 65–50 the rest of the way, and what could the Twins do but hire him? "He's so far ahead of everyone," Fowler says in his Carolina drawl. "And the only difference from Denver's he's got smarter."

Martin was saddled with a coach at Detroit he was convinced was ratting on him to the GM—never again. His four Ranger coaches are all his own men, each from a different phase of his life, so that together they know the whole man, but apart each coach knows only his share. It is Martin's wife Gretchen who says, "You see only a small portion of Billy. Of course, he must have designed it that way." Merrill Combs played with Martin in the minors 27 years ago; Charlie Silvera was with him on the Yanks; Fowler was Denver; and Frank Lucchesi was managing the Phillies and Martin the Tigers when they met. The four coaches span his career. There is a great constancy to Martin, and despite all the upheavals in his life he seems to have made each stop have some meaning. And always he keeps harking back to his childhood.

"You know, Billy," he was told the other day, "You ought to write a book."

"Someday I'm going to write a book about my childhood," he replied, although the subject of his youth had not been in the discussion.

That upbringing, despite a father's desertion and a Depression backdrop, was not really unhappy; there was much love for him and no real deprivation. He was born May 16, 1928 in the oldest house still standing in Berkeley; his mother lives there still. Eight months after his birth his father walked away. Mr. Martin is a Portuguese—*Por-to-gee* (hard g), Martin says—from the Hawaiian island of Maui, Martin's mother is Italian, and he refers to himself as a Dago, but Martin (Mar-*teen* in the Latin pronunciation) is indeed his real name. He was christened Alfred Manuel Martin, but was always Billy, which came from his grandmother calling him *bello*, cute in Italian.

Martin's mother married again, to an Irishman named Downey, but Billy lived next door with his grandmother Selvini, sleeping in the same bed with her until he was 15 and kicking so much they got him a cot. Mrs. Selvini died in 1946 when he was 18; she sang *O Sole Mio!* on her deathbed. The two major influences in the home in Billy's life were both female—grandmother and mother. As any knight would have, he felt very protective of them.

Martin can remember walking down the street with his mother when he was about 11 years old and flushing with anger when men turned to look her over or whistle. "Now you got to understand," he says, "my mother's only four-eleven, but she's the toughest little thing that ever walked. Oh, you'd like her. She's something. She was good and chesty and had one of those round little Dago heinies, and all that whistling was really embarrassing me. This is my mother. I wanted to fight these guys. She sensed that, and suddenly she turned to me and said, 'Listen, Billy, don't you ever forget that I got the best-looking fanny in town.' "

From his father, his disappearance notwithstanding, Martin seems to have obtained some other hard qualities. Martin is only 5' 11", but his father is big, maybe 6' 2", and Martin always heard that the Por-to-gee was the toughest son of a gun on Maui. But he never saw his old man until one day when he was 14, and his father showed up out of the blue, bringing him a pair of corduroy pants; then he popped up again four or five years later when Billy made the roster of the Triple A Oakland Oaks, and they had a long, even satisfying chat. His father materializes now and again in Lakeland, and Martin seems to accept him without emotion one way or the other. The real father-son devotion in his life goes the other way, to his boy Billy Joe, age 10, on whom he lavishes his time and attention. "We do as much together as we can," he says. "I try to include Billy Joe in everything I can when we're home. We have some wonderful times." He pauses and looks away, actually beaming. "Oh, it's so exciting, that kind of love."

Exciting. When was the last time you heard anyone refer to that kind of love as exciting? The thing you must remember about Martin is that he is every bit as intense and compelling about the positive emotions in his life as he is about the negative. It is just that bopping people is what he does in the sector that is being recorded. And he is gloriously candid. Of umpire Ron Luciano he recently declared, "I don't want him fined, I want him fired." When he beat up on Dave Boswell, one of his best pitchers at Minnesota, Martin graciously provided a full accounting: "He hit me in the temple and the ribs. I just held on, and then I started to hit him in the stomach. I worked up and hit him in the mouth, nose and eyes. He bounced off the wall, and I hit him again, and he was out cold before he hit the ground." But here, too, is the sort of thing Martin does: all of a sudden one day last winter he decided to write Stengel a thank-you note. "I just thought it would be nice to say something good," Martin says. "I just said that I was writing him to thank him for being a great manager and teaching me all the things he did."

Stengel, obviously, was something of a father figure for Martin, and not only because he managed him when he played for the Oakland Oaks and brought him to the majors. Stengel seemed to comprehend Martin, how to direct the furies within him. Once, when Martin was fuming about some slight, Stengel walked over, chucked him under the shin, and cooed, in baby talk: "Ith Li'l Bill-wee mad at naughty Ol' Case?" And yet as much as the two men came to prize each other—"That fresh punk, how I love him!" Casey once rhapsodized in a weak moment—Martin felt that Stengel failed to stand up for him following the Copacabana hassle, and after he was traded Martin did not say a word to Stengel for six years.

Martin was 29 when he was sent to K.C.—old enough, a man. But in context the Stengel rejection, coming as it did not long after Martin's first wife ditched him in extraordinary circumstances, really served to extend the pained adolescence of a sensitive, fatherless, unattractive boy—one who could succeed in sports and with his buddies but who could never find acceptance in the respectable grown-up world. Accounts of Martin's disputes with school officials (for fighting in basketball and baseball games) seem no different in substance from what we have 30 years later, Martin railing at Bowie Kuhn or general managers or umpires. We have often wondered what James Dean would have been like in middle age; well, Billy Martin is James Dean in middle age.

Significantly, the first decision Martin had to make in organized ball came on the day he signed with Oakland and they told him to give up his old street gang buddies. Flabbergasted, he refused. Martin is perfect for baseball because it is the belonging that counts so much, the camaraderie, the men in groups. The players who stay on in baseball as managers and coaches, even as broadcasters, are not necessarily the sagest; often they are not the type we expect, for we are looking for the wrong things in the career men. Instead, the only strain that runs through virtually all the oldtimers who stay in the game is that they can't get the club out of their systems.

The club—yessireebob, baseball is still a club with a clubhouse. Football is not a club, or basketball or hockey; they are just teams with locker rooms. So, baseball coaches and managers individually may be smart or dumb, shy or ebullient, city or country, and now even black or white, but almost all will be marked by one trait—a love of that club. Characteristically, at each of his managerial layovers, the first thing Martin has done is to issue edicts more firmly establishing the sanctuary of the clubhouse. In a letter of some 20 paragraphs to the Rangers in advance of spring training this season only one regulation is underscored: "No one, and I mean no one, will be allowed in the clubhouse. . . . "

In order to better remain a part of the club Martin has violated one of the hoariest of baseball traditions by making it his custom to drink with his players. Purists, appalled at this practice, could hardly wait to say I told you so when it was revealed that Martin and Boswell tangled after hoisting a few at the same bar. But *alone* is the worst part of being a manager, Martin says. He doesn't see why he can't have a pop now and then with the other guys on the club. "I've taken the manager off the pedestal and put the team on the pedestal," he says. "Why should the manager get the hotel bar and make 25 other guys go somewhere else? Besides, communication is the name of the game, and you get communication when you drink with someone. Don't give me that baloney about 'my door is always open' because the ones you have to communicate with won't care whether the door is open or closed. You've got to talk to these kids, learn their language. And if you can do that having a drink or two with them, so what? At Detroit I had a guy who needed five drinks. Five drinks, he was going to be MVP. He never was, that's for sure, but he was better for having five drinks with the manager."

Martin came up at a time when clubs were even closer and more homogeneous. There are more cliques now, the kids are better-educated, have more money and thus are less intimidated. But a team is still a very exclusive club that comes together every day. The one word Martin uses to characterize the year he spent out of baseball—1970—is "lonely." Oh, sure he'd love to get out there and play again, but he was never all that good a player, and the belonging in baseball still means the most.

Martin's closest friend ever, he says, is Mantle, who now lives in Dallas, a vice president of Reserve Life Insurance. "I was the happiest man in the world when Billy got the job down here," Mickey says, "because it gives me somebody to hang around with." And here is Mantle, who hit 536 home runs and made the Hall of Fame, on what he misses in baseball: "I miss the playing. I still dream of a comeback. I do. Almost every night I still play ball. When Aaron hit that home run last year, I just had goose pimples all over me. When he ran around those bases, I knew exactly how he felt. It almost felt like he was me." It was eight o'clock in the morning, seven years since he last played; Mantle stared out happily into the pale light over his backyard, savoring the old acclaim. "I miss the crowds applauding. I miss the big ovations," he said, smiling.

Billy Martin, who hit .257 lifetime, on the same subject: "What I miss when I'm away is the pride in baseball. Especially the pride of being on a team that wins. I probably was the proudest Yankee of them all. And I don't mean false pride. When it's real on a team, it's a deep love-pride. There's nothing greater in the world than when somebody on the team does something good, and everybody gathers around to pat him on the back. I really love the togetherness in baseball. That's real true love."

And with this attitude comes the territorial imperative: to protect the club, to be loyal to it, to stand up for it, to be a *stand-up* guy. Really, all you have to know about Billy Martin is what Merrill Combs, his coach, says: "All Billy wants is what is ours. And he'll fight to get it. That's all." And Combs hits another fungo. That's all.

It might seem an anachronism that suburban-raised college graduates would give a hoot about whether their managers were stand-up guys, who kicked dirt on umpires and threatened to retaliate against brushbacks and all that plug-ugly John McGraw stuff. But it is difficult to talk to any player who has ever worked for Martin who does not start off by referring to his loyalty: Billy Martin is behind you. That sort of thing still matters very much, on the clubs. It is worth noting that Frank Robinson, one of the youngest managers and the new breed, for sure, made his biggest fuss last season when he claimed that Bobby Winkles, the college coach the Angels had hired as manager, didn't fight for his men hard enough. Football coaches are generals, but baseball managers are master sergeants.

The one track Billy Martin's mind runs on in this department can best be illustrated by an incident that occurred early this season when he was thrown out of a game by a rookie umpire, Richard Garcia. Martin maintained that Garcia had called a grounder fair only after getting a sign from his colleague at third base, Ron Luciano. Martin swore he had seen his nemesis Luciano give the signal. Garcia denied it. Thus the dispute became much more than a simple matter of judgment; to Martin it was a point of honor. Garcia was not wrong, Martin said; he could tolerate that. No, Garcia was lying. "Truth," he observed to several newspapermen in his office after the game, puffing on a pipe, reflecting on a favorite theme. "Truth. I don't think you see much of it anymore." He shook his head sadly; it was as if truth were a favorite puppy dog that no longer came when he called.

The newpapermen eyed him warily, as did the coaches. Martin can do a wonderful imitation, complete with darting eyes and shuffling feet, of how strangers react around him, convinced that he is going to haul off and hit them in the nose. You can't be too sure. Certainly nobody took any chances this time. Nobody smiled at all. The newspapermen competed with the coaches at trying to outgrim one another.

Postmortems done, Martin could at last being to assess the full impact of the situation. "They're out to get me," he declared ominously. "Two National League umpires asked me in spring training why the umpires in my league were all out to get me. And if they're out to get me, it will be very difficult for my ball club to win this year. I've got to protect myself and my team."

Art Fowler came by, and Martin told him to get a microphone so he could wear it the next day and record any conversations with umpires for use in his defense in the league office's "kangaroo court." Fowler nodded and went to his locker. After so many seasons with Martin, Fowler could work earthquakes without getting perturbed.

"The really sad thing about Garcia," Martin said, picking up the thread again, "is that he had called a good game up to then. He could be a good ump. But he was out to get Martin, wasn't he?" For emphasis, he began to address himself directly to Garcia. "So you're real cute, Garcia. And now it's you and me. Let's see how you handle the pressure that way because you're going to get a lot of it now."

Martin leaned back, relit his big pipe and mused on tactics, a professor addressing a small seminar. An idea came to him. "I'm going to call him Spic or Greaser or Wetback, and see how he likes that," he said. The remark was made *sotto voce* and, understand, it was spoken absolutely without malice or racial antagonism. Indeed, a complaint against Martin is that he favors Latin ballplayers. They remind him of the scuffling minority kid he was 25 years ago—and they return the affection. No, he was not being racial at all, merely pragmatic. This just seemed to him to be the most effective way for a stand-up guy to serve his club in this particular instance.

"They called me Dago and Wop, all that, every day I was growing up," he went on evenly. "That doesn't bother me anymore. I just look through those people. But can this guy? Let's see how he takes it when I walk out there tomorrow and say, 'Hello, Greaser.' Let's see."

As it turned out, Martin decided against using this ploy because he felt that Luciano was the greater threat. He put on a lavaliere mike and went after Luciano even before the game started.

Such controversies and disputes, violent or otherwise, are simply part and parcel of Martin by now. Deadpan, he maintains that he has never started a fight, but even granting that claim he certainly has set a lot of tables. Fights aside, twice he has been fined or suspended for ordering his pitchers to throw spitballs and brushbacks. When he was at Detroit and Baltimore was the chief foe, he orchestrated a feud with Oriole manager Earl Weaver. Now that Oakland is Martin's Baltimore, he is spoiling for a newspaper scrap with the A's Alvin Dark.

In each case Martin seeks out the best weapons. As he would use ancestry to rattle Garcia, so against Weaver, a coarse little scuffler himself, Martin employed the most basic alley cat approach ("I'm going to take care of him. I'm going to hurt him"), and now for Dark he is plainly fondling his jugular—religion. Martin, who always pins a little god cross on his cap, suggests that Dark is a Pharisee who wears his Christianity on his sleeve. "Everybody's always talking about my ego or this or that," Martin says a bit testily, "but do these people really know me? The Brat, they dubbed me. But I went to church every Sunday. I prayed to my God. And those people who dubbed me, did they go to church? I gave a car to a priest once. I don't believe anybody in a front office ever gave a car to a priest."

That display of largesse came after Martin was named MVP in the 1953 World Series, which turned out to be the apex of his playing career. His hustle won games—Mantle says Martin really didn't have much besides a good arm which, for a second baseman, is the fifth teat on a cow—but his dustups hardly fit the classic Yankee tradition of dignity, and he was sometimes nearly unstable. Once, Martin broke a leg sliding in spring training. So scared was he that he would never play again that he could not eat, and dropped from 163 pounds to 132 in the two months he had to sit out.

And then one morning, two weeks after his first child, a daughter, was born, his wife woke him and said there was a fellow at the door who wanted to see him. It was a process server delivering her divorce papers. Desperately, Martin fought for his marriage—"out of love, pride, hurt, who knows?"—in the bargain suffering acute melancholia, insomnia and hypertension. A winter's stay with Mantle in Commerce, Okla., where the city boy hunted and fished and funned, ate quail and mashed potatoes for breakfast and ballooned to 185, may have saved Martin's sanity.

But at least he was with the Yankees then, proudest of them all. After he left New York nothing seemed to work anywhere, and when he slugged Cub pitcher Jim Brewer in 1960, the jig was really up. Brewer had to have an eye operation, and he and the Cubs sued Martin and the Reds for better than a million dollars—even though all the evidence indicates that Martin only bopped Brewer on the chin (after the pitcher called him "a little Dago son of a bitch," Martin says) and that it was a teammate who hit Brewer near the eye in the melee that followed. After the Reds ditched him, no one else in baseball offered support, even though the case set a nasty precedent in civil courts for intrasport conduct. Martin was saddled with suits for years, and has paid out $22,500 for legal fees and hospitalization. It was in effect the final repudiation of Billy Martin by the Establishment.

In the year and a half more he managed to hang on as a player Martin became a pariah; no longer just a brash pepperpot, in the public mind he was a psychotic who maimed people. So bad was his reputation that when Martin was cut by the Twins just before the '62 season, he turned down a $100,000 Japanese offer because he thought it was crucial to stay in the game here and try to rehabilitate his image. He signed on with the Twins as a $10,000 "troubleshooter" and settled into what became a six-year vocational hiatus.

"I had been knocked down so badly," he says. "The things they said about me. And when I was released, I was determined to come back. I thought: I got to stay in this game. I was going to eat humble pie, but I had to prove to people in baseball that I was a different person than who they thought I was. I'd let them see the real Billy Martin. But some of the stuff would follow me wherever I went. I know I'll never get completely away from it. But they've taken so many cheap shots at me, and I've won so often, I don't care anymore. I don't even take any satisfaction when I win again because it's just their own urine blowing back in their faces. It doesn't concern me."

When the offer to manage Denver came up suddenly in '68, Martin was still so insecure and defensive that his first response was to turn it down. Gretchen, a refined, small-town Midwesterner with Junior League looks, not at all the kind of woman you would expect to have been married to Billy Martin for 16 years, had to stay up with him till one in the morning convincing her husband to reach for the brass ring. Even then, he did not make up his mind until after a long prayerful session in church. Similarly, it took two days of the same sort of emotional gyrations before he finally agreed to head up the Rangers.

Perhaps he fears that it takes too much out of him, managing baseball. "I love it, I'm very happy," he says, "but I can't ever get away from it. I take it home with me, I take it to bed with me, I wake up with it. And what I feel inside you'll never see on the outside." Always, too, he is on trial in a way that other managers who may be just as obsessed are not. Martin is guilty until proven innocent, and he knows that. Rookie umpires don't throw Managers of the Year out of ball games the moment they say one naughty little barnyard word unless that is the case.

As Martin puts it, he is almost like a gunfighter now, with a reputation that invites challengers. Umpires, executives, journalists, tough guys—each in their ways are looking for a shot at him. He went into a bar not long ago, and down at the other end a guy bet his buddy he couldn't beat up Billy Martin. So he snuck up behind Billy and decked him. When Martin got up he took the fight to the aggressor, ruining his clothes and face in the process of playing catch-up ball. When he got home he said, "Gretchen, you'll never believe this, but I was just sitting there. I didn't say anything. I didn't do anything. It just happened." And what did she say? "She said, 'You're right. I don't believe it.'"

The world is always out to get Billy Martin—he is right—because the world cannot afford to tolerate Billy Martin. It would all come apart at the seams if we acted like him. This is another reason why we have commissioners. But nobody is going to do Billy Martin in, because he believes in himself as surely as he believes in the other things he fights for. "I don't care what the others think," he says. "I've always been the toughest critic of myself, and the only one I want to know me is Jesus Christ. They talk about my temper. Well, I haven't seen a good race horse yet who wasn't highstrung. And anyway, temper is a wonderful thing if you can control it and it doesn't control you. Jesus Christ took a whip to the money changers, right? Well, that's a temper, and that's not a bad guy to follow. The way I see it, my temper is a great ally. It is what has pushed Billy Martin."

And then, he has another edge on more temperate people in that he doesn't need a name on a mailbox to tell him where home is. Martin is at home wherever he pulls on a uniform and walks out there to get "ours" for the club.

Benching of A Legend

BY ROGER KAHN

The prideful struggle of an aging Stan Musial to prolong his career—a painful experience for everyone involved—was poignantly recounted by one of the game's most astute observers.

DISTURBING PARADOXES SURROUND AN AGING BASEBALL player. He is old but not gray; tired but not short of breath; slow but not fat as he drives himself down the first base line. Long after the games, when the old ballplayer thinks seriously, he realizes that he has become obsolete at an age when most men are still moving toward their prime in business and, in politics, are being criticized for their extreme youth. It is a melancholy thing, geriatrics for a 40-year-old.

To Joe DiMaggio, age meant more injuries and deeper silences. To Bob Feller it meant months of forced jokes, with nothing to pitch but batting practice. To more fine ballplayers than anyone has counted age has meant Scotch, bourbon and rye. The athletes seldom bow out gracefully.

Amid the miscellaneous excitements of the current National League pennant race, the most popular ballplayer of his time is trying desperately to overcome this tradition; Stanley Frank Musial of the St. Louis Cardinals, now 39 and slowed, intends to end his career with dignity and with base hits. Neither comes easily to a ballplayer several years past his peak, and so to Musial, a man accustomed to ease and to humility, this has been a summer of agony and pride.

Consider one quiet June evening in Milwaukee when Musial walked toward the batting cage to hit with the scrubs, dragging his average (.235) behind him. He had been riding the bench for two weeks.

"Hey, what a funny-looking ballplayer," called Red Schoendienst of the Braves, who was Musial's roommate on the Cardinals for five years. Musial grinned wide. It was an old joke between old friends. Then he stood silently among anonymous second-liners, attempting to act as though he were used to the company.

"Stash," someone said, while George Crowe, a St. Louis pinch hitter was swinging, "did you know that Preacher Roe was using a spit ball when he pitched against you?"

The question snapped Musial to life. "Sure," he said, enthusiastically. "We had a regular signal for it. One day Preacher goes into his motion and Terry Moore, who's coaching at third, picks off the spitter and gives me the signal. Preacher knows I've got it, so he doesn't want to throw the spitter. But he's halfway through his windup and all he can change to is a lollipop [nothing ball]. I hit it into the leftfield seats, and I laughed all the way around the bases."

Musial laughed again at the memory, then stepped in to hit. He swung three times but never got the ball past the batting practice pitcher. A knot of Milwaukee fans jeered as Musial stepped out of the cage, and the sound, half boos, half yahs, was harsh. Musial blushed and began talking very quickly about other games against Roe and the old Brooklyn Dodgers. "Yeah, I could really hit those guys," he said. It was strange and a little sad to see so great a figure tapping bouncers to the pitcher and answering boos with remembrances of past home runs.

Why was he doing it, one wondered. He was long since certain of election to the Baseball Hall of Fame. He was wealthy, independent of the game. He was a man who had always conducted himself sensibly. Now here was sensible old Stan Musial reduced to benchwarmer, as he waged a senseless war with time.

The answer, of course, is pride; more pride than most of us suspected Musial possessed, more pride than Musial ever displayed when he was Stan the Man, consistent .350 hitter, owner and proprietor of most National League pitching staffs.

The issues in the case of Stan Musial versus time have cleared considerably since his May benching and his dramatic July comeback. He was not through in June as many suspected but, because Musial is well-loved, few put in words. But neither was he the young Musial in July, as many said loudly, but, I imagine, few really suspected. Both the benching and the comeback represent skirmishes in the continuing battle Musial joins each time he puts on a pair of spikes and heads out toward leftfield, trotting a shade more slowly than he once did.

After a career in which he had never batted lower than .310, Musial hit .255 in 1959. Since he was 38, the wise conclusion was that he was finished, and most baseball men assumed that he would retire. In fact, most hoped he would choose retirement instead of the awkward exit that seemed inevitable if he played this season. "No," Musial insisted during the winter. "I want to go out on a good year. I'm not quitting after a lousy year like that." Athletes, like chorus girls, are usually the last to admit that age has affected them, and Musial appeared to be following the familiar unhappy pattern. His timing seemed gone—changeups made him look foolish—and he appeared to be the only man who didn't know it.

During the winter Musial enrolled in a physical education program at St. Louis University. The exercises were orthodox—push-ups and such— but placed emphasis on tumbling. He arrived in spring training splendidly conditioned and hit well, if not sensationally, during exhibition games. For the first three weeks of the regular season he played first base, batted about .300 and fielded poorly. Then his hitting dropped sharply, and over the next three weeks his average drifted toward .200. Finally, on May 21, Solly Hemus, the Cardinal manager, benched Musial. The decision brought pain to Musial and pain to Hemus, too, since what the manager did, after all, was bench a legend.

"He'll be back," Hemus said vaguely to everyone who asked. When? Solly wasn't quite sure. "I'll play whenever they want me to," Musial said cheerlessly. But he didn't start another game for almost a month.

Hemus is a conscientious, combative man of 36, who joined the Cardinals in 1949 when Musial was already a star, a factor which complicated the usual manager-ballplayer relationship. "I'd never pulled much," Hemus recalls, "and when I first came up Stan gave me some tips. He told me to concentrate on hitting that rightfield screen—it's close—at Busch Stadium. I admired him, and I guess he liked me. It got so that when he'd come home, Janet, Stan's daughter, wouldn't start by asking if he got any hits. First she'd say: 'Did Solly get any hits?'"

Discussing the Musial benching troubles Hemus. He was buffeted somewhat in St. Louis sports pages for the move, and, beyond that, it strained a friendship. But he talked about the benching at some length and with tremendous earnestness after one recent Cardinal night game.

"What's my obligation as manager?" Hemus said, staring darkly into a glass of light beer. "It's not to a friendship, no matter how much I like a guy. My obligation is to the organization that hired me and to 25 ballplayers. I have to win. Stan was hurting the club. He wasn't hitting, and balls were getting by him at first base. It wasn't something I wanted to do. I had to do it."

For all his attempts to show outward indifference, Musial hated the bench. He confided to a few friends that he wouldn't mind being traded to a club that would play him every day. A few hints appeared that he and Hemus were feuding. They weren't—they were just miserable about the situation—but Musial still says, in the closest he comes to a grumble: "Don't let anyone tell you they were resting me. I was benched."

On June 19, after Musial had spent three weeks in the dugout, Hemus said before a doubleheader: "Maybe I'll use you in the second game." The Cards won the first, and in the clubhouse afterward Hemus announced simply: "Same lineup."

Later Musial, deadly serious, approached him. "There's one thing you shouldn't ever try to do, Solly," he said. "Don't ever try to kid me along."

Hemus said nothing. There wasn't anything to say.

"He caught me," the manager remarked over his beer. "He knew me well and he'd caught me. I was wrong to kid him, but I did."

Hemus paused and gathered his thoughts. "I spent a lot of time, a lot of nights worrying about this thing," he said finally, "and I got to remember the coffin. What does he want to take with him to his coffin? Records. Something that people will remember. As many records as he can. Now what do I want to take to my coffin? Honesty. I always wanted to manage, and I want to know I managed honestly. I was right to bench him when I did, but I was wrong to kid him, and I know it makes me look bad to admit it, but I was wrong."

Hemus never evolved a plan to work Musial back into the lineup. While benched, Musial pinch hit nine times but batted safely only once. There was no indication he was going to hit any better than he had. On June 16 Bob Nieman, who had been hitting well, pulled a muscle, and suddenly Hemus needed a leftfielder. He alternated Walt Moryn and rookie John Glenn, but neither hit at all. Then he turned to Musial, hoping for batting but not really confident that he would get it.

What would have happened to Musial if Nieman hadn't been hurt, or if Glenn or Moryn had started slugging? Again Hemus speaks with absolute frankness: "I really don't know," he says. "I just got no idea."

On June 24 Musial started in leftfield against the Phils and got one hit in four times at bat. On June 25 he was hitless, but on June 26 he started again and that day took off on a devastating hitting tear (15 games, .500 batting average) that surprised everyone except, possibly, himself. What brought Musial back to batting form? "Well, one reason I didn't quit," he says, "is that they weren't throwing the fast one by me. Last year they were giving me changes, and I wasn't going good, so I kept swinging too hard. I figured that one out. Now I'm going to left real good on lots of the changeups."

Musial has also changed the unique stance that was his trademark. Remember the old crouch? Now Musial stands closer to the plate, a change that gives him better control of fast balls over the outside corner. He still crouches, but less markedly. His stance remains unusual, but it is no longer radical.

He always concentrated when he hit, but Musial's concentration seems to have deepened further. It must make up for what age has taken from his reflexes, and he now plots his swings with great care.

Nobody around the league has an easy explanation of Musial's great hitting in July, because there is no easy way to explain great hitting by a washed-up 39-year-old ballplayer. "Hell," Musial himself says, "just use that old line of Slaughter's. Just say I never been away."

One night before the Cardinals played the Braves, Charley Dressen, a man who has more explanations than newspapermen have questions, agreed to study the revivified Musial and report on what he saw. Musial lined one of Bob Buhl's inside changeups high into the rightfield bleachers for a home run.

"Ah," Dressen said later. "I know how to pitch to him."

"How?"

"Same as always," Dressen said. "Changeups."

"But he hit the home run off the change."

"Wrong kinda change," Dressen said, cutting off further conversation.

Fred Hutchinson, who manages Cincinnati and once managed the Cardinals, took up the Musial question several days later. "What can you say?" Hutchinson asked, shrugging. "He's hitting like hell, that's all. He's hitting all kinds of pitches, just like he used to."

On the field, during workouts, he tries to be as he once was, too, filled with small jokes and with laughter. "Do you know what sex is?" he may ask. "That's what Poles put potatoes into." Then, lest he offend: "You know I'm Polish."

Sometimes, while playing catch, he shows his pitches—he was a pitcher in the low minor leagues 23 years ago. "Fork ball," he'll say. "Next time I come back it's gonna be as a pitcher."

But once in a while pride, until now the unseen side of Musial, breaks through. He was chatting at a batting cage recently when Jim Toomey, the Cardinals' publicity man, approached and asked broadly if he was telling the story of his life.

"Yeah," someone said. "He's up to a Donora sandlot game in 1935."

"What did you do," Toomey asked, "get four hits?"

"I'll tell you this, buddy," Musial said, quite loudly. "You can bet I got two."

Since his July blaze, Musial has slipped somewhat. "One thing I know about him now," Hemus says, "is that when he gets real tired one day's rest isn't enough. If he needs it, he'll get a week off. If he goes real bad, he'll get plenty of time to get strong again."

The old 154-game-a-year Musial is vanished. The swift base runner, whose sloped shoulders suggested the contours of a greyhound, is slowed. The great batter, whose forte was consistency, now hits in spurts. Yet, in sum, this season makes for a graceful exit. Musial wanted to go out with a respectable year, and through concentrating on pitchers and conserving his own energies, he seems likely to achieve this.

But ahead lies one more trap—another season. Musial has not formally committed himself to 1961, but informally he drops hints that he may play again. He relishes his life in baseball, and when he hits well he seems to feel that he can go on hitting indefinitely. "Maybe my wheels are gone," he says, "but I'll be able to hit like hell for a long time."

Perhaps, but anyone who watched his prideful struggle this summer must wonder. Time presses. The benchings can only get longer; the comebacks still more labored. He has been a fine and gracious man, Stan Musial. It would be nice to see him say farewell with a wave, a grin and a double lined up the alley in right centerfield.

At Full Blast

BY JEFF PEARLMAN

Shooting outrageously from the lip, Braves closer
John Rocker banged away at his favorite targets: the Mets, their fans,
their city and just about everyone in it.

You are a disgrace to the game of baseball. Maybe you should think before you
shoot off your big fat mouth. You are an immature punk who is lucky to be in
the majors. Get some class!"
—A posting by "Metsfan4Life" on www.rockersucks.com

A MINIVAN is rolling slowly down Atlanta's Route 400, and John Rocker, driving directly behind it in his blue Chevy Tahoe, is pissed. "Stupid bitch! Learn to f----- - drive!" he yells. Rocker honks his horn. Once. Twice. He swerves a lane to the left. There is a toll booth with a tariff of 50 cents. Rocker tosses in two quarters. The gate doesn't rise. He tosses in another quarter. The gate still doesn't rise. From behind, a horn blasts. "F--- you!" Rocker yells, flashing his left middle finger out the window. Finally, after Rocker has thrown in two dimes and a nickel, the gate rises. Rocker brings up a thick wad of phlegm. *Puuuh!* He spits at the machine. "Hate this damn toll."

With one hand on the wheel, the other gripping a cellphone, Rocker tears down the highway, weaving through traffic. In 10 minutes he is due to speak at Lockhart Academy, a school for learning-disabled children. Does Rocker enjoy speaking to children? "No," he says, "not really." But of all things big and small he hates—New York Mets fans, sore arms, jock itch— the thing he hates most is *traffic*. "I have no patience," he says. The speedometer reads 72. Rocker, in blue-tinted sunglasses and a backward baseball cap, is seething. "So many dumb asses don't know how to drive in this town," he says, Billy Joel's *New York State of Mind* humming softly from the radio. "They turn from the wrong lane. They go 20 miles per hour. It makes me want—Look! Look at this idiot! I guarantee you she's a Japanese woman." A beige Toyota is jerking from lane to lane. The woman at the wheel is white. "How bad are Asian women at driving?"

Two months have passed since the madness of John Rocker was introduced to the world. In the ninth inning of Game 3 of the National League Championship Series, Atlanta Braves manager Bobby Cox called for his closer—Rocker, a hard-throwing 6' 4", 225-pound lefthander who would turn 25 two days later and who had 38 regular-season saves, a 95-mph fastball and an unhittable slider—to seal a 1–0 win over the Mets. The Shea Stadium bullpen gate opened. A smattering of boos. Louder. Louder. Then, on the fourth or fifth stride of Rocker's dash toward the mound, it started: "A--hole! A--hole! A--hole!" Fifty-five thousand nine hundred eleven fans—black, white, brown, whatever—united by a common bond: hatred of John Rocker.

> *You are a low-class, ignorant piece of scum who doesn't care about anything or anybody. You are the Neanderthal. Maybe this upcoming season Mike Piazza or any other Mets player will hit you in the head with a line drive.*
> —A posting by "Ed" on www.rockersucks.com

JOHN ROCKER has opinions, and there's no way to sugarcoat them. They are politically incorrect, to say the least, and he likes to express them.

• On ever playing for a New York team: "I would retire first. It's the most hectic, nerve-racking city. Imagine having to take the [Number] 7 train to the ballpark, looking like you're [riding through] Beirut next to some kid with purple hair next to some queer with AIDS right next to some dude who just got out of jail for the fourth time right next to some 20-year-old mom with four kids. It's depressing."

• On New York City: "The biggest thing I don't like about New York are the foreigners. I'm not a very big fan of foreigners. You can walk an entire block in Times Square and not hear anybody speaking English. Asians and Koreans and Vietnamese and Indians and Russians and Spanish people and everything up there. How the hell did they get in this country?"

But Rocker reserves a special place in his heart for Mets fans, whom he began bad-mouthing during the regular season when the Braves were battling the Mets for the National League East title eventually won by Atlanta. Although the Braves beat the Mets in a grueling six-game Championship Series (and thus reached the World Series, in which they were swept by the other New York team, the Yankees), Rocker has not allowed himself to let go of the bitterness. You try to find different topics—hunting, women, family—but it always comes back to three cold nights at Shea, when bottles whizzed past his head, beer was dumped on his girlfriend and 2,007 sexual positions involving him and a sheep were suggested.

LIKE MANY Americans nowadays, Rocker is not one to look on the bright side. He likes to bitch and moan and shred things, and his voice—deep, intimidating—is naturally suited for the task. So are the thick eyebrows, the killing-spree scowl. Want to know how Atlanta will play in 2000? Ask later. Want to know why he has Manson-like feelings toward the Mets and everything remotely blue and orange? *Heeeeere's Johnny.* . . .

• On Mets manager Bobby Valentine: "The guy is not professional. Could you see [Yankees manager] Joe Torre or Bobby Cox getting thrown out of a game and then putting on a Groucho Marx disguise and sneaking back into the dugout? If a player got kicked out of a game and did that, Joe Torre would probably suspend him for a week. Bobby Cox would probably demand that the player be traded and tell him not to come back to the team. The Mets' manager did it! That, and his college rah-rah s---? I don't like it."

• On Mets fans: "Nowhere else in the country do people spit at you, throw bottles at you, throw quarters at you, throw batteries at you and say, 'Hey, I did your mother last night—she's a whore.' I talked about what degenerates they were, and they proved me right. Just by saying something, I could make them mad enough to go home and slap their moms."

Much of Rocker's rancor traces to Game 4 of the NLCS, when the fans were especially harsh, the night especially frigid and the Braves one win from reaching the World Series. Rocker entered in the eighth inning to protect a 2–1 lead, with two outs and runners on first and second. After a double steal, John Olerud, the Mets' dangerous-but-struggling first baseman who was 0 for 7 lifetime against Rocker, rapped a bouncer up the middle, slightly to the left of second base. Atlanta reserve shortstop Ozzie Guillen, who had just replaced starter Walt Weiss as part of the double switch that brought Rocker into the game, lunged awkwardly for the ball. It hit his glove, then dribbled into the outfield. Two runs scored, and the Mets won. Afterward an angry Rocker called Olerud's single "one of the more cheaper hits I've given up my entire life." In retrospect he doesn't even allow that much credit. "If Walt is playing shortstop instead of Ozzie, that's not a hit, and we win," says Rocker. "But we had a 38-year-old guy [actually 35] playing shortstop, and he can't make that kind of play."

That's not all. At Shea, Rocker was a one-man psycho circus. He spit at Mets fans. He gave them the finger. During batting practice he would shag a ball in the outfield, fake a toss to a throng of waving spectators, then throw it back to the pitcher, smiling wickedly. Once he took a ball and chucked it as hard as he could at a net that separated fans from the field. "If there wasn't a net there, it would have smoked 'em right in the face," he says. "But they're so stupid, they jumped back like the ball would hit 'em."

Cox, who was routinely asked about Rocker's behavior, told the media before Game 3 against the Mets that he had spoken with the pitcher, requesting that he tone down the act. "That never happened," Rocker says now. "Bobby never talked to me about it, and I never talked to him. Why would he? We were winning."

> *"You are the most hideous man I have ever laid eyes on. Hope your baseball career is short. . . just like your intelligence."*
> —A posting by "Michelle" on www.rockersucks.com

ROCKER BEMOANS the fact that he is not more intelligent, and though his father says John graduated with a 3.5 GPA from Presbyterian Day High in Macon, Ga., in 1993, sometimes it's hard to argue. In passing, he calls an overweight black teammate "a fat monkey." Asked if he feels any bond with New York Knicks guard Latrell Sprewell, notorious for choking coach P.J. Carlesimo two years ago, Rocker lets out a snarl of disgust. "That guy should've been arrested, and instead he's playing basketball," he says. "Why do you think that is? Do you think if he was white they'd let him back? No way." Rocker is rarely tongue-tied when it comes to bashing those of a race or sexual orientation different from his. "I'm not a racist or prejudiced person," he says with apparent conviction. "But certain people bother me."

Rocker was into sports from the get-go; if it wasn't baseball, football or basketball, it was hunting and fishing. (He has gone hunting more than 40 times during this off-season.) His passion, though, was baseball. By his senior year at Presbyterian in 1993, Rocker—who threw three high school no-hitters and a pair of 16-strikeout games—was reaching 91 mph on the radar gun, drawing as many as 15 scouts per game.

Rocker was the Braves' 18th-round selection in the June '93 amateur draft, lasting that long because many clubs thought he'd enroll at Georgia. A starter who threw hard but was wild, Rocker was also nervous and sometimes eccentric. At Class A Danville in '94 he earned a mutant Fidrychian reputation for biting baseballs and letting throws from the catcher nail him in the chest. "He can get crazy," says Atlanta reliever Kerry Ligtenberg, who missed last season with a torn right elbow ligament. "I've played with John since '96. He's got a real short fuse. When it goes off, it's probably better not to be around."

When he signed with the Braves, Rocker and his parents, Jake, an executive at Georgia Farm Bureau Insurance, and Judy, who runs an ad agency out of her home, agreed on a five-year plan. If things weren't looking good, he would use the education clause in his contract and finish college. (Rocker has completed two semesters at Mercer.) By the end of the '97 season things weren't looking good—5–6, 4.86 ERA at Double A Greenville—and the Braves mentioned turning him into a reliever. "It didn't sound too great to me," Rocker recalls. "I was a starter my whole life." The Braves sent Rocker to the Arizona Fall League to pitch exclusively from the pen. There, "I learned that everything's about attitude," says Rocker. "I used to worry over every pitch, every batter. The coaches in Arizona talked to me about just going out and throwing. Don't worry, throw."

The following season Rocker stuck with the big club and appeared in 47 games, mostly as a long reliever. During spring training last year, after Ligtenberg got hurt, Cox named Rocker the closer, and he amassed those 38 saves (in 45 opportunities) with a 2.49 ERA and 104 strikeouts in 72⅓ innings. Still it is his mouth, not his arm, that has won him Rodmanesque notoriety. "Some of the more stoic guys on the team probably get annoyed by me," he says. "But the younger, fiery guys—we get annoyed at their stoicism. There needs to be more atmosphere in our clubhouse. I don't mean loud music and hooting and hollering. But I don't think having the atmosphere of a doctor's office helps."

In the locker room at Shea following Game 4 of the National League Championship Series, as Rocker ranted and raved, fumed and fussed, Mike Remlinger, a 33-year-old lefthanded reliever with six years of major league experience, was asked whether Rocker had gone too far. Remlinger—quiet, thoughtful—paused. "The thing is," he said, "baseball is a game of humility. You can be on top one minute, as low as possible the next. When you're young, you don't realize it. But sooner or later you learn—we all do. Be humble."

> *"My mouth is watering for that day when Rocker steps foot in*
> *Shea once again. (This time I'm bringing D batteries.)"*
> —A posting by "Metswin" on www.rockersucks.com

Me and Hutch

BY JIM BROSNAN

In one of the stories he penned for SI—*which were later included in his classic*
The Long Season—*a wisecracking righthander recalls the adjustments he had
to make when a tough old manager took over the Reds in midseason.*

JULY 8: THE PHONE RANG AT 7:30. WE WERE STILL IN BED. I
reached for the receiver. "Who in the world would dare call us
this early?" my wife said.

"Hi, Donald," I growled into the mouthpiece. "Is everything all
right?" (*It's Don Studt*, I whispered to my wife.) "Nice of you to call so
early, Don. . . . No, I didn't watch the All-Star Game. . . . No, I haven't read
the paper. We're still in bed. What's in the paper?. . . . Oh! Great. What I
mean is, *great*, I like him! Thanks for calling Don. . . . "

"We've got a new manager," I said.

"Who?" she said.

"Hutch," I said.

JULY 9: The clubhouse man warned each player not to go out of the clubhouse till after the meeting. "Hutch wants to talk to you," he said. I had
missed the workout; now I couldn't make up my mind whether or not to
apologize to Fred Hutchinson. Hutch seems to be embarrassed by apologies.
If you do wrong, you should figure out why, vow never to do it again, and
forget it. Still, I waited till the last moment, then had to take a chair at the

table right in front of him. He stood, waiting for attention. I sat down, rif-fled the envelopes containing player passes that lay on the table, and looked up to see Hutchinson staring at me with half a smile on his face. He winked at me and murmured, "Hi, Jim."

"I met most of you fellows yesterday," said Hutchinson. "Most of you I knew already anyway. Most of you know me." He paused and looked slow-ly around the room as he went on. "I like to win. That's the only way to play this game. To win. We're all like that. From now on I'm running this ball club. If you have any problems, come to me. I'll handle them or get somebody to do it for me. On paper this club looks better than the stand-ings indicate so far. I don't know why, yet. Some people say you've been playing a little too conservative, that you don't bump heads enough in the field. All I got to say to that is that if somebody bumps your head the only thing to do is bump back. Now I'm not going to say to you pitchers that you should knock somebody down just because they're takin' a shot at you. I can't say that, and I won't say that." He paused, emphatically, timing his words perfectly. "But I don't care if you brush a hitter back once in a while. Just to let 'em know you're out there."

He picked up a scorecard. "I just want to add one thing. I'm glad to be up here with you. We're going to start winning. We might as well start tonight."

JULY 16: The smile of Fred Hutchinson is a treasured one. His ballplayers vie hopefully for it. By playing well and winning they earn it. (Hutchinson snorts at plain luck.) Miserly with his laughter at all times, Hutchinson is miserable in defeat. The depth of his frown is in direct proportion to the length of his losing streak.

Hutch had little to smile about in his first week as our manager. We lost three games to the Giants. The Dodgers followed the Giants into Crosley Field, and Hutchinson met them with a cold and hungry stare. We won both games from Los Angeles, and Hutchinson led us into St. Louis with just the bare hint of a grim smile on his face. Ernie Broglio and I were the scheduled pitchers for the Thursday night game. When I came up through the Cardinal dugout with a well-oiled arm, Ernie grabbed me and asked if everything was all right. I told him he'd look good in a beard. He asked me if I'd like to trade pitches—he'd throw me a fastball to hit if I'd give him one up in his eyes. I asked for a high slider and we agreed on the arrangements—first pitch the first time up for each of us. Such friend-ly arrangements between opposing pitchers are only good as long as each thinks the friendly gesture won't interfere with winning the game.

By the time I got to hit we had a three-run lead and all I got from Broglio were good curveballs. Which I never could hit; it should be illegal to throw them to pitchers. By the time Broglio hit, I was struggling to retire the side before my lead vanished. Since he'd thrown me good curveballs, I decided to reciprocate. Only I didn't have a good curve. Broglio lined a hanging curve into leftfield for a hit, and Hutchinson growled loud enough to scare bears in the St. Louis zoo. One thing a pitcher should never do is let the opposing pitcher drive in a run.

Already I had walked four men in four innings. This is one more than I usually walk in nine innings, and three more than Hutchinson would like his pitchers to walk in 30 days. "Bend your back a bit," he said to me after Broglio's base hit. "You know you can't pitch high and get away with it." We still had a one-run lead, and I vowed to mend my pitching manners. Cunningham and White drilled two low fastballs into centerfield to start the fifth. I might have caught both balls had I anticipated them. But such good pitches shouldn't have been hit at all.

"Boyer will bunt, probably," I thought. "I'll waste a slider outside just to find out." Bailey took off his mask and walked out toward me. "Forget it, Gar, I know what to do," I thought. But Bailey wasn't even looking at me. Suddenly Hutchinson loomed up in the left-hand corner of my vision. "Make Peña get the ball over the plate," Hutch said to Bailey. He held out his hand for the ball, which I had just rubbed till it felt comfortable.

"For what?" I said, stupefied.

No one in the stands knew. The bus driver who took us to the airport and the pilot who flew us to Chicago couldn't have cared less. We won the game anyway.

When we arrived in Chicago my roomie told me to go to sleep. We had six hours to rest up before the next game. My wife sympathized with me when I called in the morning. "You just better tell Hutch that you want to start and you deserve to start and why did he take you out so quickly and why did he let Newcombe stay for 11 innings two nights before that, and. . . . " But I cut her off in time to catch the bus to the ball park.

"Don't you think you took me out a little quick last night?" I asked.

Hutchinson greeted my hesitant query with a raised eyebrow and an amused twitch of the left corner of his mouth. "You don't think you were pitching good ball up to then, do you?" he countered. "I didn't."

"Maybe not," I conceded. "But it seemed to me you don't trust me as a starter, that you think of me primarily as a relief pitcher. Is this Hook you're bringing up from Seattle going to take my starting job?"

"Let me say this," he said. "You've got good stuff and you're a pretty good pitcher. I may use you in the bullpen now because I know you can do that job for me. Not every pitcher can. Newcombe couldn't, for instance, and these two kids can't. I have to use Hook and O'Toole because they're going to develop only if they get a lot of work. They're going to start in rotation and pitch in turn if they get shelled eight times in a row. As for you, don't worry. You'll get plenty of work."

He patted me on the back, pushing me toward centerfield, where I shagged fly balls that came crashing through the wind barrier from Lake Michigan.

JULY 19: The bullpen welcomed me with cutting remarks and well-sharpened needles, which they inserted into my wisecracks. Above anything else, a sense of humor is necessary for life in the bullpen. Once admitted and accepted in camaraderie, a relief pitcher may even suggest a serious topic for conversation. Like baseball. "You know what this Hook said yesterday?" I asked. "He told me that in the Coast League they're saying it's easier to pitch in the big leagues than in the minors. That's what somebody in Seattle told him. I'll be damned if he's not proving it, too."

Hook pitched against the Cubs as if they were not quite up to Pacific Coast League caliber. Not only did he get them out with ease and dispatch but he looked as if he knew what he was doing with each pitch.

"He's got a good fast ball, a live fastball," said Clyde King, the pitching coach.

"How fast is a good fast ball?" I asked.

"Just fast enough, Broz," said Pete Whisenant. "It's not the speed of the ball alone, but the pitcher's motions and the spin of the ball, and how fast it moves. . . . Lotta things involved in a good fastball."

"Did you know that the biggest curve you can throw is 17 inches?" I said.

"Who says?" said Willard Schmidt.

"Some professor in Washington. He runs the Bureau of Standards, I think."

"Who'd he pitch for?"

"He was an outfielder in college."

"That figures."

"I believe I'd rather have a good slider than a good curve," I said. "Good hitters complain about the slider more than any other pitch. The good hitters in this league do—Musial, Mays, Whisenant, That right, Whiz?"

"Broz, take away sliders and curveballs and I'd be the best hitter in this little ol' league," said Whisenant. "And if you made every pitcher throw lefthanded they'd never get me out."

JULY 27: The Cardinals, who were having trouble beating anybody else, came back to play us four more games. In less than five weeks we had played 12 games with St. Louis. They won seven of the first nine. When Hutch took over he said we could beat them any day of the week.

Mizell started the first game for the Cardinals. He walked the first three men to face him. From the bullpen Mizell's pitches looked close to being strikes, but the bullpen is 328 feet from the plate. From the Cardinal dugout, 90 feet from the plate, Hemus swore that Mizell's pitches were close enough to be called strikes. All Hemus got for his squawks was the thumb from the umpire. "Hemus is going to lead the league for the first time in his career," I said. "I'll bet he's been thrown out of more games this year than all the other managers put together."

"You're keeping up with Solly, aren't you, Brosnan?" said Schmidt. "I was under the impression that you didn't care for him too much."

"What in the world gave you that idea, Willard?" I said.

The Cardinals didn't recover their poise for two games. That's the way it goes in baseball. Hemus also did a slow burn 24 hours later when Broglio and McDaniel lost a four-run lead to enable us to tie the score in the seventh. Quietly, I sneaked onto the mound to pitch in the eighth. The Cardinals threatened, with two outs, and George Crowe, the best pinch hitter in the league, glared at me while I reviewed my last attempt to retire him. This time he didn't get around on the high, tight ball, and I made it to the bench.

Hutchinson wisely used a pinch hitter for me as we scored two runs in our half of the eighth. Brooks Lawrence wrapped up the game by retiring three men in a row. I sat motionless in the ninth, watching Lawrence save my win. It's rougher, it seems, to wait them out. You sweat almost as much sitting down as you would pitching for yourself.

AUGUST 1: The sun was hot in the bullpen. We curled a hose on top of the bullpen roof, turned the water on, and lay across the bench throughout the game, sweating in comfort. The Crosley Field bullpens are built like battlefield bunkers. They're well-equipped, with a water fountain, a telephone and a long bench against the back wall. But you can't see the game if you sit down. Of course, it you decide to lie down, no one can see in, either, to criticize your lack of attention.

The Cubs scored two in the first, but we scored seven in the third. Our pitcher hit a grand-slam to cap the rally. We almost moved, we were so excited.

"Your roomie just hit one with the bases drunk, Willard," said King.

"He always did say he was a good hitter," Schmidt retorted. "I'll never hear the end of this, though."

"Why don't you go lay on the grass, Willard," I said, "and I'll fan you with a towel like you just fainted."

"No, no, that's too far to go in this heat. You might wave the towel around a while and stir up this air."

"It's a pretty heavy towel," I noted.

"Let it lay, then," he said. "Let us know how we make out, will ya, Clyde?"

We won.

AUGUST 7: Midsummer weather in San Francisco is comparatively cool. The wind, which dies down after dusk, had little effect on the Friday night game, which Antonelli won 3–2. But it picked up velocity in the morning, and blew briskly all Saturday afternoon. We scored two in the first inning, but Hook walked three Giants to start their half, and Hutch called for Peña, who got out of the inning with a tie ball game.

We picked up seven more runs in the next three innings. Peña gave up a homer in the third, and another to start the fifth. When he loaded the bases, Hutch waved me in. As I took my first warmup throw I nearly fell off the mound. A gust of wind had caught me off balance. Antonelli laughed loudly on the Giant bench.

Each inning as I walked through that wind toward the mound I heard myself say, "How can you pitch in this park on a day like today? It's ridiculous. You can just throw and pray." My prayers held up well except for two pitches—Alou hit a ball halfway up the leftfield bleachers and Kirkland hit a home run over the back of the rightfield bleachers to give me the league leadership in long-ball throwing. The most encouraging advice I could get from my teammates during my performances came from Frank Thomas. "Just hang in there, Brosnan," he called, "we'll get 'em somehow."

The Giant fans moaned angrily whenever I managed to retire the side. In the ninth, with two men on, they howled for my scalp. Hutchinson sat back in the dugout, apparently oblivious to the expected carnage. I was too tired or terrified to think my way out of trouble, so I threw exactly what Bailey called for, hoping he knew what to do. Brandt, pinch-hitting with two out, guessed wrong at the curveball, and Delmore called him out.

I staggered slowly to our bench, mopped some sweat from my face, wrapped a towel around my neck and waited for the official scorer's decision as to who got the win. Peña had retired 14 men and given up two runs. I'd relieved him with the bases loaded and gone on to retire 13 men. Did I get a save or a win?

"Winning pitcher, Peña," came from the field microphone.

AUGUST 13: Our chances of overtaking Pittsburgh and finishing in the first division were no less remote than the pennant chances of the three top contenders. We had to win all six games we had with the Pirates. The schedule presented a greater problem. We had to play five games over the weekend after a four-game series with Milwaukee. During the last of the Braves games on Thursday night, I had an eight-run lead when the fifth inning started. Pinch hitter Lee Maye led off for the Braves. I had never pitched to Maye before. "He'll be taking one strike anyway," I thought. "Then I'll try to jam him with the slider. It's working well for me."

I laid the first pitch right over the heart of the plate. Maye hit it into centerfield, and I turned around to look at the Milwaukee bench. How could Haney let him hit the first pitch when he's eight runs behind? It just isn't done. Avila bunted, a move that I expected even less. I waited for Bailey to come out from behind the plate to field the ball, and he waited for me. Avila got a base hit.

Mathews took three sliders just inside, fouled off two others, and then walked as I missed with a curve just outside. The fans started to grumble, and Hutchinson called the bullpen. I knew I'd be out of there if I didn't get Aaron. He'd already hit two sliders on the nose his first two times up. He was also hitting .370, or something like that.

"I'd better waste one slider and gamble on him leaning into a hummer," I thought. "If I can jam him good on one pitch, I'll be able to go back to the slider, which is my best pitch." Aaron tomahawked the high inside fastball and bounced it right back to me. Bailey took my throw to the plate and doubled Aaron at first, the grandstand collectively breathing a sigh of relief. "Hutch has gotta let me stay in here now," I thought.

Covington fouled off four sliders and I tried to outthink him. "He can't be looking for a change now. I'll slip it right by him." He hit it over the centerfield fence to make the score 8–3.

The tension of the inning plus the heat and humidity undermined whatever strength I had left after throwing 87 pitches, many of them frustratingly good ones. Pinson homered in our fifth, but I had to go back to the mound too quickly. Before the inning was over I could feel myself "pushing" the ball, and hoping for a mediocre swing. Torre popped up a high curve that he should have creamed, and he cursed so loud he woke my brother Mike, who was watching the game on television at home.

Avila singled sharply on my next pitch, a crackling noise that brought Hutchinson to the mound. He said, "It's a hot night. I'm bringing in Peña."

I showered and poured a bottle of rubbing alcohol over me to stop the nervous sweating. Peña held the five-run lead through the seventh. By that time I was driving home to watch the end of the game on TV. Aaron, Adcock and Logan singled to knock Peña out in the ninth. Nuxhall got Crandall but gave up a single to Lopata and a double to Pafko, and the score was 9–8. Lawrence relieved Nuxhall and walked Avila to load the bases.

My mother said, "You ought to be ashamed of yourself. A grown man, crying about baseball. It's only a game."

Lawrence went 3–2 on Mathews while I urged him in a hoarse whisper, "Don't walk him, Brooksie. Don't let 'em tie it up. Make him hit the ball." Mathews popped up, to make it seem like a game instead of a moment of truth.

AUGUST 14: "Hutchinson reminded us before the first game of our five-game weekend series with Philadelphia that we had a good shot at the first division, which could mean $400 to $500 per man. "That's worth putting out a little extra from now on," he said. "We can beat this club four out of five games."

The first game, at least, was a long one. With Pinson and Robinson getting five hits apiece, we scored 15 runs on 23 hits. Lawrence had a four-run lead as the Phils batted in the ninth. But he couldn't get the side out. Four singles around one strikeout gave the Phils two runs. With men on first and second, Hutch waved me in to pitch to Gene Freese. My record against Freese for the year was enough to chill any manager's heart. Hutch may not have known it. He said nothing to me except, "There's one out."

I took the ball from Lawrence and said, "I owe you one."

Freese fouled off a high slider as I gulped fresh air. "Gotta be more care-ful than that," I said. "Brush him back now and go with another slider, down and away. Or at least down." Freese jumped at the slider and hit it on the ground to Kasko. Kasko tossed it to Temple, whose throw to first beat Freese to the bag, and we'd won it.

Hutch met me with a strong grip and a little smile. "Nice going. How's your arm feel?"

"It aches. But no more than when I was out there."

Lawrence joined me at the trainer's table. "We're even," I said, as he held out his hand. "Don't shake it too hard. It may come off."

AUGUST 19: "Better loosen up, Jim," said Cot Deal. "Hutch will proba-bly use a hitter for Peña."

Stretching my arm gingerly, I heated up as Whisenant ran up to bat for Peña. The score stayed at 3–2 against us while I pitched the eighth. We scored seven runs in the last of the eighth, however, with the Dodgers using four pitchers to retire the side. With any easy win in sight I walked out to the mound in the ninth, smiling. How could I lose this one?

"We'll wipe that smile off your face," came loudly from the Dodger dugout. What vulgar emotion!

Essegian hit my first pitch into centerfield for a single. Roseboro pinch-hit and I walked him. Hutchinson jumped off his chair in the dugout. The crowd moaned. "This is ridiculous," I thought. "I'd better bear down."

But it was too late. When I reached back for the little extra it wasn't there. I panicked. My slider wouldn't break. I didn't dare try the changeup; the fast-ball moved all right, but I couldn't control it. Ron Fairly swung at a bad pitch and flied out to left. Furillo hit for the pitcher. I tried to jam him good to move him back from the plate, but he hit a soft line-drive just over Tem-ple's head. The ball fell for a single, the bases were loaded, and Gilliam came up to hit. I always have trouble with Gilliam. Either I lay it in there for him or he doesn't swing. He took a walk. Six runs ahead, and I walk a man home? Hutchinson stormed out of the dugout. I didn't wait for him to chew me out. Tossing the ball at him as we crossed paths, I headed for the dugout. But he got at me with a contemptuous snarl, "That was the worst exhibi-tion I ever saw!"

Lawrence retired the side on one pitch. The Cincinnati radio broadcast-er said, as I entered the clubhouse, "Well, we're going to wait now and see what the official scorer does about declaring the winner of this game. Brosnan is the pitcher of record, but Peña pitched outstanding ball, and he certainly deserves credit for the win more than Brosnan. . . . Here's the announcement. Well, the scorer called Brosnan the winner. But, I don't know, the rules should be changed to cover situations like this. I certainly don't think justice was done."

SEPTEMBER 14: The San Francisco papers, agog about the pennant race, hardly mentioned our fight with the Pirates for fourth place. We had beaten the Braves on Sunday, and it wasn't until we landed in California that we learned the Pirates had also won. Our win over the Braves gained us nothing in our race. When Hutchinson announced that I would start for the Reds, odds on the game jumped to 5 to 2 for Frisco, according to reliable cab drivers. "What's the story?" Schmidt said to me. "Is Hutch betting on the Giants?"

I gave him my best nervous sneer, and reported to the trainer for a pre-game rubdown. Hutchinson's last words were, "Go as far as you can. We got plenty of help down there when you need it." Not even *if* I need it, but *when* I need it! We didn't go over the hitters before the game. "You've pitched against them enough," said Hutch.

Bressoud took two pitches, then half-swung at a good slider and popped it up. McCovey usually took one pitch just to get a look at the stuff. I laid a flat slider in for a strike, then broke one off on his hands. He popped it up. Willie Mays stepped into the box, stared at me, popped up a jammer that broke his bat, and I had lasted one inning.

Antonelli had a little trouble in the second, getting Bailey for a called strike on the last out. Bailey screamed at the call, and Conlan threw him out of the game. Hutchinson charged Conlan with having a quick thumb, and Jocko threw him out, too.

I took a long look at Cepeda, the fourth Giant hitter. There's only one way to pitch to him, of course. I threw him a slider on the outside corner for a strike. He leaned over the plate looking for another one and caught a sinker on his bat handle. Cursing in Spanish and shaking his hands in pain, he jogged toward first as his little fly ball settled into Kasko's glove.

Kirkland ran up to the plate eagerly. My old homer-hitting buddy. Six home runs off me in three years. I growled a negative growl at Dotterer's sign. No sir, if Kirkland hits a home run off me on this pitch, it will be from a prone position. Down he went. My control was excellent. He fouled off the next slider, fouled off a curve and fanned on a fastball right under his chin.

Well, that pitch did it. When a pitcher can rid himself of the feeling that he can't get a certain batter out, he knows he's got good stuff. The Giants stared at me for six innings, waiting to see Old Broz, Old Nervous Broz, start to waver, start to think on the mound. They waited in vain. Mays, still looking for a slider, caught me thinking he might be taking one pitch as he had done on his first two times at bat. He hit a flat slider over the left-field fence. A man is entitled to one mistake in a game.

I didn't make another. Hutch called me into the runway behind our dugout at the end of the seventh. He said, "Now, I want you to tell me if you're tired. This is the first time you've gone this far in months." What could I say? "I had a little trouble getting loose in the last inning," I said.

"I think you're tired," he said finally. "Let's let Brooks finish this up for you."

Well, now, I thought to myself, that's good enough for me, Hutch. My bridge partner and I are undefeated so far this year. Every game we've both been in, bridge or baseball, we've won. We had a 3–1 lead. Let's let Brooks finish up. Why not.

Brooks had nothing but good cards left. We won.

SEPTEMBER 20: We lost both games to Pittsburgh.

The light of our first-division dreams flickered on Saturday as the Pirates won in 12 innings, 4–3.

I started the Sunday game. I struck out the first Pirate batter. Superstition has it that it is bad for a pitcher to retire the first batter on a strikeout. That's ridiculous, of course. It's not the first out but the last one that you should worry about.

I didn't have to worry about the last out. I never even saw it. Two walks and four singles sent Pirate runners circling the bases around me. I felt like the operator of a merry-go-round, with everybody getting a kick out of the ride but me. The base hits weren't hit very hard, and the walks were unintentional. But four base runners scored. The season ended, for all practical purposes, at 2 o'clock that afternoon.

"There goes my winning streak," I thought, as Hutch silently took the baseball from me and gave it to Willard Schmidt.

"There goes my ERA," I said to myself in the showers. From below 3.00 it soared to 3.86 in 15 minutes.

"There goes my salary drive," I thought, as I dressed and left the ball park.

"That's enough for one year," I hoped. It had been a long season.

SEPTEMBER 22: Philadelphia beat us in a doubleheader, forever quenching the aftertaste of our fourth-place ambitions. To add to the insult, the bus driver hired to drive us to the airport for our flight to Cincinnati lost his way. He drove through the midnight-quiet streets of the city, finally reaching a dead end in a railroad yard. A railroad watchman asked, in a bewildered voice, "How in the world did you ever get that big thing in here?" A cab appeared, the driver grinning as he inquired if he could guide us back to the highway. Hutchinson hired him immediately.

We won both games in Cincinnati during the final weekend, ending the season on a positive note and almost bringing a smile to Hutchinson's face. On the last day of the season, baseball is a game that professionals really do *play*; it no longer seems like work to them. It is virtually impossible for a ballplayer to convince himself that he will never play the game again. On the last day of the season, baseball, truly, is in his blood.

I stuffed my glove into a duffel bag and picked up the last shirt from my locker. That final look at the empty locker brings no smile to a ballplayer's face. On the last day there really is not much tangible evidence of the sweat, the tears, the applauding cheers of the season past that a ballplayer can take with him. A bagful of gloves, shoes and jock straps; a fistful of clippings and fan mail, a line of statistics following his name in the record book. I'd already used my line: Brosnan, James Patrick, Cincinnati, Won 8, Lost 3, ERA 3.36.

Gabe Paul offered me the contract that I was after, and I signed it. Shoving two World Series tickets into my jacket pocket next to my 1960 contract, I made the rounds of the room, saying my au revoirs. Hutchinson was last in my tour of the clubhouse. He looked up from the trunk into which he had packed his equipment, shoved a huge bear paw at me, and said, "Good luck. You did a good job for me. Have a good winter." And he almost smiled. I thanked him and went home.

❧

Totally Juiced

BY TOM VERDUCCI

With this groundbreaking story, SI documented how the use of steroids and other performance enhancers had become rampant in baseball, and how players—and their reliance on drugs—had grown to alarming proportions.

ARIZONA DIAMONDBACKS RIGHTHANDER CURT SCHILLING thinks twice before giving a teammate the traditional slap on the butt for a job well-done. *"I'll pat guys on the ass, and they'll look at me and go, 'Don't hit me there, man. It hurts,'" Schilling says. "That's because that's where they shoot the steroid needles."*
The Texas Rangers were packing their gear after the final game of a road series last year when a player accidentally knocked over a small carry bag by his locker. Several vials of steroids spilled out and rolled on the clubhouse carpet. The player, hardly embarrassed or concerned, gave a slight chuckle and scooped them up. No one else in the room showed any surprise.

STEROID USE, which a decade ago was considered a taboo violated by a few renegade sluggers, is now so rampant in baseball that even pitchers and wispy outfielders are juicing up—and talking openly among themselves about it. According to players, trainers and executives interviewed by SPORTS ILLUS-TRATED over the last three months, the game has become a pharmacological trade show. What emerges from dozens of interviews is a portrait of base-ball's intensifying reliance on steroids and other performance-enhancing drugs. These drugs include not only human growth hormone (hGH) but also an array of legal and illegal stimulants, ranging from amphetamines to Ritalin to ephedrine-laced dietary supplements, that many big leaguers pop to get a jolt of pregame energy and sharpen their focus. But it is the use of illegal steroids that is growing fastest and having a profound impact on the game.

The surest sign that steroids are gaining acceptance in baseball: the first public admission of steroid use—without remorse—by a prominent former player. Ken Caminiti, whose 15-year big league career ended after a stint with the Atlanta Braves last season, revealed to SI that he won the 1996 National League Most Valuable Player award while on steroids he purchased from a pharmacy in Tijuana, Mexico. Spurred to try the drugs by concern over a shoulder injury in early '96, Caminiti said that his steroid use improved his performance noticeably and became more sophisticated over the next five seasons. He told SI that he used steroids so heavily in '96 that by the end of that season, his testicles shrank and retracted; doctors found that his body had virtually stopped producing its own testosterone and that his level of the hormone had fallen to 20% of normal. "It took four months to get my nuts to drop on their own," he said of the period after he stopped taking the drugs.

Yet Caminiti, a recovering alcoholic and former drug user, defended his use of steroids and said he would not discourage others from taking them because they have become a widely accepted—even necessary—choice for ballplayers looking for a competitive edge and financial security. "I've made a ton of mistakes," said Caminiti. "I don't think using steroids is one of them.

"It's no secret what's going on in baseball. At least half the guys are using steroids. They talk about it. They joke about it with each other. The guys who want to protect themselves or their image by lying have that right. Me? I'm at the point in my career where I've done just about every bad thing you can do. I try to walk with my head up. I don't have to hold my tongue. I don't want to hurt teammates or friends. But I've got nothing to hide.

"If a young player were to ask me what to do," Caminiti continued, "I'm not going to tell him it's bad. Look at all the money in the game: You have a chance to set your family up, to get your daughter into a better school. . . . So I can't say, 'Don't do it,' not when the guy next to you is as big as a house and he's going to take your job and make the money."

ANABOLIC STEROIDS elevate the body's testosterone level, increasing muscle mass without changes in diet or activity, though their effect is greatly enhanced in conjunction with proper nutrition and strength training. Steroids are illegal in the U.S. unless prescribed by a physician for medical conditions, such as AIDS and hypogonadism (an inability to produce enough testosterone). Studies have shown that the side effects from steroids can include heart and liver damage, persistent endocrine-system imbalance, elevated cholesterol levels, strokes, aggressive behavior and the dysfunction of genitalia. Doctors suspect that steroid use is a major factor in the recent increase in baseball injuries, especially severe injuries such as complete muscle tears.

Unlike the NFL and NBA, both of which ban and test for steroid use—the NHL does neither—Major League Baseball has no steroid policy or testing program for big leaguers. (Baseball does test minor league players, but violators are neither penalized nor required to undergo counseling.) Any such program would have to be collectively bargained with the Major League Baseball Players Association, which traditionally has resisted any form of drug testing but now faces a division in its membership over this issue. "Part of our task is to let a consensus emerge," says Gene Orza, the associate general counsel for the players union.

"No one denies that it is a problem," says commissioner Bud Selig. "It's a problem we can and must deal with now, rather than years from now when the public says, 'Why didn't you do something about it?' I'm very worried about this."

But it is also true that fans have become more accepting of steroids as part of the game. Fourteen years ago the crowd at Fenway Park in Boston chided Oakland A's outfielder Jose Canseco during the American League Championship Series with damning chants of "Ster-oids! Ster-oids!" The game had never before seen a physical marvel such as Canseco, a 240-pound hulk who could slug a baseball 500 feet and still be swift enough to steal 40 bases. Upon retiring last month after failing to catch on with a major league team, Canseco, while not admitting steroid use himself, said that steroids have "revolutionized" the game and that he would write a tell-all book blowing the lid off drug use in the majors. Canseco estimated that 85% of major leaguers use steroids.

Heavily muscled bodies like Canseco's have now become so common that they no longer invite scorn. Players even find dark humor in steroid use. One American League outfielder, for instance, was known to be taking a steroid typically given by veterinarians to injured, ill or overworked horses and readily available in Latin America. An opposing player pointed to him and remarked, "He takes so much of that horse stuff that one day we're going to look out in the outfield and he's going to be grazing."

STEROIDS HAVE helped create the greatest extended era of slugging the game has ever seen—and, not coincidentally, the highest rate of strikeouts in history. Power, the eye candy for the casual fan, is a common denominator among pitchers and hitters, as hurlers, too, juice up to boost the velocity of their pitches.

Schilling says that muscle-building drugs have transformed baseball into something of a freak show. "You sit there and look at some of these players and you know what's going on," he says. "Guys out there look like Mr. Potato Head, with a head and arms and six or seven body parts that just don't look right. They don't fit. I'm not sure how [steroid use] snuck in so quickly, but it's become a prominent thing very quietly. It's widely known in the game.

"We're playing in an environment in the last decade that's been tailored to produce offensive numbers anyway, with the smaller ballparks, the smaller strike zone and so forth," Schilling continues. "When you add in steroids and strength training, you're seeing records not just being broken but completely shattered.

"I know guys who use and don't admit it because they think it means they don't work hard. And I know plenty of guys now are mixing steroids with human growth hormone. Those guys are pretty obvious."

If steroids are the cement of body construction, then human growth hormone is the rebar, taken in an attempt to strengthen joints so they can hold the added muscle mass produced by steroids. Human growth hormone can be detected only in specific blood tests, not the standard urine test used for other performance-enhancing drugs. It is prescribed to treat dwarfism in children, but it can also change a mature person's body structure and facial characteristics. Players joke about the swollen heads, protruding brows and lantern jaws of hGH users. "And they talk like this," Caminiti says, pushing his tongue to the front of his mouth and stammering, "because the size of their head changes." One major league executive knows of a star player whose hat size has grown two sizes in his late 30s.

Says Chad Curtis, an outfielder who retired last year after 10 seasons with six clubs, including three (1997 to '99) with the Yankees, "When I was in New York, a player there told me that hGH was the next big thing, that that's the road the game's heading down next. Now you see guys whose facial features, jawbones and cheekbones change after they're 30. Do they think that happens naturally? You go, 'What happened to that guy?' Then you'll hear him say he worked out over the winter and put on 15 pounds of muscle. I'm sorry, working out is not going to change your facial features."

"Here's one easy way to tell," says a veteran American League infielder who asked not to be identified. He grabbed a batting helmet and put it on the top of his head without pushing it down for the proper fit. "They can't get their helmet to go all the way down. It sits up on their heads. You see it all the time. You see this new culture of young players coming in, caught up in the vanity of getting big. They're bloated and ripped, and they shave their chests [to accentuate their physiques]. It's gotten to the point where more guys use [steroids or hGH] than don't use."

The infielder says that last year he asked a star teammate, whom he suspected of steroid use, why he used. The star replied, "It's a personal decision. It's like taking aspirin. Some people choose to take it and some don't. I respect somebody's choice one way or the other."

Clearly, the players who choose to use steroids do so because they believe the drugs work. "It's still a hand-eye coordination game, but the difference [with steroids] is the ball is going to go a little farther," Caminiti says. "Some of the balls that would go to the warning track will go out. That's the difference."

The improvement steroids have made in some players has been striking. Says one veteran National League general manager, "You might expect the B player to become an A player with steroids. But now you see the C player go to an A player. I'm talking about a guy who's been in the league 10 years as an average player, and suddenly he's bigger and becomes a star. That's very troublesome."

Another National League G.M. tells a story about an overweight, lumpy backup player who had kicked around the fringes of the major leagues. "We signed him, and two years later the guy looked like someone in a muscle magazine," he says. The player, by then in his 30s, won a starting job for the first time and, with a decent season, earned a multiyear contract. He subsequently suffered a series of muscle tears and ruptures and was quickly out of baseball. "He was gone that fast," the G.M. says. "But the contract probably set up him for life. Other guys see that."

Says Texas lefthander Kenny Rogers, "Basically, steroids can jump you a level or two. The average player can become a star, and the star player can become a superstar, and the superstar? Forget it. He can do things we've never seen before. You take a guy who already has great hand-eye coordination and make him stronger, and without a doubt he'll be better."

Steroids might even help a player become an MVP.

CAMINITI WAS playing third base for the San Diego Padres in a series against the Houston Astros in April 1996 when Derrick May hit a flare into short leftfield. Caminiti dived for the ball, landed hard on his left elbow and shoulder, and tore his rotator cuff. "For the next six or seven days I couldn't lift my arm," he says. "I played for a month and a half in pure pain." Finally, he says, he decided to do something "to get me through the season." Caminiti had heard of players taking steroids to help them through injuries. He knew where to go. "When you play in San Diego, it's easy to just drive into Mexico," he says.

Anabolic steroids are readily available in parts of Latin America as an over-the-counter item at *farmacias* that, in Mexican border towns such as Tijuana, cater to an American trade. Caminiti says he purchased a steroid labeled *testosterona* "to get me through the second half of the season." Then 33, he was playing in his 10th big league season. Never had he hit more than 26 home runs. He exceeded that in the second half alone, belting 28 homers after the All-Star break. He finished the year with 40 home runs, 130 RBIs (his previous best was 94) and a .326 batting average (24 points better than his previous high). He won the MVP award unanimously.

"There is a mental edge that comes with the injections, and it's definitely something that gets you more intense," Caminiti says. "The thing is, I didn't do it to make me a better player. I did it because my body broke down.

"At first I felt like a cheater. But I looked around, and everybody was doing it. Now it's not as black market as when I started. Back then you had to go and find it in Mexico or someplace. Now, it's everywhere. It's very easy to get."

Steroids are taken in what users call "cycles"—several weeks of use followed by several weeks of nonuse to allow the body to recover. Caminiti, a novice, never stopped using during the 1996 season. He wound up injecting twice as much steroids as was considered normal for ballplayers at that time. "I was just experimenting on my own," he says. "I did it wrong. My body shut down and stopped producing testosterone."

After a slow start the next season, Caminiti says he returned to steroid use, this time with the help of a friend in California who supplied the drugs. He says he continued using at various times through his career, learning from his supplier how to do cycles. "I felt like a kid," he says. "I'd be running the bases and think, Man, I'm fast! And I had never been fast. Steroids made me like that. The stronger you get, the more relaxed you get. You feel good. You just let it fly.

"If you don't feel good, you try so hard to make something happen. You grip the bat harder and swing harder, and that's when you tighten up. But you get that edge when you feel strong. That's the way I felt, like I could just try to meet the ball and—wham!—it's going to go 1,000 mph. Man, I felt good. I'd think, Damn, this pitcher's in trouble, and I'd crush the ball 450 feet with almost no effort. It's all about getting an edge."

Though he kept using steroids—in 1998, he says, "I showed up at spring training as big as an ox"—Caminiti never again approached the statistics he generated in 1996, partly because he never played another season without going on the disabled list. His injuries were mostly muscular, including a strained hamstring, a strained quadriceps, a strained calf muscle and a ruptured tendon sheath in his wrist.

"I got really strong, really quick," he says. "I pulled a lot of muscles. I broke down a lot. I'm still paying for it. My tendons and ligaments got all torn up. My muscles got too strong for my tendons and ligaments."

Caminiti was released twice last season, by the Rangers and the Braves. Upon his second release, Caminiti, who had used cocaine in the past, says he drove into a notorious section of Houston, rolled down his window and asked a man on the street where he could score some coke. Four days later Caminiti woke up in a drug-strewn motel room wearing the same clothes. Police showed up, and he was arrested for cocaine possession. He pleaded guilty and was sentenced to three years' probation and 200 hours of community service.

Caminiti lives on the outskirts of Houston, where he is tested regularly for drugs, attends support meetings three times a week and meets with his probation officer once a month. He visits often with his estranged wife and three daughters, who live about 45 minutes from him. He spends his time working out, customizing vintage cars and riding his motorcycles. He suffers from bulging disks in his back, underwent surgery last month to remove bone fragments in his right ankle and is scheduled to have surgery on his right ankle and right foot this month. He eats dinner at a pancake house near his home so often that the cooks know just what he likes: 10 egg whites. He still appears close to his playing size of six feet, 200 pounds.

"I don't think this puts an asterisk by my name," he says, referring to his 239 homers and .272 career average. "I worked for everything I've got. I played the game hard, gave it everything I had. Nothing came easy. I could sit here and lie and try to make myself look like a better person, but I'm not going to do that. I take responsibility for what I've done. I'm guilty of some bad behavior. It's embarrassing, some of the things I've done. But like I said, I don't consider steroids to be one of them."

That's not to say that Caminiti hasn't paid a price for his steroid use. He is now legally prescribed weekly shots of testosterone because of his body's continuing inability to make the hormone in sufficient quantity. "My body's not producing testosterone," he says. "You know what that's like? You get lethargic. You get depressed. It's terrible."

HE IS 5' 11" and 190 pounds. He is not a home run hitter. Pete is a speedy minor league outfielder. He is also a steroid user who has been juicing up for five years, hoping all those needles in his buttocks will finally get him to the majors. His wife knows about it. Sometimes she's the one who sticks the needle in.

"I'm not looking for size," says Pete, who asked that his real name not be used. "I do it for my fast-twitch muscles. If I don't feel good that week or if my hands don't feel good, if they're a little slow, I'll take a shot or get on a cycle. It helps immediately. I notice the difference. My hands are quicker, so my bat is quicker."

Pete began his steroid use through a familiar gateway: Latin America. He was playing winter ball in Venezuela in 1997 when, after hearing other players talk about the easy availability of the drugs, he decided to purchase a steroid, Winstrol, at a *farmacia*. A year later he was introduced to a female bodybuilder in California who made steroid runs to Mexico. Pete would place orders with her or an intermediary.

While making contacts in the steroid subculture, Pete eventually found a supplier, his current source, in the U.S. Pete places his orders by telephone with the supplier, who ships the steroids and needles to him in a FedEx package. A user of Winstrol and Sustanon, Pete says 10-week cycles of steroids cost him $300 to $400, or about $12 a shot. He says steroids obtained in Mexico are cheaper, but the quality of the foreign product is not as reliable. "You pay a pretty good price for the U.S. stuff, but it's worth it," Pete says. "The guy I have runs a fair business. He's got the needles, which are not always easy to get. And he cares about his guys. He's not just about making money. He wants you to use the stuff right. He's got just baseball players—a bunch of them."

According to Pete, steroid use is discussed so openly among players that everyone knows who's using and who's not. He says one player can walk up to another in batting practice, bring the subject up, and tell by his answers whether he's using. "There are code words or street names that everybody knows," Pete says. "Listen, this is not my choice. I'd rather not [use]. I discussed it with my wife, and she understands. When you want to get to a higher level of competition, it's pretty obvious that it's worth trying."

Last year Pete tested positive for steroids under the program administered by Major League Baseball. So did several other players on his team. Here's what happened to them: nothing.

Major League Baseball randomly tests minor leaguers during the season. The best prospects, those on the 40-man major league roster, cannot be tested because they fall under the protection of the collective bargaining agreement. (Pete was not a 40-man-roster player.) That exemption explains why players in the Arizona Fall League, which is filled with top prospects, are notorious, one scout says, for driving by the carload into Mexico to stock up on steroids for the winter.

According to two highly placed baseball sources, physicians for Major League Baseball reported at an internal meeting among doctors and trainers last December that 10% to 15% of the minor leaguers tested came up positive for steroids. The sources acknowledged that the number of users is probably significantly higher than that because baseball does not test in the off-season, when many players follow the traditional steroid training regimen: They shoot up in November, December and January, then get off steroids to start a four-week flexibility program before spring training. Two minor leaguers told SI that they attempt to cheat the tests by gulping water and diuretics when a test administrator arrives to take urine samples.

Virtually all of the 20 or so minor leaguers interviewed by SI described the use of steroids and other drugs (including amphetamines and marijuana) as rampant in the minors. They said that testing is spotty. A Class A player in the Kansas City Royals system says he was not tested at all last season. One former pitcher in the Detroit system even says, "Two coaches approached me and suggested I *do* steroids." Two players say they easily obtained steroids from contacts at their local gyms. "When you were in college, everybody knew someone who could get them pot," says one minor leaguer. "In baseball everyone knows someone who can get them steroids."

Pete says the follow-up to his positive test was familiar to any minor leaguer on steroids: A club employee told him he had tested positive, warned him about the danger of steroids and sent him on his way.

When asked why baseball doesn't crack down on steroid users, Pete replied, "I've got an easy answer for that. I'd say, You've set up a reward system where you're paying people $1 million to put the ball into the seats. Well, I need help doing that."

It may not be so easy in the future. Robert Manfred, baseball's executive vice president for labor relations and human resources, says baseball will suspend and fine repeat minor league offenders this season. The Padres have administered their own three-strikes-and-you're-out steroid policy for the past five years, though they do not test in the off-season, either. "The word's out in our organization, but the trend we're seeing is that most of the players who tested positive were in [Class] A ball," says San Diego general manager Kevin Towers. "That tells me the problem is spreading fast. I think it's prevalent in college and high school—even before we get them."

KENNY ROGERS made his major league pitching debut with the Rangers in 1989. He was taught in the early years of his career that the safest place to throw a pitch was the low-outside part of the plate. Nobody was going to hit that pitch out of the park, coaches told him. "It's not true anymore," Rogers says. "Now you've got 5' 7" guys built like weightlifters taking that down-and-away pitch and hitting it out to the opposite field. No one thinks it's unusual because it happens all the time."

And steroids are not just for sluggers anymore. They're used by everyone, from erstwhile singles hitters to aging pitchers. Says Rogers, "Just look around. You've got guys in their late 30s, almost 40, who are throwing the ball 96 to 99, and they never threw that hard before in their lives. I'm sorry. That's not natural evolution. Steroids are changing the game. You've got players who say, 'All I want to do is hit,' and you have pitchers who say, 'All I want to do is throw 97. I don't care if I walk [everyone].'" Steroids have helped even mediocre pitchers turn up the heat. "The biggest change I've seen in the game," says a veteran major league infielder, "is seeing middle relievers come into the game throwing 91, 92 [mph]. Those guys used to be in the mid-80s or so. Now everybody is throwing gas, including the last guy in the bullpen."

The changes in the game are also evident in the increasingly hulking physiques of the players. The average weight of an All-Star in 1991 was 199 pounds. Last year it was 211. "We're kidding ourselves if we say this problem is not happening," says Towers. "Look at the before and after shots, at the size of some of these players from the '90s to now. It's a joke."

Barry Bonds of the San Francisco Giants is often cited as a player who dramatically altered his size and his game, growing from a lithe, 185-pound leadoff hitter into a 230-pound force who is one of the greatest home run hitters of all time. Bonds's most dramatic size gains have come in the past four years, over which he has doubled his home run rate. Bonds, who insists he added muscle through diet and intense training, has issued several denials of rumors that he uses steroids, including one to a group of reporters in April in which he said, "You can test me and solve that problem [of rumors] real quick."

But there is no testing in baseball, and everyone continues to speculate. What's a little speculation and innuendo these days anyway? Mark McGwire was cheered in every park on his march to 70 home runs in 1998 by fans hardly concerned about his reluctant admission that he'd used androstendione, an over-the-counter supplement that reputedly has the muscle-building effects of steroids.

"If you polled the fans," says former outfielder Curtis, "I think they'd tell you, 'I don't care about illegal steroids. I'd rather see a guy hit the ball a mile or throw it 105 miles an hour.'"

Says Caminiti, "They come to the arena to watch gladiators. Do they want to see a bunch of guys choking up on the bat against pitchers throwing 82 miles an hour or do they want to see the ball go 500 feet? They want to see warriors."

It is a long way from 1988, when Canseco lost a prospective national endorsement deal with a major soft drink company because of unconfirmed suspicions that he used steroids. Many players, too, are showing more acceptance of steroids, especially when users and nonusers alike believe the health risks can be minimized if the drugs are used in proper doses. Today's user, they claim, is more educated about steroid use than Caminiti in 1996 or NFL lineman Lyle Alzado, who died in 1992 at age 43 from brain cancer he believed was caused by grossly excessive steroid use.

Pete, the minor league steroid user, says, "I've talked to doctors. They've studied [steroids], and they know if you don't abuse them, they can help you. As long as you don't go crazy with them, like Alzado, you should be fine."

Says Curtis, who estimates that 40% to 50% of major leaguers use steroids, "There are two things that might stop a person from using steroids: a moral obligation—they're illegal—and a fear of the medical complications. I was

100 percent against the use of steroids. But I must tell you, I would not fear the medical side of it. I fully agree you can take them safely."

Rogers also opposes steroid use on ethical grounds, but understands why it is so tempting. "My belief is that God gave you a certain amount of ability, and I don't want to enhance it by doing something that is not natural and creates an unfair advantage. I'm critical of guys who do it," he says. "On the other hand if I were 22 or 21 and trying to make it in baseball, I can't say for sure that I wouldn't try something when I plainly see the benefits other guys are getting. I can't say I'm 100 percent positive I wouldn't resort to that."

The first generation of ballplayers who have grown up in the steroid culture is only now arriving, biceps bulging, chests shaven and buttocks tender. The acceptance level of steroids in the game may very well continue rising until . . . until what? A labor deal that includes a comprehensive testing plan? Such a plan, unlikely as it is, given the union's resistance, might deter some players, but even baseball officials concede that the minor league testing program in place gives players the green light to shoot up in the off-season. And athletes in other sports subject to testing have stayed one step ahead of enforcement with tactics such as using so-called "designer drugs," steroids that are chemically altered to mask the unique signature of that drug that otherwise would show on a urine test.

So even with testing, will it take something much darker for steroids to fall from favor? Renowned sports orthopedist James Andrews recalled the impact of two prominent deaths on the drug culture in football. "Major League Baseball can't continue to leave this door open," says Andrews. "Steroids became a big deal in football after Lyle Alzado [died] and ephedrine became a big deal after Korey Stringer. You don't want to see it get to that [in baseball] before someone says stop. But, unfortunately, that's what it seems to take to wake people up."

Rogers has a nightmare about how it might end, and that is why he does not always throw his fastball as hard as he can. It is the thought of some beast pumped up on steroids whacking a line drive off his head. "We're the closest ones to the hitter," he says of the men on the mound. "I don't want the ball coming back at me any faster. It's a wonder it hasn't happened already. When one of us is down there dead on the field, then something might happen. Maybe. And if it's me, I've already given very clear instructions to my wife: Sue every one of their asses. Because everybody in baseball knows what's been going on."

GOOD STUFF

The Sound
Of Summer

BY STEVE RUSHIN

Television has the gimmicks, but for patter and word pictures,
you can't beat baseball on radio.

YOU CAN KEEP YOUR FLAT-SCREEN, YOUR HIGH-DEFINITION, your plasma-projection TVs. All I need is my AM radio, with its 9-volt battery, its Doobie Brothers hits, its Casey Kasem dispensing wise counsel: "Keep your feet on the ground, and keep reachin' for the stars."

The first big league baseball game that I "saw" was described to me by Herb Carneal on WCCO-AM in Minneapolis. My AM radio seemed to me then, as it does now, a technological wonder beyond words, pulling in the 50,000-watt flagship stations that have forever been affiliated in my mind with a ball club: the Reds on WLW, the Cardinals on KMOX, the Indians on WWWE ("*Three* Double-yew *E*").

Indeed, the first baseball game ever broadcast was carried by KDKA in Pittsburgh 80 years ago next week, and the electronic revolution in the ensuing decades has done nothing to alter the fact that baseball is still best experienced on the radio. It isn't merely because of the game's memorable voices, though many of them remain a marvel. (Listen to Marty Brennaman, his vocal cords smoked like a couple of cured hams, punctuate a Cincinnati win with "And *this* one belongs to the Reds.") It's not simply that the soundtrack of summer in so many cities—the background vocals issuing from taxicabs, beach blankets and backyard barbecues—has been the play-by-play of Vin Scully or Mel Allen or Ernie Harwell (or Jack Buck or Harry Caray or Red Barber).

No, there are countless reasons that baseball, unlike children, should be heard and not seen. Every ballpark is beautiful on the radio, and the great players even better when imagined. Babe Ruth, in the days before television, was whatever you wanted him to be and no less authentic for existing largely in the mind's eye. "What the imagination seizes as Beauty," wrote Keats, "must be truth." Which is to say, if the Phillies radio broadcasters *tell* you that the Vet is architecturally exquisite—and you believe them—why, then, it *is*.

Of course, baseball's lumbering pace is perfectly supplemented by radio, which abhors dead air and fills it with ceaseless sponsorships, one for every mundane moment of a ball game. So, during Yankees games on WABC radio, "the umpire's lineup is brought to you by Weitz & Luxenberg, setting the standard in asbestos litigation for over a decade."

I am a connoisseur of such promotional pairings (umpires presented by lawyers, that seems about right) and all the other rituals of baseball on the radio. I enjoy pausing for station identification. I breathlessly await the inevitable admonishment not to rebroadcast or retransmit the accounts and descriptions of this game without the express written consent of Major League Baseball. I still love—when the announcers embark on a leisurely discussion of yesterday's lunch—removing the 9-volt battery from my radio and testing its potency with my tongue. (The resulting shock was, in an age before PlayStation, the greatest thrill a kid could have.)

Lately I've been listening to baseball games broadcast in Spanish on the radio. With a few exceptions—*pelota, Heineken, Chuckknoblauch*—I cannot understand a word, but each play is described with such urgent enthusiasm (you can almost see those upside-down and right-side-up exclamation marks bracketing every sentence) that I am enraptured. *This* is baseball the way it oughta be, in which even the laziest infield fly-out is reported in tones more appropriate to the crash of the *Hindenburg*.

What else do I like about baseball on the radio? Only everything: I like falling asleep to a night game on the West Coast and waking the next morning to Weather on the Ones and Traffic on the Twos. I like the impossibly cheap tokens of appreciation given to guests of the pregame shows. ("For stopping by the booth, His Holiness will receive a $25 gift certificate from Jiffy Lube, with 27 locations in the Tri-State.") And while I can't say I like them, I have come to accept the sponsor jingles that take root in the head of a regular listener by May and soon become unshakable even by exorcism.

Which is why the swingin' jingle of Foxwoods Casino (played relentlessly during Yankees broadcasts) has played relentlessly in my brain all summer: "Take a chance, make it happen/Pop the cork, fingers snappin'/Spin the wheel, 'round and 'round we go/Life is good, life is sweet/Grab yourself a front-row seat/And let's meet/And have a ball/Yeah, let's live/For the won-*der* of it all!"

There's a second verse, and I know that too, for baseball on the radio has taught me so much—new songs, the power of imagination, a new language. So I say to you, my fellow sports fans:

¡Pelota! ¡Heineken! ¡Chuckknoblauch!

Tiger Tales

BY LEIGH MONTVILLE

It was certainly showing its age, but when Tiger Stadium fell to the wrecking ball, a lot of treasured memories went with it.

THE MANAGER SCRATCHES SOMETIMES AT THE BLUE PAINT on the walls and posts and ceiling of the home dugout. How can he not? The paint looks soft, inviting, almost as if it had been applied to cardboard. Or papier-mâché. Or—yes— it is the final layer on top of years and years of paint jobs. The manager gets a fingernail in there and scratches a little bit, and flecks of history fall into his hand. "You see the different colors," Detroit Tigers manager Larry Parrish says. "You have the dark blue at the top, and then you get other shades of blue from other years, then shades of green and then some other colors and then, well, you're at the wood. You're back at the beginning."

The beginning was 1912.

THE SON occupies the same office that the father occupied. The father, John McHale, had played with the Tigers and then worked his way up through the front office to general manager in 1958. The son, John McHale Jr., 50 years old, is now the team president. He remembers going to the stadium as a child, his family parking in a lot that is now occupied by Tiger Plaza, a collection of fast food and beer stands. The son remembers coming in the old club entrance, eating in the old club dining room. He remembers that the field and the dugout were out-of-bounds to children. He remembers this every day. "Not much has changed in the office since my father had it," he says. "It's the same dark paneling, the same desk. I think, but I'm not sure, these are the same plaid curtains and venetian blinds. I know they've been here forever."

"I SAW Ty Cobb when I was a kid," 86-year-old Arthur Brooks says. "My grandfather had a deal with the Tigers: Whenever it snowed he would hitch up the horses and plow our lumberyard, then he would plow all around the stadium. The Tigers gave him four tickets to every game for that. The best player I ever saw was Charlie Gehringer, second base. He was just smooth. He made everything look easy. At the plate—this was before all of this home run stuff, all these lunkheads with all their money—he was a place hitter. Is that a term you know? Nobody does it now. He was a place hitter. All line drives."

The lumberyard is still in business beyond rightfield: Brooks Lumber, run by Arthur Brooks's descendants. Baseball has been played at the corner of Michigan and Trumbull avenues since 1896, first at Bennett Park, built over the cobblestones of an old haymarket, then at the present stadium, opened on April 20, 1912, the same week the *Titanic* sank. The lumberyard has been the Tigers' neighbor almost from the beginning. "There's a lot of Brooks lumber in that stadium," Arthur says. "There's been a lot of changes through the years. Do you know that the clubhouse used to have one shower for the entire team? The place smelled so bad that pitchers didn't want to be taken out of games because they didn't want to go to the clubhouse.

"Before management put in the extra seats—the pavilion in rightfield [in 1936]—balls used to land in the lumberyard all the time. I remember, as a boy, when those Yankees teams came to town in the '20s. Ruth, Gehrig, all of them. I'd walk around the yard, pick up a dozen balls in a day."

"MY PARENTS were divorced when I was very young," says Mark Cunningham, a Tigers team photographer. "I lived with my mother, and she made it a point to take me to Tiger Stadium once or twice every season. It was a big adventure. We didn't have a car, so we'd take a bus to the Michigan State Fairgrounds and then the train, and then we'd still have to walk half a mile or so from the old station. Sometimes we'd bring a couple of my friends. They were kids whose parents had cars, but they liked coming with my mother and me better. It was more exciting.

"The first game I ever saw, the Tigers against the Seattle Pilots, I remember walking in here—it was a night game—and there was just a wonderful haze over the field. Everything was green. Denny McLain was standing in leftfield during batting practice, hitting baseballs into the stands with a fungo bat. We had good seats, but I remember wishing that our seats were in the second deck in left. I couldn't think of anything better in the world than catching one of those balls."

McLain, a righthanded pitcher, played for the Tigers from 1963 to 1970. He went 31–6 in 1968.

A FORMER player—no names, please—made a sentimental visit to Tiger Stadium a year ago. Wearing his business suit, he wandered through the cramped and unchanged locker room, talked with the current occupant of his old locker, then traveled through the long tunnel toward the dugout and the playing field. As he approached the dugout, he stopped at a small sink in the tunnel. He unzipped his fly. "You'd always do this during a game," he said to a local sportswriter as he whizzed into the sink. "Saved you from going back to the clubhouse."

The modern player still walks where the long-ago player walked. The sink is still an option. The extra bats, balls and uniforms are still stored in the ceiling of the clubhouse, brought down by a clubhouse attendant on a ladder every day. The manager's office still has no bathroom. The lockers are still small and crowded together. The footsteps and voices of the past still provide the directions to be followed. "I can strike out, go into the tunnel and bang on the same wall that Ty Cobb banged on," says Tigers third baseman Dean Palmer. "Except he didn't strike out as much as me."

"Guys will go to the batting cage under the stands, see the concrete falling apart, and they'll make comments," says first baseman Tony Clark. "They'll say that they heard a voice from a ghost, that Cobb told them to do this or that. Or maybe, hah, Jimmy Hoffa."

Clark, who is 6' 7", has to walk through the dugout in a half crouch, because if he stood he would hit his head. Everyone in the dugout, tall or short, sits at an awkward angle to the field. There is no way to see a ball that is hit to left, and it is hard to see a ball hit to right. A man of average height sitting in the dugout finds that his eyes are at the same level as the field.

The bullpen view is even worse. Relief pitchers sit in a pillbox along the leftfield line. They call the pillbox the Submarine. "You can't see much of the game," says closer Todd Jones. "It's a weird feeling. You're of the game, but not in the game."

THE FIELD might be the newest part of the stadium. Not one blade of grass is a descendant of the grass that was roamed by Wahoo Sam Crawford and Harry Heilmann and Hank Greenberg and Gates Brown and Willie Horton. Not according to Heather Nabozny, the head groundskeeper. "I don't see how it would be possible," Nabozny says. "There was a Rod Stewart concert here a couple of years ago, and it rained, and the field was torn apart. Everything had to be resodded."

Nabozny, 28, took over as groundskeeper this year, replacing Frank Feneck, who worked for the team for 35 seasons. She is a graduate of the Michigan State sports turf management program. Her major worry in Tiger Stadium's last season is a concert by the Three Tenors scheduled for next month.

"I WAS sitting right here one night, maybe 15 years ago," *Oakland Press* sportswriter Jim Hawkins says in the workroom of the press box. "I was typing my story. There was a big commotion on the roof. This was when people were allowed on the roof. Some cops were chasing a guy. *Thump. Thump.* All of a sudden the guy stops, bends over and throws a big bag of dope through that window. I just let it sit there on the floor. I wasn't touching that dope. No, sir."

The words that have flowed from this press box have described the exploits of most players in the American League for 87 years. They have described the work of 11 hometown Hall of Famers, from the fierce Cobb to the hardworking catcher Mickey Cochrane to the graceful rightfielder Al Kaline. They have described six of the Tigers' nine World Series, the last in 1984. ("Even then the park couldn't handle all of the cameras, all of the electricity that was needed," Hawkins says. "I can't imagine what would happen if the Tigers were in the Series this year.") The words have also described some troubled teams and troubled times.

"Actually, this is not the original press box," says *The Detroit News* columnist Joe Falls. "The old press box burned down during the winter of '77. I remember that Jim Campbell, the general manager, said he wished the fire had happened 'five months from now.' He was asked why. 'Because then all of 'em [the writers] would have been in there,' he said."

THE PARK sits at its famous corner like a large, down-at-the-heels amusement ride. The games continue, but there is the overwhelming feeling that the show soon will pack up and move along. The tiled corridors are dark and narrow. The signs on the outfield walls, the logos changing from those of pizzas to those of health-care plans by the inning, seem an intrusion, a last stab at modernization that could never work. The famous sign on one door—VISITORS CLUBHOUSE, NO VISITORS—has disappeared.

The best seats in baseball are still at Tiger Stadium, maybe 10,000 of them that put the spectator closer to the game than he would be at any other ballpark. The worst seats in baseball, too many to count and all with obstructed views, are also at Tiger Stadium. The front row of the upper deck in right overhangs the field by about 10 feet, catching fly balls and turning them into home runs. The eye can still see the transformer on the light tower that Reggie Jackson hit with his monster home run in the 1971 All-Star Game. The ear can still hear the four-man list of players who hit homers over the roof in left: Harmon Killebrew, Frank Howard, Cecil Fielder and Mark McGwire. The mind can still remember Mark (the Bird) Fidrych talking to the baseball on the mound in 1976.

The future awaits only a mile away, where the $290-million Comerica Park is being built. The Tigers' press guide details the wonders to come: the chair seats and suites; the dramatic view of the Detroit skyline; the beer garden on the third base side and the food court on the first base side, which will feature a carousel.

The old park simply sits there. One day closer to its fate.

"IT'S TIME," Parrish says. "You lose all of this history, but you gain a new ballpark. You know what I think it's going to be like? You know how you have that old reliable car that you've driven forever, really loved, and then it breaks down, and you have to get a new car? You know how you think you're going to hate the new car, and then you get behind the wheel and see all the features and say, 'Hey, wait a minute'? I think that's how it's going to be."

He admits there is one feature at the old stadium that cannot be replaced: the showerheads. Made before there was concern over the environment, before worries about water conservation, the Tiger Stadium showers are man-sized showers, torrents of water that can't be found anywhere else. "Everybody's going around talking about what he wants to take home after the final game—a locker, a bat rack, something sentimental," the manager says. "My coaches and I, we want the showerheads."

The final game in Tiger Stadium is Sept. 27, a 4:05 start against the Kansas City Royals. Tickets sold out in 33 minutes.

Waiting Game

BY JACK McCALLUM

Coming to bat cold and chafing at their second-string status,
pinch hitters often see only one good pitch per game and have to make the
most of one big swing.

I'S 3 P.M. ON A MAY AFTERNOON AT VETERANS STADIUM IN Philadelphia, an hour before batting practice, four hours before the Phillies will take the field to play the Milwaukee Brewers. "Where are Jordan and Ducey?" somebody asks in a nearly empty Philadelphia clubhouse.

"Where do you think?" answers an attendant. "Down in the cage."

To be a pinch hitter, the job being performed by Kevin Jordan, Rob Ducey and a host of other anonymous practitioners of this sweaty-palmed, knock-kneed art, is to be a member of baseball's Breakfast Club. Talk to a major league pinch hitter, and he'll offer a version of this sentiment: "As a pinch hitter you have to work twice as hard as a regular player."

Pinch hitters sneak in extra licks whenever they can because they get only one at bat per game. They take extra fielding practice because, on occasions when they remain in the game after pinch-hitting, they could be asked to fill in at one of several positions. They track every pitch because an opportunity to bat, if it comes at all, may present itself unexpectedly. All the while they hope against hope that no matter how well they perform in this role, one fine day they will be released from it.

Or they might be just plain released. When second-division teams start to trim their rosters, pinch hitters are usually the first to go, and even contenders treat them like pawns in a chess game. Witness the National League East–leading Phillies, who on June 6 gave Ducey his walking papers to make room for a power hitter from the minors; six days later Ducey hooked on with the division's last-place club, the Montreal Expos. Philadelphia's move surprised Ducey only slightly. Even when he contributed four pinch hits as the Phillies amassed a .297 pinch-hitting average (way above the league's average of .218 and second to the Atlanta Braves' .315), Ducey admitted he pored over box scores, paying particular attention to what other lefthanded-hitting reserves were doing. "When you're a 36-year-old bench guy like I am," he says, "you have to know what's out there."

What's out there is a cocktail of sweat and adrenaline, mixed in a tall shaker of obscurity. "When you're playing Wiffle ball in the park," says outfielder David Dellucci, one of a fearsome foursome of Arizona Diamondbacks pinch hitters, "do you ever hear anyone say, 'Hey, I want to be the pinch hitter'? It's a role that no one wants."

A pinch hitter is like a field goal kicker: He's often asked to help his team in a make-or-break situation. Pinch hitters, though, also have to be capable in the field. "That's why pinch hitters fade in and out pretty quick," says Phillies bench coach Greg Gross, a superb pinch hitter in his playing days (143 pinch hits, third on the alltime list, during a career that lasted from 1973 through '89). With most teams carrying 11 or 12 pitchers now, Gross adds, "they don't have the luxury of keeping someone around who can't take the field."

The first pinch hitter is believed to have been Cleveland Spiders catcher Jack Doyle, who was sent up to hit for pitcher George Davies in a game against the Brooklyn Bridegrooms in 1892. He singled, and thus was born an art. The names of the great pinch hitters, cold-blooded creatures who thrived under the pressure of the late-inning at bat, hold a mystical place in baseball history. There was Moose McCormick of John McGraw's New York Giants, who used to hold up the game for three minutes while a trainer massaged his legs, and Frenchy Bordagaray, a grandly mustachioed Brooklyn Dodger. They were followed by, among others, Dusty Rhodes, who made his name with the New York Giants; Jerry Lynch of the Cincinnati Reds and the St. Louis Cardinals; Smoky Burgess of the Pittsburgh Pirates and the Chicago White Sox; Gates Brown of the Detroit

Tigers; George Crowe of the Cardinals; Dave Philley of—who else?—the Phillies (and the Baltimore Orioles); and Rusty Staub of the Mets.

The patriarch of pinch hitting is Manny Mota, now a Los Angeles Dodgers coach and mentor to the Dodgers' crack pinch hitter, Dave Hansen. "When I stood up there as a pinch hitter, I honestly believed I was the best hitter in the game," says Mota, who claims never to have taken a called third strike as a pinch hitter in his 20 big league seasons. "That's the only attitude to have."

The art of pinch hitting isn't as celebrated—or as necessary—as it used to be, especially in the American League, where the DH is a kind of full-time pinch hitter. (National League teams used an average of 261 pinch hitters last season, compared with only 114 for American League clubs.) Nonetheless, a number of players still excel at this perilous pursuit.

What little limelight is being directed at pinch hitters this year is falling mostly on Lenny Harris and his 142 career pinch hits, as he pursues Mota's mark of 150. Last year Hansen (103 career pinch hits) got the attention when he established a single-season record with seven pinch-hit home runs. "I promise you they were seven singles that happened to go out," says Hansen. "No pinch hitter can deliver home runs on demand."

The Diamondbacks have the major leagues' highest PH level. Indeed, they present what amounts to a 13-man lineup these days. First baseman Erubiel Durazo ("the shiniest tool in the box," as manager Bob Brenly puts it) blasted four pinch-hit home runs in April; through Sunday he had run that total to five and was batting .435 in the pinch. Dellucci was at .300 with two homers, and Danny Bautista, a part-time outfielder, was at .364 with one homer. The only Arizona pinch hitter who isn't tearing it up is Greg Colbrunn, who, after 10 years in the majors, is the game's highest-paid PH at $1.5 million. The four pinchmen, who last season wore T-shirts proclaiming themselves THE STUNTMEN, are seeking a new moniker this year—the Four Amigos? Four Diamondbacks in the Rough? Four Guys Who Would Rather Be Playing Regularly?

Arizona's pinch-hitting scheme is fairly set. "If we need a pinch hitter leading off an inning, it's going to be either, depending on who's pitching, Dellucci [a lefthanded hitter] or Bautista [righthanded]," says Brenly. "If we have runners in scoring position, and a home run or an extra-base hit won't tie it or win it, it's probably going to be Dellucci. If I need a home run or an extra-base hit, it's going to be Durazo [a lefty] or Colbrunn [a righty]." Brenly admits that when Durazo kept going yard in April he factored that into his strategy. "It got to where I was going to save him until a home run would tie it or give us the lead," says Brenly. "That's how specialized it became."

Not that Brenly is complaining, but late in a tight game he does have to consider more options than most managers. During the pregame he scrutinizes the makeup of the opposition's bullpen. "If the other team's got two or three lefty relievers available, it's going to be hard for me to get Durazo in the game against a righthanded pitcher," says Brenly. So against the Braves early in the season, Brenly used Durazo as a pinch hitter in the fourth inning against righthanded reliever Jason Marquis, and Durazo responded with a sacrifice fly.

Pinch hitters would prefer that their managers spend time figuring out how to get them into the regular lineup. Those who become regular players are rather like community-theater thespians who get plucked for Broadway. They are the envy of their erstwhile fraternity brothers, a status currently being enjoyed by Pirates rightfielder John Vander Wal, who over the years has fretted about being used mainly as a pinch hitter, and San Diego Padres rightfielder Bubba Trammell, who recently proclaimed pinch hitting to be "the hardest thing I ever did." A number of great hitters might concur. Ty Cobb batted .367 for his career, .217 in the pinch; George Brett, with a .305 career average, was at .219 as a pinch hitter; and five-time batting champion Wade Boggs's numbers were .328 and .207, respectively.

Pinch hitters say that the most difficult aspect of the job is overcoming an inferiority complex: If you're by definition a pinch hitter, you're by definition not good enough to be a regular, and that gnaws at you. "Many players who are given a pinch-hitting role won't accept it," says Gross. "They end up sabotaging themselves."

Hansen agrees. "About three years ago [when he was with the Cubs], it came to me that pinch hitting was why I was up here," says Hansen, who has played all the infield positions and in the outfield during his 11-season career. "I decided to release all that hardheadedness. I was mad about not being an every-day player instead of accepting the fact that I could be a major league player as a pinch hitter. That's when I started to get good at it."

Pinch hitters estimate that they face a closer 90% of the time. Moreover, they're coming in cold against that 95-mph fastball or wicked splitter. They'll take a walk, but in the typical pinch-hit situation it's not as if the hitter has the luxury to work the count. "Athletes live for the excitement and the adrenaline," says Hansen, "but, man, when you consider the typical pinch-hitting situation—ninth inning, men on base, closer on the mound, game on the line—sometimes you get a little bit more than you need."

Further, Vander Wal (116 pinch hits and 16 pinch homers, the most among active players) has a theory that a pinch hitter gets only one good pitch to hit per at bat, which means one good pitch per game. Colbrunn agrees. "You take or foul off that one pitch," he says, "and you've got an uphill battle."

Dellucci believes the most difficult facet of pinch hitting is that your chances are few and far between. (The season record for pinch-hit plate appearances is 94, set by Staub in 1983.) "If you don't drive in a runner or move a guy along," says Dellucci, "maybe you don't get another chance to redeem yourself for three or four games. So it sits with you."

Gross used to play a mental game with himself. "I got about 50 pinch-hit at bats per season, so I'd chop them into five 'seasons,' " says Gross. "If I was, say, 0 for 9, I'd want to get the 10th real quick. It was like, O.K., thank God that's over with. Now I can start a new season."

Here's another fear, one that may be unique to pinch hitters: They worry about becoming too good at what they do. "If you do it successfully, then you're thought of as *just* a pinch hitter," says Dellucci. "That's the worst thing that can happen."

Pinch hitters fill their days and nights with routine. "Surprise is the enemy of the pinch hitter," says Hansen. "[You're always asking] Who's in the pen that day? How's he been throwing? What's my likelihood of seeing him? I learned more about the intricacies of baseball when I became a pinch hitter than I did as a regular."

In the third inning Durazo will go either to the batting cage to hit off a tee or to the locker room to swing in front of a mirror. Colbrunn and Bautista usually join him, and Durazo picks their brains for pointers about opposing pitchers. Dellucci likes to jump on the stationary bike in the fourth inning, pedaling away while he watches the game on the clubhouse TV. "One thing you worry about is getting up there, getting a hit and then pulling a muscle because you've been sitting around," says Harris, who also rides the bike during games. As with the Diamondbacks' pinch hitters, Jordan often finds himself in the locker room, stretching and swinging. He takes a lot of what he calls "dry swings" or "shadow swings," getting the timing down on his compact stroke.

With all that peripateticism during the game—Gross had a rule that he never sat still for longer than a half inning—one might think pinch-hitting lore is rich with stories of pinch hitters sneaking in a quick hand of clubhouse rummy or being in the middle of relieving themselves when the call comes. Forget it. Unlike closers, their late-game counterparts, pinch hitters tend not to be flakes. Most of them got the job precisely because they are, first, disciplined, studious hitters and, second, desperate to stay in the bigs; they know they can't afford to blow a single opportunity. "I didn't want to become a pinch hitter," says the 27-year-old Durazo, who was a regular as a rookie in 1999 but now sits behind Mark Grace, "but they know I'll do anything to stay here."

There have been pinch-hit surprises over the years. In the 1960 World Series, New York Yankees manager Casey Stengel sent Dale Long up to bat for third baseman Clete Boyer in the second inning of Game 1. Long flied out, and the Yanks were without Boyer, a sterling gloveman, for the rest of the game, which they lost 6–4.

The lefthanded-hitting Gross recalls the night in '79 when Phillies skipper Danny Ozark had him hit for righthanded-batting cleanup man Greg (the Bull) Luzinski with the bases loaded. "Other than my first at bat in the majors, it was the most nervous I had ever been," says Gross, who delivered a sacrifice fly. What was the Bull's reaction? "I can't say because I stayed away from him," says Gross. "Pinch hitters, you see, can't get too cocky."

Against
The Grain

BY STEPHEN CANNELLA

Carving a new niche in maple, a Canadian woodworker gave hitters an alternative to ash and unleashed the boutique bat business.

A S LEGEND HAS IT, KING ARTHUR OBTAINED THE MAGIC sword he used to smite his enemies from Nimue, a beautiful woman who stood sentry at a lake in which the weapon was submerged. Barry Bonds's meeting with his Lady of the Lake was less mythic but no less momentous. It was spring training 1999, and, instead of a knockout in gleaming locks and flowing robes, Bonds was introduced to a gray-haired, 53-year-old Canadian carpenter in denim overalls. Sam Holman, founder of Ottawa's Original Maple Bat Company, ambled up to Bonds at the San Francisco Giants' complex in Scottsdale, Ariz., and presented him with his creation: the Rideau Crusher, named after the canal that winds through the Canadian capital. The Crusher was carved from sugar maple rather than the white ash that Bonds and the majority of his major league colleagues had used throughout their careers. "His first reaction was," says Holman, " 'Oh, no, not another bat salesman.' "

Bonds changed his tune after a session in the cage. He reported to Holman that the bat felt harder than his ash models. True, the maple was heavier, but Bonds also thought the ball jumped off it with more zip. After Bonds gave him a few design suggestions, Holman scurried back to the lathe in the shed behind his home on Bayswater Avenue in Ottawa to tinker.

That sample bat was the prototype of a 21st-century Excalibur. By the end of last season more than 200 major leaguers had armed themselves with what are known as Sam Bats. Bonds began swinging Holman's maple full time midway through the '99 season, and last year he used a 34-inch, 32-ounce model 2K1 Rideau Crusher with a half-cupped barrel to bash his way to 73 home runs and an .863 slugging percentage, both single-season records.

When it comes to choosing bats, many hitters insist, in the words of Los Angeles Dodgers outfielder Brian Jordan, "It's not the arrow, it's the Indian." That may have been true 10 or even five years ago, but not anymore. Reason No. 1: Thanks to a slew of innovative bat makers like Holman, the Indians—and the Giants, and everyone else in baseball—suddenly have many more arrows to choose from. "People talk about the ball being juiced," says Tampa Bay Devil Rays catcher John Flaherty. "I've been saying for a while now that the wood is so much better than it was when I came up."

Holman's introduction of maple five years ago was the first major innovation in wooden bat technology in almost a century, and the heavier wood has caught on. St. Louis Cardinals slugger Albert Pujols hit 37 home runs and set a National League rookie record for RBIs (130) in 2001 using a Sam Bat. Dodgers catcher Paul Lo Duca switched to maple last year, using bats made by Louisville Slugger and by the Tennessee-based Old Hickory Bat Company during his breakthrough season. "It took me a while to try it, but now I'm a maple believer," says Lo Duca, "a full-time maple guy."

Cliff Floyd of the Florida Marlins also switched to maple—a model made by Old Hickory—last June. "I used the bat for the first time last year, and I hit 31 bombs," says Floyd, who never before had hit more than 22. He believes the new wood gives him extra pop even when he doesn't hit the ball cleanly. "I'd get jammed and instead of the bat breaking, the ball would bloop into the outfield for a base hit," he says. "That's a huge advantage of maple—strength."

Another advantage is its durability. Ash bats, especially the thick-barreled, thin-handled models most modern hitters prefer, rarely last more than a couple of games. Yet stories of seemingly unbreakable maple bats circulate like Arthurian legends. Flaherty, who still swings an ash Louisville Slugger C271 in games because he likes the feel, used the same Sam Bat every day for batting practice last year. Phillies catcher Mike Lieberthal, who uses maple Louisville Sluggers and Tuff Bats, the latter made by a small firm in California, used the same maple stick every day this off-season while hitting in his backyard cage. "Ash bats would splinter after two or three BPs," he says. "Now I'm a maple guy till the day I die. I've heard you'd better order your maple now because they're going to run out."

That seems unlikely given the glut of bat makers now catering to major leaguers. Five years ago the bats of 11 manufacturers were approved for game use by the commissioner's office. This season that number has swelled to 48. Biggies like Hillerich & Bradsby, Rawlings, Mizuno and Easton are still the most common names in big league bat racks, but in recent years bat companies have sprung up like microbreweries, sporting clever names and promising personalized service and handmade quality. There are bats from seemingly every state (Carolina Clubs, Jersey Sticks and Texas Timber) and two countries (Mash Bats and Tom Cat Bats are also based in Canada). There's Chesapeake Thunder and Thunder Lumber, Hoosier and Zinger and Reaper. Need a bat fashioned by Amish artisans? There are two choices, the Dutch Craftsman Bat Company and Akadema, which promises quality bats built "in the Pennsylvania Dutch tradition" and without the aid of electricity.

Whether they choose maple or ash, all hitters—not just the superstars—can now have their needs met by one of the bat-company reps who swarm through spring camps. While once those reps sought to match the average major leaguer to the bat, offering him his choice of any existing model in the company's lineup, the approach among the small companies is to match a bat to a player. Most companies can get hitters an order of custom-made bats within two weeks.

The days of a young player signing a 20-year contract with Louisville Slugger to get his name on a bat are long gone. Plenty of rank-and-file hitters still get their signature models, but the deals they sign are for a season or two at a time. Indeed, most hitters' lockers are stocked with bats from three or four companies, and a manufacturer will use its customized service as an incentive to get a player to use its bats. The model Bonds will use this year, for example, is the result of three years of tinkering (shifting barrel weight, fattening the knob, etc.) by him and Holman. Says Dodgers outfielder Shawn Green (Rawlings ash in games, maple for BP), "There's more competition, so it's easier to get good service."

More companies also means more gimmicks. Major league rules state only that "the bat shall be a smooth, round stick not more than 2¾ inches

in diameter at the thickest part and not more than 42 inches in length."
There is no maximum weight. The commissioner's office limits the color that
bats can come in (natural, brown, black and a two-tone stain are the only
acceptable hues), but says nothing about how many coats of finish they
can carry. Some hitters believe lacquer gives a bat more durability and,
perhaps, extra juice. But even manufacturers concede that the extra dipping
may provide only a psychological edge at best. Says Chuck Schupp,
Louisville Slugger's director of pro baseball sales, "Lacquer doesn't matter. If you want to drive the ball, use a heavier piece of lumber."

That's where Holman made his breakthrough. He was relaxing at Ottawa's Mayflower Pub, his usual haunt, one night during the spring of 1996
when his friend Bill MacKenzie, then a scout for the Colorado Rockies, be-
moaned the fragility of the wooden bat. MacKenzie turned to Holman,
who had worked for 23 years as a carpenter and theater-set builder at Ottawa's National Arts Center, and said, "You know wood. Can you make a
stronger bat?"

Holman started by slogging through 225 U.S. bat-making patents; by
the time he was done, he knew he wasn't going to make a better ash bat. He
knew that maple, with a density (or specific gravity) of between 0.63 and
0.67, is only slightly heavier than ash (density of about 0.60), yet is much
stronger and more durable.

Holman carved his first bat out of a maple newel post from the stairway
in his house. In April 1997 he descended on the Toronto Blue Jays and persuaded Joe Carter, Carlos Delgado and Ed Sprague to try maple in batting
practice. Carter fell in love; he sneaked a Sam into a game that season and
homered, and Holman was in business.

By last season at least seven other companies were producing maple
bats. The biggest hurdle for all of them is maple's wide variance in density, an obstacle to consistently producing bats of identical weight and dimensions. (That difficulty accounts for the high price of maple bats. As a
rule, teams pay for all players' bats, and Sams sell for $65 apiece, nearly
twice what most ash sticks go for.) If a hitter insists on a bat that weighs 32
ounces, for instance, some of his bats may have to be made with a thinner
barrel, maybe 2½ inches in diameter compared with a standard 2⅝ inches
ash model. If barrel size is more important, he may find himself swinging
bats of slightly different weights.

Holman insists that thin-barreled bats lead to increased bat speed,
with little or no sacrifice in the size of the bat's "sweet spot," and that

those models will be the wave of the future. "I can make a bat barrel just over two inches in diameter that will give you the same weight to the ball as Barry's bat, which is almost 2⅝ inches," he says. "I'll guarantee you one thing: If anyone beats Barry's record of 73, it will be with a narrow-barreled bat."

In January, Bonds visited Sam Bat headquarters. He tiptoed through Holman's living room, stepping around hundreds of bats waiting to be boxed and shipped to every major league camp and stepped into the second-floor bedroom that doubles as Holman's "administration room." Bonds also toured the manufacturing plant Holman opened in a converted tavern in November. Until then every Sam Bat had been carved and finished in the shed behind Holman's house. "When we were walking through the living room, Barry told me he had to stop and take a moment to wrap his mind around all this," Holman says.

Holman expects to turn out 30,000 bats this year, double his 2001 production. Nearly all will be sold to professionals in the major and minor leagues and in Mexico and Taiwan. After the tour Bonds and Holman retired to the Mayflower Pub for a reception for 150 of the bat maker's closest friends. There the home run king thanked his Lady of the Lake. "You know, it's my record," Bonds told Holman, "but it's still your bat."

YOU COULD
LOOK IT UP

☙

From the Hill
To the Hall

BY HERBERT WARREN WIND

*On the eve of spring training, a distinguished member of SI's staff
paid homage to Yogi Berra, a mainstay of the Yankees dynasty and one of the
game's most appealing personalities.*

I T IS PLEASANT TO CONTEMPLATE THE GOOD FORTUNE THAT HAS come the way of Lawrence Peter Berra. If it is coming to any athlete, he has it coming to him. Aside from being a person of unusual decency and natural charm, he has, from a fairly inauspicious beginning in the big leagues, achieved over the last dozen years a place among the memorable players in the long history of the game. Over and above this, Berra is a personality of such original force and magnetism that sometimes it has even obliterated his stature as a player. He is, as Joe Trimble has called him, the Kid Ring Lardner Missed, and possibly more—the last of the glorious line of baseball's great characters.

In this age where ballplayers have kept growing taller and more statuesque until the breed is now in appearance a combination of the stroke on the college crew and the juvenile lead in summer stock, Berra adheres to the classic blocky dimensions of the oldtime catcher. He stands 5' 8" and weighs about 192 and looks even chunkier (especially in a baseball uniform) than these figures would augur, for he has the broad and wide-set shoulders of a much taller man, a barrel chest and enormous arms. Unlike most men of similar musculature, Berra is very lithe, very loose—in fact, there is such friskiness in his movements (except when he is catching the second game of a doubleheader) that, as he approaches 34, he still conjures up the picture of a beknickered boy of 13 or 14. Berra's build is quite deceptive in other ways, or at least it has led a number of observers into glib deductions that are strikingly wayward. For example, nearly everyone decided years ago that a man with his nonmissile dimensions would *ipso facto* have to be a slow runner. Only in recent years has it been generally appreciated that Yogi has always been extremely fast, one of the Yankees' best base runners, in fact. Even stranger is that ivied slice of myopia which depicts Berra as all awkwardness at bat, a man who busts the ball out of the park by sheer brute strength. This is simply not correct. While there is assuredly little esthetic splendor about the way Yogi bunches himself at the plate, he handles the bat beautifully, with a delicacy and finesse which few place hitters approach and which is rarer still, of course, for a power hitter. He has magnificent timing, releasing his wrist action at the last split-second. This explains why when Berra is hitting, he can hit anybody or anything, including more bad balls than anyone since Joe Medwick. In the 1955 World Series—not the 1956 Series in which he hit three home runs and batted in 10 runs, but the 1955 Series in which he made 10 hits and batted .417— Yogi put on one of the finest demonstrations of straightaway hitting in modern times, meeting the ball right between the seams again and again and lining it like a shot over the infield, very much in the fashion of Paul Warner and Nap Lajoie. "There's no one more natural or more graceful that Yogi when he's watching the pitch and taking his cut," Phil Rizzuto said not long ago. "He's all rhythm up there, like Ted Williams."

Williams and Berra are alike in one other respect: They are talkative men. Splendidly endowed as Williams is in this department, he is simply not in Berra's class. In truth, no player in the annals of baseball has been, and those who potentially might have challenged his preeminence made the mistake of playing the wrong position. Stationed behind the plate, Berra has a steady flow of new faces to ask how things are going, and during lulls between batters there is always the umpire. Early this year, Casey Stengel, a fairly articulate man himself, had a few words to say about Berra's verbosity. Asked if he considered Berra to be the best late-inning hitter in the game, a claim many have made for him, Casey replied that he didn't know about that. "I'd have to look into it," he said. "He could be the best late-inning hitter in baseball because he's got to hit sometime during a game, and he is a very bad early-inning hitter. Sometimes Mr. Berra allows himself to go careless. He forgets to start the game with the first inning. He's out there behind the plate saying hello to everybody in sight. Oh, Mr. Berra is a very sociable fellow. He acts like home plate is his room."

In all of Yogi's actions on the ball field there is a beguiling spontaneity and a total lack of affectation. Beyond this, a tide of friendliness comes pouring through, and it communicates itself in a wondrous way not only to the people within earshot of his gravelly banter but also to the outlanders perched in the deep recesses of the stadium. It is difficult to think of another performer in sports who possesses Berra's particular quality of empathy: You just sense you like that guy. Viewed at intimate range—and it is a pleasure to report this since it is all too seldom true of national figures who are irresistible in their public roles—Berra turns out to be the same guy he appears to be: friendly, full of unposy vitality, marvelously good-natured. There are times when Berra's exceptional energy gets worn down and responding to his fans becomes a nervous strain, but he has absorbed the niceties of applied public relations and employs them well at these moments. What is remarkable, though, is the genuine consideration which Berra, on most occasions, shows the countless strangers who yell to him wherever he may be or who come over to talk with him—he treats them as if they were neighbors he has known all his life.

There is, however, a lot more complication in Berra than meets the casual eye. When Sal Maglie joined the Yankees, a friend asked him what if anything was different about the players from what he had expected. "Yogi," Sal replied. "Yogi worries a great deal." These periods do not last too long, but when Yogi is troubled, it goes all through him; he is not only grave, he is gloomy. He is also quite a sensitive person, which many people miss, though they shouldn't. Moreover, there is considerable shyness in him. At social gatherings away from the park, he will on some occasions hang mutely on the edge of a group engaged in conversation, keeping his distance momentarily, but when he joins in, he arrives in force. All of this makes Yogi not one whit different from you or me—except that most of us lack his buoyant good nature and the grit and instinctive soundness which knit him together—but it is rather important to mention these things in Berra's case since he has been so invariably portrayed as a happy-go-lucky child of nature.

This distortion, to a considerable degree, stems from the incomparable Berraisms which he has produced since he first came up. They are the Goldwynisms of baseball. The only qualifying point that need be made about Yogi's *authentic* Berraisms is that they are not the product of stupidity but rather of the pleasure he gets in participating on all fronts and expressing himself. He is anything but facile at translating his thoughts into words but, far from being a slow man on the bases upstairs, Berra has an essentially good mind and a very active one. If there is a fund of goodwill in Yogi, there is also a native shrewdness. He has, for instance, invested his money very soundly. He now represents himself capably in his salary symposiums with George Weiss, having matured tremendously over the years in his sense of values, his own included.

Berra's remarks can be incisive as well as comic; for example, after sitting in on a strategy conference before an All-Star Game, in which a long time was spent debating the best methods for pitching to Musial: "The trouble with you guys is you're trying to figure out in 15 minutes something no one has figured out in 15 years." He also has the gift of good taste, which he has demonstrated most markedly, perhaps, in his choice of Mrs. Berra (Carmen Short, also from Missouri), a fine-looking girl with a very crisp, perky personality. Thanks to Carmen and to his great friend Rizzuto, Yogi has long since abandoned his celebrated allegiance to comic books, which was slightly exaggerated anyhow.

As far as baseball goes, Yogi, despite the camouflage of his mannerisms, thinks well and swiftly and has become a master of the hard art of talking shop and thinking baseball. While he is gabbing away with batters, another part of his mind is setting up a pitching pattern for instant use as well as filing away for future reference pertinent dope on each hitter. Stengel, who has been known to refer to Berra as "my assistant manager" because of his veteran catcher's ever-readiness to contribute his knowledge to the common cause, not long ago meandered into an oblique shaft of revelation which recalled his famed soliloquy on the short-fingered Japanese during his appearance before the United States Senate. "Berra," said Casey, "is alert because he's got very good hearing. He has better ears than any other catcher in the game. He hears everything that's said on the field and not only there but away from the field. He knows all the scandal."

Stengel has also long been struck by Berra's knowledge of sports in general. So is everyone who knows him. Yogi's old friend Joe Garagiola, the former Cardinal catcher who currently is a highly successful baseball broadcaster and after-dinner speaker, frequently tells his audience on the banquet trail that "funny as it will sound to many of you, Yogi could have been an A-student in college." Joe then elaborates on this by stating that Yogi has an exceptionally good memory for anything he wants to remember, such as sports.

This is a very significant part of Berra—his abiding love of sports—and it explains the man directly. In a nation like ours there are literally hundreds of thousands of boys and grown-ups who are attached to sport before any other consideration, but it is really extraordinary to find an experienced professional athlete whose youthful affection for his game has not withered. After all these bruising seasons Berra has somehow managed to retain a boy's full-hearted enthusiasm for baseball. Once he enters the dressing room, that spirit of the young boy, all eagerness for the game, clutches him wholly. He loves to play ball like other men like to make money or work in the garden. And this is what makes Berra the ballplayer he is.

THE OUTLINE of Yogi's early years and his road to the top are fairly well known to sports fans, and to summarize them elliptically is probably enough for our purposes. He was born in St. Louis, May 12, 1925, the son of Paulina and Pietro Berra. Mr. Berra worked in the kilns in one of the local brick factories. The Berras lived on 5447 Elizabeth Avenue, the Garagiolas at 5446, on "Dago Hill." Yogi left school at 14 after completing the seventh grade. After this he had a long series of small jobs in various plants. He lost one after another because sports came first; whenever it was a question of whether to play in a big game or pass it by and stay on the job, he chose the former. Deep within him he clung to the obscure hope that somehow or other he might be able to make a career in sports. As he has always been the first to admit, he owes the chance he had to pursue this hope to his older brothers, Tony, Mike and Johnny. All three were fine athletes, and two showed such talent for baseball that they were approached by big league clubs to join teams in their farm system. (Yogi has always claimed that Tony, the oldest brother, was the best ballplayer in the family.) The pressure to bring money into the hard-pressed family forced the older boys to forsake their ambitions in baseball and to knuckle down to wage-earning in local plants. However, when Yogi began to blossom in American Legion Junior Baseball, his brothers insisted that he be given the chance they had never had, and they were so adamant about this that they eventually broke down the opposition of their parents. In 1942 when he was 17, Yogi was signed by John Schulte, a scout for the Yankees organization, for $500. This was the amount which Joe Garagiola, eight months younger than Yogi, had received from the St. Louis Cardinals after he and Yogi, both of them lefthand-hitting catchers, had been given a tryout the year before.

The Cardinals had also wanted to sign Berra but had not offered him a bonus for signing. Though it almost killed him to do so, Yogi had turned down their contract, not because of envy of his pal—there is no envy in Berra—but because he felt he was worth $500 too. In 1943 the Yankees assigned him to Norfolk, their affiliate in the Class B Piedmont League.

The fact that two members of their gang had been signed by big league clubs was a towering feather in the hats of the kids on the Hill. Mulling over Yogi's chances of making good, they were positive he would, for they had known him as a superlative all-round athlete, a mainstay for their team, the Stags, in their organized league games as well as in their sandlot games and street games.

Yogi was an average if clamorous basketball player, pretty fair at roller hockey and truly outstanding at soccer, a game that has long been big in St. Louis. He played halfback, and was so fond of the sport that he went on playing it even after he had definitely arrived in professional baseball, and probably would have continued to play it had not the Yankees, fearful of injury, ordered him to retire. "The main thing about Yogi that impressed us as kids," Garagiola was remembering recently, "was how fast he picked up any sport. One time the Italian-American club wanted some kid to represent them in the city boxing matches. They got Yogi. If you wanted something done, you always got Yogi. He'd never boxed before, but he turned out to be darned good at it: I think he had five fights and won them all, two by knockouts, before his folks made him quit. Another time I remember we went up to the YMCA and found a Ping-Pong tournament going on. Yogi had never played the game before but he entered. In his first match he was just trying to return the ball across the net, but he got the hang of it quick and went all the way to the final." Garagiola paused a long moment, "Just talking about those old days," he resumed, "brings back to your mind what a wonderful guy Yogi was even as a kid. He was never one to come forward and try to stand out, but he was the fellow who got the other fellows together. He was a peacemaker kind of kid. More than that, he had a lot of strength and cheer in him. When you were troubled about something, there was no one like him. Why, just to see him come bouncing around the corner half-solved your problem. 'Here comes Yogi,' you'd say to yourself. 'It isn't as bad as it looked.' "

AS FAR as baseball went (and its close relatives, softball and corkball, an offshoot particular to St. Louis), Yogi as a youngster did some of the pitching for the Stags and played every position except first base. He did little or no catching until he was 14. "I got the job because no one else wanted it," he remembers. "You took quite a beating back there. You didn't have any shin guards or belly protector." He did the catching, when he was 16 and 17, for the Fred W. Stockton Post American Legion team, and was one of the chief reasons why the team in 1941 and 1942 was the class of its section and both seasons reached the final round of the national championship finals. Up with Norfolk in '43. Yogi blew hot and cold, batting a mild .253 for the season, but in 1946, following his wartime tour of duty with the Navy, he hit .314 with Newark, the Yankees' farm club in the AAA International League, and was considered ready to go up with the big club. In the Navy, incidentally, he had seen action of the roughest kind in the landings in Normandy and later in southern France. He was a rocketman on a Coast Guard boat, one of a group of 36-foot LCSSs (Landing Craft Support Small) which on D-day were disgorged from a larger vessel some 300 yards off Omaha Beach to help open the beach for the first wave.

During his first full year with the Yankees, 1947, Berra, a very young 22, was nervous and conspicuously unpolished behind the plate. Although he drove in 54 runs in 83 games that year and a thumping 98 runs in 125 games in 1948, he made many costly errors in judgment behind the plate as well as physical errors. Work as he did to correct them, he continued to make them and was frequently played in rightfield, where he could do far less damage. These were days of anguish for him, because on top of these concerns he was the target of some brutal personal riding. In the final analysis, it was his own hardy character that saw him through, but he was extremely fortunate in the men he was associated with. He was fortunate, for instance, that his idol, Joe DiMaggio, was around to support him in many critical moments. One typical example of DiMaggio's help occurred during one of those stretches when Yogi had been exiled to rightfield. Way down in the dumps after popping up his previous time at bat, Yogi shuffled dejectedly out to right at the beginning of the next inning. DiMaggio noticed this. An inning later, as Yogi was gallumping out to his position, Joe, instead of sprinting out to center as was his hustling habit, followed out after Yogi and yelled to him to get moving. "Always run out to your position, Yogi!" Joe continued as they ran out together. "It doesn't look good when you walk. The other team may have gotten you down but don't let them know it."

Yogi has also been fortunate in playing under managers like Bucky Harris, a kindly man, and Casey Stengel, who has directed the Yankees since 1949. When Casey first took over he set about building up Berra's confidence as a catcher, and here his most valuable contribution was his decision to turn Yogi over to coach Bill Dickey, that most accomplished technician, for a full course of instruction. Dickey not only instructed Berra in every facet of the mechanics of catching, he taught him how to call a game. "Yogi before Dickey and Yogi after Dickey—the difference was like night and day," Rizzuto has commented. "Before, he was never thinking ahead like a catcher must. He hesitated all through a game calling the pitches. He didn't know how to set a batter up for the curve with the fastball, and so on. He was really shaky and the result was that the pitchers didn't have any confidence in him. After his schooling with Dickey, he started to think ahead automatically, he set up very good patterns and he began to study the hitters intelligently. Our pitchers began to lean on his judgment very quickly after this. Only Reynolds or Raschi every shook him off and they didn't do it very often."

Above all Yogi was fortunate in having Phil Rizzuto as his roommate on the road trips and as a staunch friend at all times. Yogi was (and is) stoical by nature. Never one to moan or alibi, he prefers to keep his troubles to himself. During his first seasons in the majors he simply had too many troubles to absorb and sometimes they accumulated into a ponderous burden, and you cannot overestimate the good it did the young man, so distrustful of his ability to get across what he felt in words, to find himself understood when he opened himself to Rizzuto. Rizzuto showed Berra all the ropes, additionally, but he was beautifully unpaternalistic—he never forced his advice on Yogi, merely gave his opinion when asked and let Yogi make his own decisions, which were invariably quite logical. "Yogi is an iron man and it really works against him," Phil reflected recently. "All the fellows on the team know he's caught innumerable doubleheaders after only five hours of sleep. They know that over the last dozen years he's caught many more games than any other catcher, many more. He's gotten out there and done the job despite a staggering number of painful injuries, jammed thumbs and split fingers and the rest. That's why Yogi never gets any sympathy. No one thinks he needs it."

When Yogi is learning something now, he customarily gives the impression that his mind is wandering and that he isn't following his instructor. For instance, he never gives back a paraphrase of what the other person has been saying, which is the most common method by which students indicate that they understand a new thing. For all the ambiguity of his re-actions, Yogi has a first-rate aptitude for learning. It is, in fact, hard to think of a man who has done as much for himself. Today he leads a rounded and enviably full life, at the core of which is his home in Tenafly. There is a lot of pep and sense in the Berra household. "Once in a while after we've lost a tough one or if I've played a lousy game," Yogi was saying not long ago, "I get angry when I get home. My wife doesn't let me get very far with it. Carm will tell me, 'Don't get angry with me. You played badly. I didn't.' "

The spirited Mrs. Berra has a lively interest in baseball, but her major pastime is antiques. She has acquired for the house some handsome pieces, both American and European, among them as old table of Italian walnut at which the Berras eat breakfast and their snack meals. All smiles at the shoe being on the other foot for a change, Yogi loves to tell about the morning Bill Skowron walked into the breakfast room, studied the table for a moment and then declared, "With all your money, Yogi, you can certainly afford to buy a new table."

While Yogi has indeed come a long way from St. Louis, the wonderful thing about him is that in many essential areas he has not changed a bit from the kid on the Hill. For him—and this is just one phase of that ap-pealing immutability—anybody who can play sports a major part of his hours is still the most privileged of people. His zest for reading sports and watching sports and talking sports when he is not playing sports has diminished not at all. During the autumn, when many baseball players are tapering off from the season's grind by hunting, Berra gets his mind off baseball by traveling to some spot like Pinehurst for a therapeutic week of golf, and then indulges his passion for football by going not only to the New York Giants' games but to those of local high school teams. As the colder weather comes on, Berra becomes almost as regular in his atten-dance at the basketball and hockey games at Madison Square Garden as Gladys Goodding, the well-tempered organist. Mrs. Berra has now cut down on the number of events she attends, but still goes to a few with him. On other occasions Yogi takes his two oldest boys or goes with friends with whom he also plays golf. And sometimes Yogi just drives in alone, sure in the foreknowledge that at courtside or rinkside he will run into some fellows he knows.

At the half-time interval of the first game of a recent pro basketball double-header which he went to with a neighbor from Tenafly, Yogi returned to his seat just in time to be slapped on the back by a tall, athletic-looking fellow. "Hey, you character, where you been keeping yourself?" the tall man, who turned out to be Joe Black, the old Dodger pitcher, asked with obvious affection. Yogi's eyes lighted up with pleasure. "This guy's a no-good catcher," Black explained to the friend he was with. "Trouble with him is he can't hit." Yogi and Joe gabbed about old times and new jobs until the second half got under way. In the break before the start of the second game another tall, husky fellow, circulating in the courtside section, spotted Yogi and came over for a similar reunion. "That was Doby," Yogi later explained to his friend from New Jersey, exhibiting more than a little of the same pride an average fan would take at being on speaking terms with a real big-leaguer.

This high regard applies to all athletes Berra admires, not just to baseball players. They are "his people." During the off season when Berra must endure the hardship of having no assured supply of conversational fodder presented to him in the shape of enemy batsmen, his encounters with old friends at athletic events help to provide his gregarious soul with the communication it constantly craves. On the other hand, unlike the modern sports pundit who views each event as a springboard for his own trenchant comments, Berra is a quiet, intent and excitable spectator, with what nowadays amounts to an old-fashioned point of view: he doesn't focus primarily on the stars, but on the team play and the winning and losing of a game.

Berra stays in shape during the off season by cutting down on his eating—he frequently skips lunch—and by fairly-regular exercise. One of those men who are bored by calisthenics and point-to-point walks and for whom a workout has to be the unconscious byproduct of playing a game, he fools around with a basketball on the backyard court he has set up (for the kids, of course), bowls and golfs. When Yogi warily took up golf some 10 years ago, he merely used an adaptation of his baseball swing. Hitting from the left side he was a very wild and woolly golfer, and the few powerhouse blows he got off generally journeyed in the wrong direction. Three autumns ago when he was playing a round (and an anguishingly bad one) at White Beeches with Tommy DeSanto, one of the club's best players, DeSanto suggested on the 11th hole that Berra borrow one of his right-handed clubs and see how he made out. Berra proceeded to hit his best shot of the day. He played in the rest of the way with DeSanto's clubs and has played righthanded ever since, though, interestingly enough, he continues to play his wedge shots and to putt lefthanded. Since switching over,

Yogi's golf has shown steady improvement and his club members now consider his 14 handicap about two shots too high. He is interested in the games of the people he plays with, he chirps good conversation and at the right times, competes just hard enough and without gamesmanship and, all in all, is almost the perfect golf companion.

There are few people who can match the bonhomie that emanates from Berra when he is in an expansive mood, which he was one day last November after he had finished a particularly satisfying round at White Beeches. He had played with two friends from New York who wanted to round out their safari into the hinterland by visiting the Berra-Rizzuto alleys, which lie a complicated half-hour drive away from the course. It was arranged that Berra would lead the way in his car and they would follow in theirs. "There are two tolls," Better informed them. "You'll need a quarter for the first and a dime for the second. You get it?" They had, and the abbreviated caravan rolled off.

Some minutes later Berra swung his Pontiac into an entrance to the Garden State Parkway. He paid his toll and gabbed a moment with the toll attendant. His friends then drove up to the attendant, and the driver held his hand out with a quarter in it. The attendant waved it away. "Mr. Berra," he said, "has already taken care of it."

APRIL 14, 1969

⟶

Baseball's Johnny Appleseed

BY HAROLD PETERSON

*In 1845 a New Yorker named Alexander Cartwright Jr.—not
Abner Doubleday—invented the game that became America's pastime. Then
he headed West, taking with him a ball and a missionary's zeal.*

O N A PLEASANT AND SUNNY MORNING IN THE SPRING of 1845, six years after Abner Doubleday did not invent baseball in Elihu Phinney's Cooperstown cow pasture (or anywhere else), a black-whiskered 25-year-old New Yorker named Alexander Joy Cartwright Jr. walked off the pleasantly shaded sidewalks of Fourth Avenue into a meadow on Murray Hill between Third Avenue and the railroad cut. There he joined a group of young men lightheartedly playing a game of ball remembered from their childhood— a game, like most children's games, whose antecedents were mysterious and whose rules were subject to constant change and much dispute.

This particular day Cartwright had a carefully drafted diagram in his hand. He beckoned his fellows to gather around and described his plan, which was a distillation of many vague ideas that had been proposed in the previous several years. The plan was simple. Instead of the casual arrangement of bases that had prevailed in the past, the ballplayers would be stationed at first, second and third base around a perfect square, with 90 feet between the bases. Instead of an indefinite number of players in the outfield, there would be only three, at leftfield, centerfield and rightfield. Because most balls were hit between second and third, Cartwright put one player at an entirely new place he called shortstop. There were to be flat bases instead of random posts or rocks that happened to be found where the game was played. There could be only nine men on a side. They would bat in a regular order, announced before the game started. To determine when the hitting and fielding sides would exchange places, Cartwright proposed a rule that he called "three bands out, all out." In cricket, popular in New York in those days, a side continued to bat until the whole team was out.

The game that Cartwright and his friends tried out on Murray Hill was phenomenally successful from the start. The standardized shape and dimensions of the playing field meant that ball clubs could meet each other on equal terms wherever they played. Throwing to bases to make outs—instead of throwing the ball and trying to hit a wildly dodging base runner—tightened and rationalized the game remarkably; it immediately ceased to be a mere children's amusement. The rapid succession of innings rescued the game from the dawdling pace of cricket, a game that, being of English origin, was losing its appeal among Americans, who had indicated they would fight the English rather than give up their claim to all territory south of the 54th parallel in the Northwest. But the best evidence of Cartwright's inventive genius was his placing the men at their positions on the diamond (which have remained almost exactly the same ever since) and his setting the distance between bases at 90 feet. He was exactly, uncannily right. The result was a succession of close plays at first base.

Cartwright's innovation meant the beginning of lightning-fast team play, the development of the art of the shortstop and first basemen and the stricter policing of games by umpires. The latter became suddenly important because of the closeness of plays, but their effect was to bring order into the contests in all respects.

There had been many other games involving bases and balls before 1845 (some were even called baseball). A crudely defined game known as town ball, derived from the ancient English sport of rounders, had attained some popularity in New York and New England. (The New England version, with bases arranged in a U pattern and the batter's position entirely separate, was called the Massachusetts game.) But all of these primitive exercises were static and aimless, and impossible to codify. Only after Cartwright's revolutionary innovations did the game ignite general excitement. Alexander Cartwright had invented baseball—in the same sense that the Wright brothers (and not Leonardo da Vinci) had invented the airplane, and Thomas A. Edison (and not Benjamin Franklin) had invented the electric light.

But who was Alexander Cartwright? You can read every work on baseball ever published and glean only a few sentences, most of them inaccurate, about this founding father. He is variously described in standard reference books (if he is mentioned at all) as an engineer, a surveyor, a draftsman, a New York City fireman. His father was a maritime surveyor, he was a volunteer fireman and some of his best friends sold fire insurance, but his trade, originally, was banking.

Alexander Cartwright was a big man. He stood 6' 2" and weighed 210 pounds. He had dark hair, dark eyes and was considered an excellent athlete. By 1845 he had been married for three years to Eliza Ann Van Wie of Albany, and he was prospering. He lived in a house on Eighth Street just off Fifth Avenue. He earned a good living as a teller in the Union Bank on Wall Street. The cashier there, and his superior officer, was Daniel Ebbets, an ancestor of Charles Hercules Ebbets, who, half a century later, became the owner of the Brooklyn Dodgers and laid out Ebbets Field in Brooklyn. Like Ebbets, most of Cartwright's friends were either in banking or insurance on Wall Street and they were all sportsmen.

So delighted by the new rules were the Murray Hill sandlotters that by September of 1845 a group of Cartwright's social peers—and a very few who were not—eagerly accepted his proposal that they establish a club of baseball players, to be called the Knickerbockers. Their idea was that a baseball club should be an association of gentlemen amateurs, much like the Marylebone Club that had made cricket the national game of England. Those Knickerbockers of 1845, the first organized baseball club, eventually played the first recorded match game with another team, the New York Club, on June 19, 1846.

Although he was the team's best player at several positions, Cartwright volunteered to act as umpire (as we shall see in a moment, this was disastrous for the Knicks). In that capacity he enforced baseball's first fine, a 6¢ levy for swearing. A drawing of an antediluvian encounter at Elysian Fields in the resort town of Hoboken, N.J., still exists, as well as an observer's description of the first game, "played under perfect skies" as "lady visitors sat under a canvas pavilion to protect their alabaster complexions from the sun."

The Knickerbockers took the field in a uniform of blue pantaloons, white flannel shirts and straw hats, an outfitting that was later modified to include mohair caps and patent leather belts. The New York Club beat the Knicks 23–1. (The idea of the nine inning game was not originated until some years later. Matches at this time ended with the inning in which a team had gone over 21 runs, or "aces.")

Scores of other ball clubs sprang up. Long Island workmen formed the Pastime Club; policemen organized the Manhattans; barkeeps the Phantoms; schoolteachers the Metropolitans; dairymen the Pocahontas Club. Already there were fans, called cranks, which is what losing managers still call them.

Cartwright's game did not instantly replace all other forms. There is a story that as late as the 1890s, when Rube Waddell first entered league ball, he tried to "soak"—throw at—a base runner. When the umpire remonstrated with him for this unseemly attack on an opponent, Rube protested, "That's out, where I come from."

The Civil War only propagated the game. Many Southern boys learned baseball in Union prison camps, and it has been reported that once a pause was called on the front lines to allow for a contest between Northern and Southern troops. Baseball spread west. In 1866 Peverelly's *Book of American Pastimes* (which still credited the Knickerbockers as "the nucleus of the now great American game of Base Ball, so popular in all parts of the United States, than which there is none more manly or health-giving") already mentioned a Frontier Club at Fort Leavenworth, Kans.

In 1868 Harry Wright, one of the best of the early players, reorganized an amateur club called the Cincinnati Red Stockings as the first team to play openly for money. By 1903 there were some 400 men earning fame and a fair living by playing baseball on 16 teams in two major leagues, and there were 19 minor leagues. Not a one could have told you who Alexander Cartwright was.

So completely had Cartwright vanished from the annals of baseball—the most documented of all American sports—that by the time of his death in 1892 not even an obituary in agate type appeared in *Sporting Life*, the baseball bible of the period. Reach's baseball chronology, which detailed the minutest events day by day, instead had a nice note on the passing of good old Joe Blong.

Cartwright's contribution became further obscured as a result of a report made by the Mills Commission, formed in 1904 to determine the origin of baseball. It was organized by Abraham G. Mills, who had been third president of the National League, and was a close friend of Albert Spalding, a superb pioneer professional player and the founder of the sporting goods firm. Henry Chadwick, the first sportswriter to cover baseball, had written a historical sketch in which he traced its origins to the old English game of rounders, and Spalding hated the idea that any part of the sport might have started outside the United States. The mission of the Mills Commission was to destroy that notion. It was made up of seven men. Among them were Mills himself and two oldtime players who had become manufacturers of baseball equipment, Al Reach and George Wright.

The most interesting member of the commission, and the man who could have done most to set the record straight, was Wright, who had played ball in New York in the 1860s and unquestionably was familiar with the older men who had played with Cartwright. In the 1880s, when his playing days were over, he headed the Boston club in the old Union Association, and founded the sporting goods firm of Wright & Ditson.

Among many other prejudices, Mills hated the Union Association. He called it an organization of deadbeats and played-out bums. When Augustus Busch of the brewery company backed the St. Louis club in the Union Association in 1883, Mills sneered that the new circuit was floating on beer money. Another source of chagrin was that the Union Association teams played with Wright & Ditson instead of Spalding baseballs. But by 1904 the Union Association had disappeared, and one would think that Wright, a wealthy manufacturer who was venerated as the grand old man of baseball, could hardly have been ignored.

There is no evidence, however, that George Wright ever attended a meeting of the Mills Commission. For that matter, there is no evidence that the commission ever held a meeting of all its members. Wright had become interested in golf, laying out the first course in Boston, and one of the first in the U.S. He had publicly declared that tennis was a better sport than baseball; two of his sons were national champions. He was an elegant, worldly traveler, interested in music and the theater and a golf-playing crony of millionaires at Palm Beach. Perhaps he was never consulted by Mills; perhaps he declined to participate.

In any case, whatever historical material the Mills Commission had assembled was destroyed in a fire that burned the office of the American Sports Publicity Company. Mills issued the report personally in 1907, and he was the only person to sign it. The report concluded that baseball was a purely American sport, not derived from rounders, and that the method of playing it had been devised by General Abner Doubleday at Cooperstown in 1839.

This document was a classic example of manufactured history. The report incorporated the uncorroborated ramblings of an octogenarian, Abner Graves, whose dubious claim to baseball fame was that at one time he lived in Cooperstown. Graves claimed that some 68 years earlier "Doubleday improved Town Ball to limit the number of players, as many were hurt in collisions."

GENERAL DOUBLEDAY, who had died in 1893, made an almost perfect figurehead, apart from the fact that there was no record that he ever had anything to do with baseball. Handsome, distinguished, he was the holder of a heroic Civil War record that dated from Fort Sumter, where he was credited with firing the first Union shot. He was also an excellent writer and a commanding public figure. It is unlikely that even the Mills Commission would have made up the story of his part in baseball out of whole cloth, but at most he could be credited with a youthful interest in the game and with having encouraged sports among the troops. In all General Doubleday's extensive writings, including his memoirs, there is not a single reference to baseball.

Why did Cartwright disappear so quickly from the annals of baseball? The answer lies in American folk history. To rediscover the historical Cartwright one must go back to January 1848, when gold was found in California. Within the space of one turn of John Sutter's mill wheel the placid postrevolutionary society of 19th century America was churned by greed into a great lunge westward for gold and glory. By fall rumors were spreading in New York, and in December of that year President James K. Polk made the news official in his State of the Union message. "The supply is very large," he said.

Cartwright, who had gone into the stationery business with his brother Alfred De Forest Cartwright and by this time was the father of a son and two daughters, was doing well, but he got caught up in the fever, too, and soon was making plans. The brothers sold their business. Alfred would sail for San Francisco by Cape Horn. Alexander would go by land with a party of 11. While others were mesmerized by thoughts of instant wealth, Alexander Cartwright went as a man with capital to invest. By all accounts, he was the reverse of calculating. He was sociable, hearty, devoted to his old friends, ingenious and inventive, but without ambition to profit from the things he devised. He started west for adventure and became, along the way, a Johnny Appleseed of baseball, proselytizing recruits to the game all the way from Hoboken to Honolulu.

"It took him 163 days to travel from Newark, N.J., to San Francisco," Bruce Cartwright Jr. wrote in 1938 in an attempt to restore recognition to his grand-father, a project that gained inadequate notice, partly because of Bruce Jr.'s own death soon after. "He walked the whole distance [from Pittsburgh west]. Whenever they rested and had enough people to form two baseball nines, they played 'baseball,' according to his letters to old Knickerbockers."

There had existed in Honolulu a diary along with notes kept by Cartwright of his journey and even an original ball used by the Knickerbockers, brought west by him as a memento. Bruce Jr. noted that his grandfather "told peo-ple in Honolulu that he taught people to play baseball at nearly every stop of his journey across the plains" and that "it was comical to see mountain men and Indians playing the game."

Scattered old sources can be found in Hawaii that refer to Alexander Cartwright having taught the game to "enthusiastic saloonkeepers and miners, to Indians and white settlers along the way" and "at nearly every frontier town and Army post where his wagon train visited." A secondary source mentions the New Yorkers "laughing as they watched the converts to the game attempt to imitate their own grace and skill with the bat and ball, such as catching the ball with the hands cupped and allowing the hands to 'give' with the catch." Another source declares, perhaps apoc-ryphally, that one such match was interrupted by Indian attack.

Unfortunately, Bruce Cartwright Sr., Cartwright's son, burned the diary be-cause it contained information "potentially damaging to prominent people in California and Hawaii." Before he set match to the manuscript, however, an-other son, Alexander Cartwright III, did copy out of the diary those parts that he considered of historical interest. But, more unfortunate still, few of these concern baseball, despite the fact that Alexander III was a lover of the game.

Bruce Jr. sent a copy of the notes, along with his own accompanying narrative to the Hall of Fame in Cooperstown, but by 1968 it was nowhere to be found. The Cartwright descendants had all died or left Hawaii, and considerable tracking was required to establish that great-grandson William Edward Cartwright was alive and trying to popularize a new sport called ski bobbing.

William Cartwright *did* have the last remaining copy of Bruce Cartwright Jr.'s version of the journal and would send it along "as soon as my wife, Anne, can type a copy." He added casually, "My son, Alexander Joy Cartwright IV, is following in his great-great-grandfather's footsteps as a member of the 'Indians' team of the Rincon Valley Little League. He is quite good, too."

Even incomplete, Cartwright's journal turned out to be a remarkable document. Baseball seemed new, alive and exciting then. How much so can be judged from a contemporary description: "It is a game which is peculiarly suited to the American temperament and disposition; the nine innings are played in the brief space of two and one half hours, or less. From the moment the first striker takes his position and poises his bat, it has an excitement and vim about it, until the last hand is put out in the ninth inning. There is no delay or suspense about it, from beginning to end; and even if one feels disposed to leave the ground, temporarily, he will generally waive his desire, especially if it is a close contest, from fear of missing some good point or clever effort of the trial."

Alexander Cartwright's party left Newark on March 1, 1849. In San Francisco, Cartwright met his brother Alfred, who had made better time sailing around Cape Horn. Alfred wrote to his wife, "Alick arrived . . . in good health after a very long and trying journey. They lost some of their mules and broke their waggons, and were obliged to abandon most of their truck, so that Alick says, 'They had what they had upon their backs, and a cup and a spoon apiece left.' Now where do you think he has gone to? Why, to the Sandwich Islands."

So he had, and for a time he absorbed himself completely in business in Honolulu—ocean trade, ship chandlering and banking. Cartwright became a diplomat for five Hawaiian rulers, from Kamehameha IV to Queen Liliuokalani, and handled the personal financial affairs of the monarchy. He became one of Hawaii's leading figures, founding the Honolulu Fire Department (which he served as chief from 1850 to '59), Queen's Hospital, the American Seamen's Institute, the Honolulu library, Masonic Lodge 21, Bishop & Co. (now the First National Bank of Hawaii), the Honolulu Rapid Transit Bus Company and the Commercial and Pacific clubs. Before her death, Queen Emma designated her close friend Cartwright—and his "heirs and assigns forever"—executors of her estate.

But all through these years, Cartwright was also thinking of baseball. His family joined him in 1851 and the next year he and his youngest son measured out by foot in Makiki Park the dimensions of Hawaii's first baseball field. Rebitten by the bug, he organized teams and taught the game all over the islands. By 1900, eight years after his death, a regular baseball school and club teams were in full operation.

In 1938 Honolulu changed the name of Makiki Park to Cartwright Park and celebrated Cartwright Day. Babe Ruth paid a visit to Nuuanu Cemetery to place leis on Cartwright's grave. In 1939 a plaque was dedicated at City Hall, a street was renamed and a Cartwright Series was inaugurated by the Hawaii Baseball League.

To this day Hawaii, where baseball began before its introduction in some parts of the mainland, claims to have more players per capita than any other state. The Hawaii Islanders, though usually low in the Pacific Coast League standings, are always high among the minor league attendance leaders. And nowhere in the world can one find more colorful and racially heterogeneous baseball than in the state where vendors hawk sashimi, saimin, crackseed, laulau and poi along with their peanuts, popcorn and Crackerjack.

Forgotten though he may have been on the mainland, Cartwright was scarcely underestimated in the Islands, as may be judged from this Honolulu newspaper clipping, brittle with age: "His name should be revered by posterity for all time," the unsigned writer said, "and be emblazoned on the tablets of fame somewhere near that of George Washington, the Father of his Country. Mr. Cartwright was the Father of the National Pastime. . . . Oldtimers here say that when the feebleness of age prevented him from participating actively, he occupied the seat of honor at all the matches and was always an enthusiastic rooter."

After mentioning that the original ball was still in existence, the paper continued with what it claimed were old residents' recollections of things Cartwright had told them but what in fact were pirated portions of a series of articles by Will Irwin on the origins of baseball that had appeared in *Collier's Weekly* magazine.

"It dawned upon the pitchers after a while that they could deceive the batters by certain twirls of the ball. . . . In 1848 they changed the method of putting a man out on bases to the present rule—'Catch him out at first, touch him out at second, third and home.' At this juncture the runners took to sliding bases to avoid being touched out. The batters learned that better results could be obtained by making frequent short hits than constantly slugging for a home run."

The 1850s ball, the paper (and *Collier's*) reported, was so lively that one dropped from a housetop would rebound to the roof. "The first baseball manufacturers were shoemakers. They sewed on the covers in quarter sections shaped like the petals of a tulip. The seams were always splitting and bunching. The size and weight of the ball together with its rough and uneven surface, caught without gloves, battered the players' hands all out of shape, and the game was denounced by the New York *Herald* as . . . barbarous.

"As soon as the war was over Mr. Salzman, who took the game from New York to Boston, went to Charleston, South Carolina, and the game took a firm rooting there. Savannah then 'caught' onto it, and in 1867 sent a team up to Charleston, accompanied by a bunch of rooters and a band of music, to play for the baseball championship of the South. The blacks, reveling in their release from bondage, swarmed about the sidelines and hurled epithets at the white men on the diamond. The players charged the Negroes with their bats and a regiment of soldiers had to be called out to quell the riot."

Cartwright occasionally wrote to the old Knickerbockers. In one letter, dated April 21, 1858, he asked, "What are my old friends doing. . . . How flourish the Knickerbockers?" The Knickerbockers did not flourish for long—1858 was the year the first national association of baseball clubs was organized, and the Knicks were defeated in their attempt to gain control of it.

Another letter that survives is one written by Cartwright in 1865 to De Bost, who had captained the Knickerbockers: "Dear old Knickerbockers, I hope the Club is still kept up, and that I shall someday meet again with them on the pleasant fields of Hoboken. Charlie, I have in my possession the original ball with which we used to play on Murray Hill. Many is the pleasant chase I have had after it on Mountain and Prairie, and many an equally pleasant one on the sunny plains of 'Hawaii nei. . . . ' Sometimes I have thought of sending it home to be played for by the Clubs, but I cannot bear to part with it, it is so linked in with cherished home memories. . . ."

WILLIAM EDWARD CARTWRIGHT now lives in Missoula, Mont., where he will be host to the world ski-bob championships next year, but at the time of the search for his great-grandfather Alexander he was living 50 miles north of San Francisco, high in the dry, fecund hills above Santa Rosa, with a German-born wife, Anne, charmingly earnest in her hospitality; a daughter, Anna; and 13-year-old Alexander Joy Cartwright IV. Bill Cartwright is a bluff, amiable man with a constant supply of cigars in a sports-shirt pocket. He takes pride in showing his treasures, remarkable heirlooms that speak of his family's unusual past.

Bill Cartwright has donated most of his ancestor's papers to the Honolulu Archives, but he does retain some portraits of Alexander, notably one showing him as he was when he left New York. But no one has the original Knickerbocker ball. "My father saw it once," Cartwright remembers, "but when Grandmother died the family lived in a hotel for a time, and the ball was definitely lost."

Young Alexander Joy Cartwright IV, although he likes to play baseball (he is a Giants fan), has other interests, too. "I just thought I'd try butterfly collecting, and the first day I caught 14," he explains, his eyes lighting up as he begins a tour of a bedroom walled with mounted specimens. "This blue one is a *Morpho polyphemus*, and this is an *Ornithoptera*—that means birdwing, because it looks like that for protection. Did you know most butterflies have something in their bodies that tastes yickity, and birds know it by instinct? I'd like to be a lepidopterist when I grow up. . . . "

When Alex's lecture tour was finished and it was time to leave, Bill remembered a couple more items of interest. "We have a nugget of gold Great-grandfather picked up in California," he said, displaying an astonishingly large lump of metal. "Right off the ground." The visitor exclaimed over the nugget and remarked what a fine thing it was to hand on to future generations. "Yes," Cartwright said. "I just hope Alex doesn't hock it to buy more butterflies."

"Oddly," he continued, "my grandfather never cared at all for baseball—only horses and women—and I've never played on a team myself. I was more a football player.

"The San Francisco Seals—Lefty O'Doul was their manager then—visited Hawaii in 1949, and when they heard about me they invited me to see them at the Maui Grand Hotel. 'Are you really the great-grandson of the man who laid out the diamond and all?' somebody asked. 'Yes,' I said. 'Have you ever played ball yourself?' somebody else asked. 'Yes,' I said. "What position?' 'Oh, fullback and quarterback.' Lefty O'Doul just roared. 'Get him out of here!' he said." So all the San Francisco Seals threw Alexander Cartwright's great-grandson bodily out of the room.

With Bill Cartwright's help, the visitor found the only other surviving descendant of Alexander Cartwright Jr., granddaughter Mary Check. A sweet and pungent lady in her 70s living in San Francisco south of Golden Gate Park, Mrs. Check suggests that this scarcity of kin may be another reason Cartwright's contribution was so long unknown: "Two daughters died, one of scarlet fever, and one son was poisoned."

Mrs. Check has a surprise—the actual old notebook containing an account of Cartwright's journey to California. William believes this to be the extract from Alexander's diary copied by his son, Alexander III; Mary believes it to be some part or version of the original. In either event, it contains some additional material, including a list of animals seen—"Prairie Hens, plenty; Plover, millions; Brown Wolves, plenty; Buffalo, 20,000"—and also Indians. ("We have passed through, and had intercourse with the following Tribes of Indians: Shawnee, Caws or Kansas, Delaware, Pottawattomies, Pawnees, Sioux, Crows.") "I think this is the original journal," Mrs. Check says, "because the start of the trip to Hawaii is in the back."

Mary is the daughter of Alick's son Alexander III, the one who loved baseball. "Bruce didn't do anything but wear four-inch collars and gardenias in his buttonhole and his nose in the air," she says, "but my father played baseball constantly. They played without gloves, you know, and his fingers were all out of shape.

"We used to go to baseball games every Sunday. He took me before I could talk. I played baseball myself; any old position. I still follow the Giants and get mad at them. I used to cut school in the most polite way to watch the Seals. I had bands on my teeth, and I would go to the principal and tell him they hurt. We used to root for Truck Eagan, who was built like a truck and ran like one.

"Although Father was called Little Alick, he was 6' 4" and very heavy on his feet himself. He gave up playing when, one day, he planted himself on a base and his best friend ran into him, bounced off and broke a leg. Father said never again, and hung up his glove.

"Grandfather named me, but he died when I was six months old. Mother said he looked like Santa Claus, had a very keen sense of humor and just loved life. Father remembered his talking about how he scrawled out the first rules in a notebook balanced on his knee and how he fiddled around with baseball a little while in San Francisco."

When Mrs. Check had told all she knew of her grandfather and the visitor had finished the 7-Up she had provided, the visit—and the long search for Alexander Cartwright and his invention—seemed at an end. Mrs. Check accompanied her guest to the door.

"Oh, there is one other thing," she said. "My father remembered having cut up a baseball when he was a child to see what was in it. He got the only licking of his life for it. Years afterward, he often thought that that might have been the Knickerbocker ball, the original baseball."

❧

Still a Grand Old Game

BY ROGER KAHN

Touring the baseball world, the author of The Boys of Summer
found that the national pastime retained all its charms,
whether played in suburbia, the Ozarks or at Chavez Ravine.

V ANDALS HAD SET FIRE TO THE GRASS. NO ONE KNEW HOW
they had gotten wet spring grass to burn or why anyone
wanted to set fire to a soft suburban meadow, but there
the ball field lay, grimy with ash on the 11th day of spring.
"It's all right," the boy said. "We can play anyway."

I was wearing red sneakers, a gift Lou Brock had offered along with a
lecture on quickness and traction and stealing bases. Brock's autograph is
stitched near the instep, and someone, noticing the name as I loped through
a softball game, once said, "Them sneakers have never moved so slow."
Still they are my present from a superb big-leaguer, and so a kind of totem.
I didn't want them dirtied with black ash.

"We'll get messed up," I said. "We can try again next weekend."

"We don't have visitation next weekend. Come on. Just pitch a few," he
said. Then seductively, "After that, I'll pitch, and you can hit."

His name is Roger, and he has a sturdy 12-year-old body and a passion-
ate excitement at being alive. "I'm studying the renaissance," he announced
recently as I was preparing papers for a tax audit.

"Good," I said. "The Renaissance. . . . Who was Michelangelo?"

"Wait," Roger cried. "Don't give me the answer. I know. Michelangelo put statues in the gardens of the Medici."

So, though we don't live together anymore, we can talk about the Renaissance. And we can play ball.

He hits lefthanded. We started working on that nine years ago, and now, as he took an open stance, he chattered directions. "Don't throw too hard. I haven't started working out yet. Don't throw curves. Let me get my swing grooved. O.K. Come on."

I began to throw high pitches at medium speed. Roger lunged. Four years with the Little League in Ridgefield, Conn. Four seasons under coaches who work for I.B.M. or sell insurance or pilot 727s, and nobody has taught him—or been able to teach him—that a good hitter does not lunge.

"Keep your head still," I said.

The boy's mouth tightened. He had not come to learn. He wanted to show me how far he could hit my pitching, swinging his own metal bat in his own way.

Very well, young man, I thought. Today, in the April cold, you'll get a lesson, whether you want it or not. Subject: He who lunges never hits .300.

I threw hard with an easy motion. Roger swung late. I threw easily with a big motion. He swung early. I tried to jam him, but the ball drifted inside toward his knees. Roger made a graceful arching leap. The ball skidded to the backstop. He lay face down, shaking on the earth.

I hurried to him. "Sorry. Sorry. You all right?"

He rolled over in the ash, blackening his jacket. He was shaking with defiant laughter. "You couldn't hurt me," he said.

We grinned, and at once the lesson was done. He had earned the right to pitches he could hit. Roger began scattering line drives. He looped a fly to center. There was no one to retrieve the ball but me. He bounced sharply through the middle. Another chore for an aging, chilly righthander. He lashed a high inside pitch clear to a ditch at the border of rightfield.

"Now we'll just play pepper," I said when I returned with the ball.

He insisted on borrowing my bat. Thirty-two ounces. A fat-barreled Ron Santo model. Either Roger did not know the rules of pepper, or he did not know how strong he has become. We stood 30 feet apart. I made a pepper toss. Roger whipped the big bat. The blackened baseball hurtled at my nose. I threw a glove up, deflected the ball and stumbled. Sitting on the charred grass, I remembered a transcendent reality of baseball. The ball is hard. It is something to fear. Forty years ago I learned that from my father in Brooklyn fields that have vanished under high-rises. Seventy years ago he learned that from his father on fields that have disappeared under slums. And now my son, in careless innocent excitement, has reinforced a family lesson as old as the century.

Roger came toward me slowly. The Ron Santo model seemed almost as big as he. His face was white. "Dad, I didn't mean to hit a liner at your face."

Getting up, glad to still have my nose, I fall back on an old John Wayne-Humphrey Bogart gambit. "Gosh, kid, I didn't know you cared."

"Sure I care," Roger said, and he put an arm around my waist. We started hiking to a distant house where splits of maple crackled in a fireplace. There we could sit before the fire and talk baseball.

What would I tell him? Of Stan Musial, most gentle of athletes, whose swing was like a viper's lash. Or of the day when Early Wynn brushed back Mickey Mantle, who bounced up and hit a single. Wynn was so furious that before he threw another pitch, he went into a careful pick-off move. Then he hit Mantle with his throw, knocking him to the ground alongside first base. "That S.O.B. is so mean he'd like to knock you down in the dugout," Mantle complained. Or about Victor Pellot Power of Arecibo, Puerto Rico, whom the Yankees traded in 1954 for announced reasons that are not worth remembering. The real reasons were that Power was black and Latin and reputedly liked the company of white women. When I saw Power in the hilly Puerto Rican town of Caguas several weeks ago, he demonstrated that the Yankees had been correct. He liked white women well enough to have married a compact, smoldering blonde whose name is Ada. But in between, while the Yankees employed Joe Pepitone, erratic, libertine—but white—at first, Power, a solid .285 hitter, was indisputably the best fielder at that position in the American League. Seven times he won the Gold Glove.

Or would I merely tell him about my father, a teacher and an editor, who hit a baseball hard. Two months before his heart stopped, he was lining high drives to center on Monhegan Island off the coast of Maine. He was 52 and I was 24, but I could not hit a ball as far as he. No power. He had hoped I would grow taller and stand someday beside Jake Daubert and Zack Wheat, the heroes of his own sandlot days. Then he was dead, and the people who admired his eidetic memory and his understanding of the Renaissance told me how fine it must have been to grow up at his side and to talk seriously with him about serious things, such as the gardens of the Medici. I don't believe we ever did. We talked seriously (and joyously) about baseball. That was a serious thing, and that was enough.

You learn to leave some mysteries alone. At 28 I was susceptible to suggestions that I explain—not describe but explain—baseball in America. I published in small quarterlies. I addressed a Columbia seminar, and I developed a showy proficiency at responding to editors who asked me to "equate the game in terms of Americana."

Such phrases now bang against my brain like toothaches. I never look at the old pieces anymore, but I remember some generalizations I drew:

Baseball is not played against a clock. (But neither is tennis, golf or four-handed gin rummy.)

Baseball rules have barely changed across generations. (Neither have the rules of water polo.)

The ball field is a mystic creation, the Stonehenge of America. That is, the bases are a magic 90 feet apart. Think how often a batter is thrown out by half a step, compared to instances when he outruns a hit to shortstop. But artificial surfaces have lately changed the nature, if not the dimensions, of the diamond. A ground ball at Riverfront Stadium moves much faster than the same grounder bouncing on the honest grass of Wrigley Field. Yet at last look, baseball in Cincinnati seemed to be surviving. Batters there are also thrown out by half a step.

Suppose the bases had been set 80 or 86 feet apart. The fielders simply would have positioned themselves differently, and a ground ball to short would still be a ground ball to short, 6–3 in everybody's scorebook.

I do believe this: baseball's inherent rhythm, minutes and minutes of activity erupting into seconds of frenzied action, matches an attribute of the American character. But no existential proclamation, or any tortured neo-Freudianism, or any outburst of popular sociology, not even—or least of all—my own, explains baseball's lock on the American heart.

You learn to let some mysteries alone, and when you do, you find they sing themselves.

A TOWN WHERE SOMEONE DRIVES A KAISER

Alongside the two-lane blacktop that crosses northeast Oklahoma, the land rolls bare and poor. Outside of villages called Broken Arrow and Chouteau lie shacks and rusty house trailers where survivors of the Cherokee Nation live in poverty. This is not farming country. It is hard, red, intractable soil that we have abandoned to the Indians.

Then, as the road crosses into Arkansas and into the village of Siloam Springs, a wonderland of pastureland abruptly appears. Siloam Springs is Wally Moon's domain. Wallace Wade Moon, late of the St. Louis Cardinals and the Los Angeles Dodgers. Now head baseball coach at John Brown University. Enrollment: 550. Team batting average: .362.

On the telephone Moon said he had a few more minutes of desk work to do before he could meet me. Waiting for him, I asked the lady behind the front desk of the East Gate Motel to explain the relative prosperity of Benton Country, Ark.

"It's a little embarrassing," she said. Behind her spectacles, her eyes were pale and pleasant.

"How so?"

"Chicken droppings," the lady said. "I guess that's the best way to put it." Then she explained. Northwest Arkansas had been as poor as northeast Oklahoma until after World War II, when some men decided to try chicken farming in the Ozark foothills. "That went pretty good, you might say," the lady continued, "but it sure left a lot of chicken droppings. They smelled. So the farmers spread the stuff across the fields and hills, and after a few years the soil got a darn sight richer. Real good grass grew. After that, some other people brought in cattle, and the cattle grazed good and times got even better. Not that we don't have some poor, but Benton County's doing fine right now.

"Truth is"—the lady's eyes darted to make sure we were alone—"the economy here is built on chicken. . . . "

"Yes, ma'am," I said.

Moon had talked rather less of chickens and more of a high sky and gentle streams when we had shared dinner after an oldtimers' game the year before. Moon, outfielder and batsman, played 12 major league seasons during the 1950s and '60s. He wore his hair short and his thick black eyebrows met, and he had the look of a Confederate cavalry captain. But he was a decent, tolerant man, with a master's degree from Texas A&M, wholly dedicated to squeezing a base hit out of each turn at bat.

The Cardinals called him up in 1954, just as they were selling Enos Slaughter, a portly, combative legend, to the Yankees. Two days before Moon broke in, the *St. Louis Post-Dispatch* published a front-page picture of Slaughter weeping with grief into a large white handkerchief.

Moon came from Arkansas delta country, and the first time he saw a major league game, he was playing in it. The fans in St. Louis were, at best, belligerently neutral. They loved the legend Moon had been hired to replace. In his first time at bat in his first major league game, Moon pulled a home run over the rightfield pavilion of old Busch Stadium and into Grand Boulevard. That year Slaughter batted .248 for New York. Moon hit .304 and became Rookie of the Year.

Five years later with the Dodgers, he perfected his opposite-field stroke. The Dodgers played in the Los Angeles Coliseum then, and the leftfield screen, the players said, was only a medium spit away from home. Moon hit 19 home runs, most of them to left, tied for the league lead with 11 triples and hit 26 doubles, and a Dodger team of shreds and patches established itself in Los Angeles by winning the World Series from the White Sox.

When Moon's skills eroded, he and his wife Bettye debated city and country life. They had five children, and he could earn more money in a city. But Wally remembered the good days with his father Bert, hunting and hiking through the woods of Benton County. There was an offer to try Benton County again as head coach at John Brown, a small Christian Evangelical school.

The Moons live in a rambling ranch set on 200 acres three miles east of Siloam, a town with an artists' colony, no daily newspaper, a little light industry and springs that were once thought to possess medicinal properties. A giant red oak towers over Moon's house, and inside there is a cheerful babble of children. Wally Joe, husky and 23, writes free-form poetry and studies toward a master's degree in physical education. The four daughters, ages 12 to 20, are bright, mannerly, attractive. Their interests range from baton twirling to Clementi piano sonatas. Moon said grace, and we dined sumptuously on Arkansas grass-fed beef. Then, the old-fashioned way, the ladies went about their chores, while Moon and I retired to a sunroom crowded with pictures and trophies. On one wall Moon glowers from an old SPORTS ILLUSTRATED cover that has a caption announcing: THE SPIRIT OF THE GASHOUSE GANG.

"Actually, the spunkiest guys of all were those 1959 Dodgers," Moon said. "Not the best. Some of the old Brooklyn Dodgers on the way down. Fellows like Koufax and Drysdale on the way up. But I never played on a club that wanted to win more." He had admired Walt Alston, Moon said, and he had roomed with Koufax and told Sandy that he was tipping his pitches. But those were old times, and Wally had a new story to tell.

"Do I look tired?" he said.

"You sound subdued."

"We had a tournament doubleheader across the mountains in Pine Bluff yesterday. We had to win both games, and we won them big, 12–4 and 24–8. When we finished, it was 8:20 and only one restaurant in town was open. Only one waitress was working there. By the time we all got fed, it was past 11. There's no team bus. We have no budget for that. We travel in station wagons and cars. I was driving the lead car, and coming back across the Ozarks, we hit fog. I got home, still in uniform, at 5 a.m."

The John Brown Golden Eagles come from towns like Texarkana, Texas, Paducah, Ky., and Hurley, Mo. To a man, they played Little League ball and enjoyed it. To a man, they ache to play in the major leagues. "I'm not looking for a bonus," one of Moon's best players said. "If I had the money, I'd pay *them* to sign me."

Most of the players are on scholarship. They address Moon as "Coach," often in the deferential way a man in pain says "Doctor." Coach Moon imposes rules. No beanballs. Bench-jockeying is permitted, but within limits. Moon is a devout Methodist, and none of his players "may blaspheme the name of the Lord."

"As a coach, my strongest point is batting," Moon said. "I teach them to hold their heads still and keep their bats back. Strike zone? They're not ready for that yet, and I don't believe in teaching too many things at once. Just develop a quick, compact swing. If I have a weak point, or a point where I lack confidence, that would be pitching." He looked across a darkening field.

"You're still learning baseball, aren't you?"

"I'm still learning, and I'm 46. Man, this is a difficult sport to learn."

The next afternoon John Brown played a twilight game against the University of Tulsa, which has a student body of 6,000. The Eagles use aluminum bats, which Moon says saves $300 a year. They take batting practice without a cage. There is no budget for a batting cage either. The infield is dirt, not grass. "What's the name of this ball park?" I asked Moon.

"It has no name. We call it 'the field.' "

The fans sat on wooden bleachers and on grassy banks. "A kind of Greek theater," Bettye Moon says. Two major league scouts sat among the crowd. Both Fred Hawn of the Cardinals and Milt Bolling of the Boston Red Sox had come to see Moon's shortstop, Chuck Gardner, a junior who was batting .443.

The Eagles warmed up smartly with quick infield play. The outfielders, particularly Randy Rouse, showed strong young arms. Moon started Ron

Rhodes, a junior lefthander who had won eight straight games, and his team jumped ahead when Gardner doubled home one run in the first inning and two more in the second. But Tulsa came back when Bruce Humphrey slammed a 380-foot home run over the cyclone fence in centerfield, and Tulsa kept coming.

These teams were good. Unlike college teams in the northern tier of states, they started working outdoors in February. Each club had already played 40 games. But they are collegians, and collegians make mistakes. By the first inning, Tulsa had drawn ahead, 6–5. Gardner led off with a single, a murderous drive that hurtled past the pitcher's left ear. A sacrifice moved him to second. He was the tying run. Then Rouse grounded to shortstop, and Gardner tried to go to third.

That never works. The rule is as old as baseball. A runner cannot advance from second to third on a ball hit to the left side of the infield. Gardner was out by 10 feet, and when Dave Stockstill blinked at a fastball, knee high on the outside corner, the Golden Eagles had been beaten.

Moon's lips were pressed together. He does not like to lose. "You can never advance on that play, Wally," I said.

He shook his head and spat, then looked less fierce. "But the kid wanted to score so damn bad."

Lightning interrupted the next day's workout, and a siren wailed steadily in downtown Siloam Springs. "That's a tornado alert," Moon said. "Don't worry till it warbles. A warbling siren means a funnel's been sighted." We repaired to the Quonset hut that is Moon's clubhouse, and he began to tell his 24 players about the previous day's game.

He had spoken privately with Gardner, and now he had more general things to talk about. "My analysis is that we got beat because they wanted to win more than we did," he said. "It wasn't a tournament game for us. We had a hard trip the other day. But that doesn't make any difference. No matter how you feel, when you walk through that gate and onto the field, you've got to kick yourself in the butt. I can tell you from personal experience that across a major league season your butt ends up pretty sore. But you've got to do it.

"Now, Ron," he said to Rhodes, "you remember when first base was open and I went out to the mound and told you to pitch around the hitter?"

Rhodes nodded gravely.

"In the majors I would have told you to deliberately walk him. That was the play. But we're here to learn, and I want you to learn what I mean by pitching around a hitter. In that situation, with a runner in scoring position, the hitter is eager. Start him with a fastball all the way in on his belly. He's so eager he may swing, but he's not going to hurt you off a pitch like that. Then when you curve him, get it in the dirt. Not just low. *In the dirt.* He's still eager. If he walks, you aren't hurt, and if he swings at a bouncing curve, you aren't hurt either. But you gave him a pitch he could hit, and he hit it and it scored a run, and that's what we lost by. One run.

"For you hitters, look at that situation in reverse. Control your eagerness. That's a mental discipline. There's a lot of mental discipline in the game. But you've got nothing to be ashamed of. Tulsa is a good club. They wanted the game more than you did, and they got it."

Rain beat fiercely on the iron roof. "Do you have any questions?" Moon asked me.

"I'd like to ask how many of you gentlemen hope to play in the major leagues?" The boys, 18 to 21 years old, looked at one another. Then slowly, shyly, all 24 of the Golden Eagles raised their hands.

"How many have a chance?" I asked Moon after the players had left.

"Probably none," Moon said. "The shortstop is good, but he's 21 years old. I've seen another college shortstop just about as good and he's 18. A big three years. Then you figure beyond all the college shortstops, there are all the boys already in the minors playing 140 games a year, kids from all over the country and Latin America, and you realize what the odds are against Chuck Gardner. He'll play minor league ball. So will a few of the others. But most of them will go on from here to teach and coach. I want them to enjoy the game, but I want them to learn technique and conduct and discipline as well." Moon stood up. "Maybe they can pass on what I give them to others."

We went to a Rotary meetings then. We stood to pledge allegiance, and we sang *America the Beautiful* under the fervid conducting of a doctor named John Moose. I remembered morning chapels in my grade school and how every afternoon we played baseball on a gravelly field and how we sometimes admitted that our dream was to play baseball in the majors. (None of us did.)

For all the fresh, clean-shaven faces of Moon's Golden Eagles, the trip to Siloam Springs was like a voyage into the past. Leaving town I saw a sign that read:

GUITAR LESSONS
PIANO TUNING
GOSPEL PIANO

Then I passed someone driving a yellow Kaiser car. I believe they stopped making Kaisers in 1955.

THE FRANCHISE BUSINESS

The man who owns the Los Angeles Dodgers did not like *The Boys of Summer*, a book I wrote celebrating baseball, life, the courage to be new—and certain men who spent a decade winning pennants for the Brooklyn Dodgers. A Los Angeles morning had broken summery and dense, light smog hovering under a yellow sky. Walter Francis O'Malley, a compelling 73-year-old paterfamilias who mixes Quaker parsimony, pagan ferocity and Irish-Catholic charm, looked up darkly from sheaves of correspondence. He did not say "Hello." He did not say "How are you?" Instead he growled in a Tammany bass, "This time are you going to write something positive?"

At such moments, I long to utter an infinite retort, at once deflating the critic and placing my published work beyond criticism lower than Ruskin's. But I am not any good at that. I am good at making plodding responses and later getting angry.

"It sold some copies," I said.

O'Malley waved his cigar as though it were a scepter. "Several stories involving Fresco Thompson and Buzzie Bavasi were unfortunate," he said. "They were so unfortunate that I asked my son Peter what in the world has gotten into our Brooklyn friend."

Ah, but we argued long ago in Brooklyn, too. O'Malley is a consistent man, and he has consistently believed that the first function of the sporting press is to sell tickets to Dodger games. I looked out a window. Dodger Stadium, loveliest of ball parks, had been swept and scrubbed clean of the litter and gum deposited by 52,469 customers the night before. "What a pleasant office you have," I said.

"Not so pleasant," O'Malley said. "Outside my window there's a groundkeeper standing in centerfield with a hose, and I wonder, if he's going to use a hose why the hell did I put $600,000 into an underground sprinkler system."

"Why *does* he use a hose?"

"Because we brought him out from Brooklyn, and he used a hose there," the owner of the Dodgers announced impatiently.

O'Malley and I go back four decades, not only to a single borough, but to a single neighborhood and a single private school. "You know," O'Malley said, mingling sentiment and blarney, "I take pride in being the man who handed you a diploma when you graduated from Froebel Academy. You certainly looked at things more positively then."

Like Joseph Kennedy or F.D.R., O'Malley is an indefatigable one-upman. Like them he is a master of his trade. That trade is major league baseball.

"You want to know about our success out here," O'Malley said. "First, we're not a syndicate. The Dodgers are a family corporation. Second, we don't have absentee ownership. Third, the chairman of the board, with whom you're sitting and who isn't getting any younger, comes to work at 8:30 on the morning after a night game. When the board chairman shows up that early, the rest of the staff tends to do the same."

O'Malley approaches me with suspicion because I write, as I approach him carefully because he criticizes. Still, Fred Claire, the Dodger vice president for public relations, set up a schedule of interviews that taxed my ability to assimilate and caused one cassette recorder to expire.

Al Campanis, the vice president of player personnel, opened a drawer and showed me his private treasury. Fourteen transcriptions of Branch Rickey on baseball. No one studied baseball more passionately than Rickey, and every Dodger employee now hears, directly or indirectly, from the source.

"We wouldn't want this stuff to get around," Campanis said. Then, with a Byzantine flourish, he showed me some extrapolation. "Thou shalt not steal," Rickey said. "I mean defensively. On offense, indeed thou shalt steal and thou must."

Amid such platitudes lies baseball gold. According to Rickey, the change of pace is a magnificent pitch. Instruct young pitchers in the art of changing speeds. But first let them master the fastball and control. Teach changing speeds in Double A or Triple A. On tape Rickey suggests that they will have gained confidence and sophistication at that level. Look for ballplayers who run and hit with power. Neither speed nor distance hitting can be taught. Consider the present and, simultaneously, plan for the future. Luck is the residue of design. Once Rickey assembled his staff and cried out in the voice of Job, "I stand on a cliff. On the edge of an abyss. I lose my footing. I stumble toward the yawning gates of hell. One man can save me. Only one. I ask each of you, who is that man?" This meant the Dodger bullpen was uncertain and Rickey wanted a consensus on the best minor league reliever to call up. His name was Phil Haugstad. He won none and lost one.

In the dugout Walter Alston reviewed his 22 years with the Dodgers. "How long will I keep managing? It's always been a one-year contract: I wouldn't stay anyplace where I wasn't wanted. I can teach school, you know. Used to do that in Ohio. But I'll make my decision next October. I make it every October. Meanwhile, I have a delightful job."

Dixie Walker, the batting coach, instructed Steve Yeager, a good young catcher, with side comments to a relief pitcher and me. As a batting-practice pitcher threw, Walker chattered caressingly: "Think opposite field, Steve. Think other way. They're going to give you outside sliders, Steve. No one can pull them. Don't worry about the other, the inside stuff. Your hands are so quick, you'll pull everything there, the way Babe Ruth did. I played with Ruth."

Yeager popped three outside fastballs to right. Walker winced. Then he said, "I can't push him more. Ballplayers have changed. On the old Tigers, nobody told you anything. Only Charlie Gehringer—he wasn't a coach but a player—said I should go the other way."

"You think this guy is working?" the pitcher said.

"I think so," Walker said. "But if I push him too hard—it's this new generation—he'll work against me. Against you."

Tom Lasorda, the third-base coach, discoursed on imposing team spirit. "You know, there are guys like Bill Russell, our shortstop, who will get down on their knees at parties and say, 'I'm a Dodger; I love the Dodgers.' " Lasorda gazed into a glass of soda water. "I love the Dodgers. Cut my own veins, I'll bleed Dodger blue."

Steve Garvey, the first baseman, offered his theory on California crowds. "Friday night they're mad. They've worked a long hard week. Make some errors early on a Friday night and the people at Dodger Stadium crucify you. Saturday is date night. Medium. Sunday is easy. You can play real bad, but the fathers are out here with their sons. Nobody boos." Garvey touched his chin. "Monday and Tuesday nights you get the people who know baseball."

Dusty Baker, an outfielder fairly fresh from Atlanta, discussed a difference between the Dodgers and the Braves. "In Atlanta, you *hoped* to win. Out here, it's expected."

I had come to Los Angeles to consider the Dodgers for three days, I stayed for five. On each of the first two nights they drew over 50,000 as they split a series with the Reds. Then the Braves flew in. The Braves were playing the dreariest baseball extant. Still, Dodger crowds hovered around 30,000. Friday night brought the Houston Astros and Cap Night. Buy a ticket and you get a baseball cap worth about $1 for free. Once again attendance soared over 50,000.

The Dodgers are contenders, as they have been through most of Alston's three generations of Los Angeles teams. They run well, play tight defense, gamble, hit to right. Quite simply, the Dodgers, a good team, are this: the most valuable franchise in baseball.

The Dodgers win games. They make money. They are a rousing team to watch, and that all leads back to the 73-year-old man sitting in a glass-walled office and glowering at a distant figure costing him money behind a hose.

"We have been fortunate, obviously so," O'Malley said. "We hoped we knew what fans wanted in a stadium. Good parking. We could still have done more there. Reasonable prices. We held the line, not increasing prices at all for 18 seasons. We try to keep within the image of baseball as a daily event, so a fellow can afford to bring his wife or kids or grandparents. Our demographic image is the best in sport. I see them coming in with canes, walking sticks and wheelchairs, and I see the middle generation, and I see the kids. Everybody's getting a reasonably priced evening's entertainment. The kids mean that we're building future fans.

"We've stayed in contention. That's all anyone can do. We stay in contention, and we're the only team that ever did—or ever will—fly the World Series flag on the Atlantic and the Pacific coasts."

He looks very much as he did 20 years ago. Round face, round spectacles. Dark hair. The same incredible alternation in expression between patriarch and trial lawyer.

"If they had built you a ball park in Brooklyn, would you have stayed?"

"I've got to correct you there. You're falling into the same trap the others have. A boy from Froebel Academy should know better than that." The cigar waves. O'Malley shakes his head.

"I never asked them to build me a new park in Brooklyn. I said we would build it on taxable land with our own money. We had a site at Atlantic and Flatbush Avenues where the subways intersected. There's no place back there big enough for many parking lots, so my thought was that you'd dock your car in any subway station and come to the ball park for 15¢.

"Now there was a thing in New York. Bobby Wagner was the mayor. A nice man, not very strong. I knew his father, the Senator. Robert Moses was the real power in New York.

"We had a site, and a sports authority was set up to condemn the land we needed, but Moses blocked us. He had a site of his own bounded on one side by water, on another by a cemetery, on a third by a slum and on the fourth by a parkway, which meant that everyone going to our games was going to have to pay out to the toll booths on the parkway that Moses had built. I couldn't see us drawing many people from the water or the cemetery. We *had* to come out here. We had ambitious plans for Brooklyn. We were toying with a domed stadium. We were looking ahead to pay television and hoping to get some financing that way, but they wouldn't give us the land we needed to do it.

"The writers have been snowed under by a theory that this L.A. thing was a big giveaway. This park was built for about $20 million, and it didn't cost the taxpayers a dime. We pay the county of Los Angeles more than a million dollars in real-estate taxes. They write we've got the oil and mineral rights to our land, and that's so much bunk, too. If someone struck oil back of second base, the oil would belong to the City of Los Angeles."

He turned and gestured toward the hills behind centerfield. The terrain was once arid, but now Chavez Ravine has evergreens and desert plants. "When he was working here, Buzzie Bavasi asked me why I was spending all that money landscaping when we play six nights a week and nobody can see the hills after the sun sets. I told him I was doing it for our Sunday afternoon customers. You won't believe it, but growing things are important to me.

"We took a chance. They told us Los Angeles was not a baseball town. We had a short lease on the Coliseum, then we were at the mercy of the city council. I think we won there by a single vote. Otherwise we might have been playing in the street.

"Even my son asked me why I was taking the risk of putting so much money into the ball park. I told him, 'Peter, after I'm gone—and maybe after you are, too—this ball park will remain, and it will be a monument to the O'Malleys.' "

OF GALAHAD AND QUESTS THAT FAILED

Artie Wilson's major league record appears in a most abbreviated form in my copy of *The Baseball Encyclopedia*, which contains an extensive array of statistics on virtually everyone else who has ever played in the big leagues. The abridgement of Wilson's record was intentional, but not malicious. To qualify for a full listing in the 1974 edition of the encyclopedia, a player had to have at least 25 major league at bats; Artie Wilson had only 22 for the

1951 Giants. The cursory way in which Wilson is treated says a great deal about the incompleteness of what is supposed to be baseball's basic reference work. But it says even more about the game itself, which prevented Wilson and generations of players like him from qualifying for the encyclopedia because of a single and, indeed, malicious reason. Artic Wilson is black.

When you dig further, the records on Wilson still yield only a fraction of his truth. He played shortstop, second and first with the Giants, appeared in 19 games and hit .182. Officially Wilson was 30 during his only major leaguc season. Some suggest he was four years older. Whatever, his skills had long since been eroded by having to play professional baseball 11 months a year.

Monte Irvin, who was 30 before he was allowed to begin his brief, brilliant big-league career, says, "Artie was one of the greatest shortstops anybody ever saw. In the old Negro leagues we called him the Octopus, because it seemed as though he had eight arms. He had tremendous range, wonderful speed, a super arm. Besides that, he was a first-rate pinch hitter. But by the time they let him join us on the Giants, he simply wasn't the player we'd known."

You find Wilson these days among the damp green silences of Portland, Ore., where Artie's minister, the Rev. Thomas L. Strayhand, says there are no racial problems of any kind. Pastor Strayhand smiles slightly. "That's because there aren't enough of us blacks here for them to notice."

Wilson sells Chryslers, and during our three days together he managed to mention in his quiet, relaxed way all the merits of a model called the Cordoba. Artie is a hard-working auto salesman, and, yes, I would buy a used car from that man. But mostly we talked baseball, which Wilson looks back on with a warmth that others focus on old romances.

"Oh, but I loved playing the game," he said in the tidy living room of his two-story frame house in northeast Portland. "I loved it as a little kid 'round the sandlots in Birmingham, and I loved it playing for the Acipco cast-iron pipe company. Say, you know I played against Willie Mays's daddy back then? Cat Mays played for Westfield in the Tennessee Coal and Iron League. And I loved it with the Birmingham Black Barons. We used to have an all-star game in the colored league. I was the starting shortstop most of the years I was playing for Birmingham. Except 1945. That year they had Jackie Robinson take my place."

"I never thought Robinson had a big-league shortstop's arm," I said.

"Right," Wilson said, "but Jackie cheated. He studied the hitters good and made up for the arm by playing position. He knew where they'd hit the ball. There wasn't nobody who saw me and Jackie in 1945 who wouldn't tell you but one thing. I was the best shortstop. There isn't nobody with intelligence who wouldn't tell you something else: For integrating baseball, Jackie was the best man."

What Artie loved most was his one season in the major leagues playing for Leo Durocher. "Leo had the greatest tricks," he said. "He'd carry a rubber cigar—he didn't smoke—and he'd come up to some rookie and say, 'Hey, gimme your matches.' Twenty minutes later he'd be asking the kid what he was doing in the Thunderbird Club last night. The rookie wondered how Leo knew where he'd been drinking. Leo had looked at the matches, that was how. But after a while the rookies got smart. You can't stay dumb forever. They stopped carrying matches and bought lighters. Then Leo would come up with something else. No way you could get ahead of that guy."

Artie, a trim man with a pencil mustache and a soft tenor voice, and his wife Dorothy put two children through college, which meant he always had to supplement his income by playing Caribbean winter ball. "The guys I knew in baseball," Wilson said. "Luis Tiant's father was on the New York Cubans. Best lefthanded pick-off move I ever saw. Silvio Garcia, an infielder. Durocher said he'd have been worth a million if he was white. Luke Easter. They spoiled him up in Cleveland by getting him to pull. If they'd left Easter alone, he'd of hit 'em 450 feet to any field. When I was finishing in the Pacific Coast League, I played for Charlie Dressen. He was a sharp one, almost like Durocher. But not quite. Leo was off there by himself.

"One time with the Giants, Leo came into a Pullman car where a bunch of his players were shooting craps. Leo took off his jacket, got down on the floor and in half an hour had every dollar in that Pullman. Then he stood up and told the players, 'You've already been taken to bed. Now it's time for you to go to sleep.' "

The memory made Wilson laugh softly in delight. He grew up in black poverty outside of Birmingham, but he says neither poverty nor segregation bothered him when he was a child. "I didn't know nothing else, and I was happy long as I could get into a game. For a baseball, we'd find an old golf ball somebody had hit out of bounds. We'd wrap some string around it tight and have our ball. For a bat, we'd saw down a tree branch. When I needed a buck or two for sneakers, I shined shoes.

"Later I got a job cutting pipes and playing ball for the Acipco Company, and one day I got careless in the factory and lost part of my thumb." He showed me his right hand. The thumb was cut off at the knuckle. "Didn't hurt much and I just had to adjust my throwing a little. I pitched once in a while. In the colored leagues you had to play every position. After the accident, I could make my fastball move better.

"With the Black Barons we had an owner who ran a funeral parlor in Memphis. He paid us regular. We went from town to town by bus, and I got so I slept better sitting up in a bus than in a bed. Then Abe Saperstein got the club and took us out barnstorming, and we won nearly every game we played. When we got to San Francisco, Abe wanted to take us to DiMaggio's Restaurant on Fisherman's Wharf. Then he got the word. A colored ball team wasn't welcome. I think that got me as mad as anything ever did."

Integration moved slowly. First Robinson. Then Larry Doby. Then Dan Bankhead. It was 1960 before the majors were truly open.

"But the years you were excluded from organized ball?" I asked.

"You're thinking now, not then. Then, like I say, I was just happy to be a professional baseball player anywhere."

Wilson drove me about Portland, soft-selling his Cordoba, pointing out the stadium where the Portland Timbers were playing soccer, and the Columbia River, crowded not with salmon but with freighters. "Rains a lot here and it's cool, but it's been my home for 22 years now," he said. "You have any plans for tomorrow?"

"No."

"Well, if I'm not intruding on you and interfering with your sleep, I'd like you to be my guest at church." It was a hesitant, strangely poignant invitation.

"Thanks," I said. "Appreciate that." Then, musing aloud, "Is your church integrated?"

"Of course it's integrated," Wilson said.

I attended Sunday School class at the Allen Temple Christian Methodist Episcopal Church where we read *Corinthians* and men debated whether sin began with taking a drink or getting drunk. The issue still lay in doubt when services began. The congregation sang *Come, Thou Almighty King*. Wilson, the finance chairman of the church, supervised the passing of collection plates. Pastor Strayhand preached and chanted on life's decision. After services, score of people came up to shake my hand and bid me welcome. All of them were black.

At dinner Wilson said, "You remember when you asked me if my church was integrated?"

"You told me it was."

"What I meant was that God don't know no color."

Then we were back to baseball again. Artie asked me what was happening in Seattle.

"Well, they have their dome, Danny Kaye and Less Smith have the franchise, and for the first few years the team there will be terrible."

"Is there any chance they might hire Leo to manager?"

"Depends on Durocher's health and how he's been getting along with Kaye. What makes you ask?"

The soft voice grew even more quiet. "I know a lot about the game. I can teach good. I'm fine selling cars, but I was just thinking that maybe if Leo got the managing job he might just happen to remember me."

The old Negro all-star shortstop looked out a restaurant window into twilight. "My children has grown fine," he said. "My wife's a lovely woman. I'm at peace with myself. But I didn't just love playing that game. I loved being around baseball. The big leagues is the greatest baseball in the world.

"I don't miss nothing, and I don't resent nothing, 'cept bein' turned away at DiMaggio's. But now at my age, if Leo got Seattle and hired me as one of his coaches, I could help him and be back in the major leagues again."

"I'd pray for that," Wilson said without sadness, " 'cept you just shouldn't ask the Lord for too much."

NOT QUITE GALAHAD

Outside the multipurpose stadium in St. Louis, in the vaulting shadow of the Gateway Arch, a hulking statue purports to represent Stan Musial at bat. It is a triumph of ineptitude over sincerity.

St. Louis baseball writers who watched Stan Musial play baseball for almost a quarter of a century engaged a sculptor named Carl Mose to cast Old No. 6 in bronze. Then someone composed an inscription for the pedestal:

> HERE STANDS BASEBALL'S PERFECT WARRIOR;
> HERE STANDS BASEBALL'S PERFECT KNIGHT.

The shoulders are too broad. The torso is too thick. The work smacks of the massive statuary that infests the Soviet Union. It misses the lithe beauty of the Man.

"I saw the sculptor when he was working on it," Musial said. "I told him

I never looked that broad. He said it had to be that broad because it was going to be against the backdrop of a big ball park. He missed the stance, but what kind of man would I have been if I'd complained? The writers were generous to put it up. The sculptor did his best. Look, there's a statue of me in St. Louis while I'm still alive."

A pregnant woman, armed with an autograph book, charged. "Write for my son Willie," she commanded. Musial nodded, said, "Where ya from?" and signed with a lean-fingered, practiced hand.

"Thank you," the pregnant woman said. "Willie is coming soon. After he gets here and learns to talk, I'm sure he'll thank you, Mr. Musial."

Inside the round stadium, the Cardinals were losing slowly in the wet Mississippi Valley heat. The final score would be Cincinnati 13, St. Louis 2. We had left after the fourth inning when baseball's perfect knight passed his threshold of anguish over the bad game being played by the home team.

To reach most old ballplayers, even millionaire old ballplayers like Hank Greenberg, you simply call their homes around dinner time. A pleased, remembered voice comes through the phone. "I had a good day playing tennis. How've you been? Who've you been seeing lately? Say, if you're ever in town, come over and we can talk about the old days."

To reach Musial, you call the office of the resort and restaurant corporation called Stan Musial & Biggie's, Inc. When I did, a secretary said crisply but politely, "I'm sorry, but Mr. Musial is on a goodwill tour of Europe. He'll be back briefly in two weeks. Then he's flying to the Montreal Olympics. We'll try to fit you in, but could I have your name again and could you tell me what this is in reference to?"

It was in reference to one thing. Stan Musial, neither a perfect warrior nor any sort of knight, is my particular baseball hero. I once heard a teammate who knew him well call him a choker. "Considering his ability, he didn't drive in enough runs," the man said. Musial heard about that remark, but would not stoop to make a response. During his 22 years with the Cardinals, Musial batted in a total of 1,951 runs. That is the fifth highest total in the history of the major leagues.

Musial is a man of limited education, superior intelligence, a somewhat guarded manner, a surface conviviality and a certain aloofness, because he knows just who he is. Stan Musial, Hall-of-Famer, great batsman and, 13 years after he last cracked a double to right centerfield, still an American hero.

We were rambling about baseball in one of his offices in St Louis when my wife, who can be more direct than I, interposed five questions.

"By the time you got to be 35," she said, "and your muscles began to ache, did you still enjoy playing baseball?"

Musial nodded, touched his sharp chin and said, "I always wanted to be a baseball player. That's the only thing I ever wanted to be. Now figure that I was in the exact profession I wanted and I was at the top of that profession and they were paying me $100,000 a year. Yes. I enjoyed playing baseball very much right up to the end of my career."

"About politics?" Wendy asked.

"I'm a Democrat. Tom Eagleton, the senator, says he remembers sitting in my lap when he was a kid visiting our spring-training camp years ago."

"What do you think of Jimmy Carter?"

Musial laughed to himself. "I'd have to say he's very unusual for a candidate."

"You worked for Lyndon Johnson?"

"He asked me to run his physical-fitness program and I did. I believe in physical fitness. I'm 55 years old, and I still swim two or three hours every day."

"But didn't you find Johnson vulgar?" Wendy said.

Musial looked impersonally at me, then at my wife. "No," he said, "because we only talked politics."

If I read him correctly, Musial had said in quick succession that Wendy's first question was naïve, that Carter was the prince of peanuts growers and that Johnson would have sounded obscene in a roaring dugout. Just as he hit home runs without seeming to strain. Musial had implied all these things without a suggestion of rancor.

People were always mistaking his subtlety for blandness. An agent employed by both Musial and Ted Williams once said to me, "If you want to make some money selling articles, stick with Williams. The other feller's nice, but there isn't any electricity to him." Then one of the editors at *Newsweek*, where I was working, directed me to prepare a cover story on Musial. "Pick up the Cardinals out in Pittsburgh," the editor said, "and make Musial take you back to Donora. It'll work well, putting him back on the streets of the Pennsylvania factory town where he grew up."

At Forbes Field, Musial said that he was driving to Donora the next day and I was welcome to ride along with him—provided I promised not to write about the trip.

"Why not?"

"I promised someone I'd visit sick kids in the hospital. If you write that, it'll look like I'm doing it for publicity. And my mother lives above a store there. That's where she wants to live. We had her in St. Louis, but she missed her old friends, so she went back home and found a place she liked. No matter how you write that, the magazine will come out with a headline: STAN MUSIAL'S MOTHER LIVES ABOVE A STORE."

"Well, I have to come back with a story."

We'll spend some time and maybe come up with something," Musial said.

We talked batting for three days at Ebbets Field. He remembered a day at Ebbets Field when he had gotten five hits, all with two strikes, and he remembered a year when he suffered chronic appendicitis and played 149 games and hit .312. He remembered the doubleheader at Busch Stadium when he hit five home runs. He could even recall the different pitches that he hit.

"Do you guess at the plate?" I asked.

The sharp-featured face lit. "I don't guess. I know." Then Musial spun out a batting secret. He had memorized the speed at which every pitcher in the league threw the fastball, the curve, the slider. He picked up and speed of the ball in the first 30 feet of its flight, after which he knew how the ball would move as it crossed home plate.

About 80 pitchers worked in the National League then. Musial had locked the speed of about 240 different pitches into his memory. I had asked the right question, and Musial responded with a story that was picked up by 100 newspapers.

They oversimplified, as newspapers often do. Even if you can identify a pitch 30 feet away, you are left with only a tiny fraction of a second to respond. Musial's lifetime batting average of .331 was not the product of a single secret. It was fashioned of memory, concentration, discipline, eyesight, physical conditioning and reflexes.

Going for his 3,000th hit, Musial neglected to concentrate and took his stride too early. But he kept his bat back, as all great hitters do. On sheer reflex, he slugged a double to left.

Now in his office, Musial looked much as he had 15 years before. The same surprisingly thin wrists. The same powerful back. A waistline barely thicker than it had been. The deceptive self-deprecation also persists. "I'm semiretired," he insisted, but twice he politely broke off our interview to take business calls. Stan Musial & Biggie's, Inc., a family-held company, owns two Florida hotels and a restaurant and a hotel in St. Louis.

"Are you a millionaire like Hank Greenberg?" I asked.

"Just write that I'm not hanging for my pension."

At the park, fans flooded toward his box, demanding autographs and making it difficult to study the game. Musial singled out Pete Rose for praise and said he felt embarrassed that so many major-leaguers were hitting in the .200s. "There's no excuse for that. You know why it happens? They keep trying to pull everything, even low outside sliders. You can't do that. Nobody can. If you're a major league player, you ought to have pride. Learn to stroke outside pitches to the opposite field. That's part of your job. A major league hitter is supposed to be a professional."

"Do you miss playing?" I said as Rose rapped a single up the middle.

"No," Musial said. "Nice stroke, Pete. I quit while I still enjoyed it, but I put in my time. I like to travel now, but not with a ball club. Have you ever seen Ireland? Do you know how beautiful it is?"

After the game, we drove back to Musial's restaurant, and a crowd surrounded him in the lobby. He said to each, "How are ya? Where ya from?" One 50ish man was so awed that he momentarily lost the power of speech. He waved his arms and sputtered and poked his wife and pointed. Musial clapped the man gently on the back. "How are ya? Where ya from?" Musical said to him again. The man looked as if he might weep with joy. At length he recovered sufficiently to say a single word, "Fresno."

"Does this happen all the time?" I asked.

"Isn't it something?" Musial said. "And I'm 13 years out of the business. You know what Jack Kennedy said to me once? He said they claimed he was too young to be President and I was too old to be playing ball. Well, Jack got to be President, and two years later, when I was 42 years old, I played 135 games and I hit .330."

"Ebbets Field, Stash," I said. "They should have given you the rightfield wall when they wrecked the place. You owned it, anyway."

"What do you think my lifetime average was in Brooklyn?" Musial said. "About .480."

"It only seemed that way," he said. "Actually my lifetime average there was .360."

I can't imagine Galahad, the perfect knight, as a baseball hero. He was priggish and probably undersized. That doesn't matter. Having Stanley Frank Musial is quite enough.

MAN FROM THE HALL OF SHAME

On Jan. 19, 1972, Early Wynn, the pitcher, was voted into the Baseball Hall of Fame. Such tidings generally lead to a phone call from a wire-service reporter, who asks the player for a comment, and if you follow that sort of thing, you know what happens next. In a wash of sentiment, the player thanks mother, God, truth, justice and the American way of life.

Early Wynn is not inclined toward sentimentality. Working through four decades in the major leagues, he had won 300 games and he had intimidated generations of American League batters with the best knockdown pitching of his time. He knew he deserved to be in the Hall of Fame.

The telephone rang. It was an enthusiastic young man from a wire service. "Naturally, I'm happy, and so is my wife," Wynn said. "We have had a long wait.... I don't think I am as thrilled as I would have been if I had made it the first time. I would have liked to have joined Stan Musial and Ted Williams and Walter Johnson as players who gained the honor the first year they were eligible."

A few weeks later, during a private conversation when he was less concerned with keeping in baseball's good graces, Wynn told me, "Hall of Fame? Hell, it's a Hall of Shame. I should have been voted in three years ago." He pulled the cork from a bottle of rare old Canadian whiskey. He took a drink.

That summer Wynn managed Orlando, the Twins farm team in the Class A Florida State League. It pleased him to work in the Minnesota organization under Calvin Griffith, because Calvin's uncle, Clark Griffith, had brought Wynn into the majors in 1939. Early took a few days off to attend the induction ceremonies at Cooperstown that August and did make a few sentimental comments in a speech. That may have been an error. Griffith fired him from Orlando in November, making Wynn the only man I know of who was trumpeted into the Hall of Fame and bounced out of a managing job in the same year.

Baseball offers a full quota of absurdities. In the low minors, where players are supposed to be learning, you find one man, the manager, charged with teaching 20 different apprentices. In the majors, where players are supposed to be fully skilled, you find special coaches for pitching, catching and even base running. The big leagues have expanded chaotically, and clubs that might have become intense and profitable rivals—Oakland and San Francisco, for example—play in different leagues. It is tempting to regard Wynn's dismissal as one more instance of baseball's thoughtlessness. Some, knowing that Minnesota organization, suggest that Griffith simply wanted to find someone who would manage for $500 less. I suspect other considerations were involved.

Wynn is a fierce, direct man who can take a drink. Don Newcombe took a drink, too, and he told a Senate subcommittee that whiskey had cost him his career, his first marriage, all his investments and his home. The difference is the classic borderline between drinking and alcoholism. Wynn could mix hard stuff with wine, drink throughout an evening, run at 11 the next morning and pitch a shutout.

To Wynn, convivial gatherings were a delight of big-league life. He went to parties and he gave parties, gay raucous evenings rich in baseball talk and needling, and with a single exception, he never overestimated his capacity. One night, when he was pitching for Cleveland, he visited Bill Veeck, who owned the Indians. Martinis preceded dinner; stingers followed. "Curiously, I don't remember exactly what we served next," Veeck says, "but I do recall that at 4:30 in the morning I was mixing grasshoppers. Then it struck Early. He was scheduled to pitch the next day, and here he was drinking late with the boss."

"I better go home," Wynn said. "One o'clock game."

"It's too late to worry about sleep now," Veeck said. "You better just keep going."

Wynn reached the ball park at 11, put on a rubber jacket and began to run. He sweated, showered and went out and pitched a shutout. "The reporters came," Veeck says, "and Early answered all their questions. He got somebody with the knuckleball. Someone else was fooled by a high slider. He did just fine until the last reporter left the dressing room. Then he fell over on his face."

There was nothing bland about Early, nothing subdued, nothing cautious. He didn't like hitters, and he said he didn't like hitters. He knocked them down. "Why I should worry about hitters?" Wynn said. "Do they worry about me? Do you ever find a hitter crying because he's hit a line drive through the box? My job is getting hitters out. If I don't get them out I lose. I don't like losing a game anymore than a salesman likes losing a big sale. I've got a right to knock down anybody holding a bat."

"Suppose it was your own mother?" a reporter said.

Wynn thought briefly. "Mother was a pretty good curveball hitter," he said.

That was humor, but at Yankee Stadium I saw Wynn brush back his son. Joe Early was a tall, rangy boy who was visiting at his father's place of business for a day, and Early volunteered to throw a little batting practice. Joe Early hit a long line drive to left center. The next pitch was at his cheekbone; it sent Joe Early diving to the ground.

"You shouldn't crowd me," Wynn said with a certain noncommittal tenderness.

Wynn learned rope tricks and played supermarket openings. He began a newspaper column and within a month had attacked general managers for their penury and *The Sporting News* for publishing too much gossip. Air travel bothered him, so he took flying lessons and purchased a single-engine plane. He bought a cabin cruiser and a motorcycle and a Packard and a Mercedes, leading Shirley Povich of the *The Washington Post* to comment, "Wynn simply seized life with his great hands, implacably determined to squeeze every ounce of living out of his time."

Despite that, his staying power was prodigious. He pitched for the Senators in 1939, moved on in 1949 to become a mainstay of the great Indian stuff that included Bob Feller and Bob Lemon, and 10 years after *that* pitched the White Sox to a pennant and won the Cy Young award. He was a thick-chested, black-haired man with a natural glower, which he would direct at the batters like a death ray. He seemed indestructible. But in the early 1960s he began to suffer attacks of gout. On a snap throw to first, he strained muscles near his elbow, and the gout moved into his pitching arm. His legs were weakening. It was time to quit, but he wanted to win his 300th game.

"During those last years," says Wynn's wife Lorraine, "when he'd come back from running, his legs would be so sore that we had to work out this routine. He'd lie down on his stomach and I'd take a rolling pin and move it up and down over the backs of his legs. That was the only thing that seemed to relax the muscles."

The old fastball was gone, and it was not until 1963 (it took him three seasons to win his last 16 games) that Wynn got his 300th. To do it, he had to pitch in pain and terrible weariness, but 300 was the goal and he got there. "Hell, I've lost more than 200," he said.

His rage to live persisted, and one night he asked if there were any interesting parties in New York. We tried one, which was dull, and another, which was worse. "Let's go down to the Village Barn," he said.

"That's way downtown," I said. "I haven't been there since college."

"I just want to see that place one more time."

The Barn was barren. It was getting very late. We had some drinks. "The hitters may not know this," Wynn said, "they aren't all that smart. But I know it. I can't get 'em out anymore."

"You're in your 40s, Early. You knew this was going to happen."

His face assumed a look of inexpressible sadness. "But now it's *happening*," he said.

After retiring, he drifted through a predictable mix of baseball jobs: pitching coach, scout, minor league manager. But he never became a politic man. In 1969, when Billy Martin managed the Twins, a columnist's story enraged Martin. Three sportswriters, Red Smith among them, appeared on the field. Martin began cursing at the perfidy of the press. "Anyone who talks to any of those newspaper bastards is crazy," Martin yelled.

Wynn had known Smith for 20 years. He was also Martin's pitching coach. Before Martin's popping eyes, Wynn walked over to Smith and welcomed him warmly to the field. He was not Martin's pitching coach again.

Early was a scholar of the game, and whenever I have watched him teach, he has been both stern and patient. The knockdown pitch has been curtailed by a system of fines, but I don't think that's why nobody likes Wynn. Baseball executives increasingly favor men who are corporate-bland. More and more major league teams are run by syndicates, and syndicates prefer managers and coaches who do as they are told, salute the company president and study statistics rather than spend spirited evenings talking baseball with the press.

Wynn has found work in Florida as sales coordinator for Wellcraft, a boat manufacturing company, and flying south I expected to find him depressed, or at least subdued. He lives in Nokomis, 40 minutes south of Sarasota, and commutes to his office every morning. "The traffic," he said, his old rage still intact. "What the hell do government officials think about, if they do think? What do they think the west coast of Florida is, a slum? It was no secret that more and more people would be moving here. We knew it 20 years ago. Why haven't they put in first-class roads?" In his party room, baseballs from 15 of his greatest victories hung from the ceiling. He had placed his Cy Young trophy on one wall. From another wall, three men smiled out of an old picture: Stan Musial, Ted Williams, Early Wynn.

"The Hall of Fame," I began.

"Look, I'm honored to be in there," he said. "Hartford, Alabama, that's where I grew up, and the biggest thing that happened in that town was a peanut festival. But we had baseball, and we'd ride mule wagons many a mile for a town game. They write that when I showed up at a pro tryout I was barefoot. I wasn't, but I was wearing overalls. It's a long way from Hartford, Alabama to Cooperstown, but any man who wins 300 major league games ought to get voted in as soon as he's eligible. I mean, don't people know how much hard work that is?"

I said I thought I did and asked how he liked the job at Wellcraft. "Well, I've always been fond of boats," he said. He took out a catalogue, and then the fiercest competitor I've known in baseball set about selling me a cabin cruiser.

A light checking account blocked the sale, but this wasn't precisely like a Wynn ball game. I knew I could resist his will without getting a fastball fired at my head.

THE CHILDREN OF ROBERTO

On a Puerto Rican plain, beside Avenida Iturregui and a pleasant subdivision called Country Club, 600 barren acres stretch under a pitiless sun. Part of the land is dry and caked, part is still marsh. This is Ciudad Deportiva (Sports City), one of the last dreams Roberto Clemente voiced before a DC-7, overloaded and undermanned, carried him to his death in the Caribbean on the night of Dec. 31, 1972.

I suppose sociologists would find Clemente's dream naïve. He wanted to build a Puerto Rican sports camp open only to the very poor, who would attend free of charge. He hoped that "every single child from poverty can learn to play sports and maybe make some success, as I did." More than $800,000 has been collected for Ciudad Deportiva, and on the barren plain two bulldozers work at a languorous pace that would have been inimical to Roberto Clemente.

Certain rumors persist about the death of Clemente, neither a saint nor a tramp, but a gifted ballplayer with a social conscience. "Bobby had a woman in Nicaragua," someone insists. "That's the real reason he took that flight." Another Puerto Rican suggests that the plane contained gold, or U.S. dollars, which Clemente was going to sequester beyond the grasp of tax authorities.

These are the facts. That November, Clemente had taken an amateur Puerto Rican baseball team to play a series of games in Nicaragua. He had liked riding in ox carts as a boy in Carolina, his home village, and in Nicaragua he saw ox carts again. He also met a hospitalized child without legs and asked why he had no artificial limbs.

"We don't have any money," the boy said. "Legs would cost $800."

"When I go back to Puerto Rico I will raise the money," Clemente promised.

Five weeks later Managua was literally flattened by six violent shocks. In Puerto Rico, Clemente organized a relief campaign. He appeared on television and radio, pleading for money, morphine, sugar. Although his back ached, he helped load supplies on trucks in a staging area near Hiram Bithorn Stadium. Then word reached him that soldiers in the Nicaraguan army were stealing the supplies and selling them to earthquake victims.

Clemente remembered the ox carts and the crippled boy. He had recently lined his 3,000th major league hit, a double, and he had a strong sense of his Latin fame. "If I go to Nicaragua, the stealing will stop," he said, beating a palm against his chest. "They would not dare to steal from Roberto Clemente."

A jet could have been used. The DC-7 was cheaper. A certified flight engineer could not be found to work on New Year's Eve. Instead, the third seat in the cockpit was occupied by an aircraft mechanic. Sixteen 60-pound bags of sugar were hastily loaded through the plane's forward door in the last minutes. Were they properly lashed down? According to witnesses, one engine seemed to sputter when the plane went down the runway at 9:20 p.m.

The plane took off. Another engine coughed. On a tape of the plane's radio transmissions to the tower you can hear the pilot say without panic, "This is NC 500 comin' back around." It is thought that the pilot banked the plane steeply. It could have been that the bags of sugar shifted. In the blackness, NC 500 continued to bank and then slipped sideways into 12-foot waves at approximately 150 mph. The aircraft might as well have flown into a wall of concrete.

"It was so sad for all of us," said Luis Rodriguez Mayoral, a Pirate scout who guided me about his island. "In one year we lost two great heroes. Roberto Clemente and Don Pablo Casals. But do people remember? If they did, wouldn't Ciudad Deportiva be more than this by now?"

Latins have a gift for patient melancholy, but Mayoral brightened quickly. "I will show you, *amigo*, that there is nothing else sad about baseball on our island. Our island baseball is wonderful, ¿*tu sabes*?"

We drove Mayoral's Volkswagen through San Juan, on to a village called Guaynabo, then to Caguas, a small city located along a road lined by royal poincianas, a tree with rust-red flowers. We watched Little League ball in

Carolina, now a suburb in the San Juan sprawl, and we saw amateurs play in Las Piedras (The Rocks), a town that did not even appear on my tourist map. Puerto Rican baseball is a joyous pastime played mostly for the wonders of the game.

When you are looking at a team you have not seen before, watch the shortstop, who must move laterally and charge slow, twisting ground balls and make the play. Neither 14-year-old shortstop looked promising to me; Vic Power, the old major-leaguer, agreed. We were not seeing the best of Puerto Rican games. "In New York, in what you call Spanish Harlem, do they still remember my Gold Gloves up there?" he asked.

The baseball cast is always changing, and in Spanish Harlem people now talk of Felix Millan and John Candelaria and Willie Montanez. "Sure, they remember your Gold Gloves," I told Power.

He beamed. "This team is called Café Crema after a big coffee company that gives the uniforms. It is not the best team, and Café Crema is not the best coffee. When you have lunch, order our other coffee, Café Rico."

Following lunch the next day, Mayoral drove me to the Country Club section of a Little League playoff. At Parque Angel Ramos 200 people cheered and watched and listened to Carols de Jesus broadcast over loudspeakers as the game developed before their eyes. Country Club defeated Valle Arriba 9–0, and the Country Club shortstop, Jorge Burgos, played impressively.

In the fifth inning, with Country Club's victory already safe, a Valle Arriba base runner reached second. The next pitch bounded five feet from the catcher. The runner did not try to advance, but when I looked up, there was Jorge Burgos backing up third.

"Good play," I told the 12-year-old after the game.

"Not a good play," he corrected me in Spanish. "Just the play you're supposed to make."

"Would you like to make the major leagues?"

"In my short life, I have accomplished little aside from baseball," he said. "So my answer is, yes, I would like to play there. But perhaps later, when I accomplish other things, my answer would be different."

When Guaynabo played Cayey in a game of two town teams, 2,000 fans showed up at 9:45 p.m. at the modern ball park in Guaynabo. Guaynabo's uniforms were blue and white. Cayey wore faded red. Guaynabo was leading by two runs when a cloudburst struck. The home team's ground crew moved so slowly that the field was drenched. The fans chattered and applauded and sipped beer. The Cayey manager announced that he was protesting the game "because of Guaynabo's lazy ground crew." The fans hooted and laughed, and everyone went home.

Near the ball park in Las Piedras, on the narrow road that twists toward Humacao Beach, a young man was playing pepper with his son. Their names were José Soto, junior and senior, and after Mayoral introduced us, Mr. Soto said, "Vic Power tells me my child's swing is so good I should not touch it."

"*¿Tu eres de Nueva York?*" the small boy asked me. Was I from New York? "Yes."

Had I seen the Yankees? Would I watch him?

The father chattered like a salesman, and José Soto Jr., who is seven, swung wildly, then missed six ground balls out of eight.

"He moves well," I told the father.

"If you come back to Las Piedras," the senior Soto said, "understand you always will be welcome."

Baseball came to Puerto Rico in 1900, introduced by occupying U.S. soldiers after the Spanish-American War. It is the single continental export almost every islander understands and watches and plays.

It would be hard to explain the federal budget to the Soto family, but our sense of baseball needs no explanation. For what that father and son were doing in a scruffy tropical backyard was the same thing that my son and I had done many months before on a blackened field, set among $150,000 homes, in the casual prosperity of Westchester County.

This Old House

BY WILLIAM NACK

Babe Ruth may have built Yankee Stadium, but the foundations of its legacy are the battles waged there and the great athletes who called it home.

I T WAS A BALMY MORNING IN THE HARLEM RIVER VALLEY THAT separates the Bronx from the island of Manhattan, and in the distance you could hear the clack and rumble of the elevated trains as they passed just outside the centerfield wall of Yankee Stadium. Inside the Stadium—as workers in yellow hard hats scurried about the scaffolding and pigeons pecked at the freshly planted sod—there was a sense of renewal in the air. It was Feb. 17, and George Steinbrenner's ballpark was undergoing its makeover for the 1999 baseball season, its final facial of the millennium. Only Monument Park, that brick-lined haven tucked behind the wall in left center, was untouched by the pneumatic drills and hammers.

For decades the Stadium has been one of New York's most popular tourist attractions, the Bronx's answer to the Empire State Building and the Statue of Liberty; on this sparkling Tuesday morning, tour guide Tony Morante was leading 20 visitors up the walkway into Monument Park when they all seemed to stop at once. There before them, rising like tombstones in the corner of a churchyard, were four marble slabs bearing bronze plaques depicting in bas-relief the merry visages of Yankees legends Babe Ruth,

Lou Gehrig, Miller Huggins and Mickey Mantle. Deirdre Weldon had brought nine boys from Yorktown, N.Y., to celebrate the birthday of her son, Terry; as they all gathered reverently around, staring at the faces on the monuments staring back at them, 10-year-old Chris Raiano said aloud what all his friends were wondering.

"Are they all buried here?" he asked.

"No, they are not," Weldon replied. "Only the memories are. . . . "

BACK IN 1921, not long after the New York Giants' baseball team moved to evict the Yankees from the Polo Grounds in Manhattan—the Giants were sore that Babe Ruth's Yankees were outdrawing them—the Yankees' owners, beer baron Jake Ruppert and Til Huston, announced that they had purchased a 10-acre lot across the river, in the Bronx, and that they planned to build a ballyard of their own. The Giants' manager, John McGraw, scoffed at the scheme. "This is a big mistake," said Little Napoleon. "They are going up to Goatville, and before long they will be lost sight of."

Today, nearly 80 years later, old Goatville is the richest repository of memories in American sports. It was way up there, in the wilds of the Bronx, that the New York Yankees won 33 American League pennants and 24 world championships. Close your eyes, and you can see, on the grainy film of memory, Lou Gehrig listening to the echoes of his farewell speech in 1939 . . . Al Gionfriddo twice looking over his shoulder and then reaching out for Joe DiMaggio's 415-foot drive in the '47 Series . . . Mickey Mantle's thunderous shot denting the copper frieze lining the upper deck in right . . . Reggie Jackson driving a knuckleball into the black tarp covering the seats in center for his third home run in the final game of the '77 Series . . . Yogi Berra leaping into Don Larsen's arms at the end of the Perfect Game . . . the dying Ruth, bracing himself on a bat, waving that last, long goodbye.

It was there, in 1928, in the very bowels of the place, that Notre Dame's Knute Rockne, at halftime of a scoreless tie against Army, exhorted his players to "win just one for the Gipper." It was there that Doc Blanchard ran with Glenn Davis in '44, when Army whipped the Irish 59–0, and it was there that Jack Dempsey flattened Jack Sharkey in '27, first scrambling his eggs with a low blow and then shaving his stubble with a short, sharp hook to the chin. Joe Louis fought in Yankee Stadium 11 times, and it was there in '38, in the most politically charged prizefight in history, that he knocked out Hitler's model of Aryan supremacy, Max Schmeling, at 2:04 of the first round. And it was there, too, that the New York football Giants waged all those wintery wars against the Bears, the Browns and the Baltimore Colts.

Of course, neither Ruppert nor Huston foresaw any of this when they bought the land from the estate of William Waldorf Astor for $675,000 and then shelled out $2.5 million for construction of the park. All they really had in mind, by way of mooning the Giants just across the river, was to build the largest, grandest ballpark in America. In the remarkably brief course of 284 working days, beginning on May 5, 1922, some 500 men turned 45,000 barrels of cement into 35,000 cubic yards of concrete. They made bleachers out of 950,000 board feet of Pacific Coast fir that came to New York by boat through the Panama Canal. They secured the grandstand seats with 135,000 steel castings and a million brass screws. They rolled out 16,000 square feet of sod.

When it was finished, the park had 36 ticket booths and 40 turnstiles that ticked like clocks as they counted the house. And what a house it was—a colossus, in fact, a three-tiered horseshoe that seated 70,000. F.C. Lane, in a 1923 issue of *The Literary Digest*, called it "the last word in ball parks. But not the least of its merits is its advantage of position. From the plain of the Harlem River it looms up like the great Pyramid of Cheops from the sands of Egypt."

It was the first ballpark in America to be called a stadium, which traces back to the ancient Greek and Roman word for a track for footraces, and the place had nothing if not room to run. When Ruth stepped out of the Yankees' dugout and onto the field for the first time, he looked around and declared, "Some ballyard!" It was short down the lines, 281 feet to left and 295 to right, but the fence flared out sharply in left and seemed to disappear at the 490-foot mark in dead center, creating an alley in left center that righthanded power hitters dubbed Death Valley. Wrote one bug-eyed scribbler in the *New York Sun*, "The flag pole seems almost beyond the range of a siege gun as it rears its height in distant center field."

The Yankee Stadium, as it was called then, had its grand opening on April 18, 1923, and more than 70,000 people—at the time the largest crowd ever to watch a baseball game—made their pilgrimage to see the Yankees play the Boston Red Sox. The roads around the Stadium were unpaved, and flivver dust choked the patrons massed at the turnstiles. The impatient crowd pressed forward, and it took a cordon of 200 policemen to keep it back. Baseball commissioner Kenesaw Mountain Landis arrived via the Interborough subway, promptly got caught in the crush of bodies outside the gates and had to be rescued by the cops. Inside, as John Phillip Sousa struck up the Seventh Regiment Band for *The Star-Spangled Banner*, the two rival managers, Huggins and Boston's Frank Chance, pulled the rope that raised the flag just inside the centerfield wall. The Yanks won the opener 4–1, on a homer by Ruth.

Grantland Rice, in the next day's *New York Tribune*, rolled up his sleeves and let fly with this lead: "A white streak left Babe Ruth's 52-ounce bludgeon in the third inning of yesterday's opening game at the Yankee Stadium. On a low line it sailed, like a silver flame, through the gray, bleak April shadows, and into the right field bleachers. And as the crash sounded, and the white flash followed, fans arose en masse . . . in the greatest vocal cataclysm baseball has ever known."

The saga of Yankee Stadium had begun, and it wasn't three innings old when Ruth claimed the place as his own. Because of its short porch in right, the House That Ruth Built was also known as the House Built for Ruth. While placing the centerfield fence at the outer limits—or beyond—of most righthanded hitters, the mischievous Ruppert then took an even greater edge. He made the cracking of home runs a relatively facile exercise for lefthanded pull-hitting sluggers, of whom he had the greatest ever. Ruth's 54 homers in 1920 and his 59 in 1921—many of them over the Polo Grounds' short porch in right—had established the fan appeal of the home run and had launched the Babe as America's most charismatic athlete. Ruppert designed for Ruth a porch of his own.

Over the next 20 years, first through the power of Murderers' Row and then through the teams of DiMaggio, the Stadium became a kind of secular church in the Bronx. The Grand Concourse, two blocks north of the Stadium, was the main thoroughfare for an upscale neighborhood of handsome apartment buildings that had elevators and doormen. Many of the players lived up the hill in the Concourse Plaza, and kids used to meet them coming out the door and trail them to the Stadium.

John McNamara grew up there in the 1920s, and he recalls the day the bronze door of the players' exit burst open and out swept the Babe himself, wearing his signature raccoon coat. "He looked like a bear," says McNamara. "He was trying to get into this little roadster, but he was so big he couldn't. He took off his coat, handed it to me and said, 'Here, kid, hold the coat.' I took it like the pope was handing me his cloak. When he got in, I handed it back to him. 'Thanks, kid,' he said, and drove off. What a thrill!"

In those days visiting teams often stayed at the New Yorker Hotel at 34th

Street and Eighth Avenue in Manhattan and came to the ballpark on the C-line subway. "When I was a kid, I used to wait by the subway station at the Stadium and meet the players when they got off," says Arthur Richman, a senior adviser for the Yankees, who grew up in the Bronx. "I met the old St. Louis Browns there. They used to get me in."

As those championship pennants multiplied along the the Stadium's facade—10 were fluttering there by the end of World War II—old Goatville became a national shrine. "If you'd never been to Yankee Stadium, you'd never been to the big leagues," says former big league pitcher Bill Fischer, who first played there with the White Sox in 1957. "It was like you had never lived until you played ball in that town."

Fischer's first trip there came near the end of the longest orgy of winning in Yankees history and in the history of baseball—the dozen years from 1947 through 1958—and at a time when major events in three sports had lifted the place to the zenith of athletic venues. There have been 30 world championship fights contested as main events at the Stadium. It was there that Rocky Marciano twice whipped Ezzard Charles in '54—the second time after Charles had butterflied Marciano's nose like it was a shrimp and opened a cut over his left eye; Marciano was bleeding so much by the eighth round that his corner feared the fight would be stopped. Bulling forward, increasingly desperate as the seconds ticked away, Marciano caught Charles in the eighth, dropping him with a long right hand for a count of four, and then chasing him across the ring and knocking him out with a left hook and a right cross.

Sugar Ray Robinson, pounding for pounding the greatest of all fighters, lost only 19 times in his 25-year career, but two of his most memorable losses came in that little ring set up over second base. On June 25, 1952, giving away almost 16 pounds to light heavyweight champion Joey Maxim, Robinson was hitting Maxim at will for 11 rounds, winning easily on all cards and about to take his third world title before deliquescing in the 104° heat. It was so hot that night that the referee, Ruby Goldstein, nearly keeled over and had to be replaced following the 10th round. Robinson's collapse began in the 12th, when he staggered around as Maxim pursued him and pounded his body. Robinson fell to the canvas in the 13th after missing Maxim with a wild right, and the crowd of 47,983 gasped as Robinson, slumped on his stool, was unable to answer the bell for the 14th. Thus he suffered the only knockout of his career, but it was the heat, not Maxim, that beat him.

And it was in Yankee Stadium in '57 that middleweight champion Robinson and welterweight titleholder Carmen Basilio, an onion farmer from upstate New York, skinned and peeled each other for 45 long minutes in what *The New York Times* called, "fifteen rounds of the most savage fighting at the Yankee Stadium." In a dramatic climax, ring announcer Johnny Addie called out a split decision and declared Basilio the new middleweight champ.

Bob Sheppard has been at the Stadium's public address microphone since 1951, announcing all regular- and postseason baseball games in his precise, resonant voice, but among his most cherished memories are those from the Giants' football games he worked. Sheppard was at the Stadium on Dec. 28, 1958, for the Greatest Game Ever Played, the overtime NFL championship game between the Giants and the Colts. What he remembers now is the Colts' final drive in regulation; losing 17–14, they had the ball on their own 14 with two minutes left. He can still see quarterback Johnny Unitas finding flanker Raymond Berry again and again. "It drove me crazy," Sheppard says. "We almost had it in the bag. The Colts only had two minutes and all those yards to go, and I thought, It's safe. We have a good defense. But what a magician that Unitas was! He had me saying, over and over and over on the P.A., *Unitas to Berry, first down. . . . Unitas to Berry, first down. . . . Unitas to Berry, first down!*" Steve Myhra kicked a field goal to tie the score 17–17, and the Colts won it in sudden death when fullback Alan Ameche plunged through a hole at the one to score. "A huge hole," moans Sheppard.

That game was played less than three months after the Yankees beat the Milwaukee Braves in the seventh game to win the 1958 World Series. That victory crowned a 12-year stretch in which the Yankees won 10 pennants and eight World Series—a record five titles in a row from 1949 to '53. The Stadium itself had changed very little since '23. By then the Yankees had installed those monuments close to the wall in center, the first, in 1932, honoring Huggins, who had died three years before, and then stones commemorating Gehrig ('41) and Ruth ('49). The monuments were in the field of play, and nothing tested a centerfielder more than having to run down a ball that was rattling around between the monuments and the wall. The Yankees shortened the Stadium's deepest fences in 1937—centerfield went from 490 feet to 461, left center went from 460 to 457 and right center from 429 feet to 407—but it still took a Thor-like blast to reach the bleachers. It is no wonder so many memories of those years involve outfielders dashing madly after long fly balls.

In the sixth game of the '47 Series, with the Yankees leading the Dodgers three games to two, DiMaggio came to bat with two men on in the sixth and the Dodgers leading 8–5. Leftfielder Al Gionfriddo was playing near the line when DiMaggio ripped a 415-foot drive toward the bullpen in leftfield. Gionfriddo, thinking he had no chance, took off after it anyway, head down. Twice he looked back over his left shoulder. On the rooftops of the nearby Gerard Avenue apartment buildings, men with binoculars watched him run and listened as Dodgers play-by-play man Red Barber shouted over the radio, "Gionfriddo's going *backbackbackbackback*!" DiMaggio was rounding first as Gionfriddo neared the wall: "I saw it coming over my head," Gionfriddo recalls, "and I knew I had to jump, and so I jumped, with my back toward the plate, and I reached out and caught the ball in midair, as I am turning, and I came down and hit the bullpen gate with my butt."

Barber cried out, "Oh, doctor!"

DiMaggio, that most taciturn of men, kicked the dirt as he pulled up near second base. "In all the years I played with him, that's the only time Joe showed any emotion," Yankees shortstop Phil Rizzuto says. "Ever." The Dodgers won the game 8–6 but lost the Series.

Rizzuto remembers Ruth's coming to the park long after he'd retired, even when he was sick and dying of throat cancer, and sitting in the dugout cheerily spinning tales. "He used to sit on the bench in that camel hair coat and camel hair hat with that big cigar. His voice was just about gone with cancer, but he'd tell us stories about the old days, like how he'd eat hot dogs during games. Some innings, when he wasn't going to bat, he'd just stay out in rightfield and walk to the hot dog vendor under the stands and eat hot dogs among the people. . . . "

Two months before Ruth died, in '48, he returned a final time to celebrate the Stadium's 25th anniversary, and *Herald Tribune* photographer Nat Fein got a picture of him on a stool in the clubhouse. "He was so sick, it took two men to dress him," Fein recalls. "The Yankees were playing Cleveland that day, and Ruth took Bob Feller's bat and leaned on it, like a cane, as he's coming out of the dugout." Fein took a picture of Ruth from behind, with the number 3 on his back for the last time. That picture won the Pulitzer Prize in '49.

The Stadium touched everyone who played in it. Former Brooklyn pitcher Carl Erskine grew up in Anderson, Ind. (pop. 55,000), hearing about

Ruth and Gehrig and DiMaggio and dreaming about playing in the Stadium one day. And there he was, in the '49 World Series, walking into the visitors' clubhouse recently vacated by the Yankees, who had switched dressing rooms. "We walked in, awestruck, a bunch of kids," says Erskine, "and here were two lockers with two uniforms in them: Ruth's and Gehrig's. All cleaned and pressed and hanging there. I think they did it on purpose: We'll shake these kids up *real* good.

"The Stadium had an aura. There was a feeling of privilege and almost a disbelief that you're walking on the same field as those greats of the past. I stood on the mound there one day, and I'm looking around at 70,000 people, and I had this thought: *That's more people than live in Anderson!*"

In the sixth game of the '51 Series, the Yankees were leading the Giants three games to two when rightfielder Hank Bauer struck a bases-loaded triple in the sixth, giving the Yanks a 4–1 lead that they carried into the ninth. The finish was a circus. The Giants loaded the bases with nobody out and Irvin coming to bat. Stengel called on lefty Bob Kuzava. Irvin hit a bolt to left center that Bobby Brown, the Yankees' third baseman, says traveled about 450 feet before leftfielder Gene Woodling chased it down. That scored the runner from third and advanced the other two. Bobby Thomson then struck a nearly identical shot to left center that Woodling grabbed on the run. The runner scored from third, making it 4–3. With the tying run on third, pinch hitter Sal Yvars came to bat. "I can still see it," Sheppard says. "Yvars hit a screaming line drive to right."

"I was holding my breath," says Rizzuto.

Bauer, playing deep, charged. "I saw it, and then I didn't see it," he recalls. He slid forward feet-first and snatched it off the top of the grass, ending the game and winning the Series. Brown laughs at the unlikely climax: "Monte Irvin and Bobby Thomson hit two balls 900 feet and Yvars hit a screaming line drive, and the next day one headline said, KUZAVA SHUTS DOWN GIANTS IN THE NINTH."

DiMaggio played in his last World Series that year; Mantle was playing in his first. One of the most important plays in Mantle's career took place in the second game of that Series. On a Willie Mays fly ball, Mantle, trying to get out of DiMaggio's way, stepped on a drain cover, tore ligaments in his right knee and collapsed. He lay motionless. "I thought he'd been shot, the way he went down," Yankees second baseman Jerry Coleman says. "That was the beginning of Mickey's long, agonizing problems with his leg."

Mantle was DiMaggio's heir apparent to the most venerated role in the Stadium's lore: the Yankee slugger. It was a legacy founded by Ruth from Opening Day in '23, and a parade soon trooped in his wake: Gehrig, DiMaggio, Berra, Mize, Mantle, Roger Maris. But none of them, not even Ruth, hit the ball as far as Mantlc did. Twice in his career, batting from the left side, the Mick was a foot or two short of becoming the first man to drive a fair ball out of the Yard. Over the years, the fact that no one has ever done so became a central element of the Stadium's mystique.

On May 30, 1956, facing Washington Senators pitcher Pedro Ramos, Mantle drove a 2-and-2 fastball into the copper frieze along the rightfield roof. "I first thought it was just a pop fly," Ramos recalls, "but it carried like that new airplane that's gonna take a half hour from San Francisco to New York. If it had not hit the roof, it would have been in Brooklyn."

Seven years later Mantle busted a fastball from Bill Fischer, now pitching for the Kansas City Athletics, that hammered the same filigree. "You could hear everybody suck in their breath when it was hit," says Rizzuto. "It was on its upward arc when it hit that facade, and then it seemed to hesitate a moment before it dropped." Mantle proclaimed it the hardest ball he ever hit. Says Fischer, "Six feet over and it would have gone right through the gap by the bullpen and killed somebody waiting at the train station."

Perhaps the mother of all blasts in the Stadium came two years later when 6' 7", 255-pound Frank Howard of Washington smote a Steve Hamilton fastball down the foul line and over the upper deck in left, over the exits and over the roof and out of the park. It was foul by about four feet. "Nobody's ever hit a ball that far," says Yankees third baseman Clete Boyer. "It was like a shot out of a bazooka. I wish it had been fair. You had to see it to believe it."

Which is precisely what they were saying on that afternoon of Oct. 4, 1955, as the 2,838,000 citizens of Brooklyn danced out their doors and into the streets. For Brooklyn fans the Stadium came to be the embodiment of a wicked curse—a mammoth white oracle orchestrating their fate. Coming into their '55 Series with the Yankees, the Dodgers had been in seven World Series since 1916, and they had never won a championship. The Yankees had beat them four times (two of those in seven games) in the past eight years. Going into the seventh game of the '55 Series, each team had won on its home field, setting up what Harold Rosenthal of the *New York Herald Tribune* described at the time as possibly "the most dramatic Series game ever played."

Dodgers manager Walter Alston made two fateful moves that day. First, since the Yard was friendly to lefthanded pitchers, he sent Johnny Podres to the mound. Second, in the sixth inning Alston moved Jim Gilliam, an infielder playing leftfield that day, to second base—where he belonged—and replaced him with Sandy Amoros, a light-hitting outfielder with the range of an antelope.

The Dodgers were leading 2–0 in the sixth when Berra came to the plate with no outs, Billy Martin on second and Gil McDougald on first. Amoros was playing the lefthanded pull hitter toward center. "I threw a fastball that was high and about a foot outside," recalls Podres. "He shouldn't have even swung at it! But Yogi did." Berra sliced the ball down the leftfield line. Amoros got a good jump and began sprinting wildly toward the foul pole. Martin took off for third, and McDougald raced to second. As he rounded second, he saw Amoros closing on the ball. "When Amoros got near the fence, he put on the brakes, and it looked like he was leaning backward," McDougald recalls. "When I saw that, I took off for third. I was going to score! And then Sandy stuck out his hand. . . . "

All of Flatbush inhaled at once. Brooklyn fans had seen this all before, year after year—the killing Yankees rally, the turn of the screw. Frozen now in time, that moment, that scene, is a museum piece, an autumn diorama worthy of its own corner at Cooperstown—the October light playing tricks in leftfield, McDougald racing toward third, the players in the dugouts on their feet, heads craning toward that corner, the ball slicing and Amoros reaching out. . . .

"The sun was devastating that day," says Coleman, "and there were dark shadows in front of Amoros. He never saw that ball. . . . "

"And then Sandy stuck out his hand," says McDougald, "and found that Easter egg."

Both runners skidded to a stop as Amoros turned and fired to shortstop PeeWee Reese, who fired to first baseman Gil Hodges and caught McDougald between second and third. "I felt like cutting across the diamond, but I think the coaches would have got mad at me," McDougald says.

It all seems so simple to Podres now: "Yogi hit that ball off me, and Amoros made the greatest catch in America."

The Dodgers won, their first and only World Series in Brooklyn, and Erskine remembers walking into the clubhouse when it was all over—the same clubhouse where Ruth's and Gehrig's uniforms had been left hanging clean and neatly pressed in '49—and feeling a tranquillity that he'd never felt before. "To go to their park and beat them, after all those frustrating years, just added a dimension to it," he says. "There was a quietness when we first walked in that clubhouse, almost a spiritual feeling, gratitude for this accomplishment. Then someone popped a bottle of champagne, and the lid blew off."

Just as it was about to do again on the afternoon of Oct. 8, 1956, when Dodgers pinch hitter Dale Mitchell came to the plate in the top of the ninth, the only man standing between Don Larsen and his perfect game. Larsen had pitched brilliantly, to be sure, but the elements had favored him that day. In the fall the Stadium is hard on hitters late in the day. As the sun sets behind the upper deck, a shadow gradually moves across the infield; there is a time when the ball is pitched out of the sunlight and into the shade—the ball seems to flicker on and off like a light. The glare also makes leftfield the hardest position to play in baseball at that time of year. It gets late early out there, as Yogi once famously said.

In the second inning Jackie Robinson smacked a liner off third baseman Andy Carey's glove. The ball caromed to McDougald at short. "Luck, blind luck," McDougald recalls. Robinson's foot was six inches above the bag when Collins took the peg at first. "Out!"

In the fifth Hodges drove a ball into left center, a homer almost anywhere else, but Mantle, the fastest Yankee of them all, was in full flight, a la Gionfriddo, and made a sensational backhanded catch. And then Amoros hit a long drive down the rightfield line that looked like a homer, but it hooked foul by inches.

By the sixth inning, Coleman recalls, excited Yankees on the bench began playing manager and moving players around on the field: Move here! Move there! Play up! Play back! Finally Stengel had had enough: "Shut up!" he hollered. "I'm managing this here ball club!"

By the time Mitchell, the 27th Dodgers hitter of the day, came to bat, a cathedral-like stillness had descended on the Stadium. "He was a tough contact hitter," recalls Sheppard. "I thought, Oh, no. The last out. The last player. Top of the ninth. My stomach was churning. It was silent. You don't shout, you just pray." Larsen's first pitch was outside, ball one. The second was a slider for a called strike. Mitchell then swung at and missed a fastball, strike two, then fouled off another fastball. Larsen's third fastball caught the outside corner of the plate. "I can see Babe Pinelli turning and calling, 'Steee-rike three!' " says Sheppard. "The exhalation! It filled the Bronx!"

And it still does, even though the Stadium is no longer what it was in the days when the Yankees shared the place with the football Giants and Louis and Marciano and Robinson. The Giants are long gone to Swampsville in New Jersey, and the last fight to be staged there was on Sept. 28, 1976, when Muhammad Ali feebly outpointed Ken Norton to keep his heavyweight title. In 1973, on the occasion of its 50th anniversary, the Stadium underwent major surgery. When all of King George's men put Yankee Stadium back together again, all those girders that blocked sight lines were gone, but so was Death Valley and the monuments, which were moved to the other side of the fence in left center. And with the infusion of righthanded power in the Yankees' lineup, most notably Dave Winfield in 1981, the fences kept coming in. "People want to see home runs," Steinbrenner said in 1984, as he prepared to bring the walls in again. "It hasn't been fair to our righthand hitters." Today, that original 460-foot power alley in left center is now 399 feet, and the centerfield wall, once 490 feet away, is now 408.

From the fall of '73 to the spring of '74, the men of the Invirex Demolition Co. busted up the Stadium with jackhammers and wrecking balls, turning Goatville into the greatest archaeological dig west of Cheops. Jay Schwall, the owner of Invirex, ordered the 30-ton copper frieze dismantled and melted down—including that section over rightfield that, he says, bore a dent from Mantle's bazooka shot in '63.

Bert Sugar, boxing historian and baseball aficionado, sifted through the artifacts and unearthed everything but Rockne's halftime speech. He walked away with Babe Ruth's ashtray and bat bag—"which looks like a cow's udder," he says—sheets of undistributed World Series tickets from '48, the year the Yankees finished a close third, 2½ games behind Cleveland; a set of first-down chains (*Unitas to Berry, first down*); Casey Stengel's shower door; and a full uniform worn by DiMaggio, a pair of Gehrig's pinstriped pants and Ron Swoboda's jockstrap.

Some things are immutable. The Bronx is up, and the Battery's down. And some things should never change. The old Grand Concourse neighborhood is not what it used to be. The doormen are gone, the elevators are going. The Concourse Plaza, where so many Yankees used to live, is now a home for senior citizens. There has been much talk lately of building a new Yankee Stadium on Manhattan's West Side. Or in New Jersey. For those whose lives have been touched by the spirit of Yankee Stadium, such a thought is tantamount to a sacrilege.

"Can you imagine moving the Statue of Liberty to Montauk Point?" says Sheppard.

"How about moving Carnegie Hall to Hoboken?" says Sugar. Yankee Stadium may not be the house it was when Ruth built it, but it remains on the same plot of land Ruppert and Huston picked out when they decided to stick it to McGraw's Giants, and it has been hallowed by the triumphs and failures of the great athletes who played there and were, in turn, shaped by the experience.

Mickey Mantle used to have this recurring nightmare about the Stadium: He is dressed in his Yankees uniform, wearing spikes. He can hear Sheppard announcing the lineup one player at a time, his voice echoing like Gehrig's farewell. "Catching *catching*, number 8 *number 8*, Yogi *Yogi* Berra *Berra*. . . . " Mantle is outside, on the street, and he is trying, frantically, to get in. All the gates are locked, but he can see inside. The Stadium is full. He hears Sheppard call his name: "In centerfield *centerfield*, number 7 *number 7*, Mickey *Mickey* Mantle *Mantle*. . . . " He rattles the gates, a prisoner locked outside, but no one is there to help him, and he cannot get in.

Maybe this was Mantle's final legacy, this nightmare he bequeathed to us. That we would one day go to Yankee Stadium and the gates would be locked, the monuments moved, and we could not get in. And then not even the memories would be buried there.

ↄঊ

Acknowledgments

T HE STORIES IN THIS COLLECTION REPRESENT THE CUMULATIVE efforts of several generations of Sports Illustrated writers and editors. The latter generally work anonymously, but they deserve a tip of the cap here, especially those of recent vintage whose ideas helped inform the selection of these stories for this book: Bob Roe, Kevin Kerr, Dick Friedman, Larry Burke, Greg Kelly and Peter Carry. Also indispensible were many current members of the SI staff, who somehow found time, while producing a weekly magazine, to work tirelessly on this project: Steve Hoffman, Jodi Napolitani, Josh Denkin, Linda Verigan, Natasha Simon, Joy Birdsong, Linda Wachtel, Helen Stauder and Barbara Fox. And special thanks to Terry McDonell, whose support has been pivotal in putting these magazine stories between hard covers—a neat double play.

Grateful acknowledgment is also made to the following for permission to reprint copyrighted material:

The Most Exciting 12 Seconds in Sports Copyright © 2003 by Roy Blount Jr.

Son of Ball Four Copyright © 1979 by Jim Bouton

The Worst Baseball Team Ever Copyright © 1962 by Jimmy Breslin

Me and Hutch Copyright © 1960 by Jim Brosnan

Aches and Pains and Three Batting Titles Copyright © 1966 by Myron Cope

Perfect Day—A Day of Prowess Copyright © 1956 Used by permission of the estate of Robert Lee Frost

Master of the Joyful Illusion Copyright © 1960 by William Barry Furlong

An Outfielder for Hiroshima Copyright © 1958 by Mark Harris

Benching of a Legend Copyright © 1960 by Roger Kahn

Still a Grand Old Game Copyright © 1976 by Roger Kahn

He Does It by the Numbers Copyright © 1981 by Daniel Okrent

Dream of Glory on the Mound Copyright © 1961 Used by permission of the estate of George Plimpton

A Day of Light and Shadows Copyright © 1979 by Jonathan Schwartz

The Bird Fell to Earth Copyright © 1986 by Gary Smith

Hey, Chicago, Wait Till This Year Copyright © 2003 by Rick Telander